World War II Generation Speaks: The Things Our Fathers Saw Series, Vols. 1-3

Maps by Susan Winchell.

Photographic portraits of Robert Addison, Daniel Lawler, Dante Orsini, Gerald West and Earl Morrow used courtesy of Robert H. Miller.

Front Cover, Omnibus edition: 27th Infantry Division, Saipan, July 1944. Signal Corps., United States Army. New York State Military Museum. Used with permission. Cover layout by Emma Rozell.

Back Cover: U.S. infantrymen pushing toward Itri, Italy, during Operation DIADEM, May 18, 1943. Credit: Public Domain, U.S. Army Signal Corps photograph.

Any additional photographs and descriptions sourced at Wikimedia Commons within terms of use, unless otherwise noted.

Publisher's Cataloging-in-Publication Data

Names: Rozell, Matthew A., 1961-
Title: World War II generation speaks: The things our fathers saw series boxset, vols. 1-3. /Matthew A. Rozell.
Description: Hartford, NY: Woodchuck Hollow Press, 2018. | Series boxset: The things our fathers saw: the untold stories of the World War II generation, vol. 1-3. | Includes bibliographical references.
Identifiers: LCCN 2018953391 | ISBN 978-1-948155-03-8 (pbk.) | ISBN 978-1-948155-12-0 (hbk) | ISBN 978-1-948155-02-1 (ebook)
Subjects: LCSH: World War, 1939-1945--Personal narratives, American. | World War, 1939-1945 --Biography. | Military history, Modern--20th century. | BISAC: HISTORY / Military / Veterans. | HISTORY / Military / World War II.

matthewrozellbooks.com

VOLUME I

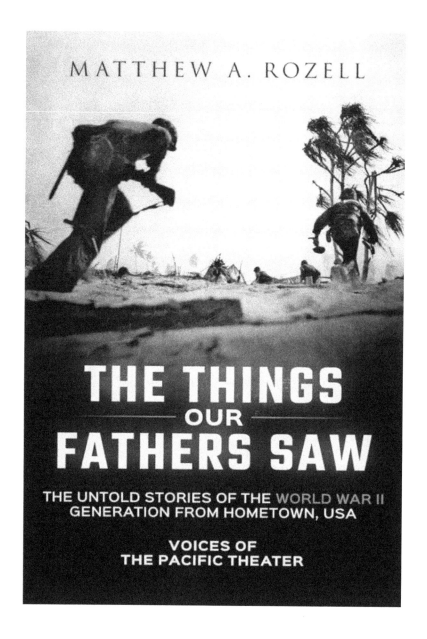

MATTHEW A. ROZELL

THE THINGS OUR FATHERS SAW

THE UNTOLD STORIES OF THE WORLD WAR II GENERATION FROM HOMETOWN, USA

VOICES OF THE PACIFIC THEATER

THE THINGS OUR FATHERS SAW

THE UNTOLD STORIES OF THE WORLD WAR II GENERATION FROM HOMETOWN, USA

VOLUME I: VOICES OF THE PACIFIC THEATER

Matthew A. Rozell

WOODCHUCK HOLLOW PRESS

Hartford · New York

 Grateful acknowledgment is made to the following: 'A Rain of Ruin' previously published by Andy Doty in *Backwards Into Battle* as 'Into Combat'/ 'They're Running Out of Gas'; and various short quotations credited to other previously published sources. Please see author notes.

Information at woodchuckhollowpress@gmail.com.

Maps by Susan Winchell-Sweeney.

Photographic portraits of Robert Addison, Daniel Lawler, Dante Orsini and Gerald West used courtesy of Robert H. Miller.

Front Cover: "Marines Under Fire, Tarawa, November 1943". Official USMC photograph. USMC Archives. Used with permission.

Back Cover: 27th Infantry Division, Saipan, July 1944. Signal Corps., United States Army. New York State Military Museum. Used with permission.

Publisher's Cataloging-in-Publication Data

Names: Rozell, Matthew A., 1961-
Title: The things our fathers saw: the untold stories of the World War II generation from hometown, USA-voices of the Pacific Theater / Matthew A. Rozell.
Description: Hartford, NY: Woodchuck Hollow Press, 2015. | Series: The untold stories of the World War II generation from hometown, USA-voices of the Pacific Theater, vol. 1. | Includes bibliographical references.
Identifiers: LCCN 2015920700 | ISBN 978-0-9964800-0-0 (pbk.) | ISBN 978-0-9964800-1-7 (ebook)
Subjects: LCSH: World War, 1939-1945--Personal narratives, American. | World War, 1939-1945--Campaigns--Pacific Ocean. | United States. Marine Corps--Biography. | Military history, Modern--20th century. | BISAC: HISTORY / Military / Veterans. | HISTORY / Military / World War II.
Classification: LCC D810.V42 R69 2015 (print) | LCC D810.V42 (ebook) | DDC 940.54/8173--dc23.

matthewrozellbooks.com

Printed in the United States of America

THE THINGS OUR FATHERS SAW

For the mothers who saw their children off to war,
And for those who keep the memory alive.

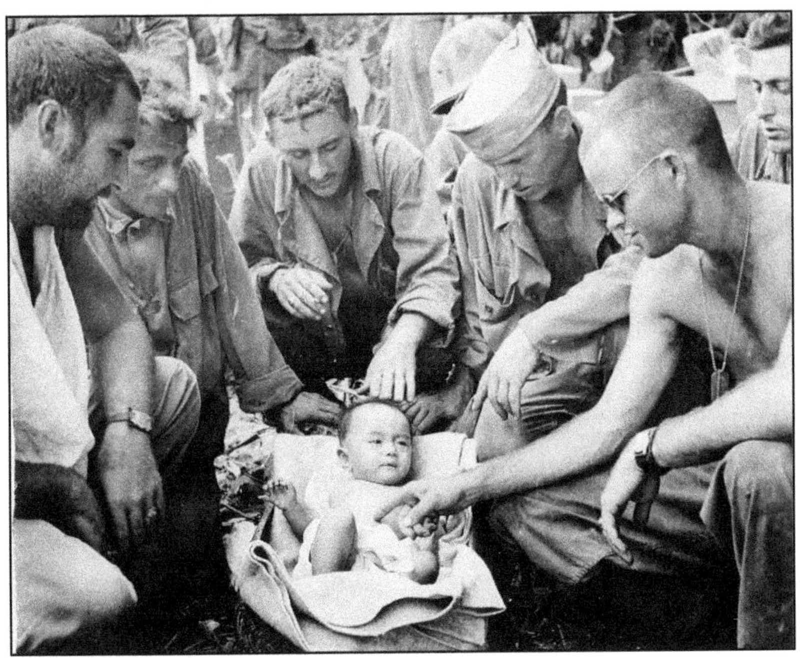

27th Infantry Division. Saipan, July 1944.
'An abandoned Japanese baby is adopted by front line medical unit of the 27th Div. The baby was found with a scalp wound, in the arms of its dead mother, by a tank crew during the fighting below Mt. Tapotchau.'
New York State Military Museum.

Dying for freedom isn't the worst that could happen.
Being forgotten is.

— Susie Stephens-Harvey, reflecting on her brother,
Stephen J. Geist
MIA 9-26-1967

I hope you'll never have to tell a story like this,
when you get to be 87.
I hope you'll never have to do it.

— Marine veteran of the 1945 Battle of Iwo Jima
to his teenage interviewer

THE THINGS OUR FATHERS SAW

The Storytellers (in order of appearance):

Harry 'Randy' Holmes

Gerald Ross

Joseph Fiore

Dante Orsini

Joseph Minder

Richard M. Gordon

Dorothy Schechter

John A. Leary

Robert Addison

Gerald West

Thomas H. Jones

Alvin Peachman

John Parsons

Ralph Leinoff

Walter Hooke

Irving Schechter

Nicholas Grinaldo

John Sidur

Daniel Lawler

John Murray

James Butterfield

Robert Blakeslee

Sanford Berkman

Arthur LaPorte

Herbert Altshuler

Walter Hammer

Andy Doty

Bruce Manell

Katherine Abbott

Mary Butterfield

John Norton

Joseph Marcino

THE THINGS OUR FATHERS SAW

TABLE OF CONTENTS

Preface

In the study of World War II, we are tempted to teach and learn the history as if the way things turned out was somehow preordained, as if it was a foregone conclusion that Americans and their allies were destined to win the war from the outset. Because we know how events turned out, we tend to read the history with a sense of inevitability. Nothing could be further from the truth. By listening to persons who lived through these troubling times, we gain critical insights that make the study of the past all the more relevant; indeed, I would argue, more urgent. More importantly, their recollections amplify crucial points that should be essential to our understanding of World War II, but are often overlooked.

It is easy to forget that during World War II the United States would be essentially engaging in two full-blown wars at the same time, taxing America's resources and families to the hilt. Many had expected to be in the fight sooner or later in Europe, where it had raged for two years; few expected it to begin in the Pacific. But that is where the story of American involvement begins, and it is also where it would end.

So imagine your world now, and turn it upside down. In this narrative, we focus on the stories of the Pacific War as told by more than 30 survivors who were fortunate enough to return. This is what they saw and brought back with them to the communities surrounding "Hometown, USA."

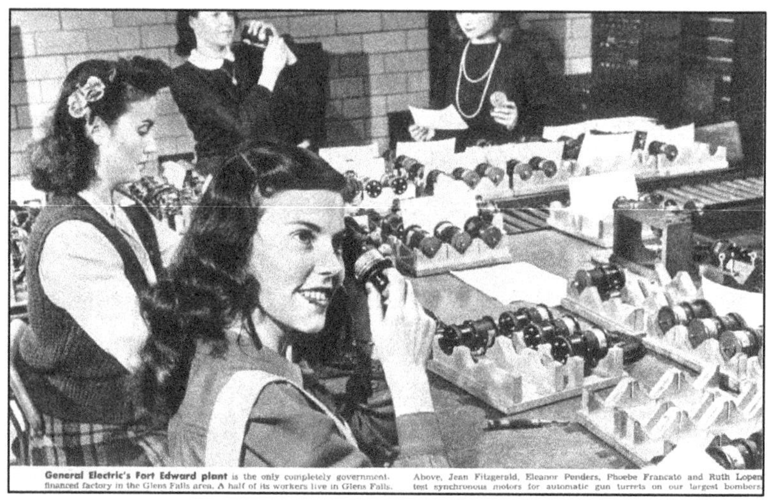

'General Electric's Fort Edward plant is the only completely government-financed factory in the Glens Falls area. A half of its workers live in Glens Falls. Above, Jean Fitzgerald, Eleanor Penders, Phoebe Francato and Ruth Lopen test synchronous motors for automatic gun turrets on our largest bombers.' LOOK Magazine, 1944.[1]

---

[1] Fort Edward High School's sports teams are still known as the "Flying Forts," after the Boeing B-17 Flying Fortress heavy bomber and the motors for the gun turrets built here.

INTRODUCTION

Hometown, USA

During the greatest conflict humanity has ever known, a cluster of small towns in upstate New York sent its sons and daughters off to war. In 1945, after six years of savage fighting, the devastation was unprecedented and incalculable. Between sixty and eighty-five million people—the exact figure will never be known—would be dead. Overseas, the victors would be forced to deal with rubble-choked cities and tens of millions of people on the move, their every step dogged with desperation, famine, and moral confusion. American servicemen, battle-hardened but weary, would be forced to deal with the collapse of civilization and brutally confronted with the evidence of industrial-scale genocide.

John Norton, American sailor at Hiroshima, after the atomic bombing: We walked around. The people, the civilians, were looking at us wondering what we were going to do to them. And, oh my God, the scars on their faces and burns. Oh God, it was sickening. Women and children—it was just sickening.

World War II would become the gatepost on which the rest of the twentieth century would swing.

Just what did our fathers see?

*

In the study of World War II, we are tempted to teach and learn the history as if the way things turned out was somehow preordained, as if it was a foregone conclusion that Americans and their allies were destined to win the war from the outset. As historian (and Pacific Marine veteran) William Manchester noted, because we know how events turned out, we tend to read the history with a sense of inevitability. Nothing could be further from the truth. It is easy to forget that during World War II the United States would be essentially engaging in two full-blown wars at the same time, taxing America's resources and families to the hilt. The story of World War II has been told many times, but only recently have we allowed those who actually lived it to speak for themselves. The narratives in this book are reflective of many of the places in the United States 75 years ago, but most have never been heard before. Most of them are drawn from those who share a connection to the communities surrounding the 'Falls' in the Hudson River, some 200 miles north of where the river joins the sea at New York City. Over a span of six months in 1943 and 1944, *LOOK Magazine* dispatched a team of photographers to Glens Falls, New York, and its environs for a patriotic six-article series on life in what was then dubbed 'Hometown, USA' to a national audience.[2]

---

[2] Assistant Secretary of War Robert P. Patterson had a hand in influencing the selection of the Glens Falls region by the magazine's editors. Born in Glens Falls in 1891, Patterson allegedly helped to steer the magazine towards the North Country in promising the availability of color film, which at the time was scarce and prioritized for military use. Over 5000 photographs were taken by magazine photographers presenting Glens Falls as a model of the home front during World War II. You can see more at bit.ly/hometownusa.

'Near Falls-Finch, Pruyn & Co., Inc. on Left'
Glens Falls-Hometown USA—LOOK Magazine, 1943-44.
Credit: Crandall Public Library, Folklife Center, Glens Falls N.Y.

Esthetically and demographically, it seemed an apt decision. The counties on either side of the waterfalls on the Hudson River, Washington and Warren, give rise to the Adirondack Mountains and the pristine waters of Lake George to the north. To the east lay Lake Champlain and the Green Mountains of Vermont; just to the south, Saratoga with its historic racetrack, a summertime destination for over 100 years. Beyond Saratoga lay the industrial city of Troy and the state capital of Albany, less than an hour away by rail or automobile. In the early days these counties played pivotal roles in the formation of the United States, given their geographic strategic importance on the Great Warpath, the almost unbroken stretch of water linking New York City with Canada. It was around the vicinity of the 'Falls' that watercraft had to be taken out and portaged. Two major fortifications were constructed here by the British during the French and Indian War, and this was the setting for

James Fenimore Cooper's classic *The Last of the Mohicans.* Half a generation later, a British army sweeping through here would be repulsed by county sons at the Battle of Saratoga.

Following the American Revolution, the early settlers engaged in agricultural pursuits such as dairy farming and, later, sheep raising. Mill-based operations on the river were centered around the upper falls at Glens Falls and the lower falls just downstream at Hudson Falls and evolved into significant lumber and papermaking operations. With the opening of the Erie and Champlain Canals two generations after the Revolution, new worlds opened up, but the 'North Country' counties remained relatively small in population. Living here required hard work in all four seasons, but it was a quiet, close-knit place to raise a family, like many rural areas across America.

Then the war came.

*

Like most every other community in America, from the outside this region seemed untouched by the war. As documented by *LOOK*, life went on to its rhythmic beat—children went off to school, the mills hummed, department stores filled their storefront windows, and farmers sowed and reaped according to the seasons. The beat quickened as young men and women stirred to volunteer, notices arrived in the post box, and many left town for the first time in their lives. Life went on but was now accentuated by rationing, victory gardens, blackouts, and paper and scrap drives. Soon, the arrival of telegrams announcing sons missing or captured, teary phone calls from military hospitals, or worse, the static rings of the front porch doorbell would drive this war home into the heart of 'Hometown, USA' with the fury of hammer blows. Things would never be the same again. Like the 'hard times' of the Great Depression in the preceding decade, this war affected every family. Few American communities would remain unscathed by the emotional detritus of World War II.

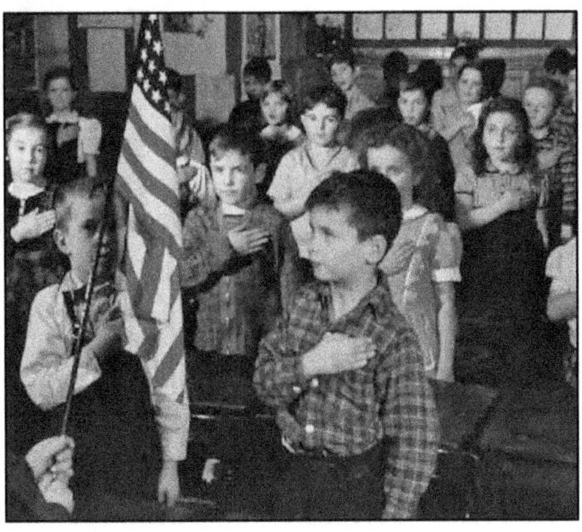

Glens Falls-Hometown USA—LOOK Magazine, 1943-44.
Credit: Crandall Public Library, Folklife Center, Glens Falls N.Y.

John Norton: There was a family that lost two sons in World War II. The family got a telegram on a Monday that one of the boys was killed, and that Thursday they got another telegram saying that his brother had been killed. There were about 35 young men from [this town] who were killed in World War II, and I knew every one of them.

Thus the war came and went. Of the sixteen million Americans who donned uniforms, nearly three-quarters of them went overseas. Most returned home to a nation on the cusp of a change not imaginable to their younger selves who had struggled through the Great Depression. The GI Bill of Rights brought new opportunities everywhere, and the economy began to boom. It was best to forget the war and to get on with normal life.

Art LaPorte, U.S. Marine at Iwo Jima: I've had a nightmare down through the years. When I worked at the paper mill sometimes I would be working on something, with all the noise and whatnot, and I would go back in the battles and I could almost smell the gunpowder. I would see all the action for a few seconds. If you had waved your hand in front of me, I would not have known you were there. I was right back there.

'Normal' life. Except maybe it was not going to be that easy.

*

Twilight

Nearly seventy-five years after the beginning of those dark days, the twilight of living memory is now at hand. Day after day we open the newspaper to see that more American veterans have passed on, and we are suddenly on the other side of the 'bell curve' of deaths per day—the downhill slope. By September 30, 2018, the U.S. Department of Veterans Affairs estimates that fewer than 450,000 will remain with us; in just 20 years, the World War II generation will have all gone the way of the veterans of World War I and the Civil War.

I don't know exactly when I was struck by the notion that this day would come, though on some cosmic level I have been planning for it for years. I was born sixteen years after the killing stopped, and I grew up in the company of men and women who fought in World War II. Probably like most kids my age, I had no idea what they did, and like most kids, I did not think to ask. I was raised in this sleepy hamlet on the 'Falls' in many ways not unlike their generation: an innocent in an intact home surrounded by brothers and sisters and community-minded parents. I seemed to draw strength from the study of history at a young age, spending my summer mornings wandering in the woods down near the waterfalls that gave the town its name, searching for evidence of colonial skirmishes and settlements of the French and Indian War and the American Revolution. As I got older I became interested in the conflicts of the twentieth century but remained blissfully unaware of the veterans who were all around me. Some of my teachers in school were veterans of World War II, but I don't remember anyone ever specifically launching into a story about their time in the conflict. It's also possible that they did, but I was not paying attention.

In the late spring of 1984, all of that would change. On television I watched as the 40th anniversary of the Normandy landings was being commemorated over in France. Thousands of American veterans joined their Allied and German counterparts for a solemn tribute and reunion tours of the battlefields where they had fought decades earlier. Many of these men would have now been just hitting their stride in retirement. It was also the first time in nearly 40 years that many would be back together to ruminate on their reawakening past. And here it was that I woke up and was moved.

I returned to my high school alma mater in 1987 as a teacher of history. I found myself spending a good chunk of time each spring lecturing enthusiastically about World War II, and it was contagious. There was a palpable buzz in the classroom. All the students would raise a hand when I would call out for examples of grandparents or other relatives who had served in the war—frequently two hands would go up in the air. Every kid had a personal connection to the most cataclysmic event in the history of mankind—and in the late eighties, many of the soldiers, airmen, Marines, and sailors who came home from the war were still with us.

A few years later my students and I watched as the nation observed the 50th anniversary of the Pearl Harbor attack. After that we had the 50th anniversary of the Normandy landings, which again attracted much interest. The films *Schindler's List* and *Saving Private Ryan* were released to much fanfare and critical acclaim. The United States Holocaust Memorial Museum, a work in progress for over a decade, opened its doors on a cold April day in 1993. These events signaled to those who had lived through World War II that it was okay to begin to talk about these things, that maybe people were finally ready to listen.

Building on that blossoming interest, I created a simple survey for students to interview family members. I had hit upon something that every teacher searches for—a tool to motivate and encourage students to want to learn more, for the sake of just learning it.

I was haunted, though, by one survey that was returned. When asked to respond to a simple question, a shaky hand wrote back in all capitals:

> *I DON'T KNOW HOW YOU COULD MAKE YOUNG PEOPLE TODAY UNDERSTAND WHAT IT WAS LIKE TO GO THROUGH A NIGHTMARE LIKE WORLD WAR II.*

He was right—nobody can interpret history like those who were there. Maybe I took that as an unconscious push to bring the engagement into the students' lives even more personally. Every spring we produced themed seminars and veterans' forums, and at every step of the way students were actively involved. We began to conduct videotaped interviews, inviting veterans into the classroom, and I also conducted dozens of interviews on my own outside of school. It seemed that for every facet of the war, if we dug deep enough, we could find someone who had lived it and would be willing to share his or her story. Young people who despised school stopped me in the hall to voice appreciation after listening to the veterans. I learned a lot about World War II, but I also learned a lot about teaching.

Shortly after the 50th anniversary of the end of the war we initiated a dedicated project, and to date, young people have fanned out into the community and collected nearly 200 stories, forging bonds and bridging generational divides, bringing happiness and companionship to their elders. They became 'collectors of memory' and brought back much of what you will read here, improving their 'people skills,' honing their capacity for sustained concentration and analytics, and sharpening their writing chops for college in the process. Just as importantly, students of history had a hand in creating new history, adding an important tack on the scholarship of World War II that would have probably otherwise been lost. In that regard, the books in this series are unlike other World War II titles on the bookshelves today.

Hardwired to History

Another early inspiration for this book is contextualized by an interview I did many years ago with Judge John A. Leary, a former Navy torpedo bomber pilot who later would go on to a distinguished legal career. Here was the young man who rubbed elbows with the likes of Joe Kennedy Jr., Pappy Boyington, Joe Foss, and others, the man who received the Navy Cross and the Silver Star for his actions in combat, but would not display the medals to the students at Hudson Falls High, instead showing me 'on the sly.'[3] Later Judge Leary invited me to his modest home, and I sat with him for hours on a warm spring Saturday night.

---

[3] Joe Kennedy Jr., older brother of the future president, was Leary's floor mate for a time while in training, and shared with his fellow Irishman a lust for life and his 'little black book' of female admirers. Kennedy was killed when his plane exploded on a voluntary mission over England in 1944. Gregory 'Pappy' Boyington and Joe Foss were 'larger than life' Marine Corps aces many times over in the Pacific and recipients of the Medal of Honor.

He settles into a comfortable chair across from me and lights up a cigarette, relaxing and clearly delighted with the company. His wife has passed, his children have long since moved on, and he and I are alone. With a twinkle in his eye, he tells me joke after joke and regales me with one incredible World War II story after the other. We laugh and pass the time; the lifeblood of this small town is being transfused as he recalls his life and his old companions in the quiet of his living room, and then he tells me something that will resonate with me to this day:

A little boy in the 1920s walks the streets of this town with his grandfather, hand in hand. They near the Soldiers Monument erected in the 1880s to remember the young men of the community who fell in the Civil War. The old man stops, points, and wipes his eye, proclaiming to the youngster that 'there stands nothing but a tribute to Southern marksmanship.'

Here is the young John Leary, who would go on to pilot dozens of harrowing combat missions in World War II, the little boy holding the hand of his aged grandfather, who had fought at terrible places like Gettysburg two generations earlier.

Soldiers Monument, Hudson Falls, on the Hudson River, in 1946.
Source: Hudson Falls High School Yearbook, 1946.

It is nearly midnight now, and it's time to leave. In shaking John Leary's hand I am suddenly conscious that I am now 'hardwired' to the past. An electric tingle goes up my spine; in my mind's eye I can see him flying as he steadies his torpedo bomber through a hail of anti-aircraft shrapnel exploding all around his plane, reciting his rosary prayers as he closes in to bomb the target. I am physically connected to the sixteen-year-old boy from our town who fought in the furious action at the turning point of the Civil War. I am just two persons removed from his fellow World War II veteran and later President of the United States, John F. Kennedy. In reaching out to other veterans, I am only one person away from FDR and Eisenhower, Chiang Kai-shek and Churchill; I'm just twice removed from the likes of Stalin and even Hitler!

A Higher Purpose

Still, as we recount these stories, the overarching question for some may be *'So what? Who cares?'*, and I suppose in our busy world that is to be expected. But somehow I believe that there is a higher purpose to this endeavor. There are always the lessons of sacrifice and service, of duty and honor, and that is enough to warrant a work like this. But in the end it comes down to simply listening, and pausing to consider all we have gone through together in a broader scope as a nation. It helps us to understand the essence of the eternal truths of the human condition, and ultimately, ourselves. World War II brought out the worst in humanity, but it also brought out the best. In studying World War II and the Holocaust, the ripples created generations ago remind us that history is not static, that these events will continue to flow and reverberate down through the ages.

John A. Leary, like most of the subjects for this book, has passed on. Thirty years after it all began, sometimes I will lie awake at night and wonder about it all. It appears that the past beckoned, and we channeled a portal. Here are the stories that a special generation of Americans told us for the future when we took the time to be still, and to listen.

Matthew Rozell
Washington County, New York
Memorial Day 2015

Extent of Japanese Control in the Pacific, 1942, featuring battles and locations in the book. Drafted by Susan Winchell-Sweeney, after Donald L. Miller.

CHAPTER ONE

A Sunday Morning

On Saturday, December 6, 1941, life was good for the average high school student in America, despite the fact that war was raging in Europe and the Empire of Japan had begun its tenth year of conquest, massacre, slavery, and rape in Manchuria, Korea, and eastern China. While many families still struggled with the challenges brought by the Depression, most 'didn't know we were poor, because everyone seemed to be in the same situation.' Holiday preparations were underway and sports or other outdoor activities filled the time for most boys and girls outside of the classroom. Teenage romance bloomed, and football and basketball practice occupied many hours that fall. The Saturday matches were looked forward to all week, as interschool rivalries were fierce and led to especially-anticipated games between certain teams. Little did the players realize just how important their ability to function as a team unit would soon become—and for some, it would be a skill essential to their survival.

'Where the Heck is Pearl Harbor?'

The world changed on a dime that weekend when the Japanese Empire launched its early Sunday morning aerial attack on Pearl Harbor. In New York State, it was early afternoon. Church services had concluded; some families heard the announcement as they were traveling to relatives' homes for Sunday dinner. Many others were at home or in a car listening to the New York Giants football game on the radio. Some young people went bowling on Sunday afternoons, and others were in the local theaters to see the latest Abbott and Costello release when the show was interrupted and the announcement of the attack made. For the young people and their elders, the response was the same: outrage, followed by the universal question—'Where the heck is Pearl Harbor?' The other universal feeling was the uneasy realization that life was going to be significantly altered from here on out.

A few of the boys from the North Country surrounding the "Falls" were well acquainted with where the Pacific Fleet was anchored; they had joined the Navy already, and on December 7, 1941, they were onboard ship in Hawaii for the attack. At the time, over 180 ships and vessels were moored in the harbor. At 7:55 a.m., the first of two waves of Japanese planes struck.

Randy Holmes

A lanky kid from Hudson Falls was serving as a fire-control man on the *USS Oklahoma*, and that Sunday morning he may have been reading in his bunk, walking a duty shift, or maybe sidling through the chow line. With his parents' permission, Randy Holmes had left high school early, and had arrived at Pearl Harbor a few months before. Just 19, he was probably one of the youngest sailors out of nearly 1,900 crew members.

Dating from World War I, the 'Okie' was an older ship with thin armor plating, but had lately made a name for herself evacuating Americans trapped in Spain at the outbreak of the Spanish Civil War in 1936. Like many ships docked at Pearl Harbor that morning, she was in a state of complete unreadiness at the moment of the attack. Having returned to port following sea maneuvers only the day before, the ship had its anti-aircraft ammunition locked away and the normally closed watertight compartments below the waterline open in preparation for a fleet admiral's inspection the following Monday, the 8th.[1]

Barely minutes into the attack, as the airbases at Hickam and Wheeler Fields billowed smoke and flames and Battleship Row was coming under fire, the *Oklahoma* was struck by three Japanese torpedoes dropped at low altitude; crew members actually saw the torpedoes in the water with virtually no time to react.[2] The explosions ripped through the port side, with Randy and over 400 others trapped below her decks. The order was given to abandon ship, but as the ship listed and more torpedoes were taken into her port side, the men below deck were plunged into darkness as water flooded into the open compartments. In desperation, many tried to make it to the shell deck (from which it might be possible to reach the top of the ship and jump overboard) as oil from the damaged machines slickened the surfaces while the ship was rolling in the water. Dozens of 1,400-pound shells broke loose from their tiedowns; sailors screamed as the shells barreled towards them and they were crushed to death. When the ship took her fifth torpedo, she capsized completely around 8:08 a.m.

A frantic rescue operation by civilian shipyard crews with jack hammers and torches along the 'bottom' of the ship, now above water, over the next two days saved some 32 men, but it was beyond hope for most trapped below the waterline, where banging would be heard for several days.[4]

---

[4] During the salvage operations for the *West Virginia*, it was discovered that three men had survived for weeks in a watertight compartment, marking time on a calendar until two days before Christmas. Gregory, Eric. "Sixteen Days to Die...Families Weren't Told Of Sailors' Lingering Deaths." Honolulu Advertiser, Dec. 7, 1995.

The destruction of the *Oklahoma* had taken all of fifteen minutes, yet it would take Herculean efforts over the next eighteen months to recover the sailors' remains. Randy and over 400 others on the 'Okie' that morning would never return home.

Japanese view as the "Okie" is struck. U.S. Navy Archives.

The Japanese aircraft wheeled and dove in again. The *USS Arizona* suffered a direct hit with a nearly two-ton armor-piercing bomb, which penetrated below the main deck and ignited gunpowder in her forward ammunition magazine, instantly killing 1,177 crewmen.[3]

When the battle ended two hours later, over twenty ships had been sunk or damaged, including the *USS Utah,* which capsized with 50 men aboard.

Hailing from just a few miles to the north of Randy's hometown, Whitehall native Gerald 'Barney' Ross enlisted soon after an eventful career on the Railroaders' 1939 'undefeated, untied, and unscored upon' football team.

Gerald 'Barney' Ross

I was standing on the deck of the *USS Blue*, a destroyer. I had gotten up early that morning and was getting ready to go to church services. We were all alone out there at this buoy, tied up. I was waiting for a motor launch to pick me up and take me to a larger ship, where they had a chaplain; destroyers did not have chaplains because they were too small. I think that because the *Blue* was a small ship it probably saved my life, because the Japanese concentrated on those battleships. I was talking to a shipmate of mine waiting for the motor launch, and all at once I saw a plane go over our ship. I did not know what it was, but the fellow with me said, 'That's a Jap plane, Jesus!'[5] She went down and dropped a torpedo. Then I saw the *Utah* turn over.

I did not really know what to do. The searchlight was my battle station, but there was no need to be on a search light at 7:55 in the morning. Not only that, but two-thirds of the crew had been allowed to go to the shore because they had weekend passes. The only ones aboard were those who had the duty. I started to help bring the awnings down. When we were in Pearl like that, in order to get out of the sun, we always had awnings over the back end of the ship, the stern of the ship. We used to sit there on Sunday morning and read newspapers. Sunday was our day to relax...

Things were happening. So, anyway, while I'm out taking that down, the chief gunner, he's coming and running, trying to get into the magazine so we can get some ammunition going. We were caught flatfooted, everything was locked up... it was really a mess, you know, and we didn't have any kind of warning that the Japanese were coming.

He started breaking the locks on the ammunition. Everything was locked up for fear that someone might go in there with a cigarette or something. He said, 'Ross, follow me.' He took me down into the number three magazine. He said, 'I want you to take powder and shells, and send it up to the gun.' He showed me how to operate the hoist, and that's what I did. I'd get a shell—they weighed about 80 pounds, I think, but when I was 19 or 20 that was nothing, I could pick one of those up easy. So, that's what I did. I'd take a shell and then I'd take a bag of powder, I'd put it in the hoist, and then I would send it up to the gun.

In the meantime, we were getting under way. All we had aboard the ship that morning was one Annapolis graduate and three

---

[5] Mr. Robert Addison, one of our local Marines, explained for our young people: "When I am referring to our enemies as 'Japs,' for us, then, well, we called them 'Japs.' Nowadays, I refer to them as 'Japanese people.'"

reserves—all the top officers were ashore! We managed to get underway, and I don't know to this day why we didn't get struck or take a torpedo, but we didn't. We got outside of the exit of the harbor and we started dropping depth charges. There were Japanese submarines out there, and we got credit for two of them and credited for knocking down four planes on our way out. We were doing this with the *Phoenix* and the *St. Louis* and four or five other destroyers; our duty was to try and find the Japanese fleet. We formed up and started out.

We were out there searching for 36 hours. We never did find the Japanese fleet, and I am awfully glad that we didn't, because they had attacked us there with six carriers, three battleships, ten or fifteen cruisers, and about twenty destroyers. The planes alone would have taken care of us, so I was grateful that we never found them.

When we came back into Pearl, it was pitch dark, and we could see the fires from the *Arizona* and the other ships still burning in the harbor. They sent this commander out to bring us in because our young naval officer ... was not acquainted with coming into the harbor, especially because it was pitch dark. Anyway, it was a terrible mess, as you can imagine, these ships blowing apart... they destroyed the *Arizona*, hit the *Oklahoma* and tipped her over, and then the *Nevada*, she got hit, and the *California*, and the *Tennessee*, these are all big battleships; they sent about 300 planes in there, and it would have been like sitting here having 300 planes come and tear Hudson Falls apart. As a nation, we were sleeping; it is a terrible thing to say, but we just—I was just standing there waiting for a motor launch to take me to a bigger ship to go to Mass, to go to church! We had no inkling, no inkling whatsoever. We were sitting there like sitting ducks! Here are men, if you can visualize, men struggling to get out of the ships. A lot of them were sleeping in because they had the day off. It was a horrible thing! This fleet was coming to blow us off the face of the earth. [6]

Back in Glens Falls, Joseph P. Fiore was a seventeen–year-old soon-to-be Marine who would later go on to be wounded several times in action in combat against the Japanese in the Pacific.

Joe Fiore

I was on Warren Street in front of Lenny Bovac's news room. He had a table with all the newspapers on it out front and a big strap across it, with rocks on it holding it on the table, so they could put the extra that the *Post-Star* put out, and the headlines were, 'Japs Bomb Pearl Harbor!' So I looked at Ted Toomey and he looked at me, and I beat him to it—I said, 'Where the hell is Pearl Harbor?'

Well, not quite a year later I knew where Pearl Harbor was, because we came in on a ship, and when we entered the harbor—I'll never forget this—you couldn't hear *a thing*. The only thing you heard was the slush of the water as the boat was going in... And we saw all these ships leaning over on their sides, and so on, and so forth. So to answer the question, that's where I was, and ended up in Pearl Harbor.

---

[6] In his remembrances, Mr. Ross's voice began to break up recalling his friends who had passed before him. Barney brought smiles through the tears as he reminded the students that, "I may get emotional, but I'm still a tough guy." Barney passed away at the age of 94 in August 2015.

The Day of Infamy

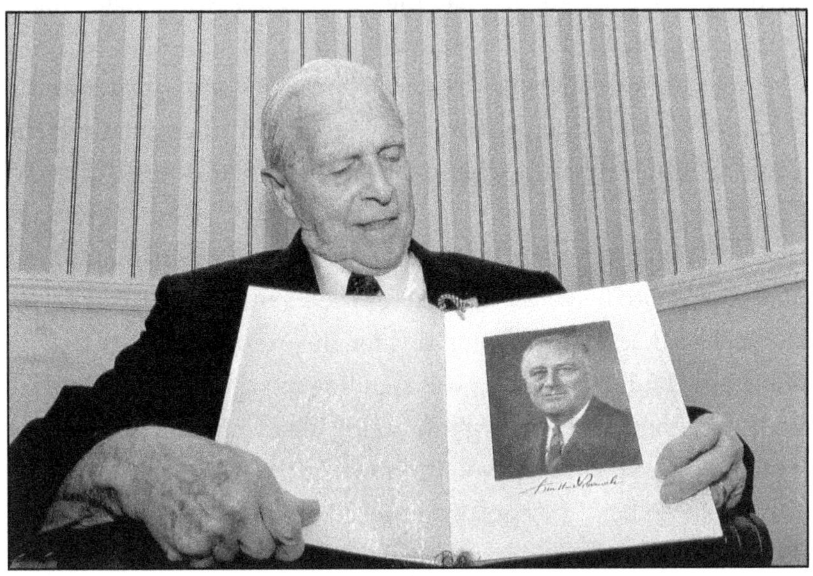

Dan Orsini, 2011. Portrait by Robert H. Miller.

On December 8, the President of the United States asked Congress for a declaration of war. Dante 'Dan' Orsini had graduated from St. Mary's Academy in Glens Falls in 1939, and like so many others, decided to go into the service, as jobs were scarce at that time. By 1941, he was stationed in Washington, D.C., attending the Marine Corps Institute for specialized training; he was also assigned to a very special detail. At 21, he was the youngest sergeant-major in the Marine Corps.

Dan Orsini

I had only been in Washington, D.C. three months; already I'm a member of the White House Guard, which was quite a thing! The White House Guard is made up of sixty guys, each with week-long duties, and our job was to be near and protect the President of the

United States and go wherever he went, wherever the White House demanded that we go. So I had the opportunity to see many, many things that the normal person in life would not see.

I went to many events with the President on several occasions. I went to Warm Springs, Georgia, twice with his train; that was the Little White House in Georgia, that's where he died in 1945. I saw FDR swimming in his pool—nobody saw that; I knew that FDR was disabled, couldn't walk. He had polio. He had to be lifted out of his chair, he had to be wheel-chaired to wherever he went—you know, things like that. He was doing this for the exercise more than anything else, and his little dog was standing next to him, barking like hell... and that was very thrilling, seeing the President go by, saying, 'Hello, sergeant. How are you this morning?'...

On December 7 I was playing basketball at the U.S. naval facility in Washington, D.C. It was about one o'clock in the afternoon, and they stopped the ball game, and they said, 'We want you to know that we just found out that Pearl Harbor has been bombed.' So we finished our ball game [*laughs*] because we weren't sure how serious this was. We found out later.

When I got back to the barracks that night—this was still December the 7th—my name was on a bulletin board, and it said, 'You twenty will be at the House of Representatives tomorrow night; the President is going to address the nation.' That's when President Roosevelt gave his famous 'Day of Infamy' Speech. It still goes on record as one of the greatest speeches ever given by a President. He knew he had a job to do; he had to bring the country together to win the war. I was about 100, maybe 200 feet to him, right in the House of Representatives when he spoke. It was very inspiring, and he had everybody. He showed his leadership abilities then as President. Politics went out the window. He brought everybody together, and it's the same thing as saying, 'Hey, guys, we've got a war we've got to win. What are we going to do?' And from then on, the world changed. That's when America loaded its gun and decided, 'Hey, this is serious, the Japanese have attacked us, they destroyed our fleet.' It was a great victory for them; now it was our turn. We had to build our country up, and that's where we started.

On that tragic day at Pearl Harbor over 2,400 Americans were killed, with another 1,100 wounded. In the following hours the Japanese struck U.S. bases in the Philippines, Wake Island, and Guam, and also began attacks on Thailand, Malaya, and Hong Kong. On the 9th, Japan invaded the Gilbert Islands, and Germany and Italy declared war against the United States on the 11th. It was a shocking start to the war, whose prospects had loomed uneasily on every American's mind since the invasion of Poland two years earlier.

In the Philippines, the attack at Pearl Harbor came at 3:00 a.m. local time. Warren County natives John E. Parsons and Joseph G. Minder were with the U.S. Army's 803rd Engineer Aviation Battalion working on survey crews building runways to beef up military locations in the Philippines.

At Clark Field in the Philippines on Dec. 8, 1941, John Parsons was sitting on the steps of a barracks with some fellow soldiers watching an approaching flight of 56 planes, which a passing officer described as a "Navy formation." In a few minutes a thunderous crash of bombs began what would become a nightmare of horrors for Parsons and the other soldiers in the Philippines. Due to confusion at high levels and conflicting reports, the Japanese bombers achieved almost complete tactical surprise, knocking out half of the U.S. Far East Air Force on the ground.[4]

After entering the service in May 1941, twenty-four–year-old Joe Minder began to keep a diary. Little did he know the tortured story his completed narrative would reveal about his subsequent three and a half years as a prisoner of war at the hands of the Japanese Imperial Army. His entries for December 1941 highlight the confused nature of the start of America's war.

Joe Minder

O'Donnell Airfield

November 3, 1941

Arrived here at O'Donnell by truck. What a rough road and place for a camp—'cogon grass' [*kunai grass*] is higher than a man's head around here. There sure is going to be plenty of work building a camp here in this jungle! [*This would be turned into the horrific POW camp several months later.*]

December 7, 1941

Returned back to camp at 8:00 p.m. after spending the weekend on a pass at Baguio [*resort city to the north near the Lingayen Gulf*]. Traveled all over Baguio with Drake, a good buddy from Louisiana. Also went up on top of the mountain near a gold mine. That sure was a beautiful sight, going up the sharp, winding, zig-zag trail, cut in the side of those steep mountains. Had air raid practice at noon in Baguio.

December 8, 1941—9:00 a.m.

Paper just came in from Clark Field—*'Hawaii Bombed! War Declared!*[7]

[7] Clark Field was the main U.S. airfield in the Philippines.

While we were eating… the first flight of Jap bombers went over our field to bomb Clark Field. Heard their explosions when the Japs dropped their bombs on oil dumps and ammunition dumps on Clark Field!

3:00 p.m.

Started tearing down tents, preparing to move all our equipment back into denser jungle to seek protection from Jap bombers.

7:00 p.m.

Just found out how much damage was done at Clark Field. Several hundred killed and injured. Much of the 803rd Engineers' equipment was destroyed; also several of our men were injured. Our surveying job broke up at noon. I have been put on a machine gun. So far, no Jap planes have come down close enough to get a shot at one.

December 9, 1941

Awakened early this morning by Jap observation plane. Thank God, no other planes came back to bomb or strafe us after he left. Just finished moving machine gun nest to the hill overlooking the airfield. Ready for action in case some of those high-flying bombers decide to come down and blow up our equipment on the field below us!

December 10 to December 22, 1941

For the past few days, hundreds of Jap planes have flown directly over our field on their way to bomb air fields, oil dumps, and ammunition dumps near here. So far, not a single plane has bothered us. We have been darn lucky! From this hill, I have seen many of the fires which they have set and heard the explosions of hundreds of tons of bombs. God only knows how many men were killed already.

December 23, 1941

Japs have broken through the lines and are now only a few miles from here. We are going to have to abandon this field and move to San Jose to construct an emergency landing field there. Things are getting hot!

December 25, 1941

Christmas Day! Sure doesn't feel like Christmas! Nothing different from any other day, except we were fortunate to have a little turkey for dinner. Sent a telegram home yesterday. Hope their Christmas at home isn't anything like this! Still on the machine gun here in San Jose.

Japanese infantry continued their steady advance from the north. The 803rd and other units, along with tens of thousands of Filipino troops, rushed to consolidated defensive positions on the mountainous Bataan Peninsula. At the tip of the peninsula at the entrance to Manila Bay lay the fortress island of Corregidor, where General MacArthur maintained his headquarters.

December 30, 1941

Japs broke through again! We are going to Orani [*on the Bataan Peninsula*] to work on another airfield.

December 31, 1941

We were bombed for the first time, as we were eating supper. Koltoff almost had his leg blown off and two other men from my company also were injured by shrapnel. Two large air corps gas trucks were also blown up, across the road from where we are. Several Filipinos were also killed. Twelve were buried alive when a bomb landed near their bomb shelter. Some of our men dug them out, but only two survived.

CHAPTER TWO

The Defenders

The degree of unpreparedness that faced the nation in the first months of the Pacific War was nearly overwhelming. Young Americans were hurled into a stratosphere of uncertain and unfolding events against battle-hardened Japanese forces. In the Philippines, a three-month death struggle would be waged as American and Filipino forces desperately tried to salvage their positions. Ordered to fall back to consolidate their lines, the defenders were confronted with the day-to-day realities of dealing with an enemy of superior numbers and experience.

By January 1942, the main island of Luzon was in the crosshairs of the Imperial Army and Navy, Japan now having a firm grip on all of Southeast Asia. After the fall of Manila on January 2, the Bataan Peninsula and the island of Corregidor were the only Allied holdouts in the region. The 803rd Engineer Aviation Battalion struggled valiantly to widen roads and repair airfields for the Allied reinforcements and counterattack that would never come. Fate would render her terrible hand to the 12,000 American troops and 65,000 Filipino defenders trapped here on Bataan. There would be no relief—only sickness and starvation, and tears of frustration and exhaustion.

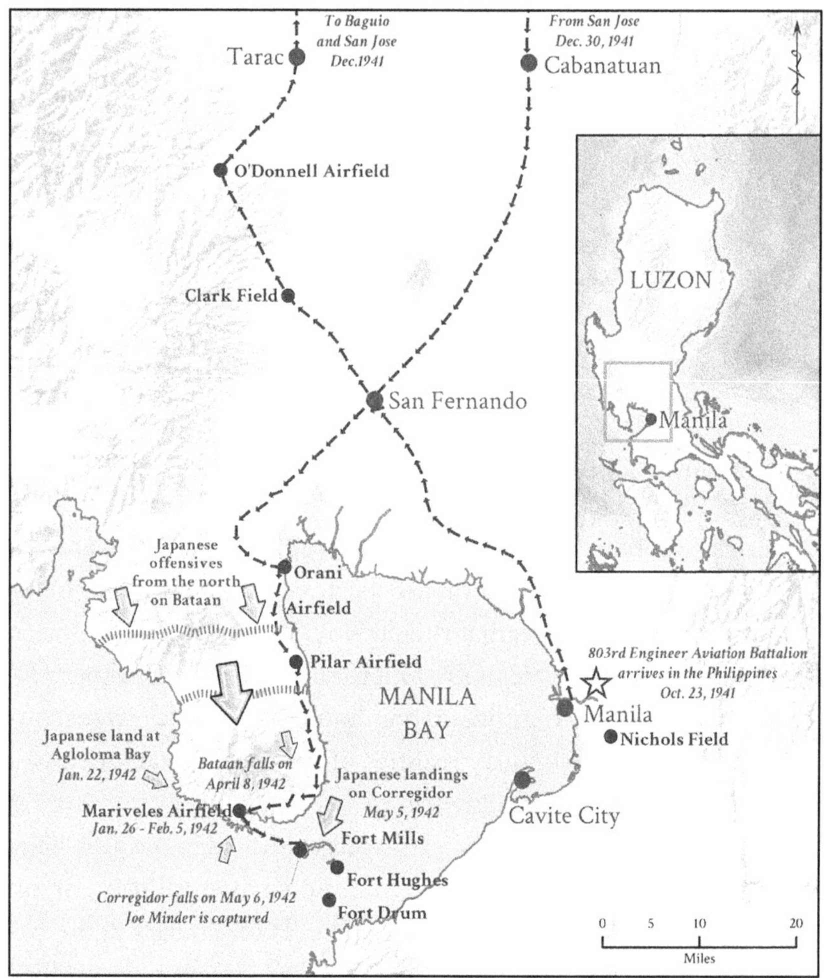

Route of Pvt. Joseph G. Minder in the Philippines, Oct. 1941-May 1942.

Joseph Minder was a country boy at heart, growing up in the Adirondack Mountains of northern Warren County with his brothers and sisters and a genuine love for people and the beauty of the natural world that surrounded him. He spent his days after school hunting and fishing or skiing on the mountain near his home. Like so many other young adults right out of high school, Joe would be literally thrust to the front lines of an unfolding titanic struggle that would engulf the entire world.

Joseph Minder, 1941.
Courtesy Minder Family.

Joe Minder

January 1, 1942

Darn tired this morning. Greco and myself celebrated New Year's Eve last night drinking warm beer in what was left of Orani. Spent the five dollars my sister Josephine sent me.

11:00 a.m.

Japs bombed and strafed while we were working on the field. Got my first shots at a Jap plane when I emptied my rifle as it came in to strafe the field. Saw the Jap plane catch fire and explode when it hit the ground!

4:00 p.m.

Japs spotted our foxholes and dropped frag bombs and strafed the heck out of us. One bomb landed 10 feet from the foxhole that John Delemater was in, knocking loose dirt from the sides of the foxhole on us. Although many bombs landed very near to many men and the entire area was machine gunned heavily, not a single man was injured today.

January 2, 1942

Spent half the night blowing up dud bombs which the Japs dropped yesterday. Darn tired but will have to work like heck today, preparing to move again, to Bogani Road on Bataan. This will make the fourth airfield that I have worked on which they have captured.

Retreat to Bataan

January 3, 1942

Started working on Bataan roads today. Shreppel and two other men were injured when Japs bombed us again today as we were working, building a bridge bypass.

January 4, 1942

Things were too 'hot' yesterday, so we worked last night instead of today, to get away from the Jap bombings. Intended to sleep today but found out we are going to have to move to Kilometer No. 201. Japs have bombed all the bivouacs [*improvised temporary camps*] around us. If we stay here we will be next...

January 5 to January 20, 1942

Although the Japs have been keeping us in hot water, bombing and strafing roads, trucks, bridges, and bivouacs areas, we have managed to keep most of our machinery running, widening the roads and building bridges here on Bataan for these past 15 days.

January 21, 1942: 9:00 p.m.

Japs must have made a deeper drive into Bataan. Heavy guns can be heard much clearer tonight.

1:00 a.m.

A lot of machine gun fire coming from the beach about a half mile from here.

The Japanese had turned a landing on the west coast of the peninsula, and now were attempting to surround and isolate American and Filipino positions. The defenders fought on tenaciously and contained the Japanese breakout, protecting the further withdrawal of troops and tens of thousands of civilians. In the Battle of the Points, these sick and hungry men killed over 2,000 Japanese invaders.

January 22, 1942

Japs landed at Agloloma [Bay] behind the lines last night about a mile from here. We have been notified to move in there this morning and help other outfits who are already fighting them.

January 23, 1942: 9:00 a.m.

First food and water since 6:00 a.m. yesterday. Fought 26 hours straight, with only one casualty!

2:00 p.m.

Many Jap snipers were all around us. I almost got it when one spotted me and started firing at me before I had the chance to get my machine gun set up! It was thick with vines that we had to cut our way through with our bayonets.

We managed to keep pushing the Japs back toward the beach till about 5:00 p.m., at which time we ran into crossfire from Jap machine gun nests. Before we could fall back, they broke the line and killed or wounded half of us. Robert Ray and Kenny, two close buddies of mine, were the unfortunate ones. Thank God, they were both killed instantly and didn't have to suffer like some of the rest did. The Japs tried to cut the rest of us off, but we waited until dark and managed to sneak back through their lines.

January 24, 1942

Found out at about 3:00 p.m. that we were being relieved by the Filipino scouts. The handful of us who were left went to Signal Hill [*the reconstituted Army headquarters near the city of Mariveles on the southern tip of Bataan*] to reorganize.

January 26, 1942

Left Signal Hill for Little Baguio [*a bit further inland, to the engineer depot at Kilometer Marker 168.5*] where we joined with Company B, 803rd Engineers to work on the roads again.

January 28, 1942

Visited men in Little Baguio hospital who were injured in Agloloma. Cappel and Peterson both lost their legs.

Retreat to Corregidor

February 4, 1942

We were notified this morning that we are to move to Corregidor tonight and construct another airfield there.

Corregidor was the fortified island at the opening to Manila Bay, about three miles off the tip of the peninsula. Dotted with bunkers and riddled with tunnels, it had nearly thirty heavy gun batteries and twice that amount of large cannons for the defense of the Philippines. Situated not unlike Gibraltar in Europe at the strait entering the Mediterranean, it was expected to be able to withstand any enemy attack.[5] *The most formidable structure was the Malinta Tunnel, a fortified tunnel complex constructed between the wars that would go on to house General MacArthur's command as well as a thousand-bed hospital.*[6]

February 5, 1942

Arrived here about four this morning. Everyplace we go, the Japs seem to follow us. Corregidor was shelled, from Cavite [*seven miles away, the by-now abandoned U.S. naval base for the Philippines*] for the first time today. Several shells landed in our bivouac area, but no one was injured.

General MacArthur was ordered by President Roosevelt to leave the Philippines for Australia to compose its defense in mid-March, leaving General Wainwright in charge. British Malaya and Singapore had fallen rapidly with the capture of 15,000 Australian soldiers, and air attacks in Australia had already commenced, shocking the world. The Japanese were simultaneously consolidating positions in New Guinea and elsewhere for the possible invasion. Meanwhile, at Bataan and Corregidor, troops continued to struggle to hold the Japanese onslaught at bay. Rations became nonexistent; many of the men were subsisting on small handfuls of plain boiled rice twice a day. Enemy pressure continued to build.

March 24, 1942

The Japs have been shelling Corregidor every day since we landed here, but we didn't lose any men until today. They caught us out on the field this afternoon and gave us a terrific bombing which lasted about a half hour. Karp and Harrington were killed and many others injured. Most of our equipment was blown up. I thought my number was up when I was bounced around in a foxhole by some large bombs which landed about a hundred feet from me! Large fires broke out, so we left for Malinta Tunnel to determine how many men were injured and killed in the bombing.

March 25, 1942

Most of the trees were blown down, so we moved what was left of our supplies to the other side of Corregidor, seeking a little better bivouac which isn't as conspicuous from the air.

March 27, 1942

Company Commander Captain Zebowski died in Malinta Hospital from shrapnel wounds, which he received March 24th.

March 28 to April 7, 1942

Bombing and shelling of Corregidor is getting heavier every day. Japs are only a short distance from Mariveles. Heavy gun fire and gun flashes can be heard and seen across the bay at night.

April 8, 1942

Bataan fell! Men arrived here this morning who managed to get away by small boats and gave us the dope about what happened when the Japs succeeded in breaking the lines on Bataan!

The Bataan Death March

On April 8, the Japanese closed on weakened American lines on the Bataan Peninsula. By this point, most of the defenders were incapacitated by malaria, dysentery, fatigue, and starvation. Major General Edward P. King, Jr., commander of the ground forces on Bataan, received assurances that his men would be treated decently.[8] *Glens Falls residents Robert B. Blakeslee and John Parsons were two of 78,000 taken prisoner on Bataan in the largest surrender by the United States Army in its history. Many men scrambled to make it across to Corregidor, where Joe was, but by this point for most it was too late.*[7]

During the Bataan Death March, American and Filipino prisoners were forced to march in blazing heat for sixty-plus miles. Many stragglers were clubbed, shot, stabbed, bayoneted, or beheaded for sport and left where they lay; some Americans were even forced to bury alive their sick buddies who had fallen near the ditches on the side of the road. No accurate measure is possible, but perhaps 750 Americans and 5,000 Filipino prisoners died along the route. Barely able to stand near the end, the survivors were

---

[8] This assurance, of course, was immediately broken. One survivor recalled, "Mile after mile the looting and the beatings continued. They cared not who they struck. High ranking officers were no exception. I watched one private attack Major General King. The soldier was so short he had to jump to strike the general in the face with his fist. He did it time and time again, and the general just stood there...Guards with pointed rifles waited for us to do something. Finally, the private gave up in disgust and walked away." Machi, Mario, *Under the Rising Sun: Memories of a Japanese Prisoner of War*. Miranda, CA: Wolfenden Publishing, 1994. 70.

forced to double-time trot to the city of San Fernando, where they were crowded into boxcars for a five-hour rail journey. They were then forced to walk again for the last several miles to the notorious Camp O'Donnell, where over 16,000 more prisoners would die over the next two months.[8]

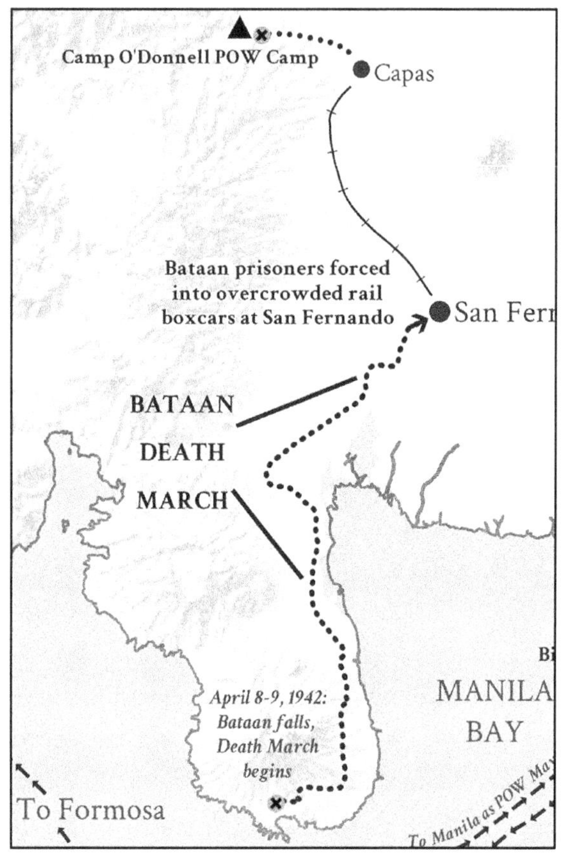

Route of Bataan Death March.

John Parsons' account was published after the war in the local newspaper.

"Of the 'Death March' Parsons says, 'It just can't be imagined.' The march was a distance of about 75 miles [*sic*], which was covered in around six days. For healthy troops that would not be exceptional, but for the sick and weak, as nearly all were, it was a cruel ordeal. It was not a continuous march, parade fashion, but rather continued over a period of about a week with groups of 500 being sent out each day. Parsons says they were forbidden to help anyone in any manner, even if he fell. To do so was to invite a rifle butt in the back. He saw three men bayoneted in the back at a rest period when they walked a few feet from their group and knelt over a puddle splashing water on their faces.

The Japanese way of feeding the prisoners, on those days when they did, was to place a bag of about 150 pounds of cooked rice at the head of the column and let them scramble for it. Those at the rear usually got nothing. More food was always promised 'tomorrow.' "[9]

In 2006, Death March survivor Major Richard M. Gordon gave an interview.

Richard M. Gordon

Words cannot really describe those days or the thousands of individual horrors. Suffice it to say, I went nine days without food and with very little water. My training as an infantryman paid off. I conserved water in my canteen by taking a sip, swishing it around in my mouth, and letting a little drip down my throat. I would do this until I reached the next potable water spot. Others, untrained and dying for water, would prostrate themselves along the side of the road and drink water from puddles. All this water was contaminated with flies and fly feces and brought on death from dysentery. Thousands of Filipinos and several hundred Americans died this way. The Japanese beat any who attempted to break ranks and obtain water, killing a number of them in the process. Japanese tanks, moving south to take up positions to attack Corregidor as we marched north, would deliberately drive over the dead and dying on the side of the road.

The Japanese were in a hurry to move in their reinforcements and artillery to pound Corregidor into submission before the final invasion. Before the march, Parsons and other prisoners were forced to excavate gun emplacements for the heavy weapons.

Joe Minder

Corregidor, April 9, 1942: 3:00 p.m.

The Japs have massed much artillery along the beaches facing Corregidor and are really giving us heck now. With only four miles of water between us and the mouth of their big guns, Corregidor is trembling as if there were an earthquake as these Jap shells tear into her sides, blowing up gun batteries, ammunition dumps, and setting large fires!

4:00 p.m.

Several boats were sunk trying to move around to the other side of Corregidor. "How long can this last, and why doesn't Corregidor fire back and quiet some of those Jap guns?" is the question in everyone's mind here.

April 10, 1942: 8:00 a.m.

Japs started their heavy bombardment early again this morning. Just found out that there are several hundred Americans concentrated in the vicinity of those Jap guns. That is the reason why Corregidor isn't firing back.

April 11, 1942

Corregidor is finally firing some of her guns in an attempt to cut down some of the intense Jap fire.[9]

4:00 p.m.

What an explosion! Japs just blew up several tons of black powder and TNT on Cavalry Point where we were bivouacked two weeks ago! Buildings, trees, and everything within a 500-yard radius were leveled to the ground!

April 12, 1942

Almost got it this morning, when I awakened to find shells dropping all around me. One of our trucks was blown up a few yards from where I slept!

April 13, 1942

Several more large buildings burned this morning by Jap shells. Our guns, which are firing at Japs, don't seem to be doing any good. For every shell which we send at them, about a hundred bounce back, cutting off telephones, roads, and all our communications here on Corregidor.

April 14 to April 30, 1942

In the past 16 days of constant shelling and bombing, the Japs have succeeded in burning about 3/4ths of the buildings and have blown up about half the gun batteries here. Dead tired! Haven't gotten hardly any sleep these past 16 days—night shelling and

---

[9] Many of Corregidor's big guns were made at the Watervliet Arsenal on the Hudson River, just a few miles to the south of the "Hometown, USA" region Mr. Minder hailed from. It has been in continuous operation since 1813.

bombings getting worse each night. We no sooner get asleep when we have to dive for a foxhole or a bomb-proof shelter! How much longer can we stand up under this terrific bombardment? Sent letter home by submarine the other day.

Soon the American gun batteries on small neighboring islands were also targeted, and they responded.

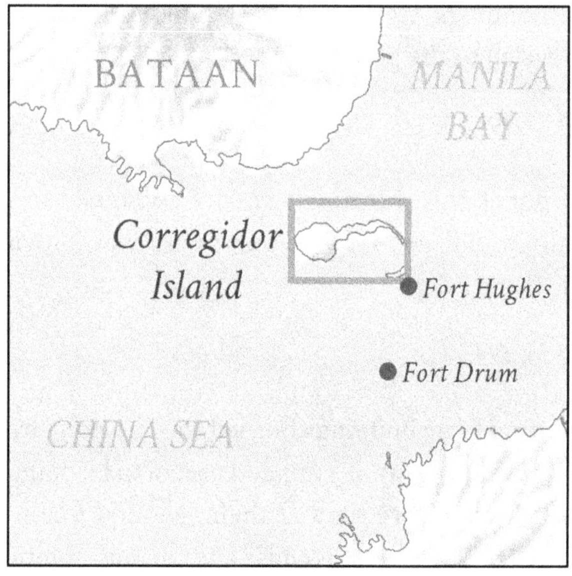

Corregidor and island forts.

May 1, 1942

Japs have lightened their fire on Corregidor a little and have started pounding Fort Hughes with heavy shelling and bombings. Fort Drum has started firing her 14-inch guns in a desperate attempt to blow up some of those hundreds of guns. Dirt and smoke rise many feet into the air as those huge shells from Fort Drum explode among the Jap guns! Corregidor is located between the Japs and Fort Drum and Fort Hughes, so we can get a bird's-eye view of the exchange of fire by the Japs and the other two forts.

May 2, 1942: 5:00 p.m.

Fort Hughes is taking a terrible pounding, in the vicinity of her large mortars, by Jap artillery. God! What explosions on both sides of us! Fort Drum is loping her 14-inch shells over Corregidor to Bataan, the Japs are sending all types of artillery shells over our heads to Fort Drum, and Fort Hughes is sending her large shells over our heads, also, to repay some of the steel that the Japs are so generously sending them. Some of those shells sound like freight trains passing overhead! With all these large shells passing directly over us, it makes our blood run cold, wondering if some of them might hit a tree, or fall short of their mark. Some of them sound close enough to touch as they go roaring over our head!

May 3, 1942

Worked late last night repairing roads, between the numerous shelling. Two more 803rd Engineer men killed by shells today.

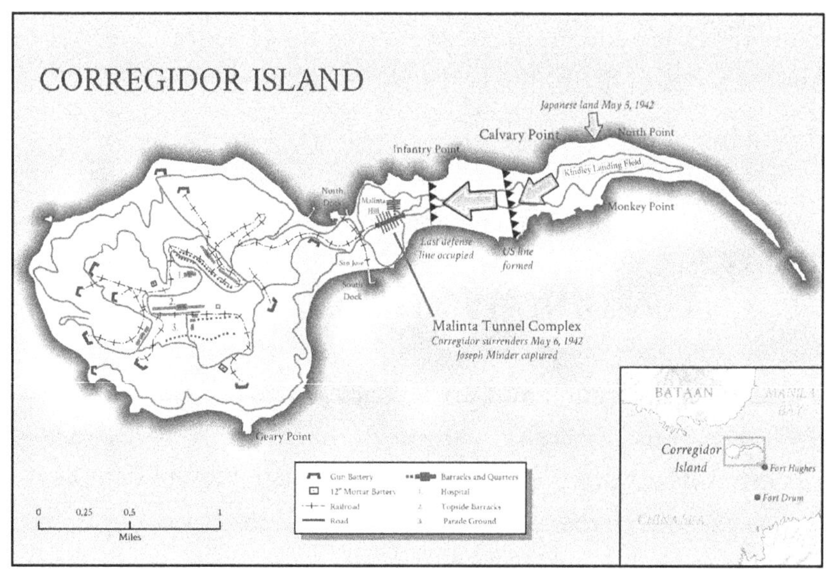

Japanese Invasion of Corregidor, May 1942.

May 4, 1942: 5:00 p.m.

Just saw the last two interisland boats sink, as the Japs scored several bomb hits by dive bombers, sinking them between here and Fort Hughes.

7:00 p.m.

Just finished helping putout fires started by Jap shelling. My clothes were blown up by a Jap shell!

Joseph Minder was turning 25 years old.

May 5, 1942

Plenty of fireworks to celebrate my birthday today! The Japs have been shelling and bombing continually since early this morning. All communications have been cut off from the other end of Corregidor!

5:00 p.m.

The Japs seem to be pounding this end of the island heavier than ever before. Marines were forced to leave the beach from their foxholes by Jap artillery.

The 4th Marine Regiment would shortly return to their positions to fight valiantly to try to turn back the invasion, claiming many Japanese lives, but at this point the enemy now had 75 big guns firing away at what amounted to point-blank range. [10]

11:00 p.m.

For the past three hours, there hasn't been a single break in the hundreds of shells which hit this end of the island!

11:30 p.m.

INVASION!

A runner just made his way over here through heavy artillery fire. JAPS HAVE LANDED, under this heavy artillery fire at Monkey Point, about an hour ago! The communications having been cut off, no one knew they had landed, only the men in the immediate vicinity of the invasion points!

A bunch of us loaded into a truck, which had all tires flat from shell shrapnel, and made our way over a shell-blasted road to site a machine gun on a small hill overlooking the beach and the airfield, only about 500 yards away, which the Japs had already succeeded in advancing to. We managed to hold the Japs at this point, except for the few Jap snipers who managed to filter through the gaps in our lines.

Artillery continued to blast away all night from Bataan and there was a fierce exchange of machine gun fire between us, but our losses were small during the night, as compared with large numbers of Japs which we killed while they attempted to mass-attack us. One of my biggest scares of the night was when an American mistook me for a Jap sniper, as I was moving up nearer to the Jap lines, and opened up with a tommy gun on me!

May 6, 1942: 5:00 a.m.

At first I thought I would be glad to see daylight, so we could see what we were doing, but when Jap planes started their daylight bombing and spotting for the artillery from Bataan, I soon changed my mind! With the cover of darkness gone, it was impossible for us to fire without being seen by the hundreds of snipers who had by this time stationed themselves all over the island!

8:00 a.m.

By this time we have suffered many losses; we managed, however, to continue holding back the main force of Japs until they started landing tanks. With no guns left to combat the tanks, we were forced to surrender at noon. Then is when I received the bad news of Drake's and Bailey's deaths, two very close buddies of mine. The last time that I saw Bailey was about midnight when he and I were firing at a Jap sniper from the same bomb crater. Dead tired, sweaty, and dirty with minor scratches and bruises suffered from diving in shell holes and going through the bush, I climbed on top of a stack of empty ammunition boxes and slept until 5 o'clock, at which time the Japs came and stripped us of most of our belongings and marched us down near the Malinta Tunnel, where we stayed for the night.

The Fall of Corregidor

The landing of the tanks finally decided the issue as they began to move up toward the Tunnel. With no possibility of relief and no good options, General Jonathan Wainwright radioed President Roosevelt, 'There is a limit of human endurance, and that point has long been passed.' The formal surrender on May 6 marked the fall of the Philippines. Like Joe, nearly 11,000 of the garrison on the 'Rock,' including 77 nurses, would now be at the mercy of their enemy.

May 7, 1942

[Forced to] work on airfield for Japs. Hot as heck!

May 8, 1942

Forced by Japs to bury American dead. God! What sights! Some were lying in foxholes bloated up twice their natural size! Buried one who had his hands tied to a tree with brutal marks all over his body, showing clearly what type of death he must have died when one of those cruel Japs got him. Some were torn up pretty bad, and after lying in the sun two or three days, the flies and smell from those poor boys' bodies was almost unbearable!

8:00 p.m.

Carried heavy load of Jap landing equipment on my back from the invasion point to top side of the island, about a three-mile hike. Thirsty as heck before I got there.

May 9, 1942

Sent to 92nd Garage [*an open-air, flat, ten-acre area on the south shore*] where about 1,200 prisoners were jammed into a very small space almost on top of one another. [11]

May 10 to May 22, 1942

With very little food and water and no sanitation at all around here, diseases started breaking out and the dead are beginning to pile up. Filth and flies around here are terrible! Dead bodies still lie on top of the hill uncovered, men who died on May 5/6. We tried to get permission to go up there and bury them, but they refused us. I guess those filthy Japs don't mind this terrible smell around here at all.

After days in the open sun, the Japanese began moving the men across the bay to Manila, parading the sick, wounded, and exhausted prisoners in a humiliating fashion down Dewey Boulevard on the way to their first prison.

May 23, 1942

Several thousand of us were packed into a small Jap freighter and landed at the end of Dewey Boulevard, south of Manila. From there we were marched through Manila to Bilibid Prison, a distance of about eight miles. Saw several men get kicked around by Japs because they were too weak to make the march.

6:00 p.m.

Received my first meal, prepared by the Japs, which consisted of plain rice. Slept outside on the ground until 5:00 a.m.

May 24, 1942

We were marched to the station, jammed into closed boxcars, a hundred men to a car, and sent to Cabanatuan [*what would become the largest American POW camp in the Far East*], where we stayed overnight in a schoolyard. [12]

May 25, 1942

Left Cabanatuan for Camp III, a distance of 12 miles. Several men were unable to carry their bags so were forced to throw them away. Others managed to drag themselves to camp but died from overexposure. I managed, however, to get through with a blanket and a few other odds and ends, suffering only from the lack of water and the intense heat of the day.

May 26 to June 15, 1942

Sick from diseases. Got very weak. Nothing but rice and thin onion soup since we arrived here. Saw four men get shot for trying to escape.

General MacArthur's Army of the Pacific had been defeated in less than half a year. Like most of the prisoners who survived, Joe Minder and John Parsons would spend three and a half years in captivity. For most of the men of the 803rd Engineer Aviation Battalion, and all of the American captives of Bataan and Corregidor, eight months to a year would pass before family back home were properly notified. [13]

According to Major Gordon, General King told his men in an assembled prison camp session that 'we had been asked to "lay down a bunt to gain time." The baseball metaphor was probably the best way to explain [the "big picture" of the tragedy of Bataan and Corregidor].' The defense of Bataan thwarted Japanese timetables and planning, and forced them to commit many more troops than was expected, unsettling their ferocious drive in their conquest of the Pacific and, perhaps, Australia.

CHAPTER THREE

Captivity

The nightmare of being a prisoner of the Japanese Imperial Army was unfolding with a stunning rapidity. Joseph Minder continued to risk taking down notes and recording the horrors, never knowing if his diary would ever see the light of day. These actions must have helped to keep him going, especially when he could open himself to finding wonder and being thankful, even there.

Joe Minder

July 1 through July 3, 1942

Many men broke out with pellagra, beriberi, and scurvy, while others started losing their eyesight.[10] At this time the Japs decided to give us a little meat and mungo beans. I feel a lot better now but still darn weak. Weighed 115 pounds on July 4.

---

[10] Diseases brought on by vitamin deficiency. Various symptoms included fatigue, ulcerations, rapid weight loss, vomiting, vision irregularities, swelling, mental confusion, and lethargy.

August 1 to August 31, 1942

Still getting small amount of meat and beans but in too small amounts to do us much good. I started suffering from pellagra and scurvy along with others this past month. Many men still dying. Jay, Brozoski, and Nelson died recently. Three large details [*men who would be used as slave laborers*] left for Japan.

September 1 to September 30, 1942

Have regained a little strength back. Worked on latrine digging details and wood details outside of camp, also went to Cabanatuan once to load rice on trucks. Managed to get a little food from the Filipinos when I was on some wood details. Pretty risky business getting food from them, when our guards weren't looking, but we took those chances anyway.

October 1 to October 20, 1942

Had several hard rains in the past 20 days, making mud ankle-deep here. Japs have allowed us to have religious services but have placed certain restrictions on the way we worship, such as denying the chaplains the right to preach the gospels. I received communion on October 4 from Chaplain Brown.

October 28 to November 29, 1942

'Fifty Men to a Bucket of Rice'

Marched to Camp I at Cabanatuan, a distance of six miles, which is the main prison camp here in the Philippines. Food is scarcer now than anytime so far. Fifty men to a bucket of rice! The living conditions here are much worse than at Camp III. This camp is located in the center of huge rice paddies with swampland all around us.

The flies and mosquitoes are terrible. Two months ago they had a death rate which averaged 30 or more dying a day. Death rate has dropped somewhat, however we still have a death rate of 18 or more per day [out] of the 7,000 men who are packed here under these horrible conditions!

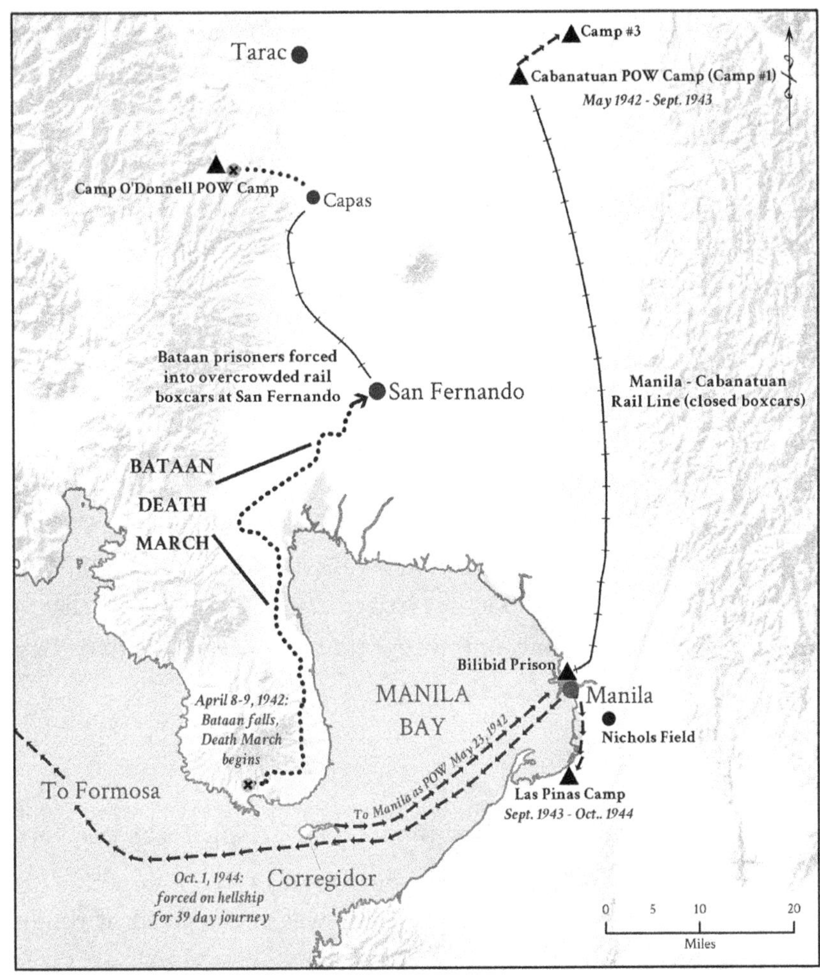

Prisoner of War Route of Pvt. Joseph G. Minder in the Philippines, May 1942-Oct 1944.

Chief Anderson and several other men from my company died. Volunteered for burial detail and have been carrying out men and burying them for the past two weeks at the rate of 15 per day. The first day was rather tough, but I don't mind it too bad now. The expression on some of their faces was horrifying at first, and not being embalmed, the smell was terrible, but I soon got used to it. Most of the men weigh less than 100 pounds when they die, but occasionally we run into one which is bloated up with beriberi and weighs twice his normal weight.

The cemetery that these boys are buried in and the improper conditions in which these darn Japs force us to bury those boys is horrible. Thank God, the mothers of these poor boys can't see any of these horrible sights.

November 30 to December 23, 1942

Things are beginning to look a little brighter around here now. The Japs have allowed the Filipinos to send us meat, mungo beans, and various other food items. Rainy season is nearly over so we go from one barracks to another without walking in ankle-deep mud. Above all, our death rate is about half from last month. My pellagra and scurvy is almost gone, but my eyes are very weak, due to certain vitamins which this diet lacks.

December 24, 1942

Attended Midnight Mass outdoors. Our arrangement was very simple, but this Mass was more impressive to me than any Midnight Mass before in my life. The altar was constructed of rough boards, the best we could get, and was covered in white sheets. Colored bottles were cut off, and candles placed in them—God only knows where they came from—served as lights for the altar. To make it more impressive and beautiful, it was an extremely clear night, with the moon and stars shining down on us as we prayed and worshipped there in our simple but heart-touching way. I'll never forget Christmas Eve 1942 as long as I live.

December 25, 1942

Christmas Day! Although we can't be home with our loved ones, we have plenty to be thankful for. This morning we all received a No. 10 package per man along with several other small gifts from the Philippine Red Cross. Much bulk food also came from the American Red Cross, which will be rationed out through the mess hall. But best of all, many new types of medicines came with the American Red Cross food. I know there were men today who offered prayers of thanks who probably never before in their life thought of thanking God for his wonderful blessings. This is the happiest day so far for most of us since the war began! Morale is sky-high around here tonight.

CHAPTER FOUR

Into the Fray

Back home, every morning brought more news. As the situation in the Philippines was deteriorating, the American public clamored for action. The President expressed his desire to the Joint Chiefs of Staff for a military response to Japan's attacks to boost public morale. Out of his wishes evolved the top-secret planning for the Doolittle Raid, where aircraft carrier-based planes would drop their bombs over Tokyo and Yokohama, and would attempt to crash land in China. The heavily modified B–25 bombers would be guided by a volunteer force of pilots who would train secretly before transferring to the West Coast to commence the operation. It was a deadly mission, as no one had attempted to fly a bomber off one of the early aircraft carriers.

Dorothy Schechter was a young civilian worker who had a ringside seat to the secret preparations for this first offensive action against Japan, a raid now legendary for its audacity and daring. She was in charge of accounting on various Army Air Corps bases for goods brought onto base to be sold to military personnel. At one base in South Carolina in early 1942, she was the only woman authorized to be on the premises, which made for some interesting moments.

Dorothy Schechter

When I got there I was the first woman on the base. They had no other women and they put me in a tent [*laughs*]. And one of the strange things about being the only woman on the base is the fact that there is no latrine for women on a base! And they suggested that I use the men's latrine, but call the military police each time I had to use it, so you can imagine what it was like for me. I had to call them up and say 'I have to use the latrine'; they would come and everything. They had to have their military arms with them, and so that's what I had to do. They were all very nice about it. But then after about a month they decided they needed to do something more than that. And so they found me a desk in the administrative building, which was very near the hangar, and they also made an actual ladies' room for me!

While I was on the base there working, there were a lot of B–25s... I don't know if you know what they are. They are military bombers, small ones, twin-tailed. And I saw there were a lot of them and I had been told this base was a transitional base, from a one-motor to a two-motor plane, which was very dangerous. There were numerous crashes. We would be working and the lights would go out and we would know that there had been a crash.

Practicing for the Doolittle Raid

I did not know at that time that most of the B–25s were for Jimmy Doolittle's group that he was forming. Of course, my whole story, it's like a jigsaw puzzle. I knew what I experienced, and then during the years that followed I learned from books what the rest of the story was, so that I had to put it together. So what I am saying to you is the combination of the two. But I have material that proves that it's all part and parcel of a real story.

So the master, the first sergeant, called me up one day and said to come up to the hangar area, up on the catwalk—you know what that is? Well, you know what a hangar is? Huge, huge, big place where they repair the airplanes. And then up along around the inside is like a catwalk. You go up the metal steps, you can walk, and you can see through it, and he said to come up to meet him and not say anything. So I went up the back way and went up on the catwalk, and he put his finger to his mouth [*makes 'shushing' gesture*]... We looked down at a group of men and that was the first time I saw Jimmy Doolittle...at that time he was going to several B–25 bases, gathering men, the best of the B–25 pilots, for the eventual raid over Tokyo off of the aircraft carrier *Hornet,* and it was the first time they had ever done that, to have bombers actually take off from an aircraft carrier. And they were sent to Columbia Army Air Base, which is in South Carolina, where I was. All of them were there for a while.

I thought there were a lot of B–25s. I couldn't imagine that a small base like that would have so many of them, but even they did not know what they ... were going to be doing. They thought they were to be watching for submarines in the Atlantic. They were supposed to be doing this sort of thing, and they didn't know until they got on the *Hornet,* at sea, what the actual thing was about...

There was some crazy training going on. And, of course, I didn't know what it was about. But they were putting chalk across the runways, with a flag on either end. And they took me out and showed me one, and the pilots had to take off before they hit that chalk mark on the runway. But the soldiers were telling me the strange part of it was, as soon as the pilots knew they could do that, they moved the chalk line closer and closer to the start point.

Well, we had no idea what it was, but they were training them to take off from the aircraft carrier—and they did it, every single one of them. And then they made a book and a movie from the raid called *Thirty Seconds over Tokyo.*

"Take off from the deck of the USS HORNET of an Army B–25 on its way to take part in first U.S. air raid on Japan." National Archives.

Launched on April 18, 1942, 600 miles from Tokyo, the sixteen-bomber raid did little physical damage, but it did bring the war home to Japan in a way never experienced before. In the United States, it was considered a success and garnered much attention at a time when America was still trying to come to grips with how exactly to stop the Japanese offensives.

Internment

Later in the war Dorothy was assigned to the West Coast, where she encountered many Japanese-Americans interned during the war.

Towards the end when my husband [*a lawyer in Army intelligence*] was shipped out to California, I followed and there I did the same job I did in all the other air bases. I had to go every morning to the satellite base, collect the money, and see that everything was provided for the soldiers. And the first few days, I didn't see anybody. But after a few days there were two ladies of Japanese descent who came to stand near where I drove my car up to the office. And they just were standing up like this and bowed, and I said, 'Good morning' and they said, 'Good morning.' They seemed happy that I was talking to them, and then I went on about my way.

But after a week or ten days there were more and more people coming to greet me with this bowing thing. And I thought, 'What's going on?' Finally one of the ladies spoke and said, 'Is there any possibility that you could buy something for us from the main base if we give you the money for it?' And I said, 'Of course! I'd be glad to do it.'

I did not know they were Japanese internees—I did later, and as it turned out, I was in the middle of it. And this is what I did for them all during the time I was there. And they were so appreciative of it, if you realize how much they lost... they had their businesses, their homes, everything was taken away from them, and they were sent into camps behind wire... And it wasn't only about 20 years ago that the United States made some attempt at remuneration, not too long ago. But they of course didn't get nearly as much as what they should have gotten.[11]

---

[11] It is not clear if the women of Japanese descent were actually interned at this instance. Nevertheless, the episode illustrates the mood of the times that targeted Japanese-Americans.

Miracle at Midway

At the same time the men and women at Corregidor were being forced to capitulate in the Philippines, the first major U.S. naval engagement against the Imperial Navy was shaping up at the Coral Sea in the South Pacific bordering New Guinea, the Solomon Islands, and New Caledonia on May 4-8, 1942. The Japanese, bent on making a landing at Port Moresby in their push for isolating and perhaps invading Australia, were surprised at sea by the carriers Lexington and Yorktown. This was the first sea battle in history where the opposing fleets never even caught sight of one another, separated by 175 miles of ocean as the carrier-based pilots inflicted all of the damage. Each side lost a carrier and had another heavily damaged, so in conventional wisdom the engagement was seen as a draw, but it highlighted the American ability to level the playing field against a more experienced and aggressive foe.

A month later the Japanese sent a strike force of over 150 vessels to attack the U.S. base in the Midway Islands, a thousand miles from Pearl Harbor. The plan was to lure the remnants of the U.S. Fleet at Pearl Harbor and annihilate it once and for all, eliminating the strategic threat of the United States in the Pacific. It was not to be; Navy cryptologists had broken the operational code of the Imperial Fleet, and the Japanese trap backfired. In an amazing show of daring, Admiral Nimitz ordered his heavily outnumbered fleet out of Pearl Harbor to try to surprise the Japanese. Despite incurring early and heavy losses, the 'miracle at Midway' allowed the United States to send Admiral Yamamoto's fleet limping back to Japan short four of the six aircraft carriers with which they had attacked Pearl Harbor six months previously. In addition to losing nearly 250 aircraft and over 3,000 men, the Japanese High Command placed wounded survivors in quarantine and kept them from their own families to contain news of this astonishing defeat.[14] Historian John Keegan called it "the most stunning and decisive blow in the history of naval warfare."[15]

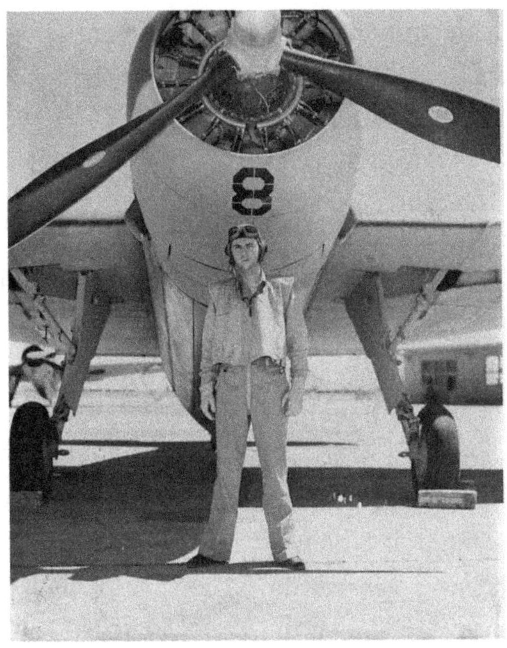

John A. Leary, July 1943.
Courtesy Leary family.

John A. Leary was born in Hudson Falls in 1919, and finished high school in 1936. As a kid he was interested with events unfolding in Europe, and kept a scrapbook of world events that would later prove to be prescient in regard to what destiny had planned for him. Like many boys, he was fascinated by flight and the dashing aces of World War I, and in hanging around a local airfield, he got the feel for the canvas-covered biplanes of that age. The old hands took a liking to him, and John was taught the rudiments of flying at age twelve.

After high school, young John tried to enlist to fly, but his father put an end to that idea, for a time. Instead, he went to Syracuse University, and immediately upon graduation in June 1941 was accepted into the Naval Air Service. A year later, he was commissioned as a Navy pilot and mastered aircraft carrier take-offs and landings, first in the Aleutian Islands, sometimes flying by instruments due to the dense fog and darkness, calculating life and death mathematical readings in his head to get him back to the ship. In a 2001 seminar, he offered his perspective on these first major naval engagements in the Pacific.

John A. Leary

Midway was the turning point of the war. We had been at the Battle of the Coral Sea where we lost the carrier *USS Lexington.* The *Yorktown* was badly damaged, but anyway, the Japanese did not continue to invade New Guinea or Australia.

Days later, after Coral Sea, when we arrived at Pearl Harbor, we thought we were going home because the *Yorktown* was so badly damaged. But Admiral Nimitz had other ideas and he outranked most of us [*laughter from audience*]. They put on civilian workers to repair the damage, and when the *Yorktown* sailed 72 hours later, it had quite a few civilian workers still aboard repairing. They never mentioned their losses in the war.

The Yorktown was lost at Midway.

Yorktown was hit again at Midway and they did abandon ship, but she stayed afloat and looked like she could make it, so about 200 men went back on board and unfortunately they were still on it when it was taken down by a submarine. But the battle was won principally, I think, from our intelligence, because we outmaneuvered and outsmarted the Japanese... But with the help of God the battle was won by the American carrier pilots, and [those] on *Yorktown* went over and landed on *Enterprise,* some on *Hornet.* So we were holding our own, and later I ended up at Guadalcanal, not too long after the Marines landed.

CHAPTER FIVE

A Turning Point-Guadalcanal

In any war, an apt metaphor is that sometimes hands are forced to be played before all the cards have been dealt. So it would be at Guadalcanal, the six-month-long battle that pitted young Americans for the first time offensively on land against veteran Japanese troops who were being reinforced on an almost nightly basis. While military planners in Washington debated these Marines' fate, they would fight on tenuously to survive. Indeed, it would be the incredible actions of these men, against overwhelming odds in the vicious jungle fighting, that would simply force the establishment in Washington to take notice.

As the first months of 1942 unfolded, an all-out military offensive against the Japanese seemed simply out of the question. General Alexander Archer Vandegrift began pulling together his 1st Marine Division that spring, and advance elements were gathering in New Zealand. It was expected that the division would have an additional six months to prepare for amphibious landings and jungle fighting, and no American offensive action was planned until early 1943. However, in mid-June, following the victory at Midway, intelligence showed that the Japanese were constructing an air base in the Solomon Islands at Guadalcanal. If they finished it, the noose menacing Australia would be complete and the Allied counteroffensive would become very difficult to implement and sustain. An amphibious landing had to be implemented immediately, the scale of which had not been attempted since the Allied disaster during the World War I debacle at Gallipoli in 1915—and with much less time to plan. 'I could not believe it,' General Vandegrift later recalled of the plan[16].

Nevertheless, the Japanese advance had to be checked, and out of these desperate times came the First Marine Raider Battalion. Schooled by Marine veterans of Central America and China operations in the 1920s and 1930s, specially selected young men became a lightly armed, highly mobile commando unit that could conduct operations in the sub-equatorial jungle, the vanguard for larger troop landings to follow. Edson's Raiders, named after their highly respected colonel, 'Red Mike' Edson, would earn combat honors in eighteen weeks of violent engagements at Guadalcanal that are unparalleled in Marine Corps history. Twenty-four Navy ships would be named in honor of individual members of the battalion before the war was over.[17]

Remarkably, out of the 900 original Raiders trained in punishing conditions, two veterans who resided around the "Falls" were members of this elite group. Robert Addison, originally from Ohio, would later spend 29 years as the Athletic Director of Adirondack Community College (SUNY Adirondack). He had a personal 'bone to pick' with the Japanese—his 19th birthday was that day of the attack on Pearl Harbor.

Robert Addison

I was home celebrating my birthday with a few of my friends. It was a Sunday and my youngest sister had gone to the movies. She came back and she said they stopped the movie and said they bombed Pearl Harbor. So that's when I heard about it. So we turned on the radio—no television during those days—and that's about all you could hear.

A month after the war started, I joined the Marine Corps, January 7, 1942, and was sent down to Parris Island for boot camp. Prior to the war, boot camp had been thirteen weeks. But they had to get a division; they had parts of a division, so they had to get a division ready quickly, so they cut boot camp to six weeks.

By this time, so many recruits were signing up that boot camp had to be cut short and advance training taken somewhere else.

Boot camp to me was not much [*snaps his fingers*] because I found that playing high school football in Ohio was harder than boot camp was. You were supposed to spend two weeks of close-order drill, three weeks on the rifle range, and a week of extended-order drill. Well, when it came close to the time for us to go to the rifle range, there was not any room down there because we recruits were coming in at five hundred a day, so after our close-order drill they gave us the week of extended-order drill and put five hundred of us on a train and shipped us up to Quantico to fire at the rifle range. When I was just about ready to finish boot camp they were filling up and forming this 'Raider' battalion.

22 Miles with a Pack and a Rifle

Addison made the cut. When interviewed by a Marine captain, he was told that the Raiders would be the 'cream of the Marine Corps' but was also warned that their mission would be likely 'first in and last out.'[18] *He was accepted and was assigned to a mortar squad in the fledgling Raiders. More training would follow. Some days they would march, fully equipped, dozens of miles in the day, only to turn around and re-navigate the same terrain in the dark, through swamps and across rivers.*

When we got into the Raider Battalion, then we really got into the force. On a Saturday morning we would go on a 22-mile, full pack, forced march in the morning and then they gave us liberty in the afternoon...And Edson was known for getting people in good physical condition. He was the type of guy, you would follow him anyplace, because what he would do when we were on these forced marches, he would stop and watch everybody go by and he would 'walkie-talkie' to the head of the column, and they would hold up and he would start jogging past the men double-time up to the head of the column... When we came in at the barracks he would stand there and watch every man go by and give compliments to us, you know, 'good job, good job.' That's the type of leader he was. Everybody practically worshipped him. He was quite a leader.[12]

Born in 1919, the other original Raider, Gerry West, pointed out to his teenage interviewer that his birth was unusual because he was born in the 'hospital at Glens Falls, and not at home.' He grew up in Fort Ann and, like many youths during the Depression, decided to enlist in the Marine Corps following high school. He was already a Marine when he heard the news of Pearl Harbor.

Gerry West

I'll never forget it. I was sitting in a barracks in Quantico, Virginia. I had the duty that weekend, and there were about ten of us

[12] Merritt 'Red Mike' Edson was born just over the border from Washington County in Rutland, Vermont, in 1897. Retiring as a USMC Brigadier General, he returned to Vermont and became the first Commissioner of the Vermont State Police.

there listening to the Washington Redskins football game which had just started; maybe five minutes they had been playing. It started at one o'clock, and something like 1:05 they broke in with the announcement saying that the Japanese had attacked Pearl Harbor. You heard so much about all these meetings [*Japanese delegation in Washington, D.C.*], but still you didn't expect something like that to happen. So I couldn't believe it really, to tell you the truth.

West would join the Raiders and under expert tutelage be the first in his battalion to qualify for specialty pay as an expert in mortars, demolition explosives, and as a machine gunner.

They came out with the $6.00 a month pay for the four guys that were gunners, and I was the first one in the battalion to get that six bucks. Well, when you're making $21.00 a month, you make six more dollars, that's a big raise... Later, I went from private to platoon sergeant in fourteen months in the Raiders.

The Raiders embarked on a cross-country train journey and were then carried across the vast South Pacific to Samoa for two weeks on reconverted World War I destroyers. Strenuous training would continue with night operations, punishing hikes in rugged mountain terrain, hot, muggy weather, frequent rain, and steep ridges with slippery trails. They practiced landings in inflatable rubber boats, survived on skimpy rations, and were sometimes pushed from five in the morning until ten or twelve at night. Judo and bayonet training, first aid, stalking, and demolition were all part of the schedule.[19]

The Landings

In order to secure Guadalcanal, the Raiders were assigned to take the neighboring island of Tulagi, where they would be up against the best of the Japanese combat forces, the rikusentai—the Japanese Special Naval Landing Forces. Coming in on Higgins boats[13] *in the morning hours of August 7, 1942, the Raiders clashed for three days in vicious fighting characterized by hitherto unknown cave bunkers, their enemies' deadly sniper actions, night fighting, and their willingness to fight to the death. Thirty-eight Raiders would die, but the 350-man Japanese garrison would be eliminated with only three prisoners taken.* [20]

Robert Addison

We went ashore eight months after Pearl Harbor to the day. Our battalion was given the task to take the island of Tulagi, which was across the North Channel. And it was only a little island about half a mile wide, three miles long. Before the war, this was the island residence for the governor of the British Solomon Islands—a beautiful little island, great grounds, great fields, and big, almost mansions there. And this is where the Japanese were...

---

[13] Higgins boats, also known as Landing Craft, Vehicle, Personnel (LCVP), were flat-bottomed, self-propelled watercraft capable of ferrying 36 men to shore. Men generally entered the boat by climbing down a cargo net hung from the side of their troop transport; they exited by charging down the boat's bow ramp. [www.higginsmemorial.com/design.asp]

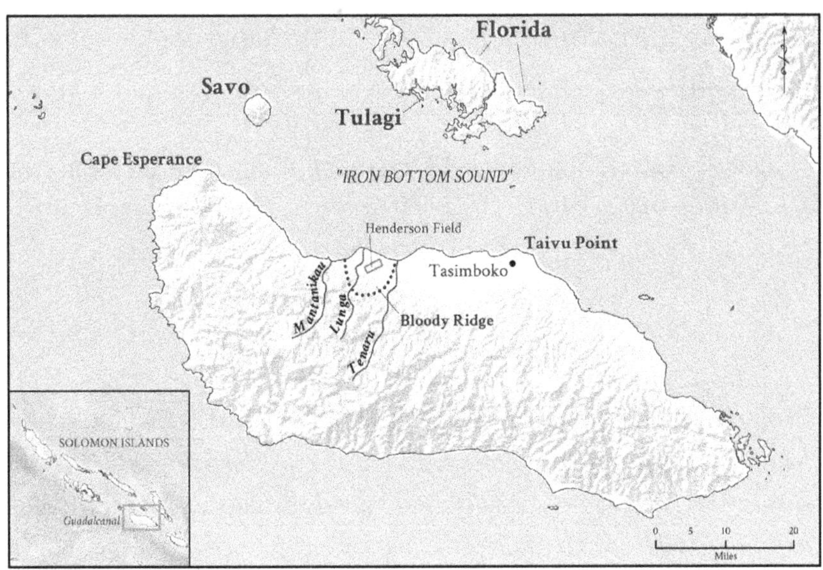

Guadalcanal, Sept. 1942.

On the first day, we had them in what we thought was a pocket... but, unbeknown to us, we had bypassed a lot of them who were in caves. And at night they came out, and then all hell broke loose in the night. They like to fight at night because they think it's a psychological thing. We think, 'Oh Jesus, they fight at night, they can see in the dark, they know what they're doing.' Well, it didn't take us long to figure out that they couldn't see any better than we could. So it took us a while to dig them out, and very few of them would surrender. We had darkened our faces. We had strips of burlap sacks painted green on our helmets, and after a few days what few Japs were left said, 'Don't let the men with the sacks on their heads get us!'

A lot of them we just left in the caves and blocked them up with explosives because they just wouldn't come out. And so it took us several more days to secure the island. Anyway, after we had taken

Tulagi, we kind of rested up a little bit, then they took us over to Guadalcanal.

Edson's Raiders, including Addison and West, were the very first Americans to engage the Japanese offensively on land in World War II.

'Confusion to the Extreme'

An hour after the Raiders landed on Tulagi, the other troops of the 1st Marine Division began to land unopposed at Guadalcanal, across the channel. Thomas Jones, another local Marine, was born in 1913, enlisted for his first tour in 1931, and rejoined later when the clouds of war began to form. His experience illustrated just how unprepared the nation was, and later, how chaotic the sea-to-land operations in the Guadalcanal campaign would be.

Tom Jones

When I was about to be drafted into the army, I decided against being drafted and reenlisted in the Marine Corps. Sometime late November or early December, we were called and sent to Parris Island… on December 7 [1941], I recall we were standing waiting in line for our noonday meal, when we got the word, someone announced the Japs were now bombing Pearl Harbor. Of course that caused great excitement with us. From then on it was a lot of speculation and wondering what would happen next.

Late in May we went aboard trains and were taken to the west coast. We left San Francisco sometime during the first week in June. We landed in New Zealand late in June or early July; we were aboard ship for about 30 days. When we arrived in New Zealand, we disembarked and I remember it was during the rainy season. I believe it started to rain every day we were there and continued until we left, and what we did was unload our ship and reload another ship[14] to be transferred somewhere north of New Zealand. What island we didn't know, but before we left New Zealand, evidently the Joint Chiefs of Staff in Washington had gotten word that the Japanese were building up an island called Guadalcanal.

Things were confused, and when I say that, it was not the homegrown garden variety of confusion, but this was confusion to the extreme... We got to Guadalcanal, then we found out we had loaded our ammunition first and all our supplies on top of our ammunition! Now this was turning out to be a combat operation and we were going to make an assault on Guadalcanal, but fortunately, opposition was not that heavy... Part of the division [*the Raiders*] was landing across the bay at another island called Tulagi. Those Marines were hit pretty hard, casualties were relatively heavy in that battalion...Anyway, to get to the ammunition, we hauled all of this material that we had above the ammunition and we threw that over the side into the Pacific Ocean! That was part of the confusion.

The Japanese, who had never before experienced defeat, were taken by surprise by the audacity of the 1st Marine Division assaults, but immediately showed their skill at nighttime naval engagements. At the battle of Savo Island off the coast of Guadalcanal, the U.S. Navy suffered one of the worst defeats in history, losing four ships and over a thousand sailors during the night. When the men on the island surveyed the carnage the following day, the Navy was gone, taking with it most of the supplies and

---

14 William Manchester clarifies: 'Wellington's [New Zealand] longshoremen chose this moment to go on strike. Drenched, sick Marines... had to load their own ships in eight-hour shifts, wrestling with soaked cardboard cartons which frequently burst open...because of the strike, they would have to attack with only ten days of ammunition and, in the words of a divisional order, other 'items actually required to live and fight.' Manchester, William. *Goodbye, Darkness: A Memoir of the Pacific War*. Boston: Little, Brown, 1987.167.

ammunition meant for the Marines on Guadalcanal. They would have to fend for themselves, and the 'Tokyo Express,' the destroyer convoys out of the Japanese stronghold at Rabaul, would be landing reinforcements nightly in the days and weeks to follow. Rabaul was the principal Japanese forward operating base in the South Pacific at New Guinea, with tens of thousands of troops in reserve.

The second part of the confusion was that a reconnaissance plane had picked up the Jap fleet headed toward us. Well, all the cargo ships got the word and left the area, but we left four cruisers behind and they didn't get the word about the Jap fleet coming down on them, so the night of August the 8th the Japs attacked our cruisers... consequently, we lost four cruisers. One of the cruisers, the *Astoria*, burnt. The next morning you looked out in the distance into the ocean and you could see the smoke. Eventually it sank.

Now we were on Guadalcanal. We had about three days' food supply in our packs, and all of our other stuff was gone. So we were now relying on Japanese supplies and equipment that we captured. Things were pretty tough for a while....

Jones was assigned to scout the Japanese.

Sometime after mid-August they sent me and Barney McCarthy and another guy out, Norbert Bush. Prior to our landing on the 'Canal,' the Japanese had landed in another spot, and it was logical that you should keep that spot in mind, because they might want to land there again sometime. So they sent us out—it was called a forward observation post. We concealed ourselves in the jungle. We arrived on the spot late in the afternoon, and no sooner than it got dark, we could see a couple of barges and they were starting to unload in that spot.

I was in charge of the post, so the next morning we kind of kept track of what we could see, and we could see they were unloading troops. And by morning the barges were gone, so I sent Bush back to report what we had seen and that left Barney McCarthy and me, and nothing happened during the day. We could look down and we could see the troops and what they were doing. Gee whiz, no sooner than it got dark again, the barges started showing up with more troops and supplies. Now I estimated there were so many troops, so I sent Barney back. Incidentally, all we had were three canteens of water and hardtack to eat.

Anyway, now Barney is gone, so it's now the third night, they are coming in again that night. And there are more troops, and I now estimated they had about 1,200 to 1,500. So I'm running out of water and hardtack, and I thought I'd better get in, so I left and went in and reported. Now that would be about the 16th or 17th of August—now I'm not sure of my dates, but anyway, we now knew… So we were expecting it [*a major attack, which came on the 21st*]. And they didn't disappoint us!

The Battle of the Tenaru

The first major attempt by the Japanese to retake Guadalcanal was to come at night. Nearly 900 battle-hardened frontline troops with over five years' fighting experience moved out silently toward Marine Corps lines.

Tom Jones

We had been able to string a single lane of barbed wire, Japanese barbed wire, we had captured. We were on one side of the Tenaru [*River, misnamed on Marine Corps maps, actually the Ilu River*], and they were coming from the other side, so they had to cross the Tenaru to get to us, and for some reason or another, I don't know, the Japanese ... attacked on a narrow front; consequently, their casualties in wounded and dead were more or less bunched. They would throw up a flare and you could see a target—boy, we laid down a sheet of steel! During the night I think I fired off a hundred rounds or better, and the rifle was an '03—it kicks like a mining mule, it's a very accurate rifle.[15] The next morning I had a jaw on me like I had the mumps, that damn rifle kicking me! Well, the next morning we counted something like 600 dead Japs and we found out it was the Ichiki Battalion; it was supposed to be the premier fighting group of the Japanese, and it had had considerable success in the Philippines and the Orient and they were hastily sent on to Guadalcanal. And that was just the first battle.

Jones was describing the first major Japanese offensive to regain control of Guadalcanal, where the enemy had 774 killed. The Marines lost 44 men. Still, night after night, the 'Tokyo Express' would continue to deliver men and supplies to the island.

Later, on another scouting patrol, he describes losing his best friend.

We were on patrol and this Jap, he shoots and he hits my buddy, Barney McCarthy. The bullet hit him in the head and knocked his helmet off. Now I'm looking around for the guy that shot. All of a sudden he comes running out of the jungle and he's about from here to the door from me [*motions*] and he doesn't see me. And he's grinning from ear to ear. Then he spots me. I couldn't get the rifle to my shoulder to aim, so I squeezed off the shot and I hit him in the

---

[15] Model 1903 Springfield Rifle, clip-loaded, 5-shot, bolt-action. It 'kicks like a mule' because the 30.06 cartridge is very powerful. Used in WWI and WWII, one WWI veteran recalled that U.S. troops in France could operate the '03 so rapidly and accurately that the Germans thought Americans had machine guns. Army Times, www.armytimes.com/legacy/rar/1-292308-269297.php.

abdominal region; he jack-knifed and he went down. He threw his rifle. I immediately reloaded.

Rage is instantaneous. He's looking at me from a crawling position. I didn't shoot him; I went and kicked him in the head. Rage does funny things. After I kicked him, I shot and killed him.

By that time, the other guys in the platoon were coming. I took Barney's religious medals off his body and put them in his pocket.

You get so that you accept death. Anyway, I didn't think too much more about it until I got back to San Francisco. Then I remembered. Barney was from San Francisco. Barney's father worked for the Pacific Industrial Supply Company.

I'm walking around San Francisco and I see this building with 'Pacific Industrial Supply' on it. So I go in, to find his father. I asked the receptionist if they had a Mr. McCarthy. He owned it. I asked if I could see him. I told her to tell him I was Barney's friend and I was with him when he was killed. Mr. McCarthy came running out and that was the beginning of a real good friendship.[21]

Tom Jones saw much more action on the 'Canal.'

For the next four months it was very heavy fighting and battles at sea. Off the coast of Guadalcanal, the waterway there, they gave the name of the 'Iron Bottom Sound.' I think that fifty-some ships were sunk within a couple months there in these naval battles with the Japs. On a nightly basis we held no more than a mile of beachfront property, and we were consolidated in that area and the Japs would come down nightly with their cruisers and battleships and shell us. They'd get out of there before morning because we still had a few airplanes that could bomb them. That went on until sometime in October, when things began to change. The Japs would attack but we were able to beat them off.

Edson's Raiders Come Ashore

The Raiders were then assigned to be transported from the now-secured Tulagi to Guadalcanal following the Battle of the Tenaru.

Robert Addison

It was four or five o'clock in the afternoon when we got towards Guadalcanal. They were debating whether to have us stay on ship overnight or take us to shore. They decided to take us to shore. We had no sooner stepped on Guadalcanal, and the ship was gone! The Japs came over and bombed it, and in three minutes, it was down. That was one of the first close calls that we would remember.

The Raiders spent the next eighteen hours trying to rescue the oil-slicked survivors of the disaster. Six nights later two other transports were cut to pieces by Japanese destroyers, and the survivors deliberately run over and machine gunned in the water.[22] *For the Marines on shore, such actions by the enemy would steel their hearts.*

The First Raider Battalion was now tasked to the village of Tasimboko, where the Japanese reinforcements were landing. They also secured vital supplies and information about the intention of the Japanese to retake American-held positions.

Gerry West

We were there about eight days and they decided we'd make a raid on a place called Tasimboko, because the Japanese had been landing troops night after night. They would send a few hundred down on destroyers, land them, and get out of there before daylight.

The general [*Vandegrift*] kind of wanted to know what was going on, so that was the only way to find out. We made a landing early in the morning of September the 8th and found out that, yes, there was a considerable force at Tasimboko, which had already left there.

Robert Addison

Prior to our landing, the main force had moved back up into the jungles, and I think there were probably about 3,500 of them, and they left four pieces of artillery there which they were going to use on us when they attacked us. So we destroyed the artillery and pulled it out to sea. We blew up an ammunition dump, and we destroyed the food that we could not carry back with us. They had bicycles and everything there.

The Battle of Bloody Ridge

Gerry West

So the colonel [*Edson*] came back, and the next morning, he told the general the situation. He estimated there were three or four thousand troops there, and that's when we went up and manned this position, which turned out to be where the Battle of Bloody Ridge was three days later.

Most of the Japanese at Tasimboko had pulled back into the jungle. The Raiders took as much food and medicine as they could carry, and destroyed the rest, cutting open sacks of rice and fouling it with urine or gasoline. They also captured intelligence documents that showed a major action was planned to retake the airstrip that the Marines held, now dubbed Henderson Field. Colonel Edson convinced General Vandegrift to allow him to set up his Raiders on the ridge overlooking the airfield. The subsequent two-night Battle of Bloody Ridge would prove to be one of the most decisive of the six-month-long engagement.

Robert Addison

We got back into that perimeter defense. There was this spot on the longer ridge that was not covered, so that's where we were, because Colonel Edson had served in China before the war with contact with the Japanese military, so he knew the Japs—in fact, sometimes he knew what they were going to do before they did! He just knew that was where they were going to attack. Again they fought at night, and the first night they were scrimmaging, they were feeling us out and so forth... [And] the more we read and learn about this today, the scarier it gets. Poor Gerry, after our book came out,[16] he couldn't sleep for three nights because he found out that first night he was out on patrol, he didn't know it, but he was within a hundred yards or so of a whole battalion of Japanese! Fortunately they didn't meet, and about that same time I was out on an outpost that night. They didn't hit my outpost, but they did hit a couple others and overran them.

Gerry West

It's kind of hard to explain because you can't say you're scared then because there are too many things going on. You're probably more scared afterwards, when you think about all the things that happened, than you are right when it's happening.

---

[16] Alexander, Colonel Joseph H. *Edson's Raiders: The First Marine Raider Battalion in World War II.* Annapolis: Naval Institute Press, 2000.The definitive book on Edson's Raiders. Both Addison and West are profiled in it.

One or two Raiders were captured, interrogated, and tortured with blades during the first night. The whole battalion could hear their screams, remembered one Marine[23]. The Japanese would also taunt the Marines, trying to get the Americans to reveal their positions.

Well, anyway, the next day, Colonel Edson pulled us back a little more, and the next night, they hit us in an onslaught! [17]Another thing that helped protect us was the 11th Marines, which were artillery, and they were lobbing in 75s, 105s [*mm shells*], within 100 yards of us. If the Japanese had probed a little bit when they attacked us that second night, they would have found that we had *nothing* on our left flank, nothing. They could have probed and essentially surrounded us, and when I looked back the next morning, I thought they had. But it was the 5th Marine Regiment who had been back there waiting, and there they started to move up forward through us.

Anyway, they did not get through us; if they had gotten through, they would've had the airstrip back. The next morning, a Japanese plane was so confident of victory that he came in to land, and you can imagine the reception he got! Anyway, so we went through off the ridge, and it became known now as 'Edson's Ridge,' or most of us just refer to it as 'Bloody Ridge.' We had 50% casualties that night, and we went back into the coconut grove [*the original base of operations*].

---

[17] Edson to his officers: 'They [the Japanese] were testing. They'll be back. I want all positions improved, all wire lines paralleled, a hot meal for the men. Today dig, wire up tight, get some sleep. We'll all need it.' Edson and Raider Major Ken Bailey would receive the Medal of Honor for their actions on the Ridge. Manchester, William. *Goodbye, Darkness: A Memoir of the Pacific War* (Boston: Little, Brown) 1987. p.189.

On September 14, 1942, first light revealed over a thousand Japanese dead on the ridge.[24] *Outnumbered five to one, for two nights the Raiders held on against Japanese shelling by sea and Imperial troops, and the battle has become legendary in Marine Corps history.*

Gerry West

It was probably the decisive battle of the whole campaign. In fact, history will record that without the Raider Battalion, we probably would not have held Guadalcanal. No question about it. I'm not saying that because I was in the Raider Battalion, but anyone who has studied Marine Corps history can attest to the fact that we saved the airfield those nights, because without it, it would have been another Bataan Death March. In the Battle of Bloody Ridge, just to give you an idea, two men in our battalion received the Congressional Medal of Honor and there were thirteen Navy Crosses awarded to men in our battalion just for that one battle, which is unheard of.

The Battle of the Matanikau River

The First Marine Raider Battalion would then be assigned to assist Lt. Col. Chesty Puller at the Battles of the Matanikau River, a jungle river about two hundred yards wide where it emptied into the bay near the airfield. It would change hands several times, and the fighting would be equally brutal. Nerves were also on edge. In total darkness, jungle noises, reptilian sounds, exotic birds screeching and calling to one another through the thick and rotting foliage increased the tension and terror—some of the men had been told that the Japanese signaled to each other imitating these sounds.

Gerry West

I think probably the strangest thing that happened to me was in the first Battle of the Matanikau River, I think about a week or ten days after Bloody Ridge when we went up the Matanikau for the first time. I was standing watch on a machine gun and it was raining when I heard a big thud. I thought of the Japanese; they [*snipers*] used to tie themselves in trees. I didn't know what it was, I heard this big thud. It really scared the heck out of me, and it was a big iguana about a foot long that had fallen out of this tree. He hit the ground and scampered off. He probably was as scared as I was!

They were on one side and we were on the other, but we were able to hold them off. We went out there a second time, on October 9 and 10, about three or four days before we left the island. In the second Battle of the Matanikau, we lost quite a few guys that night.

More than 700 Japanese were killed, and the Raiders drove the Japanese back into the jungle, suffering 200 of their own casualties.

Malaria

The Marines were exhausted. Rain was constant, bivouacs flooded, clothing rotted away. The air was hot, humid, fetid, and foul. Tropical insects and illnesses plagued the men.

Gerry West

One captain got sick, and then the next day another one got sick. By that time, we had lost quite a few to both dengue fever and malaria. They hadn't necessarily been evacuated from there; we got some of them back, but they were in sick bay, you know, to recover.

Tom Jones

Now one thing about Guadalcanal was malaria. Boy, we all got that! That is something. You get chills or a fever and you could be in the hot sun, the temperature well in the 100s, and you get those chills of malaria, your teeth are chattering and you're cold. I mean cold! And that lasts just so long and then you get a fever and you think you're going to boil over! It wasn't long after that they came out with a new drug called Atabrine, which was a preventive for malaria.[18] A mosquito carries malaria; if you had malaria in your blood and a mosquito goes in and siphons out a little of your blood and he goes and bites someone else, now he's transferred it to the next one. That's how it spreads.

By mid-November, the Navy in the South Pacific had re-grouped under Admiral Bull Halsey and won the significant naval Battle of Guadalcanal, enabling it to bring supplies and Army reinforcements to the island. Although it was suppressed from the public at the time, more than 7,000 U.S. Marines, soldiers, and sailors had died at Guadalcanal. Japanese losses were much higher. By the time the last starving and dispirited Japanese troops left in February 1943, further Japanese expansion into the South Pacific was halted.

Robert Addison

They called it Hell Island, the Japanese, because they had to live out in the jungles... They had lost over 26,000 men. A lot of them

[18] The "scuttlebutt" was that the new drug caused impotence, and it did cast the skin a pale yellow/orange. Some men refused to take it; finally, a corpsman would be assigned to the chow line to witness the men swallowing the tablet before meals.

died of starvation and diseases... When they left, they left 26,000 behind.

Bob Addison and Gerry West and the rest of the Raiders departed in October for New Caledonia for 'R & R', and to prepare for a vanguard assault on New Georgia in the Solomons. Tom Jones would be joined by thousands of fresh American troops, closing out a four-month stand of isolation. In the words of historian and Pacific veteran William Manchester, "There have been few such stands in history." Winston Churchill, in his later study of the battle, concluded with his assessment: "Long may the tale be told in the great Republic."[25] *Though the fight was far from over, and hard lessons were still to be learned, astounded Japanese strategists now thought that the situation was serious indeed: the Americans would fight.*

Gerry West and Robert Addison, 2011.
Portrait by Robert H. Miller.

Robert Addison

You know, the word 'Guadalcanal' to me is just like Hudson Falls, Glens Falls, Queensbury, and Fort Edward... [*He recites*]: 'Guadalcanal, Tulagi, Tasimboko, Matanikau, Enogai, Bairoko.' You know, engrained in me. I will never forget them—it's just like yesterday.[26]

*

Striking at the Serpent's Head

John A. Leary, the Navy pilot, was particularly fond of the Marines on the ground that he would protect, flying missions out of the newly secured Henderson Field for months and inching forward with the Marines on death-dealing raids under heavy fire.

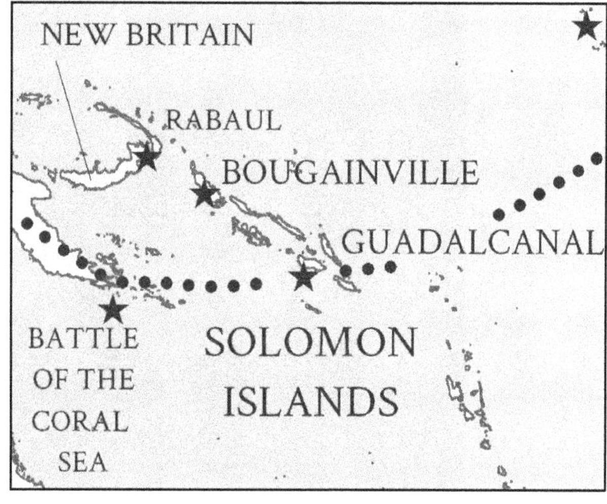

Solomon Islands Campaign.

John A. Leary

With one very short leave, we went from Guadalcanal and we ended up on Bougainville, so we covered the Solomon Islands [*by air*], all of them. And that cut the Japanese off because it destroyed their largest base at Rabaul Harbor, on New Britain. Rabaul had five Japanese airfields, a great harbor, and we could hit it from Bougainville, and we did.

Rabaul hosted hundreds of Japanese fighter planes and tens of thousands of troops. In November 1943, John Leary and his fellow pilots of squadron VC-38 [composed of fighters, dive bombers, and torpedo planes] commenced attacks in support of the Marine Corps landings below at Bougainville and hit supporting bases nearby. Bombing and strafing Japanese positions at Empress Augusta Bay on the 14th, 18 torpedo bomber fighters hit Imperial Japanese Army positions with pinpoint precision within 100 yards of the attacking Marines.

A radioman of his group recorded in his war diary: 'November 14, 1943—Attack Jap ground troops in the Empress Augusta Bay Region. Our ground troops had too much to handle so we dropped our hundred-pound bombs in their direction. We killed about 300 Japs and those who were still alive were stunned so that our troops just stuck them with a knife...[27]

Two nights later Leary was back in a night attack, sowing mines in the Buka Passage. For the next several weeks he and his radioman and gunner would be bombing and strafing Japanese positions in support of the ground campaign below. On December 13, he made a lone attack at heavy anti-aircraft positions on Puk Puk Island, scoring a direct hit with a 2000-pound bomb and successfully setting a radar building afire with his .50–caliber guns. At one point during his missions, Leary's plane was hit by anti-aircraft shrapnel, and a four-pound glowing shard lodged in his cockpit near his foot as he focused on guiding the plane back to base at Munda in New Georgia.

(L-R) Gunner L.E. Dale, Pilot John A. Leary, Radioman Dale Greslie. Courtesy Leary family.

On February 17, 1944, Leary was part of a mission of two dozen torpedo bombers to attack Japanese naval vessels near Rabaul. Diving in at masthead level, Leary's plane scored a direct hit with a 2000-pound bomb on a packed Japanese cargo ship.

John A. Leary

Those ships were reported by one of our submarines and they couldn't do anything about it because they had just finished up a patrol and were out of torpedoes. They followed these people with their naval escort into Rabaul Harbor. We were then called because we were the oldest outfit there. We were briefed, then set out somewhere around midnight. We hit them around dawn....I was probably about 55 or 70 feet above the ship...

Matthew Rozell: They could look up and see you if they wanted to. Were they firing at you pretty heavily?

Yes, they were, and it's rather difficult to fly when you have a rosary in each hand. I took more fellas in with me than I brought home that day, unfortunately. So the score wasn't 'twelve to nothing.' I was about 23 or 24. It was the principal Japanese airbase. They had five Japanese airfields defending it. They had about 200 to 250 Japanese fighters there, which could have been interesting. I was banged up a bit, but always made it back.

For his actions against Rabaul and elsewhere in the South Pacific, Leary was a recipient of the Silver Star and also the Navy Cross, second only to the Medal of Honor.[19]

---

[19] You can see Leary's flightlog, flight maps, and other bonus material at bit.ly/LearyGallery.

CHAPTER SIX

Sea Action

In 2003, I set out to interview a retiree living on the quiet boulevard leading up to our high school. I sat on his back porch with him for a few hours on a late spring afternoon. Born in 1922, he was in the Navy, serving as a radioman on a destroyer escort, and he seemed to be everywhere in the Pacific during World War II. Like John Leary, he also spent a great deal of time supporting the Marines, and saw his first action in the South Pacific in the reduction of the massive Japanese base at Rabaul on New Britain.

Alvin Peachman

I am from the coal-mining district of southwestern Pennsylvania, from a remote rural setting. I grew up in the horse and buggy days. I do remember Herbert Hoover, and I think when I was very young, a little bit about President Coolidge, too. When I was a boy we had the Great Depression, in which things were very rough. So I do remember that.

Most people then spoke of World War I. My father and his brother and my two other uncles were there. They had gone to France, and they all spoke of the western front in World War I. My great-grandfather was in the Civil War, but I didn't ever meet him. But at that time, when I was a boy, they still had Civil War veterans who were alive. I have a book from my hometown that shows them marching, and then they went by wagon, parading when they got a bit older, and then finally a few of them were in a truck or car, and then there were not any of them left; they got too old.

I was educated at a small country schoolhouse with two rooms. And then I walked to high school, three miles each way. I graduated in a class of 50; it was a fairly big school. The discipline was quite exact. I found our teachers were quite efficient.

When I heard about Pearl Harbor, I was playing ping-pong. I had just come into New York City because I had to get work. I found work on merchant ships, really as a longshoreman. I was doing it for about a week and a half when the war started. And so it didn't last long until I enlisted.

Since I had worked on ships and got to meet people, I thought I might like to be on a ship. So I enlisted in the Navy in 1942. I thought they were having a pretty good fight in the Pacific, and I was ready to get into it at that time. I was just about 20, not quite, yes, I was just about 20. A year after I got out of high school.

I went to Great Lakes, Illinois, to the University of Chicago, where I got my training, and then they gave us a lot of tests there and they determined it would be better for me to be in radio. I wanted to go into gunnery. But they gave you aptitude tests and they determine what field you should go in. I wasn't enthused about anything connected with radio at the time, but I then went into radio school. They said that was the best place for me. And I stayed there about four months for learning, and one month for guard duty; it was a very well-operated school.

Naval training was very exact. You had to march to class. You had to stand at attention before you sat down. You had to do everything just right. You couldn't speak or talk to anyone marching. I learned to swim there. And you learned how to live with people both through boot camp and school.

The Vast Pacific

From there I was shipped to California. And I got there and was very disappointed because I landed in what they call an 'ACORRN' outfit. It meant aviation, communication, ordinance radio, radar, navigation. What it involved was to get us ready for land invasions. We then were trained by the Marine Corps for rifle range and bayonet. Just like Marines, we practiced a lot of landings off the California coast, and then we set sail for the island of New Caledonia, which is a great big French island off the coast of Australia.

You see, the Pacific Ocean is so large that it encompasses about one-third of the surface of the earth. It is an enormous ocean; I think the Pacific would have more water than all the land combined in the world. It's really big! I know my first trip was 6,500 miles from California to New Caledonia.

It took us about three weeks to get there, and I know we all bathed in salt water the whole time; it was very difficult to stand it because it was like a suit of armor on you. I did not like New Caledonia because the French people there were very indifferent. They were not welcoming hosts at all.

We were jungle trained there. One day, the *President Adams,* a big troop ship manned by the regular Navy, came in. We were slated to go into Guadalcanal with the 3rd Marine Division. And they were very well equipped at that time, very fine soldiers. So, we got into Guadalcanal, which at that time was pretty well over—the battle had started a couple of months before that. As a matter of fact, two boys I grew up with who were brothers were killed in Guadalcanal.

In Guadalcanal we got further training, and I got shipped away from the Marines and got traded into [supporting the landings for] the New Zealand infantry, because they were going to make the next invasion near Bougainville at the Treasury Islands, which mainly consists of about two small islands, Mono [and Stirling]. They put us in the northern part of any land forces at that time, so our contingent supported anyone on landing ships with the New Zealand infantry division. They put on a big attack on those islands. They handled themselves really well and I got to meet a lot of good friends there. The New Zealanders were really fine soldiers, well taken care of, and we had quite a fight. They killed about five and a half Japs to one, until we secured it.[20]

We established a radio base and then they took the jungle. It was a great big rainforest. Our Seabees [*'CBs'-Construction Battalion*] came in and they took the rainforest down, and in a few weeks we had an enormous airfield there on Stirling Island, which was flat. It was not a very large island, probably about three and a half miles long and maybe a mile or mile and a half wide, but enough for what we wanted. The airfield was so large it could take two bombers at a time. The object of all of this was to knock out all the bases in Rabaul. Rabaul is in New Britain and New Britain was off New Guinea.

We were on constant aerial attack for quite a while. The Japanese at that time were very powerful. They had big airbases in Rabaul and they even controlled Bougainville. Now Bougainville was just north of us, about 20 miles, which was invaded by the Marines about, oh, maybe a week or two later [*John Leary supported this invasion from the air—see previous chapter*]. The island is about 90 or 100 miles long, maybe about 40 miles wide of rugged rainforest. They only took a small part, about 12 square miles. There was a very

---

[20] In supporting the New Zealand troops, Mr. Peachman was participating with them in their first amphibious landing since the World War I Allied disaster at the battle of Gallipoli against the Turks in 1915. So many men from 'Down Under' were lost that the anniversary of the battle is commemorated each year in Australia and New Zealand as a memorial day. After the invasion, an airstrip was built on the smaller Stirling Island.

mountainous volcano, just a very rough country out there. The natives there were very 'third world.' They were Melanesians and black people, they were very fine-looking people. They loved us and we traded with them. They got along very well with us. Only men could trade because the women were owned by the men. Boys and men would come down—they were very good at dickering.

One day, a friend and I bought an outrigger canoe so we could go out in the bay when things got safer. We stayed there from, I think it was October [1943] until early summer. And things did get better there. We fell behind the lines, things got too tame for me there. And one day, a ship came in called the *USS Witter.* Some of our men were being transferred and the captain told me and my buddy we were going to have to leave. One of us would go to New Guinea to practice what we were doing [*landings*] in the Solomon Islands. And the other would go aboard the ship. So I wanted to go aboard the ship, I wanted to get some sea action—I'd had enough of this jungle. My buddy wanted it too. So the captain gave us a game and I beat him out on it, and I got aboard the ship.

Six weeks later I got a letter from him with two pictures. That night his orders were changed and he went to Australia instead. He'd had a beautiful time on the beaches of Australia; he had two girls behind him and a nice big bottle of beer! So I kicked my own behind—I was always 'volunteered,' but this time I volunteered myself!

The Destroyer Escort

The ship duty was a lot harder than I had anticipated. On a ship you only had four hours on duty at a time and eight off, as a rule. Every morning an hour before sunrise, you had an hour duty at 'general quarters,' which was 'ready for action'; same thing in the evening, an hour after the sun went down. That's the two most dangerous times to be aboard a ship because of the cast of the ship's shadow and the silhouette out in the water; you were most apt to be attacked at that time, especially by U-boats [*submarines*], however, I was on a ship that was very deadly to U-boats. The destroyer escort had wonderful gear on it for that time. We had a crew of about 325—not a big ship, thinly armored, but we had about 26 guns on there.

Four hours on [duty] and eight hours off didn't last too long because often we'd go a thousand, or up to two thousand miles into enemy waters. Then, you would have four on, four off. Now at four off, you relieved your buddy for meals—we'd call that 'chow'—general quarters, or anything at all. You weren't off at all. Now when they put stores aboard for your provisions or ammunition, all hands had to show forth. So, if they pulled into the place at midnight, you had to get out of bed and help load these groceries or these bullets and whatever else you had. It was a lot of work. You could not backslide on anything. You had a lot of responsibility. Therefore, I found it harder than being on land.

I had a commander whose name was "Fearless Freddy." He was a very unique character who a lot of people thought was psychologically off. He loved battle extremely and he expected you to be that way, too. He wanted you to be a red-blooded American. He loved battle more than any man I've ever met. I would rank him with General Custer or General Patton or someone. He wasn't afraid of the devil! He won a big medal in the beginning of the war on the *Lexington,* and I think he was aboard every one of our group of ships when they were hit in Okinawa! They said he jinxed everything. But he loved fighting.

Rescue

I think the first thing we did, after working around Bougainville and Emirau Island, [was a rescue operation]. We got a call one day to rescue a downed Marine plane near Truk in the Caroline Islands, one of the great Japanese forward bases. This Marine plane went up there and bombed it, and it was hit by anti-aircraft fire and fell at sea. Our mission was to go and rescue them, and we were about 1,500 miles away, so we went up into that region and made a search. We would go a couple square miles in each direction, in a box-like direction. And we had no results after three days because we got another call, there had been a big wind and the plane was seen about 200 miles to the west. So we steamed in that direction and again, we could not find them. After the fourth day we were told to leave, but our captain was a very fine gentleman, and he said he could not do that. He said, 'We'll cut our power to conserve our fuel and we'll keep looking.'

On the fifth day, at night, we thought we had a submarine scare and so we started to fire depth charges; I guess it made a great big flame at night, and way out in the far distance, we noticed a flare! So, we headed out and found these Marines! Two had been killed. I believe there were five of them and their faces were three times the size of normal. They were all in the water, except for the officer who was alive but injured, and all these guys were struggling with sharks! So, we put them aboard and they were very happy and we were happy, too. One of them had my bed, later. They told us they would never criticize the Navy! It took about three or four days to bring them back to base.

They were almost on the equator. I would say I crossed the equator sixty times, being on the *Witter.* Then we took part in the New Guinea operations. In New Guinea, like everywhere else in the war, we had the 'hop, skip, and jump' philosophy. And that meant you maybe took one island out of ten, and neutralized the rest by air and sea. In New Guinea we just hopped along the coast. Now New Guinea is a very large, mysterious, beautiful island. I had been all over the coast. And it would be about from here [*upstate New York*] to Denver, Colorado, in length, extremely big and that includes great big mountains that you can see from the shore and enormous rain forests, just tremendous amounts of rain. The rain we have here is nothing. You could get a few feet in the ground in no time! I know when we lived in the tents on that island we were always wet, extremely wet. They also had large meadows and big rivers and all kinds of natives, and some of them were very black and very different.

After that, we worked that whole region and we did a lot of convoy duty, and one day after a long period of time we were to go to Australia. That night, being the radioman [on duty] taking Morse code, I found out that our orders had been changed. I think that night our captain got drunk and insulted the 'big guy' on shore! The guys were up cleaning their gear the next day to go to Australia, and I said to them, 'You're not going anywhere,' and they said, 'Well, maybe instead we will go to Hawaii,' and I said, 'Well, you're not getting in there, either.' So we had to make this long journey, 5,500 miles to Hawaii, and when we got about a hundred miles from Hawaii, we were relieved of our convoy duties! And we were ordered [back] to the Marshall Islands... [In all] it was three weeks, an 11,000 mile trip![28]

As the book went to press, I was contacted by Japan's largest news wire service, "with over 50 million subscribers worldwide, publishing articles in Japanese, English, Chinese, and in Korean..." They wanted a veteran's "reflections as we approach the 70th anniversary of the double bombings of Hiroshima and Nagasaki" (which he offers in Chapter 13, 'The

Kamikazes'). So, seventy years after the war, Mr. Peachman got to address the Japanese people.

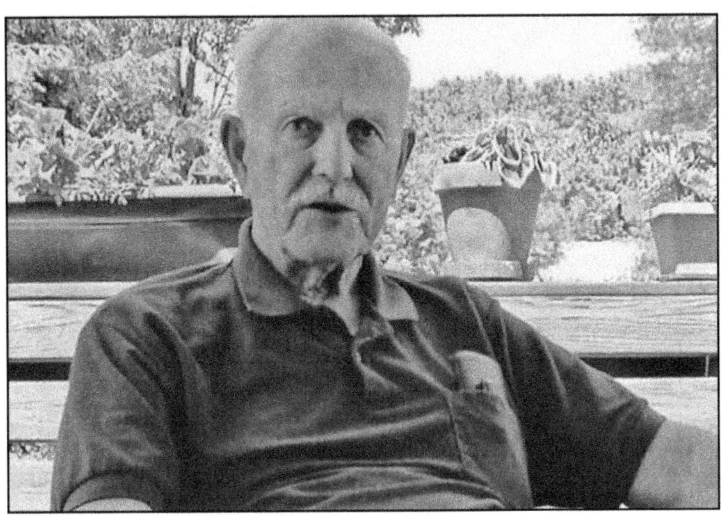

Alvin Peachman. Author photo.

Mr. Peachman was my high school U.S. history teacher. At the time, I had no idea that he had fought in World War II.

CHAPTER SEVEN

Captivity-Year 2

As 1943 unfolded, America entered its second year of war. In Europe, the Axis war machine was being confronted in North Africa and at Stalingrad. Vast amounts of men and materiel were being poured into the fight as Sicily and Italy loomed large as new Allied invasion targets, with the planning for the Normandy landings already commenced. Britain had staved off an invasion by Nazi Germany and by mid-year was resembling a floating air base as nearly a million GIs crowded encampments there to prepare for the great invasion of France.

In the Pacific, the Allies were also on the move in coordinated attacks, following up on the successes in the Solomons and elsewhere. But for prisoners of war like Joseph Minder with little concrete information, conclusions had to be teased out of scant information and the increasingly belligerent attitudes of their captors.

'Someone is Getting a Cruel Beating'

Joe Minder

January 21 to May 1, 1943

During these past four months, I have worked cutting wood, carrying hay, digging long draining ditches, planting and taking part in this useless garden, and made a few burial details. The Japs must be suffering heavy losses on their battlefronts, by the way they are treating us now. They have cut down our food again and have started beating the heck out of us, on various work details.

May 1, 1943

Every time we look around someone is getting a cruel beating for some darn thing. I got hit in the head by a bayonet, crushing my sun helmet and putting a lump on my head, which I carried for a week. My worries would be over now if that Jap would have hit me with the sharp edge of that bayonet!

May 2, 1943

Started building new garden across the road from the hospital.

May 3, 1943

Rainy season has started. The mud finished tearing up my old rotten shoes which I brought from Corregidor, so I'll have to go barefoot now.

May 4, 1943

Worked laying stone foundation for 'Burma Road,' as we called it. Several of us got the heck beat out of us for dropping large stones which were too heavy to handle as we passed them from one to another.

Joe's second year in captivity was beginning on his birthday.

May 5, 1943

Hope a year from today I am celebrating my birthday under the Yanks. I'll celebrate today by eating rice and greens soup!

May 6 to May 29, 1943

Food is constantly getting worse and these darn Formosan guards [*Japanese guards who previously had duty at the notorious island camps on Taiwan*], armed with clubs, are using them plenty every day. Saw a guy get a hose broken across his back yesterday! Two men escaped this week. So far they haven't been able to find them. That of course made things worse. After they escaped, the Japs doubled the guard and made it stricter than ever on us.

'Made to Dig Their Own Graves'

John Parsons, captured on Bataan in April 1942, described a new policy he witnessed in subsequent escape attempts.

John Parsons

Prisoners were put in groups of ten, a policy which was in effect from then on, and in the event any one man attempted to escape or made any move which might be construed as such, the other nine were put to death with him. When this did happen, the ten condemned were made to dig their own graves the afternoon prior to their deaths. Then four stakes were driven around the pit and the man was tied hand and foot spread-eagle over the hole so he was forced to stare at his own grave all night. In the morning the entire camp was turned out to witness the executions and the condemned were offered a cigarette and a blindfold, the latter of which was usually refused.[29]

'The Mothers Back Home'

Joe Minder

May 30, 1943

Japs allowed us to have memorial services for the 2,644 who have died since this camp opened, less than a year ago. About 2,100 of us attended the services. It made me shudder when I looked around at the huge crowd and remembered that there was even a larger amount than that piled on top of one another in this small, swampy half acre of ground. Only 11 months ago they were all with us, but their fear of the Japs' clubs is over now. I almost cried when I thought of the mothers back home who are waiting for their return.

May 31 to June 30, 1943

Several papers have been smuggled in from the Filipinos. We understand now why we are getting such rough treatment. Those 'Yanks' are kicking the heck out of them now! The Japs are also killing and burning down many Filipino villages now. Some Filipino guerrillas killed some Jap guards on a bridge near here and the Japs retaliated by dive bombing, and burnt the entire village.

July 1 to August 1, 1943

The Japs have enlarged this farm and are forcing the officers to work with us now. They are making everybody go barefoot now. The officers are having a heck of a time wading in this mud and walking over these sharp stones with their bare feet. I have been barefoot for three months, so my feet are pretty tough now.

August 2 to September 17, 1943

Even though we aren't getting hardly any meat or extra food from the outside, our morale is high in the sky. We found out through a paper smuggled in by a Filipino that the Yanks had landed in Italy!

This camp is much smaller now. Several hundred have been taken out to work on airfields in the Philippines, while others left for Japan. I was scheduled to go to Japan but my name was taken off. I'll be one of the first to go after the first bunch leaves here.

September 18, 1943

About 800 of us are packed and ready to leave camp to go work somewhere in the Philippines. No one knows where we are going.

12 Noon

We all made this hike of five miles pretty good and are now waiting here on trains to go towards Manila. These old shoes which I wired together are still staying on my feet. Didn't even get a blister out of that hike!

6:00 p.m.

Jap navy personnel met us here in Manila railroad station with trucks. Just found out that we are going to go to Las Pinas to work on an airfield.

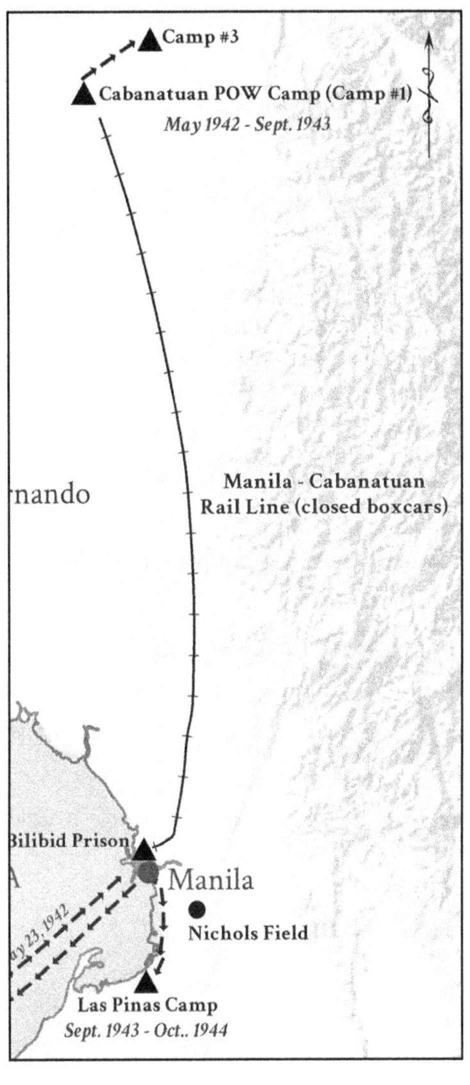

7:00 p.m.

Raining hard. We arrived here to find out this camp is only another mudhole like the grounds at Camp I.

9:00 p.m.

Dead tired. I flopped down on the floor, 50 of us packed in a small room and I got a good night's sleep. This makes the fifth prison camp which I have been in since I have been taken prisoner.

September 20 to November 15, 1943

Things have been pretty good here for the past two months. In the middle of October, 150 new men came down from Camp I to replace the 150 men who had dysentery. My buddy, Greco, was one of the ones who had dysentery, so he went back to Camp I, also.

Working conditions aren't too bad. We have been levying down rice paddies. No one has received any beatings yet. This detail wouldn't be half so bad if we only had shoes to protect our feet.

Food is a lot of fish. Although it is rotten as heck we boiled it up and made fish soup using heads, guts, and even the bones. Some of the guys can't do it, but I force it down because I know there is a lot of protein in it. In fact, I'm not suffering from pellagra or scurvy anymore and my eyes don't bother me much now. We also received a little extra food from the Philippine Red Cross.

November 16 to November 23, 1943

Started working harder now, digging deep drainage ditches. They started using their clubs. I thought these guards wouldn't be so bad, but they are as rough as those Japs at Camp I. Frank Bollinger, myself, and about 50 others got beat across the back by a raging drunk supervisor about a week ago. I'm still carrying some of those club marks.

Three and a half thousand miles away in the south-central Pacific, unbeknownst to Joe and his fellow prisoners, an intense battle was winding down at a tiny coral atoll called Tarawa in the Gilbert Islands.

November 24, 1943

Not a bad Thanksgiving. Each one of us received a No. 10 food parcel from the American Red Cross. Those candy bars and the cheese and corned beef are wonderful. We stayed up until two this morning drinking coffee and eating. We will at least have our bellies full until we finish that final bit of American food.

November 25 to December 24, 1943

We have made connection with the Filipinos out at work and they are selling our American cigarettes on the black market in Manila and are giving us food and money for them. Hope none of us gets caught dealing with them. Japs have already said they would kill us if we got caught dealing with the Filipinos.

December 25, 1943

Christmas Day! Each of us received another food parcel. Also about half of us received American Red Cross GI shoes. I have gone without shoes so long now I doubt if I will have strength enough to carry those heavy shoes, especially through this deep, sticky mud.

CHAPTER EIGHT

Islands of the Damned

As 1943 turned into 1944, the objective turned to cutting off and destroying Japanese forward positions still operating in the South Pacific while also taking the Marshall and Mariana Islands in the Central Pacific, ratcheting up the pressure on the enemy in simultaneous operations. Coral Sea, Midway, and Guadalcanal had demonstrated America's grit and mettle, but the first test of a new type of amphibious landing operations for the coral islands was at the invasion at Tarawa Atoll in the Gilberts in November 1943. It was a three-day bloodletting and a brutal lesson for the American forces; over 1,000 Marines and nearly 700 sailors were killed in less than 80 hours, and Japanese dead numbered nearly 4,700, with only seventeen prisoners taken.

The island battles of 1944 set the stage for the major operations to follow in 1945. For the Japanese, it would be do-or-die. Entire garrisons were committed to fighting to the death in a tradition that celebrated suicide before surrender, condemning them and thousands of Americans to death.

Hailing originally from the Bronx, Ralph Leinoff was assigned to the 4th Marine Division as part of a machine gun squad.

Tarawa

Marines Under Fire, Tarawa, November 1943. USMC. Public domain.

Ralph Leinoff

Tarawa was an atoll island. I don't know if you're familiar with a map of the Pacific, but it consists of a lot of underground mountains, which really, above the water, become 'atolls,' tiny little islands. And the operation before us was Tarawa, and we took heavy losses on Tarawa, because we were using Higgins boats, which were not able to negotiate the coral reefs. We got hung up on the coral reefs, which meant that the men all had to get to shore; they had to wade through hundreds of yards of water to get through. It's very shallow water in the coral reefs. And of course the coral is very sharp. It would tear your shoes, and they were sitting ducks; there was no place to get cover. So we took an awful beating on Tarawa. At that time, then, it was decided that we have to do something else.

We can't use the Higgins boats—Higgins boats were good in that they were very, very fast. They moved right along. But we needed a tracked vehicle, like a tank that could float. And they invented the...the half-track, which was a true carrier, an open-top, true carrier, and that could ride right over the coral. If you got in it, it moved very slow; it didn't have propellers on it. The cleats on the treads, the tank treads, were the propulsion device. It would push the water back and the vehicle would go forward. And it held maybe about ten men or so, but it was very, very slow-moving, and we had casualties.

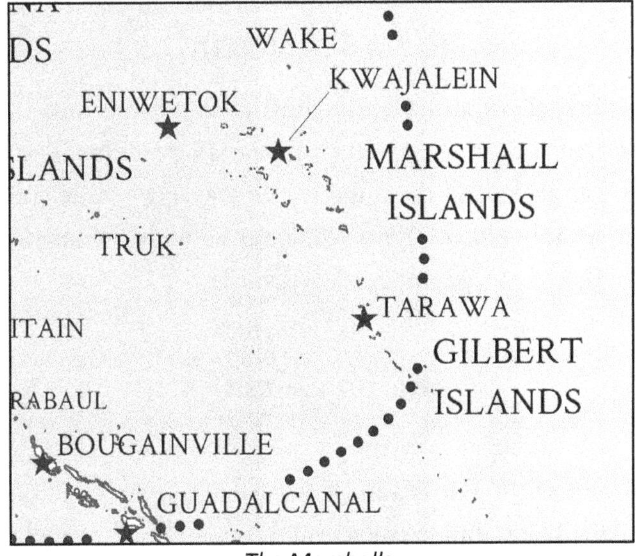

The Marshalls.

The Marshall Atolls

With its tiny airfield, Tarawa became a necessary stepping stone to the Marshall Island atoll group, and thence to the much larger islands in the Marianas, from where the sleek new B–29 bombers now rolling off the assembly lines at home would find the range to the cities of Japan. Here, in the Central Pacific, working in tandem with the burgeoning U.S. Navy under Admiral Nimitz, U.S. Marines and Navy flyers advanced on island after island in 1944 and 1945, supported by Navy corpsmen and Army units.

Operation Flintlock began in early February 1944 with a joint Marine-Army assault in the Marshalls at Kwajalein Atoll, followed by a Marine landing 330 miles northwest at Eniwetok Atoll, which consisted of about 30 tiny islands. The three largest were Engebi, Eniwetok, and Parry, and all were intensely defended; aerial photography had proven that the Japanese were slowly building these islands into defensive positions.

Alvin Peachman

The Marshall Islands were beautiful. We came into this atoll, which was one of the most beautiful places I ever saw. The interior [lagoon] was green and the outside reef was like a large ring, never too wide, no more than about a half a mile wide. In some places it was just a few yards, or one hundred yards.

Ralph Leinoff

Kwajalein was a flat island. It was of strategic value because it had an airfield on it, but there was no place for the Japanese to really dig in deep. They had their pillboxes, but they were able to resupply their own ships from Kwajalein, and we had to take it. And we wanted that airfield. So the Navy Air Force did a very good job of bombing the island, so when we got there it was comparatively light resistance. As I say, we had losses, but not on the scale with what was coming up.

The 22nd Regiment of the 6th Marine Division included twenty-one-year-old Joseph Fiore of Glens Falls. He graduated from St. Mary's Academy and enlisted in the Marine Corps in 1942. He described his first encounter with the enemy.

Joe Fiore

I made my first landing on Engebi Island in Eniwetok Atoll. I was scared—yes, I was scared. That was the first island, and the priest heard confessions aboard ship. We were up at four o' clock in the morning, and we went down to the cargo nets into our Higgins boats. But before that, they gave us breakfast, which was a steak with three or four eggs right on top of it, and that was our last meal. Everybody said it was going to be our last meal before we get to get out of here. I was in an amphib [*amphibious landing craft*] with no ramps; we had to go over the side, jump maybe three or four feet from the ground. And all I could think of was, when I jump out of this thing here, I am going to be facing a Jap holding a machine gun on me.

Well, when I hit the ground I looked around and I didn't see anything. We had landed just at the end of the runway that we were there to take because we were 'island hopping,' and every time we took an island, it usually had a runway for planes—our fighter planes. We just start walking on the runway, going up to the other end of the island where headquarters was. Three or four of us were talking as we were walking; we weren't running or anything like that because we didn't see any Japanese. All of a sudden I looked down to the ground and I said, 'Jeeper's sakes, look at those little marks there! They look like Mexican jumping beans!' Well, there were Japanese snipers way back and they were firing, and their bullets were hitting the ground at our feet! We didn't realize it, and then we started running! We made the rest of the island in no time flat. Tony Luciano[21] would've been real proud of me because I broke more records on that day!

We secured the island and spent the night there, which was hectic. That's when the Japs would try to sneak into our positions, but we had machine gunners covering us. The Navy left an awful lot of bomb craters from huge shells, 16-inch shells that exploded on the runway. So we got in those big holes in the ground—it was in the coral reef—and just dug into the side and waited until daylight. When daylight came, then they'd send us back to our ships out in the harbor to get ready for the next operation, which was in the same atoll, Eniwetok Atoll. I would say [the operation] was about four days later, Parry Island, and that's where I got my first Purple Heart.

I used an awful lot of hand grenades in those days. As a matter of fact, I have an article that a war correspondent wrote up on me and called me the 'Pineapple Kid.' I used 70 hand grenades in one day and one night on that island, blowing up foxholes. And underneath the coconut trees, the Japs would build a little nest for themselves, so I was working my way up to an installation that I was going to blow up, and my partner, Seymour Draginsky from New York, Polish Jew, he was backing me up. And a mortar came into our area, and that's when a mortar landed over to my side, and I already had pulled the pin of the grenade. But there's a spoon that goes in the palm of your hand here [*gestures*], and as long as you keep that grip and that spoon doesn't move, you can walk around the whole island all day long until you're ready to throw it.

---

[21] Legendary Hudson Falls track and field coach, also a World War II Marine veteran and Mr. Fiore's brother-in-law.

Local Marine Hero Called 'Pineapple Kid' by Buddies

(Special to The Post-Star)

SOMEWHERE IN THE PACIFIC —(Delayed)—In the action on Engebi Island, Eniwetok Atoll, Marine Pvt. Joseph P. Fiore, of Glens Falls, N. Y., was known as the "pineapple kid," according to Sgt. Benjamin J. Masselink, a Marine Corps combat correspondent.

In the two days and two nights on Engebi, he used more than 70 hand grenades.

He carried them, along with other explosives, in his pockets, fastened to his dungaree coat, and in a leather Japanese demolition bag which he picked up right after landing on the island.

He did not throw the grenades, but would run up, pull the pin, and merely place the grenade in the opening of an emplacement or underground sniper nest. Then he would step back and wait for the explosion. He put in as many grenades as he thought necessary.

In this manner, he blew up nest after nest throughout the honeycomed island.

One time he ran into a little trouble. A wide awake Jap in a hole threw a grenade back, Pvt. Fiore ducked and rolled in another. The second one came soaring out of the hole. Fiore ducked again and tossed a third. At the same time a Marine standing on a little rise above the hole fired and hit the Jap. The third grenade went off in the hole, finishing the Jap.

PVT. JOSEPH P. FIORE

Landing with the first wave on Parry Island, Eniwetok Atoll, three days later, Pvt. Fiore was hit in the leg with shrapnel. He was given first aid treatment by Navy corpsmen and taken to the hospital ship.

Pvt. Fiore is the son of Mr. and Mrs. Peter Fiore, 47 Walnut Street

Glens Falls Post-Star, May 1, 1944.

So I went down on my stomach in a depression in the ground, and before I knew it, Draginsky had jumped on me because he figured I was wounded. Then I found out later that he was wounded too but he really saved my life. He picked the grenade out of my hand, and he threw it as far as he could and then started dragging me back by my collar. And Sergeant Wolfe came up on the other side, so between them they got me the hell out of that area. A tank was coming up and they put me in the back of the tank, and this corpsman worked on me and got me in a stretcher. And they brought me to the beach, and I ended up on a hospital ship, *USS Solace,* and on my way to Pearl Harbor.

I went to Pearl. I was in there about a month recuperating from the wounds. They gave me that first Purple Heart at Pearl Harbor. As a matter of fact, Admiral Nimitz pinned that on me; someone took a picture of it, and I never saw that picture. I would have loved to have had that!

Walter Hooke had his fill with handling pictures back at the Marshall Islands. He was tasked with a difficult duty—packing up the wallets and personal possessions of those killed in battle to mail home to their families.

Walter Hooke

In the Marshall Islands [*pauses, voice breaking*], I had the job of securing the personal belongings of the guys that were killed, wallets and pictures and dog tags of the guys who were injured or killed. For instance, one of the people I remember making a little box for and wrapping up his wallet and picture of family and parents was the son of Harry Hopkins, who worked as Roosevelt's aide. His son could have been an officer, but he enlisted in the Marine Corps as an ammunition carrier. So I remember making up this little box and sending it to the White House, addressed to Harry Hopkins, with his son's dog tags and wallet....[30]

Stephen Hopkins was just 18. His father was FDR's 'go-to' man in the White House. His commanding officer, Marine Captain Irving Schechter, related the following story after noting his charge's White House address.

Irving Schechter

'Hopkins, I see you have been in officers' training and I'm somewhat puzzled as to why you should show up here. There is no mention of your flunking out of OCS [*Officers Training School*].'

'No, sir,' he answered, 'I did not flunk out; I just got damn sick and tired of getting the needle about my having some kind of an easy job because I was Harry Hopkins's son. My dad has believed in this war since it started and so have his sons. I'm anxious to go overseas and back up what my father stands for because I stand for the same things.'

'Okay, Hopkins,' I told him, 'we'll get you into machine guns in the morning.'

Well, we went into the Roi-Namur part of the Marshalls around the beginning of February. Our battalion went ashore on Namur... whenever you have to kill a few thousand Japanese, you always lose men yourself. One of the Marines we lost here was young Hopkins. He had kept his machine gun going right into the middle of a banzai charge until he took a bullet in his head.[31]

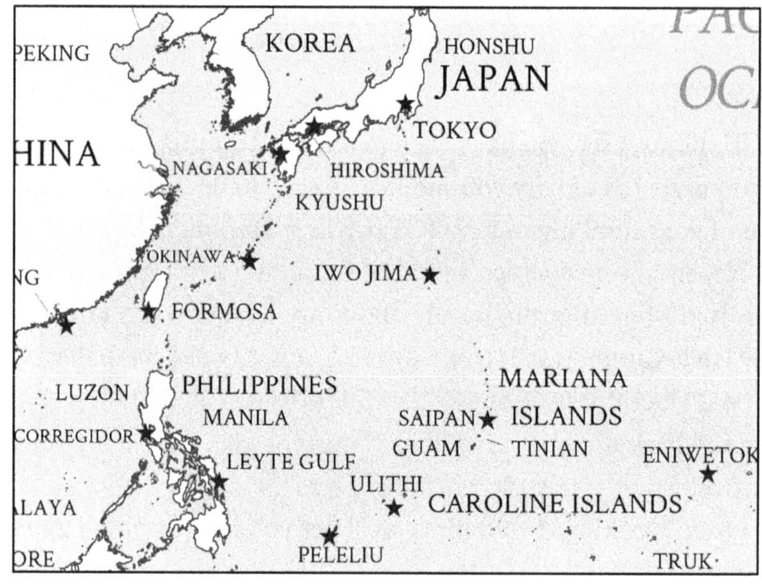

The Marianas and environs.

The Marianas—Saipan, Guam, and Tinian

Fiore lost his original outfit and took up duties in the 2nd Marine Division as a flamethrower for the invasion of Saipan in the Marianas. In mid-June 1944, just over a week after the Normandy landings in France, 20,000 Marines of the 2nd and 4th Divisions landed and suffered heavy casualties. Reserves of Marine battalions and the Army's 27th Division followed a few days later.

Ralph Leinoff

In the Marianas, we had the islands of Saipan and Tinian. Now that's getting close—they were about 1,500 miles south of Japan. You had to go up and down these valleys and there was a lot of vegetation in there. Now the island is only about 18 miles long. It's shaped something like an upside-down monkey wrench. You know what a monkey wrench looks like? You turn it upside-down you got an idea of what Saipan was like. It had a sugar mill and they had agriculture. It was a very beautiful island, actually... These are not coral islands, now. The Marianas were actually sandy beach islands, and we were able to get in with faster vehicles, but of course the amount of fire that we took was enormous, compared to what happened at Kwajalein.

The Japanese managed to stake out a number of snipers and they took their toll. And it was very hard to find out where we were being shot at from, so we took a lot more losses on Saipan. We lost a lot of men there getting on that island, and that took more than five days. It took us about three weeks or so to get up to the north end of the island, and in that three weeks we suffered casualties, but less and less each day. The worst casualties were suffered by the Army, which went up a low section of the island. The Japanese had reformed and it was a nasty battle between so-called banzai fighters and the Army. They were able to break through the Army lines and get all the way back to the Marine Corps artillery. It was Marine artillery that would stop them.

The Marines on Saipan were joined by the Army's 27th Infantry Division, a New York National Guard unit federalized in October 1940. Many of its members hailed from the mill towns north of Albany, and it was the 27th which would bear the brunt of the biggest banzai attack of the war.[32] *Before the final attack, the Marine commander expressed his unhappiness in front of war correspondents with the progress of the Army soldiers, and had the Army general relieved of his command. In fact, in the attack to follow, three members of the 105th Regiment would be awarded the Medal of Honor, posthumously.*[33]

Nicholas Grinaldo of Troy was a twenty-three–year-old sergeant who would receive two Purple Hearts and the Bronze Star for his actions on Saipan. In an interview with the NYS Military Museum's Veterans Oral History Project, he explained the situation.

Nick Grinaldo

The 27th Division got stuck in the mountains fighting. We had to fight cave to cave, hand to hand sometimes. And we had a General Smith, Ralph Smith, one hell of a good man. And he was relieved by this Marine general, 'Howlin' Mad' [*Holland M.*] Smith. From what I understood back then, the reason he was relieved of his command was that the Marines said we could not keep up with them. Well, Jesus Christ, they had tank support down in the lowlands, which we didn't have! They confiscated half of the 27th's artillery... and we were supposed to keep up with them! The best we had was 60 and 81mm mortars, and half the time you could not use them because of the terrain. There were mountains, gulches, hillsides, caves dug into them. That's the way it was, it was really rough going up through the goddamn mountains! As much as you tried, you could not keep up with them. You go past a cave so small you never noticed the opening. The next thing you know, you're getting shot at from behind.

John Sidur was a twenty-six–year-old sergeant from Cohoes, New York, and would also receive the Bronze Star for his bravery at Saipan.

John Sidur

We had this cave, and we had two Japanese [*Japanese-American*] guys from the Hawaiian Islands; they didn't carry any guns or anything, but they were smart. They walked right into the cave and talked to the Japanese soldiers. They weren't going to give up. Our two came out and told us, and then went back in and told them they had five minutes before we are going to shell them. Then they went back in and told them they had three minutes—all of a sudden we heard the screaming of women and children! We told them to let the civilians out. The Japanese wouldn't let them out—that was their protection. So it came down to... they blew the cave up! How many people were killed, we don't know, but that cave was closed. They exploded it with dynamite!

On July 7, after three weeks of fighting, the worst suicide charge of the Pacific War was about to get underway. Rather than resort to surrender, between three and five thousand screaming Japanese soldiers and sailors broke through a gap in the Army lines.

Nick Grinaldo

I remember it rained like hell that night, and the water was running down the slope into our foxholes. I had to use my helmet to keep bailing out, you know. The night before the banzai, I woke up that morning and, oh, Jesus Christ, they [the Japanese] got above us, and they were giving us plunging fire, shooting right down into the foxholes, because they were high enough to look down. Lt. Gower, he was my platoon leader, he was regular Army...he was a good man. He called us together, the squad leaders. He said, 'I think we're getting hit with a banzai. We're going to have to pull back.' Holy Jesus, there was howling and screaming! They had naked women, with spears, stark naked! They took bayonets and strapped them on the end of a pole. And they came screaming at us, figuring, 'Hey, the good-hearted Americans ain't gonna shoot a woman, you know?' Horseshit. There were so many of them, like cockroaches coming out of the woodwork. We had to pull back.

John Sidur

I saw everything, women and men mixed up, everything, and we just kept shooting. Whoever got too close, that's who got the bullet... we got to the point that there were too many casualties. So we tried to hold back as much as we could. We were getting mixed up with the Japanese, and all of a sudden we got hit with artillery. American artillery. They said it was for the Japanese, but we were on the frontline and we got hit with that. We lost quite a few men— I got hit then, I got shrapnel from artillery on my hand, not too bad.

Nick Grinaldo

I was with the lieutenant and a few of the men that were with me. And all of a sudden I turn around and I see the lieutenant go down. He took one right across here [*gestures to his jaw*], blew the whole bottom of his jaw right off... I went to grab him, to take him with us. And he said, [*shaking his head*] 'Get back to the Japanese trenches!' There were trenches at the point, that's where we headed... it was general rout, a general rout. We had them running right alongside of us. I had one running right alongside of me. Christ, he wasn't five feet from me! I don't know whether he was 'sakeed up' or what the hell was wrong with him, but I put him down quickly, I tell you![22] They were right with us!

That's when I got shot through the shoulder. When we fell back to the trenches, my rifle fell out of my hand, and I went to pick it up; I could not close my hand. I looked and I saw a trickle of blood

[22] sake-Japanese 'rice wine' alcoholic beverage

on my right shoulder. We had a guy by the name of Tony Simonds, he was in C Company before he went to a medical detachment. And [now] he was running with us, and he turned around and he said, 'Let me fix your arm, sergeant.' I said, 'Not here, Jesus Christ, not here!' He said, 'Here, you're hurt bad!' He took care of me. While he's standing in front of me, he took one [*a bullet*] right in the back which was intended for me—he took it. Nice guy, a real nice guy.

We got to the Jap trenches all right, and all of a sudden we started to get hit with artillery fire. Real bad, and it was our own! They had to be [105mm] howitzers, and they poured them into us, trying to break up the Jap banzai.

27th Division on Saipan assessing results following July 7, 1944 banzai charge. New York State Military Museum.

That's what they tried, to break up the attack. Unfortunately, we had made it back there and they didn't know we were there, and they killed [us]—half of the casualties we suffered were right there.

More than 900 men of the 27th Division's 105th Regiment would be killed or wounded in this attack. With their backs to the water, the Army survivors could see half of the estimated 4,300 Japanese dead in front of them.[34]

When the Saipan operation was declared secure on July 9, over 16,500 Americans were casualties, with over 3,400 killed or missing. Approximately 29,000 Japanese defenders had been killed, with almost no prisoners being taken. Some of the enemy survivors would live on in the hills for months and even years afterwards.[35] *To compound the horror, over twenty thousand civilians were killed, hundreds of whom committed suicide by wading into the sea or jumping off cliffs, fearful of U.S. soldiers and captivity.*

Ralph Leinoff

The native population, the Chamorros, had been under Japanese control for many years, and they were fed a lot of propaganda about how they should not surrender to the Americans, the American troops are barbarians and everything. And rather than surrender—they believed this stuff—and we tried to get women and children down, but the people were so indoctrinated that rather than surrender, they jumped from the cliffs with...with the babes. There are movies—you might've seen them, I don't know—showing people who were trying to get them down and they wouldn't trust us.

Joe Fiore

The Japanese told these people there that if the Americans grab you, they are going to torture you and kill you, especially Marines, because in order to become a Marine you had to kill either your mother or your father, which was garbage. But those people 'ate it,' and they jumped, they jumped off that cliff! Terrible!

Joe Fiore would be one of the American casualties in the battle for Saipan.

I was wounded here [*points to chin*] and took one here [*points to lower lip/jaw*], and, of course, from my ankle to my buttocks, it was full of shrapnel. That hurt! And I didn't realize how much shrapnel I had in me until they got me off the stretcher, these two hospital corpsmen, and they sat me in these metal chairs. Well, I went right through the ceiling! It was like sitting on a pin cushion... I was in isolation because of my wounds. The most serious one went in here and came out here [*points to upper thigh*]. It was a piece of shrapnel. So I was in tough shape. For 18 days, I was out of it. I was receiving morphine every 12 hours—at noon and at midnight—and it would wear off at 10 o'clock, right on the dot. And I'd beg the nurse to give me another shot, and she said, 'No way!'

So anyway, I finally got out of there and back to my outfit, and I was back in combat again. And when I left the hospital, I still had a bandage around this leg [*points to left thigh*].

My mother took it pretty bad when she got the telegram that I was wounded. So my sister and my brother said, 'Well, Ma, at least he's alive!' And I felt sorry for her when she got the notice of the second Purple Heart... [*He trails off, looks down, and softly begins to cry*].

Fiore shortly returned stateside on leave and finished out the war in the Philadelphia Navy Yard. Even before the battles had ended at Saipan, Guam, and Tinian, Navy Seabees got to work and the first B–29 bombers arrived.

The Hell of Peleliu

Working his way out of Australia, General MacArthur prepared for his assault on the Philippine Islands. Military planners decided early on that the fortified island of Peleliu stood in the way and would have to be taken. On September 15, 1944, the 1st Marine Division and Army troops began the attack on Peleliu after three days of heavy bombardment by Navy gunships. Peleliu hosted a major Japanese airfield that, in the planning stages, was deemed a major threat to any U. S. advance on the Philippines. The island was heavily defended by over 13,500 Imperial troops dug into a network of pillboxes and 500 coral caverns and caves.

Four young men from the local counties surrounding the "Falls" back home were assigned to the 1st Marine Division and had developed a strong bond even before going overseas. They now found themselves together in the thick of it on Peleliu, and later, would be in the battle for Okinawa. Daniel Lawler was assigned as an ammunition carrier in a squad for a BAR [Browning automatic rifle, a .30–caliber heavy machine gun] to K Company, 3rd Battalion, 5th Regiment.[23] *John W. 'Jack' Murray was a squad leader and heavy machine gunner. Harold Chapman joined Jim Butterfield in the 6th Company, 2nd Battalion, 1st Regiment.*

Dan Lawler was nineteen years old.

Dan Lawler

We hit the island, which was only four miles long by two miles wide. I was in the first assault wave. It was hell, and everyone was scared—it was an awful feeling. As we disembarked, I looked up and down the beaches, and all you could hear was screaming, and men were falling and dying. There was artillery, mortar, and machine

[23] One of the main outfits portrayed in the 2010 HBO series, *The Pacific*.

gun fire constantly. We fought all day, and by evening, we reached the airstrip about half a mile from the beach. We set up for the night along the sides of the airstrip. The temperature was from 102° at night to 120° in the daytime.

We went in with two canteens of water—that's a gallon of water. This island was two degrees off the equator! By noontime, we were out of water. They sent more in to us in 40-gallon drums. They brought them up to the lines, and we drew the water out. They used these for gasoline before, and didn't clean them out—so we almost got sick just drinking water.

John Murray

Luckily, we made it to the far side of the field. My squad was still intact. The first thing I saw was a Japanese machine gunner chained to his machine gun... They were not going to give up.

Dan Lawler

The second day in, I started across the airfield, and machine gun fire and shells were going by us. We were running, and what you do is run a short distance and then you drop, run a short distance and then you drop. You never want to stay running, because you do not want the Japs' machine guns to get after you. About halfway across, I heard an artillery piece go off. It must have landed behind me, and I went down—face down. When I woke up I was still facing down. I pulled my right hand down, and I looked at it [*looks at hand*]. It was all bloody, and I couldn't feel anything in it. So the corpsman came along, and he said, 'You have four fingers broken.' And my arm was broken [*points to arm*]. So he patched that much up and said, 'You also got hit in the back—you got a wound on your back.' So he patched that up, tagged me, and then I came out.

Dan Lawler, 2011. Portrait by Robert H. Miller.

Lawler was evacuated to a hospital ship, then to a hospital on Guadalcanal. He was awarded the Purple Heart and rejoined his outfit later on Pavuvu, the 'rest and recuperation' area back in the Solomons.

John Murray

Some of our men were getting hit and we were much smaller now. There was no clean water on the island, and our water was brought in old oil drums that hadn't been properly cleaned. Between the bad water and the extreme heat, many of us started to get sick with dysentery and fungus. I believe time on the island under these conditions was starting to take its toll. The 1st and 7th Marines were out of action because of casualties. We, the 5th Marines, had to take Bloody Nose Ridge.

After securing the airstrip, the Marines headed into the coral hills to reduce the Japanese defenders. The fight for Bloody Nose Ridge and the Umurbrogol Mountain was particularly brutal, and considered one of the most difficult fights of the entire war, with the 1st Division losing up to one-third of its strength. Many of the hundreds of limestone caves and former mine shafts were interconnected and had multiple entrances, housing artillery pieces protected by sliding steel doors, machine guns, and thousands of troops.[36]

Jim Butterfield

The first 200 hours at Peleliu, we lost over 1,600 people. That made our regiment the first regiment that could no longer function as a regiment! They split the rest of us up—which was about 500—into other outfits.

John Murray

My memory of what happened was of total destruction and death. Every day was the same. That damned island was all coral rock. Our movement was slow, sometimes only a few yards each day... It's hazy now but it was very vivid for so long, sleepless nights filled with emptiness, sadness, fear, and total anger, constant yelling, flares in the sky all the time, spurts from our machine guns. I know I prayed a lot, held my rosary around my neck. We prayed and remembered our relentless training and hoped the two would pull us through. And as the days went by, I realized that there was a strong possibility I wouldn't get off Peleliu alive.

We started up the ridge October 6. As we pressed toward the top, flamethrowers were necessary to get those animals out of the caves. The closer we got to the top, the more resistance we faced.

Our second lieutenant tried to go over the top, but got hit in the shoulder and had to be moved out. Machine gunners were given orders to spray the ridges, especially the caves where the bastards hid.

Our squad had been hit hard. There were 15 of us on September 15, and now there were five of us left and most of us were sick. I turned around and asked for more ammunition, and I only had five more rounds left. I hadn't realized my right knee was exposed; something made my left ear ring. I looked down and saw that my right knee had been shot off by a sniper hidden in a cave. I lay flat on the ground so he couldn't get another good shot at me. They located the cave, and a flamethrower came up and filled the cave with flames. That Jap came running out, flames all over him—completely engulfed. I fired a burst at him. It was all over then.[37]

Casualties were very heavy. The 1st Marine Division lost 1,252 killed and over 5,700 wounded or missing. The 81st Infantry Division, sent in to relieve the Marines, lost over 540 dead and 2,700 wounded or missing in action. The battle remains controversial since it was never used as a staging area for the invasion of the Philippines or any other subsequent operations, though it did draw some Japanese troops away from the Philippines. Nearly 10,700 Japanese were killed on the tiny island.

Jim Butterfield

You've got to stop and remember when you're studying about these islands that the Japanese had ten years of war before we got into it, before they bombed Pearl Harbor. They were at China, Korea, and other places over there. These people were good. On these islands, they were digging [fortifications] for years! They didn't meet you out on the beaches; we had to go get them. They knew what we were going to do, and they were good.

The purpose at Peleliu was to take that airport and securely keep it. It was also to draw troops from the Philippines. MacArthur was getting ready to go in there. I guess we pulled a couple of divisions out. Peleliu, in the last five years, has come forward to become one of the biggest battles of the Pacific. In fact, after we secured Peleliu, it came out in *Time Magazine* with MacArthur that it wasn't really necessary that we took Peleliu. Now this doesn't make you feel too good, when all your friends are gone, but it brought back some memories. I was up there for 74 days, and fortunately, I did not get wounded. I lost part of my hearing up there, but otherwise I came out pretty good. It was the [bitterest] battle of the Marine Corps in World War II. There's no doubt about it.[38]

CHAPTER NINE

Captivity-Year 3

The Hellships

As the Marines prepared for combat on Peleliu, Robert Blakeslee was herded with 750 other American prisoners aboard a decrepit prison ship for transport to Japan for slave labor. Nearly 19,000 men were transported in the stifling holds of these unmarked 'hell-ships,' destined to be used by Japanese industrialists for slave labor. At least sixty percent of these prisoners never made it to Japan alive due to submarine and air attacks, unsanitary and inhumane conditions, and the brutal treatment of their captors[39].

After 28 months in captivity and 19 days of brutal conditions in the bottom of the hold of the transport, Blakeslee's ship would be torpedoed by the *USS Paddle*, an American submarine. He would be one of only 83 survivors, as he later relayed in a 1945 debriefing.

Robert Blakeslee

During the summer [of 1944], we began to hear rumors that we might be shipped to Japan—we heard that the men in No. 2 Camp at Davao had been shipped out early in June. The Japs were getting uneasy and we were pretty sure the Yanks were getting near. We knew they had taken over the Solomons and that they were in New Guinea. This airfield they made us work on was a re-fueling point for planes being ferried southward, and it bristled with anti-aircraft guns. When we learned of bullet-riddled Jap planes arriving at a nearby navy air field, we knew for sure the Yanks were not too far away.

Finally, on August 5, they told us to get ready to move. They said we were to be taken to Japan and put aboard an exchange ship to be exchanged for Japanese nationals that were U.S. prisoners. I guess we only half-believed that story, but in any case, Lasang [*Japanese airfield*] seemed like a good place to be away from. You see, we figured if the Yanks moved in, either one of two things probably would happen: the Japs would shoot all of us, or a lot of us would get killed trying to make a break for freedom.

They gave us back the shoes we had gotten from the Red Cross way back in February, and the last of four packages of food, candy, cigarettes that had arrived at the same time. We had worn those shoes only a month when there was an escape from the camp and they were taken away. From then on, we were barefoot. Incidentally, those shoes upset the Jap soldiers. They had rubber soles and heels. Their officers had told them America didn't have any rubber.

As it turned out, we had our shoes back only for one day. The Japanese major who had been in command moved out, leaving a first lieutenant in command. Also, he cut us down to two meals a day, one of rice and salt and the other a pasty mixture of camotes, something like a sweet potato, and squash. We were on that diet for two weeks.

During that time we saw the first Allied planes we had seen since before the fall of Bataan. There were air raid alerts nearly every night, and one night a single multi-motored plane came over and we heard bomb explosions nearby. It was one of the sweetest sounds I've ever heard!

On August 20 they told us for the second time to get ready to move. They roused us at three the next morning, and after a scanty meal of rice with a little meat and salt in it, they lined us up in lines of fours with about 175 men in a group. Then they strung a heavy rope around the outside of the group, tying it to all the men on the outside of the column. Anyone who stepped outside the rope would be shot, they said.

Ringed by guards armed with bayoneted rifles and with a truck containing a machine gun detail ahead and behind each group, we marched three miles to the dock. There we were joined by another hundred American prisoners who had been in the custody of the Jap navy. They gave us back our shoes, but told us not to put them on.

The Holds of Hell

We were loaded in barges and taken out to a freighter of about 5,000 tons that was anchored in Davao Gulf. After climbing up rope ladders we were herded into two holds, about 450 men in one and 300 in the other. I was in the larger group.

As soon as we were packed in, they pulled up the ladder and covered up the hatch, all but a strip about two feet wide along each side. Each hatch was guarded by a detail of soldiers armed with a machine gun, rifles, and grenades. It was pretty obvious that if anything happened to the ship, they had no intention of letting any of us get out.

There we were, just like rats in a trap, in an area about 50 by 60 feet. The only light and air came from those two strips alongside the hatches. It was about 110 degrees down there, and to make things worse, the vessel's last cargo had been salt, which got in the cracks and sores on our feet. There was one small ventilator in the hold, but it didn't work.

We had been given a mess kit of rice before leaving the camp, and late in the afternoon they sent down some water. But at that point we weren't very well organized; some got a lot and others got none.

Some of the men had brought native brooms with them, and finally we got organized, got the hold swept out and arranged so everyone could lie down. The men lay like sardines, one man's feet alongside another's head.

There were no water facilities for washing, or for latrines. They sent down some five-gallon gasoline cans to use for latrines. The task of emptying those became a choice assignment because it gave those who did it a chance to get up in the fresh air for a few minutes.

As the afternoon wore on, it got hotter and hotter. In the evening, one man cracked and began screaming for water. The Japs had told us that if there were any disturbances they would fire on us. We were pretty apprehensive about that, but one of the men who spoke a little Japanese succeeded in convincing the guards that the man was delirious and not responsible for his actions. He was still delirious the next day and finally the medical officer in our group gave him drugs from his pitifully small stock to keep him quiet.

The next morning they passed down our first meal, a small portion of steamed rice and a watery soup made of camotes and a little water. They promised us a canteen of water per man as a daily ration, but we never got that much. Generally the ration was less than a pint. That morning the Japs began practicing air raid alerts. Each time they would cover over the hatch completely, cutting off what little air and light there was.

In the afternoon there was a real air raid. We heard the plane, then the chattering of machine guns, the boom of anti-aircraft, and finally the concussion of bombs. The concussions were near enough so that they nearly caused a panic. Then the chaplain took over. He was a chaplain who had been decorated for valor at Clark Field. Setting an example by his calmness, he urged the men to be quiet, that it was better that way, since there was nothing they could do. Then he said a prayer.

After that, he conducted a vesper service every evening, and sometimes, one of the officers, who was a first-rate story teller, would narrate the story of some book he had read.

The men were organized in groups of 25 for the distribution of food and water. That ensured everyone getting a share. Because there was so little air, four periods a day were set aside for smoking. Then we would all wave towels to get the smoke out of the hold. There were two meals a day, and actually most of our days were taken up waiting in line to be served, or waiting our turn at the gasoline cans that served as latrines.

The first night the vessel had anchored in Davao Gulf, but about 2:00 a.m. the second night, it began to move again. The Japs immediately covered over the hatches. By morning, 70 of the men were unconscious. We moved them to the area directly under the hatch where the best air was, and they were there in the morning when the Japs came down to count us—they counted us twice a day, God only knows why! I guess they realized then how bad the air was, for after that they opened up the hatch a little more. Some of the men had shelter tent halves, and they built makeshift wind scoops out of them. The Jap guards set them up above the hatch but they didn't work too well.

The second morning, they had let us up on deck in groups of 50 for about ten minutes of calisthenics, but after that air raid, they wouldn't let us up anymore. The third morning, as we were steaming out of Davao Gulf, we heard explosions like depth charges, but we never did find out whether there had been a sub attack, or if it was just an anti-submarine drill staged by the three naval vessels that were escorting our ship. To tell the truth, we weren't too worried about submarines. We figured that American submarines had been notified when we sailed—but the Japs crossed us up.

By the fourth day, we had become so dehydrated and were suffering so from thirst that we finally prevailed upon the Japs to substitute lugao, a gruel-like rice preparation, instead of the drier boiled rice. I'll never forget how good it tasted. But despite that slight change, men were passing out constantly from heat and thirst. The medical officer and the chaplain spent most of their time attending to them. About all that could be done was to move them to the area beneath the hatch, fan them, and put salt water compresses on them. They were about the only medical cases those first days. Fortunately, there was no dysentery. That would have been terrible!

Here's how the Japs crossed us up. We pulled into a harbor, lay there for nine days, then they transferred us to another freighter [the *Shinyo Maru*]. During those nine days we were on deck three times, once for 10 minutes of calisthenics and twice to stand briefly under a salt water hose.

The Shinyo Maru before 1936. USN.

We thought that first freighter was awful, but once they transferred us, things got even worse. The first carried a cargo of hemp that filled the lower part of the hold. The second had nothing but some rock ballast, and we were right down on the keel, about 30 feet below the deck. The hold I was in was about the same size as the previous one, but instead of 450 of us, they jammed in 500. It was so crowded, all of us couldn't lie down at once. We had to sleep in shifts. We couldn't even organize lines to the latrines. Instead, those cans had to be passed through our area from man to man.

The vessel apparently had carried a cargo of cement not too long before, and our movements raised a cloud of cement dust. It filled our nostrils, caked on our perspiring bodies, and went in our hair and beards. As soon as we got down there, they placed boards over the hatch, leaving a little space between them for air, and then lashed them down. We were there 24 hours before sailing.

Right after we started, the Japs began having practice alerts. Each time they would throw a tarpaulin over the hatch, shutting out the light and most of the air. So actually, the heat, filth, and air were worse than on the other ship. And in addition to the exhaustion cases, some of the men had malaria attacks and others developed skin diseases.

Torpedoed

About 5:30 on the afternoon of September 7, we heard some small arms fire, then the bugler blowing an alert. We could tell this was the real thing from the way he blew. Can you imagine how a man might blow a bugle with his teeth chattering? Well, that's just the way it sounded. I remember thinking that just before everything went blank. I heard no explosion, no outcries.

The next thing I remember, it couldn't have been more than a few seconds later, and I was fighting salt water. For what seemed like minutes, I seemed to be suspended like in mid-air, and then I shot upward! I had barely time to fill my lungs before I was sucked down again. On the way down I grabbed a piece of rope. When I came to the surface again I was near the top of the hold, which was nearly completely submerged. I just swam out and away from the side of the ship, grabbing at various floating objects. It was then that I discovered my right arm was useless. I finally caught the edge of a piece of a life raft and glimpsed eight or ten other prisoners clutching it also. Bullets were hitting the water all around us. They were fired by Japs standing in a lifeboat on the freighter!

The freighter, hit by one torpedo in the bow, apparently right in the hold that I was in, and by a second torpedo just ahead of the aft hold, sank in about ten minutes.

Just as they cast off their lifeboat, it capsized and the Japs joined us in the water. Among them was the sadistic lieutenant who had been in charge of us at the airfield after the major left. Looking at him, I remembered the pleasure he seemed to get out of meting out punishment for minor infractions of rules. Once, I recalled, he tortured a group of about 50 men by making them kneel for about 45 minutes with their shins on the sharp flange of a railway rail. Now he didn't look so brave. If I ever saw a man look afraid, he was the one.

Through an interpreter, he told us that if we would not harm the Japanese, he personally would guarantee our safety. As if we didn't know what his guarantee was worth, we saw one of the Jap escort vessels moving toward us, picking up survivors—Jap survivors! They were shooting whatever Americans they saw!

It was obvious there was no safety in numbers on that raft, and some of the men began to swim away. Finally there were three of us left. One of the men and I were constantly bobbing back and forth under the raft trying to keep it between ourselves and the Jap marksmen aboard the naval vessel. The other man was either injured or did not realize the danger, for he merely clung to the raft without making any effort at concealment. Suddenly I looked up and noted there were only two of us. Where the third man had been there was a neat bullet hole in the raft!

When darkness hid us from the Jap vessel, my companion and I climbed up on the raft, both of us pretty exhausted. I apparently went to sleep immediately. The moon was up when I awoke. We decided we had best try to paddle our piece of raft toward shore. I quickly found there wasn't much I could do because of my useless arm. And every time my companion tried, he would break into a spasm of coughing and would spit blood. Besides, the current was against us.

Through the night we floated aimlessly amid the wreckage. At daylight, we observed we were floating in the approximate area where the prison ship had gone down. Once again we tried to paddle toward shore, but made scant headway. By noon the sun was hot and blistering and we were parched with thirst. We had no food or water.

Suddenly we saw two Filipinos in a banca boat [outrigger canoe] a short distance away, and we hollered to them. They acknowledged our shouts by waving, but would not come near us. In desperation, we began furiously to paddle toward them. The Filipinos packed up their paddles and moved away. Jap planes were passing over from time to time and apparently they were afraid they would be observed aiding us.

By mid-afternoon we decided we had best abandon the raft in favor of life preservers, several of which were floating around. My companion, by this time, was getting very weak. I finally spotted a preserver and we swam toward it only to find that it supported a dead Jap. My companion removed the Jap, donned the preserver, and started off alone. To my knowledge, that is the last anyone saw him.

After experimenting with some floating boards, I finally elected to stay with the raft another night. I was on the verge of delirium by this time, and while I slept some, the night was a horrible experience. Toward dawn, however, I slept soundly and awoke refreshed and much stronger. A stiff wind had come up during the night and blown my raft down the coast about 20 miles, I learned later. I was still two or three miles from shore and headed toward the open sea. It was obvious my only chance lay in heading toward shore at once. I struggled all morning, pushing and pulling the raft, but made scant progress. I was about to give up in despair when I heard an American voice behind me.

I looked around. There was a smiling Yank, astride a big bamboo raft, with a smaller one tied behind it. He was Pvt. D.J. Olinger of Denver, Colorado. He had found the raft soon after being blown overboard.

We decided to wait until night and then try to paddle the smaller raft toward shore. Late in the afternoon, we saw some bancas close to shore, and two finally appeared behind us. After we convinced them we were Americans, they went for aid. While they were gone, some others appeared that had room in their craft and they took us ashore just as darkness fell. That was the evening of September 9.

We were taken inland and fed a mixture of raw eggs and put to bed. The next day we had a virtual banquet: rice, boiled chicken, goats' milk, and more eggs. They told us some other survivors had come ashore, and in the afternoon some guerrillas came and took us to them. There were six other survivors there, two with compound leg fractures. A Filipino doctor attended a dozen or so lacerations, but since he had no anesthetic, he could do nothing for my injured arm.

Within a few days, more survivors arrived, until finally there were 83 of us, including 25 officers. Twenty-eight of us, all of whom had been in that forward hold, had broken eardrums. As nearly as we could gather, the torpedo had struck just about midway along the side of the hold.

It was the third night, October 30, before contact was made with the sub, and shortly thereafter we saw its dark outline in the water. Some of its crew came ashore with rubber boats to take the litter cases aboard. The others were taken out in bancas. We arrived in New Guinea, where we were feted at a naval base with the most delicious steak I've ever tasted, French-fried potatoes, and cold beer from Terre Haute, Indiana.

A short time later, I was flown to Australia for hospitalization. While there, I was promoted to major. I had been promoted to captain a month before the fall of Bataan. Several of us arrived back in the U.S. together November 6 and went to Washington, where we were awarded Purple Hearts. I was assigned to Walter Reed Hospital, and it was there that I saw my wife for the first time in more than three years. A couple of weeks later, my son Stephen joined us in Albany. He was 15 months old when I left. Now he is four and a half!

I lost everything when the prison ship went down, including my most prized possession. It was a New Testament, bearing a Jap censor's stamp: 'Approved reading.'[40]

*

Joe Minder dared to hope at the arrival of American planes overhead, but would soon find himself in his own version of hell.

Joe Minder

March 29 to August 14, 1944

Morale is as low as a snake's back around here. Many men have taken sick and have been sent to Bilibid hospital for treatment, but many have died soon after arriving there because of their terrible condition when they leave here. Several other men, however, have deliberately broken their arms and legs to get away from the hard work and brutal treatment on the airfield.

August 19 to September 20, 1944

Working building plane revetments [*reinforced parking areas*]. Neck stiff as heck from blows from the fists of "Higison," a very small Jap guard. First he slapped me in the face until it was numb, then belted me a couple good 'haymakers' to the jaw.

September 21, 1944

Planes! Planes! American planes! All heck broke loose directly overhead when the Americans slipped in through the clouds, contacted Jap planes, and started several dogfights all around us! We ran from the field to a mango grove and saw what we had been waiting for. The dogfights lasted for about one hour. During that time we saw the Yanks shoot down one large transport plane, and they sent several Jap fighter planes away smoking! With all the Jap planes driven off, our Grumman Navy planes started diving on the bay and Nichols Field and all the other military objectives, strafing and bombing with no opposition air at all! Several stray 20-millimeter shells landed 25 yards from us in the mango grove, but we were so darned excited watching our planes we didn't even go for a hole. We were darn lucky that the Americans did not frog bomb and strafe under the trees where we were! When they strafed the fields, hundreds of Japs and Filipinos working on the field ran under the grove. They must have been visible from the air.

September 22, 1944

American planes came back at 8:00 a.m. and continued their heavy bombings of Nichols Field and Manila Bay. With only about five miles from the bombing point, we can feel the ground shake under us when these huge explosives go off, caused by exploding ammunition dumps and boats in the bay! Huge billows of smoke and fire rising high into the air can be clearly seen from here. Everyone is excited wondering how long it will be before the Yanks land on Luzon and free us. Many of us, however, are wondering if any of our American POW friends were killed at Nichols Field.

8:00 p.m.

The sky just lit up for a second when a terrific explosion went off in the Manila area, making the doors rattle in our barracks!

September 23 to September 30, 1944

Having it pretty easy now working in stone quarry and laying stone on airfield. Also getting pretty good food again.

39 Days in the Hole

October 1, 1944: 2:00 p.m.

Oh, what misery! Seven hundred forty-one of us are packed into the forward hold of a small, crummy coal cargo ship sitting here in Manila Bay waiting to be shipped to Japan! We are packed into a small space of 35 feet by 50 feet almost on top of one another!

6:00 p.m.

Several old letters were just brought aboard from Manila. Most of them have been here for months! I received several Christmas cards from people in North Creek in December 1943, also some letters from home; one had a nice picture of my ma and dad.

I know this is going to be hell, standing down here in this cramped position for twelve days, but after seeing those pictures and reading those letters and cards, I don't feel quite so bad now.

October 3, 1944

Finally moving out of the bay in a small merchant convoy of Jap ships. The bay is full of wrecked ships which the Americans sank in the September 21 and 22 air raids. With no markings on this tub whatsoever, we are expected to be sent to the bottom any day now by a Yank bomb or a torpedo! No one has a life belt, and there is only one small escape ladder running down to this stuffy, crowded hold, three decks below the top of the ship, so our chances of surviving are darn small if the Yanks sink this scow! With only a couple small machine guns on it, the Yanks can also strafe the heck out of us if they so desire.

October 9, 1944: 2:00 p.m.

Ten men have already died from overcrowded conditions and lack of water and have been thrown overboard. We thought we might be some more shark bait a few minutes ago when the Yank sub fired a torpedo at us, barely missing the bow of the ship, and sank an oil tanker along the side of us. When the Japs started dropping depth charges, it sounded like the sides would collapse in on us!

October 10, 1944

Carl Deamer died last night in my arms. He passed out several times last night with a high fever. I managed to bring him to several times by fanning the heck out of him, but about 5:00 a.m., Carl's worries ended. I first met him at Camp I in November 1942.

October 11, 1944

Sailed into Hong Kong harbor.

October 12 to October 21, 1944

Started sailing out of the bay for Formosa [Taiwan]. Sure glad to leave here! Americans have visited this place several times with their bombs and have bombed many of the buildings on the waterfront and have left the bay full of bomb-blasted ships. We were bombed once, but luckily the Yanks missed us again. We unloaded copra and have sugar aboard now.

October 25, 1944

Arrived at Port Takao in Formosa.

November 8, 1944

After being chased in and out of the bay by the American bombers, we are finally going ashore this morning!

10:00 p.m.

Just got on shore, most of us are so weak we can barely walk! During those 39 days of hell, cramped up in that crummy hole, we lost 38 of our men. The rest of us who managed to survive have lost many pounds. God! What [awful] looking men! With a 39-day beard, dirty, pale, and skinny, we all look like walking skeletons coming out of a dungeon!

Like Joe and thousands of others, John Parsons had arrived in Formosa from the Philippines on a hellship two years earlier. During this time the men captured with him at Bataan labored at working in rice fields, growing sweet potatoes, and making rope. He remembered that 'on rainy days, the camp would be called out and made to sit in a group on the wet ground facing mounted machine guns. [We] were told that in the event of an Allied invasion of Formosa, this would be [our] fate. This took place about once a week, and having no source of news, [we] never knew if it was the real thing or another rehearsal.'

Just before Joe Minder arrived at Takao, John was leaving that port on another hellship bound for Japan, a route that Joe would be following soon enough. The Oyroku Maru had considerable difficulty getting out of the

Formosa harbor. The prisoners were packed into their compartments with timbers wedged against the door and the hatches sealed as the harbor endured three days of consecutive bombing by American planes. One bomb struck so close that it killed 17 Japanese soldiers on the deck. The first attempt to leave the harbor ended when a submarine was detected the first night out and the hellship turned back; the men remained confined aboard and forced to wait in the harbor for another five days. On the second attempt, a torpedo narrowly missed the ship and exploded on the shoreline. The vessel finally made it out of the harbor and on its way to Japan only with the help of a destroyer escort.[41] Two months later, the Oyroku Maru was bombed off the Philippines in Subic Bay with 1,600 American prisoners on board. Survivors were forced into the water and many were deliberately machine gunned before they could reach shore.

John Parsons would spend the remainder of his captivity at the notorious Mukden POW camp in the far reaches of Manchuria. He would be liberated by Soviet troops on August 20, 1945.

CHAPTER TEN

The Sands of Iwo Jima

As the tens of thousands of prisoners were being transported to the Japanese home islands for slave labor and the Philippines was slowly being liberated, military planners focused on the next two stepping stones—Iwo Jima and Okinawa.

Iwo Jima, or 'Sulfur Island,' was eight square miles of sand, ash, and rock lying 660 miles southeast of Tokyo. It could serve as a refueling stop for the B–29s and B–24s that were now flying almost daily out of the fields in the Marianas to bomb the Japanese mainland. In late November 1944, aerial bombardment of Iwo Jima with high explosives began and continued for a record 74 straight days. The 21,000 Japanese defenders survived this with scores of underground fortresses connected by 16 miles of tunnels stocked with food, water, and ammunition. The surface was covered with concrete pillboxes and blockhouses housing some 800 gun positions. On February 19, 1945, the attack began as the landing ships brought the Marines towards the beaches of blackened volcanic sand.

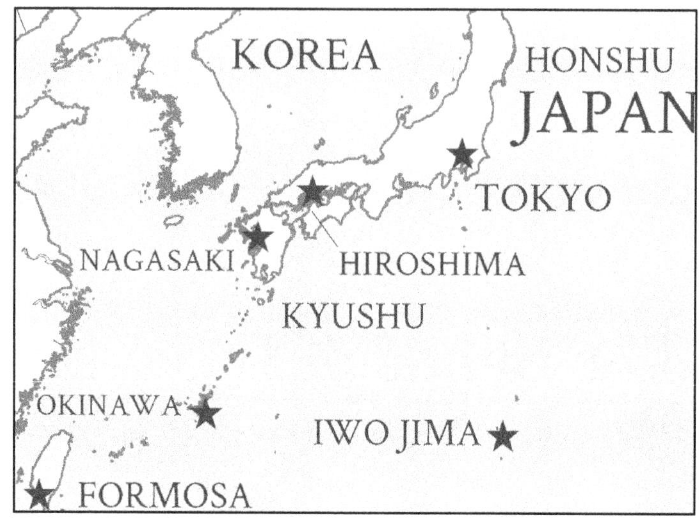

Iwo Jima and Okinawa.

At 24, Sanford 'Sandy' Berkman was the old man of his outfit, serving as a second lieutenant in the 5th Division, 26th Marines, and wound up commanding a machine gun platoon on Iwo Jima. In 2007 he sat down for an interview with the New York State Military Museum's Veterans Oral History Project.

Sandy Berkman

We shoved off from Hawaii January 1, 1945, and we were part of an invasion force—not knowing where we were going at the time, but we found out later that we were going to Iwo. Everybody wanted to know where Iwo Jima was, no one had even heard of it. There had never been a white man on that island, only the Japanese—they owned and controlled it and lived there. We were aboard ship over forty days.

Arthur LaPorte was an eighteen–year-old Marine from Hudson Falls. He had been trained on the light machine gun in the 4th Marine Division. His convoy left training at Pearl Harbor for the long journey across the Pacific. It would be his first time in combat, as an ammunition carrier for a gun squad.

Art LaPorte

We went aboard ships right to Pearl [Harbor] and stayed at Pearl for a couple weeks until they got supplies and got the convoy together, and then we headed out, not knowing where we were going, across the Pacific on a huge convoy. We did not have any Japanese resistance; we were very lucky, no torpedoes or anything. We got out to Saipan and stayed offshore. After that, when we got going again, they brought out an easel, and they told us about how the Japanese had gun emplacements and what we would meet there. And that was our first knowledge that we were going to Iwo Jima.

We approached Iwo at night, and we could hear the gunfire from the ships. We could see the flashes and the firing, but we could not see Iwo at that time. Us new guys were too nervous to sleep, and we played poker all night. And even some of the old-timers, who were shaken up going into another battle, would be there with us.

Herb Altshuler joined the Marine Corps in April 1943 and was also assigned to the 4th Marine Division. The naval bombardment preceding the landings lasted three days.

Herb Altshuler

I remember very clearly how dramatic it was, seeing for the first time TV [monitors] with all these silhouetted ships and the beach.

It was quite an impressive thing going up on deck, and seeing as far as you could see, in a circle of 180 degrees, nothing but ships lined up. Battleships and destroyers and cruisers and all, just throwing in bombs right into this little island! You wondered how anybody would be there, how could anybody possibly live, and I think the leadership thought so too. They really thought they pulverized this island. It was amazing to see the armada of ships that were just lined up around this little island, just pounding it.

Sandy Berkman

We landed on Iwo February 19, 1945, and our division was part of the assault. Needless to say, it was a very, very tough operation, very costly in human lives. You couldn't move. It was all volcanic ash. We had poured some 18,000 rounds of [heavy] ammunition into the island from the battlewagons that were out there. And they [the Japanese] sat there and laughed at us; they were dug in. [Our] intelligence was not good—it later came out, and they admitted that it wasn't. We lost a lot of men. I lost a good deal of my platoon early.

Art LaPorte

Early in the morning, they fed us a steak dinner. Then we went up on deck, and we watched the 'goings-on' over Iwo. We looked out the stern of the ship, and there was Iwo standing right in front of us—Mount Suribachi to the left and a long stretch of beach, and to the right, some higher ground. The first outfit [went in] at 9:00. They hit the beaches, and we weren't scheduled to go in till the afternoon, but they lost so many men that we went in at 11:00. The thing that really got to us almost immediately—the boats were bringing back the wounded to our ship. I guess they were at least not-so-badly-hit casualties; the worst ones were being taken to the hospital ship. But they were bringing casualties back to our ship, and of course that made us quite nervous because we knew what we were getting into.

Herb Altshuler

I can remember very clearly watching the guys getting loaded onto the boats that were coming alongside and coming down the ladder, the netting. And I remember seeing a guy slip and getting crushed between the landing craft and the ship. I also remember very clearly that night when we had the burial at sea; we held service on deck, with a bugle and the works, and him being slipped over the side. Before you even went into battle, you were introduced to the reality of the war. I went in on the following day.

Art LaPorte

Our turn to hit the beach came at 11:00 a.m.; we were called in early. And the Japs didn't fire on us as we went in; I hardly saw any shells... When we got close to shore we were told to get in the landing craft. And when we landed at the beachhead, we ran out, and there was a slight rise ahead of us. It was hard to get over it because it was a mix of that black sand and volcanic ash and it was awful hard to get over it, and we were worried about the bullets.

Sandy Berkman

It was all volcanic ash; you couldn't dig. You'd dig a hole and it'd cave back in again. There was no such thing as digging a foxhole because it wouldn't hold. You lay there and hopefully you were all right. You see, they could see us, but we couldn't see them. They were so dug in, in these [fortified] emplacements. They had all those years to get that island ready, and especially when the war broke out, they knew that eventually we'd be going there. And they were waiting for us. There were over [20,000] of them. Probably, in the entire engagement, we landed over 40,000 men. You can imagine on an island [that small] with 60,000 men on there, it was just incredible. Absolutely incredible!

Herb Altshuler

Iwo was nothing but pulverized volcanic ash, and you sank in further over your ankles as you hit the beach. Now the Japanese had registered all their weaponry onto the beach, so you were there and you were just sitting ducks. The idea was to get in and get in as far as you could, and I remember doing that. And I remember that night, I crawled in a foxhole—well, actually, it was a hole that was caused by one of their large mortars. I had been lying there, and a 'recon' came by. A 'recon' was a small vehicle loaded with rockets, and it was dark, and it pulled up alongside of where I was, and I dug in, just holding onto my rifle, scared as hell, and he let go of all of his rockets, which flashed and made a big bright spot. After he let all of his rockets go he just drove off, and I thought, 'Well, this is the end.' These guys [the Japanese] would just register on me, but I was lucky that it didn't happen. I remember lying there thinking about all of the stuff I hadn't done [in my life]. Then I fell asleep.

"Trapped by Iwo's treacherous black-ash sands."
Mount Suribachi in background.
National Archives. Public domain.

Walter Hammer had just turned 21 a few months before the landing.

Walt Hammer

When we landed, our landing craft got hit. I was a heavy machine gunner carrying a 43–pound receiver [*the midsection 'business' action of the machine gun*]. We had a tripod carrier and also a guy who carried the barrel, which had a handle on it and a little pocket. Well, when we landed, I got ashore, and the landing craft backed off and the barrel went with it! Now we were ashore, so I said to Looney, 'We can't damn do anything right now, so take that tripod and put it on the ground, and let me put my receiver on there.' First thing that had to be done [on the beach] anyway was to start finding the mines, or we wouldn't have gotten any tanks, bulldozer tanks, or flamethrower tanks in there. So for a while, that's what we were doing...We were doing engineering work to make a pass up there [off the beach], putting the white tape on the side so that we could get the heavy equipment in. Later on, about two days later, the barrel showed up!

The Japanese were dug in and they had cisterns all over the island, and those got destroyed by our Navy [shelling]. The water ran out and a lot of those cisterns became operating rooms for the doctors. Doctors took those over. And the Japanese themselves, as this campaign wore on, they started wanting for water, so they used to go out and take the canteens from the dead Marines. They'd take their [empty] food cans and they'd set them outside so that when it did rain, they could collect the water. Now I understand that [the Japanese soldier] lived a miserable life underground, and he had to get the water so that he could take his biscuits and soak them so that he could eat them. And the lice drove 'em crazy! [*Laughing*] They lived that way, and they fought that way, and they fought to the very end. They stayed in the ground and they died in the ground.

At Iwo Jima, Ralph Leinoff made his fourth invasion landing as a Marine.

Ralph Leinoff

The first wave landed, they went ashore, and apparently there was very little resistance. They started to move inland and a few minutes later the second wave hit, and they started to move inland. And the wave I was in, the third one, we hit behind them and we started moving inland, and suddenly all hell broke loose!

We were sitting there on these open beaches. Our unit had to get up to this airfield, we wanted that airfield. When I went ashore, I had seven or eight men—the table of organization for a machine gun squad calls for eight men, but by the end of the first day, I had three guys left! I went in with seven, and I lost about half of them. Not killed, but so badly wounded that they couldn't go any further. And we were only about halfway up to the airfield and I tried to get up as far as I could [with the men]. Machine gun squads in an infantry company are in support of the riflemen. The riflemen are supposed to lead the way; the machine guns are supposed to protect them, set up crossfire in front of them, so that any enemy coming at us, the machine guns could take them out. When it became apparent that we had suffered so many casualties by the end of the first day, everybody just dug in where they were, halfway up to the landing field.

We got the word to stay where we were, we were in for the night, and we had to wait for reinforcements. When dusk came the Japanese couldn't see us that well, so the firing died down quite a bit. I said, 'We are going to dig in here tonight,' then I looked at one of my men, Tom Keiser from California, and I saw him up close for the first time that day. He had a big patch on his right cheek. I said, 'What happened to you, Tom?' He said, 'Nothing.' I said, 'I want to see what is under that patch, I don't know if you should be here.' Well, I made him take off the patch and I could see a piece of shrapnel and I think it went through, but I couldn't tell clearly because it was dusk and all. He took it off and I could see a pretty good gouge out of his cheek, and I said, 'Okay, Tom, you are out of it, you go back to the first aid. You have had enough.' He said he wasn't going. So we had an argument, again—before the landing, we had had an argument about some of the weaponry that I wanted the squad to carry. I said, 'Yesterday you wanted out of my squad, now I am telling you to go back! I don't need another wounded man on my hands! I will wait until I get relief in the morning!' He said to me, 'I am not leaving you with two men.'

What do you say to that? I was about 21; I did not know how to take it. I did not know if I should thank him, or tell him to follow orders, but I needed him. I really needed the manpower, and he says, 'I am not leaving you.' I was kind of flabbergasted. To make a long story short, Tom stayed with me for the rest of the war.

Art LaPorte

Our target was an airbase. They had one main airfield, and they had another smaller one, and the third one they were still working on. That was where I got wounded, the unfinished airfield. They had Mount Suribachi, the highest peak, which the 5th Division took. We had the next highest peak, which was Hill 382—you name them by height. The day I got hit, my company went against it. They lost half of the men and had to pull back.

Mount Suribachi was quite a sight, too. There, for a while, you could watch what was going on. They put spotlights on it at night, and they were pounding with everything they had! They put 20-mm and 5-inch guns—and the 16s—they were really pounding it. I don't know if it did any good, the [Japanese] had the caves. But they were really working it over!

Flag of our Fathers

AP combat photographer Joe Rosenthal took the iconic photo of the flag-raising on Iwo Jima. As at Peleliu, mission planners had expected the island to fall within a few days. Only a third of Iwo Jima had been taken when the U.S. flag appeared over the peak of Mount Suribachi on D–Day+4.

Art LaPorte

I didn't actually see the flag go up. We were pretty far inland, by that time, from the cliffs. I volunteered with another guy to go and get some food for the platoon. As we approached the cliffs, I looked over and I saw the flag flying. I said to my buddy—not knowing that it would become so famous—I said, 'What in the devil do they have that flying for? We haven't even taken this damned place...'

Sandy Berkman

I lasted four and a half days. I got hit on February 23, about 30 minutes after the flag went up on Suribachi. Part of my outfit went to Suribachi, and the rest of us went to the airfield. We had to secure the airfield—that's the way they broke us up.

By the fourth day we'd only advanced less than a mile. We were pinned down most of the time. We couldn't even set ourselves up to meet the enemy. I was lying there waiting to pull my platoon up into a flank, and I looked over and I saw the flag up, and it was a wonderful sight. I saw the first flag. There were two flags that went up. Then they put up the second flag—that was the famous photograph. About thirty minutes after that, I guess they [the Japanese] got a little mad at us, because we got everything thrown at us, and I got hit. I got hit with a mortar shell, all across my back. I had eight pieces [of shrapnel], they found out later, that hit me.

I gave myself a shot of morphine. The officers were allowed to carry it; we were the only ones that could take it with us. And I gave myself a shot to ease the pain up a little bit. The corpsmen saw me, and they came and got me, and they took me out on a stretcher and they took me down to the beach. Then I went to a hospital ship. From the hospital ship, I went to Saipan to a field hospital, and from Saipan I went to Hawaii to a field hospital. From Hawaii I went to

San Francisco, and from San Francisco I went to St. Albans in Long Island. They tried to get you as close to home as they could. I was at St. Albans until June of 1945.

I lost a lot of people who I knew, especially in my platoon. I later found out that we had almost 100 percent casualties in my platoon. It was just a devastating place to be. The island was nothing, really, but we had to get the airfields. There was no question whether we had to or didn't have to—we had to, because by the time we completed the engagement, the first [U.S.] planes that landed were hit, and they would have never made it back to Saipan.

Ralph Leinoff

Now we were about two miles up from Mount Suribachi, where the flag was raised. We were put into a reserve position until we could get manpower; other units took over the front line, and we were put on reserve. While I was up on the airfield, I could see the mountain; I thought I spotted a little fleck of color up there at the top. I was like, 'What the hell is that?'—because you were still seeing smoke coming up. We didn't think that they had gotten up there. And I borrowed one of the officer's field glasses, I took a look, and I said, 'Son of a gun, there's an American flag flying—they're up there!' But what happened was they bypassed a lot of pillboxes to get up there; they got up there as fast as they could. They took a tremendous beating going up, and they went by a lot of Japanese machine gunners and all.

In his enthusiasm to be a Marine, Ralph had joined up, although he was still technically a member of the New York State Guard. He recalled mail call on Iwo Jima.

Ralph Leinoff, 2013. Portrait by Erica Miller.
Courtesy of the Saratogian.
(Note his painting in background.)

They brought up some fresh food, water, and supplies, and even brought up mail. At about two weeks into the operation, one of the letters I got was a postcard from the New York State Guard, threatening me with a court-martial because I had been missing the drills. So I told my sergeant, I said, 'Sergeant, I'm sorry to tell you this but I have to get back. I'm missing the drills in the New York State Guard. They want me back there.' [*chuckling*] He said, 'Get back to your foxhole.' [*He laughs again*] So it was kind of a comical relief.

So anyway, we started to get mail, and one of the things I got that was distributed by the Navy was a small edition of *Time Magazine*. And as I sat there eating a sandwich I was going through this small magazine, and I came upon the picture, the [now famous] photograph—it was all black and white, no color. I said, 'Son of a—

look at this silhouette! There's six guys here trying to raise the flag on Mount Suribachi!' So I started drawing. We had nothing else to do; we were in reserve until we got up there to the airfield. I had letterhead, I had a pencil, and so on—I was drawing it! And I kept the drawing, and finally when we got back to our base in Maui, I was serious. I said, 'I'm going to go get some paper and some paint—some watercolors.' At that time it just came out, nobody really knew [how iconic the picture would become]. The paintings that the artists made afterward with the oil, of course, were much superior. I'm not a professional artist, but yes, I used to try to paint pictures of some of the men who were killed. I would try to make a picture and send it home to the family. I didn't do too many, because some of the letters I got back in appreciation were really heartbreaking...and they wanted to know the 'when, how, and why'; they wanted all the details, how the men got killed, and, well, it's... [*pauses a short while*] War is hell, it really is, and if you try to describe it, it just—it just can't be done, can't be done.

Art LaPorte

Art's unit moved up to secure the unfinished airfield. Looking for cover, he received a shock.

We got the word that one of our outfits got the pounding pretty bad, so we were the replacements. We went up during the night, early morning, and moved into position. They told us to get in a foxhole. I got into a foxhole quickly, and there was another Marine sitting there. I see his feet. I brought my eyes up his body, and his rifle was standing beside him. So I said to him, 'I'm going to get in with you, all right?' And no answer. As I come up his body, no head [*motions across his neck*]. Some Japanese officer or somebody with a sword had taken his head off during the night. I felt the hair raise on the back of my head, and I got away from there! I found another foxhole and jumped in it.

Art LaPorte.

'I've got a good one for you, Doc.'

That morning, 12 days into the attack, Art was hit.

I was kind of in a shallow place, I was going to run up and join my outfit—they were a little ahead. All of a sudden a sniper was putting shots right by my head. I could almost feel it, so I figured I better run. So I zigzagged. Of course, if you zigzag, you make yourself a harder target. Next thing I know, I'm flying through the air. A machine gun burst had gone by me, and they were using explosive bullets. And so, luckily, I landed in a 5-inch shell hole; our guns on the destroyers were 5 inches in diameter across the shell, like the battlewagons had 16-inch diameters across that shell. Now the 16-inch shell was about across-my-body wide [*motioning*], 2,000 pounds, and you can imagine what explosive that is. You could put about 15 or 20 people in the [crater made by the shell on impact],

I'd say. So I looked down at my leg, and I could see the bone, and you could put your fist into it. I could hear some guys in the next 16-inch shell hole, so I think I hollered over to them, 'I'm hit.' I wasn't feeling any pain, I was in shock. As bad as it is, it was no pain that I remember. And so, I heard somebody running, and somebody popped down on me, and the machine gun was trying to get him. And it was my sergeant, section leader. And he says, 'How bad you hit?' And I said, 'Pretty bad.' I think he said, 'Jesus,' and he ran into the 16-inch shell hole. And this time, another body landed on me, and it was a corpsman this time. And he tried to patch me up, but that machine gun kept trying to pick him off. So he says, 'I can't work on you here, I haven't got room enough,' because it was very shallow. And he said, 'Would you take a chance? We can push you across to the 16-inch shell hole.' It was a short distance, maybe 10 feet. I said, 'Sure, I got to get patched up.' So he pushed against my good leg, and I'm trying to crawl. And the other guys in the 16-inch shell hole are reaching out for me. And one of them got a graze against the wrist.

They got me down in the hole; it was pretty deep, probably six or eight feet deep. Quite wide, too. They worked on me—patched me up. Then they left; they had to go to Hill 382. So all day I was there, I tried to drink water. But I couldn't, I'd throw it up. Tried to eat food, same thing. I noticed a funny sensation, like something wet. I knew that they had bound up the wounds good. I was worried about hemorrhaging, so I pulled up my pants leg, and there was a fountain—about an inch or two high—coming out of my kneecap. A piece of shrapnel had gone in and hit an artery or whatever is in there. I had used my bandage on my wounds; the only thing I had was toilet paper. So I put that on with some pressure, and it stopped the bleeding.

I was by myself in the shell crater. I was all alone. All kinds of weapons were firing because they were trying to pick our men off.

My company was going against 382. And, of course, I was right in line with it. I'd peep up and try to see how they were doing, but I didn't dare to stand up on my good leg. I looked back toward some rocks behind me. Some of our men were there, and stretcher-bearers, but they didn't dare send anyone because there were so many bullets flying around. And they didn't want to lose four men to save one.[24]

I was there about eight hours. I was concerned that they would leave me there and the Japanese would get me. Then, my sergeant came by and asked if I was still there. I don't know how he got me out of that 16-inch shell hole but he asked me if I could stand on the good leg. He put me in a fireman's carry and carried me out under fire.

On the hospital ship, LaPorte waited his turn for surgery.

From where I was I could watch the doctors operate. It was a table, and around the table was a trough. What fascinated me was when the trough was filled with blood, and when the ship would rock, the blood would go back and forth in unison with the ship.

They finally got to me, and I believe I said to the doctor, 'I've got a good one for you, Doc.' Because the one that was ahead of me apparently couldn't take the pain too good. And he was screaming and hollering, and I could see the doctor. They were working right around the clock, and they looked awful tired. And I said to myself, 'I'm not going to give them a hard time'—they had enough trouble. So when he got to me, I watched him. It really didn't bother me. I could see him clipping with scissors around the wound, taking the jagged edges off. Then, when I got done, they put me out on the

---

[24] As on Peleliu and in other battles, the Japanese would target corpsmen and stretcher-bearers.

side where I could look out and see Iwo. Like a sundeck or something. That was the last time I saw Iwo—we sailed for Guam.

The Guys Left Behind

Herb Altshuler

One thing I will always remember is the day or two before we left the island, before we got back on that ship, they had services and they dedicated the cemetery on Iwo. I remember sitting on a hill looking down and there was a flag pole—they used dogs for bringing messages back from the front forward to the firing units in the back, and they had the [dead] dogs lined up around the flagpole where they were to be buried... You see a large area of your [dead] men just lined up, and... then I saw heavy equipment, and that [the ground] was plowed, and all the dead bodies were laid out. You could see dead bodies as far as you wanted to look, and then you realized that war was not fun and games. These were the guys that were left behind.

A total of 27 Medals of Honor were awarded for individual acts of heroism under fire at Iwo Jima. The island was deemed secure on March 25—25 days longer than planners had counted on. Nearly 7,000 Americans and 19,000 Japanese died at Iwo Jima. It was the Marines' costliest battle ever.[42]

CHAPTER ELEVEN

Captivity-Year 4: The Copper Mine

As 1945 dawned, Joe Minder and 500 other prisoners would depart from Formosa for the Japanese home islands. After nearly two weeks, they arrived in Kyushu, where they would then be shipped north in boxcars to arrive at a freezing copper mine, slaving for Japanese industrialists. Many of the major Japanese corporations lobbied the government intensively for the opportunity to exploit American laborers, especially skilled ones, though the prisoners were routinely starved and abused. Nearly forty percent of the 27,000 American slave laborers died in captivity.[25] Joe's journey was far from over.

---

[25] U.S. Congressional Research Service. To date, out of the 60 Japanese corporations that profited from American slave labor during the war, just one has formally apologized. Said one daughter: 'This isn't going to end even when all of the former POWs pass away. Their children and grandchildren have heard and lived with the stories, and they haven't forgotten. This isn't about money. It's about acknowledging what was done to these men.' [time.com/3334677/pow-world-war-two-usa-japan]

Joe Minder

Hell, Revisited

January 12, 1945

Hell again! Found out last night that we're going to be shipped to Japan.

Americans are much more active around here now. We have seen many planes fly over our camp and have also heard the rumble of bombs and strafing from the Yank planes. I hate to think of dodging those torpedoes and bombs on the open seas again, but God saved us on that last trip and if he answers our prayers, we will make this okay, also.

4:00 p.m.

Arrived at Port Takao by train and went aboard a little larger ship this time, named *Melbourne Maru.* After loading on sugar and salt, we sailed for Moji, Japan.

January 22, 1945

We didn't have contact with any Yanks until today when we had another attack by an American sub. Several depth charges were dropped and drove it off. Now we are wondering if American planes will be after us!

January 23, 1945

Sailed safely into Moji.

January 25, 1945

Disembarked at Moji, got on train and started for Hanaoka on the northern tip of Japan.

January 29, 1945

After a four-day bitter-cold train ride, we finally arrived here at camp, where we will work in this open copper mine as soon as a little of this snow melts. What a different climate—in the south of Japan there are oranges on the trees, here there is about four feet of snow and it is cold as heck!

Mittens Made of Grass

February 20, 1945

Started working in the mine today, loading dirt into four-wheeled steel cars and pushing them about one mile by hand. With only shoes and mittens made of grass, our hands and feet are about to freeze in this bitter cold!

March 6, 1945

Had our first bath in 54 days today! They broke down and even gave us wood to heat our water with!

What a camp this is! We have to carry all water from outside the camp and carry the wood in on our backs, about two miles from here. They ration the wood out to us every day. Those 15 sticks which they give us don't even take the chill off of our barracks. Several men are suffering from chilled feet and hands.

April 1, 1945

One hundred men arrived in camp from Kawasaki.

April 4, 1945

Received one American Red Cross food parcel per man. I enjoyed this better than any other chow that I have ate in my life!

April 19, 1945

Received second Red Cross parcel, less a half can of butter, due to stealing by new men in camp.

May 5, 1945

Celebrated my birthday by having a can of pâté baked into a rice loaf. Also had some coffee, which I saved from my Red Cross parcel.

June 18, 1945

Four men escaped from camp!

Working conditions are steadily getting harder and our food is getting lousier every day. When we first got here, we received a little fish and horse bones to flavor our soup, but we have to work on plain watery greens soup and a small bowl of barley.

Several men have gotten so weak out in the mine that they have fainted and tumbled off of the ledges while picking at the dirt!

June 28, 1945

Our morale went up today when 45 Australian officers joined our camp! They gave us the dope as to how the Yanks were blasting Tokyo and other large cities south of here. Where their camp was located in southern Japan, bombing became so terrific that the Japs were forced to evacuate the entire area!

CHAPTER TWELVE

A Rain of Ruin

Strategic bombing raids to Japan began in earnest from the newly liberated Mariana Islands as the fighting ended in the early summer of 1944. By early 1945, wave after wave of the sleek new B–29 Superfortresses began to arrive in the skies over Japan. A quantum leap in aviation technology, the B–29 was much longer, wider, and faster than its predecessor, the B–17, and capable of carrying a much larger bomb load over vast expanses of ocean over thousands of miles. Additionally, the densely populated industrial areas of Japan and the dispersal of Japanese industry into domestic settings (i.e., people's homes) would have grave consequences for the populations within the areas to be targeted.

The coupling of the B–29 with the development and deployment of incendiary "firesticks," six-pound cylinders filled with napalm, or gelatinized gasoline, was a very serious development for the enemy, indeed. While few were willing to face up to the inevitable, the death and destruction brought by the B–29s would plunge the country into a feeling that it had never felt before in its thousand-year history: a mixture of desperation and quiet despair.[43]

Andy Doty, a 1943 graduate of Hudson Falls High, was tasked as a tail gunner on 21 combat missions in the B–29 in the skies over the vast Pacific in these raids on the Japanese home islands. Landing in Guam for the first time as part of an eleven-man crew, he recounted his first missions and the horrors of war as witnessed by a twenty-one–year-old kid from Hometown, USA.

Andy Doty

My earliest impressions of our new home were of jungle, rain, and mud. We lived in tents surrounded by high rows of uprooted trees and got about on wooden walkways. After a few weeks we moved into newly constructed Quonset huts that were high and dry.

Not long after we arrived, the pilot and co-pilot went on a mission to Japan as observers. They were strangely noncommittal when they came back.

'What was it like?' I asked the lieutenant, our co-pilot, a day later.

'It was interesting. Spectacular. You'll find out soon enough.'

The First Mission

Our turn came not long afterward. On March 30 we were alerted for our first raid. We made our way to the briefing tent that was filled with combat crews sprawled on rows of benches. At the front was a huge map. The Marianas were at the bottom. Iwo Jima was halfway up, and the Japanese homeland angled across the top, 1,600 miles away.

A red string led from our base straight to Nagoya, on the main island of Honshu. It was to be a high altitude daylight mission against the Mitsubishi aircraft engine factory, one of the two largest engine plants in Japan. It was a heavily defended target that previous missions had failed to destroy. Briefing officers told us about the importance of the complex. We listened closely to reports about the weather, the location of enemy anti-aircraft batteries, the positions of rescue submarines and aircraft, the tactics of Japanese fighter planes, and other details. A chaplain concluded the session with a short prayer. We sat with heads bowed.

We gathered up our parachute harnesses, parachutes, inflatable 'Mae West' life preservers, survival vests, helmets, oxygen masks, hunting knives, sunglasses, and other items, and climbed into a truck with benches along each side. There was little talk in the darkness as we rode to our hardstand.

Much to our disappointment, the new bomber we had flown to Guam had been taken away from us and assigned to a more veteran crew. We inherited an older plane, No. 43 92996, and unloaded in front of it. We climbed aboard to check our equipment and positions, then returned to sit on the pavement near the front landing gear, our backs against the big wheels.

A long hour later, it was time to go. We paired up to pull the big propeller blades down and through, twelve turns per blade, to make certain that no oil had accumulated in the lower cylinder heads. I climbed up the rear ladder and started the auxiliary generator.

'Putt-putt started and on line,' I reported.

'Roger,' the pilot, our captain, replied. The men up front closed the bomb bays and switched on the first engine. The propellers slowly began to turn. The engine coughed to life, spewed smoke, and settled into a steady roar. Three other engines followed in turn.

Into the Air

Few wartime scenes can be more dramatic than dozens of heavy bombers departing on a mission. I will never forget the sight. One at a time, on a precise schedule, the B–29s inched out of their paved revetments and fell into line, brakes screeching, high tails bobbing in the moonlight like some prehistoric monsters. Nose to tail, the bombers edged ahead in a slow parade to the head of the runway. The air was filled with noise and fumes.

The large flaps at the back edge of our wings were slowly extended as we moved ahead, adding a fifth more surface area to the bomber's narrow wings. The flaps allowed take-offs and landings at lower speeds.

'Left flap, twenty-five degrees,' the waist gunner reported to the pilot. 'Right flap, twenty-five degrees,' the opposite waist gunner added.

A wooden control tower lay ahead, to the right of the runway. Red and green lights from the tower triggered a take-off every minute. When the green light flashed, the captain opened the engines to full power and stood on the brakes, holding us fast as the engines roared. He released the brakes, and we began lumbering down the long runway. It was a dangerous moment, with little margin of safety; the temperamental engines had to haul a thirty–five-ton bomber, four tons of bombs, eight thousand gallons of gasoline, thousands of rounds of ammunition, and eleven men into the air.

We slowly picked up speed, engines roaring, wisps of vapor trailing from open engine cowlings that reminded me of the laid back ears of a running dog. We seemed to hug the ground forever. The captain held the nose down to gain as much speed as possible, then eased us into the air. He touched the brakes briefly to stop the wheels from spinning once we were airborne.

The lieutenant quickly retracted the wheels into the inboard engine nacelles [*housings*] to rid ourselves of the air resistance. 'Gear up,' he said. We sagged over the rocky headlands at the end of the island, adding speed as we dropped. The captain 'milked' the flaps back into the wings as we sped on.

Seated in the tail, I watched the bombers behind us, the runway, the cliffs, and the island disappear. We were on our way. After a time I test fired my guns, went back through the unpressurized section to turn off the 'putt-putt,' and joined the others in the waist compartment for the long trip. We had left at three in the morning to reach our target seven hours later. That timing would give us several hours of daylight for our return to Guam after the bomb run.

Three and one half hours later we passed over Iwo Jima, a brown pork chop-shaped island halfway to Japan. Marines had taken it from the Japanese only a few days earlier after a monumental battle. The island's new landing strip, built while the fighting still raged, already was a welcome haven for bombers in distress.

Although the B-29's top speed was 358 miles an hour, it actually was flown more slowly when loaded with bombs and gas, and when a long trip lay ahead. The average indicated airspeed was closer to 220 miles an hour, which meant that the crews had to spend more than fifteen and one half hours in the air on every mission. The trip from Guam to Japan and back covered some 3,200 miles.

Three hours after we passed over Iwo, the captain announced that he was starting the climb to our bombing altitude of 25,000 feet. I returned to the tail and settled in. Ahead of us a lead bomber, its nose wheel extended for identification, circled above a tiny volcanic island off the coast of Japan. Arriving B–29s cut across the wide circle to catch up to the leader and other bombers. We edged into a formation of twelve planes. Once we had assembled we joined 256 Superforts in a long bomber stream, headed for Nagoya.

B–29s over Mt. Fuji, 1945. USAAF. Public domain.

The Bomb Run

The side windows of my tail compartment flared out slightly. I could crane my head around to see the wings and engines. Looking down, I saw the coast of Japan appear beneath a wing. The enemy territory appeared dark and foreboding. There was no turning back. We were being drawn inexorably toward a point high in the sky above Japan's second largest city.

My stomach was tight as we continued on and turned into our bomb run. We were flying in close formation, keeping each other company as we maximized our fire power and bombing pattern. One B–29 was just behind and below our plane, only yards away. I looked into the front cabin, where the bombardier, pilot, and copilot were hunched tensely in their flak suits, oxygen masks, and helmets.

I kept my guns angled straight up in the air, knowing that the men in the following bombers were frightened by friendly weapons pointed in their direction.

It was quiet in our bomber as we bore ahead in perfect weather. The first puffs of anti-aircraft fire began to appear. I strained to watch in every direction for enemy aircraft.

'Twelve o'clock level,' the lieutenant shouted, and the guns chattered up front. A Japanese fighter flashed through our formation, the pilot's head swiveling as he looked about. I fired as soon as I could without hitting any bombers behind us. Someone had hit him—I hadn't—and he bailed out. He drifted to earth far to the rear.

As we neared the target area, the anti-aircraft fire increased. Our introduction to the war was a sky filled with ugly black bursts of fire, each burst sending jagged bits of steel flying in all directions.

I tried to shrink my body into the smallest possible target. The deadly puffs contrasted with the long, almost beautiful white tentacles of phosphorous bombs that were dropped into our formation by a Japanese plane flying above us. It was a surrealistic scene. Several bursts walked silently in a line toward our plane, but stopped short. Out of range to our right, a twin-engine Japanese fighter radioed our speed and altitude to the ground batteries.

I was struck by the unreality of it all, although nothing could be more real. Perhaps all warriors are somewhat traumatized by their situations. We were in the thick of it, five miles above Japan, and yet I was observing myself and our situation almost with detachment. The cool interior of my compartment, the gleaming bombers all about us, the clear air outside, the vicious bursts of flak, the masked and helmeted men huddled in the plane close behind, all seemed from another world.

We were suspended in time on a steady bomb run from which we could not deviate. Flak described as 'intense and accurate' crashed all about us. Finally our bombardier called out 'bombs away' and our plane surged upward, relieved of its burden. Looking around, I saw schools of fat, 500-pound bombs drop from the other bombers and begin their long slants to earth; looking down moments later, I could see explosions twinkling in the target area, much like strings of tiny Chinese firecrackers.

Our formation wheeled into a long turn to head back home. Off the coast, the individual bombers spread out to begin their solitary flights to Guam. The feeling of relief in our B–29 was palpable.

'My,' the left waist gunner said. 'That was quite a party!'

'Only thirty-four more to go,' the radioman added. No one answered.

Post-strike photos showed 'excellent' results; *The New York Times* reported the next day that the target had been hit squarely by our bombs, resulting in the 'virtually total destruction of the vast works.' All but twenty-four of the 140 buildings were destroyed, some 3,446,000 square feet of roof space.

The anti-aircraft fire was 'the heaviest yet encountered,' according to the reports of veteran crew members, and fighter opposition was severe. Five aircraft were lost and more than half the bombers were damaged by flak, but I did not see any Superforts go down.

'Look what you did to my airplane!' our ground crew chief said after we landed and returned to our revetment. He mounted a ladder to poke the end of a screwdriver into one of the small holes that had been created by bits of flak on the underside of our right wing.

'Sorry about that,' said the captain.

Perdition

If the bombing run over Nagoya seemed interminable, the next one seemed even longer. It came over Tokyo on April 13, during the second low-level incendiary raid on that city.

Although our high-altitude Nagoya mission had been successful, earlier precision bombing from that height had been largely ineffective because of the dense clouds and strong winds above Japan. Clear weather was found over the target only four to seven days a month. General Curtis LeMay, head of the 20th Air Force, concluded that individual B-29s, flying in at 5,000 to 8,000 feet at night, would be far more accurate than if they bombed from 25,000 to 30,000 feet. They could burn out large areas of the Japanese cities, 'de-house' the population, and destroy the many cottage industries that supported the war effort.

Another major advantage was that the bombers would not have to make the long, demanding climb to high altitudes that strained the engines and drank up fuel. Nor would they have to assemble in formation and jockey about on the way to the target. Consequently, they could carry twice the bomb load. Engine maintenance would be reduced, which would result in more bombers over the target.

LeMay's decision had dismayed the B–29 crews. The low-level raids obviously were much closer to ground anti-aircraft and searchlight batteries, and left less room for crewmen to bail out if their plane was shot down. Many B–29s were seen to catch fire, explode, and plunge to earth. The incendiary raids against major cities were not welcomed by the airmen.

We took off late in the afternoon on a mission appropriately code named 'Perdition'—hell, utter destruction, entire loss, ruin. Our target was the arsenal area of the city, six miles northwest of the Imperial Palace. It was a sector that contained housing and factories that made or stored machine guns, artillery, bombs, and other arms. An estimated 30,000 to 80,000 people lived in every square mile of that area.

Each of the 348 bombers carried between five and eight tons of incendiary bombs, depending upon the distance they had to fly. Guam was 125 miles south of Saipan, so our ground crew loaded fewer bombs and more fuel. Each of our main bombs contained a cluster of fifty-five smaller bombs filled with jellied gasoline; the big bombs opened at 5,000 feet to scatter the smaller ones. One bomber could create a flaming swath a half-mile wide and a mile and a half long.

The Death of the President

As we flew north that night, we heard on our headsets that President Roosevelt had died suddenly while vacationing in Georgia. The news shocked us, for we were fond of our president and respected his steady leadership. We buzzed about the development for a time, speculating about the little known vice president, Harry Truman, who now would move into the White House. We put the news behind us and concentrated again on the mission ahead.

Inferno

We arrived off the coast at midnight. Looking ahead, I could see the glow of the burning city. We had heard about the three hundred anti-aircraft guns awaiting us, and were fearful. The report was that bombers caught in the searchlight beams above the city often were goners.

'This is it,' someone said as we bore ahead.

'Stay off the intercom,' the captain ordered.

Once over the city, I looked down into an indescribable scene. Tokyo was an inferno. Block after block of buildings were aflame. The fire covered eleven square miles of the city, and smoke towered thousands of feet into the air. The smell of burning wood and other materials came through our open bomb bays. A violent updraft suddenly drove us hundreds of feet higher, pinning us to our seats. I could hardly lift my hand.

Searchlights swept the sky and tracer fire laced through the night. I strained to watch for other bombers and Japanese night fighters. A few thousand feet above us, and to the rear, I saw a silver bomber caught by the searchlight beams. It shone brightly in the night sky. Bombs began tumbling down from its open bays, shimmering in the light of the fires and the beams.

Suddenly a beam fastened on our own bomber, and it was quickly joined by others. It was bright enough inside my compartment to read a newspaper. I felt naked in the grip of the beams as we plunged wildly ahead, waiting for our load of bombs to be dropped. They finally fell free, and the captain nosed the plane down to gain speed.

'Let's get the hell out of here!' he said as he banked swiftly down and away. We were greatly relieved as we headed home. More than one hundred miles from the city, I could still see the red glow in the sky. Beneath that glow, thousands of people were dead or dying.

Some 2,100 tons of bombs fell on Tokyo that night. *'B–29s Set Great Tokyo Fires; Explosions Heard 100 Miles,'* the *Times* reported afterward. A correspondent who flew in a 314th Wing bomber wrote:

> 'A very large task force of B-29s swarmed over Tokyo, a minute apart, in the darkness early today with millions of pounds of incendiaries. From my vantage point in this battleship of the sky, it appeared that the Army Air Force had achieved its goal of wiping out the fire-able sections of the Japanese capital. The sight of the capital aflame would thrill any American, and it was especially exciting for me, marking my first combat mission in the Pacific air theater.'

Seven bombers and seventy-seven men failed to return. Our crew had emerged shaken, but unscathed.

The 15th Mission

I wrote home to my parents before our fifteenth mission. 'This should all be over pretty soon,' I said. 'The Japs can't keep it up. They're running out of gas.'

We took off for Osaka early in the morning of June 7. Our regular radar man was ill, and was replaced by a young radar officer. He was quiet on our flight north, a handsome fellow among strangers, intent on the green radar screen in his dark room.

We were fairly confident it would be an easy run, for we had seen few fighters in recent weeks and the anti-aircraft fire was growing weaker. The flight was even easier than we expected; all of Japan was blanketed by heavy clouds. We saw no land from the time we neared the coast until we left it. We bombed by radar and saw only a few bursts of flak well away from our bomber.

A hundred miles off the coast on our way home, we began to relax. I was still watching behind us when something caught my eye. Far to the rear, to my lower right, a twin-engine fighter plane popped up above the clouds, and then dropped down. He was on the prowl, hoping to catch us by surprise.

'Tail to crew,' I called out. 'A fighter just came out of the clouds at seven o'clock low and dropped back down. Get ready.'

It was an Irving, the name that had been given to a night fighter that was equipped with radar and heavy armament. I entered his wingspan into my gun sight and waited. The black plane suddenly emerged a few thousand yards to the rear, climbing rapidly at my lower left.

'Five o'clock low,' I cried out, and found him in my sight. I narrowed the circle of dots down to his wing tips, and began squeezing off bursts. He opened fire at the same time. The machine guns in his wings flared again and again as he closed in. His glowing tracer bullets flew lazily by, looking almost harmless. He kept coming until he was a few hundred yards away. The image of that black fighter, his winking guns, and the slow motion tracers will stay with me forever.

I slowly opened the ring to hold it around his wing tips, and continued firing. I was aware that I was spacing my bursts, letting up for a few seconds as he bore in. My bullets were striking his right engine, sending parts flying. Smoke began pouring from the engine, and the pilot broke off his attack. He banked down into the clouds, a long, black plume trailing behind. I have often wondered if he made it home safely, and where he is today. One of his engines was still operating, so he probably was able to return to his base.

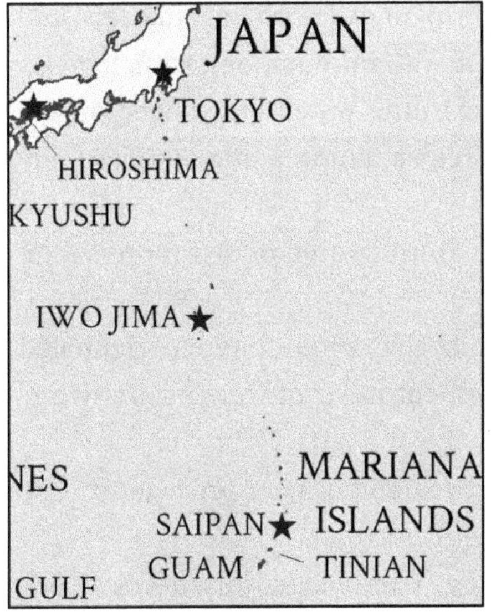

Late that day, as we were nearing home, I became aware that something was wrong. The captain and our flight engineer were talking about headwinds and the amount of fuel that remained in our wing tanks, as they so often did. But this time I could tell they were worried. Finally the flight engineer said, 'It's going to be close.'

Not long after, the captain came onto the intercom.

'We've got a little problem up here,' he said. 'We've hit some headwinds, and might not be able to make it back. Y'all should get ready, in case we have to ditch or bail out.'

By that time, we were well south of Saipan and forty-five miles north of Guam. So not only the Japanese were running out of gas. I scrambled quickly back to the tail, where my life raft rested in its canvas pack within the seat frame. I snapped my chest parachute onto my harness. Listening from the tail, I could hear that the situation was worsening.

I lifted out the life raft pack and attached it to the rings on the bottom of my parachute harness. A long strap hung from the raft inside the pack. I pulled the strap underneath my harness and snapped it onto my Mae West. It was an ingenious arrangement; once I shucked the chute harness in the water and yanked on the strap, the raft would be pulled free of the pack and automatically inflate.

I folded my seat back and slid it up to give myself more room. The intercom clicked.

'No time left', the captain said. 'Everybody out!' A frightened voice broke in. It was the replacement radar officer. 'I can't swim,' he cried out. 'I can't swim!'

'You don't have to,' I said. 'Just remember your procedures. The life vest and raft should be enough.'

The bailout bell began ringing. I unplugged my headset, unsnapped my throat microphone, and opened the escape window. The air whipped by in a fearsome roar. As I moved to dive out, I found I could not; I was caught by the life raft strap, which had become snagged in the folded seat. I felt a wave of panic, and began tugging desperately at the strap. It would not come loose. The bell kept ringing. I thought of cutting the strap with my knife, but told myself to calm down to work the strap free. I unfolded the seat, slid it back down, and released the strap. I pushed the seat up, and went out the window.

Into the Ocean

First there was a rush and roar of air, then I tumbled over and over. Suddenly the parachute opened above me with a 'pop' and I was jerked to a halt. I have no memory of pulling the ripcord handle, or where it went afterward. My helmet was gone. It was strangely quiet except for the hum of our disappearing bomber. The evening sky was still pink from the sunset as I floated down.

I could see another chute against the black sea below, and called out to its owner. I undid my chest and leg straps and inflated my Mae West so that I could get out of the harness as quickly as possible after landing. I dangled there like a kid on a swing. As I watched, the horizon quickly closed in. For the first time, I realized that I would be alone in the ocean. I landed with a hard splash on my back and sank far deeper into the water than I ever imagined. It seemed a long time before I came up to the surface, even with an inflated vest. But I kept my mouth closed and held my breath until I surfaced. I threw off the parachute harness and pulled the life raft strap. The raft came out of its pack, and a gas cylinder opened it with a 'whoosh.' I drew the small raft to me and climbed in.

The waves were rolling monsters, flecks of white spray whipping from their crests. I rode them up and down as if on a roller coaster. Even when I was carried high on a wave, I saw no other crew members. I spent the night trying to sleep, being tipped over by the big swells, climbing back into the raft, and drying off only to be tipped over again. I was glad I had not cut the strap, for it kept the raft from blowing away when I was spilled into the water. Each time I was dumped into the sea, I thought about the possibility of sharks being in the area and scrambled back into the raft as quickly as I could.

A squall moved in. I collected rain in the rubber raft cover, washed the salt away as best I could, and drank all I could hold. I did not know how long it would be until help arrived.

Just before dawn, I noticed a dark shape in the distance. For a time I thought it was Rota, a small, Japanese-held island just north of Guam that had been bypassed [by our forces]. I did not want to be washed ashore, for B–29s that had to abort their missions dumped their bombs there before returning to Guam. The soldiers were not likely to be kind. I reversed the yellow side of the cover to the dark blue side and snuggled down even lower in the raft.

After a time, I heard the muffled chugging of an engine. The dark shape was a merchant ship that was looking for us. A searchlight swept the ocean. 'Ship ahoy,' I called out, as they did in the movies. The beam came my way, and I waved my arms. It lighted on me. Soon the side of the ship loomed high above. A sailor came down a cargo net, grabbed my hand, and helped me out of the raft. I scrambled up the side, only to find my legs weak when I climbed over the railing and stood on the deck. Members of the ship's crew stood watching the strange scene. I was led below, given a hot shower, a shot of whiskey, an officer's underwear and bunk, and fell asleep.

Our waist gunners were picked up before I was. One said later that someone told him that another member of the crew had been found, and that 'he came up the side of the ship like a monkey.'

'That must be our tail gunner,' he said.

Three other members of the crew were not as fortunate. Our navigator and the flight engineer failed to open their life rafts and had drowned. They were found floating in their life vests, unable to keep their heads out of the choppy waves all night. Our radioman was able to do that; he did not get his raft open, but he fought to keep his head up. His neck was scraped raw by his life vest, but he survived.

I assumed that the replacement radar man who could not swim had leaped from the plane after I did. In the most bizarre aspect of the entire tragedy, I did not learn otherwise for many years. In actuality, he had gone down with the plane, refusing to jump despite the pleas of the waist gunners and our central fire control gunner. They considered throwing him out the rear door, but the central fire control gunner thought he could persuade him to jump by himself. He argued as long as he could, and then had to leap before it was too late. The radar man preferred to die in a crash rather than risk drowning in the sea.

The Unwritten Rule

They never talked about those awful moments, nor did I ever ask about them. Their need to deny or forget was complete, and I must have undergone the same subconscious process. It was only after I was reunited with one of the waist gunners, Jim Dudley, forty–five years after the war, that I learned the true story.

We could only speculate on what had happened to our navigator and flight engineer; possibly they had left their rafts behind. Possibly they had forgotten to attach the raft straps to their life vests, or had attached their straps over their chute harnesses instead of underneath them. Nor did we ever find out why we had not stopped at Iwo, Tinian, or Saipan to refuel. There was an unspoken agreement that the enlisted men should not press the captain too much on the subject, so we did not. We knew our place, and stuck to it.

My impression was that the captain disliked the long fueling delays, and enjoyed the attention that early arrivals from a mission received. He may have been eager to get back to report that we had beaten off an enemy fighter at a time when few were left in the skies. Whatever the reason, three young men paid with their lives.

Our encounter with the Irving was never reported; the damage inflicted on a Japanese fighter was incidental in light of what had happened to our bomber and the three men. I have since wondered if other B–29s that mysteriously disappeared off the coast of Japan without a trace during the war had fallen victim to surprise attacks such as ours.

A few days later we gathered at a military cemetery outside of Agana. The burial ground was located on a hillside, overlooking the Pacific. The sun was shining, a light breeze was blowing, and clouds were piled high in the sky. It was a glorious summer day. Our lives were continuing on; three others had come to an end.

An olive-drab Army ambulance with a large red cross arrived, bearing the remains of our navigator and flight engineer in wooden coffins with rope handles. I wondered where the radar man's body was. Thinking that he also had drowned, I assumed he was to be buried by members of his own crew at another time.

We opened the rear doors of the ambulance and slid the flight engineer's coffin toward us. As we did, the box tilted, and blood trickled from a crack onto the ground. The officers bore our navigator to his open grave as we carried our flight engineer to his. The graves were located side by side, approximating the way the two men had sat across an aisle from each other for hundreds of hours in the air. After an Air Force chaplain performed the funeral service, our central fire control gunner stepped up to the graves and wailed a Hebrew funeral chant. It was one of the saddest refrains I had ever heard. None of us dared look at the others. Our crew was sent on a one-week rest leave in Hawaii. Still stunned, we flew back in a comfortable Navy Douglas C-54 passenger plane. Seated close together on the long flight, we did not discuss what had happened. We dealt with our emotions by avoiding the incident altogether. Just as it was an unwritten rule not to question our captain, so it was that we did not revisit our experience. We were glad to be alive.

The Morality of War

Over sixty Japanese cities had been incinerated by the B–29s. Howling firestorms devoured civilians and workers in sheets of flames, burning hundreds of thousands to death.

When asked after the war about the morality of his orders to the crews of the B–29s, General LeMay responded, 'We knew we were going to kill a lot of women and children when we burned [Tokyo]... Killing Japanese didn't bother me much at the time. It was getting the war over with that bothered me.'

'We had to kill in order to end the war,' one pilot remembered. 'We heard about the thousands of people we killed, the Japanese wives, the children, and the elderly. That was war. But I know every B–29 air crewman for the next two or three years would wake up at night and start shaking. Yes, [the raids] were successful, but horribly so.'[44]

Aftermath of March 9–10, 1945 Tokyo raid. Ishikawa Kouyou.

While the population reeled and staggered, the Japanese High Command showed no signs of giving up the fight.

It would go on.

CHAPTER THIRTEEN

The Kamikazes

'People of the Philippines, I have returned... Rally to me. Let the indomitable spirit of Bataan and Corregidor lead on! As the lines of battle roll forward to bring you within the zone of operations, rise and strike!'[45]

On October 20, 1944, after three years of Japanese conquest and occupation, General Douglas MacArthur dramatically strode forth through the surf to arrive in the Philippines from Australia. The campaign for the liberation of Manila and the rescue of the prisoners, many of whom had felt abandoned by his abrupt departure two and a half years earlier, began even before Peleliu Island was secured. On the first day, more men would land at Leyte than the numbers put ashore that previous June to invade 'Fortress Europe' at Normandy on D-Day.[46]

Alvin Peachman was part of the naval force that put 200,000-plus American liberators ashore, and would also be a part of the Battle of Leyte Gulf, in which the Japanese Navy set into motion a complex 'oceanic banzai charge' to destroy the landing fleet and isolate the Americans now on land.[47]

Alvin Peachman

On the destroyer escort *USS Witter,* we made another trip to Saipan, and I got off there for a night. The captain was a good guy, because I had a brother there in the Army crew, and I asked if I could visit the Army anti-aircraft crew where he was. He said, 'Yeah, take the night off,' which I did. He was a good fellow. I went up there with the soldiers for a night with my brother.

Then we left there and October 1944 we made a lot of fleet exercises, and we invaded Leyte in the Philippine Islands. We carried in a bunch of soldiers there and I witnessed the battle both on land and later on the sea, because the Japanese closed in on us. We picked up and escorted several ships filled with ammunition, and several with fuel oil. We were under great aerial attack coming in and out. We got through and brought them to the fleet and they unloaded them in great haste to get ready for the Japanese Navy.

The Japanese Navy was converging from three different directions to take the gamble at destroying the invasion fleet.

Crossing the 'T'

Admiral Oldendorf was there with the 7th Fleet and crossed the 'T' on them and sank the whole Japanese fleet. They had to come up for what was called the Surigao Strait, which was a strait between Samar and Leyte. Every ship coming in in that division, in that area, was sunk.

'Crossing the T*' was the ideal in classical naval warfare. The battle line of the enemy's ships steams ahead in single 'vertical' file just as its attackers cross the top of the line horizontally, the bar of the '*T*' allowing all of its broadside guns to be brought to bear while the enemy can only fire its forward-facing guns.*[48]

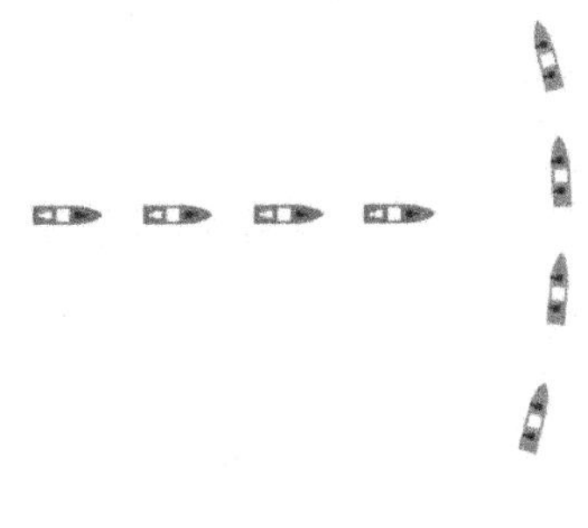

That didn't occur in other places. The Japanese Navy never attacked one spot. One of their fleets came through the center and Admiral Halsey had left that area, exposing our DEs [*destroyer escorts*] and light carriers, which we provided in force for Leyte, and it almost upset the whole invasion! He had gone further north, hunting the Japanese carriers; the Japanese had provided the bait for him to do that very thing!

The Japanese are not dumb people. Not only are they clever, but they are very brave and very fanatical. Every island we invaded had very few prisoners taken; they fought right to the last man. If they would have had our resources, it might have been a different story.

We then left that area because we were needed elsewhere. Before the rest of the Philippines were invaded, we went back down to New Guinea and we got ourselves ready there.

The greatest naval battle of the entire war had cost the Japanese nearly all of its Imperial Navy. However, at the conclusion of the three-day Battle of Leyte Gulf, a sinister new development began to harry the weary American crews. Out of the skies came suicide planes, armed with bombs, often closing on a target in pairs, intent on crashing into ships. The kamikazes, or 'divine wind,' took their inspiration from the typhoons which had saved Japan from Mongol invasions centuries before.

Back on land, 65,000 Japanese soldiers were killed at Leyte, with over 15,000 American casualties. The worst scenes of urban fighting in the Pacific took place for Manila, where in the month preceding February 1945, over 100,000 Filipino civilians died at the hands of the Japanese. The battles in the Philippines lasted until June 30, 1945. By this time, Alvin and the crew of the Witter were conducting tactical exercises and escort duties in the run-up to the massive Okinawa campaign, which would prove to be the last great amphibious operation of World War II.

Ulithi

Then we set sail for Ulithi. Ulithi Atoll was known as 'Shangri-La' to us, because it's a deep-water lagoon in the Carolines [*where sailors could rest, swim, and get beer*]. The Caroline Islands cover an area about as large as the United States, but if you put all of the land area together, you'd get about the size of Rhode Island, very small atolls but in a very large area.

In Ulithi we had an anchorage; it looked like a large ring. We had a net to cross where we'd go in, and we had our fleet in there [it could hold up to 700 ships] for this invasion of Okinawa. And I knew what was taking place right along, because I was on the radio.

The ships that were coming in there were unloading to the other ships right from the water. They couldn't even put it on land. There was just very little land for a staging area, you know? And one night, two suicide planes came in unannounced. I don't know if the Japanese fixed them in some nearby island, because we neutralized them all.[26] They hit this one carrier while they were watching movies. The other airplane came down and he saw an island lit up right

[26] March 11, 1945. Nearly two dozen planes had taken off from Japan, a distance of nearly 2,500 miles. At 10 p.m. at night, only two kamikazes arrived at the target area. The *USS Randolph* was the stricken carrier.

beside us; he thought it was a super dreadnought. He smashed into the island, and that was the end of him [*chuckles*].

Setting Sail for Okinawa

We then set sail for Okinawa in March of '45, which was over about 2,000 miles, patrolled by Japs. See, things happen quickly; we had the Japanese on the run, we were hitting them hard. The Philippines were still going on when we hit Okinawa—there were troops in Luzon, still in battle. As I remember it must have taken five or six days. We had such a force; I thought we'd go right to Japan! It was 60 miles long, protected with submarines and DEs like ours, for Japanese U-boats.

The Japanese spotted us, we knew it, and we could see that they were here. We pointed them out on radar, but they didn't dare attack. We shot a few planes down on the perimeter and knocked off a few subs. So I thought, boy we're going to take on Japan now, this will be the end. But when we got up there near Okinawa, it was on my birthday on March the 25th, there was a big bombardment. Okinawa was protected by the Japs for fifty years before we came! They had seven huge airfields there at that time. So we bombarded that that day and created quite a few fires; I think we hit oil tanks. Then we'd leave at night and come in early in the morning. One morning when we came in, they were taking off in the airstrips, and we gave them all the anti-aircraft fire we could. We got a few—not only our ships were firing, but so were many others.

We were the escort ship for the *Indianapolis*, you might have heard of it.[27] As a matter of fact, we would go in like a beagle dog,

---

[27] The *USS Indianapolis* was the heavy cruiser which would go on to deliver the parts for the first atomic bomb to the take-off base at Tinian Island. Sailing later for Leyte, she was torpedoed on July 30, 1945, sinking in less than 15 minutes with 300 men. The 900 other crew members spent the next five

close to the shore, and if a shell was fired, the *Indianapolis* fired a big one in. Our heaviest gun was only three-inch; that's about as heavy a shell as you can carry. It's nothing compared to what naval shells are. The *Indianapolis* had eight-inch. You couldn't handle an eight-inch shell yourself. So the *Indianapolis* was with us and we were with a sister ship, the *Bowers*, and two of the Japanese suicide planes aimed for the *Bowers* and us on the *Witter*; they were concentrating on our escort ships. One came for the *Bowers*, he came in a straight dive. Just before he hit, the *Bowers* made a quick turn, so just part of the wing hit it. And when the plane meant for us came, our ship did not fire quickly enough, and the *Indianapolis* did. Aboard the *Indianapolis* was Admiral Spruance, who was the Commander of the 5th Fleet. He gave our captain heck, so he got it for us that day, though we had gotten other suicide aircraft ourselves in the Philippines, under big attacks.

'We're Going to Be the Target'

On Easter Sunday, it would have been April the 1st of 1945 as I remember, the big invasion started, and on that day it wasn't too bad from what I would have expected, because troops and Marines were able to cut straight across the island. But now, pretty soon we found ourselves all alone. We were assigned to what was called 'roger [radar] picket duty.' We had to protect the island against the Japanese coming in to attack our troops; the attacks started getting worse and worse by kamikazes. One of my friends told me that battle was not so bad. He had only come onboard two months before, just coming from the States. I said, 'Yeah, that's true, until you're the target. We're going to be the target one of these days.'

---

days in a nightmare of battling sharks, exposure, and thirst and hunger. Only 317 survived the ordeal. [www.ussindianapolis.org/story.htm]

USS BUNKER HILL is hit off Okinawa by two kamikazes, May 11, 1945. National Archives. Public domain.

On April the 6th we were under great attack all day. Our ship had to have oil [*refueling*], and we finally got it on. We had lunch about four o'clock, and right after that we had a big attack. Two of them came out of the skies and we fired like mad and got the first one. The other one was coming straight for us and we had him on fire. He hit into the engine room, fire room, and kitchen. He blew out about half of the ship with a thousand-pound bomb in the plane! Luckily he missed where I was, because on the other five ships in our group, most of the radiomen were dead, unless they were manning guns. You see, the kamikazes would aim for the bridge because it was the communication part of the ship, and they wanted to exterminate or get rid of all the destroyer escorts and destroyers so that they could come in and torpedo everything else. It was a good idea, but it didn't work out.

The kamikazes were coming from Japan. Okinawa might be just a few hundred miles from Japan, very close to Japan. So we were hit heavily and I saw quite a bit of action that day. One or two suicide planes went right through the noses of our ships, but several were shot down. When our ship was hit, I helped the gunners out all I could. One of our sister ships came up and towed us in to a little anchorage called Kerama Retto. Kerama Retto was not really controlled by us, except we used it for our ships. The Japanese planes would show up, and we'd fire at them. So we had the bait, and if we were under attack there, the Navy would use PT boats and make a big smoke ring, put in white smoke; you couldn't see anything, so they couldn't see us. But some of our ships would open up on the planes right through the smoke—our radar was so good that we'd shoot them right down. As a matter of fact, the radar on our ship was so efficient, we could spot a plane three hundred miles away! And we just traced them; if they came within 20 miles, we were all ready. That was a very good thing, we had good radar.

So we were in there from when we got hit at the beginning of April until June of 1945. There were so many ships that had been hit that we could not get a guy to weld it good enough to take us back to the United States. Finally, my lieutenant came up to me one day and he said we were going to take casualties back to the United States on the troop ship *USS Hocking*, a big ship, and that I could go with them because I had been there the longest. He said, 'When you get to California, you will take a leave, and then you will come back to California and our ship will be ready, and you will take it through the Panama Canal with the men who are [going to the East Coast].' So I went back on the *Hocking*; we were under great attack in a big convoy. We brought back a lot of amputees to Tinian to a big hospital there. Many of the men had legs off, arms off, maybe even all limbs off, a pitiful sight.

We got down there and we also put aboard the Seabees. We then went to the island of Kwajalein and then to Hawaii. We got off on a little base and they gave the destroyer escort men two beers every day. That's all I needed, I was drunk on two beers! I was 'landsick'; instead of being seasick, I was landsick. I was aboard a ship too long; I thought the land should hit me in the teeth! Then we came to San Francisco, and I had leave and came across the country, which I had to pay for, by the way. When I came back I found out the *Witter* had beaten me and had made it to California [*and then departed for the East Coast*], so they had to send me back again across the country!

Right about that time, World War II ended. And on September 28, 1945, I had enough points. I was in Philadelphia when the *Witter* came in, and I asked to get out. I got out and on October 1, I was in college! I wasted no time, one weekend.

'I Lost Many Friends'

Matthew Rozell: So what did you think about the atomic bomb?

Best thing that ever happened to us. If it wouldn't have been for the atomic bomb, I think we would have had a catastrophic amount of men killed, and probably the elimination of the Japanese nation as a whole. It would have been a terrible thing to conquer. I think it did a great deal in helping to save a million or two men, as well as the Japanese. I believe Harry Truman was a wonderful president in that regard; he really did a great favor to us. But I do not understand why we had to wait so long to figure things out! We shouldn't have gone into Okinawa if we knew we had the atomic bomb, because in Okinawa, we had 50,000 casualties! Our whole division was hit, except for the *Wilmarth*, as I told you. Two hundred and fifty ships were hit at Okinawa by kamikazes. The day we got hit, 26 ships got hit, and six were sunk to the bottom! I believe the Japanese had over 500 aircraft against us that day, suicide aircraft. Have you ever been startled by a partridge suddenly trying to fly into you? It is really a scary thing! They were nuts, like [angry] bees! Although you weren't thinking of it at the time, it was a scary thing that these people would give up their lives like that. It was the most Navy lives lost in one battle. I lost many friends.

Destroyer Escort USS WITTER
following kamikaze attack. Alvin Peachman collection.

As the land battle for Okinawa raged toward its crescendo with the fury of a storm, the kamikaze attacks would claim over 15,000 American casualties for the Navy alone.

CHAPTER FOURTEEN

Typhoon of Steel-Okinawa

After three years of fighting across 4,000 miles of ocean, the United States was finally poised at the threshold of the Japanese home islands. The island of Okinawa had been colonized by Japan in the early days of her imperial might; at a mere 340 miles from mainland Japan, the coming assault on the island would be an attack on her inner defenses. Sixty miles long and nearly 900 square miles, the island hosted perhaps 120,000 defenders, but once taken, planners reckoned it would be big enough to support 800 heavy bombers. As the winter of 1945 gave way to spring, it was clear to the Japanese that the island had to be held at all costs. Taking it was not going to be simple or easy. Planning for the largest combined operation in the Pacific War took months, and over half a million Americans would be committed to the battle.

Early morning on Easter Sunday, 1945, the invasion of Okinawa began. The first Marines and soldiers to hit the beaches that Easter morning were somewhat perplexed, however, to find little or no opposition. Others noted the irony of the date: besides being Easter Sunday, it was April 1- April Fools' Day.

Bruce Manell, a combat photographer from Whitehall with the 6th Marine Division, remembered the invasion.

Bruce Manell

They gave us a good time before we went to Okinawa. The Navy gave us all the beer we wanted to drink all day long. Oh, what a place that was [*Mog Mog, the island set aside for rest and relaxation at Ulithi*]!

When we hit the China Sea going into Okinawa—it is supposed to be one of the roughest seas in the world, and I won't deny that a bit—you would see ships go out of sight under the waves and coming back on top of the wave! The screws in the propellers came out of the water, and the whole ship vibrates because there is no water there, and you go back down. It was pretty rough. Anyway, we pulled up off Okinawa during the night, and about 1:00 in the morning, they woke us up to get ready to go ashore. I said I would go up topside to see what was going on. So I went up topside and—my golly!—guns were going off. That Navy, they really knew how to spit that stuff out! There were times when you could see the shape of a hill—with all the explosives going off at once. They were hitting a hill, and you could see the shape of the hill silhouetted in the dark. That was a tremendous barrage. Just about daybreak, they let off on that. And fighter planes and dive-bombers came in, and they did an awful job on the shore. That was a spectacular sight also. Then, at 20 minutes after 8:00, I went ashore with the first wave. You go to shore in one of these LCMs or LCVPs.[28] You have this big metal door in front of you, and they ram it into the shoreline. And as soon as it stops, the door flops down, and you wonder what's

[28] LCM was Landing Craft, Mechanized, capable of carrying one small tank or 100 troops. LCVP was the Landing Craft Vehicle/Personnel, also known as a Higgins boat; it could carry 36 troops or a small vehicle such as a Jeep.

going to be on the other side. There was nothing there! We were surprised. So we went ashore and started doing our job like we were supposed to, and guys were saying, 'Where's the Japs? Where are the Japs?' No one seemed to be able to find the Japs!

Then we started to get reports, a couple hours later— well, such-and-such has found some Japs south of us a ways. Then they started to get heavier and heavier resistance down there. So we found out where the war was...

Our job was to cut the island in two and then proceed north from there, which we did. We got scattered resistance here and there—except for one night, we had a banzai charge all over the island. They just seemed to come out of the ground, and it was 11:00 at night. It was a horrible night! I shot my first Jap then on Okinawa, and I have the grenade that he was trying to throw at me as a souvenir.[49]

'Mud and Total Extinction'

The Japanese were refining a defense–in–depth tactic that brought the battle up the island to the ten–mile-long Shuri Line. In the space of a very constricted area, some places no more than 600 yards wide, 300,000 fighting men were waging a death struggle that seemingly turned the area into a moonscape of exploding shells, knee–deep mud, denuded vegetation, sewage, and rotting corpses.[29]

[29] Author William Manchester, present at the fight, thought back to his father's experiences in World War I on the Western Front: *'This, I thought, was what Verdun and Passchendaele must have looked like. Two great armies, squatting opposite one another in mud and smoke, locked together in unimaginable agony . . . there was nothing green left...* 'See William Manchester, *Goodbye, Darkness: A Memoir of the Pacific War* (Boston: Little Brown, 1987) pp. 359–360.

Dan Lawler had recovered from his wounds at Peleliu and was back in the thick of things at Okinawa with his outfit, which included a friend of his from Alabama, Eugene B. Sledge. Sledge's war memoir would be published in the 1980s to vast critical acclaim.

"Souvenirs". Dan Lawler (L) and Eugene Sledge (3rd from left) and others from 'K' Company on Okinawa. Courtesy Dan Lawler.

"Heavy rains began on May 6 and lasted through May 8, a preview of the nightmare of mud we would endure... until the end of the month. On May 8, Nazi Germany surrendered unconditionally...we were told the momentous news, but considering our own peril and misery...'so what' was typical of the remarks I heard around me. We were resigned to the fact that the Japanese would fight to total extinction on Okinawa, as they had elsewhere, and that Japan would have to be invaded with the same gruesome prospects. Nazi Germany might as well have been on the moon."[30]

---

[30] Sledge, Eugene B. *With the Old Breed at Peleliu and Okinawa.* New York: Oxford Univ. Press, 1981. 223. Mr. Lawler was well acquainted with the mild-mannered Alabamian Eugene Sledge (1923–2001), whom he would

Jim Butterfield recalled the island.

Jim Butterfield

Okinawa was a beautiful island, really. Gardens, a lot of farmlands, and one of the problems we ran into there was civilians, which we never had before. You've got a lot to learn here, I think.

Our orders were that if we took anything—we were issued invasion money, and we were supposed to pay these people if we took a chicken. But some of those chickens we would put a .45 [cal. bullet] through, and we kept on going [*laughing*]. But it was pretty nice up there. It was hard with the people, because you did not know what... patrols would go out into the villages and stuff and get ambushed. The people that were living there, you'd think they were defending. So that is when we were ordered to take them out—put them in stockades. That wasted a lot of our time—slowed us up too.[50]

The Children in the Cave

It should also be noted that over 100,000 native Okinawan civilians were caught in the crossfire and killed.

Dan Lawler

We hit the middle of Okinawa. The Marines went north, and the Army went south. There were some civilians in a cave—we

---

tease as 'Rebel.' Unbeknownst to Lawler and his fellow infantrymen, Sledge was keeping notes of what was happening to them in his pocket-sized Bible. On publication of *With the Old Breed* in 1981, Mr. Sledge would be hailed as the most influential war memoirist of World War II. Ken Burns' PBS series, *The War* (2007) and the HBO series, *The Pacific* (2010) are based in part on his work. It is highly recommended for further reading. [*bit.ly/OldBreed*] couldn't get them out. So we talked to the interpreter. He said something in Japanese that meant 'Come out; we'll give you food and water.' So I went up to this cave and said that. No one came out, but I knew they were in there. They were talking very low. All of a sudden, a boy and girl came out... they came out of the mouth of the cave. And I could see that it was quite a ways away, so I stopped. They were about that tall [*gestures with hands, about three feet from ground*]. They finally came out a little bit closer. I moved a little bit closer. I got to where I could see they were shaking—they were shaken up. Their clothes were all blood—no socks, no shoes. And they were a mess—faces all blood—but they didn't have anyone around. So anyway, they would get just so far, and they wouldn't come any closer. I couldn't figure out what was the matter with them. And I figured, well, wait a minute, it might be the weapon. So I laid the weapon down, and I came back over.

And we had these candy bars... so I offered them that, but they wouldn't take it. I figured, well, maybe they figured there was something wrong. So I bit a piece off, and I gave the rest of it to him, and he bit a piece of that. Finally, he started talking to me in his own language, and grown-ups started coming out... so they all came out of the caves. And I picked the little girl up—she let me pick her up. It was rough—it was rough... [*pauses, then speaks in barely audible voice*] I still remember—I remember well... I can still see the two little kids... the Japanese told them that we were going to kill them, all those civilians: 'The Marines are going to kill all of you.'[51]

Evacuating the Wounded

Katherine Abbott was born in 1917 and wondered about her future upon graduation from South Glens Falls High School. Soon enough, she would find herself in the U.S. Army as a flight nurse during the Pacific War.

Katherine Abbott

I just wanted to do something. I wanted to be a school teacher, but we did not have enough money for me to go on to graduate school. We had a large family and we did not have that much money—we did not have student loans then. So someone suggested I would like nursing. I did apply and I went to Memorial Hospital in Albany for three years' service.

I think a friend of mine, a classmate, talked me into [the Army]. So we decided to go in, and after we heard about the Air Evacuation Squadron, and once we had our basic training, we applied for the School of Air Evacuation. It was six to eight weeks. Then we went overseas, this was 1944 and '45, and I was discharged in February 1946. My five brothers and I went into the service, and, as I said, my classmate talked me into going in, and, well, I thought it was a good idea.

In the Pacific, we shuttled from island to island, and [the wounded were] transferred from nurse to nurse, as you would in the wards when working shifts. Since there was only one nurse and one medical technician aboard the plane, we shuttled and changed planes and we rested until we were called again. So, we just kept things going—Hawaii, Johnson Island, Guadalcanal, Guam, Saipan, Tarawa, Biak, Leyte in the Philippines, and Okinawa; we would just be 'island hopping' with our planes. We had nothing to do with the Navy or the ships; they had their own Navy nurses and Navy nurse corps. We flew day and night, so where we were all depended on how the war was going and [where we were needed in] getting the patients ready to be transferred.

We were on call as the patients were being transferred and brought in by ambulance. We would be there to see that they were put on the plane and to secure their litters to the walls of the plane. They had hooks with a certain snap to them to make sure they were safe. The [aircraft] were four-motored cargo planes. On cargo planes, all the way back, there was nothing but space, and that is where we put the patients, on each side of the walls of the plane and down the center, and it was just the nurse and the technician, the medical technician. There was no doctor.

We had 28 patients on the plane. We carried three tiers of four patients on each tier on each side, and four patients on the center of the plane on the floor. We had some patients who were ambulatory and others that couldn't move, but they were on the top layers. We did not have anyone who was really, really bad, because our planes were not pressurized and [had] no oxygen, so we could not go any higher than 9,000 or 10,000 feet. That is what you call 'primitive,' because we were the pioneers in air evacuation and they had just started. Today I believe they are much improved, and they have the helicopters.

Mostly we were looking after them and administering pain medication. We had one tuberculosis patient, bleeding, coughing up blood, and he was the only one we had sitting up on the one seat we had there. Usually, most of it was pain; codeine and morphine were the only medications we carried, and then we had penicillin. We gave penicillin shots every three hours. We had no 'facilities,' you might say, for any medical treatments or anything aboard plane; this was mostly for transport and keeping them comfortable. As I said, that was ancient. We were just starting out and it was the best we could do. I believe today they must have everything more so than we did. Of course that was quite a while ago, but you know, we did the job.

The patients were on the plane continuously until they got to Hawaii, then I do not know what they did. They probably rested, and once they had been checked out, they would take the long trip home. This was definitely discharge; they would not be going back into battle. We also had prisoners of war. Once I had a plane full of prisoners of war, 28, they were all ambulatory and walking around; I remember that one plane full.

They tried to have the safest planes for us. Sometimes something was wrong with the plane and we had to go back and change all of the patients and had them all moved into the new plane, but that didn't bother me. I was not scared of enemy fliers, because they had fighter pilots on call or on the alert all the time.

We were not at the battle areas at all except for the trips to Okinawa. We went in at midnight and we flew in from Guam or Saipan or Tinian for eight hours. We took off at midnight, so we landed at 8 o'clock in the morning, daylight, and on the first trip I had, our Navy was shelling the southern tip of Okinawa and that is the closest I ever came [to the battle zone]. The Japs did fly below the radar on the island at Biak as I was stationed there. I had taken off with a load of patients at 7:00 p.m. and they flew in at 7:30 p.m. while we were loading another plane! They just dropped the one bomb, but no one was really injured. They hit the area, but that is the only time I came close to any actual fighting. But we had to make it pretty safe for the patients, you know at the time, as we were transporting them.

Nurses relaxing, Guam. Donald P.Quarters collection. Courtesy Jackie Quarters.

'You've got nothing to work with, Jimmy.'

Within the space of seven weeks, the band of 1st Marine Division brothers from the North Country near the "Falls"—who had forged their bonds at boot camp and in combat at Peleliu—would be broken up for good. Jack Murray of Hudson Falls was stateside with his knee wound sustained on Peleliu; Harold Chapman of Gansevoort and Jim Butterfield of Glens Falls would be the next to fall.

Jim Butterfield

On Okinawa, you have to remember, we were only about 150 miles from Japan itself. Japan was next on the list after Okinawa. So every day and every night you would get air raids. They had young kids flying these planes—they were dying for the Emperor. It was a great thing to do. You were going to go up there to heaven, or so they said.

When you looked back on Buckner Bay at night, you would see all our ships would go back out to sea—because it was dangerous to stay around. We had two hospital ships there. The hospital ships would be lit up at night, and the Red Cross was supposed to be on them. These guys [*the Japanese*] weren't supposed to hit the hospital ships. But I was up on the ridge, and I said to my friend Chappy, 'If I get hit, Chappy, you make sure they don't put me aboard one of those things.' But Chappy got it before that.

Harold Chapman and Jimmy had been through boot camp together, and were in the same outfit, G Company, 2nd Battalion, 1st Marines, where Jimmy was the squad leader. Jim usually checked in with his friend every morning, but on May 5, Jim was tending to one of his badly wounded men and did not see him. Word came to him later in the day that Harold was killed.[31] *The loss affected him deeply. Sixty years later, he recalled,* 'It really took the wind out of my sails.' *Not even the letters from his steady girlfriend back home, Mary, cheered him much in the weeks to follow.*[52]

Still on the Shuri Line, Jim was severely wounded in the head two weeks later. Over 60 years afterward he came to my classroom with his

[31] Harold Chapman's remains were repatriated nearly four years after he was killed on Okinawa. He joined the Marine Corps in 1943 at the age of 17. He was survived by three sisters and his mother, whom Jimmy Butterfield and Danny Lawler visited upon their return home in 1945. 'Body of U.S. Marine Being Returned Home', *The Glens Falls Post-Star,* March 7, 1949.

wife Mary and good friend Dan Lawler. His humor still intact and on display, Jim poignantly recalled the experience of struggling to accept the fact that he would never see again.

Jim Butterfield

I enlisted into the United States Marine Corps the seventh of December, 1943. I was seventeen years old then and I went because I wanted to help fight the good war. My mother didn't want me to go. Mary didn't want me to go. But I heard they threw a party after I left. [*Laughter*]

Mary Butterfield:

Yes, we went to school together and Jimmy left six months before graduation. I told him, 'Don't go until after you graduate,' but he wanted to go. He was afraid the war would be over before he could get in. So he went in, in December, and I graduated in June.

Matthew Rozell: You were high school sweethearts?

Jim Butterfield:

Mary and I have been palling around for over 60 years now.

Mary Butterfield:

Well, we've been married 61 years.

Jim Butterfield:

She couldn't wait to get married, but I think she's changed her mind a couple times since then... [*Laughter*]

It was an exciting time, it was an adventurous time, and it was a proud time. I lasted 61 or 62 days up to Okinawa before I got hit. Danny was fortunate—he got all the way through. Right, Dan?

Dan Lawler: Ninety-eight days I was there.

Matthew Rozell: Mary, do you remember getting the news that Jim was wounded?

Mary Butterfield:

Yes, I remember. This girl who lived on our street was going steady with this Navy corpsman, and he wrote a letter to her, telling her that Jimmy was very bad, that he was wounded through the eye. She came over that Saturday morning, I remember, and she told me. I was surprised, and I called his mother. And she said that she got a letter from the government only telling her that he was wounded. But that's the way that I found out about it, about how he was wounded on Okinawa.

Jim Butterfield:

Well, the first letter that they got was telling them that I was temporarily blind at the time. When I got hit, we were going to take Shuri Castle, because the 6th Division was already in there, and they were catching it real bad. So they decided to put us in there to pull some of the people away from them—to give them a hand.

We were doing very well. It was a beautiful day when we started out. I had gotten seven Japs when they attacked the perimeter that night, and I thought I had a good day in front of me. So as we were moving along, somebody behind me yelled, 'Whitey just got it!' He was a friend of ours.[32] So I turned around, and I saw him rolling down the ridge. He got it in the head, and the face too. So I told this Marine next to me to take the squad, I'll be right back. I figured it was an easy job to do because it was downhill. So I ran down and grabbed Whitey by his belt. We went over a little ridge, and I thought we had enough shelter.

[32] Marine Corporal 'Whitey' Hargus.

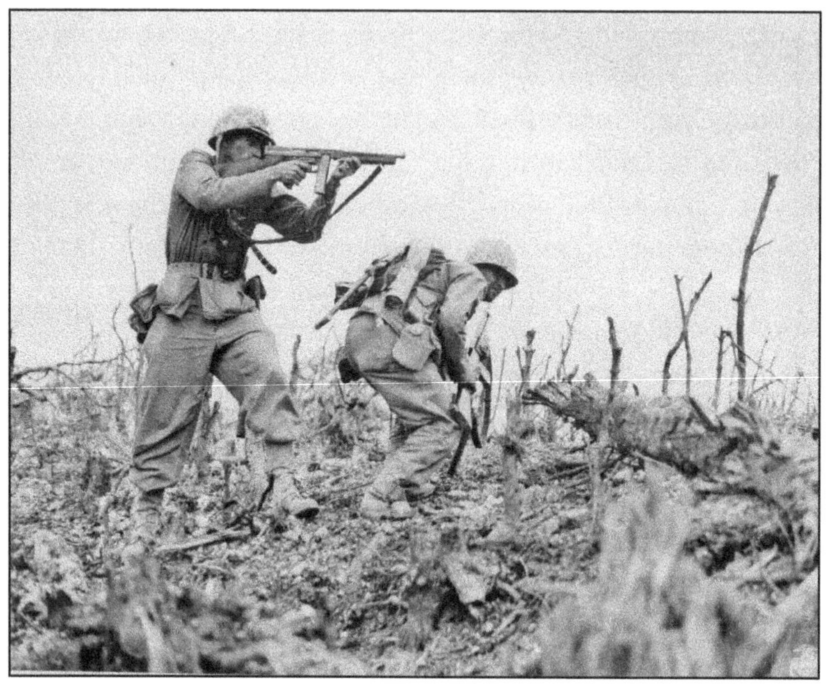

Wana Ridge. Shuri Line. "A Marine of the 1st Marine Division draws a bead on a Japanese sniper." National Archives. Public domain.

Then a couple of other guys came. I said, 'Look it, we have to get a corpsman up here, I think Whitey's going to go into shock.' You see when you got hit, you didn't always die from the wound. Sometimes you went into shock. Shock could kill you. So I turned around to say something to him, and that's the last I remember. I don't know where that guy, the shot, came from. I got it with a rifle [shot].

I lost part of the right side of my face. I don't know if it was a day, or two days later—I don't even know really what happened to me—the enemy laid a mortar barrage when I was on my way to the hospital at the beach, and I got hit again, in the face! That took care of the other side of my face. I was 14 months in the hospital having my face rebuilt, and that's why I am so good-looking today. [*Laughter*]

This is a small world we live in. A guy named Joe Gavita from Glens Falls was the corpsman at that station. Of course I knew Joe before that, and Joe was taking care of me! I don't remember this at all. He said I carried on a conversation with him. I was telling him how bad it was up there. I don't remember that. The next thing I remember is I woke up in that station and what a headache I had! Oh! Talk about a hangover!

The corpsman came and said, 'How are you doing?' I said, 'How about loosening up these bandages, they're killing me.' He said, 'No can do.' So I sat up in the sack and started to unroll it myself. The next thing I know, I got a shot in the arm and I was knocked out again. The next time I woke up, I woke up in an aircraft. A C-54 transport. I never flew before. I had no idea where the hell I was! I put my hand out on the deck, and I just could not put it together—that I was in a plane! Someone must have had a word out to keep an eye on me, because the next time I reached out there, there was a patent leather shoe. I moved my hand a little bit, and there was a nice ankle with a silk stocking! [*Some laughter*] I thought, 'Jesus, I have died and have gone to heaven!' [*Much laughter from students*] I started running my hand up that leg, and she said, 'I think you've gone far enough.' [*More laughter*]

She said to me, 'Jimmy, would you like a turkey sandwich and a glass of milk?' I said, 'Real milk?' She said, 'Real milk.' I said, 'You bet your life!' She brought it down, and there had to be something in it, because I was out again. I woke up in Guam, in the hospital. I was there about three weeks, I guess. I got an operation there. I didn't know they did it. But what was left of my left side of the eye and face, they took out. Now see, these people knew that I was not going to see again.

The doctor came up. I said, 'How am I doing, Doc? I have to go back up there. They're short of people.' He said, 'You're doing fine, my young boy.' That was all I would get, see? Do you want to hear this whole story? [*Teenagers: Yes!*]

They took me to Honolulu. The nurse said, 'You're going to like it.' I said, 'Yeah, that will be nice. Now how about a cigarette?' [*To the young people*] We smoked them then; we didn't know they killed you... So she said, 'No, you can't. They're putting fuel in the plane.' I said, 'I'm dying for one—let me have one.' Then she let me have one.

We flew into Hawaii, and it was a beautiful hospital. It was overlooking the Pacific. Down below you could see Diamond Head. Now, I couldn't see any of these things. But I was told all of this stuff.

I still had the bandages on. They were teaching you little things, like to sit down at the tray, how to eat. Now, the first thing they teach you is, you work by the clock—like your milk would be at 1:00, your bread at 9:00, your potatoes at 6:00. Things like that you had to start learning, see... I went along with this, still not thinking—and this is how stupid that you can be—that I wasn't going to see again. Nothing in my mind thought that [being blind] was going to happen to me. I was getting around. I always had somebody with me.

So this one day, we were sitting there, and this guy said, 'Jimmy, I bet you five bucks you can't go to the head and back in five minutes.' Five dollars is pretty good money. I had done it before already, so I said, 'Yeah, I'll bet you.' So I did a good job—I got to the men's room, the head. But when I came back, I took a quarter of a step wrong, and I ended up in a long, not-too-wide closet, and I didn't know how the hell to get out of there! Then I start sweating. I was all bandaged up, and underneath my bandages was Vaseline, gauze. I thought, 'Geez, I've got to get out of here!' Five bucks is five bucks, and I had lost it already.

I finally got out of there, and I went over and sat down. I said, 'How about a cigarette?' Someone handed me a cigarette. There was a Zippo lighter. Guy goes like this [*holds hand up, makes flicking motion with thumb*]. My whole face goes up in flames! [*Laughter*] I had this guy who was nearsighted next to me, trying to put it out [*he laughs*], and all he did was fan the flames... you'd think you were back in the foxhole again! The nurse comes running over, and off go the bandages. Fortunately, I did not get burned. So she says, 'Give me your lighter! Give me your cigarettes!' She took them away from me. So all day long, I'm bumming cigarettes and a lighter. Then I'm going over and putting them underneath my mattress. Now that nurse is standing there watching me do this, and I don't know she's doing this. So I get up about 4:00—I feel under the mattress. There was no lighter, no cigarettes. The nurse says, 'You want a cigarette, Jimmy?' [*Laughter*]

I'm sitting there one day with one of the guys that was just in from Okinawa. I was asking how they were doing and stuff, and this guy sticks his head in the door. He says, 'I'm looking for Jim Butterfield.' I said, 'He's right here, what do you want?' He says, 'It's Dick Barber, Jim.' Now this is Dr. Barber from Glens Falls.[33] I had no idea how he knew I was there. He was stationed there. I get a nice lieutenant-colonel walking into my room—my stock automatically goes up! He says, 'Let me look at your face.' I said, 'Dick, you can't do that. This is a Navy hospital, I think they'll frown on an Army guy doing this.' He said, 'I want to see what they're doing to you.' So he looked. This man knew right there that I was never going to see again. He never said a word to me. I don't think he ever told anybody back here at home.

---

33 Well-known Glens Falls doctor Charles Richard Barber (1914–1999).

I didn't know, until they told me there.

So here's the climax. Every morning there was inspection with the doctors. So the doctor came around that morning. He said, 'How are you, Jim?' I said, 'Fine.' He said, 'You need anything?' I said, 'Nope, I'm doing fine.' He says, 'Well, are you used to the idea?' I said, 'Used to what idea?' He said, 'That you're not going to see again.'

Well, you could hear a pin drop. I said, 'I don't think I heard you, Doc.' He said, 'You're not going to see again.' I said, 'What?' He said, 'Didn't they tell you in Guam?'

I said, 'No! But it's a good thing that [first] doctor isn't here, because I'd kill him!' I got so mad! I couldn't really grab the idea. I'm not going to see again? ... What the hell did I know about blindness? Nothing!

I said, 'How about operations?' He said, 'You've got nothing to work with, Jimmy.'

So a pat on the shoulder, and he just walks away. The nurse comes over and says, 'The doctor wants you to take this pill.' I said, 'You know what the doctor can do with that pill?'

Mary Butterfield:

Don't say it.

Jim Butterfield:

I'm not going to, Mary.

So I had a hard... two months, I guess. I kept mostly to myself. I wouldn't talk to people. I tried to figure out what the hell I was going to do when I got home. How was I going to tell my mother this? You know what I mean?

So they come around and said, 'You've got a phone call.' So I went in to where the phone was. They were calling me from home. They got the message, see... This one here was on the phone [*points to Mary*]. I said, 'Looks like things have changed, kiddo.' She said,

'No, we'll discuss this when you get home.' She was already bossing me around. [*Laughter*]

But that's how I found out, and that's how it happened. And after a while, I just started to live with it.

There are not days—even today—I go to bed and I wish I could see. So much I miss. I miss watching a nice girl walking down the street. I miss seeing my daughter, my wife. I even miss looking at Danny. [*Laughter*]

Mary Butterfield:

But you see, I'm only 17 to you now. That's a good thing.

Jim Butterfield:

Since we got in the conversation, when I dream, and I do dream, everything is real. Everything I knew before, I see it as it was then, not today. My wife and daughter would never get old in my eyes. When I dream of Mary, she's still seventeen years old.

Mary Butterfield:

But you never saw your daughter.

Jim Butterfield:

I dream about my daughter. Mary's caught me doing this. We lost our daughter a year and a half ago. But I sit right up in bed and I'm trying to push away that little cloud of fog in front of her, but I can't quite make her out.

Mary says, 'What are you doing?' I say, 'Just dreaming.'

Jim Butterfield was nineteen years old at the Battle of Okinawa. [53]

In the final push at the Shuri Line that cost him his eyesight, the Marines lost over 3,000 men and the U. S. Army even more. When the island was declared secure near the end of June, in Lawler's K/3/5, only 26 Peleliu veterans who had landed with the company had survived Okinawa. It had been the bloodiest campaign of the Pacific, with over 12,500 Americans killed or missing and nearly three times that number wounded. For the Japanese, no accurate counts are possible, but perhaps 110,000 were killed.[54]

Jim Butterfield, 2000.
Author photo.

CHAPTER FIFTEEN

Redemption

As spring 1945 turned to summer, Okinawa had fallen, the war in Europe had ended, and the air raids over Japan were reaching a crescendo. In Japan, the prisoners tried to hang on. For many men, punishment was becoming more severe, and resignation and despair set in to overwhelm them. Joseph Minder was still slaving in the copper mine in northern Japan, but was determined to remain focused on survival, and getting home.

Unbroken

Joe Minder

July to early August, 1945

Johnson and Milchesky started working at the shop. I started working at the bottom of the mine. Very dangerous down there, because of many cave-ins and rocks rolling down from the four levels above, however the work there is much easier than pushing and loading dirt carts, so I'll take my chances.

More air raids every day now. Getting soya beans in small amounts. We got so weak last month and so darn many men passed out on the job that the Japs realized they wouldn't be able to get any more work out of us unless our diet was picked up a bit. No one has gained any weight, but at least we aren't passing out on the job anymore.

'A Question Until The End of Time'

Well before the fighting on Okinawa was over, planning was complete for the invasion of Japan. The invasion, code named 'Downfall,' was to be in two stages. The first, Operation Olympic, would take place on the southern island of Kyushu on November 1. Phase two, Operation Coronet, would use Kyushu as a staging area for the invasion of the Tokyo plain in March 1946.[55]

In this narrative, we must suspend for the moment arguments about the moral legitimacy of the bomb, and focus on the facts of the day and the voices of the veterans themselves. When President Truman and the Allies demanded Japan's unconditional surrender after the successful July testing of the atomic bomb in the sands of New Mexico, the reality was that up to one-third of the American invasion force in the battle for Okinawa was killed, wounded, or missing. Invasion planners were certain that the coming invasion figures would be grimmer. It is also true that the Japanese prison camp commandants, since 1943, had been given the "kill-all" order in the event of imminent invasion, a policy which was carried out on numerous occasions and updated, reinforced, and clarified as time went on.[56]

From the Potsdam Conference in defeated Germany, President Truman warned the Japanese to surrender. On August 6, 1945, a single bomb tumbled from a B–29 Superfortress flying from Tinian in the Mariana Islands. Hiroshima was devastated by both the blast and thermal and radioactive effects that would lead later estimators to put the death toll at 140,000.

John W. Norton, a seaman on the repair ship USS Vulcan, was there shortly afterwards.

John Norton

We were in Hiroshima at the time they signed the official surrender. I was there almost six months, anchored off Hiroshima, and I spent a lot of time in the city. When we got there it was just leveled, and there were two shells of buildings—one was a hospital and one was a school—and those were the only buildings that looked like they had been buildings. We walked around. The people, the civilians, were looking at us wondering what we were going to do to them. And, oh my God, the scars on their faces and burns. Oh God, it was sickening. Women and children—it was just sickening.

Asked if he thought the bomb was necessary, Mr. Norton replied, 'Well, that has been the question, and it will be the question until the end of time, I guess, but it saved many lives.'

Ralph Leinoff was resting up from combat at Iwo Jima and preparing for the inevitable.

Ralph Leinoff

I was tired and I was disgusted. I knew that I still had another landing to make, and while out in the field at Maui doing the training exercises for Japan, we got word that something happened, that a bomb wiped out an entire city of people and that the bomb may end the war.

I couldn't believe it. We had been fighting the Japanese for three years and I felt no one bomb is going to make them turn around and change their mind; they're going to fight to the death. Everyone in the Japanese Army was told, 'You're going to die, but you have to take ten Marines with you; before you die, you take ten Marines with you!' So when the word came about Hiroshima, suddenly it seemed like maybe there was a chance we would not have to do that landing.

We had a new company captain at that time—he called us together. He said, 'Look, fellas, this is just a rumor, we can't go by it. We know how tough the enemy is, we're going to put all our heart and soul into these training exercises, because as far as we know, we're going to have to land on Japan. It's going to be a brutal, brutal thing. Japan is going to be really bad.' Three days later word of Nagasaki came and he called us together again. He said, 'Well, there is a possibility we may not have to do it, but just for old times' sake, go through the exercises you're supposed to do.' [*laughs*]. So we went through training exercises, but I never got to Japan.

With no answer to the call for surrender coming from the Japanese High Command, on August 9 the second (and last) bomb was deployed against Nagasaki in southeastern Japan. The death toll was at least 70,000. Marine Walter Hooke had occupation duty in Nagasaki.

Walter Hooke

We landed in Sasebo [the major naval base in Nagasaki Prefecture]. Every city in our first few months there, we went from one end... to the other, and every city was flattened, you know. I have some pictures I can show you. There is nothing in the cities—they were wiped out, they were worse than Nagasaki—but Sasebo, the town we landed in, appeared more devastated compared to Nagasaki—except I saw the difference.

When I got to Nagasaki, there were all these people around that had been burned and injured, and the hospitals were overflowing. They could not take care of people, and you know, I did not get there in Nagasaki until October—and from the bomb [I could see] there had been people with skin hanging off. It was awful.

Roman Catholic cathedral on a hill in Nagasaki. National Archives. Public domain.

On the radio the Japanese Emperor Hirohito spoke to his people and said, 'The time has come when we must bear the unbearable.' It was the first time they had heard his voice. Shaken prison camp commandants awaited word of whether or not to carry out the "kill-all" order within their camps.

Joe Minder recorded his observations as the prisoners dared to hope that their redemption was near.

Joe Minder

August 15, 1945

Heavy bombing near here all last night. Terrific explosions. *12:00 a.m.:* All Japs went to town. We didn't go to work until 3 p.m.—something is darn funny around here. Guards are very quiet today.

August 16, 1945

Many peace rumors floating around camp today.

August 17, 1945

Australian officers received paper written in Japanese. They say the war is over from what they could interpret in the paper.

August 18, 1945

Worked in garden near camp a half day. Heard loudspeakers blaring away downtown.

August 19, 1945

Camp commander announced we would not work in the mine anymore. War must be over?

August 20, 1945

War's end was officially announced by interpreter, 'Mosiki,' at 1:15 p.m.! Still hard to believe![34]

---

[34] Lester Tenney, a Bataan Death March survivor and fellow slave laborer at a mine in Japan, recalled testing the guards to get a feel for whether or not the war was really over. He left his barracks and offered a "Hello" in Japanese to the nearest guard he could find, a move that normally would have resulted in a severe beating, as he deliberately did not bow. Instead, the

August 21, 1945

Four prisoners who escaped from camp June 18 returned and were turned loose with us. They told us of the horrible brutal treatment they received after being captured by Japs.

Now, the moment of liberation was at hand. It would stay in the ex-prisoners' minds for the rest of their lives.

August 22, 1945

After three and a half years of starvation and brutal treatment, that beautiful symbol of freedom once more flies over our head! Our camp tailor worked all night and finished our first American flag! The blue came from a GI barracks bag, red from a Jap comforter, and the white from an Australian bed sheet. When I came out of the barracks and saw those beautiful colors for the first time, I felt like crying!

I know now, like I never did before, what it means to be able to live in a peaceful nation like the U.S.A. with its unlimited amount of liberties and freedom.

Japs increased our chow. An 800-pound bull was brought in camp. Had fried fish and fried greens and fried tomatoes, also a level bowl of barley/soya bean/thick blood soup for supper.

August 25, 1945

Twelve American planes flew over near camp! Large *"PW"* signs were nailed onto the roofs, and also a huge sign made out of blackout shades and white paper by the Australian officers saying

---

guard returned the salutation in English, with deference. In a 2014 interview, Tenney recalled with emotion, "He bowed to me. He bowed, to *me*!"

"SMOKES—CANDY—NEWS—300" was placed on the ground in front of our barracks, in the hopes that the Yanks would spot our signs and drop us supplies!

6:00 p.m.

Capt. Beadstine just announced that our parents had been notified of our whereabouts.

Bundles from Heaven

August 28, 1945

What an exciting day!

This morning we were waiting anxiously for the two cigarettes which the Japs issue each day, as their daily issue, and wondering if we would receive a level bowl of barley and beans for dinner. Our food, clothing, and cigarette worries finally ended at 4 o'clock this afternoon. About 2:00 p.m., two American planes zoomed real low over our camp, then circled around again and dropped a note saying, *"OK boys, read your message. Stand clear, supplies will be dropped shortly."* About 20 minutes later they returned escorting Grumman dive bombers and a B–29 and started dropping tons of candy, smokes, food, clothing, and medicine, with large parachutes. I don't think I have seen a more beautiful and exciting sight in my life! We could watch the men in the rear of the plane tumble those huge bundles of blessings out, then huge cargo parachutes of all different colors opened, and the food which we have been waiting for three and a half years started falling like rain all over our campground!

This continued until 4:00 p.m., when the B–29 opened and closed its bomb bay doors, signaling us, 'that is all,' and flew away. Men started running around, excited as heck, gathering up the large bundles scattered inside and outside the compound on the roofs and downtown, where one heavy load was dropped by a B–29 in a muddy rice paddy, burying many large drums deep in the mud when they broke loose from their parachutes. Several large bundles also broke loose from the parachutes over our camp and riddled many barracks full of large holes as if bombs had been dropped on us.

Bill Fisher and an Australian officer were killed by falling bundles. Bill was killed instantly when two large 55–gallon drums broke loose from the parachutes and crashed through the side of the barracks about eight feet from where my bed was located![57]

5:00 p.m.

Left camp to help dig supplies out of rice paddies and haul them back to camp. Much food was broken open, so I filled my gut with candy, canned fruit, army ration, and God-knows-what-not. I'll never forget the first taste of American food I had! I salvaged a small amount of cocoa, a cube of pineapple, and Type-C crackers on the road on my way downtown.

8:00 p.m.

It started raining hard, so I returned back to camp, barefoot, wet, muddy, and cold, but with a full gut and as happy and excited as a kid would be just after Santa Claus left!

August 29, 1945:

About 10:00 a.m., a B–29 dropped a large load of supplies outside of camp. I helped haul it back to camp. Got several candy bars from boxes of candy which Mayhue and Johnson carried in.

August 31, 1945:

Very sick this morning and last night from overeating. Just don't know when to stop; this food tastes so darn delicious!

11:00 a.m.

Truck just brought in another big load of supplies dropped by mistake by a B–29 at a Japanese camp about 80 miles from here!

The View from Tokyo Bay

On September 2, 1945, Admiral "Bull" Halsey's flagship USS Missouri was in Tokyo Bay awaiting the arrival of the Japanese delegation with General MacArthur and Admiral Nimitz aboard, positioned in the exact spot where Commodore Matthew C. Perry had anchored on his first visit to Japan in 1853, and flying his original 31-star flag.[58] The Japanese delegation was escorted promptly aboard at 9:00 a.m. and signed the terms of surrender. In the United States and Europe, it was six years to the day that the bloodiest conflict in human history had begun. Joseph Marcino, a Marine tank commander on Iwo Jima from the North Country, was on board one of the many ships in the bay as a witness to history.

Joe Marcino

What a sight that was! When daylight came, you could not see a place on the ocean where there was not a ship. The bay was just filled with all ships—massive, a lot more than Iwo Jima. At that time, we had some inkling we were going to make a landing on Japan. And so we were in that position, with ships as far as you could see on the horizon. The ocean was just full of destroyers, battleships, cruisers, and landing craft—just everything.

Surrender ceremonies, 2,000 plane flyover, USS MISSOURI left foreground. National Archives. Public domain.

The Redeemed Captive

As the Japanese delegation signed the instrument of surrender, General MacArthur concluded the ceremony: 'It is my earnest hope, indeed the hope of all mankind, that from this solemn occasion a better world shall emerge from the blood and carnage of the past.' Present just behind him on the deck for the honor of the occasion was the newly liberated General Jonathan Wainwright, who had spent much of his captivity leading his men (including John Parsons, who was imprisoned with him on Formosa) in defying the Japanese. Once the signatures were all in order, the 11-man Japanese delegation was immediately escorted off the ship. The awesome task of reconstructing and restoring civilization could begin, but for most of the prisoners of war, the journey towards home and healing had not even gotten underway.

Joe Minder

September 1, 1945

Feeling good again, going to try and take it a little easy on that rich food. Had pictures taken and got weighed this afternoon. Gained four and a half pounds in seven days.

September 3, 1945

Many men sick from overeating. Camp baking oven completed today. Had 20 doughnuts for supper, first since May 1942. Had baggage inspection this morning. We are getting packed ready to leave!

6:00 p.m.

Had chocolate-covered cupcakes for supper—they were delicious!

September 4, 1945

B–29s dropped supplies at Camp 6 and 8 today. Still waiting for our food drop. Had biscuits for supper. First type of bread since April 1942. They were made out of Jap barley flour.

September 5, 1945

Fifteen large sacks of potatoes and a dressed horse came in this afternoon. A B–29 circled over camp several times but didn't drop anything.

7:00 p.m.

Just finished hearing my first American voice over the radio since the fall of Corregidor in May 1942. [The commander was] urging us to remain in our camps and we would be evacuated from Japan as soon as possible.

September 6, 1945

Heard our first American news broadcast at noon: 4,000 POWs have already been liberated, 14% of the total POWs here in Japan.

September 9, 1945

Killed fat horse this morning. Had delicious horse steak and horse blood gravy for supper, also few Irish spuds and rice.

September 11, 1945

Stayed up until 12:30 last night with Bradley eating and drinking coffee. Got weighed, gained 13 pounds in the past 19 days!

3:00 p.m.

Waiting here in the camp yard, packed, ready to march to the train to meet the Yanks at the sea coast. God, what a crazy-looking bunch we are! Baggage of all sorts strapped to our backs. Some are packs made of different colored parachutes, blankets, Red Cross boxes, and some even have their belongings in old packed barracks bags which originally came from Bataan or Corregidor. Our pockets and shirts are crammed full of candy, gum, cigarettes, canned food, God-knows-what-all. Wish I had a picture of the entire bunch!

6:00 p.m.

Just got on train for our 13–hour train ride to the coast!

Like scores of others like it, the ex-POW train clacked and snaked through the Japanese countryside, slowing to pass through firebombed cities, which were now just charred husks of their former glory, peopled in some places only with the silent, dazed, and desperate. At the port of Yokohama, the soldiers disembarked and began the second leg of their long journey home.

Joe made it back to the Philippines, where he found he had been promoted to corporal. He was booked on a troop transport with 3,200 other Americans and headed for home.

October 10, 1945

We are sailing past Corregidor, Fort Hughes, Fort Drum, and the Bataan peninsula now. Although we are quite a distance from these fortified islands, we can still see the result of the terrible bombings and shellings which these forts took from both the Japs and Americans. I can see Monkey Point on Corregidor very plainly from this side of the ship now. That is where the Japs finally forced us to surrender after battering away at us with bombs and shells for five months.

6:30 p.m.

In a few minutes now we will be able to get the last glimpse of the battlefields where our buddies lie, unfortunate not to be going home with us. Never thought when I sailed into this bay on October 23, 1941, that these small green tropical islands would be hot battlefields within two months.

Three weeks later, Joe arrived in San Francisco.

November 1, 1945

Up ready for breakfast, couldn't sleep very much last night. Thinking of landing kept me awake!

8:30 a.m.

There she is! Off in the distance we can see a faint glimpse of the Golden Gate lying in a dense bank of fog. A beautiful day! In a few minutes the beautiful, tall buildings in San Francisco will be visible!

8:45 a.m.

Shouts and cheers rang out all over the entire ship as 3,200 men and army nurses clung to every possible point from deck to top mast, watching the boat pass under the Golden Gate! Boy, what a wonderful feeling!

11 a.m.

Tied up at Pier 15 now. Mothers, sisters, and friends are going wild down on the pier as they spot men that they know, who are clinging to the rails, life boats, and what-not. Boy, there are some swell-looking girls down there! Those Yank gals are as good-looking as ever!

12:15 p.m.

Officers have started down the gang plank. Major Warmuth's sister and mother are kissing him and going crazy with joy! There are also a large bunch of newspaper reporters around, trying to get a story from him.

1:00 p.m.

Arrived at Letterman Hospital by bus from pier! It's a great feeling riding up a modern city street again!

Thanksgiving, 1945, would find Joe at home in North Creek, New York, with his family for the first time in nearly four years. The joyful reunion was tempered with his learning of the passing of his mother while he was in captivity, but after months in and out of hospitals he would find solace in the quiet of the mountains, streams, and lakes of the Adirondacks. He found skiing, which he had taken up at the age of seven, to be particularly therapeutic as he slowly gained back some of his strength. During his visits to his doctor, he noticed a young lady who worked in the office, and began to offer her a ride home after his appointments. In 1948, Joe Minder and Hazel Allen were married and settled down to raise two boys. He worked out of the office of the local garnet mine and also in the fledgling ski industry that began to take off after World War II. He gave back to his community with a commitment to his church, fire department, and other civic organizations, and patiently taught the youth how to ski and even how to properly cultivate a garden. Despite the physical effects of those Japanese clubs or the 16-hour days carrying 70 pound bags of Japanese copper ore, which took their toll on his body as time progressed, Joe never harbored any bitterness or hatred for the horrible suffering he had experienced as a young man. He did not talk often about his prisoner experience, but his ethos of patience, kindness, and compassion for others shines forth in his journal and was confirmed in the way he lived out his days. The entire community grieved when Joseph Minder passed away in 2006 at age 88; the little town's ski bowl lodge would be named after him.

*

'Lost is the Youth We Knew'

A poem composed by Lt. Henry G. Lee, a Bataan survivor and fellow prisoner, was discovered during the daring American rescue raid on Cabanatuan Camp at the end of January 1945. Perhaps Lee's feelings, written so near to the end and hidden in the journal of poems he was forced to leave behind, sum up the conflicting emotions of so many of the young defenders of the Philippines, and all the men who fought in the Pacific.

Westward we came across the smiling waves,
West to the outpost of our country's might
'Romantic land of brilliant tropic light'
Our land of broken memories and graves.

Eastward we go and home, so few
Wrapped in their beds of clay our comrades sleep
The memories of this land are branded deep
And lost is the youth we knew.[59]

Lt. Henry G. Lee never got to go home; he had been killed in one of the American air raids on the unmarked hellships in Takao Harbor in Formosa, just three days before Joe Minder began his own voyage from there to his final destination at the mine in Japan.

World War II had formally ended, but back in "Hometown, USA," the returning survivors, their families, and the families of those who did not return would see the legacy of the war last far beyond the end of 1945.

John Norton

There was a family that lost two sons in World War II. The family got a telegram on a Monday that one of the boys was killed, and that Thursday they got another telegram saying that his brother had been killed. There were about 35 young men from Granville who were killed in World War II, and I knew every one of them. Some of them were older, and some of them were younger; most of them were good friends of mine.[35]

Ralph Leinoff

I was one of the lucky ones who managed to escape essentially unharmed physically; but there is no doubt that when you see men die around you and when you're holding dying men in your arms, it has an effect on you. Even when things calm down you start to think about it, you see things that happen when a man is begging to see his wife and children one more time before he dies, you can't help it. I mean, that has an effect on you.

When I was able to come home, I married the girl I knew from infancy. We had a good life and I got a job, we had children, but I slept for the first two years of marriage and children with a Bowie knife beside my bed, because I could still see Japanese coming at me in the dark. It was just something that I felt secure about; I had to have a knife beside me, but I got away from that.

Physically I was in good shape, but psychologically, there is some trauma. If you're fortunate, other things in life come along and they crowd out the trauma. Only in retrospect do I look back on the war and I get to feel it again. When I talk about it, see, I get teary-eyed—I can't help it. There's a lot that happened in those three years, a lot happened.

At age 94, Walter Hooke summed up his feelings about the legacy of the generation that experienced the most cataclysmic war in the history of the world for his young interviewer.

---

[35] Mr. Norton continued: 'That was real sad. Fortunately, my parents wrote me a lot, and I would write back. My father used to go down to the post office, every night, looking for the mail. He would be there waiting for a letter from me, every night, you know. The parents were concerned.'

You know, it is about the future of the world for you young people, and you have to keep everyone honest. I think that is one thing I learned with the atomic bomb, that there is no future in war, so as far as I am concerned...the worst thing that is happening is that young people are brought up to be in fear, and you should not be.

Kids should not grow up cynical—they should grow up like the world is theirs, and enjoy it and have a decent world.

EPILOGUE

Resurrection

The bell rings. The students take their seats. The lesson of the day is about to commence.

A hand shoots up.

Yes, Jessie?

Mr. Rozell, I am leaving school early on vacation and won't be here for a few days. May I have the work I will be missing?

My blood pressure ticks upward, slightly. With exams pending in the days before our Easter break, my tenth grade history student informs me that she is leaving for a vacation to Hawaii—a tad early—and she wants her assignments in advance. Since she will be missing a few classes (and she's heading to Hawaii and I am not!), I give her an extra task, never dreaming that she will actually pull it off.

Finding Randy

Randy Holmes was a couple years older than Jessie when he died. He was the first kid from our high school and all of the North Country, and quite possibly all of New York State, to be killed in World War II. Randy, you will recall, was on the *USS Oklahoma* when the Japanese torpedoed it at Pearl Harbor on December 7, 1941.

By the time I walked the halls of this high school as a student in the 1970s, no one remembered him. Today, as then, there are no plaques, no memorials on display here, outside of the local cemetery. I certainly did not know about him.

He was gone.

*

Nearly sixty years after he went missing, I've returned to the 'other side of the desk' at my alma mater. In the high school library, World War II veterans from the communities near the "Falls" have gathered on a warm spring afternoon. We're here to put on a seminar on the Pacific War for maybe a hundred excited students. During a break I'm listening to the casual conversation between our guests, and by chance I catch this snippet between Navy pilot John Leary and the Marines sitting around the table:

'There was a young man from around here; he hounded his parents to let him enlist because he was only 17. Do you remember Randy Holmes?'

'Why yes, didn't the Class of 1942 dedicate their yearbook to him?'

I'm intrigued. My next step is to search the dusty yearbooks in the district vault, and sure enough, in the back of the slim 1942 volume, I find him. Randy is decked out in his white sailor's suit and cap. He is at home, on leave, crouching before some bushes in the backyard, smiling for the camera as his mother or father proudly snaps the picture. He looks happy, and proud.

And I feel like he's beckoning to me. It's similar to the picture that my father snapped of me, less than a mile away, shortly before I ventured out into the world, like Randy, for the first time.

RANDOLPH HOLMES-
MISSING IN ACTION

The photo was probably taken in the summer of 1941, after his schooling and shortly before he was assigned to the *Oklahoma*. That fall, his classmates started their senior year of high school. Everyone's world would change shortly before Christmas, and Randy would never be heard from again. His classmates would compose a final tribute to accompany the photograph:

'RANDOLPH HOLMES—MISSING IN ACTION'

'Word was received soon after the Japanese bombing of Pearl Harbor, by Mr. and Mrs. Randolph Holmes, that their son was 'missing in action.' The young sailor was on board the steamship Oklahoma, when it was struck by a Japanese bomb. Randolph would have been a member of this year's senior class if he had remained in school.

He enlisted in the Navy New Year's Day, 1941, and was sent to Newport, R.I., where he was in training as a machinist. Later he was transferred to the Great Lakes Training School in Chicago. He graduated with the rank of Seaman, Second Class.

In August of last year Randolph was ordered to report for duty to the S.S. Oklahoma. He was stationed on this boat in Pearl Harbor when the attack was made by the Japanese.

This young sailor was a popular student in Hudson Falls High School and both faculty and students keep in their hearts kind thoughts and happy memories of his manly qualities and sterling character.'

*

According to the 1940 federal census, Randy had a sister, but she left the village, as far as I can tell, becoming a nurse in the war. His parents passed away, brokenhearted. The family homestead on quiet James Street was sold. The trail just ended.

He was gone.

In the years that followed my trip to the vault, I told the story of the 'Okie' and showed my classes Randy's photograph. I would talk about him, and wonder about him. Who were his friends? How did this news affect the community? What did his death do to his parents, and his sister?

Do you realize he was your age when he died? Where is he buried? Did his body even come home?

Finally, one of my students, Mackenna, took me up on the challenge, conducted her own research, and discovered the following from the National Park Service website: 'Resting in the main channel of the harbor, a major salvage operation began in March of 1943. This massive undertaking involved the use of winches installed on Ford Island, which slowly rolled the ship back into place in an upright position. The ship was then pumped out and the remains of over 400 sailors and Marines were removed.'[60]

The remains.
Underwater.
Eighteen months.

As World War II raged on, the bodies of the men remained entombed in the ship. Parents grieved as logistics were studied and the salvage operation planned. What was left was recovered and buried in a mass grave at Pearl Harbor. Only 35 men have ever been identified.[61]

In 1947, the *Oklahoma* was sold and began its last journey to be cut up for scrap at a salvage yard in California. Not long into the journey, she began to take on water and the tow lines had to be severed; the 'Okie' slipped away into the abyss 540 miles northeast of Pearl Harbor. A former crew member summed up the feelings of many who had served aboard, and those who perished on her, when he wrote these lines:

'Good for you, Oklahoma!
Go down at sea in deep water, as you should, under the stars.
No razor blades for you!
They can make 'em from the ships and planes that did you in.
So long, Oklahoma! You were a good ship!'

The *Oklahoma* did not even have its own memorial at Pearl Harbor until 2007. But every December 7 in our school, since I found the yearbook, we make an effort in our history classes to remember the day Randy Holmes went missing.

Resurrection

My heart is gladdened when I arrive in school the day before the Easter holiday, open my e-mail, and find this photo.

I smile. She did it.[36]

Maybe my eyes brim for a brief instant.

Maybe Randy and all of the soldiers, sailors, and Marines and airmen are resurrected.

The kids remember.

In the words of Susie Stevens-Harvey, who lost her brother in Vietnam and advocates for all those still missing in action, or prisoners of war:

'Dying for freedom isn't the worst that could happen.
Being forgotten is.'

The veterans featured in this book

A Sunday Morning

Harry 'Randy' Holmes: Randy was born in 1923. He and his sister lived on Rogers Street in Hudson Falls. When the author was a kid, he would visit a neighborhood mom-and-pop grocery store on

[36] Later, after this episode has passed, I discovered that Jessie was born exactly 56 years after the day Randy died. She is a 'Pearl Harbor baby'.

his way home from elementary school on the adjacent Maple Street. After the publication of an article related to this book, the editor of a local newspaper followed up with a note on the passing of Mrs. Nickie Piscitelli, the late owner of that store:

"1941 was Mike's Grocery's first year in business. [Following the article's publication], Nickie said that the Holmes family lived around the corner from the store. She said Randy's mother came by that day, December 7, 1941, and when the news came on the radio that the USS Oklahoma *had been bombed—Nickie then pointed to where the radio had been on the shelf—Mrs. Holmes said, 'My son is on that ship!'"* As noted, Randy was killed on the *USS Oklahoma* and his remains have yet to return to his hometown to rest near his parents.

Gerald Ross: 'Barney' was born in 1921 in Whitehall, New York. He enjoyed hunting and fishing with family and was very active in community activities, especially projects and organizations related to helping veterans. He passed away at the age of 94 in 2015, a few months after this book went to press.[62]

Joseph Fiore: After the war Joe returned home and raised his family, running a liquor store and later becoming director of the Warren County Veterans Service Agency. In his civic activities, Joe Fiore worked with many veterans organizations. He was instrumental in the establishment of the local chapter of the Marine Corps League, and with the help of many of the Marines in the book, began the annual 'Toys For Tots' Christmas drive for underprivileged children. Joe Fiore passed away in May 2015 at the age of 92.[63]

Dante Orsini: Dan became a friend of the author late in life and loved to visit with the kids in the author's classroom. Besides being in the White House Honor Guard, he also fought at Guam and Okinawa. After serving in China protecting that government against the communists immediately following the war, he was awarded the 'Order of the Cloud and Banner' by Chiang Kai-shek himself. He served his community in many ways up until the week before he passed in 2013 at age 93.[64]

THE DEFENDERS/ CAPTIVITY

Joseph Minder: Joe Minder's POW experiences as recorded in his diary form the backdrop of this work; the bulk of it is published here for the first time. He kept his notes on cigarette paper and other scraps and managed to keep them hidden from his captors. Joe sent the author a typewritten copy of his diary in the late 1990s, and it was reformatted in the spring semester of 2015 for use here by the author's students as a class project. Joe was repatriated and returned home to North Creek, New York, marrying and raising 2 sons and working for the local garnet mine. He became an expert ski instructor in the fledgling downhill skiing industry. Joe Minder passed away in 2006 at the age of 88.[65]

Richard M. Gordon: Major Gordon retired from the U.S. Army and became one of the founding members of the 'Battling Bastards of Bataan,' an organization committed to honoring the memory of the soldiers of the Philippines and to educating future generations. He led many tours back to the authentic sites and helped erect several monuments to the fallen. Major Gordon passed away in 2003 at the age of 81.[66]

John Parsons: John Parsons, having survived the Bataan Death March, gave an interview to the local newspaper in 1946 recounting his experiences. At Mukden POW camp in Manchuria, he was subjected to beatings and starvation. The Japanese also conducted a secret program that included bacteriological experiments, which the Japanese and American governments today do not acknowledge.) Parsons was liberated by the Red Army on August 20, 1945. He suffered greatly from his wartime experiences, and owing to a lack of 'documentation' at the hands of his captors, he was denied full disability benefits by thc U.S. Government, not an uncommon occurrence for POWs. He passed away in 1965 at the age of 53, having been bedridden for the previous five years.[67]

INTO THE FRAY

Dorothy Schechter: Dorothy Schechter was born in 1919 in eastern Pennsylvania. She attended Pennsylvania State University and married in 1941 before the war broke out. Mrs. Schechter, a civilian, was working at various bases in the United States because her husband, in military intelligence, was frequently on the move. After the war, she went with her husband Joe to Europe where he attempted to find members of his Jewish family in Poland and Austria, but they had all been murdered in the Holocaust. Soon after returning, Joe was diagnosed with a genetic disorder and passed away a few years later, at the age of 39. Mrs. Schechter was just 34, but never remarried. After his passing, she worked for a law firm and became a tax attorney before retiring. Mrs. Schechter loved reading and travel and her beloved dachshund was a constant companion.[68]

John A. Leary: Judge Leary was a recipient of the Navy Cross and married while in the service during World War II. He returned from the war and earned a degree in law, setting up practice in Hudson Falls, New York. He later served as Washington County Court judge and district attorney with an illustrious career of public and civil service. He passed away in 2003 at the age of 84. For most of his life he loved flying, and his original flightlog and various maps and photographs from the campaign against Rabaul and other targets can be seen at bit.ly/LearyGallery.[69]

A Turning Point/Guadalcanal

Robert Addison: Bob Addison served as the first Director of Athletics at Adirondack Community College and later became a full-time professor and beloved coach. He enjoyed attending reunions of Edson's Raiders long after the war with his friend Gerry West. He passed away in 2013 at the age of 90.[70]

Gerald West: Gerry West was a life member and past president of the Edson's Raiders Association. He served in Korea and later joined the U.S. Army after his time in the Marine Corps. He had a career in retail, where he ran into Bob Addison again in 1962, recognizing him as he was selling him kitchen appliances. Gerry West passed away in 2014 at the age of 95. Before their passing, the author was instrumental in helping the New York State Senate to induct Gerry West and Bob Addison jointly into the Senate Veterans Hall of Fame in May 2013..[71]

Thomas H. Jones: Tom Jones was born in 1913, in Wilkes Barre, Pennsylvania. Orphaned early in life, he served in the U.S. Marine Corps from 1931 to 1935, then again during World War II in the South Pacific with First Marine Division at Guadalcanal, Cape Gloucester, and Peleliu, where he received the Purple Heart. In retirement, he enjoyed fly fishing with his own tied flies in the Adirondacks. He was 99 years old when he passed away in 2013, and wished to be remembered as a proud Marine and true gentleman.[72]

Sea Action/The Kamikazes

Alvin Peachman: Mr. Peachman taught history for over thirty years after returning from the war and getting his teaching credentials. He still lives in the small house where he raised his family near the high school where he taught, and spends his winters in Hawaii, which he was introduced to in World War II and where he and his late wife had many friends. At 96 he can still be seen taking his daily walks and talking to the people he meets, and can still almost instantly recall the names of students he had in class nearly 60 years ago upon meeting them.[73]

Islands of the Damned

Ralph Leinoff: After the war, Ralph married and raised two sons with his wife. He worked as a salesman and graphic designer. Ralph also spent 27 years in the service of the New York City Fire Department. He was a consummate artist and raconteur throughout his life, expressing himself in painting, pencilwork, ceramics, videography, sculpture, acrylics, lyrics, and composition. Mr. and Mrs. Leinoff supported many community causes. They also pursued a host of other interests, including world travel and community service and patronage. Ralph became close to several of the author's student interviewers, even buying their textbooks for their college pursuits. He passed away in 2014 at the age of 91.[74]

Walter Hooke: Walter Hooke was born in 1913 and joined the Marine Corps in 1942. Serving in Nagasaki with the occupation forces solidified a passion to work for peace. He became close to the Catholic Bishop of Nagasaki, Paul Yamaguchi, and upon returning home, became a vocal advocate for the National Association of Radiation Survivors. He was also instrumental in lobbying legislators for benefits for the Atomic War Veterans; he thought the decision to use the atomic bombs had been misguided and wrong. He passed away in 2010 at the age of 97. An admirer noted on his passing, *"I regret that I shall not hear again, Walter's intoning on the answering machine, 'Have a gentle day.'* "[75]

Nicholas Grinaldo: For his actions on Saipan, Nick Grinaldo received the Bronze Star. He was honorably discharged in 1945 with the rank of staff sergeant. After the war Nick returned to Troy, New York, where he operated Nick's Shoe Store, a store that was first opened in 1917 by his uncle. He enjoyed time with his family and was active in many civic organizations. He passed away in 2012 at the age of 92.[76]

John Sidur: Due to the fact that he was treated by a Marine corpsman on Saipan and not an Army doctor and the subsequent confusion and loss of records, John Sidur was denied a Purple Heart for his actions on Saipan, but would receive one for suffering a wound at Okinawa—very belatedly—in a special ceremony in 2010, 65 years after that battle. 'It almost makes me cry,' he said at the time. 'It's a long time coming.' He passed away in 2015 at the age of 97.[77]

Daniel Lawler: Dan Lawler was a frequent visitor to the author's classroom, bringing his Marine scrapbook and various souvenirs and funny stories from his time in Okinawa, Peleliu, and China as a member of the First Marine Division K/3/5. He was awarded the Purple Heart, which he highly treasured. While in K Company, Dan was honored to serve with future author Eugene B. Sledge, whose book, *With The Old Breed*, captured the experiences of the Pacific battlefield. Other Marine brothers of the company included Sen. Paul Douglas of Illinois, who Dan visited in Washington after the war. Dan passed away at the age of 90 in September 2015.[78]

John Murray: John Murray, severely wounded at Peleliu, was evacuated and later awarded the Purple Heart at a hospital in San Diego. Through his life he remained close to his Marine buddies in this book, notably Jim Butterfield and Dan Lawler. Like many veterans, he raised his family but did not speak about his wartime experiences. His account here in this book was written in a 1995 letter to his son, which was shared with the author after he died. He passed away in 1998.[79]

James and Mary Butterfield: As noted, Jim and Mary were high school sweethearts who married soon after the war, despite Jim having been blinded for life in May 1945 at Okinawa. After the war, Jim endured many reconstructive surgeries on his face but overcame his disability, and he and Mary became the proud owners of Butterfield's Grocery Store on Bay St. in Glens Falls, New York, for 40 years. It was said that Mr. Butterfield could tell the denomination of the bill that was handed to him by its texture and touch. They loved traveling to Hawaii and Florida; Jim particularly enjoyed needling the Japanese tourists and businessmen he encountered in Hawaii, joking that the sniper who shot him on Okinawa probably owned a hotel in Honolulu. They were married for 67 years and cherished the time spent with their family. Mary passed in October 2012; Jim passed the following summer at the age of 87.[80]

CAPTIVITY—YEAR 3: THE HELLSHIPS

Robert Blakeslee: Hellship sinking survivor Robert Blakeslee passed away in 1976. His daughter Nancy Blakeslee Wood recently discovered a collection of her mother's letters, which were always marked 'Returned to Sender,' and also his postcards, which amounted to a short checklist regarding his health status and what he could receive from her in the camps, but never did.[81]

THE SANDS OF IWO JIMA

Sanford Berkman: Sandy was born in Cohoes, New York, in 1920. After the war, Sandy was the owner and operator of Kaye's Catering, a business he ran with his wife. After his career in the catering business, Sandy worked for the Commissioner of Jurors in Albany for many years until his retirement. He passed away in 2017 at the age of 97.[82]

Arthur LaPorte: Art LaPorte was interviewed on many occasions for this project, both at his home and at classroom symposiums. Like many World War II veterans, LaPorte would go on to serve in Korea, sustaining additional wounds there; he was not shy about rolling up his pants leg or sleeve to show students where chunks of muscle were missing, though that did not stop him from working hard at the mill and literally digging his own basement by hand with a shovel after the war. Like many veterans, he still can recite how to field strip/clean his weapon, memorizing the parts and the sequence, decades after combat.[83]

Herbert Altshuler: Herb and his wife retired to the North Country by the 'Falls' after a successful career. He enjoyed giving freely of his time to our high school students and was interviewed on several occasions, and maintained relationships with them after the interviews were over. They are always in the audience when the author gives a lecture or slideshow locally.[84]

Walter Hammer: Walter Hammer was born in 1924, and along with the other Marines in this book, was a frequent contributor to the panel discussions set up by the author at his high school. Nicknamed 'Sledge' by his buddies, Walt went on to receive the Silver Star for his brave actions under fire at Iwo Jima, which he never brought up in our panel discussions with the students. He passed away in 2008 at the age of 83.

A Rain of Ruin

Andy Doty: After the war, Andy Doty married his high school sweetheart, Eleanor Baker, the daughter of the local druggist, and raised three girls, settling in Palo Alto, California, and retiring as Director of Community Affairs for Stanford University. You can read more about his World War II experiences in my second book or by searching for his out-of-print 1995 memoir with the information provided in the 'Source Notes' in the back of this book.[85]

Typhoon of Steel/Okinawa

Bruce Manell: Bruce Manell enjoyed a storied career in area law enforcement, retiring as Deputy Chief of Police in the Hudson Falls Police Department. He loved photography and bowling and wrote a column for the local newspaper on the bowling leagues. He passed away in 2009.[86]

Katherine Abbott: Kay Abbot was born in 1917 in Glens Falls, New York, and received her training as a registered nurse at Albany Memorial Hospital. Along with her five brothers, she served in the U.S. Army during World War II. While serving in the Army, Kay was a flight nurse and would help many soldiers on the flights from the Philippines to Hawaii and San Francisco. After the service, Kay worked for Albany Veterans Hospital as an RN, retiring in 1980. She was an active member of the World War II Flight Nurses Association, and really enjoyed their reunions. She was also a charter member of the World War II Memorial Society. She passed in December 2007 at the age of 90.[87]

Redemption

John Norton: Mr. Norton returned home from sea in 1946. He became involved in local politics and civic organizations, and later served as the mayor of Granville, New York.[88]

Joseph Marcino: Joe Marcino joined the Marines after graduating from Whitehall High School and was awarded the Bronze Star for bravery under fire at the battle of Iwo Jima. He went on to become a celebrated and much loved football coach and athletic director. He passed away in 2014 at the age of 91.[89]

VOLUME II

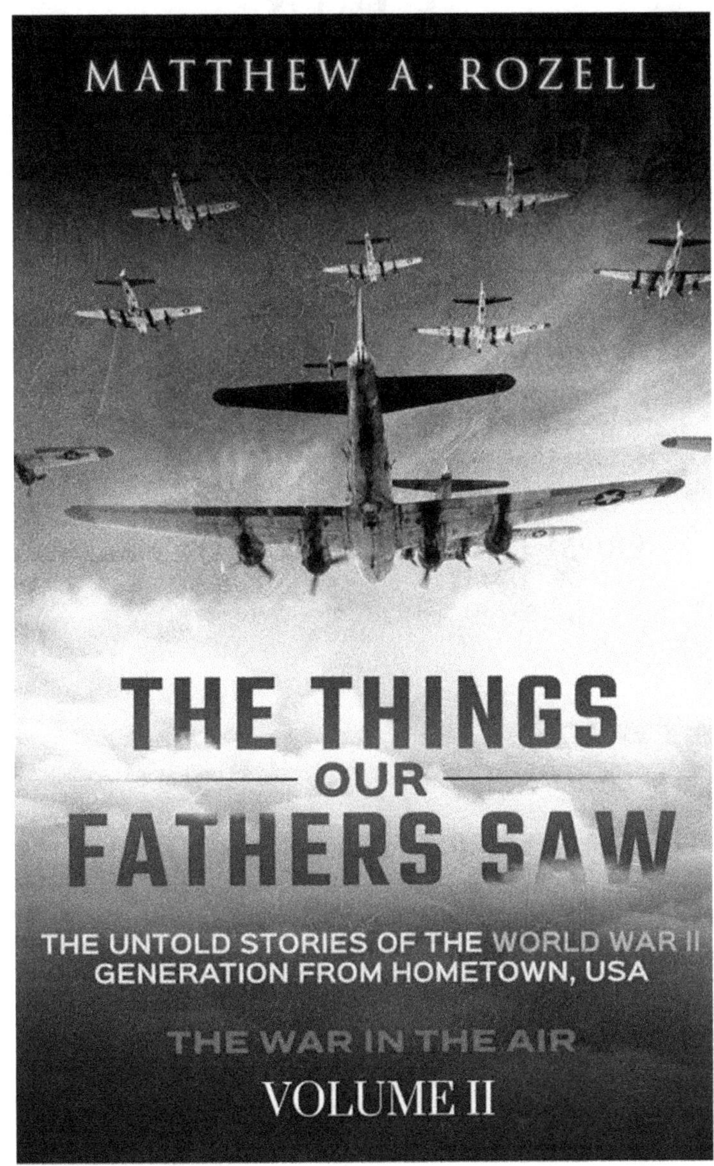
MATTHEW A. ROZELL
THE THINGS
OUR
FATHERS SAW
THE UNTOLD STORIES OF THE WORLD WAR II
GENERATION FROM HOMETOWN, USA
THE WAR IN THE AIR
VOLUME II

THE THINGS OUR FATHERS SAW

VOLUME II:
THE UNTOLD STORIES OF THE WORLD WAR II GENERATION FROM HOMETOWN, USA

WAR IN THE AIR:
FROM THE DEPRESSION TO COMBAT

MATTHEW A. ROZELL

WOODCHUCK HOLLOW PRESS

Hartford · New York

 Grateful acknowledgement is made to the following: Andy Doty in *Backwards Into Battle* and various short quotations credited to other previously published sources. Please see author notes.

Information at woodchuckhollowpress@gmail.com.

Photographic portrait of Earl M. Morrow used courtesy of Robert H. Miller.

Front Cover: B-17 Flying Fortresses from the 398th Bombardment Group fly a bombing run to Neumunster, Germany, on April 13, 1945. Credit: Public Domain, U.S. Air Force photograph.

Additional photographs and descriptions sourced at Wikimedia Commons within terms of use, unless otherwise noted.

Publisher's Cataloging-in-Publication Data

Names: Rozell, Matthew A., 1961-
Title: The things our fathers saw : war in the air, from the Great Depression to combat : the untold stories of the World War II generation from hometown, USA / Matthew A. Rozell.
Description: Hartford, NY : Woodchuck Hollow Press, 2017. | Series: The things our fathers saw, vol. 2.
Identifiers: LCCN 2017912885 | ISBN 978-0-9964800-5-5 (pbk.) | ISBN 978-0-9964800-4-8 (ebook)
Subjects: LCSH: United States. Army Air Forces. Air Force, 8th--History--World War, 1939-1945. | United States. Army Air Forces--Airmen--Biography. | World War, 1939-1945--Personal narratives, American. | Bombing, Aerial--History--20th century. | Military history, Modern--20th century. | BISAC: HISTORY / Military / Veterans. | HISTORY / Military / World War II. | HISTORY / Military / Aviation.
Classification: LCC D810.V42 R691 2017 (print) | LCC D810.V42 (ebook) | DDC 940.54/8173--dc23.

matthewrozellbooks.com

Printed in the United States of America

THE THINGS OUR FATHERS SAW II
WAR IN THE AIR:
FROM THE DEPRESSION TO COMBAT

For the mothers who saw their children off to war,
And for those who keep the memory alive.

MY BEST 4 FRIENDS
of our Crew all Killed in
action But me

I get a little emotional. I'm almost 93; I hope to see them all again in heaven.

— John Swarts, B-17 Tail Gunner

Dying for freedom isn't the worst that could happen. Being forgotten is.

— Susie Stephens-Harvey, reflecting on her brother,
Stephen J. Geist
MIA 9-26-1967

I think we shall never see the likes of it again.

— Andy Doty, B-29 Tail Gunner

THE THINGS OUR FATHERS SAW II

THE STORYTELLERS (IN ORDER OF APPEARANCE):

ANDY DOTY

DICK VARNEY

RICHARD ALAGNA

KEN CARLSON

EARL MORROW

MARTIN BEZON

SEYMOUR SEGAN

JOHN SWARTS

THE THINGS OUR FATHERS SAW II

TABLE OF CONTENTS

Twenty-year-old waist gunner Clarence McGuire,
(tallest in back row, center)
and the crew of the 'Pugnacious Ball'
England, springtime 1944

Author's Note

Twenty-year-old Clarence McGuire was always lurking around the periphery of my childhood. My knowledge of my father's older cousin begins with the memory of a familiar far-off sound. From several blocks away, my brothers and sisters and I could pick out the bass drums punching faintly into the air. Our eyes traveled the length of Main Street, lined with cars parked on either side for as far as we could see. A police officer stood in the intersection, arms folded, with little traffic to direct, and turned towards the thickening beat. Kids began scampering for the best car rooftop positions, though our neighborhood gang had the best seats all around. Our family address was 2 Main Street, Hudson Falls, and for one day of the year, we were the kings.

In our small town near the falls, the traffic began thinning out in the morning hours. Our front porch steps were prime real estate for the parade, and my parents' friends in town would come over with lawn chairs for the best views in the village. The front door of the house led directly from the porch into the foyer and thence the kitchen, where my mother had her crockpot cooking up hours in advance with hotdogs; rolls and condiments and sides were piled high on the table nearby. Our American flag on the white front porch column fluttered softly in anticipation in the late May morning breeze; the maples that lined our street gently sent their seedlings helicoptering to the pavement below.

An All-American Memorial Day morning was underway. Soon enough, a crawling police car with its flashing emergency lights appeared in the distance as the marching band grew louder and the first flags swayed forth in a rhythmic cadence in step with the beat. The firemen in their snappy uniforms with brass buttons and white gloves waved out of their gleaming red trucks, following the rescue squad and their ambulances, the Little League teams, the pickup trucks pulling the flatbed floats, adults flinging penny candy from baskets into the street at the children's feet. My father's friends in the fire company and ambulance corps tipped their caps in our direction. The parade climaxed as the grand marshal for the year was chauffeured past in a gleaming convertible, waving to the crowd. We knew he was important, but had little idea who he was from year to year: just an important old man, decked out in his finest, a military-style cap peaked on his head.

All this meant that summer was finally here. The holiday known originally as "Decoration Day" originated at the end of the Civil War when a general order was issued designating May 30, 1868, *'for the purpose of strewing with flowers or otherwise decorating the graves of comrades who died in defense of their country during the late rebellion.'* When Congress passed a law formally recognizing the last Monday in May as the day of national celebration, we effectively got our three-day weekend and our 'de facto' beginning of summer.

As American schoolchildren of the 1970s, we had a vague *'something is important here'* feeling, but like a snake that slowly winds away and retreats out of sight, that feeling dissipated with the rearguard of flashing police cars, the highway truckers, and the 'stuck behind the damned parade' summer travelers anxious to get to wherever they were in a hurry to go. The cars lining Main Street started up almost on cue, pulling away from the curbs as our family and friends made their way to the kitchen to gorge on my mother's picnic fares. But Cousin Clarence never came to our Memorial Day get-togethers. He was dead. I never even knew him; I was born twenty years after the war that killed him began.

*

I don't quite remember the year that it dawned on me. I forsook the family picnic and folded in with the tail end of the parade after it passed the house, walking a few blocks on slate slab sidewalks to the black wrought iron entrance to Union Cemetery. Here I was notified by a volley of shots that I was too late for the words of wisdom from the town fathers, but that was okay. Amidst the parade flotsam on the side of Main Street, I saw a small American flag lying in the sand. I stopped to pick it up, and continued on further to the smaller cemetery behind Union where I knew a special grave marker was located, the one my father would bring me to on our occasional walks in my boyhood:

SGT. CLARENCE B. McGUIRE
A COURAGEOUS AND GALLANT GUNNER
WHO GAVE ALL FOR GOD AND COUNTRY
JULY 29, 1944
MAY HIS SOUL, AND ALL THE SOULS
OF THE GALLANT MEN WHO DIED, REST IN PEACE

Clarence B. McGuire. Dad remembered Clarence coming to visit and teasing him in a playful manner when Dad was only in grade school. We had a crew photo of him, which I saw from time to time growing up, and which I rediscovered while cleaning out Dad's desk after he passed. It was the only photo I had ever seen of Clarence: tall, centered in the rear row, just beaming and smiling. 'Clarry' was one of the waist gunners in this B-17 crew; you get the impression that they all got along, that maybe they were pals, teammates, probably friends for life. But somebody—maybe his mother?—anointed this picture with a cross over his head. He didn't come back, you see. The entire crew in this picture was killed on a bombing mission when the plane exploded on July 29, 1944, somewhere over Germany.

Friends for life. Blown out of the sky, just parts of twisted metal and burning chunks tumbling to the German soil. Even as an adult, the photo always haunted me a bit. All died in an instant, probably only months after this was taken. Flowers scythed down in the springtime of life. All gone.

Or so I thought. I planted the tiny flag at his memorial, and walked away. A seed was also being planted. I would be back.

***

I've given a good deal of thought on how to approach telling the story of the Air War in Europe in World War II. In my first book, I unfolded the War in the Pacific through the words of the veterans, specifically using the wartime prisoner diary of Joe Minder as a chronological guide. My original goal was to do something similar here, but it was proving more difficult. I had different airplanes my subjects were on, different theatres and Army Air Forces, different times and objectives during the European war. Some readers may be disappointed by a lack of technical detail or a political history, but my focus wound up being drawn to an entirely different path.

As it turned out, most of the veterans interviewed for this book served in the U.S. Army Eighth Air Force based in England. But rather than serve up to the reader another rehashing of the Mighty Eighth's story (there are already many detailed books out there—and I'd probably recommend Donald L. Miller's *Masters of the Air* over most of the others), I decided it would be fairer to our storytellers if they could share their own experiences individually. As I racked my brain for a narrative thread, I walked away and sat down to do some proofing. Then I noticed something. As it turned out, each of the men I was drawn to held a different crew position on the heavy bombers of the B-24 Liberator or the B-17 Flying Fortress. I had a new angle; I went with that.

*

In this and the upcoming books in *The Things Our Fathers Saw* series, we visit with more of the people who were forged and tempered in the tough times of the Great Depression and went on to 'do their bit' when even rougher times came calling. Most hailed from or later settled near or otherwise have a connection to the 'Hometown, USA' community where I grew up and taught in for over 30 years. (So that readers of all the books in this series can start in any place, the background chapter on the origins of the 'Hometown, USA' sobriquet from the first book is condensed and re-presented in the introduction.)

I don't know how to explain the feeling of sitting down and going back to re-listen to and edit these conversations, which in many cases took place years ago. As the writer/historian you spend days, if not weeks, with each individual, researching their stories, getting under their skin. You really have the feeling that you are doing a kind of cosmic CPR, taking their original words and breathing new life into them in a readable format that places readers at the kitchen table with that person who had something important to say. The reader shares the intimate moments with them as he/she gets absorbed in a real story being told. As an interviewer it happened many times to me directly with our World War II veterans, in living rooms, kitchens, and dining rooms all over 'Hometown, USA,' in the classroom, and at reunion 'hospitality rooms' and hotel breakfast tables across America. As a history teacher I also turned loose a generation of young people to bond with their grandparents' generation in the same way. We gave all of our first-person interviews to research institutions so that they might not be lost. The New York State Military Museum was the primary beneficiary, with over a hundred interviews deposited for future generations to learn from. As one of the most active contributors to the program, I also leaned on them for video recordings of some of the interviews I edited for this book. My friends Wayne Clarke and Mike Russert, the workhorses of the NYS Veterans Oral History Program, traversed the state for several years gathering these stories under the leadership of Michael Aikey; they know the feeling of bonding with these extraordinary men and women well. In bringing these stories back to life, I hope I did a service to them as well as to the general public.

But memories are short. A World War II memoirist once wrote, 'Ignorance and Apathy are the greatest dangers to Freedom.' I agree, but as a lifelong history teacher, I contend that it begins with people simply not being exposed to the history to begin with. For how could one not be drawn into these stories, the human drama, the interaction and the emotion that goes into putting an ideal first? After sitting at their table, how could you not give weight to what they have seen, and where they think we are going, as a people, as a nation? I saw this spark kindled time and again in my classroom, when we got to hear from real people who had a front row seat, who acted in the greatest drama in the history of the world.

Perhaps now I ramble. Now it is better to have them tell you themselves, about the world they grew up in, the challenges and obstacles placed on life's course, and how a generation of Americans not only rose to the challenge but also built the country and the freedoms that we enjoy today. They truly saved the world. Be inspired. Share their stories; give them voice. Lest we forget.

Matthew Rozell
August 2017

8th AF B-17 Flying Fortresses, 396th Bomb Group, 1943.
Credit: USAF. Library of Congress, public domain.

CHAPTER ONE

Air Power

The transition of the young men in this book from the Great Depression to aerial combat, from boyhood to manhood, paralleled the American development of air power and the emergence of new tactics and philosophies of coordinating and waging 'air war' on a scale that had never been done before in history. The concept of waging war from the sky on a large scale after World War I was not a novel idea, but it was met with resistance by the established branches of the U.S. services. During the 1930s, proponents like Billy Mitchell, Jimmy Doolittle, and Charles Lindbergh made gains at home, as did the Royal Air Force in Britain. The German Air Force, or Luftwaffe, under Air Marshal Herman Goering, increased in size and range with the growth of Nazi militarism; these terrible weapons were tested during the Spanish Civil War and then the invasion of Poland to great effect. During the lull in the fighting between the fall of Poland in September 1939 and the German attacks in the west the following spring, Germany and Great Britain geared up for the battles that loomed on the horizon. The British had established the Royal Air Force, or RAF, as an independent wing of their armed forces. Led by independent thinkers who believed that air power and strategic bombing would be the key to winning the next conflict following its emergence in the First World War, RAF Bomber Command began their first missions with daylight attacks on German warships in the North Sea. In the course of a December 1939 daylight raid, half the bombers sent out as a force of 24 were shot down by the faster German fighter planes. The RAF quickly switched to experimenting with flying at night; survival rates for the planes dropping propaganda leaflets and the occasional bombloads thereafter improved dramatically, although bombing results were far less satisfactory.

After the German invasion of the Low Countries in the spring of 1940, British Prime Minister Winston Churchill issued a cautionary warning to the Luftwaffe that any attack on civilian populations would lead to an 'appropriate' response.[90] On May 14, the Germans bombed Rotterdam in the Netherlands, killing 800 civilians. Although part of the rationale for the Allied use of air power was precisely to avoid the constant slaughter that ground on and on along the stalemated Western Front for four long years in the First World War, no one could predict how much air power, once unleashed, would be difficult to contain. The first strategic targets were aircraft factories, synthetic oil plants, and marshalling yards for rail transport.[91] Wildly inaccurate, bombing by night led to much collateral damage.

After the fall of France in the summer of 1940, Britain stood alone. Hitler's plan, in simple terms, was to have the German Luftwaffe wreak havoc and terror from the skies, and have the U-boat fleet blockade the island country. Once Operation Sea Lion's first phase was completed, an invasion by navy barges and infantry troops could occur.

It never got that far. While London was initially avoided by German bombers, on August 24, 1940, two German pilots veering off course jettisoned their bombloads before heading home, hitting areas of the city. This gave Churchill the opportunity to order up an

81-plane retaliatory nighttime mission on the German capital. Though it did little damage, it was a public relations success, and was also sure to bring German retaliation, which would in turn garner American public opinion towards helping Britain in some way.[92] Outnumbered four to one, the pilots of the RAF, the use of newly invented radar, and effective anti-aircraft flak kept the German bombing campaign at bay.[93] In the ensuing Blitz of London, where German bombers appeared over the city in a daily parade of terror bombing, the RAF claimed 56 bombers over the city on a single day in September.[37] Even the royal family's quarters were not spared, but Londoners did not fold. Hitler called off the invasion indefinitely two days later, though the onslaught would go on at night for the next two months. Forty thousand had been killed in the Battle of Britain, and the notion that 'civilian populations be spared' rendered almost quaint. The strategic air offensive against Germany would last for five years, 'the most continuous and grueling operation of war ever carried out.'[94] Hitler turned his attention to the East, convinced that the conquest of the Soviet Union, with its teeming agricultural lands and resources, was paramount to Germany's ultimate victory in the war.[95] He could return to finish Britain off later. And now, on December 6, 1941, with Hitler's legions literally at the gates of Moscow, came Marshal Zhukov's massive Red Army counterpunch. A world away, Japanese fliers were conducting last minute preparations for launching their strikes against a place most Britishers, or Americans for that matter, had never heard about—Pearl Harbor. Germany declared war on the United

---

[37] *the RAF claimed 56 bombers*-The number of RAF kills on September 15, 1940, is frequently cited as 185, but both sides were obviously prone to exaggeration; nevertheless, the punishment dealt the Luftwaffe that day stunned the German High Command. See Dodds, Laurence, 'The Battle of Britain, as it happened on September 15, 1940' *The Telegraph*, September 15, 2015.

States on December 12, and the sleeping, lumbering giant stirred. The Americans would finally be on their way.

*

In January 1943, Franklin Roosevelt and Winston Churchill met in Casablanca, French Morocco, to hammer out a rough blueprint for the Allied invasion of Europe. One of the first priorities was to destroy the German Luftwaffe, and as such, a 'Combined Bombing Offensive' was to be undertaken, with the Americans bombing German targets during the day and the British following at night in an unrelenting bid to soften German resistance. The goals were clear—in order to bring the war to an end, the effects had to be total and overwhelming. That meant bombing not only industrial targets but also densely populated urban centers where the working people lived; a skilled worker was more difficult to replace than a machine, and many machines escaped destruction in the bombing raids. Euphemistically termed 'de-housing,' British strategists in Bomber Command never denied that those efforts constituted an attempt to terrorize the population.[96] In Operation Gomorrah, the repeated attacks by the Royal Air Force and the Eighth Army Air Force targeting Hamburg during the last week of July 1943, more than 45,000 people were killed and 400,000 left homeless in conflagrations that resulted in manmade 'firestorms'—howling tornado-like updrafts which conducted superheated air skywards, drawing oxygen out of subterranean bomb shelters and incinerating human beings by literally sucking them into the flames.[97] In this one raid alone, more civilians died than in all of Germany's air attacks against English cities, though neither Bomber Command nor Churchill felt any moral qualms; many pointed out that the Germans had begun it with their raids over London during the summer nights of 1940. Given the brutal nature of initial German attacks and the necessity of defeating Hitler, this is hardly surprising.

'Typical bomb damage in the Eilbek district of Hamburg, 1944 or 1945.' Royal Air Force Bomber Command, 1942-1945. 'These were among the 16,000 multistoried apartment buildings destroyed by the firestorm which developed during the raid by Bomber Command on the night of 27/28 July 1943.' Source: RAF, Imperial War Museum, public domain.

More direct efforts to hit specific industrial targets fell primarily to the American air command. By the end of 1943 there were more than a million Yanks in Great Britain laying the groundwork for the destruction of Nazi Germany, with the American air bases dotting the eastern English countryside. From here, the Eighth Air Force mounted raids with her heavy bombers, the formidable B-17 Flying Fortress and the B-24 Liberator.

Boeing B-17G Flying Fortress "Shoo Shoo Baby" at the National Museum of the United States Air Force. Credit: USAF. Public domain.

The first mass-produced model, the B-17E, was heavily armed with nine .50 caliber machine guns mounted in Plexiglas 'blisters' and could carry a 4000 pound bomb load.[98] Subsequent models made various improvements, and from the beginning, the B-17 'Flying Fortress' was a workhorse of the American air campaign over the skies of Germany, with nearly 13,000 manufactured for the U.S. Army Air Corps. Improvements would gain the crews of the B-17 the capacity to carry three tons of bombs to the target, up to 2000 miles. The aircraft was also armed with thirteen .50 caliber guns.[99]

The B-24 Liberator was the most heavily produced bomber in history, with 19,000 manufactured; at one point, a mile-long assembly line at Ford Motor Company's Detroit plant cranked out a B-24 every 63 minutes.[100] It sported a twin tail and four engines, with a top speed of 303 miles per hour, ten .50 caliber machine guns, and the ability to carry 8,800 pounds of bombs. It was also used in a variety of capacities throughout the war. Complex tight bombing formations kept these bombers together to increase their accuracy and firepower against German fighters rising up to attack them, and several missions involved more than a thousand bombers carrying 10,000 or more airmen into enemy territory.

Consolidated B-24 Liberator from Maxwell Field, Alabama, 1940s. Credit: USAF, public domain.

By the time the European bombing campaign ended in mid-April 1945, nearly 10,000 of these bombers would be lost, along with another 8,500 fighters and almost 80,000 American airmen.[38] Manning these planes and others, it would be up to the boys of the United States Army Air Forces to get the job done. They would come from the depths of the Great Depression, and they would become men.

---

[38] *nearly 10,000 of these bombers would be lost*-British losses were even higher, having been in the war longer. Miller, Donald L., *The Story of World War II.* New York: Simon & Schuster, 2001. 481.

Hudson Falls, on the Hudson River, in 1946.
Source: Hudson Falls High School Yearbook, 1946.

CHAPTER TWO

Hard Times

Andy Doty was born in 1925. A 1943 graduate of Hudson Falls High School, he compiled the memories of his World War II experience at the fiftieth anniversary of the war, remembering growing up during the Depression and the inevitability of entering the service. Andy became a B-29 tail gunner, completing 21 combat missions in the skies over the Japanese home islands (detailed in my first book on the Pacific War) and even surviving an emergency crash landing in the vast Pacific—all before his 22nd birthday. He recounts the tempering experience of being raised in small-town America during the Great Depression, an experience that played out all over the United States:

'I present to the reader my memories of that era—the impact of 'hard times' and a world war on a quiet village, the experiences of one of the last truly innocent generations of Americans, and the transition of a young man who hated fist fights into a seasoned tail gunner. Throughout my wartime training, I was aware of what was being done to prepare me to kill or to be killed.'

Andy Doty

Our town stretched for nearly two miles along the high east bank of the Hudson River, fifty miles north of the state capital at Albany. Main Street runs parallel to the river; along its length during the 1930s were the public library, the village fire and police stations, five churches, three department stores, a bank, three drug stores, one hotel, the tiny Strand theater, the high school, the post office, and a mysterious 'cigar store' where you could buy cherry bomb fireworks and where men 'played the horses' in a dark, smoky poolroom in the back.

Extending east at right angles to the main thoroughfare were the usual small town streets—Maple, Elm, Willow, Chestnut. By pedaling a single-speed bike half a mile out Maple Street you could see far across the broad valley to the Green Mountains of Vermont thirty miles away. Looking down from Main Street, you saw the wide river tumbling along the long terrace of rocks that gave the village its name.

Hudson Falls, formally known as Sandy Hill, was a peaceful place where there were no serious crimes, scandals, or disasters to mar the slow pace of life. Snow sifted down onto the homes in the winter, lilacs bloomed beside long porches in the spring, katydids chirped on soft summer nights, and the scent of burning leaves filled the air in the fall. The best part of the village was the tree-shaded streets at the center of town, at right angles to Main Street. The poorer sections were at the north and south ends of town, and 'under the hill,' an area near the falls and the Union Bag and Paper Company mill.

My fraternal twin Chuck and I were born on October 12, 1925. Our family lived at the south end, seven of us, in a large, two-story rented house. A porch ran along the front and one side. Inside were a parlor and front room, the kitchen, dining room, and several bedrooms. The furnace stood in the center of the cellar like a huge oak, its big pipes spreading upward to the hot air registers in the rooms above. A dark coal bin stood nearby; there was a small garden in the back of the house.

My father was a lean, angular, quiet man, proud of the fact that he had become a night shift 'back tender' on one of the paper company's big machines. He made sure that wide swaths of paper rolled smoothly through without tears or wrinkles, and he wrestled huge rolls that were half his height in diameter. He earned eighteen dollars a week and was happy to have it.

Mom was a pretty, pink-faced, somewhat disorganized woman who engaged in long, dull monologues that we learned to let slip by. She was not a gifted cook; she would become so engrossed in reading the *Ladies' Home Journal* that countless smoking dishes had to be hurriedly retrieved from the oven. Mom would scrape away the burned portion, telling her children that carbon was good for them. She raised a large family while taking in sewing from the local shirt factory to augment Dad's income.

Three older children and a set of twins lived in the house—Bill, a taut, wiry replica of his father; Agnes, who continually drank coffee and smoked cigarettes; and Ann, as pretty as her mother. The twins—Chuck and I—came along years later, no doubt to the great dismay of their parents. Two older sisters, Betty and Ruth, had left home earlier after dropping out of school to go to work.

Chuck and I turned out to be quite different. I did all the 'right' things—finished my chores, studied hard in school, and earned Boy Scout merit badges. In high school, I played on four sports teams, had leading roles in dramatic productions, and was named president of our senior class. I was the fair-haired son, and knew it—something I still feel guilty about. Chuck marched to his own drummer. He was taller and stronger than me but he cared little about sports. He was self-taught in many ways; I was amazed by the store of information he acquired about nature, animals, electricity, and many other subjects. He quietly handled the lighting and other electrical details of our high school drama productions.

It was not at all unusual that my older brother and sisters had dropped out of school early. The vast majority of Depression-era children did not proceed beyond eighth grade, for they had to work or marry to ease the economic burden on their families. Agnes proudly showed us the razor-sharp, crescent-shaped blade attached to a ring that she wore on her finger while working on a production line at the paper company. Her job was to bundle paper bags as rapidly as she could. She tied up the batches, and then cut the cord with a sweep of her razor, losing little time in the process. Ann, Chuck, and I were the lucky ones in the family; we were able to continue into high school, thanks to our older brother and sisters.

Our family was poor, but lucky to have jobs. Forty million Americans had no work or regular income in the mid-1930s, and unemployment ran as high as 80% in some cities. Fortunately, the paper products of the mills were in demand. Dad worked six days a week, and Mom sewed when she was not cleaning, washing, or scorching dinner. We had no car, no telephone, no family vacations, and no bicycles for many years (the Montgomery Ward model cost a staggering $29). I have a clear memory of dinners consisting of a slice of bread in a soup plate, covered with milk and sprinkled with sugar. At one time we ate dandelion greens that Dad dug up from a field. We complained about the bitterness but were told that the greens, like charred cake, would make us strong. We needed only to add some butter and salt.

Doctors were too expensive for casual use. One winter night I was sliding down a hill at the same time a girl was pulling her Flexible Flyer sled up the slope. The sled was behind her, trailing at the end of a long rope. Without her realizing it, the sled strayed out into my path. I was flat on my stomach, hands extended out to the steering handles as I sped down the hill. There was no time or room to turn. I smashed into her sled, the bridge of my nose catching the steel frame at the front. I rolled off my sled as blood spilled onto the snow. My companions placed me on the sled and pulled me home, where my mother applied her favorite remedy, a 'cold poultice'—a bandage soaked in cold water. No doctor was called, nor did we ever visit one. I still bear the scar and skewed nose.

Chuck and I asked Dad for a dime apiece one Saturday to attend the afternoon matinee at the Strand Theater. 'I just don't have it, boys,' he said, and turned his pockets inside out to show us. Although disappointed, I felt an even deeper sadness for him. Waitresses were averaging $520 a year in income, construction workers $900, textile workers $435, and secretaries $1,000. Wages were routinely reduced at the same time work weeks were extended, and no one dared complain. In fact, Dad had been 'let go' from an earlier paper mill job in another town when he dared talk about the need for a workers union.

Christmas brought few gifts. Chuck and I could expect a new penknife each year from Betty, knitted mittens (with our initials on the cuffs) from maiden Aunt Gertrude, and an article of clothing or two and a homemade toy from Mom and Dad.

The announcer during the 'Fibber Magee and Molly' radio show would tantalize us with his descriptions of Mars candy bars. He spoke in slow, mellow tones of the 'rich, creamy caramel,' the crunchy almonds,' and the 'smooth chocolate' that made up the candy we could not afford. As we walked the sidewalks of Hudson Falls our eyes scanned the pavement ahead, searching for lost coins. A penny was great, a nickel was a real find, and a quarter would send the finder into ecstasy. I dreamed of finding that much money.

The Delaware and Hudson railroad tracks were not far from our house. My father called the D & H the 'Delay and Halt,' but it did succeed in carrying some of that era's one million homeless—men called 'hoboes'—into northern New York. They stole rides in railroad boxcars, cooked food in tin cans over wood fires, and slept in 'jungles' in the woods. They chalked secret codes onto village curbs and sidewalks to direct others to hospitable homes—or to warn them away from unfriendly ones. Some made their way to our house, where my mother gave them a slice of bread and butter when it was available. They were courteous, grateful, and subdued as they sat on our back steps. Chuck and I stole glances at their bearded faces, grimy clothes, and worn shoes.

'Where are you from?' we asked one.

'From all over. You name it, I bin there.'

'Where you going?'

'Wherever I can catch onta something.'

When we were able to go to the theater, we watched the Fox Movietone News coverage of bloody strikes in automobile and steel factories. There were other scenes of men in black overcoats standing stoically in block-long bread lines, and of former executives selling apples, pencils, and shoestrings from tiny sidewalk stands. There were dirty, seamed 'Okies' fleeing the dust storms that had overwhelmed their farms. We saw an army of World War I veterans march on Washington to demand early payment of bonuses due them in 1945.[39] Those were 'hard times' indeed.

---

[39] *We saw an army of World War I veterans march on Washington*- the so-called 'Bonus Army' of 17,000 veterans who arrived in DC at the height of the Depression to demand early payment of WWI certificates. On July 28, 1932, President Hoover ordered his Army Chief of Staff General Douglas MacArthur to clear the gathering; supporting roles in clearing the marchers were played by then Majors George S. Patton and Dwight D. Eisenhower. At least two people were killed and over a thousand injured; the 'Bonus Army' was dispersed with their demands rejected, and it became a public relations nightmare for Hoover, one more notch that would lead to his re-election bid disaster the following November.

A new president came into office, his cigarette holder cocked at a jaunty angle, and announced a 'New Deal' of relief, recovery, and reform to lift the nation out of the Depression. Among Franklin Roosevelt's programs was the WPA (Works Progress Administration). It created jobs for the unemployed all over America. An empty corner lot near our house that lacked sidewalks and curbs was targeted for improvement. One day a truck and a dozen men arrived, hammered a WPA sign into the ground, and began shoveling. They worked leisurely that summer, stretching out the job as long as possible. 'Do you know why the WPA needs a crew of eight and a portable outhouse to hoe a field that two men can handle?' my father would ask with a slight smile. 'Because there are always two coming, two going, two peeing, and two hoeing.'

Our village was the perfect place for boyhood. The river, vacant lots, and nearby ponds and wooded areas were our playgrounds. Riding two on a bike and carrying a scruffy football, we challenged other gangs to Saturday morning battles. We tangled in the dust and mud without benefit of Pop Warner League helmets, padding, or cleated shoes. There were no obnoxious 'high-fives' or show-off victory dances after a touchdown. Neither a coach nor a parent was in sight. Our school classes were small, and our summer vacations were delicious. Sprung free in June like colts turned out to pasture, our gang of boys hiked across a bridge to roam the wooded Fenimore banks, named after James Fenimore Cooper, whose *Last of the Mohicans* was set in our area. We tried to run silently along paths through the trees and walk with our toes pointed straight ahead, as we were told the Indians once did. We swam naked in the river at a remote shale beach. An old row boat washed up onto the shore after a storm; we lugged it home, where we replaced broken bottom boards, pounded rope into the cracks, and sealed it all with chunks of tar melted in a tin can over a small fire. We paddled about happily on sunny afternoons in our resurrected craft; we fished for slippery, long-whiskered bullheads. My father told us his favorite recipe for preparing river carp; 'You put the carp on a board, bake it in the oven for an hour, pull it out, throw the carp away, and eat the board.'

The seasons dictated our activities—football in the fall, ice hockey and basketball in the winter, baseball and track in the spring. We entertained ourselves in many ways—by building, defending, and storming snow forts in the winter, by racing match sticks down a street gutter in the spring runoff, or by nudging a small wheel along the street with a T-shaped device we had hammered together. A kite could be built from strips of wood, string, newspaper, some paste, and a tail of torn rags. It was serviceable and was no great loss when it tangled inevitably in a tree or telephone lines.

We believed our gang to be unique. 'McGoosey' Walsh was a freckled imp who could drop two-handed set shots into a hoop almost at will. Bob Burns was a skinny Irishman. He was a choir boy in the Catholic Church, but was far from angelic. Bob could swear with the best of us, but he could go to confession on Saturday to be absolved of his guilt. As a Methodist, I envied the protection he gained by dipping his fingers into the water to cross himself before we went swimming or before he took a foul shot in basketball. Later in life I wondered if a controlled experiment would show that Catholics who crossed themselves drowned less often or made more foul shots than Methodists who did not.

Bill DeCamillo could not look more Italian than he did. So we called him 'Irish Bill.' Later on, in high school, he affected a 'zoot suit.' He wore a bright yellow, absurdly long jacket. His lavender pegged pants, supported by bright suspenders, reached up to his rib cage. A key chain drooped nearly to the ankles. His wide-brimmed fedora hat would have done justice to a Chicago gangster. His were the first male fingernails I ever saw that were an inch long.

'Bud' Reed was devilishly inventive. One dark night, as we were liberating apples from someone's backyard trees, the owner heard us, turned on a light, and looked out the door. As we ran away, Bud called back: 'Get down out of that tree, Mark LaRue, son of Reverend LaRue.' Mark was a popular boy who of course was not with us. The next day, his kindly father received a phone call from the angry owner.

Although we grew up in a small village and came from humble stock, we were surprisingly literate. We prided ourselves on the nicknames we devised for village characters—'Shufflefoot' Gleason, 'Choo Choo' Trayne, 'Carstairs' Lethbridge (after his favorite whiskey), and 'Commodore' Logan. The Commodore was tall, handsome, and distinguished in his castoff clothing. He had no job, and, as far as we could tell, no home. He was allowed to sleep at night in a barbershop chair or in the back of Harry Baker's Square Deal Drugstore.

Our days were enlivened by the arrival on our street of the ice man, the rag man, and the vegetable man. Their coming was announced by loud calls, bells, or whistles. The ice man's truck was piled high with large, clear blocks covered by bits of sawdust and wet canvas. He snagged the blocks down with his tongs, chipped them to the right size, hoisted them onto a leather patch on his shoulder, and bore them to the ice boxes in our homes. While he was away, we sucked on the ice shards on hot summer days.

The rag man was a shrewd old fellow who offered a few coins for all the cloth and scrap metal we could collect. 'Rags, rags, rags,' he called, and we dragged to his truck a burlap bag half filled with rusted nuts and bolts we had dug up from the Sandy Hill Iron and Brass Company yard. He was engaged in recycling long before the word was invented.

A ringing bell told us when the vegetable man was in our neighborhood. His wares were displayed on slanted racks in the back of his truck, shaded by an awning. A scooped scale dangled from a chain. Our mothers came out, wiping their hands on their aprons, to select from the fruits and vegetables when they could afford them.

As soon as we could, we found jobs. Three of us weeded Mr. Bushbaum's yard and garden at fifteen cents each for the full Saturday morning. Ten cents got us into the afternoon movie, leaving five cents for candy. 'Vaht robbers!' he roared one day when we gathered the courage to ask him for twenty cents a morning. We did not pursue it further; his was a buyer's market.

At age fifteen, Bob Burns, McGoosey, Chuck, and I obtained our working papers and began caddying at the Glens Falls Country Club. After two years we worked our way up to the highest 'Double A' status. That qualified us to advise golfers on which clubs to use, and to carry a heavy golf bag on each shoulder for thirty-six to forty-five holes on a good day. If we were polite, quickly handed out the proper clubs, and complimented our clients for their solid shots, we could expect a modest tip. As we trudged up and down the hills on those summer days the voices of the Andrews Sisters carried across a lake from a pavilion loudspeaker. They sang 'I'll Be With You in Apple Blossom Time' and 'Bei Mir Bist Du Schon,' and my heart sang with them. We were young, healthy, outdoors, and earning money.

Between rounds, we sometimes walked through the pine woods to the tenth hole, where we hid in the low-hanging branches, over a hill from the tee. As the golfers' drives came bounding over we dashed out, picked up the balls, and threw them far down the fairway. Back in the trees, we laughed as the resplendent bankers, doctors, dentists, and lawyers marveled at how far they had driven their balls. What wonderful clubhouse stories must have followed!

My friends and I were caught up in building model airplanes and in identifying aircraft of all kinds. We knew the name of virtually every plane in the world, ranging from tiny American Gee Bee racers to giant Italian Caproni bombers. Balsawood kits could be purchased for fifteen to twenty-five cents. The models were built from scratch—ribs cut out with a razor blade; stringers glued into notches with airplane cement to form the fuselage; wings and tails assembled, covered with tissue paper, and attached. A World War I Spad, a Sopwith Camel, and a tri-winged Fokker took shape on my table, as did a Piper Cub, a Seversky P-35, and a Gloster Gauntlet biplane. The Gauntlet cost a dollar, my most expensive purchase. Tears came to my eyes the night an entire wing burst into flame when I held it too close to the stove to make the doped skin tight enough to impress my friends. It took hours to reconstruct from surplus balsa.

Our schoolteachers were dedicated women, mostly unmarried, who demanded that we diagram the structure of sentences properly, recite the multiplication tables without a slip, and remember the outcome of the Peloponnesian Wars. Their right to grab an unruly boy by the ear and hustle him out the door and into the principal's office was unquestioned.

I was filled with the ambivalence of youth—quite confident at times, but insecure and uncertain at others; sometimes terribly shy, but pleased by attention; gregarious, yet often preferring to be alone; able to lead, but quite willing to follow.

I dreaded the fist fights that broke out after school or during our sandlot games. Honor required a boy to fight when challenged, so I often found myself taking a longer route home from school to avoid one thug in particular whose major reason for attending class seemed to be to pick fights afterward. There was a chip on his shoulder at all times. It actually came to that. He would place a bit of wood there and dare another boy to knock it off. Of course the other had to; great loss of face would result if he did not. Then the scuffle would begin, starting with wildly swung fists and invariably ending up with the two grappling in the dirt or snow—one, if not both, hoping all the while that they would be broken apart by their friends or a teacher or a mother who happened on the scene.

Although our gang engaged in pranks, stole apples from trees, and later found ways to sneak into the Strand Theater without paying, we were among the last truly innocent generations in America. We did not drink or smoke, or gamble. Drugs were unheard of, except for the rumor that certain big band drummers used something called marijuana. We did not swear in front of girls or insult them in any way. When an opponent took his foul shots in a basketball game, fans and players alike remained silent and unmoving so as not to disturb him. We fought fair. Two boys never picked on one, nor one boy on a smaller opponent. Kicking was not tolerated. Anyone caught carrying a knife was subject to permanent banishment. Firearms were totally out of the question.

*

Over the years our attention shifted from bicycles and ice skates to how we combed our hair, to our clothing, to shaving—and to girls. We watched the movie actors shave—men lathering, screwing up their faces, tugging at a cheek with one hand as the other drew a broad razor through the thick, white cream. We timidly roller-skated with girls to organ music at Brennan's Roller Rink on the Lake George highway, hands sweating and minds groping for a few words of conversation. There were later games of 'Spin the Bottle' and 'Post Office,' with chaste kisses at stake. We knew next to nothing about sex, even though some of our high school classmates told us they were experts on the subject. Our parents avoided the topic and our schools taught us little. The movies were discreet, songs were discreet, and magazines were discreet. The most salacious material available to us was the silk stocking ads in the Montgomery Ward catalog. Hand-holding and kissing were allowed after several dates with a girl, but a boy did not try to go 'too far' if he really cared for her. Parental wrath, peer disapproval among the girls, and the fear of pregnancy hung over our era.

Sports brought many rewards. I was not big, but could run fast and far. During my high school years I ran the mile in track, played guard on the basketball team and second base on the baseball team. The eleven starters on our football squad played the full game, on offense and defense. We received only rudimentary football training, had a slender playbook, and did not confuse our opponents with a sophisticated offense. The team photo shows uniforms that did not match perfectly and helmets without face masks. Nevertheless, we were a good, solid team, and went undefeated in my senior year. We beat the fearsome Golden Horde of Granville in a War Bond benefit playoff game before a monster crowd of 2,100 at Derby Field—with most of the fans standing along the sidelines. 'Tex' Bailey, the owner of a village saloon, bet an astronomical fifty dollars on the game, an unheard of amount in those days. He happily pummeled us all the way back to our tiny, cement block locker room.

The summer before that final season, Bob Burns and I went to work at the Imperial Paint and Paper Company in Glens Falls. We were assigned to the yard gang, where we unloaded by hand railroad box cars filled with knee-high stacks of cement bags that weighed one hundred pounds apiece. We stood on a high platform in the oppressive heat and fumes, shoveling heavy, tinsel-like shreds of lead into wide vats of acid as the metal dropped relentlessly from a conveyor belt onto a steel plate. We pushed carts of crushed ice up to the paint mixers—men whose hats, overalls, shoes, faces, and hands were red, green, blue, or yellow. They must have sweated primary colors. It was at the Imperial factory that the name of Eleanor Baker, daughter of our town pharmacist, first came to my attention. A fellow worker from Glens Falls said he had noticed her and thought she was 'cute.' Had I ever thought of dating her? I had not. Her family was high on the Hudson Falls social ladder, while ours was out of sight on the rungs below. But the seed was planted. Eleanor sat in front of me in history class that fall and I finally worked up the courage to ask her to go on a hayride. She accepted and other dates followed. She was pretty, poised, intelligent, and totally unpretentious. Freshly washed, light brown hair fell to her shoulders. She wore soft, baggy sweaters, a pearl necklace, pleated plaid skirts, bobby socks, and saddle shoes. I was hooked. The day after our first date, I dramatically announced to my teammates that I had found the girl I would marry someday.

Life was good that fall of 1943, except for one thing—the guns of war had been rumbling over the horizon during most of my boyhood, and the sound was coming closer.

CHAPTER THREE

'Ye Shall Hear of Wars'

The war had come to our small town. Like all of those who would soon find themselves in the thick of it, Andy Doty was forming his youthful impressions of a world careening out of control, and finding his place in the swirling storm.

Andy Doty

Hardly a week passed during the 1930s when our school *Weekly Reader*; the local newspaper, the *Glens Falls Post-Star*; or *LIFE Magazine* failed to carry news of some far-off conflict. Aggressors were on the march and little stood in their way.

Japan invaded Manchuria and China, Italy subdued Ethiopia, and the Spanish Civil War ran its cruel course. We were shocked by a *LIFE* photograph of a naked Chinese baby crying in bombed ruins, by the Japanese rape of Nanking, and by photos of Nipponese soldiers bayoneting and beheading bound Chinese prisoners. An Italian pilot—the son of Dictator Benito Mussolini—casually observed that when his bombs exploded among Ethiopian natives, a 'beautiful' pattern resulted that reminded him of the petals of a flower slowly unfolding.

Hitler came to power in Germany and began building one of the most formidable military machines in history. He annexed Austria in 1938 then demanded that Czechoslovakia's Sudetenland be turned over to Germany—even a thirteen-year-old boy could see war coming to Europe. The major nations made no secret of the fact they had tested their weapons in Spain's Civil War, and Hitler's appetite seemed insatiable.

'Ye shall hear of wars, and rumors of war,' my father told us fatalistically, quoting from the Bible. Although Matthew went on to say, 'see that ye not be troubled—for all these things must come to pass, but the end is not yet,' I understood Dad to mean that war was an inevitable fact of life. I could see no reason to disagree.

Later in 1938, Prime Minister Neville Chamberlain of England returned from a meeting with Hitler in Munich, smiling as he waved a signed agreement he declared had won 'peace in our time.' Chamberlain had given Hitler the land he wanted, over the protests of the Czechs. Half a year later, the German dictator scrapped the agreement and occupied the rest of the country.

World War II broke out on September 1, 1939, after Germany invaded Poland. England and France, finally realizing that appeasement had failed, declared war. Poland fell in a matter of days, the victim of swift panzer tank divisions and Stuka dive bombers.

A long lull—the so-called 'Phony War'—followed, during which little fighting occurred. America debated whether or not to take sides. My youthful sympathies clearly lay with England and France, but the memory of World War I was still fresh in the minds of older, wiser men and women. 'What did we get from the first world war but death, debt, and George M. Cohan?' the isolationists asked; their cries of 'Never Again' and 'America First' held strong appeal. Congress passed yet another Neutrality Act as public opinion polls in December of 1939 showed more than two-thirds of the people opposed involvement in Europe's problems.

An amazing reversal took place during the next six months. German troops occupied Denmark and Norway in April of 1940, paused, and then swept across the Netherlands, Belgium, Luxembourg, and northern France in a devastating 'blitzkrieg' attack. After only ten days of battle, Hitler stood on the shores of the English Channel. Newsreels showed long lines of British troops at Dunkirk, farther to the west, waiting to be evacuated by a flotilla of every English naval or pleasure craft that could cross over to France. England was standing alone, and a surge of pro-British feelings resulted. A survey that May revealed a dramatic shift in public opinion—more than two-thirds of Americans favored active aid to England.

Shortly afterward, Congress passed the Selective Service Act of 1940, and the nation began arming itself. In the next two years, the Army grew from a force of 190,000 men to 1.5 million. Isolationism had been a persuasive force, but it gave way to America's instinctive support of freedom and democracy. The feeling slowly grew that England had to be saved and Hitler defeated.

Photos began to appear of raw recruits at the Plattsburgh Army Base practicing with wooden cannon, or with trucks bearing signs that read 'Tank.' Real equipment was not yet available in any great number. In Glens Falls, a hotel was taken over to house fledgling aviation cadets. We saw the uniformed young men marching to their preflight classes on the way to becoming pilots, navigators, and bombardiers.

The 'Battle of Britain' swirled over England that summer. To pave the way for an invasion of the island, Hitler sent out his bombers to hit military targets and destroy the Royal Air Force. After suffering heavy losses—and not knowing that his Luftwaffe had worn the RAF down to its last reserve squadrons—he changed tactics and ordered the blanket nighttime bombing of London and other cities. That shift saved the RAF. London could absorb the terrible punishment, but the RAF could not have fought much longer.

'This... is London!' was Edward R. Murrow's dramatic introduction of his nightly radio broadcasts. We listened as Londoners huddled in deep underground shelters, bombs erupted, and smoke shrouded St. Paul's Cathedral. But Hitler had missed his chance to invade England after Dunkirk, and failed to subdue England through bombing. He called off the invasion, and turned his armies and air force south and east in 1941 to attack North Africa, Yugoslavia, Greece, Crete, and the Soviet Union. Britain drew a sigh of relief.

*

A Sunday Afternoon

One Sunday afternoon in December of 1941, Chuck and I came into the house to find our parents close to the radio.

'The losses have been heavy,' the announcer was saying.

'What's happening?' we asked.

'The Japs have bombed Pearl Harbor,' my father said quietly. 'They sneaked in this morning. We're going to have to fight them.'

Living in the east and watching Europe, we had not been following events in the Pacific as closely. The United States opposed Japan's expansion into Southeast Asia and had embargoed steel and scrap metal shipments to them. Japan struck back while it was strong and America weak. What made the attack even more despicable in our minds was the fact that Japanese emissaries were in Washington to negotiate peace at the same time their aircraft carriers were slipping across the Pacific toward Hawaii.

The grim reports continued throughout that day and the next. Eight battleships and three cruisers had been sunk or damaged, 188 airplanes were destroyed, and over 2,400 men had been killed. The next day, newspapers showed sunken battleships at their berths, damaged buildings, and the smoldering ruins of airplanes on the ground. It had been a devastating blow. December 7, 1941, branded by President Roosevelt as 'the day that will live in infamy,' propelled the United States into war against both Japan and its allies, Germany and Italy.

I did not feel great concern at the time. Hawaii was far away and we had faith in our nation's ability to recover. A commonly held view was that the Japanese were poor fighters, possessed inferior equipment, and could be 'licked' in a matter of months. We took satisfaction in a popular story that the Japanese once faithfully copied the stolen design of an English battleship, not realizing that the plans had deliberately been altered to make the ship top-heavy. When the ship was launched it promptly turned turtle, and floated bottom-up in the water—or so the story went.

The years pass by slowly at age sixteen, so it seemed possible that the war could be fought and won before Chuck and I reached draft age in October of 1943. If not, we would serve without question. We had to do our duty—the nation must be defended, and Pearl Harbor had to be avenged.

We drifted slowly toward the vortex as the months passed. Red, white, and blue service flags began to appear in the front windows of village homes, a star for each son in uniform. In time the village was drained of virtually all of its able-bodied men between the ages of 18 and 36. Everyone was expected to take up arms, and those who did not—the physically unfit ' 4-Fs' and those in essential occupations—were looked down upon. 'Draft dodger' and 'slacker' were bitter epithets. 'Why aren't you in uniform?' older adults demanded of young men who appeared to be of service age. The question could have stemmed from patriotism or jealousy, or both. 'They're either too young or too old,' actress Bette Davis sang in a movie, referring to those who remained behind: 'They're either too gray or too grassy green—What's good is in the Army, what's left can never harm me.'

McGoosey Walsh quit school to join the Navy, where he became a radio operator on a submarine in the Pacific. Bob Burns' brother Ed entered an officers training program at Rensselaer Polytechnic Institute and became a naval gunnery officer. My older cousin, a plumber by trade, was assigned to duty as a mechanic in a P-47 fighter squadron. Eleanor Baker's brother entered an Army Officer Candidate School. Our school's music director was stationed in Washington, where he led a Marine Corps band and returned home often on leave, resplendent in full dress uniform.

In time, gold stars that symbolized lost sons, husbands, and fathers began to replace service flags in the windows. Chuck Eagle, the center on our football team, worked at night behind the soda fountain at Moriarty's Drug Store. The store also housed a Western Union office. When telegrams from the War Department arrived, it was Chuck's duty to deliver them to village homes after work. Mothers and wives fearfully opened their doors to him those nights. 'The Secretary of War desires me to express his deep regret,' the telegrams began, 'that your son or husband has been killed or wounded, or is missing in action.' The telegrams seemed to arrive far too often. Chuck hated the task. A total of 126 young men from our sparsely populated county were killed in the war, two dozen of them from our little town. Untold numbers were wounded or captured.

The wounded began drifting back. Pat DuPell, the big, strong, red-haired brother of one of our gang members, came home from the Navy badly scarred, nearly blind, and breathing through an opening in his throat. A depot of depth charges had exploded next to his barracks at an eastern naval base. We were shocked by his appearance. Word came back that Chuck LaFountain, a bright young classmate who had entered the Army Air Force before his graduation, had been killed in the crash of an experimental aircraft called a flying wing.

At the Sandy Hill Iron and Brass Works, machinists began making base plates for machine guns, then turned out heavy winches for landing ships. The firm proudly floated a Navy 'E' for Excellence pennant from its flagpole. Married and too old to be drafted, my brother Bill left the paper mill to spray paint the heavy tanks coming off a new assembly line at the American Locomotive Works in Schenectady.

Meat, coffee, butter, cheese, sugar, flour, and other foods became scarce. Our parents took their ration books of stamps to the stores, 'spending' points for a pound of butter or a slice of ham. Gas was rationed, as well. An 'A' card allowed the owner three gallons a week. A 'B' card enabled a driver to obtain a few more gallons if truly needed. The 'X' card was granted those in essential enterprises; Bill obtained one for his daily trips with other workers to the tank factory. At night, Chuck Eagle would take his father's car out to drain any remaining drops from gas pump hoses at closed stations. Hudson Falls High School canceled all track meets to conserve gas, but the baseball season went on.

A collection center for items vital to the war effort was set up near the fire station. Villagers brought in scrap metal, vegetable fats, empty toothpaste tubes, rubber tires, metal foil, silk stockings, flattened tin cans, and waste paper. *'Lucky Strike Green Has Gone to War!* a cigarette company proudly proclaimed. I assumed that it was doing its part by abandoning the use of scarce tinfoil in its packages. Victory gardens sprouted; war bond drives were mounted; women wrapped bandages; older men volunteered to be air raid wardens. Wearing armbands and helmets and holding a page of silhouettes of German bombers, the wardens stood ready in case the Luftwaffe targeted Hudson Falls.

*

The saddest hours of the war occurred during the spring of 1942. The Axis powers—Germany, Italy, and Japan—were invincible. Their armies were spread across Europe, were approaching Egypt and Moscow, and ranged in the Pacific from Burma south to New Guinea, east to the Gilbert Islands, and north to the Aleutians. Axis navies were in command of the high seas. German submarines torpedoed American tankers within sight of the East Coast, and America's old P-40 and P-39 fighter planes fell quickly before Japan's excellent new Zero—so much for the belief that the Japanese could only copy designs developed by others. Nevertheless, it was inconceivable to me that 'our side' could lose. I was certain that someday, somehow, the Axis armies and navies would be halted and thrown back.

The tide slowly began to turn soon afterward. Japan's mighty fleet of aircraft carriers—the same ships that had launched the planes to attack Pearl Harbor the previous December—was defeated in June at the Battle of Midway. British troops routed Rommel's Afrika Korps in the Libyan Desert and sent it reeling back toward Tunisia. The Soviets halted the Germans at Stalingrad after a ferocious struggle. American troops landed in Algeria. The long, hard, costly march to Berlin, Rome, and Tokyo had begun. We traced the movement of the Allied forces on newspaper maps, unaware that the salients and advancing lines on those pieces of paper were made at a cost of thousands of dead or wounded young men. Once again, Chuck and I thought the war might be over by the time we reached our eighteenth birthdays on October 12, 1943. It wasn't.

When that date arrived, *The New York Times* reported that the American Fifth Army, after making its way across North Africa, through Sicily, and into Italy, was inching toward Rome against fierce German resistance, hampered by rain, mud, and flood waters. Our Eighth Air Force in England was flying raids deep into Germany that were so costly in men and machines they had to be suspended, although that was not announced at the time. One mission, mounted against the ball bearing factory at Schweinfurt, Germany two days after my birthday, resulted in a loss of 60 aircraft out of the 291 that participated.

I registered for the draft after my birthday, ready to enter the service when I completed high school in January. There was no way of knowing at the time, but that delay of three months—from my birthday to my January graduation—later was to play quite an important part in my life.

The three months passed swiftly. I had been taking commercial courses in high school rather than college entrance subjects because I had no hope of attending a university. In the fall of 1943, I enrolled in classes in math and physics in the hope they would better prepare me for one of the armed forces. On weekend evenings, Eleanor Baker taught me dance steps at parties in homes with the rugs rolled up. I clumsily fox trotted to *'People Will Say We're in Love'* and haltingly jitterbugged to Glenn Miller's *'String of Pearls'* and Tommy Dorsey's *'Boogie Woogie.'* By November, we had agreed to go steady.

Andy Doty, first row, right, and the crew of the "City of College Park," 1944. Source: Andy Doty.

CHAPTER FOUR

The Tail Gunner

(Notes to the heavy bomber pilots and commanders)

Duties of the Gunners

All gunners should be familiar with the coverage area of all gun positions, and be prepared to bring the proper gun to bear as the conditions may warrant.

They should be experts in aircraft identification. Where the Sperry turret is used, failure to set the target dimension dial properly on the K-type sight will result in miscalculation of range.

They must be thoroughly familiar with the Browning aircraft machine gun. They should know how to maintain the guns, how to clear jams and stoppages, and how to harmonize the sights with the guns. While participating in training flights, the gunners should be operating their turrets constantly, tracking with the flexible guns even when actual firing is not practical. Other airplanes flying in the vicinity offer excellent tracking targets, as do automobiles, houses, and other ground objects during low altitude flights.

The importance of teamwork cannot be overemphasized. One poorly trained gunner, or one man not on the alert, can be the weak link as a result of which the entire crew may be lost. —Duties and Responsibilities of the Airplane Commander and Crewmen, 1943[101]

***

Around the holiday time in 1943, some friends and I were in Glens Falls when the bus from Albany arrived. Two young men in leather Army Air Force jackets got out, picked up their green B-4 bags, and stood waiting for the trip to Hudson Falls. We knew them; they had graduated from high school the previous June, and were home on leave after finishing gunnery school training. They were dashing in uniforms bearing colorful shoulder patches, silver gunner's wings, and fresh corporal's stripes.

The dramatic return of those men, as well as my early interest in airplanes, made me quite receptive when 'Muff' Nassivera, our football quarterback, suggested that we enlist in the Air Force rather than wait to be drafted into the Army. We would become pilots, of course; every boy worth his salt wanted to be one. I quickly agreed. The infantry held little appeal.

I told my father that I intended to join the Air Force. 'Do what you think best,' he said. There were few other choices. I don't remember telling Chuck my plans. I assumed that he would go into the Army.

Booklets that contained tips on ways to pass military tests were available in the 1940s. I bought one and studied it carefully. There were drawings of blocks stacked in uneven rows in a corner, and of interlocking gears. One had to calculate how many blocks were in the pile and the direction in which the last gear would be turned. It was rather basic stuff, but I did not want to take a chance at being rejected.

I rode the bus to Albany for the first time. The Air Force recruiting station was located in a downtown office building. After taking the written exam, I was interviewed by a young lieutenant.

'What's the equation for the area of a circle?' he asked.

'Pi R squared.'

'Have you ever driven a motorcycle?'

I knew what he was looking for: an adventurous future fighter pilot. 'No, but I loved open field running in football.' That should impress him, I thought.

'What's an isosceles triangle?' I was stumped. I knew it well, but for some reason it just wouldn't come. He nodded and said nothing. On the bus on the way home, I remembered that it was a triangle with two equal sides, of course. I went home feeling disappointed.

It made little difference. I was accepted, and told to wait for further orders after my physical examination and high school graduation. The examination took place in the National Guard Armory in Albany, a grim, old stone fortress of a building. Several of us boarded a bus to go down for the tests. The group included a man who was both our high school track coach and commercial studies teacher. He was married and nearly beyond draft age. We entered the armory, stripped down to our undershorts, and spent the day being probed, weighed, and measured.

At the end of the day I walked down a long stairway. A Marine officer was at the bottom, looking over the men as they descended. He caught my eye.

'Are you sure you don't want to be a Marine?'

'I'm sure,' I answered. I was patriotic, but not to that degree. I have since wondered what would have happened had I accepted that invitation, for the bloody amphibious landings at Saipan, Iwo Jima, and Okinawa still lay ahead.

When we gathered for the trip home, the teacher was beaming.

'How did it go, coach?'

'I didn't pass,' he said. 'Flat feet.' Despite the ignominy of 4-F status, he was happy to have it.

Basketball season followed, as did long walks with 'Bake' (for Baker) on crystal clear winter nights. We held mittened hands and I stole frosty kisses as we crunched over the snow. A week after my high school graduation my first draft notice arrived. It was a mimeographed form letter from a major in the headquarters of the Second Service Command on Governors Island, with only my name and the date filled in. It sent a chill through me.

'Private Andrew M. Doty

1. This is to advise you that you are being called upon to active duty on or about 31 January 1944.

2. Orders will be sent to you within the next few days.'

Soon after that, my induction notice arrived. 'Greetings,' it began. 'You have been chosen by a board made up of your friends and neighbors to serve in the armed forces of the United States of America for the duration of the war. You will report to the Induction Center at Ft. Dix, NJ. on January 31, 1944.' It was signed by the elderly chairman of our local draft board on behalf of his elderly fellow board members.

Bake and I walked to her father's drug store that night and took our places in a rear booth. I showed her the two letters.

'They don't waste any words, do they?' she said.

'Not at all. They didn't even say 'please' report.'

'I'm glad that you have a few weeks left.'

Other than that, she said little. We were still in the formal stage of our relationship, and had not spoken of love. We did not ever admit how greatly we would miss each other. My time simply had come.

'I have a feeling this will take about two years,' I said as we walked slowly back down Mechanic Street.

'Oh,' she said. 'That long?'

The Waite Hose Company fire hall on Main Street was the scene of frequent farewell parties in those times. One was held for Chuck and me the week before we were to enter the military. We received some gifts and said goodbye to our friends. Chuck left the week before I did, bound for Camp Upton on Long Island. As his train pulled out of the D & H station he pretended to wipe tears from his eye, hiding his sorrow with humor.

The night before I was to leave I visited Bake at her house. We had known each other only a short time, but I cared for her and was sorry to say goodbye.

My mother and father watched silently as I packed my new toilet kit and stationery into a bag, along with a small Bible that my sister Ruth had sent me. What were my parents thinking? How it must have torn them to see their twin sons leave within a week of each other, but they did not say a word. It was our turn, and there could be no complaint. Thirty years later I fought off tears as my oldest daughter left home safely to attend college only one state away. How did our parents keep from breaking down as Chuck and I went off to war? Perhaps they did after we were gone.

The last day of January was bitterly cold. Mom, Dad, and I silently ate breakfast before Ken Howe arrived in the early morning darkness to drive me to Glens Falls to catch the bus to Albany. I said goodbye to them as quickly as I could. As Ken and I sat in his car waiting for the bus, a boy rode up on his bicycle. He was Gerry Ellsworth, a classmate who lived two miles outside of the city. He had ridden in to see me off, despite the frigid weather. I was touched by his thoughtfulness.

The New York Central Railroad station in Albany was an exciting place in those days. It had marble floors, hardwood benches, and towering ceilings. There was a USO area on a balcony where uniformed women volunteers passed out coffee to the servicemen. The station teemed with soldiers, sailors, and marines and echoed with their clamor and train announcements. It was the first time I had been there. I felt that I was entering the serious world of adults.

Alone on the train to New York, I saw my reflection in the window and wondered what would become of that young man. I wore the gray and white Hart Schaffner Marx suit I had proudly bought with my summer earnings, a tan shirt, and a wine tie. I was sad and apprehensive and excited. How long would I be gone? What lay ahead?

'Take Care of Yourself'

What lay ahead, indeed? Sixteen million men donned uniforms in World War II; the experience of leaving home for the first time was exhilarating and terrifying all at once, especially knowing the possibility of being in harm's way was very real. Adulthood was coming on, like a quickening freight train careening towards the unknown.

The train sped down the banks of the Hudson River, past the old Dutch towns and cities, and into New York. We dove underground with a roar and emerged in cavernous Grand Central Station. The huge, vaulted area was crowded with hundreds of servicemen and women of all kinds and ranks. The Albany station that had impressed me so much would be swallowed up in this one. At Ft. Dix, the huge, multi-floor concrete barracks contained several loud, vulgar men, seemingly all from Brooklyn or New Jersey. I consoled myself with the fact that they were Army recruits, not Army Air

Force. Then I remembered that my brother Chuck had gone into the infantry.

After arriving at Ft. Dix I took off my new suit, packed it in a box, and mailed it home. I traded it for more clothing than I had owned in my entire lifetime—duffel bags filled with khaki shirts, trousers, socks, and underwear; a heavy overcoat, gloves, a knit cap, and GI shoes. We shuffled past warehouse bins filled with metal mess kits, ponchos, and light helmet liners, tossing the items into our bags as we moved along. I also gained a new identity: serial number 42120238, embossed on metal 'dog tags' to hang around my neck.

A piercing bugle call on the barracks PA system shocked us awake early every morning that week. Knit caps pulled down over our ears, overcoats hanging to our ankles, we stumbled onto the dark, frigid company street. We fell into formation, slapping our arms, stamping our feet, our breath billowing out in front of us. Then came the first of many manglings of a name that goes far back into English history. But the hard-bitten master sergeant was not aware of that. 'Dotty?' the sergeant called. 'Duty?' 'Here!' I answered, before any more damage could be done. It was hard to understand how he—and his successors at later roll calls—could butcher a name so badly.

The indignities of military life have been well chronicled—hair shorn almost to the scalp, long rows of toilets with no partitions between them, 'short arm' inspections by doctors at our bunks at unannounced times, and demands of unquestioning obedience. Our individual identities were being stripped away. We received a battery of immunization shots, learned to count off and march in formation, and attended an irrelevant lecture on the dangers of venereal disease.

Our orientation completed, we boarded a troop train bound for basic training at Greensboro, North Carolina. As the miles clicked beneath the car, I speculated on how long it would be before the distance was retraced. We disembarked at the camp. Spread out on the red, sloping hills were row upon row of low-lying barracks. Squads of men marched along the streets, counting off cadence and chanting songs. As we formed up and moved off, the others shouted, 'You'll be so o o o r r y!' and 'Here come more gunners.' The latter was a shock; we thought we were destined for preflight training. The shouts were another touch of reality. Later on, we took pleasure in repeating them to the new batches of recruits we saw arriving.

The smell of burning soft coal will remind me forever of our six weeks at Greensboro. It came from the two iron stoves in each building, and clung in the wet air as we marched from class to class in our ponchos and helmet liners. We would sit on the hard floor of an empty barracks to hear lessons about poison gases, camouflage techniques, and carbine nomenclature. Our drill sergeant was a ruddy-faced Southerner who wore sharply creased trousers and shirts, and highly polished shoes. His cap was set at a precise military angle, and he insisted that ours be positioned exactly the same way. He stood straight and tall. He briskly herded us about, shouting commands and calling out the cadence:

'Hup, two, three, four
Hup, two, three, four
Hup, two, three, four.
You had a good job and you left;
You had a good job and you left;
Your left, your left, you had a good job and you left.
You had a good job and you left—your right,
You had a good job and you left—your right.
You had a good job and you left.'

The beat was strong and irresistible. So were the marching songs, which made long hikes about the base almost pleasant. We had become a unit, and actually enjoyed it at times. We struck up a steady rhythm as we swung along, singing *'I've Been Working on the Railroad,' 'Into the Air, Army Air Corps,'* and *'Around Her Neck, She Wore a Yellow Ribbon'* (for her airman who was 'far, far away'). The second verse was quickly corrupted to 'around the block, she wheels a baby carriage.' Singing, marching, chanting, joking, and griping made our lives much more tolerable.

The sergeant was an Army career man who shaped batches of clumsy civilians into fairly respectable soldiers. He taught us to run through the manual of arms smartly with our carbines, to salute properly, and to don a gas mask in minutes. When we failed to measure up, he chewed us out unmercifully.

'What a piss poor excuse for soldiers y'all are,' he told us early one morning for some good reason. 'Y'all don't fall out on time, ya don't get the drill raht, ya don't salute raht, ya don't do nothing raht. We're gonna lose this goddamn war sure as hell if it's up to the likes a y'all.'

'That's a double negative, Sarge,' someone offered.

'What? What'n hell do you mean?'

'That we don't do nothing right—that means we do something right.'

'You do like hell. This is the saddest lookin' bunch that's ever come through here. I swear to hell we're gettin' to the bottom of the goddamn barrel. The krauts must be lickin' their chops to get at the likes a you sad bastards.'

A member of our squad was standing in the darkness in the back row. With his lips pursed and unmoving, he muttered, 'Blow it out your ass.'

'What? WHAT? Who said that? Who said that?' the sergeant demanded, glaring into the formation. He paced in front of us, staring at each man.

'Somebody's buckin' for a year a KP, and he's gonna get it. Who's the smartass? Who's the smartass?' There was no answer.

'All right, you guys—twenty-five push-ups, ev'ry goddamn one of ya, raht nahw.'

We dropped to the ground to do as he said, but we were smiling among ourselves. Even a touch of revenge felt good.

A Greensboro boy would come into the barracks at night to sell newspapers. He was often met by a chorus of cries.

'Here comes another rebel,' someone called out. 'Nail everything down!'

'Grab your wallets, men.'

'Don't let him outta sight.'

The boy strode down the long aisle between the double bunks, looking straight ahead. 'Fuck-in' Yan-kees,' he said, drawing out the words with a marvelous drawl.

Our turn came for KP. [40] Innocent as a babe, I showed up at the mess hall on my assigned morning. The older hands on the base disappeared magically into jobs that lasted only through each meal, ladling out oatmeal or scrambled eggs. I ended up at a huge sink, washing pots and pans by hand. The sun rose on the far side of the building as I stood there, and it set behind me as I scoured. I was at the sink most of the day. Just when I thought those of us who remained were finished, an officer came into the kitchen, tested the silverware with a glove, and ruled that it was so greasy that it had to be washed again with vinegar.

---

[40] *KP duty*-'kitchen police' or 'kitchen patrol,' enlisted men performing menial kitchen tasks under supervision, like peeling potatoes, washing dishes, etc.

Mail call was the high point of each day. We went down to the mail room and waited to hear our names, or renditions of them, called out. 'Yo,' we shouted, and picked up our letters. There often was one from Bake, for we had begun to write frequently. I saved her letter for last and looked for some sign that she cared for me. She generally signed them 'Love.' Later, it was 'All my love' or 'Much love.' 'SWAK'—Sealed With a Kiss—began to appear on the back of the envelopes, along with a lipstick imprint. I was pleased by that show of affection. After a while, she sent me a photo of herself, auburn hair falling to her shoulders. I kept it in my box of writing materials and studied it often.

Pay day saw long lines of airmen waiting in front of a table. An officer sat with a log book containing our names and serial numbers. As we stood there, a soldier glanced at the sky.

'Looks like it might cloud up and rain,' he said.

A big, black sergeant stood behind me. 'I don't care if it cloud up and shits,' he said. 'Ah'm gonna stay here and get my money.'

That night men gathered in a corner of the barracks to shoot dice. Some walked away with fistfuls of bills. Others had lost all, or most, of their monthly earnings, and soon were borrowing from their friends. I did not understand how they could be so foolish.

We set out one day on a twelve mile hike to a rifle range, carrying carbines, packs, and gas masks. It was a long, hot trip. As we neared the range, tired and sweaty, a Jeep roared past, releasing a cloud of tear gas. Eyes burning, we fumbled for our gas masks and swore vigorously at the disappearing vehicle. It was a good lesson, but we failed to appreciate it.

At the range we lived in tents, ate from mess kits, and spent the days firing rifles and pistols at targets. We were eighteen years old. Stretched out in our cots at night, we could hear far-off train whistles and were homesick.

*

Back at the main camp, we took tests to find out if we could enter preflight training. The end of the war in Europe was in sight, so fewer cadets were being chosen for the lengthy program. Only one man from our group was selected. I was so ashamed that for days I could not bring myself to write home that I would be going into gunnery school instead of preflight classes. We packed our gear, shouldered it all, and marched off to the railroad tracks and a waiting train. Our sergeant shook our hands and wished us well.

'Y'all are going to do okay,' he said. 'You shaped up good.'

We boarded a 'cattle car' troop train that contained rows of bunk beds. I liked the arrangement; instead of Pullman berths that forced two men to share a wide lower bunk, there were rows of individual bunks on floor-to-ceiling steel legs. In between the bunks were wide aisles. We could move about freely in the open areas, and nap or read on our bunks during the day. No serviceman will ever forget the smell of the smoke that wafted back from the engine, or the grit that sifted through cracks and covered everything.

Standing patiently in the long chow lines with our mess kits, we were jostled by the movement of the cars. Looking out the windows, we were introduced to the poverty of the rural South. As I watched the shacks and small towns of Georgia, Alabama, Mississippi, and Louisiana slide by, I realized how fortunate I had been to grow up in our river valley village. The railroad crossing arms would be down as the train sped along the drab main streets, bells ringing as we shot past, the men waving and shouting at the girls as the girls waved back. Sometimes the train would halt in the middle of a town; the most adventuresome men would race to a nearby store and run back with all the beer they could carry before the train moved on.

We were on our way to the air base at Harlingen, Texas. The school was near the Gulf Coast, just above Mexico. We arrived at night, picked up our bedding, and retired. I awoke in the morning to find myself in a world unlike any I had ever seen. Suddenly it was summer—there were palm trees, soft, warm breezes, and suntan uniforms. High in the cloudless skies, four engine bombers droned continually on their training flights.

Our six weeks of gunnery school was a fascinating experience. There was no KP or other drudgery; we were a privileged class being readied for war. It was a grand adventure, still unrelated to the deadly aerial battles then taking place over Europe. Our instructors told us about the piercing cold in a bomber at high altitude, about the damage that anti-aircraft fire can inflict, and about the way bullets were deflected by the shielding on the front of an attacking Focke-Wulf fighter, but it did not really sink in. Much of that was due to the matter-of-fact way in which the information was presented, without reference to death, wounds, or downed crews. I had a distinct feeling that one of our instructors in particular, a staff sergeant who had flown twenty-five missions with the Eighth Air Force over Germany and looked older than his years, was sparing us the worst details. He held himself apart, and I sensed that he felt sorry for us.

One day at a range where we learned to fire machine guns, I asked an older ground attendant if he had ever flown. 'Are you crazy?' he answered. 'I've seen them wash too many of you guys out of a crash with a hose.' It was a sobering statement, but we laughed when I repeated it that night in the barracks. We were seated in an auditorium another time when an officer casually told us that a third of the men in the room would be killed, wounded, or taken prisoner. I felt sorry for the others, for surely nothing could happen to me. Youth is optimistic, feels indestructible, and sees life as infinite. Thus young people ride bicycles blindly around corners, drive cars too fast, and fight wars.

I wondered how they would teach me to kill another man. I hated fist fights, never hunted animals, and always tried to be kind to others. What would they do to change my nature? The answer is easy—they simply give you the training, the equipment, some indoctrination, and the opportunity. You can either shoot back, or regret it. And of course you could not let your buddies down, or be seen as cowardly.

Whatever was needed, we worked into gradually. There were slide shows of German, Japanese, American, and British aircraft. We called out the names of the Zeros, Spitfires, Me-109s, Lightnings, Nicks, P-47s, P-51s, and Focke-Wulfs as they flashed by. As a model builder and an airplane freak for so many years, I found it all very familiar.

Then came a turn with guns that fired a stream of BB pellets at a model airplane that moved on a track across a painted canvas sky. What adventurous boy could resist that game? It was good, clean, harmless fun. We peppered the model as it emerged from behind a 'cloud' and sped across an open expanse. Later we went out to a skeet range, where we fired shot guns at circular clay pigeons as they were catapulted in front of us. Leading the black saucers by a radius or two, we shattered them by the hour. There must be a stratum of broken birds several feet thick at that site today. We graduated from the stationary skeet range to the back of an open truck that circled an oval track. Catapult stations were located at various points along the route. We stood in the back of the vehicle and took turns firing our shotguns at the skimming targets as we drove along, compensating for both the movement of the truck and the trajectory of the birds.

One morning we were marched to a large classroom building. Inside was an area that contained several metal-topped tables. Mounted on a pedestal at one table was a large, black, lethal-looking machine gun. An instructor stood in front of us, his arm resting on the gun.

An armorer working on a .50 M2.
Credit: browningmgs.com.

'Men, this here is a .50 caliber, Browning M2 machine gun. It is a belt-fed, recoil-operated, air-cooled weapon. It can fire twelve to fourteen rounds a second, maximum, but that would burn out the gun barrel fast if you kept it up for long. So don't ever do it. Instead, we rapid-fire forty rounds a minute, in bursts of six to nine rounds, at five to ten second intervals to save the barrel. Before you're done, you're gonna learn this baby inside out and backwards. If you don't, it could be your ass, and I don't mean maybe! So listen careful.'

We did just that in the weeks that followed. The .50 caliber was a brute of a weapon, heavy, accurate, and rapid-firing. It weighed eighty pounds, and could shoot half inch diameter bullets more than four miles with a muzzle velocity of 2,900 feet a second. Its most effective range was up to 600 yards.

Day after day, we took the gun apart, learning the name and function of every piece. I removed the rear buffer plate, examined the buffer discs, released the driving spring rod, and withdrew the shiny steel bolt assembly. I could not help but admire the smooth, beautifully machined unit that pulled the rounds steadily into the gun, slammed them into the breech, fired, recoiled, ejected the clips and cartridges, and then repeated the process. We were shown how to keep the gun oiled and in good repair, and how to clear malfunctions. The day finally came when I could put on a blindfold, dismantle the weapon, spread the parts out on the table, then put them all back together. I smiled with satisfaction after the job was completed.

A machine gun firing range was located in the sand dunes near the Gulf Coast. Rows of .50s were mounted on steel pedestals, facing targets half a mile away. Holding a bucking gun by its two handles, I sent a torrent of bullets into a target area, creating geysers of sand and dust. The noise hammered my ears and the brass cases spewed into the air as long belts of ammunition were devoured. I did not let myself think about a similar stream of enemy slugs that someday could come flying back in my direction.

The next step was a visit to a large hangar at Harlingen that contained heavy wooden platforms. Mounted on them were the electrically driven nose, ball, and tail turrets that were found in B-24 Liberator bombers. Each turret contained two .50 caliber machine guns. We learned how to operate each of the turrets, swinging the units from side to side, and the guns up and down. The nose and tail turrets were like tiny greenhouses perched out on the edge of nowhere. I felt highly vulnerable sitting in them, surrounded only by thin, clear plastic.

The Sperry ball turret hung below the fuselage of both the B-24 and the B-17 Flying Fortress to protect the underbelly of the bombers. The turret was a metal and Plexiglas 'goldfish bowl' about three feet in diameter. It called for smaller men who could curl up inside for long periods of time. The B-24 ball had to be raised from its position beneath the plane so that the gunner could enter. The turret then was lowered into place. We practiced the routine on the platform. The ball would be brought up, secured, and the hatch opened. I would climb in, the hatch would be closed overhead, and the ball would be eased downward. Today, the memory of the practice gives me claustrophobic shivers; at that time, it was simply another command to be obeyed.

In still another classroom an instructor described the famous Air Force clock system for reporting the positions of attacking aircraft. 'Twelve o'clock' was directly ahead of the bomber, 'three o'clock' was off the right wing tip, 'six o'clock' behind the tail, and so on. Accordingly, a fighter closing in at 'seven o'clock low' was to the lower right of the tail gunner, and one at 'twelve o'clock high' was approaching the pilots from above.

The instructor held up a model of a German Me-109 fighter. 'Suppose I'm a German sittin' out here like this at three o'clock, checkin' you out and gettin' ready to come in,' he said. He positioned the model as if it were flying parallel to the front row of our class, the nose pointing to our left. 'Here's what to look for. You watch his inner wing tip like a hawk. If the guy is really serious, the wing will tilt up, and he'll come sweeping in and drop back toward the tail of your plane, like this.' He tipped the wing up and let the plane fall off to our right, the nose pointed steadily at us.

German ground crew pushes Me-109 onto tarmac, fall 1943, France. Credit: Bundesarchiv, Bild 101I-487-3066-04 via Wikimedia Commons.

'That's called a pursuit curve. It holds the fighter right on target every inch of the way. If the guy is a little chicken—sometimes they are—he'll dip the inner wing down and cut around behind you, like this.' He showed us how the fighter would bank sharply down and away to its left.

'That's a fly through. It means that his fire will be scattered and much less accurate, like a hose sweepin' across a lawn instead of being pointed straight at you all the time. You'll like that. And for God's sake, don't waste your ammunition on a fighter flying alongside you way out here, doing no harm! Hold your fire until he starts coming in. You're going to need every round you've got!' With those heartening words, we were ready to take to the air.

Several AT-6 training planes awaited us on the flight line at Harlingen one morning. They were low-wing, single-engine aircraft with an open cockpit in the rear. A thirty-caliber machine gun—the 'little' brother of the fifty—was mounted behind the cockpit. We were handed leather helmets, goggles, parachute harnesses, and parachutes, and told how to use them. A sergeant gathered us around a trainer. He told us we would be flown out to the Gulf, where we would fire at targets as we flew low over the water.

North American AT-6C-NT Texan trainer, 1943. Credit: USAF, public domain.

'Two things,' he said, holding up his fingers. 'One, don't shoot the tail off the airplane. If you do, somebody's going to be mad as hell, including the pilot. Second, remember to space your bursts. If you don't, you'll burn out the barrel, and then I'll be mad.'

Several of my companions flew first. Some returned swallowing hard, or with less color in their faces. When my turn came, I put on my equipment and climbed into the rear seat for my first airplane ride. The bored pilot sped out to the runway, paused as briefly as a bird on a bush, then roared into the air. Looking down at the countryside, I was exhilarated. The houses, barns, and cars were small toys far below. We continued toward the Gulf. Suddenly the plane banked, dropped, and swooped across the shallow water. I fired at the floating targets, taking care to do as I had been told. The bullets tore into the water, coming near a Mexican fishing boat that had strayed into the area to pick up stunned fish. A man dove overboard, not knowing that I had no intention of hitting the boat. We repeated the run, then returned to the base. In retrospect, the main objective of the flight may have been to see if we were fit to fly. If we managed to hit the water, did not get sick, missed the tail, and spared the gun barrel, we passed.

We began flying in different kinds of bombers as the pilots practiced piloting, the navigators navigating, the bombardiers bombing, and the gunners gunning. We donned fleece-lined helmets, jackets, pants, gloves, and boots and clambered into an old B-24 Liberator bomber. It roared down the runway, lifted from the ground, and slowly climbed upward. After a time, we put on our oxygen masks and plugged the long hoses into the ship's system.

Standing beside an open waist window some 25,000 feet in the sky, I marveled at the clarity of the air, the brilliance of the sunshine, and the vapor trails that formed long streamers behind our plane. Flight at those altitudes in those days was an adventure requiring heavy clothing and oxygen masks. Today it is commonplace to fly comfortably six miles above the earth in pressurized cabins.

High above Texas one April afternoon, a B-24 ball turret was raised, and the hatch opened.

'Your turn,' our instructor said to me. 'In you go.'

Sperry ball turret, retractable model. Credit: browningmgs.com.

I settled myself into the compartment and connected my oxygen tube and intercom line. The hatch was closed and latched above me. The twin fifties and I were pointed straight down at the ground, thousands of feet below. The turret was slowly lowered into the sparkling air. Using upright hand levers that pivoted in all directions, I leveled the turret and rotated it so that I could look all about. Overhead was the fat underside of our bomber and its big, oval twin rudders; around me was the vast sky. A camera was mounted in the turret to record simulated attacks by friendly fighters. One appeared from below—an old Bell P-39 Airacobra, coming straight on. I fixed him in my gun sight, pushed the firing buttons on top of the levers with my thumbs, and 'shot' him with my camera. It was an exciting moment.

Between flights we went to classes, learned survival techniques, and studied our manuals. I remember sitting in the lighted stairway of our barracks one night, reading a lesson after the rest of the building had been darkened. To 'wash out' of gunnery school would have been a terrible disgrace, far worse than missing out on preflight training. If I failed I could be sent to the Air Transport Command, where I would spend the war safely loading freight into cargo planes instead of flying missions over enemy territory. That was a fate to be avoided. The boy who never hunted animals now was willing to shoot at other men—or would be chagrined not to be shooting at them. I had not hardened or developed a killer instinct; I was simply responding to the pressures of the time.

I did not feel fear while suspended below the bomber, nor did I question the assignment. I should have; the turret was top-heavy, and could swing violently if not locked into place inside the airplane as I was sliding in or out. And if the ship's electrical system was knocked out, the ball turret could not be retracted. Worst of all, there was no room in the ball for a parachute. One was totally dependent upon the crewmen above to raise the turret, secure it, and help one get out, in order to put on a parachute. It occurred to me that if my bomber was aflame and spinning to earth, the crewmen above might well decide to save themselves rather than lose time retrieving me. How many ball turret gunners plunged to their deaths in World War II in the same fetal position in which they had begun their lives? Their casualty rate was high. Despite the problems, I continued on, and was destined for duty beneath a bomber when our training period came to an end. I had inherited my parents' stoicism, or their optimism, or both.

Our daily calisthenics exercises saw acres of lean, tanned men, wearing white shorts and black sneakers, swinging arms high and legs wide in chanted unison. Watching them, I speculated on the thousands of other young men at other bases around the world who at that same moment were preparing in the same way to do battle against their enemies.

'Look!' someone called out as we were returning from our mess hall after dinner one evening. He pointed to a B-24 with a smoking engine that was swinging low over the base, racing toward the landing strip. We stopped to watch the bomber bank sharply downward and drop from sight beyond the barracks. Soon a pillar of black smoke rose high in the sky. As I lay in my bed that night I imagined myself in the place of that crew in their terrifying plunge to earth. Later we learned that the bomber had leveled out to land and burn, and that everyone had escaped unhurt.

Soon, we took a battery of tests, received our silver wings and corporal's stripes, and were ready for assignment to a combat squadron. We were rolling out of gunnery schools across the south and southwest every week by the hundreds, ready to join the shiny new bombers that were steadily flowing off their own production lines.

Andy Doty went back to 'Hometown, USA' again on leave, and on his return to base he was assigned to the crew of a new bomber, the B-29 Superfortress, destined for the skies over Japan. It had been developed secretly and was well suited to the demands of the Pacific theater: long, overwater missions without fighter escorts. Before shipping out to the Pacific, he returned home one last time.

Once again, the two weeks vanished in a flurry of visits, movies, high school basketball games, and trips to the drug store. I picked up Bake at her house on those frosty evenings, and we walked briskly down Mechanic Street to the corner of Main Street to catch the bus to Glens Falls. The bus was crowded, its windows coated with steam or frost. A man gave up his seat to Bake, and I stood proudly beside her in the aisle, swaying slightly as I held onto an overhead strap. As the bus moved along, its lights showed high snow banks on either side of the road and dark clusters of people waiting in the cold at the bus stops ahead. We were on our way to Glens Falls to see 'Since You Went Away' at the Paramount Theater. It starred Jennifer Jones and Robert Walker as young lovers in wartime. Bake and I held hands in the darkened theater and identified with the two characters.

We ended the evening in the Baker family's warm front room, where we waited for her parents to go to bed after we had finished our ice cream ritual. When they were gone, Bake sat on my lap in a large, blue easy chair. Soft dance music, broadcast late at night from a hotel in New York City, formed a romantic backdrop. We kept the radio low so that we would not disturb her parents beyond their closed door. But after a time, Mrs. Baker's call emerged: 'Eleanor!' Once again it was time for me to leave. I walked home in my heavy overcoat, cupping my ears in the cold, running to slide across patches of ice in the street.

The farewells this time were much harder, for we all knew I was going overseas. Again I left Bake early the night before departing, and went through the routine of packing with my parents watching. Ken Howe drove us, Agnes, and Bake to Albany in a Buick that held three people in the front seat. Mom, Bake, and I sat in the back. It was a sad ride, but we tried to be cheerful, talking about anything but the future.

Standing on the slushy pavement in front of the railroad station, we said goodbye. I hugged Mom and shook Dad's hand. He had been taking nitroglycerin tablets for an angina problem for years and puffed after the slightest effort. I looked into his eyes and wondered if I would ever see him again; I imagined him wondering the same about me.

Dad was not given to long statements. 'Take care of yourself,' he said. 'I will—you, too.' We did not embrace, for men did not do such things in those days. I wish I had, for I never saw him again.

I gave Bake a brief kiss, picked up my bags, and disappeared into the station.

*

Andy Doty survived 21 combat missions in the Pacific late in the war, detailed further in my first book, The Things Our Fathers Saw: Voices of the Pacific Theater. *He returned home in December 1945 and pursued higher education. His brother Chuck also survived the war, and went to work in the mills like their father. Andy and Eleanor Baker married in July 1950.*

*

Andy Doty

I think we shall never see the likes of it again. The nation was fully united and mobilized in a popular military effort. The youth of America was under arms, generally willing, and often eager to serve their country. Young men who had never traveled more than fifteen miles from home fought land, sea, and air battles in every quarter of the globe.

Richard 'Dick' Varney, flight engineer, first row second from left, and the crew of his B-24 Liberator. Source: Richard Varney.

CHAPTER FIVE

The Flight Engineer

Richard 'Dick' Varney was born in 1911, and was already an 'old man' when he was drafted at age 32. Mr. Varney lived on the corner of the block where I grew up, with his wife Anne and two children. He always had a smile on his face and a loving twinkle in his eye when I saw him; his wife Anne came into the house and minded us as young children when my mother started to work as a school nurse-teacher. When I started sending my students into the community to do interviews with veterans 40 years later, two of my students happened to meet him at a garage sale and got to talking. Though he had been a part of my own family's life for decades—he was even my youngest brother's godfather—I had no idea that Richard Varney had been in the war; he flew 28 missions in the B-24 Liberator. He gave my students a wide-ranging interview in his home in December 2003. Here he is, at age 92, talking to two seventeen-year-olds, and passing advice and his take on the current state of the world with the same smile and sparkle.

***

Duties of the Flight Engineer

Size up the man who is to be your engineer. This man is supposed to know more about the airplane you are to fly than any other member of the crew.

He has been trained in the Air Force's highly specialized technical schools. Probably he has served some time as a crew chief. Nevertheless, there may be some inevitable blank spots in his training which you, as a pilot and airplane commander, may be able to fill in.

Think back on your own training. In many courses of instruction, you had a lot of things thrown at you from right and left. You had to concentrate on how to fly; and where your equipment was concerned you learned to rely more and more on the enlisted personnel, particularly the crew chief and the engineer, to advise you about things that were not taught to you because of lack of time and the arrangement of the training program.

Both pilot and engineer have a responsibility to work closely together to supplement and fill in the blank spots in each other's education. To be a qualified combat engineer a man must know his airplane, his engines, and his armament equipment thoroughly. This is a big responsibility: the lives of the entire crew, the safety of the equipment, the success of the mission depend upon it squarely.

He must work closely with the copilot, checking engine operation, fuel consumption, and the operation of all equipment. He must be able to work with the bombardier, and know how to cock, lock, and load the bomb racks. It is up to you, the airplane commander, to see that he is familiar with these duties, and, if he is hazy concerning them, to have the bombardier give him special help and instruction.

Your engineer should be your chief source of information concerning the airplane. He should know more about the equipment than any other crew member--yourself included.

You, in turn, are his source of information concerning flying. Bear this in mind in all your discussions with the engineer. The more complete you can make his knowledge of the reasons behind every function of the equipment, the more valuable he will be as a member of the crew. Who knows? Someday that little bit of extra knowledge in the engineer's mind may save the day in some emergency.

Generally, in emergencies, the engineer will be the man to whom you turn first. Build up his pride, his confidence, his knowledge. Know him personally; check on the extent of his knowledge. Make him a man upon whom you can rely. —Duties and Responsibilities of the Airplane Commander and Crewmen, 1943

***

Richard Varney

I grew up during the Depression. I remember that day in 1929 [when the stock market crashed] very well. I was about 17 or 18. I had been working for two years; I went to work at fifteen years old with working papers. My parents, God bless them, they grew up in an era when school was not that important. You went to work as soon as you were able to help the family. I don't think you people understand what I am saying or what that means, but it meant a lot. But I wish that I had gone to school. I did later on, but I made it in life without [a formal education]. I had to do it my way. I worked at the sawmill on Haskell Avenue in Glens Falls; it's not there now. I also started playing at dances in a band when I was 17 and did it for a long, long time; it was a lot of fun. It was quite necessary then because the wages then weren't what they are now. I took lessons for a little while on the violin, but I played by ear from then on. I also taught myself to play the alto and tenor saxophone, which I still have, incidentally.

You have to realize that when I went to work at the Imperial factory, later, if you weren't late or forgot to ring in and out, you got 40 cents an hour. Can you imagine that? You worked 40 hours, you got sixteen dollars a week! Now on this, you had a family to support—it isn't like what it's like today. In the Depression era you could buy a home for 1,500 dollars. You couldn't hang a door for that now! Money was something you didn't have, but you didn't feel deprived in those days because nobody else had any money. No, you probably had one change of clothes, maybe one pair of shoes if you were lucky. You didn't wear them in the summer because you didn't want to wear them out. I'm not exaggerating, because you just didn't have the money. You made do. You didn't eat a lot of prepared food, you [improvised and] cooked your own. You ate a lot of things... [Have you ever had] dandelions? We used to go and pick them.

Clean them, cook them, you make do. You just didn't always have money with those kinds of wages.

*

On December 7, 1941, I was working at the Imperial Color paint factory in Glens Falls. It was a shock—I was outraged naturally, because it was a sneak attack. But it was not unexpected; believe me, we had been heading towards it. In fact, in my opinion we were already in an undeclared war; we were actually in it because we were supporting England. We had been giving them everything they needed; from then on it was just a matter of time before we all got into it. But Germany and Japan declared war on us first.

I was not a kid; I was thirty years old at the time. I was married and I had no idea what the future was going to bring for us, because I did not know what they wanted to do. I don't think anybody relished the idea of going to war; nobody does. But nevertheless, I think we had a level of patriotism at that time that we won't ever see again; certainly we don't have it now. Everybody was behind it, the whole situation, at that time. I don't think you heard anybody wondering whether we should go in or not, because we were in. In retrospect it was so long ago now, a lot of the details are not as sharp as they should be maybe, but I can remember most of it.

*

I was drafted in April of 1943, I think. Then we went through God knows how many schools, how much training, to prepare us for it.

I took my army basic training in Miami Beach. It was tough duty in Miami Beach. [*Laughs*] After that we were assigned to air mechanic school, and there I was trained for the B-24 Liberator. I was being trained as the aircraft flight engineer, and my job at that time was everything mechanical on the plane. It was the flight engineer's responsibility, so you were taught everything about the airplane. Then after we graduated from there, they sent us to Panama City for air gunnery. After that we went to various places and to Westover Field, and from there our crew was formed. Now this crew, when it was put together, was the first time that I had met most of these people, the enlisted men I met. Then we went to Walker Air Base in South Carolina, and there we met our pilot, co-pilot, navigator, and bombardier; from then on, we were a unit—we stayed together, we trained together, all our practice missions and everything. Then we went to Langley, Virginia, and from there we took radar training. And that was the last duty in this part of the world—from there we flew to Goose Bay, Labrador, and then to Iceland and from there to Wales. We flew all the way over. Now as a unit, we stayed that way. And then when we got there, we were assigned to our bomb group. And there we went through even more training—that's all you ever did, you train, train, train, and train.

*

'There Are No Heroes'

The B-17 crews were the glory boys. The B-24 flew faster, carried more bombs, and flew higher, but the B-17s were the glory boys. We didn't name our planes like they did. We had ten to a crew in the 24s, yes. Originally they had a ball turret on the bottom but when we got over across the ocean they took that out and they put the radar transmitter in the bottom, where the belly turret was. That left the engineer free to do everything mechanical, and the assistant engineer flew the top turret [gun] in my plane.

Finally we were scheduled for our first mission, to Hamburg. It was a vital mission, in the sense that Hamburg had all their oil refineries. And without that, they couldn't fly, they couldn't have gasoline, they couldn't have anything, so you could destroy it because it would certainly limit their supplies. It was a very important mission. And because of that they concentrated their [fighter] aircraft and anti-aircraft guns to protect it. So that's a target I really remember, believe me.

I've seen planes go down, naturally. And the only things you'd look for were how many 'chutes came out of it, because when an airplane gets spinning, you couldn't get out. Sometimes because of centrifugal force, the spinning of the plane would kill you, because you couldn't get out. As I said before, I never got hurt. It was always the other guy. And the frame of mind that you have is something that most people can't understand—you can see this happening, but it's not you. It becomes an impersonal thing; it has to be, because you would go crazy if it wasn't. Not that you didn't have sympathy for the people, but still, it wasn't you. I don't know how to explain it. But there are no heroes, contrary to what people may think. It's like a job. I don't think there are any heroes up there, because you're just doing your job, you have to—you either did, or you didn't come back. You don't have time enough really to be scared a lot.

*

Our missions were all over. They were over the Rhineland, yes, sure. And Cologne, Dusseldorf, whatever you can think of. And we hit them wherever they were—we bombed as far as Austria and Czechoslovakia; in fact, we even hit Berchtesgaden, which was Hitler's retreat.

I was looking at the calendar and today is the date, incidentally [December 16], that the Ardennes offensive started, the day when Hitler tried to break through to split the Allies. They were going through the [U.S.] First Army. They did go through pretty well. And we stopped them at Bastogne. Have you ever seen that movie about that? Well, that's where General McAuliffe was the commander there. The Germans had them pretty well surrounded and beaten. The German commander asked for his surrender. Then General McAuliffe made the very famous remark [*laughs*]—he says,

'Nuts,' the General did, when asked to surrender. That's all there was to it. That actually happened. And that was of course the time when Patton was racing across France to relieve Bastogne, and he got there. But in the meantime, we're bombing. We couldn't get off the ground for about a week when that started because we were socked in with the bad weather, so we couldn't take off, we couldn't land. And of course it didn't bother you once you got in the air because we didn't have to see the ground to bomb, because we bombed by radar. The cloud cover didn't matter, but you did have to land. So we couldn't get off the ground. But when we did, we just bombed everything in sight.

Most of the missions we flew were around 20,000 feet, and believe me, in the winter time at that altitude, it's about minus 70 degrees. That's cold. But we did have heated suits, heated clothes. And of course, under those circumstances, we still had our job to do. As an engineer, I had duties at the time. I had to check to make sure the generators were synchronized, I opened the bomb bay doors, and I transferred fuel. All of these things were part of my job. I won't speak for the other people; they had their own jobs. But that is what I did.

*

'Something Always Goes Wrong'

Interviewer: Did anything ever go wrong during your job?

Did anything ever go wrong? [*Chuckles*] Oh, something always goes wrong. Yes, I remember one time when we got ready on the 'IP,' which is the Initial Point, where we start the bomb run to the target—I forget where the mission was to—well, they loaded the bombs all right. But there's a propeller on the back of it, and when you drop the bomb, the wind screws the propeller off. When that propeller comes off, that bomb is armed; it won't go off otherwise.

But when the group crews load them, they're supposed to put a safety wire through it, in each thing. Well, somebody on that mission [*laughs*], they didn't put the safety wires in. So when I opened the bomb bay doors, the wind hit them, and I called the pilot on the intercom and I said, 'I got news for you, we got 10 thousand-pound bombs here that are now armed. The propellers are all off.' Any piece of flak coming through would hit the nose of them and... [*Makes the sound of an explosion*] that would be all she wrote, you wouldn't find anything! It didn't, though. But that's one time I sweated a little bit, I can tell you. [*Chuckles*] You couldn't fix anything. We were on the 'IP.' You couldn't take evasive action, you couldn't do anything, and we're flying right through that flak. But when they dropped the bombs, it was fine.

That was one system that they used—the other system, that's visual bombing. They had two other systems; they had one where you bomb by radar, and the other, I forgot what they called it, but they used radio signals [radio navigation]. What they would do was pick a point, say, in England somewhere, and put a directional beam. And you would fly along this leg [*motions with fingers*], and this one would maybe be giving you signals like 'Da-da-dit. Da-da-dit.' And then this other one over here would be, 'Dit-da-da. Dit-da-da.' So as you came closer, they joined all of a sudden and that was your target. You didn't have to see the ground. As soon as you hit those signals together, you dropped because you were over the target. Does that make any sense to you?

Flak

I learned more about the German anti-aircraft than I did about anything else because that was the only way you could defend yourself against anti-aircraft. Oh yes, we picked up holes, sure, flak holes. They used their 88s, they called them, and at different levels, and they generally fired in bursts of three. Each battery of anti-aircraft was three guns, usually. The first gun would be [set for a range of] 18,500 feet, and another one would be at 18,700, and so on; three. They're like steps. And they would try to bracket you with the target, and they had so many of those batteries at some of our targets! When they started firing, you would have thought there was a thunderstorm up there, you know what I mean? Our protection was a skin of a piece of aluminum about that thick, and that was it [*Holds two fingers together closely*]. And those planes were all aluminum, except for the engines, of course. But it didn't provide much protection. We did have flak suits, flak vests they called them. I always used mine to sit on because that's where the flak was coming from. [*Chuckles*] But they were very heavy, very cumbersome. And of course the gloves were heavy too. But I never lost it, I never lost an engine. I did lose the oil out of one when we landed because there was a hole in the oil reservoir, but the pump in it was strong enough so I didn't lose the engine in the air. No, I made sure the engines were all right before we went up.

As I said before, I don't make that much of that because there's not many heroes up there. You're doing your job, that's all. But for flying personnel, we had the highest rate of casualties than any branch of the service, because there's no foxholes up there either, no place to hide, but [we were lucky]. Out of our original crew of ten, we only lost two. There was a bomb group that was short a copilot and a tail gunner. And we weren't scheduled to fly that day, so they assigned them to that other aircraft, from the other group. And they got shot down. They didn't come back. But, outside of that, there's not much I can tell you. You didn't do too much worrying because it's something that you were trained to do, and you had to do it, and you're busy and taking care of the duties of the job. You didn't have much time to think about anything else. No, I don't think we always wondered—of course, it crosses your mind naturally, why wouldn't it? When you look out the side window and see a plane going down, it isn't you, but naturally you're going to wonder about it, you know… But as far as that, that's all there is to it. I mean, the way the job was—what, in retrospect, what I did like about the air corps was that despite the hazards, if you went over and came back, you did have a place to sleep. You weren't like an infantryman sleeping in a foxhole! You ate in the mess halls; you did get your hot food. But outside of that, as I said, I don't think there were many heroes flying up there. I can't say I worried too much—because what are you going to do? If you don't like it, are you going to get out and walk? You're going where the plane goes, that's all there is to it. And that's it. But I can't say I got to take much credit for that. The only thing you can take credit for is being able to function under those conditions. You take 70 degrees below zero and you've got murderous work, and if you take your gloves off, it wouldn't be for two minutes and your hands would be frozen.

As the air crew, of course, we couldn't afford to get sick. But one time I went up with a cold, and I was stone deaf for a week when we returned. You see, you could take a balloon at ground level and it'd be about that big around [*puts hands together showing a small width*]. And you tie it out there in the plane where you can see it; when you get up to 20,000 feet that balloon is that big [*shows with hands a much bigger width*]. The air pressure is so much less, but the air pressure inside the balloon stays the same because it can't escape, and that's what happens to you when you have a cold. Your ear tube—your Eustachian tubes—you can't clear them, so you can't balance the pressure in your outer ear, so what it does is it stretches your ear! That happened to me and you can't turn back and it's very painful—you can't turn back because you can't abort the mission for that! That happened to me, and that's why I am having difficulty hearing you today, probably. They grounded me for a week until I could hear again, then I sat through missions. And then the stupid commander at that time, when I couldn't fly missions, they had me out there at nighttime manning machine guns to guard the base! That wasn't a good thing. In the wintertime in England it is damp and miserable, cold, and they have a longer night. People don't realize that, but it's true. But what are you supposed to do? It's like everything else—you either do your job, or else. Every member of that crew has a job to do, and he has to do it because everyone depends on everybody else.

Interviewer: Did your heated suit ever malfunction?

[*Chuckles*] There isn't anything ever made by man that didn't malfunction at some time, but not very often. Not very often, because you were careful to test them before you went out. If you had any brains, you tested it. And your oxygen, you had to have oxygen. We went on oxygen at 10,000 feet, and from 10,000 feet on up, we stayed on oxygen. Otherwise, hypoxia is a horrible thing. If you didn't have oxygen at 20,000 feet, you'd pass out never knowing it. It's amazing; you wouldn't even know it. You'd just go to sleep and that would be it, if anything ever happened to your oxygen supply and you didn't know it. But like anything made by man, it is going to malfunction occasionally. We didn't have the technology in those days that you have now.

*

Incidentally, sometimes for a mission the only warning you got was when the C.Q. in charge of quarters would come along and shake you about 4:00 in the morning. That's the way my day started, although we may not take off until 8:00. But we went and got our breakfast. We went to our briefing, where they explained where the target was and how we were going to get there. They explained the route they picked out, to eliminate as much flak interference as possible. And they told you all this sort of stuff. If everything worked right, we were back by 1:00 anyway— if you came back.

After the morning briefing, I pre-flighted the plane, checked it out all over. Our crew assembled and we got into the plane and took off, and we went up and circled around until we got all the other elements of that particular group together. So we would fire a color-coded flare and these other planes then would see that and they would come and join us. When we got all assembled and took off over the Channel, then we really started climbing to our altitude. From then on, nothing else mattered, because you were busy.

*

We were the lead crew from our seventh mission on. I don't feel we were doing anything heroic or anything like that. We were doing our job, but the job had risks. Statistics ruled.

There was another mission that I remember when we were establishing a bridgehead across the Rhine.[41] The front was only about a quarter-mile wide. Two hundred and fifty Liberators were sent up for this mission with no bombs, but we had wicker baskets filled with ammunition and supplies and food, and one thing or another. And we flew that mission over the Rhine at about 500 feet in the air, right down in the deck. And they were throwing rocks at us, we were so low! [*Laughs*] And we were the elite crew in that mission. We had everybody and anybody important in the squadron who wanted to go on that mission, all the 'big wheels.' So we could have a full colonel as a copilot, or something like this, because all the brass wanted to go, you know? We dropped these baskets of supplies in that perimeter, but they were so low half the time the chutes didn't fully open. They'd hit the ground and they'd start

---

[41] *a bridgehead across the Rhine*- On March 7, 1945, the 9th Armored Division found the only intact bridge remaining across the Rhine River at Remagen, which the Germans had neglected to destroy. For ten days American troops poured over the bridge into the German heartland before the damaged Ludendorff Bridge finally collapsed. Miller, Donald L., *The Story of World War II.* New York: Simon & Schuster, 2001. 496.

bounding across, and we would see people running for dear life every place we could look. I remember that one. We lost 25 planes in that mission because before we could even turn, we were over the German lines. And they were throwing everything at us! Fortunately I was in the lead plane so they'd shoot at us, but it would hit the plane in the back of us, I imagine. I remember I wasn't too concerned about it at the time. That's part of history, that bridge at Remagen. We did take that bridge—the ground troops did, but I guess we had a hand in it.

*

At the debriefing after the mission, the first thing they did was they gave us about three ounces of Irish whiskey; the beautiful part of that was we had six members of our crew who didn't drink. I always brought my canteen with me and they took their whiskey and we poured it in my canteen. I shouldn't tell you that, but it's true. [*Chuckles*] Incidentally, the bombardier became an Episcopalian minister. His name was Marshall V. Minister, and he became a minister!

They wanted to know everything that we saw in the flight. How heavy the flak was, how many fighters were in the air, anything that had to do with anything, but they were more concerned with the flak than they were about anything else. And, well, they should have been, because I think we lost more planes to flak than we did with anything because you couldn't defend against it. But they wanted to know everything about the flight—they had officers debriefing in one group, and the enlisted men in the other group. They got every opinion on what happened, and that's what they used to plan the next mission.

Interviewer: Do you recall your feelings when FDR died?

FDR? He was a great president, great president. Now I see they got some jerk who wants to take his picture off the dime and put Ronald Reagan's on it. Yes, that's what these [politicians] are trying to pull now. And what they're doing today is ridiculous, and I'm not going to get into that, but anybody that can read ought to know what I am talking about... I get disturbed. I find it hard to watch—why are we doing it [Iraq War, 2003]? How long are we going to be there? Do you see the end of it? I can't understand it. We've seen troubles over there for over 2,000 years, so what makes [the president] think we can change it? You can't. I don't know what the answer is; I don't know when the end of it is going to be, either. I do know there's going to be a lot more people killed before it ends.

Interviewer: What do you think about Truman's decision on dropping the bomb on Japan?

Well, I don't think it was necessary at the time because Japan was already beat, and so was Germany. But I never knew of any weapon that was ever made that wasn't used. It probably did save a few hundred thousand American lives because they wouldn't have had to invade the Japanese mainland, which would have been costly—so for that part of it, maybe. But I think that we could have done the same thing with conventional bombs, because, actually, they had no defense against the B-29 anymore. No, I don't think it was really necessary—but I don't think anybody ever made any bomb that they didn't use. When they developed that, there were a lot of worries about it—some scientists were even afraid that it would set the atmosphere on fire, with the hydrogen in the atmosphere and one thing or another. They never knew what it exactly was going to do, but they did it anyway. Now what do we have now? Now it's proliferated all over the world, and we can't stop it. Why did Truman use it? I don't know. Thought he was going to save some people, and I guess that's what he did. We were the only ones that had it. We thought we were, but we had a lot of people in this country that sold us out. They gave it to Russia, some of our own patriots. If there's a buck in it, they'll do it. I hope that answers your question.

*

'The Guy Who Will Kill My Son'

There was a British lieutenant colonel I was talking to in London. That's the period when they were bombing London with the V-2s. That was the rocket bomb; they went up into the air and came down. [*Motions with hand*] A big sign on the building fell down. I sit there looking at it, and this colonel is looking at it.

'Boy, they got that one.'

'Yes', I said, 'it happened nearby the day before, so it was weakened, so it finally fell on a bus.'

He says, 'Tell me, Yank, what do you think about this anyway, when you're dropping your bombs?'

I said, 'I don't think anything about it. I never see it; it's impersonal to me.' But I said, 'I know that we probably killed a lot of innocent people. Women and children, they didn't do anything.' I said, 'I kind of feel sorry for them.'

He said, 'Why?'

I said, 'My God, they didn't do anything!'

'No, but you want to remember something: out of their bellies will come the guy who will kill my son 20 years from now.'

They had 20 years apart, World War I and World War II, so he had no sympathy for them at all. That's the way the British felt about it. Of course, they took a lot more punishment than we did; remember, they got bombing and everything else you can think of. We didn't get that in this country. This country never had that. And our attitude would change a lot if we ever did, believe me. And it could happen today. With the kind of technology we have today, there's no place in this world that's out of range. And we're not exactly loved in this world, and we did that to ourselves. We can't run the world. I don't want to tell you my politics, but...

*

I was in Liverpool Street Station in London when they announced that the Germans had surrendered. I was just coming back from a three-day leave. So I got right off the train, turned around, and got right back to London and stayed three more days. [*Laughs*] I knew I was going to catch hell, but I did it. So they took care of me when I got back to the base; they asked me if I had a good time. I said, 'Yes.' [*Laughs*] Every day from then on, for two weeks at 4:00 in the morning, they had me flying with every pilot there was, up in the plane. They kept me going, I'm telling you. I didn't say a word. I shouldn't tell you that, but it's true. [*Laughs*]

We loaded our planes up with ground troops, people who didn't fly, non-flying personnel. Did you know that it took seven people on the ground to keep one man in the air? That was the ratio. So the people who flew were actually 12 or 13 percent of the fighting force. But these people on the ground who serviced our plane, who loaded the bombs, rebuilt the engines, all this sort of thing, they never flew. So after VE Day we loaded as many of them as we could get into the bomb bays, and we flew them at 500 feet in the air up the Rhine Valley so they could see the different places that we had bombed.

'Cologne Cathedral stands intact amidst the destruction caused by Allied air raids, Germany, 24 April 1945.' Source: U.S. Department of Defense. Department of the Army. Office of the Chief Signal Officer. Public domain.

We could see the railroad tracks all twisted, and at Cologne, the only building that had a roof on it was the cathedral.[42] Everything else was destroyed, it seemed—all the way up the whole Rhine Valley. The ground crews had a chance to see what their bombs did. Of course, a lot of them got airsick, because at just 500 feet it's pretty rough, because the plane bounces all over the external draft and one

---

[42] *The only building that had a roof on it was the cathedral*-After the 8th Air Force's last combat mission in late April 1945, planners were working on a May operation called 'Trolley,' *'to provide all ground personnel with an opportunity of seeing the results of their contribution in the strategic air war against Germany.'* One GI remarked, "The remarkably statuesque Cologne Cathedral was still standing with very little, if any, obvious damage to it... right directly across the street from it, one could see that the Cologne train station and rail yards had been completely and literally obliterated from Allied bombing! I am certain each of us privately wondered at the time (and perhaps even now) just what 'message' of war which this scene offered." Source: WW II Trolley Flights Overview, www.b24.net/trolley-missions-overview.

thing or another. So I had given each one of them an empty ammunition can, and they asked me, 'What for?'

I told them, 'You just keep it with you—pretty soon you won't have to ask me, you'll know.' [*Laughs*]

*

'I Don't Brood About It'

I was relieved when Germany quit; I felt pretty good, but that wasn't the end for us. That was only the end for the European part of the war. We were still at war with Japan, of course. So I went from there; finally we came back to this country. We landed in New Hampshire and then they transferred us to Fort Dix, then from there we went to Sioux Falls, South Dakota, to continue our training, in preparation for going to Japan, to the Pacific theater. See, in my original training, my graduating crew was split right into two, and half of us went to the European theater, and the other half went to the Pacific theater. So now, we were waiting then to see if we were going to be called to go to the Pacific theater, but the war ended when I was in South Dakota. That was VJ Day, and then it was a matter of time trying to get out because they were demobilizing so fast that they didn't have enough bases. I went to Lincoln, Nebraska, stayed there for a while. I went to Victoria, Kansas, stayed there for a while. Finally I wound up in Maryland, and I was discharged from there. But it took quite a while even after that to get out.

I liked Truman as president. He was very direct, and very honest, which is a rare commodity today. He didn't lie to us. Certainly what we have now lied to us for the reason for going into Iraq... Pardon me, I don't know what your politics are, but I'm just telling you what I think.... Why would we get into something with no idea how we're going to get out of it? We didn't learn our lesson in Vietnam?

We had no business in there, either. Those people didn't do anything to us. Nothing! That attack on September 11 had nothing to do with Iraq. The people who did that were Arabs; they were from Saudi Arabia, and it's one of our friends! They're friends as long as we got the bucks to buy the oil. I don't know. This world's a mess right now. I don't know where the end of it is, and you young people are the people who have to grow up in this. And I hate to think what is going to happen now.

*

It's not a very exciting thing, not to you. It was to me at times, but I have to tell you just like it is. I'm just telling you that I don't feel that air combat was such a personal thing. It only gets personal when you're flying through flak or got another plane coming at you or something—then it gets a little bit personal. So, like I say—what are you going to do? So I don't pretend to be a hero; I just did my job, and I was good at my job, too. I made it a point to be, because I wanted to learn everything about that plane that I could. [When I entered the service] I never expected to fly. I thought I'd be a mechanic at my age. Instead of that, I wound up over places; I'll never know how, but I did. I was in pretty good condition physically, I guess. Not very exciting, but that's the way it is.

I don't brood about it, I don't miss it, but I can remember most of it. What is different about it so much was the attitude of the people. It isn't like Vietnam, where you had people taking to the streets protesting a war or one thing and another. These are the things that I remember. It was quite an experience. I'm glad I went, but I'm not going again. Besides, I'm too old for that stuff now; I couldn't take it.

I have my problems—physical problems, naturally. I have such a high blood pressure now, I have to watch my diet; I see food, and I eat it. [*Laughs*] That's my diet. I figure I got this far doing what I want to do; I think I can go the rest of the way. Thank God I'm not senile, though. I lost my wife in '82; I was married to my wife in 1936. Oh, I wrote to her every day [during the war]. Every day. Oh yes, she was a wonderful girl. She was too good for me, and I've been living alone here since then. You could probably tell that just by looking around. You want to know what time it is? [*Motions to his collection of cuckoo clocks on the wall, laughs*]

*

Interviewer: Do you have any questions we could answer for you?

Your project, I think it's good. [I hope] it will get people an idea of what went on in those days. I don't think that it will make much of an impression, because it's not the way people think today. As I said, I don't think we'll see the level of patriotism that we had in the 1930s [and 40s]. I just don't. When you get to be my age, you look at a lot of things and wonder, you know? Of course, I've seen a lot in my lifetime, way back to the time of Herbert Hoover, and well before him. But I never saw anything like what we have got now. You think this invasion of Iraq was a good thing? Can you think of any reason for us being there? I mean, honestly. You're the people who are going to have to live with this, not me... It's not what you think. I don't really have questions except that I hope I have given anything you need; have I helped at all?

Interviewer: Yes, we appreciate it a lot. Thank you.

Well, you're nice kids. I wasn't going to do this, believe me.

Dick Varney passed away on April 28, 2008, just shy of his 97th birthday.

Richard Alagna, World War II.
Source: Richard Alagna.

CHAPTER SIX

The Ball Turret Gunner

I found Richard Alagna living in Saratoga Springs, New York, just to the south of 'Hometown, USA.' At 91, he was excited to hear of my interest in his story; he invited me down for a drink. 'You ever hear of the movie actor Jimmy Stewart? He was my commander.'

Richard Gregory Alagna was born on November 16, 1925, and was attending college in Brooklyn, New York, when the news of Pearl Harbor reached him. My wife and I went to visit with him and his wife.

'Did you know that my father served in the Navy, and then the Army? In World War I and World War II? He wasn't around much; I was an only child, and my mother raised me; she was a strong woman. She signed the papers for me, and said, 'Don't do anything stupid.'

Richard was anything but stupid. He went to Brooklyn Law School after the war on the GI Bill, passing the bar exam in New York. Only after that did he go for his undergraduate Bachelor of Arts degree! I asked him why.

'I just wanted to learn. I basically had gone into the Army at seventeen and a half years old. After the war and law school, I didn't really have a major; I just took classes, all kinds of subjects I was interested in. I racked up 132 credits in college; they kicked me out because I had too much.' Later, he also became a highly regarded painter and collected art.

He asked me about my world travels; I mentioned I had been to Germany. He said, 'Me, too. Actually, about 20,000 feet over it, dropping bombs.'

This interview was recorded in 2002 when he was seventy-seven years old. He served aboard the B-24 Liberator. I asked him if he kept in touch with his crew.

'No. I think they are all dead. I'm the last one.'

***

The Turret Gunner

Without the men who invented the turret, today's great bombing missions would be impossible. For without turrets, the bomber would be almost as helpless over enemy territory as an ordinary transport plane without a single gun.

The modern power turret-driven by electricity and mounted inside the bomber-was developed after many experiments in the 1930s and proved its worth in action in the second year of World War II. Its effect on air strategy was spectacular. At last the bomber-heavier and slower than the fighter plane-could really fight back. For turrets-little blisters of Plexiglas or safety glass, bristling with caliber .50s, swinging around to meet enemy fighters no matter where they come from-enable the bomber to match the enemy slug for slug in an air battle.

The top turret swings in a full circle; its guns move up and down from straight out to nearly straight up; it protects the whole top of the plane. The lower ball turret swings in a full circle and points its guns anywhere from straight out to straight down; it can fight off any attacker who comes from below. The tail turret throws out a big cone of fire toward the rear, and the nose or chin turret a heavy cone of fire straight ahead.

The turrets are spun around, and the guns raised and lowered, by electric motors or by hydraulic pressure systems run by electric motors. All the gunner has to do is hold on to the control handles of his guns and move them to steer the turret; the mechanism does the rest.

Armor plate or bulletproof glass will protect you as much as possible-though your best defense, like a good boxer's, will still be the offensive power packed by those caliber .50s.

If the turret power should ever fail, you will usually have a MANUAL SYSTEM for operating it by hand cranks. Some turrets even have foot pedals which enable you to fire the guns while using both hands to crank the turret into position. This is an important emergency protection; use it to keep your guns pointed at enemy fighters even though your fire cannot possibly be so accurate as when the power is on, for a motionless turret is an invitation for fighters to attack.

Even if the guns are out of order, keep tracking the enemy; if you can't hit him, you may at least scare him away. —Air Crewman's Gunnery Manual, 1944

***

Richard G. Alagna

The Funny Things

I like to tell the funny things that happened. I got into lots of trouble. Every time we went some place, they wanted me to do something I didn't want to do, like stay. [*Laughs*] But I never went AWOL in my life. I [just] didn't like the Army, I didn't like playing soldier.

I recall [the bombing of Pearl Harbor] was a Sunday morning; I was born in 1925, so I was still a kid, pretty young. Quite frankly, I didn't know where Pearl Harbor was. I think that everybody knew that we were going to go into a war, and it was as simple as that; I think the government and Mr. Roosevelt prepared us for that.

I enlisted [soon after]. I always wanted to fly; that was my goal in life. I wanted to be a bird, just fly in an airplane. I read all about the exploits of the World War I aces, and that's what I wanted to do. I was seventeen and a half when I graduated from high school, and I wanted to fly in naval aviation—the Navy flyers, Marine flyers were the best. They had to be very good because you had to be able to land a plane on nothing, on a boat that is going up and down. [*Makes wavelike motion with hand*] Then I found out that I had 20/20 vision in one eye and 20/30 in the other eye and none of the flying units—Army, Navy, or Marine—would take me. I was real depressed about that.

Then they came around with an exam called the 'A-12 exam,' and if you passed this examination you were qualified to be an officer; you had the mental ability to be an officer, which was minimal, as I would learn. They would send you to college, and this is where I have the big bone of contention with the government—which doesn't always tell you the truth, and everybody knows that. But I didn't know that at seventeen and a half years old, because I played it straight. They said they would send me to college, and I distinctly remember being given a choice of [studying about] political affairs, government—you know, what's going to happen when we take over a country, what are we going to do there, and so on. I had a great liking not just for flying but also for history and political science, and later I became a lawyer.

So I took the [officer] test and I passed. I managed to convince my mother that this was the thing to do, and she signed for me. I graduated high school and took another exam and was admitted to day session at Brooklyn College, which was a bit of an honor. I was only there a month or so [when the Army] papers finally came through, and I was to be sent to Alfred University. I did not know where Alfred University was, but I knew they had bells up there; they would wake you up and put you to sleep with bells.

When I got up there [to upstate New York] with all these other seventeen-year-old kids, they handed me some books and they handed me a very strange instrument, which turned out to be a slide rule. Now I don't understand mathematics, or whatever it is called. 'Two plus two' I get, [but other than that, you lose me]. They told me I was to be an engineer. I said, 'This is not what you told me.' They said, 'You're going to be an engineer.'

This was a reserve program. I was not sworn into the Army at the time, but I took the oath of allegiance. We plodded along, and I did not want to be an engineer; I didn't understand it, just hated it. I should have had prerequisites for some of the courses that they gave me, and I played catch-up like you wouldn't believe. It was very trying, even though I have a little grey matter. So we grumbled and mumbled our way through, and then we got good news—the Army Air Corps was lowering their eye requirements, so that if one eye was 20/30 they would take you into their flying program. I was in seventh heaven, and there were approximately twenty other kids with me who were in seventh heaven! You would think that the commander of this unit, who was a major, would be delighted to think that twenty young kids are willing to go out and fly. He was furious! We had gotten this information from a second lieutenant who had crashed and was on limited service. He had told us about this deal and that we were all pretty smart boys and that if we wanted to, we could take the air cadet test. Twenty of us went to the major and said we wanted out; he was furious. One boy said he wasn't going to go to classes anymore, so the major had him marching up and down, up and down. We all took an oath among us that we'd all fail, which was very easy for me because I hated what I was doing. I didn't have to study anymore, right?

We went to Fort Dix and we went en masse. Everybody who was in our unit went down there. The kids up there who had already passed their courses were razzing us—they said we were foolish, this and that, 'stay in the program.' Well, did they ever make a mistake, because the program they were in dropped dead right about then and there. They did not go back to Alfred University, they went into the infantry!

We were the boys they didn't know what to do with; we couldn't take orders. We were all very rebellious, bright boys; it was hard to push us around. The twenty of us passed the exam, not one of us failed, and they gave us a little card that said, 'Welcome to the Air Corps.' We went to our little barracks in Fort Dix.

I have to digress for a second because this is kind of important. I was bitten by a dog when I was very young, and I had the rabies injections with a big hypodermic needle. It was not a shot in the arm but a needle that would go into the wall of your stomach. Men would hold my arms and it was very painful. I don't like pain. So we're at Fort Dix and we get our [first set of] injections, and I don't like injections because I keep thinking about needles, and I get very upset. Anyway, we fall out into the street, and some of the guys who had passed the test were sent to Greensboro or someplace, and some guys were sent to some other place, and I'm waiting for my name to be called and it hadn't been called, about five or six of us still milling around. If you were there for a quarantine period you could get a pass. I got a pass, and where did I go? I went home, naturally.

I got home and my mother said to me, 'You don't look good.' My mother had been in training as a nurse. I said, 'I don't feel very good.' I was perspiring. She called the family doctor, and he came and he said, 'He has the measles.'

He said, 'I can't treat him, he's in the Army.' He made a phone call and they sent an ambulance. I went down in the ambulance. I don't think they let me sit up; they made me lie down. I got the chills and all kinds of nonsense, and they took me to Staten Island. They put me in a dark room and they told me I had the German measles; I think the quarantine period was fourteen days. So there I am, in the hospital. They promised that they would send a message to Fort Dix. They said I was cured. I asked, 'Can I go back home?'

They said, 'Absolutely not, private, you must go back to Fort Dix immediately.'

I went back to Fort Dix. Now when you get back on an Army post, the first thing you do is show them your papers, which I did, and then you sign a book that indicated that you got in and the date—this is very important. Signed the book, went to where I was sleeping; naturally all my gear was gone now, so I had to get more stuff, blankets or whatever. All the fellas who I had been with had left; they're gone, they're on their way, flying planes, they were killing Germans, I don't know. [*Laughs*] The weeks dragged on, they never called my name. Every day I would go out and stand in the street.

By the way, I was now a barracks chief. When I was in Alfred University, it was a cadet program. We had military procedure, how to write communiques, how to read the book. We knew the Army regs, we were officer material, and we were going to be officers of some sort. I knew how to march, how to do all the fancy nonsense. So when the new guys would come in, I'd teach them how to make beds and all kinds of things, where to go and all that. Come the weekend, I go home, got a pass, come back, comes the weekend, I would get a pass, go home, come back. I'm in Fort Dix, nobody's bothering me, I'm a king. Except the problem was, if you miss the [scheduled sequence] of injections, you have to go through them again. There was no way that I was going to have anybody stick a needle in me. I finally decided that this is ridiculous, and I began to ask, 'How about me? When am I going out?'

They said to relax.

I wandered down to the medical unit, and I said, 'I think it's time for me to get the second series of shots.'

They said, 'Who are you?'

I said, 'I'm Richard Gregory Alagna, 12228219.' The serial number is exceptionally important, because if you don't know it you can't get off the base. I have forgotten everything else, I sometimes have to look up my own zip code, my telephone number, but I will never forget '12228219,' because you can't get a drink, you can't go play with the girls. Well, all hell broke loose! This officer came over and he started to scream at me. He said I was 'absent without leave.' I was not AWOL.

I said, 'I was in the hospital, they sent you a telegram. I was in an Army hospital, [and when I returned] I signed the book.'

He was real nasty, and he said to me, 'You're going out on the first shipment.'

I said, 'Where to?'

He said, 'What did you say?'

I said, 'Where?'

Understand, I had had three months of being a cadet; I realized that nobody tells you the truth, they knock you around, and you have to grow up awful fast.

He said, 'You're going into the infantry. You don't have any service records, we have no record of your passing the exam, and we have no record of you. When your service records catch up with you, they'll transfer you to the Air Corps.'

I said to him, 'May I talk to you man to man?' I was all of eighteen years old. 'You know in your heart that once the infantry gets me, they're not going to let me go. They're not going to transfer me after they teach me what to do in the infantry. I have this booklet.' I had this booklet that said I was an air cadet.

He said, 'Anybody can get one of those.'

I said, 'It's typewritten and I don't know how to type. Give me the [air cadet] test. I can take the test blindfolded.'

He looked at me and said, 'You really did pass that exam, didn't you?'

I said, 'Yes, sir, I did, and all I want to do is fly. I got a shot at it; you have to let me do it.'

'I will send you out in the first group to the Air Corps, and I hope to God you're not lying to me.'

'I swear I'm not lying!'

Here comes the fun and games. They send me out to the Air Corps without any of my permanent service records, my hospitalization stuff was lost, and I don't even remember if I went through the second series of needles. I didn't care at that point. I was with men who were thirty-eight up to forty-two years old; they were going to be the laborers in the Air Corps—they were going to build the barracks, grade the roads, and do the menial things. Remember I was eighteen at the time. Every time I fell out, an officer would come by and say, 'What are you doing with these people?'

I would say, 'You don't want to know, unless you have my service records.' I would talk to everybody; anytime a captain, a major, anybody, came by, I'd plead with them, 'Find my records, I'm supposed to be on the other side of the field taking air cadet training!' I wrote letters for these men, I listened to them cry at night. They had never been away from home. One man had a funny story; he and his son both went down to the draft board—his son was rejected, and he went in.

Finally the major called me in and said, 'I've got some good news for you and some bad news for you, private.'

I said, 'Let's hear the good news, sir.'

'We've got your service records and you are an air cadet trainee.'

I said, 'That's wonderful!' I was in seventh heaven; I'd already gone through basic training. The bad news was I think it was 47,000 cadets were now washed out, summarily; zap, gone, finished! They weren't killing enough of us, so they cut the program down.

I said, 'What does it mean?'

He said, 'Well, I've got a problem. We don't know what to do with you.' These air trainees were being sent back to their old units. They had transferred from the infantry or the ski troops or God-knows-what.

'But you've never been in a unit other than the Air Corps. How would you like to get back [in line] as a flyer? If you volunteer to be an aerial gunner, when you finish your missions and you come back, you can get to be a flyer. I will personally see to it.'

I'm listening to this guy and I'm saying to myself, 'Who the hell is he kidding?' Although I did know a navigator who finished his missions, came back into training, and became a pilot. It wasn't such a bad deal.

'Malfunction'

So I'm now going to fly. They sent me to the place to become an aerial gunner. You have to understand, I really did want to fly, wanted to see what it was like, wanted a taste of this. Because of my height, they said I'd become a ball turret gunner. They told me later that the tail gunners wouldn't go down in the ball. I had to gain a little proficiency, mechanical ability. If you recall, I said I can't add 2+2; that is, I don't like to. They made me learn the machine gun, which was the basic thing. There was a group of two flight engineers, two radio operators, an armorer/gunner, and myself. I was the only career gunner, I think it's called a '612' or something like that.[43] You had to learn how to field strip the machine gun, you had to be able to take the machine gun apart and put it together, and we were supposed to be able to do it blindfolded. I was always very rebellious and always liked to make a joke. I would put the machine gun together and there would be a couple of parts left over and the sergeant didn't like that.

I said, 'It looks okay to me,' because it's flipped in the case. 'Why do I have to do it blindfolded?'

He said, 'If you're flying a night mission and you burn out a barrel'—we had extra barrels on the plane, we could put them in—'you have to be able to do that.'

I said, 'If it's night time and [whoever is trying to kill me] can't see me and I can't see him, why do I have to do this?' My concept was if we just keep the lights off in the plane, he'll go away. [*Laughs*]

---

[43] '612'-Military Occupational Specialty (MOS): MOS: 612 Armorer/Gunner

The gunner on a bomber is not supposed to be looking for trouble; he's supposed to make the trouble go away. [I had to keep doing it]; I went at night on my own time, and they gave me the nickname 'Malfunction' because I couldn't get the thing together. It's important that you know that I understand how things work, I just don't seem to have the ability to hold on to a screw without dropping it six times. I don't know the nomenclature of the tools that most men know, certain screwdrivers and certain bits. I just have no interest in that.

*

Now I'll tell you about people. When you fire a machine gun, it's not like a pistol or a rifle. It jumps all over the place, and a lot of guys would be quite frightened of it. Everybody had to fire this weapon. They had them fix mounted on a tripod, and they had a track that [a target] would go around towed by a Jeep with a governor on it to make the Jeep go around without anybody in it. It would go around and around, and when it would come by, you would shoot the machine gun. It was a .30 caliber gun, and the first time I went out to this range, it came by, I went 'bang-bang,' and a cartridge exploded in the barrel, in the breech! I had no glasses on, and I was hit in the face with the cordite, and it caused little blood spots; some of it was indented in my face, and when it kicked back like that, I went right down to the ground. The sergeant came over—if I ever met him today, I'd kill that son-of-a-bitch. I mean it, because he said to me, 'What are you, a coward? Get up, clear it, and do it again.' I knew later what was wrong with the weapon, but I didn't know at that time. Naturally, everybody's looking at you, peer pressure, and I want to do this thing, so I started again, and it blew up again! This time when I'm on the ground, I saw a pair of saddle shoes and pinks.[44] The only ones that wear pinks are officers, and this officer said to me, 'Are you all right?'

There were little specks of blood on my face, and I said, 'Yes, sir, I'm fine, it happens all the time.'

He said, 'What happens all the time?'

I said, 'The thing opens up, it explodes, the bullet comes out all over your face.'

He said, 'This happened more than once?'

Well, he dressed that sergeant down. The sergeant came over and whispered in my ear, 'I'll kill you if you ever come back here.'

I could have lost an eye, could have lost both eyes! I didn't realize until later that [he knew] the gun wasn't put together properly. What possesses somebody to be that callous? I couldn't put my finger on it; I didn't know why this guy would do this, at the risk of having some kid lose an eye. He had a cushy job, not being shot at, some place in the States, Florida, Texas, wherever the hell we were. Why did he do that? I couldn't figure it out. I couldn't figure out a lot of things.

*

Cute story. I was still in gunnery school at the time, but we're sitting around not doing anything, not going anyplace. They said that they needed some volunteers—that's a bad word, by the way, as everybody knows. The deal was that if you pulled guard duty for a week, you'd get a pass to go to New Orleans. I said, 'Okay, fine, I'll do it.' They gave me a carbine; I checked it out. I was very good with weapons now, and I now got live ammo. I'm marching back and forth, back and forth, in the heat. There were some tents there, not too far away, about 100 feet, and there were some guys who had been flying Catalinas, they were doing submarine patrol down in

---

[44] pinks- 'Officers' pinks,' so-called for the pinkish hue of the stripe on their American uniform khakis.

New Orleans. I'm going back and forth, back and forth, back and forth, sweating like a pig. I can't see this nonsense about marching, because to me, all you had to do was stand in one place and you could turn your head and look back and forth, but that was what the Army wanted you to do. So I noticed a kitten, and the kitten was spitting at something. I got closer to it, and it was one of the biggest rattlesnakes I have ever seen; it was a doozy! The kitten is going to get bitten and die, so I'm calling the kitten, but the kitten won't come over. I figured I never missed anything in my life when I shot, so I pulled back the slide on the carbine, took aim at the snake. This guy in the tent sees me, and he's calling me a son-of-a-bitch because he thinks I'm shooting at the kitten! I pulled the trigger, nothing happens. I eject the bullet, do it again, and nothing happens. They're lying to me again! I then yelled for the sergeant of the guard. This snake is a goddamned big snake. I figured that if the snake gets into the tent area, they're going to have a hell of a hard time. The sergeant comes over in a Jeep, and I'm trying to figure how I can hit the snake, move the kitten off to the side; I'm beside myself. He pulled out his .45, but this guy couldn't hit a goddamned barn if he was sitting next to it. He pointed it at the snake and missed, shot three times.

'Sergeant,' I yelled, 'let me have the gun, I can hit the snake.' I could hit anything; I hit the target all the time. He got pissed, managed to kill the snake. Now I'm complaining about why my carbine wouldn't go off. I found out they had filed the firing pin so it wouldn't strike. What the hell was I doing with a gun that couldn't work? He got mad at me and he made me stay in the barracks. He said he was going to have me up on charges, and I didn't know what kind of charges he was referring to; I didn't do anything wrong, I tried to kill the snake. He couldn't shoot worth a damn. Maybe I said something, but now I'm in trouble and I don't know what it is.

I went into the latrine, and guess who's sitting there? The latrines have no stalls back then, and there he was, sitting there on the throne. He glared at me; I didn't say anything to him. He got up and left.

I relieved myself and I looked over to where he had been sitting, and he had taken off his heavy canvas belt that had his .45 on it. I was delighted because you can't lose your weapon, you cannot lose your weapon. I picked up the .45, and I said to myself, 'Richard, heave it into the jungle, no one will see you. Let him sweat to figure out where his .45 is.' Then another voice went off in my head, which said, Just because he's a son-of-a-bitch, you don't have to be one.'

I went over to where his office was, knocked on the door, and he snarled at me, 'What do you want?'

I said, 'I want to give you this.' [*Extends hands*] He went like this [*Moves hands to sides*] and realized his cannon was missing, his .45.

I said, 'You left it in the latrine.'

He realized that I wasn't such a bad guy, and he said, 'Forget about the charges, you're free to go back to your unit.'

I said, 'Wait a minute, how about my pass to New Orleans?'

He said, 'You kids from New York'—he was a Southerner—'you have a pair of balls on you that I can't believe.'

He gave me a pass to go to New Orleans; he laughed, I laughed. He would have been in a lot of trouble not to have had his weapon. I went to New Orleans and had a very good time. I went with another guy who was a gunner; it was fun, we had a fun time.

*

After learning how to strip and fix a machine gun and all that, I had to learn how to work the ball turret. The ball turret was an instrument of death, torture, the most ridiculous thing they thought of. It was self-contained, it was held on by a big ring, and on the B-17 it was permanently out of the plane. On the B-24 there was a shaft, and hydraulically you'd drop it and then you'd get in it. It was exceptionally tight—you could not wear a parachute in it; you could wear your harness but you couldn't wear the parachute. When I had to get in it, I always had to turn my face sideways and put my face down on the gun sight and then signal the guy above to slam the door, and invariably I'd get hit on the head with the door. It was not very comfortable.

Let me digress again. If you recall, I desperately wanted to fly. I'd been with men that were thirty-eight, forty years old, and our training was nothing, and I'd gotten fatter and fatter and lazier and lazier because I wasn't really doing anything; I was so badly out of shape that I was a good twenty pounds overweight. I was about 185 at the time. When we got to gunnery school and I'm taking the machine guns apart and all that, I had to play catch-up with the physical part. I was never much of an athlete when I was young, but I would run with everybody and do everything they did, except I just couldn't get over the wall. I'd hit the wall and my nails would scrape on the wall. I'd always get just my fingers up there. I'm short; some of these guys were six foot, and they could just bounce up and grab it and pull themselves up.

There was an officer who thought I was horsing around. I said, 'I'm trying,' and I hit that wall. He did catch me once going around it. When I was in high school the coach always yelled at me because they used to make me go around the track, and I used to go around, then cut across, and then go in the back and read a book. I was the kid who liked to read, and I didn't want to play any of their games.

On my own I went out at night after we did everything we were supposed to damn-well do and I ran, losing weight. I even put crap in a knapsack to try to lose weight. I think I got over the wall. The officer was going to wash me out, but it got to the point where he realized that nobody in their right mind would hit the wall like I hit that wall; I would have gone through the goddamned wall if I could have. I couldn't get my hands up there! Forget about going up the rope. I could not go up the rope, but I did build my chest up; my arms were pretty strong. Anyway, he passed me on that.

*

I wanted to fly, and now we had to get into a plane, a B-17, and do our stuff that we were taught on the ground. Underneath the seat of the ball turret was an oxygen tube. We wore an oxygen mask with a certain length of tubing to connect to the oxygen supply. We went up in a B-17 and they outfitted it with long benches. My last name begins with an 'A' and I was always first, which was lots of fun, because it would have been nice to learn by watching the other fellow go first for a change. [We're in the air] and I'm supposed to go down into the turret, hook up to the oxygen, and I'm supposed to stay down there and then they'll tell me come on up. We're flying above the level at which you could breathe on your own well; you could get anoxia, get brain damage, and die. You get silly, too. I went down into the turret, put my head down, [had the hatch] slammed shut, but I was not breathing the oxygen, just breathing the air that was in there, pretty thin. I reached for the tube and I got it in my hand, and I can't make contact. I was breathing heavily and I'm nervous and I don't know how many minutes went by, but I do know that I can't stay there because I'll pass out, and frankly, I didn't know how they would then get me out from above. The sergeant was saying to me on the radio, 'Aren't you going to get it going?'

I said, 'I can't breathe, I can't connect.'

He called me a coward. I was mortified. I was really very upset.

I heard the pilot saying, 'Get him the hell out of the turret.'

I got out and I hooked up to oxygen in the plane and guys are looking at me kind of funny. The pilot orders the sergeant who's training us to go down and see if what I said was true. He said it was true. Nobody else went down in the turret. We landed, and the sergeant was a very good kid; he made all the men stand there and he apologized to me. It seems that some schmuck idiot jerk cut the tube too short. It had frayed, and no one was even thinking that the oxygen mask won't connect; some of these guys just didn't think these things through. That was the reason, and the sergeant apologized, and I felt pretty good.

Speaking of anoxia—stay in the middle and never volunteer, right? We go into the pressure tank and they simulate the altitude that you're going to go up to, and what the pressure is. The sergeant says, 'We need three volunteers.'

I thought, 'Boy, this is great, this time I'm in the middle.'

He says, 'You, you, and you,' and I was right in the middle.

One guy had to write with a pad and pencil, the other guy had to do something, I forget what, and I had to do exercise, because this will show how a guy will pass out. They started the simulation, you get giddy, you begin to laugh, because it's a great high. The lights got dim in the place, it looked like it was a rheostat, and I'm getting giddy and they slap an oxygen mask on me and give me pure oxygen. The other guy who was writing, his handwriting was going up and down, and he finally passed out and they gave him oxygen.

*

The Crew

I met my crew; now, the crew is very strange. The pilot was an old man. At that time I was nineteen or twenty, the pilot was 28 or 29, and that was very old. He didn't take the wire out of his hat, his garrison hat—there was a wire that if you took it out and crunched it, you got that fifty-mission Air Corps look. He had transferred from the infantry, and was Southern, and I don't think he realized that the Civil War was over.

The second officer was from Kansas; he went to the University of Kansas, and he couldn't fly worth a damn. He was probably the worst pilot in the Air Corps; he was obnoxious. The navigator was a nice guy, he was a couple of years older than I am, he was an accountant. He was a flight officer, not an officer—that's the difference between an enlisted man and an officer; you're some place in limbo, they gave you a bar with a little color in it, some nonsense like that. We had a bombardier who was afraid. He got us up to 30,000 feet one time and said his bombsight didn't work and he couldn't use it. We went back down; it takes a long time to go up to 30,000 feet. It turns out he just didn't plug it in. We went on a practice mission, supposed to hit a target on an island surrounded by water, surrounded by a federal reserve park. He hit a farm; he was worthless! He didn't go overseas with us. I thought he was stupid then; later on, I realized that he just liked to walk around in an officer's uniform with a pair of wings. He always wanted everybody to call him 'Lieutenant.'

The nose gunner was a delight. I don't know if he had a high school education, but he was an engineer, he had mechanical ability. He loved to smoke cigars. The radio operator was a millionaire's son. They owned a big, well-known fish cannery. Jimmy was Catholic and he couldn't make up his mind if he wanted to be a priest or marry a girl. He showed us a picture of the girl and it reminded me of the center for Notre Dame. [*Laughs*] On the very first mission—and this is one of my anti-Catholic stories—Jimmy took his Saint Christopher's medal and he hung it in the cockpit, and the navigator had a fit because the pilot couldn't fly the plane correctly because it demagnetized the compass. There was good old Saint Christopher, leading us around in circles. [*Laughs*] Needless to say, that medal wasn't used on any more missions.

The engineer, his name was Brockmeyer; he looked very young but he was competent at what he was doing. He could fix anything on the plane, did all the magic things. He was a slight kid and he was a wise guy. Once he picked me up in an automobile and said he had hot-wired it. I got out of the car instantly; this kid had stolen the car!

The armorer/gunner, Neil, was a nice guy. Neil was from Connecticut and Cornell. Most of the kids on the crew were college men. He was in advanced training and I could have killed him, I hated him for this. He had it! He was in advanced training for flying, he was the cadet officer, and they gave him his orders to go to heavy bombers, to fly multiple engines. He wanted to be a fighter pilot, as we all did; we all wanted to be Eddie Rickenbacker.[45] He got to a guy who wanted to go to bombers; he wanted to make a switch [to fighters]. He must have said it in a loud voice because the Army brass got wind of it and they washed him out. You don't tell the Army what to do. He ended up in heavy bombers. [*Laughs*] But when I heard his story, I nearly died because I was just dying to get my hands on the controls of the plane, though I did fly the plane once or twice, but just when we were in the air. I liked him; he was a very nice guy.

The tail gunner was a ski trooper; they were going to send him back, and he became a tail gunner. He was from the University of Chicago; we had Harvard, we had college men on the crew. The only two non-college kids were the nose gunner and the engineer.

Westover Field

We were in training and we're up at Westover Field [in Massachusetts]. We're flying very old planes; these were not the ones we flew in combat. Now we had some old planes in combat, but these were bad planes. While I was there, one kid from the Bronx, nice kid, said to me—I was looked upon as a guy who had the training before, and I could handle some of the officers by giving them what

[45] *Eddie Rickenbacker*- Medal of Honor recipient and America's top fighter ace in World War I with 26 kills, 1890-1973.

they wanted—he said, 'I can't take it.' He said every time he got into the plane he thought it was going to blow up, and he couldn't go near a plane again. I told him it's not a disgrace because we're supposed to be in a team, and if a unit can't function together, you're not helping the guy next to you, and you're going to let him down when it's important. I told him to go see the commanding officer, which he did, and tell him exactly what he told me. Later, I met him at Fort Dix when I was being discharged. He ended up as a sergeant in the infantry; he saw hand-to-hand combat in the Philippines. The point I always made is that everybody had a point where they'd snap, where they just sat there and couldn't function.

Now I'll tell you about this great co-pilot we had. We're still in the States, and I'm down in the ball turret. In this turret, you lower it down, it comes out the belly of the plane, you have to jump down in it, open it up, get in, and it's all hydraulic and electric. I'm listening on the interphones and I don't hear anything except the engines. It's deafening, by the way, flying in a four-engine bomber. There are some portholes, and I had my hands on the handles to make my turret turn, and it wouldn't go. It was dead in the water. I looked up in the portholes and I saw some of the guys running around and I thought I saw one of the guys put on a parachute! Normally we just wore chest chutes and the parachutes were kept separate, because it was an additional weight you had to stand up with.

I turned on the radio and tried to speak and I couldn't hear my own voice—if you can't hear your own voice, it's not coming through your headset, ergo, something's wrong. I realized that now I had to go back to my training, that there's a way to get out of the turret. You cannot drop out of the ball turret when it's in the air, but there were some cranks and you could manually crank the turret around and it would come up to where you could get out. Your memory has to be 'A' perfect because you had to then lock it. If you didn't lock it, when you got up to get out, it would spin and you would lose your legs. Thank God the sergeant who trained me told me that. I did exactly what he told me to do, and that's what comes with training. Training is a very important thing; you must do what you're supposed to do, what you're trained to do, and improvise when you have to. So I locked it, got out, pulled myself out of the well. Everybody's got their parachutes on! I put my parachute on. One of the guys said, 'We have lost electrical power.' The plane will still go, like an automobile, because the gasoline is flowing into the engines. The pilot's going crazy; the engineer is running around trying to figure out what the hell is wrong with the damn thing. He had rung the 'get ready to bail out' bell, and that's what I saw through the porthole, but I didn't hear it; there's no bell in the turret. I immediately thought that there should have been a bell in the turret or that somebody should have taken a wrench and whacked on the shaft three times or whatever so I would know to get out!

Now don't forget, this story is about the co-pilot. The co-pilot's supposed to be in charge of the gunners, that was his job. He was supposed to coordinate things that we were supposed to do. So they got the problem fixed, the music goes back on, the radio's on, everybody's happy. Up comes the turret; I'm not going down there again, not that day. Now I can't tell other guys what to do, I don't have the rank, but I was slightly pissed at them. They had to think for themselves, because when they say, 'get ready to bail out,' they're going to go—they're not going to come and hold my hand.

We landed, and the first thing I did was walk up front, and I said to the co-pilot, 'They rang the bell to get ready to bail out, but there's no sound in my turret. I would like you to instruct the gunners back there to give me some kind of a signal when that happens, so I can get out.'

This is what the son-of-a-bitch said. 'When I bail out, I'll wave to you as I go by.'

He was a big football player; I'm five foot seven and a half, but I'm from Brooklyn, and you don't say things like that. I grabbed him. You're not supposed to touch an officer, it's against the rules.

I turned him around and said right to his face, 'As God is my witness, if I get my guns around fast enough, I'll blow you out of the sky, and if I get down on the ground, I'll hunt you down and I'll kill you.'

I let go of him. Now I've got a problem, because you don't touch an officer and you don't threaten him. I went back to the barracks and told one of the guys from another crew what happened.

'I'm going to be called up, I'm going to go see the commanding officer.'

He said, 'No you're not, he's not going to say a word. Did he say that to you? Will you say that to the commanding officer? He's not going to say a word.'

So he didn't say a word, I didn't say a word, I don't think I ever spoke to him unless he asked me a question. We put in a system where you bang on the turret.

*

They always had to test your ability to function as a gunner, and they would put film next to your machine gun and it would film through your gun sight. We had very special gun sights, a Sperry invention. It had a line [*draws imaginary horizontal line with index finger*] and you had to do all kinds of crazy things. It was very unique. You had to recognize the aircraft you were firing at, it had to be a certain length, et cetera, and you'd set it in quickly into your gun sight, which is actually a computer. Then you had to cross it. You did everything—you did it with your feet, with your hands, it was quite a complicated thing but allegedly it was very accurate. The first time [all the gunners had to use it], I'm down in the ball turret. One of the gentlemen, I'm sure it was an officer, used the relief tube. A relief tube is a funnel, and you would urinate into this funnel and the urine would go out the plane and it would come back and splash over the turret. Now a little urine is not going to hurt you, but it colored the entire area of the turret where my gun sight would function. I had a problem, because they brought this plane up and they wanted me to shoot at the target, and I couldn't very well shoot at it, so I used my finger and I went like this [*waves index finger in air*], and I made some film [for them]. When we went to the briefing, everybody had good grades, and they said, 'The ball turret gunner is very creative, but we figured out it had to be his finger because we played it over and over again.'

Up we go again, and I told them in the front of the plane, 'Don't use the funnel until I'm out of there.' Well, they did it again. This is no joke because we had to go up pretty high and we had to be on oxygen. You piss on me once, you piss on me twice, the third time you don't get a shot at it.

The third time I heard the co-pilot say, 'I wet my leg, my leg is wet!'

The pilot said, 'What do you mean you wet your leg?'

'I had to use the relief tube and it's been cut.'

The pilot said to me, 'Did you cut the relief tube?'

I said, 'Me, sir? Not I, sir.' I cut it. [*Laughs*]

When we got the film back for that run, I got a commendation, which made me very happy because they used my film for a training film.

The tail gunner was a character. He had a knife; he was Jewish and he always carried a knife. My father was Roman Catholic and my mother was Greek Orthodox. I joined the Protestant Church because I was fed up with all the fighting in the family about which church I should belong to. In the barracks one time, a drunk came in and he called me a dirty Jew.

I got up, and one of my crew members grabbed me and said, 'You're not Jewish.'

I said, 'Fuck him.' The point of the story is that anti-Semitism permeated the Army and all of our lives back then, and it just wasn't very nice.

*

We hadn't gotten overseas yet. At that particular time I bought a fountain pen, a Waterman, guaranteed for life, and it broke. [*Laughs*] I was very superstitious, most guys were superstitious. And then there was the fire [on the plane].

Everybody on an aircraft had to be trained to do somebody else's job in case they got sick. My nickname was 'Malfunction,' so they made me the assistant engineer—perfect, right? For example, they taught me how to transfer fuel, which is very important on a plane, even though I had absolutely no concept of where the fuel went [after it was transferred]; it just made the engines go around. I also learned to stand behind the pilot when we would land, and I would call off the air speed because you had to land at a certain air speed or you were in deep trouble. Back then there was always someone standing when you landed a plane, I don't think they do that anymore. But then my job, what the engineer did, I would then leave, go past the turret gunner, radio operator, drop down into a well with a catwalk where the bomb bays would go to the back, and I would go forward. At that point, everybody in the nose of the plane is out. That would be the nose gunner, navigator, bombardier; three people would be out. There was a machine there like a lawn mower, which had a pull, and it was called the 'putt-putt,' for want of another name. It provided the auxiliary power to run the generator on the aircraft so that you'd have electricity. When the plane lands, the nose wheel opens up; this was a B-24, and the wheel goes down and all the papers in the front of the plane would be blown all around the place. It was not my job, not that I'm saying 'not my job, I don't do windows,' but I had no knowledge that this was an important factor. It was up to those people that had their loose papers, whether they were maps or anything like that, to have them secure. So you pull the string and the machine starts. I pull it and it belched fire! On an airplane, like on a boat, fire is not a nice thing. By the way, I heard a story that one guy got a Congressional Medal of Honor, at least the story went, because he pissed on a fire, which I thought was a very cute story; I don't believe it. Anyway, I put the fire out with my hands, and when I got it out, naturally I wouldn't turn the machine back on because I still didn't know what the hell was going on. I went up and I screamed that there was a fire, and the radio operator, Jimmy Broderick, jumped down, took a fire extinguisher, and completely encased the machine in [fire retardant].

We were now traveling on the runway. The pilot rang a bell when he heard 'fire,' and the nose gunner went out the bomb bays and luckily he didn't get killed; he went into a rolling position—we had on leather suits and stuff like that. Well, it turned out that what had burned was a comic book—I have no idea whose comic book it was, but it had blown and caught in that machine! I think I told you that my pilot wasn't a very forgiving person—he accused me of having the comic book. I didn't read comic books. I was into reading whatever books I could carry, but I didn't read comic books. I was slightly incensed that I was accused of starting a fire on a plane. This man would accuse me, if it was raining outside, that I had ruined the day.

I'll tell you more about the navigator. We're in Westover Field and we are told that we're going to go on a night mission to Ohio, with no radio and only wing lights on. We had to navigate our way out to someplace in Ohio and practice bombing something out there, without actually dropping bombs. I [tried to convince] the pilot that it wasn't necessary for me to go on the trip. It's a night mission; there's nothing a gunner can do in the back. He said, 'You're flying!' So on the way back we get to the area of Westover Field and we drop down. He dropped his wheels down, and we gunners were supposed to use flashlights and look at the wheels to see if the pins came out, because if the pin didn't come out, it meant that the landing gear was not locked and it would collapse on landing. It's dark and I'm looking out and I've got the headset on, the wheels are down and locked, and the pilot said to the navigator, 'Are you absolutely certain that's Westover Field?'

The reason he asked is that there was an airfield at Hartford; I believe there was a Navy field there.

The navigator said, 'I'm reasonably certain.'

The pilot then pulled the plane up, and everybody went on their ass, and then the fight started.

He said, 'What do you mean? If I land the plane on a commercial airfield or a Navy field, I will be the laughingstock of the Air Corps!'

I look out the window and I said to the pilot, 'I know where the airfield is.' That's when the second fight started.

The navigator said, 'He's only a kid.' He was right, I was nineteen; he must have been about twenty-one or twenty-two, so really we're all in that category of being infants.

'You are going to listen to him?'

The pilot said, 'He said he knows where the field is.'

We're practically at treetop level now, and I told him what direction to go—straight ahead, to the left, to the right—and I said, 'The airfield is directly ahead.'

He made the signal, the lights went on, and we landed on our field.

The pilot came over, and he said, 'How did you know where the field was?'

I said, 'I followed the bus route.'

Any flyer will know that old-time flyers used to do sight navigation, and you would go down and read railroad crossings, and that's just what I did. I knew where the movie house was, and in Springfield, I'm positive that it's still there, is a good restaurant, the

Student Prince, good sauerbraten. The navigator wouldn't speak to me; I guess he didn't want to be put down.

Then there was the time we went on another night mission in Springfield, and as I told you my job was to look out the window and see if the wheels were up or down or if anything was wrong on the plane. We had windows in those old planes that lifted up. I had my Class A uniform on; it was the only way you could get off the post. I looked out this window and I was blinded, couldn't see, and I had a mouthful of gasoline! I fell to the floor, I was really in pain. I don't remember if I threw up or not.

The other gunner said, 'What's wrong?'

I said, 'I can't see, I'm blind, there's a gasoline leak!' Gasoline was just gulping out of the wings! He passed the word on; down we went, we landed.

I was sitting there, there was a canteen of water, somebody either put water on my face or I had washed my face, so now I could see. It turned out that when they fueled the plane up it wasn't level, it was at a tilt, and they put too much gasoline in. The mission was off. I unzipped my flight suit, put on my hat, and my pilot said, 'Where are you going?'

I said, 'I'm going to town.' He did not appreciate that; he thought I set that whole thing up because I had a pass to go to town.

Passes—it always annoyed me that the officers could go wherever they wanted but the enlisted men could not, so we created our own passes. We got a book of passes and we were under the impression—which was wrong, I found out later in law school; I thought that if you signed a phony name, it meant nothing. I remember once I was stopped by an MP [checking passes] in Times Square, and he said, 'Captain Midnight?'

I said, 'Yeah, that's my name' and got away with it. We would do things like that.

It's been often asked of me if flying was voluntary. Nobody would believe me when I said it was, you did not have to fly. At any time you could have just gone in and said, 'I'm out.' That wouldn't mean you'd be out of the Army, you just didn't fly. Where they would send you, God only knows. They'd send you some place; the Army wasn't going to let you go.

Ken Carlson, first row second from right,
and the crew of 'Myrtle the Flying Turtle.' Credit: Ken Carlson.

CHAPTER SEVEN

The Navigator

Kenneth R. Carlson was born in 1921 in New York City. As a boy in the Great Depression, he spent his summers at Glenburnie at the Lake George Camp, the northern fringe of the communities surrounding 'Hometown, USA.' He called me at home one evening, shortly after I had returned from swimming near there.

'Tell me about yourself, your family. I myself was from a middle-class family, but we were lucky in that I was able to attend what was probably the best private school in New York City. Incidentally, my tuition in grade school in the '20s was $250 a year; today a kindergarten slot is $45,000. I had a terrific education, even though I had to fight my way through the Irish gangs on 69th Street when I came back home from school.'

He tells me that the man who cuts his hair was an eight-year-old boy in occupied France. He would look up, see the twin tails of the B-24 Liberators coming or going to attack Germany, and wish them a silent prayer, hopeful that one day he would indeed be free.

'I think what you are doing is very important. I still go to speak to the students here a few times a year; when we got out of the service, I joined the 8th Air Force Historical Society here in New York and vowed to speak to kids. At 96, I'm still keeping that commitment. Years ago the

Smithsonian put out a book, High Honor, *of inspirational stories with World War II veterans, myself and twenty-nine other fellows. Get the book, but I wouldn't try to contact any of the other fellows. I'm the last one left.'*

The interview was recorded in 2003 when he was 82. He served aboard the B-24 Liberator.

***

Duties of the Navigator

Navigation is the art of determining geographic positions by means of (a) pilotage, (b) dead reckoning, (c) radio, or (d) celestial navigation, or any combination of these 4 methods. By any one or combination of methods the navigator determines the position of the airplane in relation to the earth.

The navigator's job is to direct your flight from departure to destination and return. He must know the exact position of the airplane at all times.

Pilot and navigator must study flight plan of the route to be flown and select alternate air fields.

Study the weather with the navigator. Know what weather you are likely to encounter. Decide what action is to be taken. Know the weather conditions at the alternate airfields.

Inform your navigator at what airspeed and altitude you wish to fly so that he can prepare his flight plan.

Learn what type of navigation the navigator intends to use: pilotage, dead reckoning, radio, celestial, or a combination of all methods.

Determine check points; plan to make radio fixes.

Work out an effective communication method with your navigator to be used in flight.

Synchronize your watch with your navigator's.

Miscellaneous Duties

The navigator's primary duty is navigating your airplane with a high degree of accuracy. But as a member of the team, he must also have a general knowledge of the entire operation of the airplane.

He must be familiar with emergency procedures, such as the manual operation of landing gear, bomb bay doors, and flaps, and the proper procedures for crash landings, ditching, bailout, etc.

After every flight get together with the navigator and discuss the flight and compare notes. Go over the navigator's log. If there have been serious navigational errors, discuss them with the navigator and determine their cause. If the navigator has been at fault, caution him that it is his job to see that the same mistake does not occur again. If the error has been caused by faulty instruments, see that they are corrected before another navigation mission is attempted. If your flying has contributed to inaccuracy in navigation, try to fly a better course next time. —

Duties and Responsibilities of the Airplane Commander and Crewmen, 1943

***

Kenneth R. Carlson

I'll never forget where I was when I heard [about Pearl Harbor]. My father had died in 1939 unexpectedly when I was 18. The only asset that we had was a brownstone home on 73rd Street and Lexington Ave. So I had my mother and grandmother to support and we lived in a 4th floor tenement, a walk-up. It was Sunday, and I was in the front room listening to the radio. Being a former athlete, I was listening to the Giants football game, and during that game there was an announcement that the Japanese had bombed Pearl Harbor. Even though I'd had a great education I wasn't sure where Pearl Harbor was. As a matter of fact I thought it was in the Philippines. So that's how I found out, and that's where I was. With no television, we had to wait for radio reports and read about it in the newspaper the next day. So it really didn't make that big an impression on me at that moment; I had no idea of what the magnitude of this bombing was until a day later. I felt this was unbelievable, because although I was well educated and was aware of the problems we had been having with Japan over the last few years, I felt that this could not have happened.

I decided to enlist. It took me a couple of days to think it all through and to read and to see newsreels and see what really had happened and the damage that had been done, what was really going on and how it related to the war in Europe. We declared war on Japan, and they were negotiating in Washington when the surprise attack took place. Two days later Germany declared war on the United States. That made my decision to go to war. I picked the Air Corps, I guess, because my father had taken me to see Charles

Lindbergh take off when I was seven years of age, to fly across the Atlantic. Being Swedish-American like me, he was a hero figure to me. And with my education I understood all about Billy Mitchell and the power of the Air Force and how it was going to be the future of any war. So in my own mind, I decided the best thing I could do was to become a fighter pilot and shoot down the Japanese who had attacked us. So two days later, I enlisted in the Air Corps, [even though I had never flown before].

When I enlisted I was just about to be married; I was 21 when I got married. But the Air Corps did not call me until January 1943, so it was a little more than a year before I was called to active duty. The reason for that was that they had very limited training facilities. So in January 1943 I got on a train with orders to report to Nashville, Tennessee, which was a reception and classification center. When I got there they took away my civilian clothes and gave me my uniform, which was two sizes too big. It was a GI uniform because at that time you enlisted as an Army private at $21 per month until you were accepted as an Air Corps cadet. That meant that you had to qualify as a pilot, a navigator, or a bombardier. Though I qualified to be a pilot, based on my gifted mathematical skills they wanted me to be a navigator. I didn't want to do that because in my own psyche I was set on being a fighter pilot and shooting down Japanese. But they told me I would have to wait six to nine months to get into pilot training, whereas if I accepted navigator training I could go immediately. So I accepted navigation.

I had no feeling for bombers and I had no idea where that was going to take me. They sent me to San Marcos, Texas, which was a navigation school. It had just opened, located between San Antonio and Austin. There I underwent six months of navigation training. In August 1943, I was commissioned a 2nd lieutenant. From there I was sent to Boise, Idaho, where the crew would be assembled; when I got to Boise I found out who my pilot was. He became my best friend and was just an unbelievable pilot. He was a small guy; his parents were from Czechoslovakia and his father was a bartender in Hollywood, California. All he wanted to do was fly, and his instructor was Jimmy Stewart, the actor. He didn't drink, he didn't carouse, and he was single. I met the rest of our crew and we were sent to a new air base in Mountain Home, Idaho, south of Boise. It had the longest runway in existence, and that is where we did our crew training. From Mountain Home we were assigned to Wendover, Utah, a little town one hundred miles west of Salt Lake City at the end of the salt flats right on the Nevada border. We lived off base in this place called the State Line Hotel. On the Nevada side they were drinking, gambling, and doing anything they wanted, but on our side, because of the Mormon influence, it was ice cream sodas and going to bed early. This is where we learned to operate as a bomber crew. Wendover later became the secret training base for the crew that dropped the atomic bombs on Hiroshima and Nagasaki.

The scary part about training in those days was that so many of us had [been brought up] to do things individually, but were hard-pressed to learn how to work together. We lost a lot of airplanes through poor maintenance, false navigation, and pilot error into the surrounding mountains of Nevada, so we experienced losses right there in training and we understood that not everyone was going to go down because of enemy fire. After we completed that training we were then sent to Harrington, Kansas, where we would pick up our own airplane and fly it to wherever it was ordered to fly. In Harrington the thing I remember most was sitting in the room while the pilot, Joe Roznos, signed a piece of paper that said he was responsible for a B-24J, which was a four-engine Liberator bomber. The J signified that it was a later model, which had a turret in the front with two machine guns instead of just two flexible machine guns that the navigator shot. He signed a paper for $250,000 worth of government property and that we would return it, and the question was, what if we don't come back? [*Chuckles*] They said, 'Don't worry about it.' When we picked up the plane, said goodbye to our wives or girlfriends (five of us were married and five were single), we were given orders to fly it to West Palm Beach, Florida, to Morrison Field. When we got there our passes were taken away and we were confined to the field, awaiting orders to see where we would be sent. At that time we were all hoping that we would be sent to the South Pacific and that we would be killing Japanese. When we got down the runway and opened our orders, we were sent on a southern route; our final orders indicated that we were to report to the 8th Air Force, which was headquartered in England, so we knew then that we were not going to be killing Japs—we were going to be killing Nazis.

The trip over was an unbelievable experience. As navigator I had to plot our southern route, which took us into Trinidad, then Brazil, and over to Africa. It took us 45 days because there were weather delays all along the route. This was the first time that I had ever left the U.S., the first time this city kid was about to see the world. The thing I remember most when we got to Brazil, where we saw three different towns before flying to Africa, was the tremendous poverty, disease, and filth. Young people were walking around naked; they were going to the bathroom in the streets, and had diseases such as elephantiasis, which I had never heard of.[46] So that was a big shock. When we left Brazil it was the moment of truth for me as navigator, using celestial navigation.[47] We had no radar or radio

---

[46] *elephantiasis*- symptom where parts of a person's body swell to massive proportions.

[47] *celestial navigation*- ancient science of finding one's way by the sun, moon, stars, and planets and the visible horizon, using a sextant to measure the angular distance between two visible objects to establish a 'fix' on a location.

or anything like that. We would see if I could navigate our way across the South Atlantic, which was eleven hours, and arrive where we were supposed to. So that memory remains a very dramatic one for me, of being alone in the nose of that plane with my sextant; I felt so alone and so at peace at the same time. The stars were so bright over the South Atlantic Ocean! I had this tremendous worry about knowing where we really were when I looked down at that ocean. So when I would plot these fixes that showed where we were according to the stars, that's when I found that we were not on the course that was planned. So now the moment of truth was, do I accept that as fact and correct it, or do I pretend that maybe I didn't shoot the stars correctly and stay on the course? I decided to do what I was taught, and that was to correct the course based on the star sightings taken. After doing so, eleven hours and some odd minutes later, on the far horizon there was Africa, and there was Dakar, and we were on target! We landed and everybody thought I was just terrific. Five of them thought so because they couldn't swim, and all they could think about was that we were going to run out of gas before we got to Africa!

There again it was the poverty. There were young people who were pimping their sisters, pre-teens almost, to make a living off of those who were passing through there. They were sailors and soldiers, Americans, British, or Dutch. Leaving Dakar, our next stop was Marrakesh, which took us over the Sahara Desert and over a mountain range called the Atlas Mountains. We flew through them and into Marrakesh, which was in a beautiful area of Morocco. That trip I will never forget either. I plotted the course, and, it being daylight, I went to sleep. When I paid more attention to where we were and looked at the maps, it seemed to me that we weren't really where we were supposed to be. This was not looking at the stars—it was looking at the mountains and fixes on the map. So I found that I had made a mistake. Instead of taking the deviation between true north and magnetic north, adding it, I had subtracted it, so I was basically twice as far off the course as I should have been! So I didn't notify anybody else and made a correction and the correction worked, taking us into the mountain pass through the Atlas Mountains and into Morocco. So once again my navigation was working, what I had been taught was working, and I was becoming relatively confident. The last leg was to go from Morocco up over Portugal, the Atlantic, and on to Prestwick, Scotland. That was a long flight, and gas was a factor. It was uneventful until we got to Prestwick, where there was fog and drizzle and it was difficult to get clearance to land. One plane in front of us ran out of gas and crashed, but we landed okay and that was it.

They took our plane away from us, and that we didn't expect. Then they put us on a train and sent us to a reassignment center for the 8th Air Force in England. So we lost our plane, which we had named 'Myrtle the Fertile Turtle.'[48] That was our first disappointment. The plane that we thought was going to be ours for our missions was not going to be ours. When we got to the center where crews were assigned to established bomb groups, we waited and finally got our assignment. We were assigned to the 93rd Bomb Group. We were sent to a little town about twenty miles south of Norwich in East Anglia, which is where most of the heavy bombers were stationed. They were all within about a 50-mile radius around Norwich in the northeastern part of England. It was easier for them to form up and go out on a mission together. When we got there we learned two things. First, that our airplane was an old airplane

---

[48] *'Myrtle the Fertile Turtle'*- Mr. Carlson came up with the name. 'The reason I did it was that people were talking about wives or girlfriends, but our pilot was Joe and he didn't have a girl or a wife and he wasn't interested in doing that. So I said, 'Let's give it a girl's name.' The B-24 is a very slow, lumbering thing, like a turtle, so I said, 'Let's call it Myrtle the Turtle.' The 'fertile' part came from the plane's ability to carry the biggest bomb load of any of the four-engine bombers.'

that had survived 25 missions. At this point in the war, late 1943 to early 1944, if you completed 25 missions you were promised that you could go home and become instructors for new cadets who were learning about combat.[49] We did the math at that point and we were losing airplanes at the rate of 5 to 10% every mission. The actual math worked out that most people either got killed, wounded, or captured by their eighth mission. So we got this old airplane called the 'Judith Lynn' that had no nose turret. It just had the two flexible machine guns, one on either side, that the navigator used, or the bombardier if he wasn't at the bombsight. But it had been a lucky ship because it had completed 25 missions. So that was our first shock, that we had an old airplane.

We were in the 93rd Bomb Group, which, by the way, was called 'Ted's Traveling Circus,' because it had moved from England to Africa, where it had made raids on the Romanian oil fields at Ploesti, then back to England, and back to Africa again. This takes me up to what I guess was the moment of truth, which was our first mission.

'Your First Mission'

Your first mission is one that you never forget because it starts with a wake-up call. People talk about how we got a wake-up call at Pearl Harbor or on 9/11. A real 'wake-up call' began in the 8th Air Force with a hand on your shoulder while you were sleeping on a little cot in a cold Quonset hut. A hand shakes you and someone says, 'You're going to fly today' and you have to get up. So it's 3:30 a.m. and you get up and go to a cold stove and try to find water to shave, because you have to be clean-shaven in order for the oxygen mask to fit closely when you are up high in the air. So your wake-

---

[49] *if you completed 25 missions*-the required number of missions for bomber crewmen went up to 30 missions in the spring of 1944, and then to 35 missions after D-Day in the summer of 1944.

up call starts with a soldier waking you up, shaving, going to eat breakfast, and then going to a briefing room. By this time it's 4:30 to 5:00 a.m. [*pauses*], and there you are, locked in in a secret way, and the map is in front of you and uncovered [*makes sweeping gesture with hand*]. The commanding officer and intelligence officer show you where you are going and what the route is. So now you find out what your first mission is, which in this case was Nuremberg, which was far inside Germany. That was where the war trials were held later, but it was also near an industrial city with factories that made ball bearings. So this was our first mission. You get up, get dressed, and put on your electric flying suit, and heavy clothes after that. The navigators go to a special briefing where they plan their course. Then you go to your airplane. You are in your airplane by 7:00, and you look for the weather. It is normally rain or drizzle, or snowing, as it is never clear in the morning in England. You wait to find out if you are actually going to take off, because many times the operation is what they called 'scrubbed.' If it never takes off, it is scrubbed; if it takes off and then the whole mission is called off, it is called 'aborted.' So you are waiting to see if the mission is scrubbed and never takes off. There was nothing worse than having a mission scrubbed and knowing you were going to go back and have to do the same thing the next day. So, we took off. On that first mission [you get a feel for] the power, and it makes you feel terrific. A B-24 starts down the runway, and it only gets halfway down the runway when another starts down the runway, and then your plane starts down the runway, so at one time there are three B-24s on the runway, one taking off, one halfway, and one starting out. This sense of power that you have, going down that runway with four tons of bombs, is quite overwhelming. From there you work your way through the clouds and come up above, and there is an airplane up there with a big yellow body on it with zebra stripes. That is the plane you are going to form on. It doesn't go with you; it just circles up there until you get into formation and ready to go, and then you are on your way over the Channel. And this sense of power really is overwhelming. You are happy that you made this decision, and you see all the hundreds and hundreds of bombers that you have with you. And you have air cover. In those days it lasted for 50 to 100 miles over the coast, and then they run low on gas and have to return to base, and then there is no air cover. That is when the German fighters of the Luftwaffe would begin to attack the bomber formations as they came in. Then you begin to see the losses of your power because you look and see planes on either side of you being shot, being on fire, going down. Or you feel that yourself, which we fortunately did not on our first mission; we did not feel any hits directly. But I did see planes going down that were in formation with us. So the mission was long and it was successful. We hit the target, everything worked, we came back, and we landed. It was a very powerful experience.

When you come back, however, the letdown is tremendous. There is nothing to look forward to except doing it again, and you don't really want to do it again. You wanted to do it, and you did it, and it was terrific, but knowing that you have to do it another 24 times, knowing what you have seen, is not something you look forward to. So in between missions, one of the paradoxes is that you are at death's door and the next night you are down at a British pub drinking yourself silly because you are not going to have to fly the next day. You are with other fliers, British, free Poles, and you are having a great time. So from that experience you learn that maybe today is the day you are going to live or today is the day you are going to die. Most people drank a lot when they weren't flying. Alcohol became pretty much a way of life for people in the Air Force who were not on missions. I won't bore you with other missions, but we were on the first three raids on Berlin. March 6, 1944, was referred to as 'Bloody Monday' because we sent 600 airplanes up and 69 did not come back. That was not the worst experience I had because our group was not damaged. A lot of groups were, so we were very fortunate. But on our eighth mission we were sent to Freiburg in southern Germany, near the Swiss border. And it was there, just as we were going over the target...

Flak

Let me tell you a little about flak. I have carried this with me ever since, because this is what flak looks like [*digs into jacket pocket, pulls out a jagged flak fragment about the size of two fingers*]. This is a piece of flak from a German 88mm artillery shell, which is fired from the ground and explodes at 25,000 feet, which is where we were flying. It is designed to destroy the plane or the engines or blow up the gas tank. And on my eighth mission, just as we were flying over the target, through these black clouds of exploding shells that you had to fly through, and just as the bombardier released our bombs, I hit the salvo handle, a handle right next to the instrument on the navigation table. That would release the bombs in the event that the bombsight did not release the bombs. The second the bombardier says, 'Bombs are away,' the navigator hits the salvo handle so if any bombs did get hung up, they would automatically go when you hit the salvo handle. So as I hit that handle this piece of flak nearly took my right arm off. And all I felt was no pain, just the feeling that someone had hit me with a sledgehammer. I felt total peace. It was the most unbelievable experience I'd ever had in my life. I didn't talk to God or see God, but I had absolutely no fear.

I looked down and there wasn't much left of my right arm; I saw it hanging there. I called the pilot and asked him to send somebody down to put a tourniquet on. Meanwhile I was checking instruments, because now we were on our way back and navigating was part of what I had to do, and I was still capable of doing it; I had no problem with it. The radio operator came down, took one look at it, and fainted. So I called again and the engineer came down. He revived the radio operator and sent him back with his portable oxygen mask. He then put the tourniquet on and stayed with me for the three or four hours it took to get back to base. An engine was on fire. Joe put the fire out and we lost a second engine. He brought it back, we landed, and I was brought to the hospital. They repaired my arm. I was on the operating table for eight hours. I didn't wake up for 72 hours due to an overdose of Pentothal, which was the drug they used in those days.

Ken Carlson holds up the flak fragment that nearly took off his right arm.

While I was in the hospital, our plane had 150 holes in it [to be patched up], and the crew was given a leave to go to London and relax. Joe came in and brought this piece of flak to me. [It had been lodged] in the instrument panel, and it had a piece of my wire suit and my blood on it. So it took part of my arm and then went on to demolish part of the instrument panel. Joe said to me, 'Sorry you are so unlucky, Navigator. We're going to miss you,' because there was no way I was going to fly again.

They came back from leave to fly the repaired airplane on the next mission, and they flew and they never came back. The crew next to them saw them explode, just like the Space Shuttle did on my 65th birthday. They were officially declared missing; [only] one parachute was seen coming out. For years I assumed they were missing rather than the fact that they were killed. About two years later, the government declared them killed in action. But up until about four or five years ago, [it was assumed that] there were no bodies ever recovered, because there was no indication otherwise. Then, through a German internet source, I discovered that they had been found by the Germans and were buried in a small German-occupied cemetery just north of Paris, but there were only body parts and one piece of wing that had a star on it. That was their identification. So they [turned out to be] in a cemetery in a little town northwest of Paris.

That was the end of my combat career. My arm was repaired by a doctor who, by fate, I met thirty years later. When my hand began to contract again I was sent to an orthopedic man. As I was sitting across from him he was questioning me about where this had happened, and he was the doctor who originally had put my hand back together again. He was the only doctor in that hospital, which had just opened the week before I was shot.

'The Nine Old Men'

When I came back from combat I was sent to a rehabilitation center in Pawling, New York. There we had the company of people like Lowell Thomas, the famous commentator, and Tom Dewey, [the former governor], and Norman Vincent Peale, who came over and played softball with us. So here we were with missing legs and arms, and we were called the 'nine old men.' This was the wonderful part of convalescence, and they were great people.

From there I was sent back to San Marcos as an instructor. All of us there would devote our time and energy to trying to tell people that what they learned in school would take them only so far. That what they needed to learn in combat was how to operate under conditions that were not classroom. That's how we made most of our contribution to those people before they were sent to Japan.

*

When President Roosevelt died, I was an instructor in Houston on special assignment. Having been a 'peacenik' before the war, I would never have gone to war unless we were attacked by Germany. I had studied enough about World War I and understood there was no way in the world that America should get trapped in another European war with France and Britain, who had allowed Hitler to build himself into a dictator over ten years. So I was always an 'America First' person; Lindbergh was one of my heroes, saying, 'Let's take of America first,' and that is [originally] what my politics were.[50] Pearl Harbor changed all that. When I went to war and served Roosevelt, I was doing that coming from a family where my father thought Roosevelt was the worst thing that had ever happened to America, because [to my father], the free enterprise system was going to go down the pike. I would have tremendous arguments with him. I would say, 'Look, the banks are closed and the Republicans have not done a thing, and this guy is doing something!' I had a fondness for FDR, so when he died I was relieved because I was aware of the fact that he was a very ill man. I remember thinking, 'Thank God that he lived to the point where he knew the war had been won.' And he did know that, and I knew that. And

---

[50] *'America First'*- Founded by Charles Lindbergh and others in 1940, the America First Committee opposed any U.S. involvement in World War II, and drew the ire of FDR, who was portrayed as pushing the U.S. into the European war. After Pearl Harbor, Lindbergh recanted his stance.

I learned to have a tremendous respect for Harry Truman, who I didn't know anything about prior to Roosevelt's death.

I think all of us who had been in combat felt that Harry Truman did the right thing, [when he decided to use the atomic bomb]. I was aware of the fact that Einstein, one of my heroes growing up, said that you have no idea what you are doing when you set off this weapon, that it is beyond anyone's wildest imagination. I still think that, politically at that point in time [to invade Japan], it would have been unconscionable as to the number of Americans that would have been killed, knowing that [the Japanese] would have fought, as they did in the islands, to the last man. And I had to put it all into perspective. And this is the thing people, including my own children, who are in their fifties, don't understand—when we dropped bombs on Berlin and other cities, I understood that not only did we hit our target, we also killed hundreds of thousands of women and children. But at the same time there were nights when I sat in a bomb shelter in England with a woman and her child right next to me while Germans were dropping bombs on England. So I saw it both ways. I was in a bomb shelter seeing the horror those women were going through and remembered that Hitler had been doing this to England for a year without any real target—he had just leveled London and Coventry. So in doing what I did, it seemed that what I was trapped into had nothing to do with soldiers. It had to do with civilizations and cultures, so whatever it takes is what a president has to do. So I thought that Harry Truman made the right decision, one that I would have made. And I would have taken the bomb [to the target] had I been the navigator. I would have had no problem delivering the bomb.

*

I had enough points to get out, so in September of 1945, I was sent to Fort Dix, New Jersey, and that was the end of my Air Force career. I resigned my commission at the beginning of the Korean

War; I felt that I was no longer young enough or capable enough to keep up with the modern technology to be of use to the government in Korea.

[After the war, I did not go to reunions.] I had lost my crew and it was something I didn't talk about for many years. I had no desire to go back and share memories with crews that had survived. It wasn't until much later that I decided to do this book for reasons that it would be helpful to young people in understanding what World War II was like. Not so much understanding it in its entirety, but how it affected individual people's lives. It wasn't until then that I had any real reason to try and recapture people who had been there. Then I joined what is called the 8th Air Force Historical Society. And through that I have maintained contacts at both the national level and at the local level in New York City. I found that very rewarding.

[I think my time in the military affected me] in a very dominant way. People talk about religion and believing in something; the moment of truth comes to you. I was raised and schooled in the Christian church. I don't go to church anymore, but I do have the faith that came to me when this piece of flak hit me. There was just no question in my mind that I was coming home, and that I was going to be safe and go to work and just do the job that I had to do. It is a feeling that has stayed with me all my life. So, from that standpoint, there is no fear. So many people today seem to be afraid of so many things. The fear of doing things or fear of failing has never been with me since I left the service. I have continued to look at my own life as one of missions, a series of missions and not just adventures, and it has worked for me.

Meeting the Enemy

After the war I was lucky enough to be able to open my own business on Madison Ave. doing advertising, marketing, and public relations. I started with Milton Bradley, the game company, and helped make them very successful. And for my second client I had the opportunity to make a presentation to BMW motorcycles and cars. Here was a German company and 33 other organizations were making [potential sales] presentations. I flew to Munich to meet the director of BMW. In talking with him after making my pitch presentation, he asked me where I was during the war. I said I was in the 8th Air Force bombing Germany. He said he wanted to show me what we did to Munich. He drove me out to a park and he said they had to bulldoze all of Munich out here and raze everything. So I pulled out my piece of flak and asked him if he knew what that was.

He said, 'Jah, German 88.'

I said, 'This went into my right arm and almost took it off, and another one on its next mission went into my airplane, and my whole crew blew up.'

He looked at me and said, 'You see this missing earlobe? American .50 caliber machine gun bullet.'

From that moment on, we would drink together and he would say, 'We should have been on the same side. The Russians were the enemy.'

But I reminded him that they had a little guy with a mustache named Hitler.

Then he said, 'What could we do? We had Hitler and you had Roosevelt.'

See, in his mind it made no difference; to him, in either case we had to do what our leaders said. Anyway, he became a good friend and I did get the account. I became very successful. I drove the first

BMW that came in from Munich for $2,300, drove it to Maine, wrote the marketing plan, and you know the rest.

Later, in working on a consulting job with the game company Milton Bradley in the 1970s, I had to go to Tokyo. In another marketing company I met a man who told me he was the last kamikaze pilot. I said, 'What do you mean, you were the last kamikaze pilot?' It was the last day of the war, and he was on a suicide mission to crash his plane into an American ship. Halfway there he decided he didn't have enough fuel and turned back. He said he got back, and the war was over. He was seventeen! So I had met the head of BMW who had been an SS trooper, and had met the last kamikaze pilot during my business career.

It has been a fun trip. In 1972 when I retired from business, the war then had become the war on drugs. By 1972 it was a problem in all of the high schools in New York or Maine, or wherever. President Nixon had declared war on cancer and then a war on drugs, so most of my effort has been talking to people in the school systems and helping young people in finding some kind of career guidance. That is my current war. When I work with young people in the school systems, both public and private, I try to use the book *High Honor.* I talk further about the drug problem and why the war on drugs is so vital to the future of this country; that word 'honor' is difficult to define, not just in reference to World War II, but easy to understand when read in relation to what the Founding Fathers said when they signed the Declaration of Independence. The final sentence said, *'And for the support of this declaration, with a firm reliance on the protection of Divine Providence, we mutually pledge to each other our lives, our fortunes, and our sacred honor.'* My chapter is entitled 'Borrowed Time,' and in that chapter there is a photo of me and my crew taken in 1943. [*Pointing out crew*] Frank Caldwell was the bombardier, from Anderson, Indiana; 'Johnny' Johnson, the co-pilot, from Houston, Texas; Joe Roznos, the pilot, my greatest friend, from Hollywood, California; 'Wally' Waldmann, waist gunner, from Houston, Texas; Hal McNew, waist gunner, from Montana; Ed Miller, tail gunner, from Wyoming; Frank Dinkins, the engineer; John Rose, 'Rosie', our ball turret gunner—he could shoot a squirrel, or a German fighter pilot, from his shoulder or his waist, it didn't make any difference; and Cleo Pursifull, our radioman. He is the one that came to help me and fainted. And he failed to go on that last mission. He had just had enough.

The thing that haunts me is that I can't put a face to the guy who replaced him. He was an eighteen-year-old Jewish kid named Henry Vogelstein from Brooklyn. It was his first and last mission. And when you think about it, an eighteen-year-old boy was put as a replacement in a crew that he did not know; we were an all-Christian crew. We all had our little New Testament that the Air Force gave us, and he would have been given an Old Testament. He made his only mission with a crew of strangers. Now that's bravery!

We all want to be free, but very few of us want to be brave. For all of us to be free, a few of us must be brave, and that is the history of America.

Earl Morrow, first row, far left, and his B-17 bomber crew. 1944.
Source: Earl Morrow

CHAPTER EIGHT

The Pilot

Earl Montgomery Morrow was born on June 27, 1921, in West Pawlet, Vermont. His father, a schoolteacher, decided to take up farming across the border in Washington County, New York.

Earl first came on my radar when he called me up twenty years ago, having heard of my interest in World War II veterans and their stories. 'I just had to call you and ask—why are you doing this? Why are you interested in our stories?' Later, he would be a frequent visitor to my classroom, and I even got to introduce him to the granddaughter of the man who liberated him, General George Patton. I would also be invited to sit with him and two other B-17 veterans at his dining room table as they reunited after many years to swap stories of the day they were shot down and about their prisoner of war experience, to be detailed in the sequel to this book.

This interview was recorded in 2009, when Earl was eighty-eight years old, in the rural farmhouse he grew up in, B-17 memorabilia and photographs adorning the walls.

***

<u>Duties of the Pilot</u>

Your assignment to the B-17 airplane means that you are no longer just a pilot. You are now an airplane commander, charged with all the duties and responsibilities of a command post.

You are now flying a 10-man weapon. It is your airplane, and your crew. You are responsible for the safety and efficiency of the crew at all times--not just when you are flying and fighting, but for the full 24 hours of every day while you are in command.

Your crew is made up of specialists. Each man--whether he is the navigator, bombardier, engineer, radio operator, or one of the gunners--is an expert in his line. But how well he does his job, and how efficiently he plays his part as a member of your combat team, will depend to a great extent on how well you play your own part as the airplane commander.

Get to know each member of your crew as an individual. Know his personal idiosyncrasies, his capabilities, his shortcomings. Take a personal interest in his problems, his ambitions, his need for specific training.

See that your men are properly quartered, clothed, and fed. There will be many times, when your airplane and crew are away from the home base, when you may even have to carry your interest to the extent of financing them yourself. Remember always that you are the commanding officer of a miniature army--a specialized army; and that morale is one of the biggest problems for the commander of any army, large or small.

Crew Discipline

Your success as the airplane commander will depend in a large measure on the respect, confidence, and trust which the crew feels for you. It will depend also on how well you maintain crew discipline.

Your position commands obedience and respect. This does not mean that you have to be stiff-necked, overbearing, or aloof. Such characteristics most certainly will defeat your purpose. Be friendly, understanding, but firm. Know your job; and, by the way you perform your duties daily, impress upon the crew that you do know your job. Keep close to your men, and let them realize that their interests are uppermost in your mind. Make fair decisions, after due consideration of all the facts involved; but make them in such a way as to impress upon your crew that your decisions are to stick. Crew discipline is vitally important, but it need not be as difficult a problem as it sounds. Good discipline in an air crew breeds comradeship and high morale, and the combination is unbeatable.

You can be a good CO, and still be a regular guy. You can command respect from your men, and still be one of them.

Crew Training

Train your crew as a team. Keep abreast of their training. It won't be possible for you to follow each man's courses of instruction, but you can keep a close check on his record and progress.

Get to know each man's duties and problems. Know his job, and try to devise ways and means of helping him to perform it more efficiently.

Each crew member naturally feels great pride in the importance of his particular specialty. You can help him to develop his pride to include the manner in which he performs that duty. To do that you must possess and maintain a thorough knowledge of each man's job and the problems he has to deal with in the performance of his duties. —Duties and Responsibilities of the Airplane Commander and Crewmen, 1943

***

Earl M. Morrow

I went to school in Hartford, New York, and I graduated in 1939 as the valedictorian. It was a small class; I think there were 19 of us or something like that. I stayed around for a year and took post-graduate courses and tried to pick up some of my grades a little bit, and then I went to Iowa State College, studying mechanical engineering. I got through the first year there and I started the second year, and that Sunday, when Pearl Harbor was hit, I sat there and listened to that on the radio, and I made up my mind right there and then that at the end of the semester, I was going home and getting in the service.

As soon as the semester was over I got out on the road and hitchhiked from Iowa State and made it in three days to the farm up here in New York. Back then, people would pick you up. [*Chuckles*] I got home and told my dad what I was going to do, and my dad informed me that I wasn't going to do that—I was going back to school! He was the director of the Selective Service for Hartford, and he told me he knew the rules and regulations, and he informed me that he would have to sign it, for me to go in the service, and he wasn't going to do it.

'I'm Not Going Back'

I was 20. Dad was the kind of man that, well, you did what he wanted. Put it that way. But this was the first time that I [went against his wishes] and told him that I wasn't going back to school. So I went down to Schenectady, and got a job at General Electric as an apprentice machinist, and I enjoyed it. The instructor picked me and another guy up and we were doing real serious work on the lathe in the machine shop. But the day I turned 21, I went down to the Armory in Albany and I applied for the Aviation Cadet Program; there were thirty-some of us that went in that morning. Six of us out of the thirty-some got in and the rest were rejected. They told me, 'Be down to the railroad station ready to depart on Wednesday at 0900.' This was on a Friday. So I went home and told my family what I had done, and Mother was all upset.

I told her, 'Look, there was one boy in that group who was athletic, played every sport that there was, and they found he had a heart problem and he could drop dead at any minute. I'm one of the few that got through, and I'm healthy, and I'm going!' And that made her feel better.

The next day I got my orders to report to the draft board, and Dad couldn't do it, so I had to go to Granville to their draft board.

So I went over there and I told them what I was doing and I showed them the paperwork, and they didn't do anything except tell me 'Good luck!' Wednesday morning came, and Mom and Dad took me down. And one of my little girlfriends went with us. Walked into the station, and a guy in uniform had a pack of manila envelopes, and he walked over to me, and he said, 'You have 30 people you need to get down to Fort Dix in New Jersey.'

And I looked at him and said, 'Why me?'

He said, 'Because you had ROTC in college.'

Well, I got them there, but I don't know how. [*Chuckles*] We had to change trains down in New York City, and I got all thirty of them there and delivered the papers to the proper people, and that's the way I entered the service.

There were delays with the Aviation Cadet Program, so they sent us over to Aviation Field on Long Island and gave us a .45 automatic, showed us how to use it, and put us on guard duty. I had never fooled around with guns—Dad and I had a little rifle I shot once in a while—but they gave us pretty good instruction on the .45, and we'd go out there at night and you couldn't see your hand in front of your face, it was so dark out there. And they said, 'If you hear movement or anything at all that's not right, you holler 'HALT' three times, and then shoot!' And so I killed a cow one night. [*Chuckles*] It was just outside the line—I hollered 'HALT!' three times, and it didn't stop! But there were some fellas that actually shot people trying to come over the fence, and what happened was they were tried, found guilty, and fined a dollar and shipped out. I made up my mind early on that I wasn't going to be shipped out of this Aviation Cadet Program. So I was real careful, and eventually they shipped us out and sent us down to Nashville, Tennessee, on another train.

'You Did The Right Thing'

We're still in '42. And I'm down there, and that's where you get classified whether you go as pilot, bombardier, or navigator. And everyone wanted to be a pilot, of course, including me, and I made it, and they shipped us out of there to California. And this was a real enjoyable trip, because the train didn't go straight to California. It would go south, and then it would go north, and then it would go south, and so if the Germans were watching, they wouldn't know that this was a troop train and they wouldn't know exactly where it was going. And it took about seven days to get out there, so I got to see a whole lot of the U.S. on that trip. Once we were there, we went through pre-flight school where you took courses in theory of flight, weather, meteorology, and so on and so forth. Then about January 1, I guess it would have been in '43, I got my first flight. I had never been in an airplane before in my life, and this was a single-engine, open cockpit, and the instructor was sitting in the front seat, and they showed us how to start it.

The second day after I had been up twice, the instructor told me I would never make it. I asked him why, and he said, 'You're afraid of the airplane.'

And I asked him, 'Well, can't you do something about it?'

He said, 'With your permission, we'll make or break you this afternoon.'

I said, 'Fine, let's go.'

Man, I've never been afraid of an airplane since. We did everything that an airplane can do in that airplane. We rolled, we looped, we dove, we flew straight up and then let it fall back down, and then he went down and actually landed on a big truck going down the highway, just touched the wheels down to the truck long enough and let it sit there a few seconds! And then we found a farmer down there, and he threw a hammer at us and it went over the top of the airplane, so you know how low we flew! And within two days I had soloed on the airplane.

I think I had about six hours total [in the air] when I soloed. And we had class work and we had flights. We did night flying, we did day flying, we did short landing, and I learned in a hurry! The first time right after I soloed, I'm out there flying by myself, and here comes a thunderstorm, came right up on me, sitting right there, and I said, 'What do I do now?', and I looked around and I spotted another plane with two people. That told me that one of them was an instructor, so I got right on his tail and stayed there and we went into another landing field. And he said, 'What are you doing following me?'

I said, 'Look, I just soloed; I didn't know what to do. I saw two people in the plane, and I figured one was an instructor and I figured he knows what to do, follow him.'

And he said, 'You did the right thing.'

I got through the primary training and then we went to Chico, California, for basic training, into bigger airplanes, enclosed cockpits now. The instructor sits behind you and you sit up front; a bigger airplane, it's got more power. It's a fixed gear, though, a P-13, and it's a real nice airplane. Now I got a little more of formation flying, quite a lot of night flying, and a lot of maneuvering, precision flying, so on and so forth. I got through that. But I couldn't get through lazy eights the way I should have been doing them.[51] The instructor had me out there, and we were working, and we were just about to do the lazy eight and smoke started pouring up into the cockpit from underneath the plane, and he said, 'Get back to the field!' So I turned around, and we flew back to the field and I had a good landing even with all the smoke, and he said, 'If you can fly

---

[51] *lazy eights*- changing combinations of climbing and descending turns at varying airspeeds used to develop and demonstrate the pilot's mastery of the airplane

under those conditions, you've passed.' From there we went down to Marfa, Texas, and got into a multi-engine, five or six passenger aircraft with retractable landing gear. And this is where I was really learning to fly now; I had a whole lot more to handle. The day we got down there we had a hail storm and all these planes had fabric wings, which got all torn up. My last day there a new plane came in; it was really nice to fly around in, an airplane you could do things with. This was at the end of June, exactly six months from when I first got in an airplane, and I got my wings and a rating as a 2d Lt. They sent us down to Roswell, New Mexico, and had me doing takeoffs and landings and in a B-17; I had never even seen one before in my life! But after two months I was qualified, but instead of sending me overseas, they sent me up to Las Vegas to fly gunners in training, which was a real plush deal. When you come out of the B-17 training, you're listed as a 1st Pilot. I was a 1st Pilot all the way through, but up there in Las Vegas there would be times I would be sitting in the co-pilot seat. We had a lot of fun up there training gunners—you'd get 10 or 12 guys on Monday morning and they'd never been on the airplane before, so we just flew around and got them used to flying. The next five or six days would be real serious—they would be towing targets behind airplanes, and they had to shoot and hit stuff, and they had cameras so they could tell if they were hitting it or not. We had a lot of fun—we would go and fly down in the canyon, and go into Death Valley and fly below sea level, and let them see what the countryside looked like, and so on and so forth. Then all of a sudden they picked five crews to go fly some new B-17s down to Tyndall Field in Florida, so now the only people that I had on the airplane were a co-pilot and a flight engineer.[52] We flew from Las Vegas down somewhere in Virginia or

[52] *Tyndall Field*-on the Gulf Coast of Florida, it opened as a gunnery range. and school in 1941.

somewhere—I forget where it was—but before we landed there, we really dragged it down below because my co-pilot's hometown was nearby, and we flew real low over there. We saw people were running out of their houses and falling on their face, because they were wondering what the heck [the roaring of the multi-engine bomber was]! After we landed, that night we went to see his family and we stayed over there. Then we went over to where he went to school, and one of his teachers saw him and said, 'I was on the third floor when you went by, and I was looking down on you!'

From there, we went down to Tyndall Field and we trained gunners down there for a while. We couldn't get Pullman railroad car to get back to Vegas straight away, so I eased up there up to the farm in New York and visited my folks, and then got out to Vegas. From there, I got my overseas orders, and I went to Kansas to get my crew. All the pilots who went there got new crews; it was people coming right out of school who had just gotten their wings. I now had my crew, and I was really happy with them—they all seemed like a really great bunch of guys. There were four officers, myself, the navigator, my co-pilot, and the bombardier, and the rest of the crew had a staff sergeant rating, enlisted men. I got all my enlisted men off to the side on the first day where no one could hear me, and I said, 'I don't ever want one of you guys to salute me, unless there's someone standing over there expecting you to salute me, then you do it.' I never once had a problem with discipline, and I think the guys really appreciated me doing that. When my officers found out about it, they fell right in with it, and we never had an issue.

We started training, hard. We did night flying, long distance flying, we did high altitude and a lot of formation flying. We were practicing dropping bombs and doing navigating flights, and one night we had something break on the instrument panel, and hydraulic fluid just came flying out into my lap. The boys had an idea, and we took our parachutes and put them up under the pilot and co-pilot seats, where we could reach them easily but they would be safe. But those parachutes got soaked with hydraulic fluid, so we had a situation where we had a very flammable fluid all over the aircraft and I decided we had to get this thing on the ground. Luckily there was an emergency field up there right close by, in one of the middle states, but they didn't even have a radio there, so we had to call our home base in Louisiana and they had to call on the phone to the emergency landing field. It was just a field with a flare on each end of the 'runway.' We got the flares spotted and came in really low, and at about fifty feet off the ground a light turned on just below us in a house! So I gave it full power and we went around again; we went over the house again and got it down on the ground. We went to a hotel where we could sleep, and they said they would send parts up to us the next day. There were small crowds gathered the next day because it was a small town, so everyone came out to see us—we showed them through the aircraft, but we covered up the bombsight because that was secret, so the boys were telling the people to buy war bonds. That morning a stripped-down B-17 came in—there were no guns on it—and it made three passes over the field in daylight before it finally landed. A major was flying that and he had been in combat, and he came over and said, 'Who the hell landed this thing in here at night?' It was probably the best thing that could have happened before we went overseas, because after that the crew had absolutely no concern whether Bill and I could fly that thing or not—they didn't have to worry about [our abilities], which helped a lot. Shortly after that we got on a boat with all of our equipment, and we get in a boat in New York, and a whole fleet of boats go across.

Now that was '44. It was about two weeks in the boats going across. And the closer we got over there, I began to get a little nervous about what are we getting into over there. Especially when one of the guys mentioned about submarines being in the area. But it was a really nice trip over there, because we were on what used to be a French luxury liner—but they pulled out all the luxury, and put in all the bunks. They kept all the crew, and I've never eaten so well in my life—three and four course meals, every meal. It was great. [*Chuckles*]

'People Were Shooting At Me'

We got over there and we got in a couple of days of training. The first mission I went out on, I sat in the co-pilot's seat and I was with a crew that had been out there for quite some time. I saw all these little puffs of black smoke, and I was wondering what it was—I figured it out real quick that people were shooting at me! We sustained some battle damage to the airplane that day, but we got back okay. The missions I was on were all over lower Germany, in the 457th Bomb Group, out of the little town of Glatton, close to Peterborough, probably about 40 miles or so north of London.

I had my own airplane, but in 17 missions I flew it three times. The rest of the time they were putting it back together. The boys named it 'SHAD'; I had gotten married just before, and I had skinnied down to just a shadow of what I was, so it was short for 'Shadow.' [*Chuckles*] For my second mission, I had all of my crew, except I had an experienced co-pilot in the right seat. So we had a little battle damage on the plane, but what was bothering the crew were those short runways in England. The bombardier and the navigator had stayed down in front, but that was the only mission they stayed down in front on. We were carrying heavy loads, you know, and I had been told not to let the crew sit in the nose, but to sit in the back. You had to use every inch of the runway. We moved them back after that. We always left one man home, because there was a gun in the radio room that they had taken out, so they figured that the radio man could always get out and get on the gun.

I don't remember too much about these missions specifically, with the exception of three. Once we were going pretty deep into Germany, and on the way in, we lost the number one engine and it must have been a fuel pump or something, the way it just quit on us. So we were going in light on the power and feathering it in, because we only had the three remaining engines. We were in a formation of probably about a thousand airplanes and were in a squadron of twelve airplanes, in a group of 36 planes. We had to keep working on staying in the formation—you have to use full power just to stay in it if you're on the outside, and low power if you're on the inside.

My co-pilot was going to make this bomb run on this day. We came down in altitude, and just before we dropped our bombs, we got a direct hit on the number three engine! I went through the feathering procedures. What I mean by that is, you shut the engine down and then set the propeller blade parallel to your flight, so they're not creating a windmill and drag. I shut everything down, but we started windmilling. So now we had to get out of the formation, because there's no way we could have stayed in. Luckily we had been able to drop our bombs and get rid of them.

The dome of the number three engine started to get red-hot, then white-hot, and the engine started to break apart; pieces of it started flying into the aircraft and coming through the thin skin on the aircraft. So Bill and I decided to put the plane into a dive and then pull up to try to break the propeller free.

We dove twice and we lost a couple thousand feet, and I said, 'Look, Bill, we can't lose any more altitude, we're going to just have to leave it as is.'

That engine was still windmilling. So number two was running and number four was running, but number one is feathered and number three is out. We were now losing altitude all the way, and we had to come across occupied Belgium to make it home.

The Germans were shooting at us all the way, so we were turning every ten seconds; our fighters stayed up above us and covered us in. We had a spot about a mile and a half wide to come out of Belgium over the English Channel—there was a swamp or something there, and if you came out over the swamp, there were no guns there. My navigator brought me out right over that spot dead center, and we were flying real low now, heading for home, but we have got to get over the Cliffs of Dover when we get across the Channel. Now just as we got out over the Channel, we lost the number four engine! Unbeknownst to anybody, the Germans had flak barges out in the Channel, and they knocked out number four... It feathered; we had one engine running, two feathered, and one windmilling, so we weren't doing too well.

So now we're over the Channel and we're throwing everything out to lighten the weight. We threw the guns out. We all had flak suits and we dumped them, and everything we could throw out. And we finally got over the Cliffs of Dover, and right in front of us there was a field, and a plane was in front of us! I told the engineer, 'Throw him a flare!', and the plane got out of the way. And I got it safely down on the ground, and the guys were getting out of the airplane, kissing the ground, running around and stuff like that. I couldn't even get the plane off the runway with one engine! By the way, my bombardier had professed to be an atheist but he became a good Christian after that, and he was one until the day he passed away.

The boys got out and they started counting up the holes in the airplane—we had well over a hundred holes in the airplane. Most of them were small holes, but one of them was as big as a bushel basket. And there wasn't one of us who was scratched, but the medical people showed up and they grounded us right there, and they said,

'You boys are going to a rest camp for a week.' So we went down to some place in southern England; it was old and a real big place where they had a lot of bedrooms. The Red Cross people were running it and we had to come to dinner every night in Class A uniforms; other than that, we could wear what we wanted. They had bicycles you could ride out in the country with, and so on and so forth.

The Final Mission

Earl and his crew rested their nerves. When they returned to base after a week of much-needed relaxation, they were briefed on the next mission—a heavily defended target that would test their abilities yet again and end in disaster.

We found out we were going to Merseburg, which is a synthetic oil plant, and it was a rough one. And when you went down to breakfast in the morning and you got fresh eggs, you knew it was going to be a rough mission. If you got powdered eggs, you knew it was going to be a 'milk run,' but I never did get one of those milk runs.

This was my 17th mission. So we knew we're going to Merseburg—we've been there before and we know it's going to be rough. We took off and we got over there, and there was [heavy cloud cover over the target area]. We dropped our bombs on what we thought was the synthetic oil plant, and then there was some mix-up—I don't think anyone really knows what happened for sure, but for whatever reason after we dropped our bombs, our group was going one way [*gestures towards the right with one hand, points towards the left with the other hand*] and the rest of the strike force started turning the other way! Nine hundred and some airplanes turned right, and thirty-six turned left, and which ones do you think the

German fighters were going to hit? They picked us, and they pulled our fighters, who were supposed to be protecting us, off in a dog-fight.

I told the guys, 'Keep your eyes open, we are about to be hit!' And sure enough, they came down in groups of fifteen right behind us—I never saw a fighter at all—and they started pumping 20mm rounds into us. After they started to run out of ammunition or whatever, they would just peel off underneath our planes.

The crew told me my rudder, my vertical stabilizer, was gone. I could hear the shells exploding in the back of the airplane and I could feel the hits, but we never saw the fighters from where we were in the front—I'm flying formation, that's my job. The next group of fighters came in, and I saw about six or eight feet go off my left wing, and again I could feel the shells exploding in the back. The third group came, but kind of missed us. The fourth group came in, and we got two 20mm rounds right in the cockpit beside my co-pilot.

I didn't know if he was hurt real bad or what, but now the plane was on fire, so the top turret gunner came down and grabbed the extinguisher and he put the fire out. We thought it was out, but it flared up again, so now the only thing to do was to get out. I rang the 'bail-out' signal, and I reached out and grabbed William out of his seat, yanked him out. I didn't know whether he was hurt bad or what. The top turret gunner bailed out and went down.

I got out of my seat, grabbed Bill, and started down the gangway. But I felt the airplane climbing, and I thought to myself, 'If this thing stalls out, and starts falling down backwards, no one is going to get out.' So I crawled back up—I didn't get into my seat, but just pushed the controls forward enough to get the nose down. So I went back down to jump clear, and Bill was sitting down there with his feet hanging out. I just put my foot in the middle of his back and kicked him out—and then I sat down there and rolled out, and just as I dropped clear, the plane exploded! I could hear it and feel it, but did not see it; when you jump out like that, your eyes automatically close. You're jumping out and you're moving 160 or 170 mph, so your eyes aren't going to stay open.

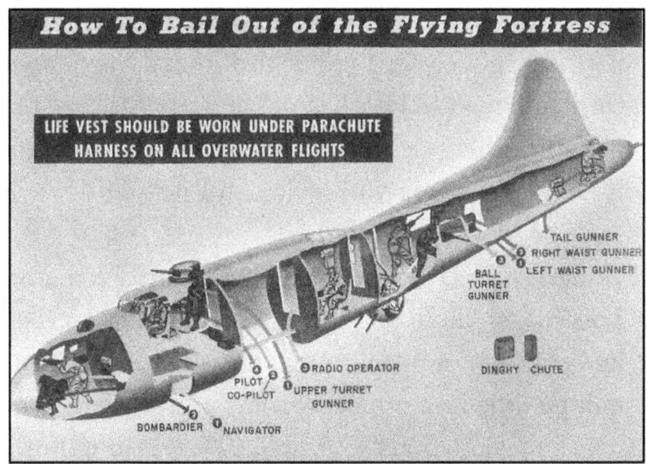

'How to bail out of the Flying Fortress.' B-17 training manual, U.S. Government. Source: www.cnks.info/b17-flying-fortress-interior

So now I was out there in the clouds, and I'm thinking, 'What's going to happen if I rip this cord and I get pulled up into everything, with the updrafts in these clouds?'

I was falling and had the wind on my face, trying to look down, so when I broke out of the clouds I could know how far I was above the ground. I figured I was above ten thousand feet when I broke out, but in fact I was well below that when I did break out—I was pretty close, and I ripped my cord [*motions across his waist with his hand*] and the parachute worked perfectly, and I swung over one or two times and I was on the ground. I almost stayed on my feet, but the chute dragged me and I went over on my behind.

Prisoner

I was trying to get out of the chute as fast as I could, because about thirty feet away were three women with pitchforks coming toward me and they weren't friendly, so I had to get out of that harness as fast as I could. I had a .45 strapped against me. I didn't take it out, but as they got closer I unbuckled it, and they backed off. I was real close to a road so I ducked down onto this road below me and ran up to the other side and started to cross this field. And German civilians were coming with rifles, so I just sat down and put my hands up.

We had been told to get under military control if we could, [as soon as possible, if there was no opportunity to escape]. Men, women, and children came up to me; the women were spitting in my face and the little kids were throwing stones at me. I saw a guy in the distance that I thought looked like he was in uniform, and I tried to tell them that was where I wanted to go, and I pointed. I couldn't speak German, [although I think the kids at least knew some English]. I got knocked down three or four times before I convinced them I wanted to get over there. The Germans then took me into a small town and the first person I saw from my airplane and crew was my tail gunner. He was so glad to see someone else from the plane, because, you see, he came out of his turret, way at the back end of the plane.

The tail gunner had got out, and he told me that the escape door was gone. Now little Joe Salerno was the waist gunner and he was a little eighteen-year-old kid. He was standing there [as the plane was going down], my tail gunner motioned for him to go out, and he shook his head, 'No.'

That's not Joe; Joe wasn't afraid of anything. When the tail gunner told me that, I realized what Joe had done. He was in the waist gun and Bob Koerner was in the ball turret, and they had this agreement that if Bob was in the ball turret, Joe would wait until Bob got out, and Bob didn't get out, and Joe just lost it. And we think that because the main door was gone, that possibly the radio operator might have gotten out.

Later, while we were on the ground, I was informed by some Germans that one of my 'comrades' was bleeding, but they wouldn't let me go to him. I got the feeling that it could have been my radio operator. But those are three boys who were killed from my crew.[53]

I didn't see my co-pilot until three or four days later. They had us in [what seemed to be the] backyard of a house for some time. The count in our squadron was twelve airplanes, and we lost nine that day. Now that's 81 men, and I only saw thirty-something of us alive.

The two Germans [who took me into custody] must have been on sick leave, though they both had rifles. One had a patch over his eye, and the other had his arm in a sling. They took me and another one of our boys who I never knew before; his name was Jerry Silverman.[54] They put us in a car and we started cross country; we had no idea why or where we were going. I didn't realize that Jerry was Jewish. They drove about 10 minutes and then the car quit. They got out, opened the hood, pulled the wires, cleaned them out real good, and we went another 10 minutes. Now at the next stop one of these guys turned around and he wanted my pilot wings. He reached out and started to touch them, and I slammed his arm down on the seat!

---

[53] *three boys who were killed from my crew-* Radio Operator: Charles Lindquist, Ball turret gunner: Bob Koerner, Tail gunner: Joe Salerno. Source: American Air Museum in Britain, www.americanairmuseum.com/aircraft/11772. Mr. Morrow states that Salerno was on a waist gun at the time of this last mission.

[54] *Jerry Silverman-*I met Mr. Silverman, the lead navigator for this raid, when he came up to visit with Earl's bombardier Sam Lisica and Earl in 2001. Their B-17 PoW reunion is a main focus of the sequel to this book.

Jerry was sitting over there yelling at me to give them what they want, saying, 'You're going to get us both killed! Just give him anything he wants.'

But you see, what I had been told before was that if you stand up to the Germans, you'll do a lot better than if you cater to them. So I'm just playing the game—that's not the way I really am—but I got away with it, I slammed his arm down on the back of the seat.

So they got out and cleaned their plugs again and we went on to the town, so their families could see that they had captured us. That night they took us out and put us in something like a one-room schoolhouse, and there were two guards there for about thirteen of us. One of the guards would take a couple of us and go into town to get food; we had a little kid's wagon. I might be pulling the wagon, and the other guy would be back there pushing the wagon, and we would argue with the guards. When one of us was arguing with the guard, the other was sticking everything he could in his pockets for the other guys who were sick—we were manipulating the guards the whole time, so we could get the food for the guys who were really in bad shape. One boy, a tail gunner, his back was broken in three places; one of the other pilots had his head severely burned going out of his airplane. I don't know what actually happened to these people who were hurt so badly.

We stayed there about three days, and they brought my co-pilot in to me while we were there. He said that a farmer and his daughter had picked him up and hid him for a couple of days, but they got scared and they turned him in. He was not bleeding, but he was in bad shape.

The Germans wound up moving us out of there on a train and I don't know where they took him, but they moved the rest of us to Frankfurt to an interrogation center.

I think the reason we got away with [our uncooperative behavior toward our guards] was because they were under orders to make sure we got to interrogation—the Germans wanted us over there badly, so they could find out what was going on. So we rode this train and we got into Frankfurt, and we had to run/walk from one end of Frankfurt to the other side to catch another train to take us out to the interrogation center. Now I never saw a full building standing; everything was shattered in that town of Frankfurt. We got over to the other station, and there was a little while before the next train, and there was a good-looking German gal there, but she got a rioting crowd rounded up in a hurry, ready to come after us. The guards finally locked us down in a room in the basement because they couldn't hold the crowds off.

Eventually the train came in and it was just a short ride to the interrogation center. We were there about three days and we gave nothing but name, rank, and serial number. About the third day in, the interrogator said, 'Well, if you won't tell me, I'll tell you.'

He proceeded to tell me things that I didn't think my parents even knew. He told me that when I was in fifth grade, I was sent to the principal's office! They knew that our bombardier had made major, which we didn't know. They had [an intelligence] system and they were working on it a long time, and the only way I can figure out how they got this information is my folks would be sitting up there on the farm, and the college kids would come through selling magazines. Mother would invite them in for dinner, and then she'd sit there and talk to them all afternoon. I think that they were spies—that's the only way I can figure out how they got this information, but I didn't think my dad or my mother knew that I had gone to the principal's office for a little offense like going down the slide headfirst; they seemed to know everything. But I just told the guys, just don't talk; name, rank, serial number, and that's it.

The third day there, they pulled us out and put a gun on a train with us. We went to the town of Sagan, southeast of Berlin. That was the camp—if you saw the movie 'The Great Escape,' that's the camp that the movie took place in. And all the time that we were in there, we were working on escape deals. But the commanding officer in there made rules—we had our own government in there, and if you wanted to escape, and you had a plan, then you took it to them and told them what it was, and then the whole camp would work on it. And they made it a court-martial offense to try and escape on your own. There were two or three escapes that went on when I was in there, and one of them failed because of exactly what I said. There was a [guard] tower with search lights and machine guns on it, and then they had a barbed wire fence and a warning fence inside of that. You didn't go over the warning wire, never. So it was winter, and we had eleven guys dressed up in clothes they had made out of white sheets, and they were hiding in the latrine, and they knew there was a space right under that tower that [the guards in] the tower couldn't see. So they went out that night and got out clean and free, and made it out. But two other guys decided they were going to try it, and they got caught. So immediately the Germans were looking for a count, knowing that some were gone. So these other guys totally screwed up the deal for the eleven that got out.

[They got recaptured], but what happened to them, I don't know.

When you first get in there, no one will talk to you until someone identifies who you are. They figure you might be a mole or a spy. I ran into my roommate from basic training, and he okayed me and then I okayed the rest of my crew.

These were all officers in the camp I was in. The enlisted men went to another camp somewhere else, and they were staff sergeants, so the Germans couldn't make them work. But we were in there and we were in barracks. And my barracks commander was Colonel Gabreski, you've probably heard of him—fighter ace in World War II, and then a jet ace in later wars; he passed away just a short time ago.[55] But every evening they would put us out on the parade ground by the barracks, and the old German major commander from the camp would come around and give the 'Heil Hitler' salute and [Colonel Gabreski] would give the accountability report: 'One's in the hospital,' so on and so forth.

Death March

[It got to be January 1945], and we began hearing guns; the Russians were getting close. Around January 10, I didn't know exactly what day it was, but one morning they routed us out of there. There were ten thousand of us in that camp, and one o'clock in the morning they rousted us out of there and put us out on the road, running. They had guns and they had dogs, so when they said, 'Run!', you ran. Blizzard, thirty degrees below zero, and we would run ten minutes and walk ten minutes, run ten minutes, and at the end of the hour they would give us a five-minute break. And this kept up all day, and somewhere on the route down there machine guns started going off, and I just dove into a snowbank until things quieted down—never did find out what it was about.

Now they put the word out that if we fell out for any reason, they would run us through with the bayonet. And as we left the camp they ran us through a warehouse and threw us a Red Cross parcel that had food in it. Well at thirty below zero we didn't have gloves and couldn't carry it, so I just busted mine open and stuck everything I could in my pockets, drove my hands in there, and proceeded on down the road.

---

[55] *Colonel Gabreski*- Francis Stanley "Gabby" Gabreski, January 28, 1919 – January 31, 2002. He was the top U.S. Army Air Force fighter ace over Europe in World War II, with 28 kills before surviving an accident that made him a PoW. He was also one of seven pilots who went on to 'ace' status in Korea as well.

We had a break at 5:30 in the morning; I had a clean pair of socks in my pocket and I thought it would be a good idea to change them, so I did, but while I tried to change them, my shoes froze and I couldn't get my feet back in. So I had to try to walk around for a while to heat them up enough until I could get my feet back down in.

We started walking again, and it was still dark, and, well, I was just so tired I figured if I just sat down I'd fall asleep and that would be it—I just felt like I couldn't go any further. So I sat down.

We had two guys who were up and down that line; one was a Lt. Col. West Point graduate. The other played football for Penn State—big guy, Polish guy, and we couldn't pronounce his name so we just called him 'Smitty.' And Smitty got to me, and he's just slapping the daylights out of me and cursing at me, 'Get your 'blankety-blank' up and get moving!'

I thought to myself, I have to get up to get away from him, so I got up and started moving again. Well, then they brought my bombardier, Sam, to me, and Sam was completely out of it. He had no idea where he was or who he was, so they wanted somebody who knew him to take him. I got well in a hurry—I snapped out of it because now I had to take care of Sam. And you'd be surprised how well it worked. So I grabbed Sam by the shoulder, and we kept him going down through [that part of the ordeal]. We stopped again, and he looked up at me and he said, 'I know who you are. You're the best damn pilot in the world!'

I never let him forget that—I told him later that when you're really down and out, the truth comes out. [*Laughs*]

But if you think about it, it was Sam who really saved my life, because up until then I was just bound and determined that I just couldn't do it. When you see somebody else who really needs your help, it really makes a difference; when you have to do it, you just do it.

*

I can't remember the names of the towns anymore, but we got into a town and they put us into churches, and they were concrete floors and it was cold. The next morning the burgermeister of this town—we heard he had a son who was a PoW in the U.S.—he [appeared to] take over from the military. They had pottery factories there in that town and they opened up the drying rooms and put a bunch of us in there. We were warm! We stayed in there two or three days, and then we marched out of there, not too far, to a railroad station, and they put us in these little boxcars—fifty to a car, you couldn't even sit down. I still had my blanket, and two or three other guys had their blankets, and there were rings in the tops of the cars, and we managed to get five or six hammocks up to get some of us off the floor and make some room for the others. We were in there probably a day and a half, something like that, and we pulled into Nuremberg and went into a camp there.

Nuremberg was nasty, filthy, and dirty. We were there for a while. We'd walk into our barracks room and we'd see rats come running down the wall and walk across the guys who were sleeping. We got a cup of soup every day, and if it was bean soup there was a worm in every bean. I had seen my dad throw that kind of stuff out; he wouldn't feed his cows what we got. But if you're hungry you'd eat it anyway.

We had to get in a line to get water, and all we could get was a tin can, though we were probably in that line for an hour. I got bitten from head to foot by bugs, and swelling all settled in my feet, and I couldn't walk, I couldn't do anything. They put me in a barracks, they called the hospital, and there was an American soldier there, a doctor who was running the hospital. He put a hot water bottle on it overnight, and the next morning, they sat me up in the chair, and he said, 'Hang on,' and he had someone hold my shoulders. He cut a hole in my knee and squeezed out a cup of stuff.

He had penicillin tablets and he didn't know what they were because they were new, and he just stuck tablets in there. Would've done more good if he had fed them to me, but he put them in there and tore up a sheet and just wrapped it up.

He said, 'Now, we're going to move out of here in a couple of days, so I'll fix it up so you can ride in the train.'

I told him, 'No way!' See, we had a radio in the camp—the Germans knew we had the radio, but they could never find it—and you could get the BBC. We had the information now that our boys [fighter planes] were shooting everything up even if it had a Red Cross on it. We had seen it as well; we saw the Germans load tanks on trains and cover them in sheets with a big Red Cross sign on it so they could move them to the front lines. Our boys had gotten wise to that, so I wasn't going to get on any train at all. I'd rather walk. And afterwards, the doctors told me it was the best thing I could have done for my leg anyway.

[We had been in the camp near Nuremberg] for a month or so, and sure enough, the first day out, we got strafed by our boys. A couple of our guys got nicked, but they then flew right down the side of us, to see what we were and who we were. We just pulled our clothes off and made a big 'PW' sign, and from then on we had a fighter escort all the way down into Bavaria, and this was a four to five, or maybe six-day trip. By then we were actually bribing the German guards to stay with us, because there were SS troops in the area, and you didn't want a bunch of Americans just floating around down there, because those SS troops would just mow you down.

So we were bribing the guards and even the civilians then; I saw a bunch of civilian women attack our German camp commander and they knocked him down, and were knocking him around pretty good. Before we got down there to Moosburg, we could have just walked off if we wanted. I found some kids in one town and bought some eggs off them with a couple of cigarettes that the Red Cross had gotten to us—one of the home guards came out and followed me to make sure I left the town and didn't stick around, but by then the Germans were screaming and hollering, 'When are the Americans going to get here?', because they wanted the Americans to get there before the Russians did.

One night we stayed in a farmer's hay mound. It was nice and really clean hay. It was a nice place to stay. The war is still going on but the kids are out there playing, and you can see the kids' ribs. And I asked him, 'Why don't you kill one of your chickens and feed your kids?'

His answer was, it's a death penalty to kill that chicken without a government permit.

'He Saluted Me Back'

We finally got down to Moosburg; I guess all the PoWs in Germany were in there—I think that there was over 100,000 in that camp. It was a Sunday morning, and we knew General Patton was coming. We got the information on our radio. Matter of fact, they had it set up so that if the Germans were going to move us again, we would put sheets on top of the building and signal to a particular place. Well at exactly ten o'clock that Sunday morning, the first tank rolled over the top of the hill—the tank drove right through the fence, they didn't open the gate or anything, and behind the tank General Patton was standing up in the back of [a vehicle], pearl-handled pistols at his sides and all. [*Gestures where the pistols would have hung on his waist; chuckles*] And I threw him a salute, and he saluted me back, and he pulled off and made a little speech to us, and then he said, 'See you, gentlemen—I have a war to win,' and he pulled off and was gone.

Coming Home

We 'pulled spades' to see who would come out first. And my commanding officer of this area pulled out the ace of spades, and I came out on the seventh airplane. The C-47s or the DC-3s were coming in with supplies for Patton, and then they would load them up with PoWs and haul them out to France. So I came out early. We stopped in Paris to refuel, and while we were there I ate nineteen doughnuts! I was trying to get even more, but they wouldn't give me any more. They brought us to the place where they were bringing all the PoWs in, and they gave us a chemical bath. We threw all our clothes away, and they gave us enough pants and underwear and clean stuff to get on, and then they ask us if we would give up our quarters on the next ship going home. We figured they would probably put sick and wounded in those decent quarters, and then we would be in other quarters. So we weren't in the best quarters, and when we pulled out we were very disappointed because they had [given our quarters to] a bunch of British war brides. They got the good quarters, but I didn't care by then, they could have put a log under me and I would have ridden that home. [*Laughs*] But we came home, and came into Camp Myles Standish up in Boston.

This would have been May. There were a whole bunch of German PoWs in there, wearing brand-new American uniforms with 'PW' on the back of them. We ran after them; they had to get all the MPs after us and round us all up. We went in the mess hall that first night, and I'm right behind that big guy Smitty, you know, the one who was banging me around on the march. The Germans were serving the food. We're in line and they put a steak on each tray as we went through, and you're supposed to move forward. Smitty tells the guy, 'I want three more steaks!' The German shakes his head no, and that German went flying across the room! They got the brass in there, and they informed everyone that these guys get anything that they want. And a couple of days later we got on a train and went down to Atlanta, Georgia. From there they put us on a thirty-day leave, so I got a bus and went up to my home here and spent some time on the farm. After that, I went to Plattsburgh for a while and went to an Army hospital. Then I came back down here to try and get into the swing of things again, went down to General Electric again, where I was working before I went in the service. I didn't stay there but a couple of weeks—I don't know how we won the war from what I saw going on there, but maybe it wasn't going on during the war, but some of them in there were putting out the least amount of work—well, that's another story.

*

The Last Close Call

[When the war ended], the airlines wouldn't talk to us right away—they said we 'flew too rough.' But eventually they found out maybe we weren't so bad. So I flew a couple of years for a non-scheduled airline, which wasn't bad, but then I was gone all the time—you didn't know where you were going or when you were coming back.

I was living in Nashville. On one of the trips out we had a long layover or something in Michigan, so I caught a train into Chicago and talked to American Airlines, and they hired me. I couldn't have had a better job. I loved flying; I never had any big problems with American. I was in the co-pilot seat for eleven years, but that was because it was all based on seniority and right after I got in, they quit hiring for quite some time. But then, when I was flying out of Nashville, I wanted to get on the bigger airplanes, especially now with the jets coming out. Then I got to Chicago and I was flying co-pilot, but very soon I was flying captain. I flew the old piston air-planes for a little while and then I started working my way up—at the end, I wound up flying on the DC-10, a 289-passenger jet airplane. I loved it.

I had stayed about eleven years on a three-engine jet so I could be pretty senior. I loved the 727; it was a nice airplane. But then someone told me for retirement purposes you better get on a bigger airplane, so then I went to the DC-10 and I really enjoyed it. That 727, you could push the throttles up and roll down the runway to make the turn to line up, and then you'd take off. But with the 10, you couldn't do that; you had to line that thing up straight off because when you pushed the throttles up, it was going where it was pointed, with no turning at all. It would push you back in your seat, and I really liked that. But it turned out I had a close call on it. I took a flight from Chicago to Phoenix on a 10 and left it there, and brought another back to Chicago and went home and went to bed.

I got home at about six in the morning—it was a night flight. About noon my wife woke me up, and she said, 'You've got to get up and see the TV!'

I went in there, and a DC-10 airplane had crashed on takeoff at O'Hare Airport, killing everyone on board.[56] Worst accident they had ever had.

I looked at it, and I said, 'That's the airplane I flew last night to Phoenix!'

Now I had brought a different plane back. And shortly after that, the phone rang, and it was the chief pilot, and he said, 'Guess what!'

I said, 'I know, I flew that airplane last night!'

He said, 'I just have one question: What kind of landing did you have last night?' You see, right off the start they have to try to nail it to somebody.

---

[56] *crashed on takeoff at O'Hare Airport, killing everyone on board*- On May 25, 1979, American Airlines Flight 191 from Chicago to Los Angeles crashed moments after takeoff, killing all 271 on board and 2 persons on the ground. It remains the deadliest aviation accident in U.S. history.

I said, 'You call the co-pilot and ask him.'

The co-pilot was a young fella, and he had flown with me a lot on the 727, but never on the 10. We were coming in to Phoenix [on that same plane], and I thought, 'I better show this young fella something,' and I touched down and we never even felt the tires touch, we never even heard them.

He looked over and said, 'You can really slick them on with the 10 too, can't you?'

So that eliminated [any theory that the previous pilot had anything to do with the problem]. It turned out there were thirty-something airplanes with the same problem. The engine just broke off, but instead of just breaking off and falling to the ground, it broke off under power, and it came up over the leading edge of the wing, and tore off the lift devices, so the left wing quit flying and the right wing was still flying, and it [careened over and crashed right after takeoff]. The amazing thing is it could have happened on that airplane at any time, and I don't know why it didn't happen when I flew it. But it made me wonder if that had happened to me, what would I have done? I think I probably would have done better than they did. I had a really good chief pilot early on in [my airline career], and he always said, 'If you get in trouble, you don't worry about the trouble; fly the airplane.' The captain was rated as one of the best. He might have been trying to figure out what was going wrong, when he should have been making sure the airplane was flying properly. There was just no procedure at all for what happened; they also pulled the nose up, and let the airspeed back, following a different emergency procedure, but if they had kept the speed they had already, it might not have gone so quick.[57]

---

[57] *There was just no procedure at all for what happened* - In researching this incident, one of the worst aviation disasters in U.S. history, the author discovered that the lead federal investigator at the Chicago crash site was none other than Elwood P. Driver, a former Tuskegee Airman who flew with

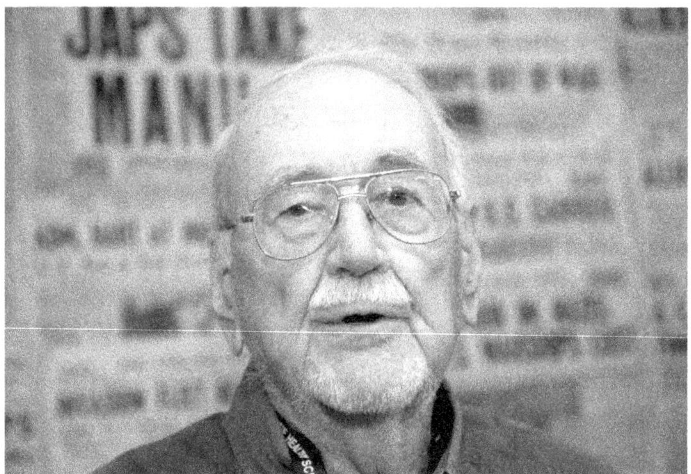

Earl Morrow in the author's classroom, May 2011.
Credit: Robert H. Miller

My time in the service was the smartest move I ever made.

To be frank with you, I was flunking out of college. I got to see the wheels turn; this thing opened up and I didn't figure I would ever make it, but I applied for it, and I made it—out of thirty-something of us who went in, I made it. And I couldn't have had a better job after I got back home. It was just never boring when I was flying. I had a little motto: 'If I don't learn something today, I'm going to quit flying.' And I never had to quit flying, because I was always learning something.

Clarence Dart, who is profiled in the sequel to this book. Mr. Dart and Mr. Driver appear together in a wartime photograph there; after the war, Mr. Dart and Mr. Morrow were great friends. *"Tuskegee Airman Heads Chicago Crash Site Probe," Jet Magazine*, June 17, 1979.

CHAPTER NINE

The Extra Gunner

We first met Richard Alagna in Chapter Six. Here, he brings us up-to-date on his later duties and adventures near the end of the war. He told me that his ball turret gunner days ended when they decided at some point to take the ball turret out of his B-24 completely.

'Did you know the ball turret was adding about a thousand pounds to the weight and drag on the airplane? Manned with a gunner like me, about 1,200 pounds. So they took it out and I became an extra gunner.'

Richard G. Alagna

'Dropped Into An Insane Asylum'

I think this brings us up to when we're going to go overseas and to show you the mentality of my flying officer. We were about to go over by ship and we had an opportunity to go home—we were in New Jersey, I don't know what port it was—and he volunteered his crew for KP duty. Nobody else would have done a thing like that but a first-class rat. We all had a chance to go home, call your mother or your girlfriend, but he volunteered us for KP. We did not become sergeants until we were overseas so therefore we could pull KP.

On the ship going over I wrenched my back very badly and I couldn't bend over at all. I went to the medics and they taped me up; they put tape from here [*points to upper chest*] down to my belly button and tied me up. There was no fresh water on the boat to shower, only salt water. When we were in the Irish Sea, we were on the top deck of this luxury liner and we're all standing there looking at the Irish Sea, and everybody screamed, 'Fighters coming in!' and they all fell to the deck. I couldn't move because I was taped. I wasn't mesmerized—the only way I could fall would be to fall on my ass or flat on my face. Before they skimmed by, I said, 'Three Spitfires,' and they thought that was wonderful, what tremendous aircraft recognition this kid had.

So now we're overseas and I'm all taped up and I'm itchy. We get off and we're in England, and we go to a place where we're going to be assigned to a squadron. I'm desperate because I can't get at this tape. You must also remember that I was issued a .45; a lot of people wondered about that, because in the Pacific I understand crew members were issued shotguns or carbines, but I was issued a .45 sidearm. As soon as we got to base and we dumped our bags, I immediately went to sick call. You have to picture it: I had on a flight jacket and I had a .45 under my armpit.

I go in and I said to the corporal, 'I just got here. I didn't have time to sign the sick book, but I really have to see the doctor. I've got to get rid of this tape; it's driving me crazy.'

He said, 'Don't worry, I'll get you in.'

I heard a voice say, 'Are there any more? No? That's it, nobody else on the sick book.'

'No, sir, we have one more man out there.'

This is what this officer and gentleman says: 'I don't care if he has appendicitis; if he hasn't signed the sick book, I'm not seeing him.'

He stepped out of the office, and I said, 'You son-of-a-bitch, they told me that when I got overseas, you guys were going to lighten up a little bit. I wouldn't let you touch me with a ten-foot pole!' He wasn't being shot at; he was in England. He was taking care of guys who had colds, athlete's foot, et cetera; I don't know what his problem was. Well, my jacket was open and his mouth was agape; I think he saw the .45. I was slightly beyond the edge at that moment.

The corporal was dumbfounded, and I turned around and walked out. Nobody came after me.

I went back to where I was billeted, and I said, 'I think I'm going to be arrested,' because that's what they do to people—you don't yell at officers.

A nice kid from Brooklyn said, 'Don't worry, you stay here in the barracks. I'll bring you food; you'll stay hidden.'

I said, 'But the tape!'

He said, 'Come with me,' and we went into the shower. He grabbed the tape, he took off every hair on my chest, on my back, and then I managed to get some sleep.

*

Now here comes more fun and games, and this is an important one. We end up in the 445th Bomb Group, 700th Squadron. The very first night we get there, I honestly thought I had been dropped into an insane asylum. The crew that had been there had been wiped out, and these fellows were absolutely bonkers, at least that was my impression. One fellow had a bolt from a .50 caliber machine gun, and he slipped a .50 caliber bullet in the facing, and he had a hammer and he's going to hit it. When you do something like that, it's going to explode, the whole thing is going to rupture, and you're going to be in trouble. It didn't explode, but the slug went into the door. I didn't know that he took all the stuff out of the thing; it was a gag.

They also had set up a guy that would come in the door, and just before he'd come in, some guy would throw a knife and it would hit the door. I turned to one of my fellow gunners and said, 'I think they're going to kill me before the Germans do.'

Later they told us that it was sort of like an initiation to their barracks. I had never belonged to Greek societies or anything like that; I vowed that I would get my revenge.

After being there some time and flying quite a number of missions and being slightly insane, I took a belt of .50 caliber machine gun rounds; there must have been about twelve of them in metal links. I pulled all of the cordite out of them, but I kept the caps and I put back the slugs. I had it draped over my bed as a souvenir. I have Romanian and Sicilian blood coursing through my veins, and we all believe in getting revenge.

They were playing poker. It was the afternoon and nobody was flying; it was raining like hell. I went through my act, 'I'm too young to die'—it was a pretty good act. They're playing poker and paying no attention to me.

I said, 'I can't stand it, it's driving me crazy, sooner or later it's going to kill me, I'm dying' of this and that.

Somebody said, 'Shut up!' I took the ammo, walked over to the potbelly stove, said, 'To hell with all of you,' and I dropped it into the stove.

Well, one guy went through the window and into the mud, into the rain. [*Laughs*] Guys hit the doors, they went all over, and I'm standing there screaming, 'What did I do, what did I do?!' All it did was go pop-pop-pop, and fortunately none of the slugs went through the stove. They chased me and threw mud pies at me, but I didn't care because I got my revenge. [*Laughs*]

We used to play poker, and when they played poker, the guys would sit with their cards up close. We would steal—'take home,' let's put it that way—the Very pistol cartridges; we didn't sell them to anybody. It goes in a Very pistol—it's a flare gun, the flares would either be red-red, red-green, whatever colors, and we'd snap off the shotgun shell part and I'd roll it up in newspaper, and we'd feed the fire. When they're playing poker, we'd just drop it in and suddenly the entire barracks room would turn full of red smoke, green smoke. When it cleared, [they would still be sitting there] with their hands on the cards and the money; it was hilarious. One hand was always on the cards, the other was always on the money, because we were all conditioned to this gag. Gags, there were quite a few. When we'd go to the latrine at night, we'd take a Very pistol out, load it, and fire it. The MPs would come, and they'd say, 'Who did that?'

We'd say, 'The guys over there,' and they would roust those guys and give them hell. [*Laughs*]

The 'ground-pounders,' the ground personnel, disliked us immensely. They had a perpetual hate because we made more money than they did. I was a staff sergeant and I made the equivalency in pay of a captain. Overseas pay, flight pay, and we threw our money around like it didn't matter for the simple reason that the next morning you might be eating sauerbraten someplace. There was [one of them] who I hated, a guy who came up after a mission and said, 'Thank God you got back!'

He was an armorer. I never heard anybody say, 'Thank God you came back.' I was really quite thrilled.

I said, 'That's very nice of you.' Now he was going to take out the guns and do the dirty work in the plane.

Then he said, 'Because I left my coffee cup in your plane and I couldn't get a cup of coffee.'

Aborted Missions

Let me tell you the story about the oranges. An aborted mission means they send you back, something happened, somebody changed their mind. We went to the briefing, then we went to breakfast, and they came in and said the mission was aborted. That was very good, marvelous, and all hell broke loose in the mess hall. As we were very privileged, we did get fresh eggs, I think, and good meat and all that nonsense. We got oranges. They started to throw the oranges around. I grew up during the Depression and I didn't think that was funny. They had just gone bonkers. I kept picking up the oranges that weren't spoiled, and I had a gas mask kit that the first thing I did when we got to England was throw the gas mask away and put my underwear and socks in and use for an overnight bag. I stuffed it full of oranges. When you weren't flying, there was nothing to do. The only duty that we had would be at night, to guard your airplane—they would trust us for that—but we had no KP and we didn't pull guard duty other than on the plane. I went back and I got into my Class A uniform and I went to town. I changed trains at Ipswich and went to Norwich, which was a delight because I liked old things and castles and to go around and see things. I figured I'd spend the day at Norwich, have dinner there, and then come back. I took the oranges and I got off the train, and I'm there on a corner and I called the little kids over. The kids always wanted chewing gum and chocolate and cigarettes, and they wouldn't take the cigarettes that we got for free; they wanted the good cigarettes. The English didn't have oranges or any kind of citrus; we didn't bring in anything for the English. I'm nineteen or twenty, and I'm giving away oranges, and a woman comes out of a house with an umbrella and she starts to beat me with it! My mother always said you never ever hit a woman; you can restrain a woman, but you never hit her. I ran into a pub and I'm out of breath, and guys there are laughing, and I said, 'What did I do wrong?'

An Englishman said to me, 'She thought you were a dirty old man.' I didn't know what a 'dirty old man' was, and when they explained it to me, I was furious, and that time I came close to hitting a woman. I didn't think it was funny that she would accuse me of something like that.

Another time, we were in the air and they aborted that mission. It was a bad one to begin with because planes were running into one another. We didn't see the planes hit; you just saw the big explosion, you saw the big red, you felt the vibration. We took off in fog, and you got up to six thousand fog, ten thousand fog, twelve thousand fog; you're going up there and there's nothing but fog. And then it wasn't fog anymore, it was contrails. We had to form on the flares, the flare color. That's when I discovered all the fun things we did with flares. That's also when we found out that our nose gunner was colorblind. [*Laughs*] He had joined the Air Corps because he figured he would not have to worry about mixing up the color of friendly and enemy uniforms.

So the pilot was pretty smart. He was a good pilot, he was just not a nice person. He decided that we'll fly around, burn up gasoline and do whatever we have to do with the bombs, [and return home]. So we're flying around in the North Sea all by ourselves and the navigator is getting upset, and rightfully so, because the fighters are going to pick up a single aircraft and you're a dead goose. So he sees a bastard squadron—we all had different tail markings, and you could tell from the tail markings that these guys were doing the same thing; they had the smarts to say let's stay together. He tacks on and the navigator was still pretty bright.

He said, 'What if it's a German weather ship?'

Sometimes when B-24s went down, they didn't always break up completely and some of them were actually captured with just the landing gear broken. They would rebuild them, fly them up, and try to infiltrate our squadrons. They would find out where we're going, listen to the conversation. You'd just be stuck because if this was a German leading us around on a merry goose chase, we're in deep trouble. He goes up front, writes down all the data on the guy's tail, all that crap. I think they talked to one another with something or other. He said we're going to pull the pins on the bombs. So we went into the bomb bays—you had to take the cotter pins out of the bombs. Then all hell broke loose. The place turned into a shooting gallery, and we were hit and we dropped our bomb. We didn't know who we hit, what poor stupid bastard on the ground was so upset that he decided to fire. If he didn't fire at us, we wouldn't have dropped the bomb. Our pilot was very upset because he wanted to be, and he did eventually become, a lead pilot. He wanted a promotion so badly.

Anyway, we get back and all the other members of our squadron had gotten back much earlier. We come back, one engine's out, all kinds of holes in the plane, the crew chief is mad as hell because he would rather we'd gone down so that he wouldn't have to repair the plane. It's true, that's the way the guy felt, that's what he said: 'Look what you did to my plane—do you know how many hours I'm going to be working on this?!'

I wanted to kick his butt. Now you have to understand that I'm dead, and I go back to our barracks and everything is gone. The bedding is gone, my footlocker is gone, my shirts, pants, my stuff that's hung up—everything gone. What's going on? It seems that the practice was that when a crew went down, they immediately took the footlocker because they were going to send things home to the families and they would go through it to make sure there wasn't anything in it that would upset a wife—girlie pictures, whatever some idiot might have in his footlocker. Everything was fine; I got everything back except my tunic. There were no tunics to be had on my base. This is old Catch-22 again—you can't get off the base unless you were in a Class A uniform. You can't get a Class A uniform because they don't have any, right? If I could get off the base, I could buy one, because the English had these Army-Navy shops, and I could go in and for 30 to 40 bucks I could get another jacket, but I can't get off the base. I was very upset.

Along comes a guy with my jacket on. I could tell my jacket because I could not sew, couldn't do any of those girl things. I was actually the worst soldier in the world; I would take cotter pins and put the buttons on with cotter pins and hide it so no one would see it. I had a special pair of silver wings that I had bought, a little fancier than what the other guys had because I thought it was kind of cute. Also, the jacket had my name stenciled in the back with my serial number.

I said, 'That's my jacket!'

He said, 'But it fits me.' It was an invitation to a fight; he wanted me to fight him for my jacket.

I just looked at this guy. I put my hand in my jacket, pulled out my .45, pointed it right at him, and I said to him in a very nice, calm voice, 'On the jacket is a marksmanship medal for the .45. I'm going to cock it, I'm going to take the safety off, and I'm going to shoot you, and I'm not going to get any blood on the jacket.' I had it pointed just where the jacket ended. He took the jacket off immediately, threw it down, and away he went.

I've been asked by many guys would I have shot him. I think I would have. I honestly think, at that point, after the aggravation I had that day, that this clown is stealing something that belongs to me right in front of me and he wants me to punch him in the nose, I think I would have shot him.

Somebody said, 'Why didn't you call an MP?'

I said, 'I never called a cop in my life.' When I was a kid, the cops used to hit us with billies, make us move, because we were playing stickball or we were disruptive or we were too noisy or this or that.

*

I became an extra gunner. My pilot did some silly things but he got away with them. They promoted him; he was a good flyer. The tail gunner went, I went, the engineer went, everybody off the crew went, and he got other personnel to train him to be a lead pilot. I'm doing nothing now. I'm without a crew, walking around, having fun. I could do anything I want, but I couldn't go home until I finished my tour. It's driving me slightly crazy. The war was coming to an end and I wasn't going to see it, but I really did love to fly.

An Old Friend

Let me tell you about meeting an old friend. I had a buddy who was in the infantry and he got lucky. Just before going to France, they discovered he had flat feet. Just like the Army, [they all of a sudden] discover you only have one leg or something like that. They had him at a repo depot someplace in England.[58] I wrote to him, he wrote to me, I didn't know where he was, he didn't know where I was, and I'm not supposed to tell him where I am because God forbid the Germans would find out, although the Germans knew exactly where we were every minute of the day. Every night before a mission the Germans would tell us where we were going [before we were even briefed]. That was very nice, I enjoyed that immensely. We'd go into a room with MPs and a screen and they'd lock the door, just like in the movies, and then they'd pull it up and you'd find out what the mission is for the day—except I knew what

---

[58] *repo depot*-replacement depot located near the battle fronts, so that individual soldiers could be sent to infantry companies to replace the men who became casualties.

the mission was for the day because the German with the best jazz program told me where we were going. [*Imitates radio broadcaster*] 'The 445th, you will be our guests,' blah, blah, blah. The cook knew where we were going; the guys in the hallway knew where we were going.

Getting back to my friend, I wanted to find my friend. I went to London, to headquarters, which was a mistake. All I wanted was for them to tell me where my old buddy was. I got into headquarters and when I told them what I wanted, they threw me through the door, they literally kicked me out. They told me I was insane and that the Army doesn't function that way.

So using what knowledge I had, I had an officer un-censor my letter. I go to him and I [had written], 'Sal, I'm at this base, I'm at this telephone number. You can reach me, that's where my squadron is. Kindly tell me where you are.' This officer was nice enough. He said, 'You're absolutely right, it's stupid,' and he signed it and stamped it. It went V-Mail all the way to the States and all the way back again. Sal finally got it. He phoned me, and I got on a train because I had all the time in the world, because by that time I was an extra gunner. I went to see him, and he was in a repo depot, which means all these poor guys who had gotten broken up had to be rehabilitated and reassigned, things like that.

I said, 'Get on your Class A's, let's get out of here and have dinner.'

He said, 'The food here is better than the food in town.' It was hospital food but it was beautiful food.

I saw some guys in black uniforms; I didn't like the black. We were told if you got shot down, you didn't surrender to anybody but a guy in a green uniform, never to a man in a black uniform—they were the SS and they were bad news. So we're sitting at this table having coffee, and I said, 'Who are those people?'

He said, 'They're ex-paratroopers that are broken up, and they're here training everybody to get them in shape, and they wear these black gym suits.'

Then I said in a very loud voice, 'You mean that stupid son-of-a-bitch over there is an ex-paratrooper, the one with the big nose? That god-awful-looking piece of shit?'

My friend Sal is now going crazy, he says, 'He's going to hear you!'

I said, 'I want him to hear me!'

The guy came over. It was a kid I knew from grade school, and we hugged each other and we all had coffee and laughed. He had jumped the day before D-Day, when they put guys on the ground.

Guard Duty

We're in England and we're in the war. I think I told you that you had to pull duty by taking care of the airplanes at night just before they took off; that was the only duty you had to do. One time I was called to do it, and it was cold and wet and I was very tired, and I had been carousing and I couldn't keep my eyes open. I knew that if you fell asleep you could be court-martialed. It wasn't very nice to fall asleep because the Germans were doing very nasty things. They were dropping paratroopers down, espionage kind of guys, and they would drop fountain pens into our airplanes. They looked like fountain pens but they were altimeter bombs, so that when the bombers got up to a certain altitude this thing would explode and the plane would go down. It was a very good method. We had to make sure nobody got near the planes. I broke into an escape kit and I took out the stay-awake pill. When you were shot down you had certain things in this thing. You had morphine, which was never there, and you had other stuff, and you had this pill. I guess it's what the kids use in college to stay awake, but this was a super pill because this was supposed to make you feel like Superman. I did not want to be court-martialed so I took the pill, took some water, and I felt great. I'd never taken drugs in my life, but this was marvelous. They told me they weren't going to come for the plane until 4:00 or 5:00 in the morning, and wouldn't you know it, at 2:00 in the morning they come over and they say, 'You can leave now.' I asked why and they said they had changed the mission to something else. I went back to my barracks and I put my head on the pillow. I closed my eyes and it was like when you snap a window [shade] up, it rolls up. I couldn't keep my eyelids closed; my eyelids would not close. Around 4:00 that afternoon it was like somebody hit me with a baseball bat; I just collapsed. That was a great pill.

Sergeant Grayboy

Going back, we took off on a mission to Berlin. Berlin's a nasty place to go; it had a bad reputation. We were the first wave over wherever the hell we were going, the target area. It's a long, long flight, and when you flew in those planes you got down on the ground, and you always knew who flew that day, because they would be shouting, everybody had to shout. Nobody could hear, your hearing had gone. Those engines—you were eight hours, maybe nine hours, who knew how long you were in the plane.

This guy runs up to me and says, 'You were in the first wave, how many went down?'

I said, 'We were lucky, they caught hell behind us.'

Well, he cursed like a son-of-a-bitch—he had the book on us, he was running a pool. This was Sergeant Grayboy, my buddy, one of my favorite friends. Sergeant Grayboy would book on anything.

Now, Grayboy—he was into black market, he was into everything—he had a beautiful leather jacket. I never got a leather jacket,

I'm a deprived person. We had a deal. He wanted my camera, which I wouldn't sell him—oh, the camera story...

When you were flying, when planes got hit, guys would bail out. They would want to know how many guys got bailed out, but everybody had a different count so taking a photograph was rather important. Photography was very strong with me, and I picked up this K-20 camera, like a Speed Graphic, and I took some beautiful pictures. When we came down from the mission, I went to the photographic unit. I knocked on the door, wanted to see my pictures. They said it was classified.

I said, 'What are you talking about, I took the pictures, I want to see how they came out!'

He said, 'Sergeant, if you don't go away, we're calling the MPs.'

I'm banging on the door, I want to see my pictures, I don't see anything wrong with just looking at them—give me one little snapshot for a souvenir. Under the threat of calling the MPs, which I knew would be trouble, they gave me a batch of pictures and they sent me away, but none of the mission I flew!

Anyway, back to Grayboy and the camera. He wanted my camera; I wanted his jacket. We couldn't make a deal so we made an announcement in the barracks that if Grayboy got killed, I got the jacket, and if I went down, he got the camera.

One morning he went up to fly, and he had on the jacket and I told him to take it off.

He said, 'It's cold outside.'

I said, 'I don't give a goddamn, take the jacket off.' I made him take the jacket off and wear a sweater, because we had that deal!

Let me tell you the story about Grayboy and flying the last mission. Everybody wanted to go home, be a hero or whatever you want to call it. One night in bed, Grayboy slept in the bed next to me, and he was doing something I have never seen anybody do. He was putting out his cigarettes with his fingertips, and then he'd throw the cigarette down on the ground and light another one. He had plenty of cigarettes. He's lighting cigarettes and putting them out with his fingers.

I said to him, 'Grayboy, you've got a problem; you want to talk about this?'

He said, 'This is my last mission, this is it.'

I was a poor kid; he had money, he was into the black market, and he could get you anything you wanted. He wanted me to fly his last mission.

We had different deals; I was an extra gunner, [with time on my hands]. You ask how could a guy do that? Well, it was very easy. When somebody was sick and you were flying their mission, your name is Grayboy, mine is Alagna, so they know on the roster that Sergeant Alagna is to fly in Tom Jones' plane. Or you'd show up and you had your helmet on, you had your goggles on the top of your head, the pilot never saw you before; this is wild, dark, and wooly. All he wanted was a body at a machine gun or in a turret. When I come back, he gets the credit and I get the money, so yes, it was done. How many times it was done, I have no idea, but it was done.

I'm sitting there with Grayboy and I said, 'I'm not afraid of flying and I don't think I'm going to get killed. If I thought I was going to get killed, I'd stop flying.' It was a voluntary thing, and if you really wanted to get out of it without going through any nonsense, just walk into headquarters and punch the officer right in the mouth. You want a nice place to eat and sleep where it's nice and safe? They give you a nice little cage. You just walk in and pop him in the nose. And they say, what did you do that for? And you say, 'I don't know, just don't like officers.' The MPs will take you away.

I said to him, 'I don't think I want to fly your last mission because I really don't know if I'm going to have to bail out,' which I didn't look forward to, ever. If I had to bail out and I float down to Germany, they're not going to look lightly upon me. I'm not a woodsy kind of guy; I'm not going to be able to run through the woods and eat the berries. I would probably end up being in some stalag someplace.

'So now, Grayboy, think of this—I'm in a stalag somewhere, and you are now me. Being me, you have to fly the balance of my missions, you have to answer my mother's mail that's coming in, my girlfriend's mail that's coming in, and when the war is over and they come and get me out of that prison, do you honestly think they're going to give me a hero's welcome? I will be AWOL, as simple as that. I'll go from a German prison to an American prison, for a couple of bucks. I won't do it.'

He got on the plane. I put him on the plane with a bottle of Scotch. He was drunk; he flew his last mission. He was as nutty as a fruitcake.

Patches

Let me tell you about my time on Patches. There was a plane called 'Patches,' and they should have made a memorial to that plane. They renamed it 'Patches' because it had literally over 100 flak holes in it. It flew at a tilt, which was funny. It sounds silly but it seemed like one of the wings went just slightly out of tilt. If you managed to get Patches, if Patches was assigned to you, you knew you were coming home. I flew home in that plane. Nobody's going to take that plane down, that was a good luck plane.

[When it was about time to come] home, before I got onto Patches, the adjutant officer in the squadron said I would fly with him and I would fly in the nose on the B-24. We didn't know where we were going to go—we had no idea whether we were going to go to India or we were going to go home—but they said we're going to have to do some navigational flights. I'm [going to be] flying in the nose, and first we're supposed to go up to the tip of Scotland, turn around, and come back and land. I'm in the nose, there's no more Germans—by the way, all the Nazis died, they disappeared, there wasn't a Nazi left in Germany. [*Joking*] I assure you, the United Nations knows this for a fact: they all went to Sweden. Anyway, something hit my eyes, sunlight. I was resting, I was probably asleep, nothing to do because there's nothing to see. I see sunlight, a rim of sunlight, and we're supposed to not be flying at night but up there it's always very bright. I look forward and I see nothing but water, look to my left, water, look to my right, water. We are no longer over Scotland. This I knew; you don't have to be a bright boy to know that Scotland is not inundated with water. This is the North Sea or the Atlantic Ocean or God-knows-what.

I turn my head around, and the navigator, I have no idea who he was—it wasn't my old navigator—he was sound asleep. True story, not a joke. In the B-24 from that angle, you could see up into where the pilot's and co-pilot's seats were, and both of them were out like this [*closes eyes, stretches legs*]; they were relaxed, they were asleep. Now the rest of the guys in the back, I don't know what the hell they were doing; they were playing cards or they were asleep, who knows what.

I put my hand to my throat mike, and I said in a very low, quiet, controlled voice, 'Hi, is there anybody in this aircraft that's awake? I don't want to upset anybody, but is there anybody in this aircraft...'

Then the fun started. The pilot yelled to the co-pilot, 'You were supposed to be flying, you were supposed to be.' They had it on 'George.' George is the automatic pilot, and we were flying out to God-knows-where. The navigator woke up, and they were yelling at one another, and I'm saying to myself, 'What a bunch of fuck-ups.' This, to me, wasn't practice, practice, practice; this was screw-up, screw-up, screw-up.

Now we get down on the ground, and I don't know how many days went by, but this [new] pilot said to me, 'Richard.' By the way, he was a decent guy, he called me Richard. He said, 'Richard, do you have a wife?'

I said, 'No, sir, I do not.'

'Do you have a real girlfriend that you want to get home to?' I'd only been overseas for a couple of months.

I said, 'No, I don't mind.'

And he said, 'Look, I've got a young pilot that is willing and who wants very much to fly the nose to come home; he's married, he wants to see his wife. I'll get you on somebody else's crew.' Because he was the adjutant, he could do all this paperwork.

I said, 'Okay, but please, no boats. I've had it with the boats, I don't want to go on another boat.'

He said, 'No, I'll get you on another crew.' And that's how I got onto Patches again.

Let's move ahead. I get home, I get fifteen or thirty days [furlough], and I get back to this airfield; the war is still going on in Japan. Some of my buddies came over, and they grabbed me and they said, 'How the hell did you get out?'

I said, 'Out of what?'

'The adjutant went down in the drink [in the other plane].'

I said, 'That's the way it goes, that's the way it goes.' So sometimes you get lucky.

Let me tell you one last thing. When I finally got home—not swimming the Atlantic—I was asked by a nice corporal, 'Sergeant, I have to ask you, would you like to fly against the Japanese?' I couldn't believe anybody would ever ask me that question, ever.

He said, 'Now you have enough combat hours, you don't have to fly against the Japanese.'

I said, 'Thank you very much, you've made my mother very happy. I would like very much to walk around in my Class A uniform with my ribbons, my wings, chase after all the girls that you've been chasing. That's what I want to do.'

Then I tried to get out of the Army, and that was next to impossible. The war was over, I wanted to go home. I did what I was supposed to do, I volunteered, it's over. Just send me home.

Martin Bezon, World War II.

CHAPTER TEN

The Radar Man

In researching this book, I came across Martin 'Hap' Bezon of Port Henry on Lake Champlain, just to the north of 'Hometown, USA,' and about 110 miles north of Albany, New York. Near here is a statue to Samuel De Champlain, who came down the lake from New France (Canada) in 1609. Martin's grandparents emigrated from Poland; little did he know that he would find himself unexpectedly there during the war, trying to convince advancing Red Army soldiers not to shoot him after he bailed out of his B-24 Liberator. This interview was given at his home in 2012 when he was ninety years old.

***

There is one man in particular who is supposed to know all there is to know about this equipment. Sometimes he does, but often he doesn't. And when the radio operator's deficiencies do not become apparent until the crew is in the combat zone, it is then too late. Too often the lives of pilots and crew are lost because the radio operator has accepted his responsibility indifferently.

Radio is a subject that cannot be learned in a day. It cannot be mastered in 6 weeks, but sufficient knowledge can be imparted to the radio man during his period of training in the United States if he is willing to study. It is imperative that you check your radio operator's ability to handle his job before taking him overseas as part of your crew. To do this you may have to check the various departments to find any weakness in the radio operator's training and proficiency and to aid the instructors in overcoming such weaknesses.

Training in the various phases of the heavy bomber program is designed to fit each member of the crew for the handling of his jobs. The radio operator will be required to:

Render position reports every 30 minutes.

Assist the navigator in taking fixes.

Keep the liaison and command sets properly tuned and in good operating order.

Maintain a log.

In addition to being a radio operator, the radio man is also a gunner. During periods of combat he will be required to leave his watch at the radio and take up his guns. The radio operator who cannot perform his job properly may be the weakest member of your crew--and the crew is no stronger than its weakest member.

—Duties and Responsibilities of the Airplane Commander and Crewmen, 1943[59]

---

[59] *Radio operator*-Marty Bezon qualified for many positions on the heavy bombers. Many of his duties outlined in this chapter parallel the

***

Martin F. Bezon

'The Black Cloud Arrived'

I was born on November 8, 1921, here in Port Henry. As a matter of fact, the house that used to be at the foot of this hill is where I was born. I attended the Champlain Academy Parochial School kindergarten through eighth grade, and I went to the Port Henry High School and I graduated from there in June of 1941.

I went to work for Republic Steel. I had hopes of stepping out in the world and getting a better job, but this job was available. So, we started working at fifty-five cents an hour, but come December the 7th of the same year—'41—the black cloud [arrived]; the Japs attacked us at Pearl Harbor and it changed my whole life around.

I was walking up to the village and somebody stopped and said the Japanese attacked Pearl Harbor. The full force of that didn't hit me yet, but I got home and got the news and all that, and I realized that it wouldn't be long before we'd get in the war too. As a matter of fact, it was the next day that Roosevelt [asked Congress to] declare war.

So I waited a little bit, then I went to Albany to enlist and I joined the Marine Corps. They said okay, they'll accept us—there were three of us there—but we have to get home and have my folks sign some papers.

I was still seventeen, too young. I came home and found my father sick. My mother was alone and my brother was in the third year of high school here, and the doctor says, 'No way are you going

---

expectations for the radio man, though much of his crew activity centered on the radar set, duties which were still highly classified.

to the service yet, because the responsibility of the entire family is on your shoulders.' I tried to talk to my mother and the doctor, but they said no. So that fell through.

I waited and worked for Republic. Eventually, I just couldn't take no more and told my mother that I got to go in. In December, I went back to Albany and signed up because they dropped the requirements for the Army Air Force Cadet Program to high school graduate. There was no Air Force at the time, so it was the U.S. Army Air Force. This would be in '42. So, they gave me the physical and the complete tests like they did to everybody. I went down to join the Air Force, and they asked me, 'Are you anxious to get back in?'

I said, 'Yeah, I'll come back tomorrow. I just need to go home for a day.'

The sergeant said, 'All right, I'll give you some advice.' He says, 'We'll accept you as an Air Force reservist, and as soon as the cadet class opens up, they'll put a call out and they'll look into the reservists first.' He says, 'If you really want to get in quick, I'd advise you to get in on the next draft that you can and join the Army Service and get in the Army. When the call comes out for cadets, they will take the ones who are on active duty first.'

So I said, 'Oh gee, I'll do that.'

So as we left Albany, we didn't even come straight home. We stopped in Ticonderoga, because [for us] that's where the draft board main office was. We went into Mr. McLaughlin's office, and he looked up and said, 'What can I do for you boys?'

I said, 'We'd like to get into the next draft, sir.'

He said, 'Great, I need three more men.' He stamped three forms and said, 'Be back here tomorrow morning.'

So, the next day, I went back to Albany, and he said to tell them that you were a reservist in the Air Force and that you wanted to join the Air Force. So, we got examined. They lined us up on the street and raised our right hand to take the oath of allegiance that we'd be in the Army. Then I didn't even have a chance to ask to be assigned to the Air Force. They just announced that anybody who wants to join the Air Force, to take one step forward. I stepped forward with a guy who later became my brother-in-law, but eventually he dropped out. He got a little leery of being up in the air so far.

I went in and went to Camp Upton at Long Island. I was there for about three days and shipped out of there to Camp Croft south of Spartanburg, South Carolina. I went through six weeks of basic and seven weeks of advanced training. They tried to keep me in as a sharpshooter, but I said, 'No, I'm waiting for the Air Force.' I had to wait a couple of weeks and then the call came out. I was happy that we were picked out of, I think, eight of us; before we left, three of the boys didn't pass. So three of us did go from Camp Croft to Nashville, Tennessee. We had one week of written tests and one week of physicals. I was accepted into the cadet program then. There were just two of us left.

'As Long As I Fly'

Even though I qualified for pilot and navigator, I was asked to be a bombardier; they needed bombardiers badly. They were building a huge armada of bombers and they said they were getting ready to just bomb Germany off the face of the map. So I said, 'It makes no difference as long as I fly.' They promised when I put in a tour and came back that they would put me into pilot school.

We wound up training and went to Santa Ana, California, for preflight. They had our curtains closed [on the train] because they said we were too valuable; we were the cream of the crop that they could pick. We weren't allowed to raise the curtains on the train until we got way out around Arizona out in the desert. Then we headed north. Everybody was guessing where we were going. We were headed northeast rather than west; we were going to Chicago or something. Nope. Then we headed south and then headed back east. We crisscrossed the country that way until we got out to Arizona. Then the officer in charge comes through and raised curtains now and said, 'You guys are going to Santa Ana, California, for preflight.' I remember that there was quite a 'whoop.' They all liked that idea. So we went to training up there.

I think it was about six weeks. I remember a sergeant coming in the barracks one time and he said, 'How many people have never flown in a plane?' I thought I was going to be embarrassed that I would be the only one standing, but quite a few of them stood up. So, we all got a ride in a plane to get the feel of it.

On weekends, we went to Hollywood, Los Angeles, and Long Beach. Every Friday night there used to be about fifty buses outside the gate to take the cadets wherever they wanted to go.

When we finished preflight, we were sent to Kingman, Arizona, for air-to-air gunnery. That was a seven-week course out in the desert. You had to shoot the .50 caliber machine guns way up in the air. You can imagine how far those projectiles would go.

We had different types of training. We had a huge screen coming over for a machine gun that fired only BBs. There were thousands of BBs falling back, and they would just put them back in. Then you would have planes going across and you would try to hit them. Then we were on the shotgun range every day. We had to fire fifty rounds of 12-gauge shotgun at clay pigeons going through the air—some going one way and some the other. That, I loved too.

The final week, we had to fire from the back side of a pickup truck. The guy shooting was tied down so he wouldn't fall, and you had two men with you. So, as you went around the track at, I believe, 30 miles per hour, they had underground cement places that they made with the front secure so you couldn't get hurt or anything. It had a small slit in it, and you looked through the slit. When you see a truck coming and hit a certain spot, you just lean back and pull the thing there, which throws it out. You had to work that for the other crews that came on. It was hard to hit with you moving, with the target coming at you and going away from you—going to the right and going to the left, going straight up. If you got six or seven hits you were lucky.

But the last day, I don't know what happened. I couldn't miss—just couldn't miss. I know a lot of the boys from the city, they didn't know how to fire a weapon, so they used to keep it loose [to their shoulder]. When that recoiled, it would hit them, so they were black and blue all over the arm and the chest. This one guy, he couldn't fire anymore, his shoulder hurt so bad. You're not supposed to do that. So, I fired mine. I couldn't believe it. I think I got 21 out of 25. We got through with gunnery, passed, and got the certificate as 'air-to-air' gunners, and then we were given a seven-day furlough.

We headed down to Albuquerque, New Mexico. We got our advanced bombardier course. There we learned all about the Norden bombsight.[60] We learned everything about the ins and outs, and made our practice runs. We flew AT-8s on a bombing run. I had a close call there. We did have one man killed. One of our cadets was killed on training. A couple had to bail out.

---

[60] *Norden bombsight*-The physics involved in dropping a bomb from thousands of feet to hit a target on the ground are astoundingly complicated. Carl Norden, a Swiss-born engineer, developed a 50 lb. analog computer that was so valued by the U.S. military that it invested 1.5 billion in 1940 dollars in it (for comparison, the Manhattan Project came in at around 3 billion). Bombardiers went to school for months to learn how to use it; it was installed in the bombers under armed guard and set to self-destruct upon the crashing of the aircraft. Unfortunately, its accuracy was highly questionable, given all of the combat conditions and high altitudes; the bombardier also had to be able to visually sight the target. See www.ted.com/talks/malcolm_gladwell, for an interesting discussion.

After we got through and everything was good, we had time on our hands. The pilots liked to fly up through the canyons. One time we saw one plane coming out while we're going in. We had enough room, but in the planes you don't know. So, as they were ready to pass, they both flipped over and flew by. It turned out good—no problem.

We enjoyed our weekends in Albuquerque. Sunday, we had to come back, because every Sunday they had a huge parade and everybody on that base had to be in that parade, even the KPs, no matter who it was. If you were on toward the tail end of the parade, you had to stand out there for a few hours, just standing [at attention] for your turn to go. It took that long—at least two hours before the last few would get to march. Whoever was picked the best would get an afternoon off to go to town at twelve noon the next Friday instead of five o'clock. Finally, we got close one day; we felt we were going to make it. We came out there and everything was good. Then they gave 'eyes right' and we did, but there was a little Italian guy who had a little bit too much to drink the night before. He snapped his head right and his hat flew off and he stooped to pick it up. They gave us a good mark, but it kicked us out of first place! But we graduated—graduated as 2nd lieutenants. This was January of '44.

*

We were sent to a place called Boca Raton, Drew Field in Florida. It was on the east coast of Florida near Tampa. As a matter of fact, we used to live on the spring training grounds for the Cincinnati Reds; we had our tent pitched on second base.

We flew missions. A bunch of bombardiers came in, a bunch of navigators and a bunch of pilots, and they formed crews—our crews that we were going to go into combat with. I ended up with Lt. Tuttle as pilot and Lt. Burkes as co-pilot. We had a good crew. Then there is Zielinski and Donovan. We were really like a family and blended together good.

'Who's Our Navigator?'

The first [training] mission, we didn't have a navigator, and I looked up on the board and we had a navigational mission that night. We had to take off at midnight. I went back to the pilot and said, 'Bob, I think we got a navigator.'

He said, 'How come?'

I said, 'Because we're going on a navigation mission.'

We went up to the instructor there and said, 'Who's our navigator?'

He said, 'What crew?'

I said, '92.'

'You don't have a navigator,' he said.

I said, 'But we've got a navigation mission.'

He said, 'Who's your bombardier?'

I said, 'I am.'

He said, 'You'd better know what navigation to learn because you're the navigator.'

I said, 'Oh boy.'

So, we had to fly from Tampa over to just below Miami, I'd say 20 miles. You could see it all lit up, and then out in the ocean, out there 50 miles or so, the land disappeared. I had to head north in pitch darkness to a point where we'd turned a little bit north-northeast and we headed down toward the Alabama area—the swamplands down through there in Florida, and then we had to go out into the Gulf of Mexico. From there we turned into our home base.

Where we were stationed, St. Petersburg was not too far away, and they had a long bridge there—I think it was the Gandy Bridge—and way off in the distance as dawn was breaking, you could see that string of lights. So Tuttle says, 'Marty, what's those lights ahead?'

I said, 'If that's not Gandy Bridge, we're lost.'

So we landed right on course and I felt pretty good since it was the first [navigation training] mission, and we did that good on it. But we had some trouble on the bombing runs—it was B-17s that we were flying; we were dropping bombs. No matter what I did, I followed all procedures and did everything we were supposed to do to make the bomb run, but the bombs wouldn't leave. I think it was about three missions we wasted where we never could get the bombs off.

I remember the co-pilot was getting a little grumpy about it. They were short of instructors, and we were one of the few crews that never had an instructor. They take you out of an AT-6 and put you into a B-17, which was quite a difference. They finally gave us this one plane, and we went up night bombing. We had to fly to Orlando, Florida, and the targets were all around Orlando. My job was to call the station as soon as we reached the area. They taught me how to do that, and they would say, 'Bezon, ask permission for bombing the target'—you couldn't go on a target until they gave you permission and told you which one. They would have to tell you what elevation so you wouldn't be on the same elevation as some other plane; the planes going around the target would be pretty close to each other at times. There was one time the pilot happened to go down to see if there was a broken wire or something. I didn't realize that and looked ahead of me a few miles. I saw lights, and when I looked up, I said to myself, 'Holy Jesus, where the heck am I? What position?' I see the lights below me, and that's a plane coming. He kept coming head-on, and as all pilots know, standard operational procedure they follow—that no matter how distant, even 10 miles away, you need to make a left diving turn, both of you, so you go away from each other. I'm waiting for him to make the turn, and I look and he's getting a lot closer. I'm looking and thought I can't make it now, so I grabbed my parachute and put it on, which was foolish, because if we were going to hit then we're not going to have time to parachute. In the meantime, somebody there woke up, and they did the dive but didn't flare off to the left. So him and I are still coming right together, and it was close. At the last minute the pilot was underneath us and saw our plane, and he revved it right up. I could see that plane. It was closer than that wall [*points to wall in room*]; we went belly-to-belly. So it shook us up, because in just a matter of another few seconds we would have all been killed.

In the meantime, I'm over my bombsight and look up to see the lights down below, over here or over there. So I knew the plane was twisting around, but you don't realize it right away because they are not sharp turns.

So we landed, and the instructor came out and asked, 'What's the trouble?' And we told him.

He said, 'Get in the Jeep. Get another plane. You're getting back up.' He said, 'Don't land for six hours.'

We flew up with another load, and this time the plane worked good. I dropped the bombs quick—twenty of them, twenty runs. So I asked the pilot where we could go to get loaded up for twenty more. Like I said, we were two missions behind already. We landed again, and they loaded up quick, and I dropped 20, 40 bomb loads that day, and from then on, I had no problem.

*

We graduated from there and we're ready to go overseas. We went up to Langley Field, and they took me off the crew. I didn't know why, but they said, 'You'd be notified.' But then I noticed all of my buddies that were bombardiers from several of the crews. So there were about ten of us that knew each other, and we were all taken off, and the rest of our crews left.

We were taken into a church, and they used that for a hall. All of the officers had to be there. They said, 'You're here for a four-week course in radar, and after that, you are going to have two weeks' furlough. I am going to name all of the guys first who are going to start school, and then I'll name the guys who are going to go on furlough for two weeks first.' I wasn't in either group! So after they got through, I walked up to the front of the church and asked the sergeant, 'Sarge, you didn't read my name.'

He said, 'What is your name?'

So, I told him, 'Lt. Bezon.'

He said, 'You're going overseas right away.'

I was happy as heck. He put me with my buddy 'Broadway.' He and I went through everything all the way. They told us, 'They are out on Langley Field waiting for you.'

'The Last I Would See of My Mother'

So, we left. We didn't get in the training program there; we got to Langley Field. We were going to fly a brand-new B-17 over in a few days. We went out that night and partied up pretty good. We had to take the plane for a thousand-mile hop. They named three places—one west, one down towards the south, the other up here near Burlington, Vermont, going right by the town here. So, I asked the pilot, if nobody has any choice, I'd like to make one. I said, 'How about going to Burlington?' I called up my mother on the phone and told her that I would be flying over Port Henry and we had permission to drop a little bit low. We could get down to ten thousand feet. I said that I would be in a little window in the middle of the plane, the waist, and I'll be waving a white flag. I said, 'I'll drop something from the airplane with a little white chute on it.'

I made a parachute out of some silk I found there and put a little gift for my mother in there and calculated the wind; I knew how to drop it. We were coming up and we flew across the bridge [over Lake Champlain, connecting New York to Vermont] and made a few circles. We dropped down over the village of Port Henry to about two thousand feet with the B-17—I see my mother! She is shading her eyes, looking up, waving, and I'm waving back. Then I threw the thing out and I saw that she got it. That was the last I would see of my mother for quite a while.

Then we flew around the bridge once more and I tried to get the pilot to go underneath the bridge. He said, 'Geez, Marty, we won't fit.' We had second thoughts and decided we better not, so we went to Burlington. Everything was good; everybody checked his position to make sure that nothing was wrong with it. That was the reason for the test flight [to Burlington].

The next day we took off for Bangor, Maine. We still didn't have a navigator; I was doing the navigation with my radar set. We got to Bangor, Maine, and stayed overnight and loaded up our plane with a bomb bay full of mail for the GIs overseas.

We took off the next day to Labrador—Goose Bay, Labrador. We had a near miss up there. They gave us a navigator; he'd never flown with us before. My orders were not to use the radar and to help the navigator. We started and got up to elevation and all of that and headed down across the ocean, to go across the ocean quite a long time before landfall would be seen. I went up and asked the navigator, 'What do you want me to help you do here?'

He said, 'Never mind, you're a bombardier. I don't need no help.'

I said, 'Okay, I'll be down in the radio room.' After I got thinking about it, I thought we'd been flying quite a while. We should have seen land.

I waited there and then I went back up and said, 'Are you sure you don't need help?'

'Nope, I don't need help.'

So, I told the pilot, Bill Tuttle, 'We should be seeing land somewhere. It seems like we've got quite a-ways to go from land yet.'

He said, 'Lower the radar set.'

I had to get the enlisted men to lower my scope. In the bottom of the ship, the scope hangs way down. Inside of it, it's a scope enclosed in this cylinder that they lower down. I warmed up my radar set; it takes five minutes for the first switch to go on. You wait five more minutes before you throw the primary in. [*Points to documents on his desk*]. If you see land, you see all of that light. Water, you see all black. When I send the pulse out, if it's water at 90 degrees, none of that comes back [to me]; that's always black. Over cities and ground and terrain and all of that, a lot of them come back to you. The rest go up. So, you could see well-lit areas. When you hit a city, about 75% or better of them come back at you. So, the city's much brighter. It's a great navigation tool. We never got lost.

He said to lower that down. So, they lowered it down. By the time they got it down there to about 15 minutes later I got it set. You have gradations on your picture and you can make these settings 10 miles, 50 miles, 100, 150, 200 miles.

I put it on 50 miles each and looked out 200 miles. There was nothing in sight but water. I finally went up to 500—nothing—and then 600. All I see is a boat out there 550 miles away from us. We were over 600 miles away from shore and we'd been flying too long!

I went back up to the pilot and said, 'Something's wrong. I can't get landfall.'

He said, 'Go up there and I'll call him on the speaker to let you look at what he's doing.'

So, I went up. In the meantime, the Air Force got a new type of compass. Flying over here [in the North Country], there is so much ore in these mines up here in the hills that the compass is off fifteen, sixteen degrees. If you don't realize it, you get lost flying around here. All over the world, there are these little deviations plus or minus. Up here in the Champlain Valley, it is high. The new compass that we got had a little furl nut on the side and a little window on the inside of the thing and you could preset the variation. Then you read the true heading. If you didn't use that, on our log, the first thing we would note is our observed heading. The next column down is deviation, and it was subtracted or added on to it. That's your true heading. If you don't use that, you could see how far off you're going.

I looked down and saw that he's got the fluxgate compass [an electromagnetic compass]. Good. I said, 'Let me see your log.'

He said, 'What's the matter?'

I said, 'What's the first column?'

He said, 'Heading.' I said, 'What's the second column?'

He said, 'My deviation.'

I said, 'What did you put it in the compass for? You've got it both places. You're going off 16 degrees since we left Goose Bay!'

We were way off course. I said, 'I am going to tell the pilot take it 270, give another heading.' So, I went up and told the pilot to take it 270 degrees, and to start praying.

We made it. The land came in, and we came in right on target. We landed, and the engines all conked out after we stopped—we couldn't even taxi to our revetment. As a matter of fact, we would have all died [if we had not seen land within those few minutes]. They got rid of him pretty quick when we got overseas.

Radar Man

From there we went from Goose Bay to Reykjavik, up in Iceland. We landed there and had something wrong with one of the engines, so we stayed there two or three days. Then we took off and headed down to England and landed there, and they took me off the crew again. I was sent to a one-month English radar school to learn their type of navigation and everything. I remember when we were first taking radar classes, they told us that if we ever say the word 'radar' in town, we would face a court-martial. It was very secretive. You had one classroom where you had to go through an MP. If you want to go from this classroom to the other one, there would be an

MP just across the hall. You would have another MP checking you very close. The radar man was known as a 'Mickey operator,' 'H2X operator,' or 'Pathfinder.'

We arrived in England about July of '44. We were all stationed just outside of Norwich—all of the bases of the 2nd Division. I used to meet my buddy there every time I went into town; we went to the same pub. I don't think I ever got into trouble with anybody. I had an argument with one of the guys in the barracks but we settled it all up. That's the way we lived.

The Quonset huts were very cold huts, just a little metal inside and outside covering it. It had one stove in the middle. They would give you a quota of just so much coal. You would burn it up in a day or day and a half and then you were going to be cold for a while unless you could find wood, and where were you going to find wood in England? So, you had to kind of conserve it. Toward the evening just before you go to bed, you just had to warm it up a bit. It was cold in the barracks. Somebody came up with the idea of taking the discarded oil from the oil changes on the airplane engines. They had barrels and barrels of it available. It took a certain amount of oil and a certain mixture of high-octane gasoline. We stirred it all up and put a can up near the top of the roof and piped it into the stove. Oh, that was good. We rigged one up and we had a red-hot stove all day, twenty-four hours a day. Then somebody put too much octane in one of them and it blew up, so they made us take them down. [*Laughs*]

*

We were assigned to the 466th Bomb Group in the 8th Air Force. I went up to headquarters the next day after I got settled down and asked if I could get on a plane and start flying my missions as quick as possible. I said that I'm a qualified navigator and qualified bombardier. I'm a qualified air-to-air gunner and I said that I would sure like to start 'em up. They said that they can't do it, that there was 'too much money spent on you radar guys'—that there was a lot of expense to train one of us. Then the officer said, 'Are you that anxious to start your missions?'

I said, 'Yes, I am.'

He said, 'The next group to us—the 467th—has a crew that is waiting for a radar man. Do you want to transfer?'

I said, 'Yes, I do.'

That was the first time Broadway and I split. I went over to the 467th and got on with [pilot] Bill Chapman and his crew and flew my missions with Chapman. We flew together until our 18th or 19th mission, when we got shot down.

What they would do is get these planes for radar men, planes that have proven themselves a little superior to the rest of them. They pick them out for lead planes, the first or second planes. They both are equipped identically alike, so if one gets knocked out, the other can take its place. So, they were all lead crews, and all lead crews were in the 791st Squadron of the 467th Bomb Group. And that's how I went into the 467th Bomb Group as a radar man in a lead plane.

I met the crew and all of that and we started our missions. I was not very happy with the navigation. With radar, you couldn't really navigate. You would see little spaces sometimes on the map with a small channel to go between two cities. On the way to a target, you would pass pretty close to the different cities or towns. They've got flak guns around a lot of them. They know the distance that the flak could reach us at the elevation we're flying. You can only be so far; if you get closer to them, they are going to reach you. If you head right between those areas, marked with the red, you were okay. There was one [corridor] that was very narrow, but [my crew] always liked to go through there because I always hit it dead center.

For our targets, the objectives were in different phases. First of all, it might be oil, and then we would only have oil production facilities as our targets. Next would be industrial, and we would bomb only industrial targets. So, I think there were three different phases that we went through. Later on it was some pinpoint bombing, like bombing a bridge going over some waterway. They kept sending squadrons to a target until they finally blew it up.

The Buzz Bombs

The English wanted us to bomb to kill people, because [their cities had been attacked]. Then the Germans turned around, got the 'buzz bomb,' and started sending them over to England.[61] It was a great big bomb with wings and it had a motor on it. I remember the first day that I got to England, I was standing in line going in the movie house, I heard the 'bzzzz.' Everybody said a buzz bomb was coming. I didn't realize that we were the closest air base to where they launched the buzz bomb. Every buzz bomb went over our base, and if it kept going we didn't worry about it. But if it sputtered and stopped making noise, sometimes they keep going through the air, other times they would turn and come right down. When it stops, you head for the bomb shelter. This one is going and it started sputtering and stopped and everybody ran. Somebody looked up and said we were okay. Then, we just watched it. It got down behind the hill, and all of a sudden [it detonated] and you could see the concussion coming before you felt it.

---

[61] *buzz bomb*- In mid-June 1944, the Germans began launching a new type of weapon—a small, medium-range cruise missile—from bases in northern France, the Netherlands, and western Germany. It was the forerunner to the modern rocket; indeed, some of the German scientists involved in the program later worked on the U.S. space program. The loud noise that the primitive pulsejet engine of the V-1 ('Vengeance Weapon 1') made could be heard approaching from more than ten miles away. See www.museumofflight.org/Exhibits/fieseler-fi-103-v1.

One night, they were sending a lot of buzz bombs, and it had rained and it was muddy outside. They had the planks to walk on. Somebody said 'buzz bombs,' and we all ran out in our pajamas and jumped into the shelter and went back. We weren't then sleeping another fifty or sixty minutes, and then another buzz bomb came, and another one. By the time of the fourth one, I said 'the heck with it,' and I slept the rest of the night. They kept coming up every night [for a while].

*

Most of the missions you'd get flak—some more intense than others. A couple of times, we had fighters come in. The CO of our group, Colonel Shower, was a stickler on tight formations. The tighter the formation is, the less the fighters bothered you because you have too much concentrated firepower. So, we weren't attacked as bad as the other groups flying with us. Once in a while they'd come over, but didn't bother us too much. But outside that, like Dresden and Nuremberg and places like that, they had a lot of flak.

Dresden, 1945.[62] *'View from the city hall (Rathaus) over the destroyed city.' Taken between 17 September 1945 and 31 December 1945, by German photographer Richard Peter. Credit: Deutsche Fotothek*

Dresden

Dresden was a bad one, one of the worst missions. It was one of our early ones. Well, what happened there was we got hit bad, and [we got off course]. We were leading three hundred planes. I loved the crew that I was on. They were great—Chapman, Wallace, and

---

[62] *Dresden, 1945*-One of the most 'notorious' missions of the war was the February 13/14 raid to Dresden, where at least 35,000 people, mostly civilians, were incinerated. American PoWs were used to remove the bodies, among them Kurt Vonnegut, Jr., where the incident would feature prominently in his novel *Slaughterhouse Five*.

our other navigator. We had two navigators on the lead ship—a DR navigator [dead reckoning] and myself, a radar navigator.[63]

We're in the front and all the planes have to go where we go, so we have to [be very accurate]. We're on the flight deck. The pilot was here [*points to table*] and the DR man was sitting right next to him back-to-back, and I was here [*motions again*], just cut in behind the co-pilot.

We had signals [because it was very loud on the plane], and the DR man said, 'Okay, five minutes, take a fix.' I would check my watch quickly and he would get a fix with the radio, and I'd get a fix with the radar and he would compare them and then give me the okay. He never gave me a sign that we were off.

Dresden had heavy, heavy flak, and we got hit with flak the size a little bit bigger than a softball; I would say about a six-inch piece of shrapnel came up through about the middle of the plane. The fuselage was open. Thank God nobody was hurt.

[There was some confusion on the bomb run.] I called out the first course correction on the bomb run, an eight-degree correction when we went from the rally point heading for the target. That eight degrees would have been okay. It's like you turn here and the target's up here [*points to piece of paper*]. I came to eight degrees. I was supposed to be heading there, and the bombardier calls up and says, 'I don't want that. I'm making a visual bomb run.' Okay, so I'm going to kill the course for him. Two minutes later, I gave him a ten-degree [approach] and he still wouldn't take it.

He said, 'No, it's a visual bomb run.' So, I wouldn't navigate the bomb run for him. He's going to make it visually.

I said, 'I can kill the course for you.'

---

[63] *DR navigator*-'dead reckoning' is the process of calculating one's position by estimating direction and distance traveled by using a previously determined 'fix' (position) and advancing that position based upon estimated speeds over time and course, rather than by electronic navigation methods.

He said, 'Never mind.' So what happened was, we kept going way off course instead of coming up. Instead of doing about a 45-degree course to the target, we got off so far that when the bombardier found out where he was, he had to almost turn it north. Now what happened was all these other planes came up, and they were now underneath us! I looked out the bomb bays to see the bombs drop. I looked down when they were ready to drop and saw a plane right below us! So, I hollered, 'Don't drop the bombs!' It was too late. They went; one bomb went between the wing and the fuselage of that plane and almost killed ten men.

Coming back, we ran into a [weather] front. We were advised to look out for it, but where they told us it was going to be was way off. I checked my radar continuously to take a fix on it. We hit the front, but it was a lot earlier than we had been briefed on. I realized something was wrong and I found that we were being blown way off course. So, I got on to the rally point where we had to meet and head home. I called up the pilot and said we were about 15 miles off course.

I said, 'We got a new heading we should take.'

Now we were flying deputy lead and there was the wing lead. Everybody wants credit for the big lead because you get promotions that way—to Wing, to Division. We had a pilot and co-pilot and a command pilot. The command pilot is there to make sure that everything is running. He is in charge of everything.

Our pilot evidently called up and nothing was said. I never got a response, so I called up again, 'Mickey to pilot.'

He said, 'Go ahead, Marty.'

I said, 'We're twenty-five miles off course. Something better be done.'

I marked the heading that we were going towards, and we're heading right for the Ruhr Valley, and that's an all-industrial place. There must be a thousand anti-aircraft guns around there. It was heavily, heavily, heavily defended. They make their steel and everything else down there.

He didn't say anything, and I called up again, 'Mickey to pilot. Chappy, we've got to get something done. We are thirty-five miles off course, and we're heading to an area that we will be getting flak soon and we are going to lose several planes.' There was going to be forty or fifty men killed, guaranteed.

He said, 'I checked with everybody, and everybody said we were on course except for one guy who said we're fifteen miles off.' All the other planes said we're on course, and we weren't! We were thirty-five miles off, and I was right!

We got over the Ruhr, and I said, 'We were going to be getting flak soon.' The guys in the waist said, 'It's already popping out ahead of you, waiting for us!'

So, the lead plane finally said, 'Since you know where we are, take over!'

So, we swung up to the lead, and I said, 'Take it up north quick and get the heck out of here!'

The Germans would have shot many of our planes down. I headed north and got on our old track that was on the map to follow home, and we went across the French coast across the Channel. You could see the White Cliffs of Dover coming up, and you know you're home. I finally relaxed a little bit.

'I Cried Like A Baby'

We got in and had a meeting, and they had all of the officers from the base. I said to myself, 'Geez, they are probably going to pat me on the back for doing a good job.'

I got up there and they wanted to crucify me, take my wings, and they said they wouldn't let me fly. They said, 'What's the matter, were you sleeping to get that far off course?'

I had a good crew and I didn't want to lose them. I didn't want to tell [the brass] that I gave the course [correction] several times to the pilot. I didn't want to tell them that when I gave the first course correction on the bomb run [which was not accepted], we first made a big 'boo-boo.' I gave an eight-degree correction when we went from the rally point heading for the target. That eight degrees would have been okay, but now I was blamed for [that mishap, too]. The plane [below us] didn't get hit [with the bomb], but it was close. It was the command pilot's fault, really. He should have told Chapman to go with that angle. By the time the bombardier gets a target in sight, it's got to be about a seventy-degree angle. Hell, if we were forty miles away from there, I could kill that course dead. You don't have to correct it more than one or two degrees with the bombsight after. They didn't do it.

I didn't want to say what I did, but I thought one of them would stand up and speak for me—the pilot, the command pilot, or any member of the crew, the bombardier. They'd heard it all. I suppose they were all scared that I might say something; I didn't want to say something. So, [the brass] said to me, 'One more move like that and you're off your crew.'

I went back to the barracks. I felt bad, real bad, because I could have blown the whistle but I didn't want to get off my crew. I took my shoes off and went to bed with my clothes on; I covered my head and cried like a baby. Then I heard my pilot and Captain Sidney come in. Sidney was in charge of all radar men.

He said, 'Chappy, I don't know what happened up there but I know this man wasn't to blame.' He said, 'He's the only one that comes to this shack after every mission to find out if he could have done better with the radar. If anything's wrong, he wants to find out. He's the only guy to ever come up there! He's very interested in his bombing. He's good. I know it's not his fault. I know it.'

Chappy said, 'No, it wasn't. It was my fault as well as the bombardier.'

I woke up in the morning and everything's okay. I went up to see the commanding officer and asked him if I could have a meeting with our crew. I would like to talk to the crew about my position and what I am there for. He gave me permission.

I went up there and we had the meeting there. I told the guys what I could do. I could navigate when all other systems are down, or blacked out by the Germans; they can in no way block off my signals. I said I've got perfect navigational equipment. I said that I'd never been lost and don't intend to be lost. I went up to [one of the crew] and said, 'If you ever countermand a correction that I give you, I am going to punch you in the head and there'd be another hole in this plane! Don't you ever do that again. It's your fault!'

He said, 'I know.'

Everything was forgotten. We had a great crew, flew some great missions. After that, when I gave corrections to them, they took them.

Berlin

[Our last mission was on March 18, 1945.] It seems like our worst mission was on a Sunday. They gave fresh eggs, so we knew it was going to be a rough one. If it wasn't going to be a rough mission, you usually get powdered eggs for breakfast.

We went outside after the briefing. There was a Catholic priest there. He's there at every briefing—not at the briefing but outside waiting. We would come out, and a lot of us Catholic boys would kneel down and some received communion. He gave us the blessing, then we all jumped in the wagons and went out to our planes. The target was Berlin. By the looks on their faces, a couple of guys kind of almost knew it was going to be a bad one.

Going over was good; navigation was super—we were leading the squadron at that time. We were coming up on the bomb run. We had a little plane that attacked us for a while and then the flak started greeting us; up ahead we could see it. The sky was black with flak. You can't swerve [or take evasive action]. You've got to go right through it.

We got right into it. I had my bomb bay doors open. I was ready to turn it over and get the bombs off. We got an explosion; I thought it was inside the plane, it was so loud. Directly underneath the plane we had taken a direct hit. We had fires in the bomb bays. Up where the pilot was, there was some kind of white-hot metal that landed. The co-pilot stamped on it. It burned right down through the ship, and a hole was left behind.

The pilot and co-pilot had bucket seats made out of heavy steel. The rest of us had safety vests that sometimes stop the flak. There was fire where I was, around my legs. I turned around and grabbed the extinguisher; the plane went into a dive, and of course, it was hard to maneuver. It forced me down on the deck. I finally got the fire extinguisher and stood up and started to put the fire out. I got the fire pretty well out and looked around; my navigator wasn't helping me. I noticed he was lying down and his eyes were very grey. His brains were hanging down the side of his head. All I could think of is that they looked like frog eggs. I went over and picked up the brains with my hands. They were warm yet. I didn't know what to do. Hell, he's dead. So, I spread some sulfa on it and went up to the pilot. [The engineer was supposed to be] in the bomb bay just below me where I could [normally] tap him on the head. I looked down. He was gone. I could see a piece of his clothes and stuff on the side of the plane; he was shot off when it hit. He just dropped out of the plane without a parachute.

The nose was burning pretty good. They got that fire out with the wind that was coming through the nose; it put that fire out. The waist wasn't hurt too much. Nobody got hurt back there. The steel seat the pilot was sitting in was hit so hard that [he had a minor injury on] his backside, but nothing serious at all.

'Thanks, Van'

We were blown into a dive, and to this day, I don't know how we could have managed to pull out of that dive, because the number one and number two engines were shot out altogether. The number three engine was only pulling half power and was running at around twenty; number four was the only good engine, and he was pushing it to the limit, about sixty-two, sixty-three. If we had flown another hour, that engine would have blown up. There must have been terrific pressure. They pulled it out of the dive.

We were also still carrying a full load of bombs in to the target. Because the explosion tangled up the releases and everything so bad, they asked me to go back in the waist into the bomb bays. I took my parachute off. It was only a six-inch walkway; there was nothing underneath me but a six-inch catwalk. I had a big screwdriver and I put all the weight that I dared to put on it to try to open the releases and drop the bombs.

I unhooked the arming wire. The arming wire goes from the nose of the plane up to the little place you hook on, and down to the point where it's going to the arming pin. When the bombs hit with the nose, the arming pin drives it in and makes the explosion. I unhooked that wire so they wouldn't go off when they dropped. I fixed the ignition and all of that so they wouldn't explode, and shut a cotter key in it so there's no way they could slip forward. So if the plane did land, [hopefully] none of the bombs would explode.

We were over the middle of Berlin. I remember when we pulled out of the dive, I put my parachute on. Of course, the navigator [who had been killed], his parachute was okay. Mine had a hole in it; it was just burnt a little bit but I knew I couldn't use it. So, I took his and remember saying, 'Thanks, pal. Thanks, Van.'

I'm up talking to the other navigator and the bombardier. I was kneeling right between them. I tell the pilot that Van [DR navigator] is gone and George Fuller [engineer] is gone. I contacted the waist. The waist was okay. I said, 'The waists are all okay.' So I said that we had two killed in action. I told him where we were, and I gave him a heading to pull and said, 'Take it 90 degrees for the time being.'

The Russian Lines

I went and set up and used my drift meter and all of that, and I gave him a corrected heading more south because that's the closest the Russians were to us, to the German boundary line, or rather the frontlines. As we were heading there, the plane stayed level but she kept losing altitude. So, it was only a matter of time before we would have to bail out, and there was no way we could land it because everything was shot up on the flight deck—the controls and everything. How he kept it level, I don't know.

We got over the lines and we started getting strafed by a German plane; he had one landing gear down, I remember, the other one was up. He made a pass and turned around to get another pass at us. Then, three Russian Yaks came in. The German flew away and they circled us a couple of times, and then they came in and started strafing us to knock us down!

The emblem was American on the plane, but I don't think they could tell [from the angle]. After years went by, I think they must have seen the bomb bay doors open and saw the bombs in it, so probably figured maybe we were on a bombing mission. However, that day we were bombing Berlin, three American ships were knocked down by Russians. So, the Russians did it every once in a while. Of course, a couple of Americans knocked down a couple of theirs, too.

They started strafing us, and Chapman asked me to give the waist gunners the signal to bail because the radio system between the waist and the flight deck was out. So, I had some object there that I heaved at the doors, so they opened up the door going into the waist and I patted my parachute and said, 'Go!' He nodded okay.

We got ready. I went over and touched my dead navigator again and went out and sat down by the bomb bay. I climbed down the bomb bay and sat on the walkway there—that six-inch beam. I sat with my feet dangling out. I never jumped out of a plane before. I waited for the co-pilot to come close to me, that way we'd be close enough that when we landed, we'd find each other quick.

The waist gunner, Twyford, jumped first. I bailed out and put my head between my legs and rolled out and fell far enough to make sure that I wouldn't be around the plane. I pulled the rip cord and nothing happened, and I started clawing at the thing and then finally it popped open—there's an auxiliary parachute in there. It's under spring tension and that popped a little parachute out; that auxiliary chute is fitted into your main chute, and it pops out first and drives the main chute out. All I remember was an awful jar.

As I was going down, I see the three Russian planes come down again. One picked on the pilot. One picked me, one was on the waist gunner. He started strafing me while I was falling, and I waved my hands at him and everything, and he's coming right at me. I saw him and thought, 'Lord, what am I going to do?' What you should do if you are far enough from the ground, you pull the cord on one side and it collapses the chute right away, and you freefall and just let it go and you get away before you hit the ground.

I chose to play dead. I waited until he went around, and he came back around and he's heading square at me. I see the guns going off.

I slumped down, put my hands along my side, and hung my head down to my chest. He circled me two or three times then flew off.

Then I heard popping and looked on the ground, and I could see it looked like a hundred people on the ground shooting at us! I heard the bullets, maybe two or three went through the canopy. I [later] cut that piece out to take it home, but somebody on the ship coming home stole it from me. I was not hit.

We were dropping down, and as I looked down there was a sharp-peaked house coming up right in front of me. I moved over a little bit with the shroud line.[64] Down along the side of the house, there's a little cavity in the ground, like some kind of excavation, I would say maybe three feet deep. I landed right in there, and, of course, it cut the wind, so my chute collapsed there and didn't have to be dragged along or anything.

I see the emblem on their hats and uniform that they're Russians, so I started yelling. My mother and father came from Krakow, Poland, back in 1911, so as we were growing up we had to learn Polish, because that's the only way we spoke. I knew enough of Polish to say, 'I beg you, do not shoot, I am an American.' I said, 'I have some papers, easy, easy!' [*Speaks in Polish*]

I reached in. We had these papers. They were small—you fold it, you take them out and open it, it's a big poster. It had a picture of Stalin and a picture of Roosevelt on it, and underneath them it says 'Komrades,' then it had a lot of Russian writing underneath it saying that we're American and all of that.

A couple of Russians started saying, 'Americans, Americans!' Then a big, black 'Cadillac' lookalike limo came along and had three officers in it. I could see that they were high-ranking officers, and they were told we're Americans. One reached down, took my hand,

---

[64] *shroud line*-parachute suspension line

and pulled me up out of there. That was the first time I had a sigh of relief.

They found Wallace almost immediately. I told the Russians that the guys falling out of the sky, they're all Americans. So, they sent word around to make sure that they're all right. They were able to find my navigator. His body was burned up but they found he was all in one piece.

Chapman collapsed his chute, then free-fell and opened it up again. When he hit the ground, they put him in a truck, and some Russian on a horse came up to him with a pistol and put it to his head and pulled the trigger three times, but the gun wouldn't go off. Then the truck pulled away; he could see the guy working on his pistol. He finally fixed it, but the truck was too far away so he didn't chase it.

So, Wallace and me and Twyford, they brought us to this building. They had some interrogators there. They asked me first; I told them I spoke some Polish. They brought a woman over to act as an interpreter, but I couldn't understand her and she couldn't understand me. They then brought in a fella by the name of Walter. He was a big, gangly guy and the type of guy that you see that you like him. We spoke to each other just like talking to my mother or father. He told the Russians that he knows what he is seeing.

They asked through the interpreter what were we bombing. Of course, generally you don't give information to the enemies except the name and serial number. But in this case, the newspapers would be blasting that, I think it was, 2,000 planes would hit Berlin that day in an all-out effort.

I told him we were bombing Berlin. He said, 'Good, good. How many planes?'

Again, I knew the newspapers would give the amount of planes. I said, '2,000.'

They were pleased with that. He said, 'How come you didn't shoot us down when the Russians were strafing you?'

I didn't tell him all our guns were all knocked out and that we couldn't shoot any of the guns. I said, 'We knew you were Russians so we didn't want to shoot back.' I had to lie a little bit.

Then they brought out a bottle of some kind of white liquor. He said, 'Have a drink.'

I said, 'Yeah, I need one.' So, they gave me a little shot. Then some woman there said to put some water in it.

The Russian said, 'No, he can drink it.' I drank it and, boy, was it strong! It went down and I felt better after I warmed up. The waist gunner [drank his] and almost went down to his knees. They put us up, and the next day got the rest of the crew together. There were two more missing but we were going to meet them at the end of the day. They said we were going to bury the navigator. They found him and they found my log. I was hoping that they'd give it to me. It was partially burnt but you could still read it.

They picked us up in two trucks. One of these flat-bottom trucks with green cloth or something over the bottom had a casket on the front. There were two Russians in the front and two in the back with rifles riding with them. The other truck had three seat benches. We sat on that and rode backwards.

We went up to a cemetery in Landsberg and they had a ceremony there. They said something in Russian. They asked me through my interpreter if one of us wanted to say something. I told Chapman they wanted to know if anyone wanted to say the last few words. Chapman said, 'Yeah, I would.' He gave a nice talk about Van Tress being a good navigator. He had been just married for one month; he married an English girl. He was a wonderful man, not only a great navigator.

He ended up having a great big tombstone there. They came to see me and asked me what I wanted on it. I put *'Harold B. Van Tress, born 1923/Killed in action today March 18, 1945/bombing mission Berlin'*—they had that all inscribed overnight, they had it on there. That was a big stone that stood up there at least four or five feet. I asked the girl taking the photograph of everything if she would send me or give me a photograph. She said she'd try, but I never got it.

'Crazy Amerikanski'

We stayed there in Landsberg for a couple of days. Then we went to [Posen]. From there, we were taken to Lublin, Poland. That was a pretty good size city. The Russians came in and told us at 9:00 there is a curfew—nobody on the streets. They said, 'If you listen tonight you might hear the Russians holler '[*speaks Russian*],' which means 'halt,' and then you hear a shot. The next day looking out of your window, you will see a funeral going by.' He says, 'We're not fooling.'

We said okay. Chappy and I walked around and found a nice English pub. It was a nice clean place run by a husband and his wife and they had a young daughter about eighteen—a beautiful girl. She's kind of the receptionist. She met everybody at the door. We went in and had a few vodkas. The next night we went down again, but this time we overstayed. It was 10:00 before we came out. I said, 'Oh boy, Chappy, this is going to be a lulu.'

We were walking up the street; he was a little bit pie-eyed. We kind of leaned on each other and then heard a son-of-a-gun Russian holler, 'HALT!'

Chappy hollered, 'Halt your butt,' but he didn't use 'butt,' he used the other word. I was just waiting to feel the bullet go through my chest; I was just wondering how it was going to feel. Two Russians came up and said, 'Crazy Amerikanski,' and they helped us up to the hotel. So, every night they'd meet us down there—they knew we were coming out—and escort us back.

*

I went to church on Palm Sunday. Over in Poland they have what they call a continuous mass. It starts from twelve midnight Sunday morning to twelve midnight Sunday night. There were no Saturday masses then. Anytime you walk into the church, whatever part of the mass was going on, when that part came up again, you walk out.

There were people going in and out all the time. It was full. I went in. I don't remember if any of the other crew were Catholic or not. I took, I think, 20,000 of those zlotys [that I got on the black market for my watch], and a bearded priest came in; he had a nice big beard on him. He was slowly passing down and you could see people giving a bill or some coins to him. He comes to me and I chuck 20,000 of them in there. He bowed three times to me and took off. I never saw him again.

I stepped out of the church that day and two guys came up to me. One talked English pretty well—very well. I said, 'Where did you learn English?' He said that he was a professor at the Lublin University, and he said, 'I'd like to talk to you sometime.' He invited me to come down to his house the next day for dinner. It wasn't too far from the hotel we were living in.

They sent a guy to take care of us, and I asked him for some food because I was having dinner with this Polish family. I said I would sure like to get some food I could give them, because food is scarce to them and I didn't want to go down there and eat their supplies. He gave me a lot of K-rations and a chicken that was still frozen, cans of different vegetables. So, I went down and gave it all to them. You would think I gave him a million dollars!

We had a nice visit and he asked me if I would take a letter for him and smuggle it back to the country; the Russians wouldn't let him mail it out. As a matter of fact, while I was walking the streets of Lublin, I must have got about eight letters from people who begged me to send them to their relatives in the States. So, I took them all.

A couple of incidents happened while we were there in that hotel. The hotel was just a bombed-out half-building, and we had a nice woman come in every day to straighten our beds, which were just two planks with hay on them. She would straighten up the hay and fold the parachute on them [that we were still using as a bedroll]. Eventually, I cut off a little piece of the shroud lines and I pulled all these threads out of it—very fine threads just like you sew clothes with, and I said, 'You can't break it. It would be good for sewing. You take this parachute too.' She brought me something to cover myself that night, and she took and hid everything I gave her so the Russians didn't see her taking it from there. I hope she finally got it out of there.

Another time we were in the room and in come three Russians. You could see they were a little bit looped; I guess they wanted to fight. One came up to me and said, 'Me, boxer.' I said, 'Me, football player.' He went to the next guy. Then he went over to Chapman. I looked at Chapman. He was a little Southern boy, and I could see he's not going to take it. So, I told Yarcusko [the bombardier] to get ready.

This Russian hits Chapman on the chest, and Chapman hauled off and belted him one. I belted one and somebody else grabbed the other one. So, there we were fighting, and somebody fired a pistol. Some big shots came in—big officers, high-ranking. We all stopped when the shot went off. My interpreter came in and asked me what happened. I told him that we were resting and relaxing here and these guys busted in and they wanted to fight. Well, they threw them out of the place. I don't mean pushed them. They threw them out! One gave me a Russian pistol, and he said, 'The next time somebody comes in to bother you, don't talk to them, don't answer them, don't ask them questions—just shoot them. Don't drag them out in the hallway, throw them out the window and we'll pick them up.' So they left and I took the bullets out of the gun and said, 'Don't fool around, boys.' The next day they came and took the pistol away from me.

*

We weren't prisoners. Though we were kept in confinement by the Russians, we had quite a bit of liberty. Whenever we pick up a Russian girl to take her to her house to talk with her, they would pick up the girl the next day. The KGB, they would question her and tell her we were spies. But none of them believed it.

One time, they came in and said, 'We can't ask you officers to do manual labor.' I guessed by the rules of the Geneva Convention, the enlisted men were going to work today.

I said, 'Doing what?'

He said, 'Shoveling some fill onto the truck.'

I said, 'I'll go with them.' [The Russian] said, 'No, you're an officer.'

I said, 'I want to go with my men.'

He said, 'Okay.'

So I went with them, and I took a shovel and helped them fill up a big truck; there were two trucks to load up. So, they're going down to [deliver] the first load, and I said, 'Can I go with you?'

He said, 'Sure.' It was into a prison. They dumped the load there. I went in where all the prisoners were; I had never seen anything so sad in my life. I see one guy there with nothing but bones sticking out of his face. You could count his ribs so easy and his face was nothing but bones sticking out. His eyes looked at me, and here I am fat as a hog and smoking a cigarette. I see he is looking at me. I took a cigarette and walked over to him. The guards said, 'No, no,' but I said, 'The hell with you, you're not going to shoot me.'

I see some of the others looking around. I had about twelve cigarettes left. I broke them in two into twenty-four and gave everybody a half cigarette. There was no filter so they could smoke either end.

'We're Going To Crash!'

It was a lot of fun. I wanted to go to Krakow but they had no way of transporting me there. I knew that I had relatives all over the area.

They finally flew us from there to Poltava up in the Ukraine over Russia. We were trying to take off. We were on a grass field—just a meadow. They had a Jeep loaded on there already and all of us went on. I sat in the seat just behind the steering wheel. They started going on the grass and all of a sudden hit a hole. They pulled it out and tried again; it hit [another crater]. I said, 'Holy cow!' Finally, they took us off and sent us down a few miles away, where they had a cement runway—a hard-top runway. They had heavy screens over the thing. When we got there, they loaded us on the plane and flew us to Poltava.

We finally found a plane there over in Poltava that was in good shape except the landing gear was pretty badly mangled. What had happened [at Poltava] a year or so before was that there were these 'shuttle missions'—they take off in England and bomb Germany, then Poland, and over to Russia. The next day they take off loaded with bombs again, hit the southern part of Germany, and land in Italy. The third day, they fly from Italy, bomb Germany again, and then land back at the base. They called it a shuttle run—three runs. You'd get three missions in three days.[65] They had had seventy-five

[65] *shuttle missions*- Operation Frantic was a series of World War II shuttle bombing operations conducted by American aircraft primarily based in Southern Italy, which then landed at Soviet airfields in Poltava, in the Soviet Union (Ukraine). The operation began in June 1944 and ended in September. The Germans contributed to the discontinuation of the program with a

of these planes come in. They lined them up in two rows. The Germans came in and demolished all of the planes. Never took off again; that's where we got our landing gear and stuff. We found landing gear on one of the other planes there that was in pretty good shape, and, with Russian help, we jacked the plane up, got the thing off, and put the other one on. We worked on the engines—whatever we knew about it. We never had any experience with them.

Each plane had a small generator on it because you don't have any electricity in the plane until at least one engine is going. So, we start them up to give us power while checking the position that we were flying. When we got that all done, the Russians took all seventy-five auxiliary engines—they called it—and put them all in the bomb bay—all seventy-five of them! Then they said, 'We've got sixteen more men we want you to haul out of here.' There's eight of us left, so there would be twenty-four men.

We went up to test-op [our rebuilt plane]. Chapman, Wallace—the two pilots and myself acting as the engineer. I knelt between the pilot and co-pilot. It was one of these steel mat runways—you could hear that rippling noise as you go over them. Usually, you should get over 100 miles, 115 miles, 110 miles an hour before you like to take the plane off. I watched the speedometer. I leaned. Both of their heads are close by me. I hollered, 'You're doing 60, 65,' but when I got around 80, it didn't climb very high. 'Eighty-four, eighty-five!' Oh boy, I looked up and we were at the point of no return, and gone too far.

When I got up around 88, 89, Chappy pulled back on the plane and said, 'We're going to crash!' The plane took off and he quickly folded his landing gear. That worked, thank God. We started going

---

German air attack on the Ukrainian bases; deteriorating relations with the USSR also hastened the demise. See www.history.com/this-day-in-history/united-states-begins-shuttle-bombing-in-operation-frantic

down again, and just before we hit the ground she picked up enough speed and kept going—success!

We landed right away. The Russians gave us heck. They thought we just taxied down the runway to turn off, but here we are going full speed. So, we told them, 'We've got to do some more work on those engines.' We have to take all those auxiliary engines out of the bomb bay, and the other men—we can't take off with 16 more of them—they've got to wait for somebody else to come in. So, they fixed the plane up, and they said, 'Okay, take off this time, and don't come back.'

All the guys assembled there. Something told me this time when we got on that plane, we're going to be searched. As soon as I got to my navigation position up there on the flight deck, I opened a big huge fuse box about that wide and about that high [*makes gesture with hands*] with all the fuses in there. I opened it up. It had two screws on top and one on the bottom. I took the bottom one off and loosened up the others, and removed it and put the letters in it and put the screw back in quickly. I went to my position, and then they came on and said, 'Everyone out.'

We all had to go out of the plane. They took about four men and they went in and searched that plane from one end to the other. So, I kind of held my breath.

Then they said, 'All right, get on, close that door, and don't come back.' They said, 'You're going to Bari, Italy.'

He gave us the elevation of the flight at ten thousand feet and gave us the wind. I forgot how many knots it was and the direction the wind was coming in. Like anybody flying an airplane, you've got a heading, and if the wind is coming [a certain direction] and you want to go there, you better go this way so the wind would blow you on the right track.

So, I told the Russians, 'One minute, when I go up in the air at ten thousand feet, I am going to take three different headings. I'll only be a minute—a minute or so on each one.'

He said, 'What do you want to do that for?'

I said, 'I want to get my own wind and the knots.'

He said, 'We gave you winds.'

I said, 'That's all right, I want to get my own.'

He said, 'All right.'

So, I took a heading so-and-so and I told Chapman to take another thirty, forty feet the other way and then the third way. Each time, I marked our heading and how much drift we were making. I put all this on the E6B computer. We carried a small computer. I set them all on there. I could turn the dials and show you exactly what degree the wind was coming from, the exact knots up to half a knot; I think it was five knots an hour. Anyway, I put the wind on the E6B after I erased it and put my heading on there and applied the wind. I put the course on there, the exact course I wanted to make. I put the heading on and it showed me how much correction to make into the wind. I put that all down and we took off. They told us if we get one mile off course, we've got to shoot you down.

We went down across Yugoslavia over the mountains. We came over the top of a mountain and looked down and saw the bluest body of water that you've ever seen. You couldn't see the other side, and I remember the co-pilot saying, 'Marty, what's that blue water?'

So I told him, 'If that's not the Mediterranean Sea, I don't know what country we're in.' We flew across it, and once we got over the Mediterranean, we still couldn't see land yet.

He said, 'What's our ETA and course?'

I said, 'The course looks pretty good, but I have been taking a drift of the top of the white caps on the Mediterranean,' and I could see we were drifting a little bit more than we did before. I gave a one-degree correction and checked my ETA and gave the time we should be there. We came into Bari right over the runway, and our time was off by half a minute. It was a perfect hit.

We landed, and they gave us hell for coming in with that plane. We had no parachutes, nobody had a parachute. They told us to get out of the plane and gave somebody orders to tow that out to the junkyard and junk that plane. Everything was beat up on it but we made it.

*

[The war wasn't over yet.] They took us up to Naples and they deloused us. They put us naked into a shower with a strong stream of water and they deloused all of us—head, ears, everything, any crevice in the body, to make sure. There was a lot of lice; we were loused up from Russia. They put some kind of powder on us and put it under our armpits and stuff like that.[66] Before we went into the shower, we had to take all our clothes off and shoes and stockings and put them in this rubberized bag, and then they sealed it off so no air could come outside of it or anything. Inside of it you could feel a little tube, a hard metal cylinder. They said, 'Put it on the ground and put your heel on it.' That was before we went in the shower. We had our shoes on yet and stomped on it. [The cylinder] opened up and put whatever [is inside of it all over inside of the rubberized bag], to delouse our clothes. Everything was clean. We then went in the shower and put our clothes back on. It did a good job.

In Naples they gave us a couple of days there and we went into town—Chappy and I. We got a little bit looped. We were so happy to be back in American hands.

---

[66] *put some kind of powder on us*- DDT, an insecticide used late in WWII to control malaria and typhus among civilians and troops. A white powder was generally sprayed on the subject; it was banned for agricultural use in the USA in 1972 as a threat to wildlife.

'We Were All Killed'

[We flew to England and] we went back to the base. It was about eight weeks that had gone by; [we got there] at supper time. Of course, we weren't dressed in Class A uniforms. We went up into the hallway, and they lined up to go into the mess hall outside, and the line goes into the door. You pick up your metal plate. We were walking up and everyone turned around looking at us. They were all young kids; Christ, they looked like they must have just gotten out of school or something! I didn't see any of the old-timers. They were all gone. When we got shot down, word came back that we were all killed. As we turned to go in the mess hall, I could see inside. There was a long table in the front. It had the CO, Colonel Shower, and all the brass from the base, all on that long table. They were waited on while the rest of us had to go through the line.

The minute I walked in, I noticed this Captain Novak looking up. He said something to Colonel Shower, and Colonel Shower jumped up and came running over to us. They had been notified that we were dead. He took us back to the table and we were waited on that night. Captain Novak asked who spoke Polish. I said, 'I did.' He said he was Polish, too. I asked where our clothes and all our belongings were.

He said, 'I think they are up in the post office. I hope they haven't sent them out yet.'

I got out of there as quick as I could, and Chappy said, 'Where are you going, Marty?'

I said, 'I am going to see if I can get up to that post office.'

So, I took a bicycle; I don't know who it belonged to. I rode off because the post office was on the outskirts of the base. I knocked on the door. It had a screen wire mesh glass on the front of the door, and way in the back, I could see one guy working. He points to his watch and says 'No.' I kept banging and banging and banging. He finally comes up to the door and says, 'Sir, we're closed.'

I said, 'No, no, I just want to ask you a question. Do you have any boxes of clothes that are going to be shipped out here yet?' I gave him the names.

He said, 'Yeah, we've got ten boxes out there.'

I said, 'What's the names on them?'

He went back and said, 'There's a Chapman, there's a Twyford.' And he named three or four.

I said, 'Geez, don't ship them. Please don't ship those clothes out. Ship Van Tress and Fuller. George Fuller and Harold Van Tress. Ship them home, but the rest of them, we're all back on the base.'

He said, 'I'm glad you came here because in the morning, they were going out.'

I still have the board where the address was marked 'Killed in Action' that they were going to mail to my mother. I hadn't been able to get in contact with her. I did send her some letters from Italy and England. She finally got two of them. The rest of the letters, I gave to the guy that used to audit all of the mail going out. They checked the Polish letters and said that they were all right. So, we mailed them out.

I went to town that night. I knew my old buddy would still be worrying the hell about me. He was over in the corner of the bar crying his head off...he jumped up [when he saw me], and boy, did he cry! We saw each other then, but it was the last time that I saw him. We were supposed to head out. They weren't going to form any more crews here. The front lines were moving so fast, they did very little bombing after that.

After the war [in Europe] was over, everybody went celebrating, but they restricted us to the base and wouldn't let us go out. But we all had .45 revolvers and we went around shooting the smoke stacks on the buildings. Then they thought they'd better let us go into town or we'd kill ourselves.

*

Coming Home

I asked to go back by boat. I flew over, and I'll never be able to cross the ocean on any kind of ship again. I got on this ship, I think it was the *USS Frederickson.* We did see a whale. I was seasick for about three days. I lay on my cot and never moved. We slept eight above on little cots. I think it was eight above each other—one on top of the other. I was on the very bottom and only had about that much room [*makes gesture with hands*]. So I came back on that, and put all of the clothes down in the hold. Somebody, during the trip, took whatever they wanted, and that's how I lost a lot of the stuff.

I came home and landed in Boston. They had to give us furlough papers to go home for a month. I went home and then back to Langley Field. There was a sergeant interviewing all of us, getting information from us. He said, 'Where do you want to go? You can be based any place you want.'

I said, 'No, I got a little more [fight] left in me, I would like to go to the South Pacific.'

He said, 'You don't have to go down there.'

I said, 'I want to go down there.'

He said, 'Wait a minute, you were missing for over six weeks.'

I said, 'Yeah. Missing in action. Eight weeks.'

He said, 'You can't go. You have to go home for two months—one month at home and one month in the recuperation center. You can go to Long Beach, Atlantic City'—of course, there were no casinos there then—'or Lake Placid, New York, for a week. Do anything you want. Say anything you want. Dress the way you want.

You just have to have one month of recuperation. Then you come back and get reassigned.'

I said, 'No, skip that. I want to go to the South Pacific.'

He said, 'You're crazy!'

So, they assigned me to a group in Boca Raton—B-29s. I was going to be trained there for combat in the South Pacific.

I was going down. I was a couple of days ahead of schedule, so I stopped in Atlanta, Georgia. The guy that sat next to me in preflight—he was a kid that was killed; Devine, I think his name was. Him and I used to talk many a time lying in the bunks at night. I thought I would find his folks and go over and visit with them and tell them about their son, and maybe I'll get a supper out of it.

I bought a quart of whiskey first— $2.49. I put it up in my room and I went downstairs and was going down to have dinner, and thought I would make the phone calls first. I went into the phone book and I thought that there would be two or three, but there were a couple of pages of Devines, so I said forget it. My God, there must have been fifty of them.

I went down to order a steak dinner, and I put the fork in and I noticed going in that there is a package store across the street—a liquor store. I was just ready to cut the steak when Harry Truman came on the air and announced that the war in Japan was officially over. We are now at war with no one.

So, I didn't even cut the steak. I went across the road and bought eight more quarts of whiskey and took them up to my room. Ten minutes after it became known—maybe fifteen minutes—liquor went up to $20 per quart. I got them for $2.49!

I went outside and saw a Marine and said to come on with me. We hugged each other and said that we did it!

I said, 'Listen, this hotel room's going to be open and I got all the liquor in the world. You come here and take a drink any time you want.'

He took me in the poolroom and there were quite a few rows of tables. He said, 'Third table. Third table up, look on the upper left leg, reach down there, you'll see a bottle of booze at the leg. You come in here and take a drink any time you want.'

Then I met some sailors and I took them up. I wasn't doing that much drinking, but they were. The next day, they were really celebrating there. I got tangled up with five other people celebrating and dancing and eating and all of that, so I was a day late coming down to my base in Boca Raton. The little sergeant says, 'Sir, you're a day late. I've got to mark you AWOL.'

I said, 'Oh, come on. The war's over. I did my duty.'

I pleaded with him, then I made up a story. 'My car broke down up in Ft. Lauderdale and my wife's there with two kids, and you're going to give me AWOL.'

He said, 'I'm sorry, sir, that's what the rules say.'

The master sergeant came walking in. I look across his chest; he's got his name—Polish, a 'ski.'

He said, 'What's going on here?'

I said, in Polish, 'I got drunk as hell and I'm a day late coming down for my arrival. He wants to mark me AWOL.'

He said, 'Write in here that he came in two days ago.'

He signed me in two days early. I hung around for a while and asked for a discharge, and I came home.

*

'They're All Gone'

[Near the end of World War II], I was put in for a captain rating. It had to get approval of headquarters. I don't know if Doolittle had anything to do with it or not. Then we got shot down and word came back that we were killed. So, they put all that off. When we got back to England, all promotions were frozen. I got like a belated captain rating, which considered [the possibility] that I would have made captain, to appease me a little bit. I never got it. I was a first lieutenant [at the end].

I came back at the end of '46 and went back to Republic Steel. In between strikes and all of that, I worked construction here and everything and never drew unemployment. I had 31 years credit with Republic Steel. It wasn't the actual time I spent there, because our service time was counted as years worked and they called me back during the Korean War. I had to go back again to serve. So, I trained on the B-29s. Then I became an instructor. I became the staff officer of the radar men. I know they grumbled at me, but I put them through the paces every week. I said, 'By God, I want to get home, and I know most of you want to get home, too.'

*

Van Tress had a son born. He was married for a month. Chapman and I tried to talk him out of it, to wait until the war was over. He married this girl he was wild about. Then he died.

After we got shot down and then came back to base, there were a couple of guys who came over from some other base and wanted to talk to me about Van. His mother asked them to go see me because Van slept right next to me. I gave them a whole bunch of pictures of Van and his new wife and all of that. So, they took them with them. The last time I talked to Twyford, he said he heard from Mrs. Van Tress. Her son's wife and his son are coming over. So, he would be her grandchild.

I could never find the co-pilot, Wallace. He sent me a letter in 1947. He was taking engineering up in college. He let me know that he and his wife Betty are good and he hoped that I go to college too. I wrote him a letter back and then we kind of let time slip by a little bit. One time heading out to Las Vegas I landed in St. Louis, where I last knew he lived. We had about a three-hour layover and I called up his home. The people who were living there then never remembered him. My son found around ten Wallaces around the area. I called three but none of them were there. The next night I called three more, so I gave it up. I even put an inquiry in *American Legion Magazine* and the *VFW Magazine* to see if anybody knew his whereabouts; called the 2nd Air Division Association, which I belonged to, and they tried to find him and they couldn't.

All the rest of the men are gone. Chapman was the last one. I used to call Chapman several times. We talked to each other quite a bit. I know the first time I sent him a Christmas card, he sent one back. He wrote, 'Please, if you ever come down and see me, don't ever talk to my wife about what we did in the service.' [*Laughs*] He lived in Alabama. He became quite wealthy. He had a crew of men out—carpentry work, anything. He worked the whole of Alabama and even part of Florida doing construction or anything he'd want or excavating or whatever. He owned a local Howard Johnson franchise and he owned a big share of the local bank. He had a loan company and a motel. He said, 'If you ever come down, I don't want you paying for any meals or rooms. You come here; I've got a place, and I am looking forward to seeing you.' We tried a couple of times, but something happened. He wasn't feeling good or I wasn't feeling good or something.

I called him up. Every Christmas Day I'd call him up after twelve noon; I'd just call him up and have a talk. The last time I called just a few years ago—it can't be over five years ago—his wife answered. Of course, down there they don't use your first name. They just go by your last name.

She said, 'Who is this?'

I said, 'That Polish Yankee from upstate New York.'

She said, 'Oh, Bezon! Just a minute. I'll see if Bill can get on the phone.' I said to myself, 'Oh, sounds like he is not good.'

He got on and he said, 'Martin, you don't know what this means to me when you call.' I think it bothered him what happened the time that I was [reprimanded] and got chewed out, and I think it might have bothered him quite a bit later in life.

I said, 'What's the matter with you, Bill?'

He said, 'I just had open-heart surgery and I'm recuperating.' And then he had something wrong with his leg.

I said, 'Geez, Bill, we've got to get together at least once.'

He said, 'Boy, we've got to!'

I got worried about him. A few days later I called up again.

I said, 'I just want to know how Bill's doing.'

His wife said, 'I am sorry to tell you, he died last night.'

So then Twyford died, and that was the last of them.

Anderson was on the police force and died from a heart attack. Yarcusko was out in California laying rugs and he died. So they're all gone, and I stay here.

*

Marty Bezon passed away at the age of 90 in April 2012, only three weeks after this interview took place.

Seymour 'Sonny' Segan, World War II.

CHAPTER ELEVEN

The Bombardier

I got to know Seymour Segan during a visit to his house in the fall of 2002. A former student worked at the local copy center, and Mr. Segan had brought in some World War II era photographs to be reproduced. 'He asked me if I'd be interested in talking to you. Even the manner that he asked me was with the right courtesy, you know? Not imposing—he thought it was very important. I think you had an influence on him; he was on the ball.'

He invited me to his home on a chilly November evening in 2002, about a week before a planned symposium on the air war at my school, which I had invited him to be a part of. We sat down in his living room; his wife Shirley joined us.

On December 7, 1941, Mr. Segan was nineteen and leading a troupe of Boy Scouts in New Jersey on a camping trip. A forest ranger told him about the attack, and he decided to enlist. He went into the Aviation Cadet program. 'I'll bet you that three-quarters of the guys in my crew, if not all, volunteered. Definitely the pilot, the co-pilot, the navigator, and myself. Because you weren't drafted to get into the Aviation Cadet Program. When I went into the Aviation Cadet Program, you had to have two years of college or an equivalency test to do it. Originally, it was four years of college, in order to become an aviation cadet. Ford Motor Company's Willow Run plant was knocking out B-24s like crazy. They needed you fast, so they made it two years of college or an equivalency test, which I was able to pass. I didn't have any school or college at the time.'

Segan wound up in the 485th Bombardment Group flying missions on the B-24 Liberator out of southern Italy with the 829th Squadron. He opened up about the trauma of World War II, and the miracles that saved him.

'I ended up in I think 22 or 23 different hospitals. Service-related, but mostly for my leg. Post-traumatic war syndrome was the worst. A combination of that with alcoholism—I found AA. That was a deciding factor in my [post-war] recovery.'

***

Duties of the Bombardier

Accurate and effective bombing is the ultimate purpose of your entire airplane and crew. Every other function is preparatory to hitting and destroying the target.

That's your bombardier's job. The success or failure of the mission depends upon what he accomplishes in that short interval of the bombing run.

When the bombardier takes over the airplane for the run on the target, he is in absolute command. He will tell you what he wants done, and until he tells you "Bombs away," his word is law.

A great deal, therefore, depends on the understanding between bombardier and pilot. You expect your bombardier to know his job when he takes over. He expects you to understand the problems involved in his job, and to give him full cooperation. Teamwork between pilot and bombardier is essential.

There are many things with which a bombardier must be thoroughly familiar in order to release his bombs at the right point to hit this predetermined target.

He must know and understand his bombsight, what it does, and how it does it.

He must thoroughly understand the operation and upkeep of his bombing instruments and equipment.

He must know how to set it up, make any adjustments and minor repairs while in flight.

He must know how to operate all gun positions in the airplane.

He must be able to load and fuse his own bombs.

He must understand the destructive power of bombs and must know the vulnerable spots on various types of targets.

He must understand the bombing problem, bombing probabilities, bombing errors, etc.

The bombardier should be familiar with the duties of all members of the crew and should be able to assist the navigator in case the navigator becomes incapacitated.

After releasing the bombs, the pilot or bombardier may continue evasive action--usually the pilot, so that the bombardier may man his guns.

—Duties and Responsibilities of the Airplane Commander and Crewmen, 1943

***

Seymour 'Sonny' Segan

'In Maxwell, Nebraska, there's a separate cemetery just for group burial—lots of men are buried there. There were ten of us on that plane. Three of us survived. One got out before the plane went into the dive—it was in a straight dive from about 13,000 feet—one was blown out of the plane when half of the plane blew up on the way down—and I got out just before it hit the ground, maybe a second or two; I think I was pushed out. I have a 1947 [area search investigation] report that says, 'Were fingerprints taken?' 'No.' 'Why not?' 'No hands.' You know, that type of thing where they bury thirty-five pounds of a guy that weighed 200 pounds.'

*

I was one of the original 485th Bomb Group. We trained in the United States, in Nebraska. We went overseas; we flew from Nebraska to Florida, then we flew down to Trinidad, and then we flew to Brazil. And from Brazil, we flew across to Dakar. Then we came up to Marrakesh, where we lost a crew in the Atlas Mountains—they flew right into them.

When we flew the group over, the ground crew came by ship. One squadron lost their ground crew because the ship was one of the largest [troop carriers]; the Germans got them in the Mediterranean and sunk the delivery ship. We were in Tunis for about four or five weeks, and then flew across to Venosa, Italy, where we started our missions.

The first mission to Yugoslavia was a 'milk run.' A milk run is an easy mission where you don't run into fighters and have little to no flak. It was probably planned that way, because at the time the group was a whole bunch of neophytes. Later on, when you have a mixture of [more seasoned crews] and replacements, that's where it gets tougher. When I was in North Africa [before the missions in

Italy], we'd go into Tunis, and you'd run into some guys who had already finished their fifty missions. You got a hold of them right away and you would try to pick their brains the most you can. And the usual question we always asked was, 'How many guys made it all the way through?' It was usually two, three, and occasionally four crews or so. Out of eighteen planes in a squadron. There were four squadrons in a group. We were the 828th, 829th, 830th, and 831st. The group commander was Colonel [Walter] Arnold, a very famous leader at that time. His uncle was Hap Arnold, the head of the United States Army Air Corps in those days. He got shot down, too; he was shot down after I was.

We were there for about four or five weeks. You hear of two, three, four crews coming through. And I got cocky. Because you go on a mission, and you lose one, you lose two, sometimes three or four planes. You start to look out when you're flying and...

By the way, we flew to Africa in the planes that were [painted] 'ODs.' You know what OD is? Olive drab. Our planes were all painted that dark green, but later on they found out that the paint was hundreds of pounds of weight, and also the friction against the rough paint was reducing the air speed. So they would start to leave them straight shiny aluminum. But it really didn't change things; the Germans found you either way. [*Laughs*] Olive drab was not camouflage, not while you're up there.

We'd be in the air and I would look out and I would see all these silver planes around me. I'd say, 'Hey, I'm one of the ones that's going to make it'; there's always a few that make it all the way through. You look around at all the replacements and you're one of the originals! You know some of the originals are going to make it, it's a good chance it'll be me. After 25 missions, we were down to that. That was the mission before my last mission. It was a false sense of security I had.

'Controlled Fear'

Still, it might sound funny, but you always accepted the fact that you might not make it; you were stupid if you didn't. You flew with what I would call 'controlled fear.' You were scared stiff, but it was controlled. My ball turret gunner—he couldn't take it anymore. As a matter of fact, he tried to shoot his leg, but he didn't hit his foot; he just took a piece of skin off it. He didn't want to fly anymore, but they wouldn't ground him. I guess he was right. He's dead now. But he had lost control of the fear. Ball turret is a tough place to be, too. He never got out of that ball turret; he died in that ball turret. You have to depend upon somebody else getting you out. You got to crank it up [*makes hand motions*]. It goes down below the plane and you can't land with the turret down, otherwise you'll be scraping along the runway. Somebody has to crank him up and then you turn yourself around to be able to come out the hatch.

But I really thought I would complete the fifty missions. You'd get to go home. [But] the fifty missions is a fallacy. The reason they called it 'fifty missions' was because anyone who had 25 missions in the Eighth Air Force was okay. The reason we had fifty is because on some missions we got credit for two, depending on the severity of the mission. Ploesti was two. Wiener Neustadt, Austria, was two. Neunkirchen, Austria, was two. Munich was two. But when you hit, like, Bologna in Italy...

[*To wife*] Should I tell him the story about Bologna?

[*To interviewer*] You know the [local Italian-American restaurateur family]? She had her Italian restaurant; one night we went in with another couple, and on the wall was a pictorial map of Bologna, Italy.

I looked at it, and I said, 'Oh! Bologna! I bombed that in World War II!'

And she said, 'My father was killed in that raid.'

She wasn't upset or anything; there were quite a few raids on Bologna, it was hit quite a few times. Anyway, that was a shorter run, and would be credited as one mission.

The worst targets were in Ploesti and Budapest, where the oil refineries were. Those were the worst, in the same category as Wiener Neustadt in Austria, which was where aircraft factories were. Those were rough. There was heavy, very heavy anti-aircraft flak and fighter planes.

On D-Day, we were sent to Ploesti early in the morning. We were like a diversion to pull fighters to the east instead of to Normandy and that area, on June 6. Your Tuskegee Airman, is he coming [to the air war symposium]?[67] They were great; they were great. I want to compare notes with him about missions we were on. Any time we saw our American fighters coming in, it was one of the greatest sights.

The problem was, on our long missions, most of the time our fighter planes couldn't go all the way [to the target with us]. A fighter plane usually had a belly tank [with extra fuel]. But they couldn't fight in combat with the German fighters with their belly tanks on—it would decrease their maneuverability. So the minute they would come in contact with any fighters, they had to drop their tanks. [They were with us] in Italy, depending on what the mission was. We even went to Munich [together], which was a long mission. And we went to Czechoslovakia, you know, those types of places.

These were long missions, in those days. Today it's not. Our airspeed wasn't that high, maybe 150, 160, sometimes 170 mph, you

---

[67] *air war symposium*-In November 2002 the author organized a panel discussion at our high school on the air war featuring Mr. Segan, pilot Earl Morrow, and Tuskegee Airman Clarence Dart. Mr. Morrow is also featured in this book, and both Morrow and Dart are featured in the sequel to this book.

know. The fighters can go much faster. But they couldn't use their belly tanks; they'd have to jettison them for combat.

'Maximum Effort'

The missions to Ploesti, Romania, had begun in earnest in midsummer 1943, when in the first disastrous low-level raid flying out of Libya, 54 bombers were destroyed by German fighters and flak; over 660 men were killed or shot down and taken prisoner. As strategy was refined, sustained attacks on 'Hitler's gas station' over the next fourteen months crippled the flow of oil from what had once supplied at least a third of the Reich's supply.[102]

On the day we were shot down, we were not even in our own plane. Our plane had been badly damaged in the mission before this one, badly banged up from flak and needed a lot of repair. They wanted the maximum effort on this mission so they sent us up in an old plane from the 831st Squadron. I was the 829th. That plane should not have been flying. We had trouble with one of the plane engines; it started to go out, that number three engine. Later, when I was brought out of Romania back to the hospital in Bari, Italy, one of the crew members of that ship said, 'We would not fly in it. I don't know why they sent you up in it, that plane was not in a condition to fly.' That's why we got shot down.

The day we were shot down, the target was the oil refinery in Bucharest. Normally it would have been about a seven to eight hour mission; you lose a lot of time getting off, and then you have to circle until you get into formation. Don't forget we were taking a lot of ships up; you have to get into the other groups' formations. The whole concept of that type of combat we flew in was to have as many planes as possible all bunched together.

'A B-24 flying over a burning oil refinery at Ploesti, Romania, 1 August 1943.'
United States Army Center of Military History, public domain.

You have an upper box, a middle, and a lower box of planes together. When you have the firepower of all those .50 caliber machine guns concentrated, an Me-109 or Fw-190 will not come in on you. Each ship has a nose turret gun, which is two .50 caliber machine guns; a top turret, two more; a ball turret gunner, two more; two waist gunners, one each—they would hold them out the waist window; you also had the tail gunner. So you have got 2, 4, 6, 8...10. Ten .50 caliber guns, but when you're flying in a formation of 18 planes, and close by that is another formation of 18 planes, that is multiplied. There are 180 machine guns from that one box, and you have those three boxes, one right there with the other one. We flew formations so close that you could see the faces of the guys in the plane off-setting you. It took flying skill, it took coordination over the radio and everything like that, and that was the best protection you had from enemy fighters.

From flak you had no protection. The only way we had protection from flak was we would throw out tinsel to try and screw up the radar that they had, so the air would be full of metal. But still, you know, [in daylight] they more or less could figure us out. Flak was a deadly, deadly thing.

Once you go up to your 'IP,' the initial point to begin the bombing run, the plane cannot veer or take evasive action from the flak. As a matter of fact, the pilot is not even flying the plane at that point; it was my job as the bombardier, taking over. When we made that turn to the target, we have to stay in that course until I dropped the bombs. Then we had to [turn, in formation] as fast as we could to get out of the flak.

Now their fighters would be ready. They did not want to go into their own flak, most of these German fighters. So, one good thing was, when you were over the target with all of that flak, you were not being hit by fighter planes. Although on some missions they did come in to attack us through their own flak, the majority of times they did not. When we began the group turn, after we dropped our bombs and started to turn to go home, that's when we lost our group. That is when fighter pilots attacked us. They will always go after the stragglers.

We could not keep up with the group; we had that one engine out, and another one was not in good shape. We had also lost our radio communication as we were being attacked by the Me-109s. We had lost altitude from about 22,000 feet to 13,000 feet when they hit us. Some reports say nine, some reports say seven; I remember that there were a lot of them coming in. I was dry in the mouth. I was in my bombardier compartment, there was a nose gunner in front of me, and then there was a bubble over the top of it that I could put my head up in to call out the fighters: 'At twelve o'clock,' 'three o'clock,' 'two coming in at three,' 'two coming in at two,' you know, that type of thing.

The ironic part about it was that I was the best gunner in my crew. I had gone to gunnery school and I was an excellent machine gunner prior to going to my advance training as bombardier. That's a frustrating feeling, not having a gun.

I had to give testimony when we got back. [*Reads from an official 'Reports of Death' identification memorandum dated June 10, 1949*]:

Date: June 28, 1944

Time: 10:30 AM

The location was approximately 35 miles southwest of Bucharest, Romania. The plane was in a dive when I bailed out. It went into a dive at 13,000 feet, stayed in it all the way down.

I was hanging out the escape hatch when it went into the dive and managed to bail out just before it hit the ground. I bailed out approximately 300 feet from the ground. To my knowledge, none of the crew were killed or wounded before she crashed.

The plane was on fire when it went into the dive. The fire was in the bomb bay command deck and waist. All engines were shot out. In the dive, the tail blew off. While on the ground, I saw part of the stabilizer floating down. This was confirmed by radio operator, Tech Sergeant Scott, who was blown clear when she blew. Lieutenant M. J. Hirsch, Navigator, Tech Sargent Scott, and myself bailed out and our chutes opened. The plane exploded and smeared all over the ground when it hit.

After reaching the ground I saw Tech Sergeant Scott, whose parachute came down after me. He came over to me and tried helping me with my leg, which was injured upon hitting the ground. Near the fire of the plane was a parachute, and Romanians who picked Scott and I up told us that this man was dead. I did not see who it was but I have reason to believe it was Sergeant Peterson, who had been the only one reported killed.

While in the prison camp I heard from Lieutenant M.J. Hirsch, whom I later saw being freed. As for the rest of the men I heard nothing. I did not examine the wreckage, and all I could see was fire along the ground. We did not land in water.

I believe my other crew men are dead as the ship was in a straight dive down, making it nearly impossible to bail out. I (barely) got out as I was hanging out the escape hatch when we went into the dive, having only inches to go, and it still took me 13,000 feet to get out. Sergeant Scott was holding on the waist gun and was blown out the waist window. Lieutenant Hirsch got out before she went into the dive. Another reason I believe they are dead is because no one ever saw their parachutes and they never showed up at the prison camp after we were freed.

*

Last year I got a really interesting phone call from Milwaukee, Wisconsin. The nose turret gunner came from Milwaukee, he was married, he had just had a little baby girl; she was about six months old when he died. He got killed in the crash; he might have pushed me off and out of the plane. You have to understand, it's like centrifugal force. It was like a stone wall that you are up against. You got to get out—I can't get out, I die. I don't want to die, I got to get out! I can't get out, that type of thing, and then all of a sudden, bam,

I am out! He was a big, powerful guy. I don't know. I was hanging out the escape hatch of the nose wheel.

His grandson called. The nose gunner was killed on June 28, and a few months later his wife died from tuberculosis; this little girl was left alone. Her family brought her up. She had five sons. One of her sons called me, his grandson.

I said to him, 'I am almost 90% positive that your grandfather saved my life.' To be honest with you, I do not know. The pressure when the plane went into the dive was so great, it was like pushing us back. This man who called me never knew his grandparents; his mother never knew her own mother and father. I didn't even know about that until he called.

*

I don't remember pulling the ripcord, but when I hit the ground, I smashed my left leg. I was about 50 or 100 feet away from the burning plane. I took off the Star of David from around my neck and tossed it as far as I could; Romania was also very anti-Semitic and working with the Nazis. My radio operator, Scotty, came over and then the Germans arrived. They took us to an airfield. Because my leg was so bad, they took me to a civilian hospital in a small town, Budesti; Bucharest was in flames at the time from bombardment.

The first day I was there they brought in this big guy; he looked like he was cast for a beer wagon driver in the 1890s with the big handlebar mustache, the big cheeks, you know. [*Chuckles*] They were telling me that my bombs injured him! I was a little scared, a twenty-one-year-old kid. Then he starts yelling at me, 'For Vayne! For Vayne!'

I did not know what he was saying but I figured it was the F-word. [*Laughs*] One of the nurses spoke a little French and I spoke a little French, my high school French. It turns out he had a brother in Fort Wayne, Indiana; he wanted to know if I knew his brother! [*Laughs*] He gave me a big smile. He wasn't angry with me.

They had girl Russian prisoners, paratroopers, working in the kitchen there. The Romanians shaved off all of their hair so they could not escape, so they would be able to find them, you know, looking for a bald girl. [*Chuckles*] They heard that there was an American prisoner there, and they came to my bed with some food that they took from the kitchen, some fruit, and gave it to me. I liked it there but they did not keep me there long; they sent me to a Russian prison camp. I was there about four or five days until some [Romanian] officer came in one day. The men in the camp, the Russians, were enlisted men. Most of the Romanian officers were all members of the nobility. They were second and third and fourth sons of the nobles, so being an officer in the military in Romania was a very high echelon thing. Civilians in the street, as they passed, would have to salute them. So, it would be against their whole belief system to put an officer, even an enemy officer, in with prisoners who were enlisted men. So they put me in a hospital with another Romanian officer, who treated me very nicely, gave me extra food and things like that. The only thing that was bad there was the doctor. There was a three-inch gap between my tibia and fibula and he told me to walk on it. I didn't know; I was a twenty-one-year-old kid. A young Romanian intern, who couldn't speak a word of English, made me understand not to. He did it secretively, afraid of getting caught. Then, a nun brought in a picture of Jesus Christ and hung it on the wall. And I found out that the Romanian officer was anti-Semitic. I am Jewish. Finally, I told him I was Jewish. He never spoke to me for the next couple of days, and they moved me out into Bucharest.

We had a French doctor, who was interned, who took care of us in Bucharest. He took X-rays of my leg. He saw what had happened to my leg. He put me on a table and he got some guys from the camp downstairs. Real strong ones, you know, six-footers and 200-pounders. Three on each side, they held me down, and he re-broke the leg so it could have a chance to heal properly. It worked, although much later, I had to have a bone graft. I had a bone taken out of this leg [*touches right leg*] and put into that leg [*touches left leg*]. She healed beautifully. She healed so well that—you can feel it right here [*pulls down sock to show the area where the bone was grafted*]—that even in November 30, 1947, when I turned a car over five times, my car landed on top of the leg. If it had landed on [the rest of] me it would have killed me. I was thrown out as the car was turning over. It didn't break here *[points to the graft area]*; it broke here *[points to higher on leg]*.

As the Red Army poured into Romania, the pro-fascist government was overthrown in a coup d'état near the end of August and Romania joined the Allies. The PoWs' situation was precarious; as the Red Army approached the capital, the Germans carried out a series of reprisal terror bombing raids.

The bombings started by the Germans. As a matter of fact, the guys were looking up in the sky thinking maybe it was our boys, and it turned out to be Dorniers, which are German bombers. When the bombings started as the Russians were coming in, all of a sudden there were Romanian tanks around the hospital ward we [Americans] were in, to protect us, because we were their greatest asset at that time.

We were terror-bombed for three days and three nights. Before that, we were bombed by the Americans and the British. The first night we were in the basement of the hospital. This was a very, very, very old building. The rats were all over. We decided to go out, and I was starting to fall on my crutches when a couple of guys grabbed me. My radio operator had come out of a building that most of the GIs ended up in. It was the tallest building in Bucharest; it was a sixteen-story building, steel and concrete, owned by the Franco-American Oil Company. [*Laughs*] They also had two 40mm anti-aircraft guns, on the roof. Our guys had taken it over [with the Romanians' blessing].

He had come to look for me, and I thought that he should have gotten a medal for that. They grabbed me. They had no stretcher, so they used a door that had been blown off, and they carried me to the safety of this building, which was a few blocks away. We were on the eighth floor, we took over the whole eighth floor. Our officers went to the Bank of Romania and they borrowed $75,000. We got equipment and rifles, things like that. We had our guards around the perimeter. We set up our own kitchen there. It was the safest place to be because you were in the middle of a building. You had the anti-aircraft guns on the roof. Not only did we go there, but as many of the Romanian people who could get into the building got in to there. The only difference was we had food.

'Like Ants Scurrying Back and Forth'

One of the saddest things I ever saw, after the third day of bombing by the Germans, these people had not had food at all. Bread trucks came to the courtyard of the building; this building had a courtyard in the middle of the building. The bread trucks came in and the Romanians started to cue up the civilians. All of a sudden, the sirens went off again and we could hear the German planes in the air. I watched from the eighth floor... [*hesitates; gets choked up*] I'm sorry. It was like ants scurrying back and forth... [*pauses, composes himself*] I'm sorry.

They were... [*pauses*] they wanted the safety of the building. But they needed bread, they were hungry. You could see them [*motions his hands back and forth*], they were torn—do we go to the building for safety, or for the bread? [*Takes a deep breath and regroups himself*] When you fly, you don't see that. You are up at 20,000, 25,000 feet. All you can see is the landmarks and soccer stadiums, the oil refinery you are going to hit or the marshalling yards, the railroad yards that you are going to hit. When I saw that I just broke down, and at that time I swore I would never drop another bomb. But I came to terms with that; if I had to do it again, I would. But actually seeing it was a very, very traumatic experience for me, still is.

*

I was a prisoner for two months. In early September, the first and largest evacuation of American PoWs during the war occurred; they flew us back to Italy.

Over a thousand American PoWs were flown out of Romania on converted B-17s. On September 4, 1944, the commanding officer of the 15th Air Force, Major Gen. N.F. Twining, wrote to the evacuees:

> **You are going home. You are the returning heroes of the Battle of Ploesti. Your safe return to my command marked the culmination of an outstanding campaign in the annals of American military history. The German war machine's disintegration on all fronts is being caused, to a large extent, by their lack of oil-oil that you took from them. I only have one regret on this jubilant occasion. I wish it had been possible to bring out of Romania every officer and man who went down in that battle.**

Of the 3,781 men shot down trying to destroy Ploesti, only 1,185 came home.

'Missing in Action'

When I came out of Romania, I was in the hospital in Italy. A neighbor's kid from home came up to see me. He had heard that they had brought us guys back. His family had been writing to him to see if they could find out about me, where I was, how I could be reached.

I asked him right away, 'How are my mother and father?'

He said, 'Well your mother is dead, don't you know it?'

I just broke down. I was in bad shape; I weighed about 100 pounds at the time. I had just gotten out of Romania. So I sent a telegram. It said, 'Know about mother, don't worry.' [*Begins to cry softly*]

I'm sorry, sometimes I get a little emotional, I can't help that. The chaplain was supposed to tell me, but he never did. [*Hands the interviewer some World War II era telegrams*]

'Missing in action.' If you look at some of these telegrams, none of them have my home address; they were addressed to my father's place of business. I purposely didn't want the telegram to go home because I knew my mother had very, very high blood pressure. My father and I had a deal where I'd have it sent to my father's place of business so he would make arrangements to have a doctor come out and be handy, if need be. I got shot down June 28. It came to my father during the July 4th weekend, and they couldn't deliver it because the place of business was closed. So they went through the trouble to find out the home address, Strauss Street, which was delivered on July the fifth. My father was already in Manhattan working that day and my mother was home. The telegram came, that I'm missing in action. According to the way I heard it, she started to walk up the stairs and she keeled over. They called the doctor from down the block. She died of a cerebral hemorrhage.

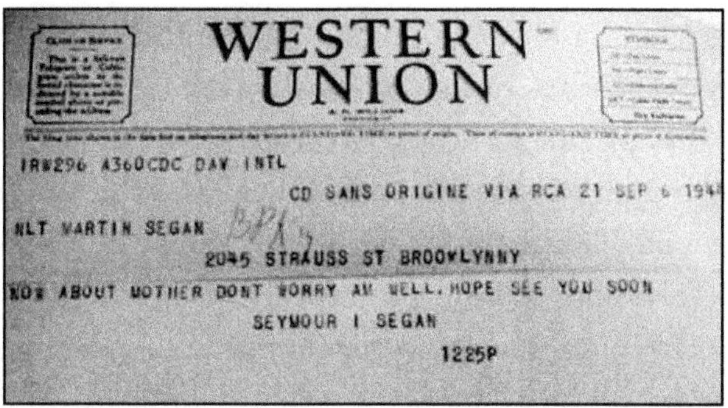

WESTERN UNION

IRW296 A360CDC DAY INTL

CD SANS ORIGINE VIA RCA 21 SEP 6 194[illegible]

NLT MARTIN SEGAN

2045 STRAUSS ST BROOKLYNNY

NOW ABOUT MOTHER DONT WORRY AM WELL. HOPE SEE YOU SOON

SEYMOUR I SEGAN

1225P

I spent a lot of time in hospitals. I had a lot of trouble reconciling how my mother died from the telegram. How do you think you feel when you find out you killed your mother?

Wife: He was 'Sonny.' He was the youngest and he was the only boy.

Seymour Segan: I used to blame myself that I didn't explain to her the fact that 'missing in action' is not necessarily 'killed in action.' You know? I didn't even think about that. One of the reasons I didn't want to be in a foxhole or be a foot soldier was because, at least in the air, it's often quick and over with, the ship blows up or crashes. Maybe that's what she was thinking. In my case, seven out of ten died and three of us lived.

Did I give you the letter where I'm dead? It was a letter from the Veterans Administration. Let's see if I can find it, it's here someplace. [*Shuffles papers around*] Here it is. 'We regret to inform you of the death of the above-named veteran.' [*Laughs*]

Wife: It came to his parents, but his mother was already dead.

Seymour Segan: That was cleared up very fast. I had a brother-in-law at that time who was very much involved with the military, and he was able to go outside of the channels and find out what was going on.

*

[I experienced a lot of troubles], but I've found, in a way, that everything sometimes turns out for the best. [After the 1947 car accident], they put me in Brooklyn Jewish Hospital and then transported me to the Veterans Hospital. When I had recovered enough, the doctor said, 'Go home for ten weeks, then come back and we will take X-rays and see how it healed.' I said, 'I can't go home; I live in a furnished room. I have no way of making food; I will have to walk in the winter on crutches for seven, eight blocks to find a restaurant for breakfast, lunch, and dinner.' So, they sent me up here, near the Adirondacks, to a veterans hospital at Mt. McGregor. [68] It was originally built in 1903 by Metropolitan Life for tuberculosis patients. It's on top of the mountain there—fresh air, cold fresh air, porches all the way around. They could take the patients and put them out in the cold air so they could breathe. They thought maybe that would help with their tuberculosis, and they did the same thing in Denver, and in Saranac Lake [Adirondacks]. So they also sent me up there.

It was January of 1948, the beginning of January. I fell in love with Glens Falls, just to the north. To me, the whole town was welcoming me from Brooklyn, New York. In 1961, December the 18th, we moved up here. It was a wonderful move for us. We were very happy. The children were brought up here. We have had a wonderful life up here; I am going to be buried up here. I hope it's not

---

[68] *Mt. McGregor*-Mt. McGregor has an interesting history. It is located in Wilton, New York, about 10 miles south of Glens Falls. Originally settled by Native American survivors escaping King Philip's War, it boasts spectacular views. Duncan McGregor built a hotel called the Mountain House in 1876; in 1885, the new owner, Joseph Drexel, loaned the use of his personal cottage on the mountain to his friend, then seriously ill former president Ulysses S. Grant, where Grant finished writing his war memoirs in just six weeks before he died there that July. Today, the Grant Cottage State Historic Site is preserved exactly as it was at the time of his death. In 1945, New York State used it for convalescing WWII veterans like Mr. Segan, and from 1976-2014 it was used as a minimum security state prison.

for a couple more years. [*Laughs*] Sometimes bad things can lead to good things.

*

To tell you the whole story is almost impossible. Because sometimes things come back to you that you haven't thought of in years. All of a sudden you think of it, and what makes you think of it, you don't even know. I'm one of the lucky ones. It took me a long time, but I was able to put it behind me and go on with my life. Not right away. For quite a while, I was at every veterans hospital in New York City. [*Lists various hospitals*] I was doing life. I was on the installment plan. [*Laughs*]

Wife: He was in and out of every veterans hospital in New York...

Seymour Segan: I ended up in I think 22 or 23 different hospitals. For my leg, for my finger that I lost—and that happened in on-the-job training, so it was covered by the government. One of the machines took it off. Post-traumatic war syndrome was the worst, a combination of that with alcoholism. I found AA. That was a deciding factor. I carry one of these around with me all the time, and maybe I'll be able to cope with everything. [*Takes a card out of his pocket*] The important thing is right here. *'God grant me the serenity to accept the things I cannot change, courage to change the things I can, and the wisdom to know the difference.'* And once I was able to accept a lot of those things, I was able to reach my potential.

Wife: You can't blame any of these fellows who nearly self-destructed. The main thing [to remember] is that they have the wisdom to know the difference.

***

Mr. Segan lost his wife of 59 years, Shirley, in 2007, about five years after this conversation. I visited again with Mr. Segan from time to time at the retirement community he settled into. He passed away a month after his 91st birthday on January 12, 2014.

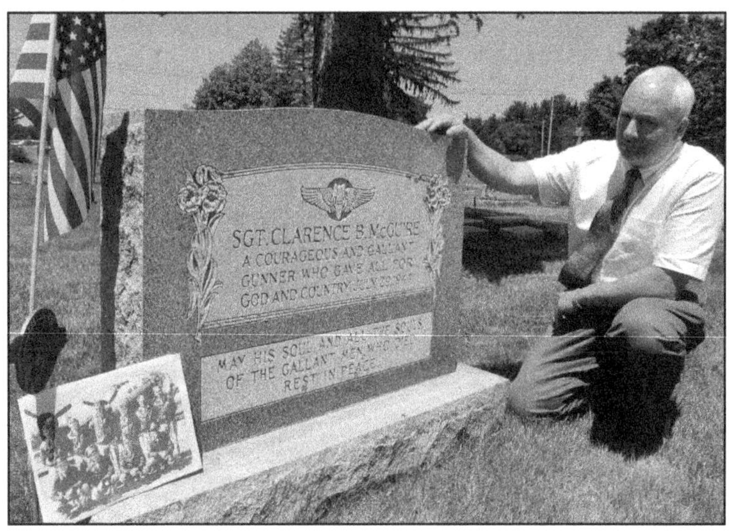

The author at Clarence McGuire's gravesite at St. Mary's Cemetery, Fort Edward, NY. 2010. Credit: Kris Dressen.

EPILOGUE

Resurrection

The phone rang on a beautiful summer evening. It was the cap to another long day at the keyboard and perhaps the answer to a long-shot query letter I had mailed a week earlier, to parts hitherto unknown.

Just a day before mailing the letter, I had had a shock. I wondered what the odds were of finding the exact same photograph that had haunted me all of my life—but now labeled with names!—on the internet. And the webpage it appeared on at the American Air Museum in Britain looked like it was a tribute to the crew. I looked closely at the caption:

A bomber crew of the 351st Bomb Group with their B-17 Flying Fortress. Handwritten caption: 'Technical Sergeant James E Ellis, Staff Sergeant Maurice J Franzblau, Sergeant Clarence B McGuire, Sergeant Fenton D Strohmeyer, Sergeant Guido Signoretti, Sergeant John Swarts, Second Lieutenant John M Morton, Second Lieutenant Donald Fish, Second Lieutenant William J Fuerth and Lieutenant McCaleb D Taylor of the 351th Bomb Group, 511 Squadron.'

I looked for the sponsor.

IN MEMORIAM

B-17 #4238146-Killed in Action (KIA) Shot down by flak and crashed near Beendorf, Germany.

Remembered by John S Swarts, Summerfield, FL

Here was another shock. The tribute appeared to be sponsored by the man who is labeled as the tail gunner on Clarence's plane. He's in the photo with Clarence that has been with me all of my life—but weren't they all killed? The webpage also says:

> '2nd Lt. Warren J Bragdon filled in as Co-Pilot for Lt. Donald Fish as he was flying lead ship on 570 Bomb Group in Polebrook, England.'

So there were two survivors of the crew photo, who had not gotten on the plane that day. On the internet again, I tracked the tail gunner to an address in Florida, and sent off the letter to what I hoped was the right address. I included the graveside photograph; I suppose if I had my man, it might come as a bit of a surprise to him.

I picked up the phone to answer the call. Some feedback interference hummed momentarily on the other end of the line, but even before he began to speak, I just knew that my hunch had played out. I found him, an actual survivor of the B-17 bomber crew in the photograph. Or should I say, he had found me.

John Swarts, World War II.

Source: John Swarts

'This is John Swarts,' said the voice with the distinctive Southern twang. 'Me and Clarence were pretty good friends.' A pause. 'You got it right, address and everything. I knew him well; I went with him to his home up there in New York. Me and him even rode horses together; I got some pictures I can send you. His mother used to write me letters afterwards. I'll look for that, too.'

John was the tail gunner in that crew photo. He hailed from Missouri, and later settled in St. Louis.

'Things worked out all right for me. Was married twice, got a boy and a girl. Spent 33 years on the railroad, and then had my own business. I'll be 93 on February 11. I don't get around good like I used to; fell three years ago and broke my pelvis and hip. But it was just me and the co-pilot who survived that day.'

'I was burned in the eyelid by flak a couple days before. I was in the hospital and didn't go on the last mission.' Because of a snafu, his mother got a telegram stating that he was missing in action—'The Army didn't know I was in the hospital. It took three months to clear up; she thought I was missing for two weeks before I was able to get word to the family that I was not on the plane.'

The plane went down on July 29, 1944. This weekend in the summer of 2017, the 73rd anniversary is upon us as we speak on the phone. 'The name of the plane was *Pugnacious Ball.* Flak got it. Blew it up. But I think they recovered a body bag to send home to his mother.'

'I watched for the planes coming back; you always do when they are out on a mission. You count them. We waited and waited. They didn't come back.'

'It was the worst day of my life. Still is.'

John sent me some material back in the mail—some photographs, scrapbook pages, even a letter from Clarence's mother.[35]

---

[35] *a letter from Clarence's mother-*

May 1, 1946

Dear Corporal [sic-Sergeant] Swarts:

I am the mother of Sergeant Clarence B. McGuire who was a member of the crew to which you were attached, and who was killed in action on his 6th mission over Germany (Merseberg) on July 29th, 1944. Only Providence knows the mystery which surrounds the entire crew. I had never received any further particulars from the Government, but Clarence's only brother, Jack, was the E.T.O. at the same time, and he worked hard to get any information to be had.

When Jack reached Versailles, France, he went directly to the Graves Information Department there, and found that Clarence had been buried in an isolated grave in Benndorf, Germany, from July 29, 1944 to June 18, 1945 – at which time he was reburied in the U.S. at Margraten, Holland. Jack went to his grave in July 1945. You may be sure that what he was able to accomplish was the source of much comfort to me. I hadn't heard a word from the Government, but in checking with them in December last, they confirmed the information I already had. Clarence's brother and I have erected a very lovely memorial to Clarence's memory, in our own family cemetery, and I have requested that Clarence's remains be sent to me, just as soon as this procedure is possible.

I am particularly anxious to get in touch with Captain James P. Tounley who was the Commanding Officer of your crew at the time of Clarence's last mission. Captain Tounley wrote my son Jack immediately after, and it was such a kind, fine letter. I wrote to Washington to get Captain Tounley's address, but one of their form cards said the department for such information was closed, and they could not be of assistance. However, it may just be that you know of his whereabouts, and would let me have his address if you know it – I would be appreciative of your kindness in forwarding it to me.

I am addressing you under your military title, though I earnestly hope you are now out of service and have returned to civilian life – in which I wish you much more happiness. If ever you come to New York, do make it a point to come and see me. I should like so much to have you do so; Clarence spoke so highly of all of the men attached to the crew; said they were all such a fine lot.

Thank you again and again for the above address if you can get it for me, or already have it, and with my best wishes to you,

'We were a very close crew. This is a photo of us horseback riding in Denver, Colorado, in cadet school training. We enjoyed our time together. We then went to gunnery school in Kingman, Arizona.' Clarence's nickname was 'Barney.' He was the biggest one on the crew. We all got along good. Oh, we had a lot of fun, going to Piccadilly Square and all...'

Riding horses in Colorado. John is on the right with the child; Clarence is on the left. Source: John Swarts.

Over in England, they called themselves the 'Ball Boys' after their commander, Col. Ball. Clark Gable, the movie actor, was also in the 351st Bomb Group at the time, enlisting and flying operational missions over Germany.

'He flew with us six times; I got to be with him a few times. He was a nice man.'

Most sincerely,
(Mrs.) Helen Y. McGuire.

John also met the eighteen-year-old Princess Elizabeth and her parents.

'She was pretty quiet. I had a year on her. That's General Doolittle and the King and Queen, too. We talked for a couple minutes; I was just coming off a mission, and they were there to greet us. Somebody took a picture; it says on the back, *NOT FOR RELEASE,* but I suppose it's okay now.'

From left: John Swarts, General Jimmy Doolittle, The Queen Consort Elizabeth Bowes-Lyon, King George VI, and Princess Elizabeth, 1944. Source: John Swarts.

'I flew six missions with the crew Clarence was on, and seventeen altogether. We flew a support mission on D-Day, knocking out a German ammo dump. I saw a lot of guys getting killed on the beach, getting shot on the ground on that day. It was awful.'

John also sent me newspaper clippings. *'Vet Feels Guilty Because Buddies Died,'* declares one. 'I feel so guilty. They were buried in Germany the same day they were shot down.'

'When they shipped me home, I was training on the B-29 in California when the war ended. I was lucky a lot. Somebody was with me.'

'Everybody was answering their call to duty. I wanted to go; you do it and that's it. I made a lot of friends; I lost a lot of friends.'

'I don't know what to make of the world today. Wars are different. Today you drop a bomb from 8,000 miles away. All the countries think different; always somebody wants to be a dictator. People are trying to divide us—there should be more unity in America.'

I asked John what his nickname was.

'Mickey. I don't know why. I was the youngest, like Mickey Mouse I guess,' he chuckled.

I asked him if he knew who took his place on that fatal mission.

'I don't know. I wondered for a long time...nobody knows, and I'm not sure I'd want to know, now. It could have been anybody—lots of times a mechanic or somebody from the ground crew would jump in, if they were short somebody last minute. Oh yes, that happened quite a bit. They wanted to go, they wanted to fly. Kids are crazy, you know that... anyway, it'd break my heart to find out now.'

John Swarts at the World War II Memorial, Washington, DC.

Our time grew short. We said our goodbyes.

'I get a little emotional. I'm almost 93; I hope to see them all again in heaven.'

'My Best 4 Friends of our crew, all killed in action but me.'
L-R- Clarence B McGuire, Maurice J Franzblau, Fenton D Strohmeyer, Guido Signoretti, John Swarts. Source: John Swarts.

*

I copy the letter Clarence's mother sent to John after the war. I fold it up and return to the grave of my youth, and leave it under a memorial pebble inscribed by my students:

'We Will Never Forget'

I turn and leave this cemetery to go back out into the world, having gone again to see a hometown boy whose future ended on July 29, 1944. And I take another memorial pebble the kids inscribed not so long ago for such an occasion, and drop it into a padded envelope.

'We Remember'

I taught my students to stop and remember, and I think they remain genuinely grateful for that. John S. Swarts, SN 37619276, tail gunner on the B-17 #4238146, has another surprise coming in the mail soon, from the young people of this 'Hometown, USA,' from the grave of his friend. Time marches on, but the ripples go forth.[69]

***

The Airmen featured in this book

Andy Doty: After the war, Andy Doty married his high school sweetheart, Eleanor Baker, the daughter of the local druggist, and raised three girls, settling in Palo Alto, California, and retiring as Director of Community Affairs for Stanford University. You can read more about his World War II experiences in my first book or by

[69] John called me a few days later to tell me that he had managed to get in touch with the co-pilot mentioned in this chapter, that he was still alive, over 100 years old, in Minnesota. He gave me the number, but as of this writing, I have been unable to reach him.

searching for his out-of-print 1995 memoir with the information provided in the 'Source Notes' in the back of this book.[103]
Richard 'Dick' Varney, Sr.: After the war, Dick Varney was employed at Imperial Color, later known as Ciba-Geigy. When he retired in 1976, he had worked himself up to the plant supervisor. He was active in his church and a local VFW post and also was an avid New York Yankees baseball fan. He also enjoyed talking politics. Dick passed away on April 24, 2008, at the age of 96.[104]

Richard G. Alagna: After the war, Richard completed law school and was admitted to the New York Bar Association in 1951. Active in community organizations, Richard also enjoys painting, photography, and etching. He has won many awards and his works are in numerous private collections and galleries across the United States.[105]

Kenneth R. Carlson: Ken Carlson enjoyed a successful career in advertising and became a youth advocate after the war. He still speaks about his World War II experiences to inspire young people and is a strong supporter of his alma mater, the Collegiate School in New York City, the oldest school in the country.[106]

Earl M. Morrow: Earl Morrow was a career airline pilot for American Airlines. He retired to the family farm in Hartford, New York, after his career, and was a sought-after speaker in local schools and community events.[107]

Martin F. Bezon: After the war, Martin worked for the National Geological Survey in Alaska. After being called up for service in the Korean War, he resumed his former job at Republic Steel until the mines closed in 1971. He later worked for the Amerada Hess Corporation. Martin was very active in his local VFW, American Legion, and his church. He enjoyed spending time on Lake Champlain, hunting, and fishing in the Adirondacks and Vermont. He passed away at the age of 90 on April 16, 2012.[108]

Seymour 'Sonny' Segan: Sonny worked in New York's menswear industry and opened a number of successful retail stores, first locally and then throughout the Northeast. In 1989, Sonny was named president of the Menswear Retailers of America. He was active in his temple and community organizations throughout 'Hometown, USA.' He was also instrumental in helping many people in their recoveries through AA. He died on January 12, 2014, at the age of 91.[109]

****

VOLUME III

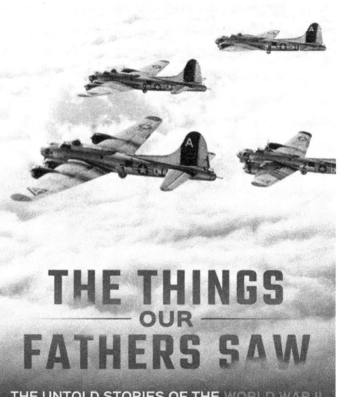

MATTHEW A. ROZELL

THE THINGS OUR FATHERS SAW

THE UNTOLD STORIES OF THE WORLD WAR II GENERATION FROM HOMETOWN, USA

THE WAR IN THE AIR 2

VOLUME III

THE THINGS OUR FATHERS SAW

VOLUME III:
THE UNTOLD STORIES OF THE WORLD WAR II GENERATION FROM HOMETOWN, USA

WAR IN THE AIR:
COMBAT, CAPTIVITY, AND REUNION

MATTHEW A. ROZELL

WOODCHUCK HOLLOW PRESS

Hartford · New York

Information at woodchuckhollowpress@gmail.com.

Front Cover: B-17 Flying Fortresses from the 398th Bombardment Group fly a bombing run to Neumunster, Germany, on April 13, 1945. Credit: Public Domain, U.S. Air Force photograph.

Additional photographs and descriptions sourced at Wikimedia Commons within terms of use, unless otherwise noted.

Publisher's Cataloging-in-Publication Data

Names: Rozell, Matthew A., 1961- author.
Title: The things our fathers saw, war in the air : combat, captivity, and reunion : the untold stories of the World War II generation from hometown, USA / Matthew A. Rozell.
Other titles: War in the air.
Description: Hartford, NY : Woodchuck Hollow Press, 2017. | Series: The things our fathers saw, vol. 3.
Identifiers: LCCN 2017915746 | ISBN 978-0-9964800-7-9 (pbk.) | ISBN 978-0-9964800-6-2 (ebook)
Subjects: LCSH: United States. Army Air Forces--Airmen--Biography. | World War, 1939-1945--Personal narratives, American. | World War, 1939-1945--Aerial operations, American. | Military history, Modern--20th century. | Air warfare--History--20th century. | BISAC: HISTORY / Military / Veterans. | HISTORY / Military / World War II. | HISTORY / Military / Aviation.
Classification: LCC D810.V42 R6911 2017 (print) | LCC D810.V42 (ebook) | DDC 940.54/8173--dc23.

matthewrozellbooks.com

Printed in the United States of America

THE THINGS OUR FATHERS SAW III

WAR IN THE AIR–BOOK TWO: COMBAT, CAPTIVITY, AND REUNION

How can I be a hero? I was lucky to get out.
— CHARLIE COREA, POW, STALAG 17

Dying for freedom isn't the worst that could happen.
Being forgotten is.
— SUSIE STEPHENS-HARVEY, REFLECTING ON HER BROTHER,
STEPHEN J. GEIST
MIA 9-26-1967

I think we shall never see the likes of it again.
— ANDY DOTY, B-29 TAIL GUNNER

THE THINGS OUR FATHERS SAW III

WAR IN THE AIR—BOOK TWO

THE STORYTELLERS (IN ORDER OF APPEARANCE):

CLARENCE DART

JOHN G. WEEKS

RICHARD J. FAULKNER

GEORGE T. FITZGIBBON

CHARLES P. COREA

EARL M. MORROW

SAM LISICA

JEROME SILVERMAN

THE THINGS OUR FATHERS SAW III

TABLE OF CONTENTS

B-17 Flying Fortresses from the 398th Bombardment Group fly a bombing run to Neumunster, Germany, on April 13, 1945.
Credit: Public Domain, U.S. Air Force photograph.

Author's Note

The rooftop of a hundred-year-old valley farmhouse holds special delights as a midsummer's twilight approaches. I go out to sit back on the porch roof, watching the wind surf through the cornrows, the river flowing quietly in the background, maybe tapping my pack and lighting a cigarette before thinking about the day's events. Supper has ended, and the sun begins to quicken its march towards the horizon. And then I think I hear it. Far off in the background, a lone drone is steadily growing louder, creeping ever closer, steadier and steadier, like the slow but deliberate advancement of the shadows across the valley panorama. And suddenly she is here, almost treetop level overhead, her four engines roaring as she passes slowly, confidently, right over the top of me with a magnificence so bold I reach up as if to touch her underbelly overhead with my fingertips. An unrehearsed and authentic joy springs up from deep within me, for I have just witnessed something that future generations will never be able to even imagine: this lone sentinel gliding across the sky, the sudden manifestation of American air power and guardian of the memory of a past generation of Americans who once saved the world as the 'masters of the air.' My eyes locked upon her until she was nothing more than a speck in the sky.

I knew I would never forget that sound. Years later, three hundred miles away from the college town airfield in western New York where my rooftop reverie was broken, I heard it again from inside my classroom on a spring afternoon. I instantly knew just from that approaching low drone that it was my old Boeing B-17 Flying Fortress. I dropped the chalk and hurried away from the lesson, signaling to the kids to 'Follow me!' outside the schoolhouse doors. I'm sure they thought I was nuts, but I was just in time to look up and see that old girl once again disappearing over the treetops as she flew in for an exhibition at the local county airport.

I made my way out to the airport on Saturday morning to see my college town B-17. I had not seen her for years since returning back to the hometown that raised me, but I knew I would find a special person out on the tarmac—my old friend Earl. There he was, smiling, his cap embroidered with the emblem 'B-17 Pilot- WWII,' arms folded for the photographer.

Earl M. Morrow, 2000, Floyd Bennett Memorial Airport.
Credit: Rob Barendse for the Glens Falls Post-Star.

For years I had been collecting World War II narratives with my history students, and it had gotten newspaper attention. So he called me up and said, 'I just had to call you and ask—why are you doing this? Why are you interested in our stories?' Earl Morrow came into my classroom over the years, and I visited with him at his home in upstate New York, close by the communities that were dubbed 'Hometown, USA' during the war. He introduced me to his Army Air Force friends, and I had great conversations with them.

Earl held court on the tarmac that weekend, even going up again in the B-17 he once commanded over the skies in Europe, the aircraft he brought in 'on a wing and a prayer' over the White Cliffs of Dover, the plane that he and the survivors of his crew were forced to bail out of before she exploded in the leaden November skies over Nazi Germany. Little did he know he would soon share quarters with over 100,000 other prisoners of war of the Nazi regime, and then go on to reunite decades later with the men he was imprisoned with right back in this community not far from the waterfalls on the Hudson River in upstate New York.

*

In this and the upcoming books in *The Things Our Fathers Saw* series, we visit with more of the people who were forged and tempered in the tough times of the Great Depression and went on to 'do their bit' when even rougher times came calling. For those of you who may not be familiar with the background, most of these people either hailed from, later settled near, or otherwise have a connection to the 'Hometown, USA' community where I grew up and taught for over 30 years.

It's always been my philosophy that history is best understood when it is relayed by those who were actually there on the front lines. I was lucky enough to recognize this early in my career as a public high school history teacher, which began at a time when America was waking up and beginning to notice the deeds of the men and women who had saved the world only a generation before. Many of these men and women had never spoken of their experiences before, but on some instinctual level I sensed they were ready to talk, and more importantly, ready to share their experiences with our young people who were about to go out into the world themselves. So we began, slowly at first, to seek them out and invite them into the classroom. We taped our conversations and later wrote them out. I began to teach and write more intensely on the subject, and taught my students the value of communication with their elders. As time went on, my kids and I fanned out into our community on a greater scale; just 50 years before, at the height of World War II, it had been the subject of *LOOK Magazine's* multi-issue photographic profile of life on the home front, appropriately titled, 'Hometown, USA.'

After nearly three decades of teaching, I finally set out to keep the promise I had made to my students to write about the people that we had met and interviewed. My first book, *The Things Our Fathers Saw: The Untold Stories of the World War II Generation from Hometown, USA*-was well received and inspired me to continue with the series. In the second book in the series, we headed to the skies over Europe in *The Things Our Fathers Saw:*. Several additional volumes are planned, including the war in North Africa and Italy, the D-Day invasion of Fortress Europe, and the piercing of the Third Reich itself to the end of the war in Europe. This book picks up where *The War in the Air* left off, with additional interviews about the air war over Europe that I could not include in that book.. So that it is not necessary to read the books in order, the background chapter on 'Air Power' from that book is re-presented in Chapter One.

*

As I also previously noted, as the writer/historian you spend days, if not weeks, with each individual in your book, researching their stories, getting under their skin. In composing their stories in their own words, you feel like you are giving them new life and placing readers at the kitchen table with that person who had something important to say. The reader shares the intimate moments with them as he/she gets absorbed in a real story being told. As an interviewer this happened many times to me directly with our World War II veterans, in living rooms, kitchens, and dining rooms all over 'Hometown USA,' in the classroom, and at reunion 'hospitality rooms' and hotel breakfast tables across America. As a history teacher I also turned loose a generation of young people to bond with their grandparents' generation in the same way. We gave all of our first-person interviews to research institutions so that they might not be lost. The New York State Military Museum was the primary beneficiary, with over a hundred interviews deposited for future generations to learn from. As one of the most active contributors to the program, I also leaned on them for video recordings of some of the interviews I edited for this book. My friends Wayne Clarke and Mike Russert, the workhorses of the NYS Veterans Oral History Program, traversed the state for several years gathering these stories under the leadership of Michael Aikey; they know the feeling of bonding with these extraordinary men and women well. In bringing these stories back to life, I hope I did a service to them as well as to the general public.

*

In the study of World War II, we are tempted to teach and learn the history as if the way things turned out was somehow preordained, as if it was a foregone conclusion that Americans and their allies were destined to win the war from the outset. As historian (and Pacific Marine veteran) William Manchester noted, because we know how events turned out, we tend to read the history with a sense of inevitability. Nothing could be further from the truth. It is easy to forget that during World War II the United States would be essentially engaging in two full-blown wars at the same time, taxing America's resources and families to the hilt.

Most of these men grew up very fast. Some left school in their early teens to work, some lied about their age to enlist or got a parent to sign off for them. Others found themselves commanding men at a tender age, where today they would not be afforded a legal drink. Listen to them tell you about the world they grew up in, how they surmounted challenges and obstacles placed on life's course, and how their generation of Americans not only rose to the challenge of defeating the greatest threat the world has ever seen, but also built the country and the freedoms that we enjoy today. Be inspired. Share their stories; give them voice. They have some lessons for us all, and we forget their stories at our peril.

Matthew Rozell
October 2017

Clarence W. Dart, Tuskegee Airman.
December 2003. Credit: Author.

CHAPTER ONE

The Tuskegee Airman

P-51 Mustang flown by the Red Tail Project. Credit: Max Haynes

The Tuskegee Airmen, or 'Red Tails,' as they came to be known, were a special group of airmen who trained at the airfield near the famed Tuskegee Institute in Alabama and would become the first African-American aviators in the United States military. Still segregated before 1940, the military had previously denied young black men the opportunity to fly for their country in combat. Historically, this was nothing new. The prevailing attitude that African-American recruits lacked the intellectual capacity and stamina for battlefield and leadership roles went back centuries; a mid-1920s military report reinforced age-old falsehoods and stereotypes about the combat readiness of the African-American soldier. Still, as war loomed on the horizon, the training of young black pilots, bombardiers, navigators, and supporting personnel began as a U.S. Army Air Corps 'experiment'—would these young people of color really be able to hold their own? Nearly a thousand men completed the Tuskegee advanced flight training program and went on to compile a distinguished record as the 332nd Fighter Group (eventually comprised of four fighter squadrons—the 99th, 100th, 301st, and 302nd) flying nearly 1,400 combat missions over war-torn Europe.[70,110]

Twice shot down by the enemy, Captain Clarence W. Dart managed to make it back to friendly lines safely, racking up 95 missions and receiving two Purple Hearts and the Distinguished Flying Cross with four oak leaf clusters, one of ninety-six fellow Tuskegee recipients of the DFC.[71] The Tuskegee Airmen were groundbreakers and paved the way for the ratcheting up of the civil rights movement and the eventual desegregation of the armed forces in 1948.

I interviewed Mr. Dart on several occasions. In December of 2003, he gave me and my class a wide-ranging interview that lasted several hours.

*

---

[70] The 447th Bomber Group was activated in January 1944, comprised of black aviators, several of whom were veterans of the 332nd who had completed their fighter tours and had rotated back home. They trained for the B-25 bombers, but the war ended before they saw combat; significantly, they distinguished themselves in standing up to overt racism at home. See 'The Tuskegee Airmen Story: The 447th Bombardment Group (M) (Colored)'; http://ecctai.org/tuskegee-477th-bombardment-group.

[71] *Distinguished Flying Cross with four oak leaf clusters*- the recipient has 'distinguished himself or herself in support of operations by heroism or extraordinary achievement while participating in an aerial flight, subsequent to November 11, 1918'-U.S. Department of Defense. Each oak leaf cluster represents an additional act subsequent to the first award.

'I live in Saratoga Springs [New York], a couple of blocks away from the racetrack.[72] *But no, to answer your question, I don't go there; in fact, I have never been there. Well, I could tell you why I've never been in there. When I first came back from overseas, they used to bring the horses in on Pullman cars all padded out with running water and everything, and compare that to what I saw in Italy, and in parts of this country, I said, 'They're treating those horses better than people,' and I said, 'They do not need my money.'*[73] *So that's why I have not been to the racetrack.'*

*

Clarence Dart, Tuskegee Airman

'A Tough Time'

The Great Depression was a tough time. To think of the way people had to live. People who had good jobs and lost them overnight because of the Crash in 1929, when the stock market crashed on Wall Street. Overnight, millionaires became paupers. No money, period. A lot of people, believe it or not, jumped out of those windows down there in New York City and committed suicide; the shock was just that great. To think that they were penniless overnight because they bought stocks on what they call 'margins.' It wasn't enough to cover or reserve when the market collapsed, and so they just became penniless overnight.

---

[72] *the racetrack*- Saratoga Race Course is one of the nation's oldest thoroughbred horse racing tracks, opening in the summer of 1863.

[73] *Pullman cars all padded out with running water*- specially-padded railroad boxcars were equipped with feeding and watering apparatus specifically for transporting racehorses; the purpose was to reduce the stress and fatigue of travel for the horse, which sometimes had to compete shortly after arrival.

It affected everybody. People were selling apples for a nickel on street corners. My father, fortunately, didn't lose his job because he worked on the railroad, but he kept taking pay cuts all the way through the Depression until the time it started to turn around when World War II started; I think he was down under twenty-five dollars a week, take-home pay. We had just bought a house, and boy, did we struggle during that time! I could take the whole afternoon telling you how we lived and what my mother used to do to keep me in clothes. My mother would buy shirts from the Salvation Army store. She would turn the collars because they would get frayed. She would take the collars off, turn them, and sew them back onto the shirts. It was a time when people really had to be on their own.

I could remember, especially in the winter, we had what you called garters, but they were rubber boots, no insulation in the darn things. We would go out and play until we couldn't feel anything in our feet and hands. You could come home and first thing [my mother] would do is put you in tepid water, supposedly to warm you up. As soon as you hit that water, you would start screaming. I don't know if any of you have had frostbite or anything like that, from being out skiing or ice skating until your hands get so cold you don't feel anything anymore. It lasts practically forever! Once it happens to you, you will always feel that cold. I experienced it again, so to speak, when we were flying—switched to the P-51s, at high altitudes, around anywhere from twenty-five thousand to over thirty thousand feet. There wasn't much heat in the airplanes. The heat in the P-51s would come in on one side and that foot would get warm, but you would have to sort of cross your feet [*laughs*] to defrost the other foot. I'll get to that further on to make a continuity.

Of course, it also brought people together. There was some welfare help, but it was tough, especially in the wintertime. We kids used to go down and stand next to the railroad tracks. The firemen on the locomotives used to shovel coal off of the engines as they went by. We would pick up the coal and take it home. Of course, we burned everything; we didn't have central heating in homes in those days. Everybody had either a fireplace or a big central furnace with one duct on the top that supposedly was to heat the whole house. We used to go out and pick wild mustards and stuff like that for food. Everyone had a garden also. There was a lot of implementation to survive.

Real Airplanes

When the war started in 1941, I had just turned twenty-one. I was singing in our church choir at our radio station that afternoon when they came in and said that Pearl Harbor had been bombed. I had just turned 21 on December 6, and it happened the next day. A friend and I were talking about going into the Navy. But my mother put a stop to that right quick. She said, 'You're not going into any army, navy, or anything.' Well, you know how mothers are; they're still that way today.

As a kid I always built model airplanes because I was an airplane fanatic. It was after I saw the first airplane fly, then they started selling these kits. First, it was mostly these little gliders you can throw around. Then I graduated to building replicas of real airplanes. There were a lot at fairs then, not like nowadays. I can remember being angry with my mother because when I was a kid they used to have these hobby shows; kids would get prizes by being judged on their workmanship. I had built this model of a Curtiss Goshawk, a Navy fighter. There were a few mistakes in the thing, so I didn't want it exhibited, but my mother, she was so proud of it [*laughs*] she took it to the show and put it in there. I didn't win anything, but she was proud enough that she wanted it exhibited. Anyway, I was always fascinated with flying.

When the war started, and after a lot of pressure started from politicians, Mrs. Roosevelt and other people decided they would train black pilots. I have commentary on this because in spite of what black soldiers and sailors have done in the history of this country, it was always convenient just to forget what they did, from the Revolution right on up until this day. They fight in Albany about getting the Congressional Medal of Honor for Henry Johnson.[74] It shouldn't have happened. He did as much as what's-his-name [Sergeant York] did in World War I. I guess he killed about ten German soldiers that had attacked his group. At the end he was fighting with a knife. He used up all of his ammunition and saved a lot of his squad.

But when they decided to train black pilots, the assessment team came through, well, let me back up...

After high school, there were no jobs, so I went to what they called Elmira Aviation Ground School. The state figured they would start all these training schools for people to learn how to be mechanics, machinists, and radio operators. I took all the classes that I could. I figured I was set to do anything, but you go around, and how things were in those days, you were rejected for one reason or another. When the assessment team from the Air Corps came around with their tests, I passed all their tests, except my medical. Most of my medical was all right, except I didn't pass the depth perception test. That was because I was so excited I didn't get sleep

[74] *Medal of Honor for Henry Johnson*-Johnson, a New Yorker, fought with the 'Harlem Hellcats' on the front lines in France, the first American to receive the Croix de Guerre, France's highest award for bravery. At the time of our 2003 interview with Mr. Dart, a renewed effort to have Johnson formally awarded the medal had just been blocked. On June 2, 2015, President Obama presented the MOH to the head of the NYS National Guard, as Johnson had died in obscurity in 1929.

the night before! My eyesight was kind of fuzzy. In those days, the depth perception test used two sticks. One of the sticks had a line on it, and you had to move the sticks until they were opposite each other. This was supposed to demonstrate your depth perception so when you came in to land [*laughs*], you knew how far the ground was below you or something like that. But it was a rudimentary test. Anyway, they told me, 'You go back and get rested. So when we come back again we'll give you another test.' That happened about eight months after that. So I came around and passed the test. They said, 'Go home. When your class is called, we'll cut orders and give you the oath of office. We will see you get to Tuskegee for training.' Well, they were still building the field down there in Tuskegee, so I didn't feel too bad about it. I told my draft board that I was going into the Air Corps.

I guess they didn't believe me because I was around for almost six months, and next thing I knew, I got my 'Greetings from Uncle Sam.' Have any of you heard your father or grandfather talk about greetings from Uncle Sam? Well, that's what the letter said: 'Greetings.' [*Laughs*] Next thing I knew, I was on a train to Fort Niagara, which was the classification center for our part of the state where they decided where you were going to go. The first thing they told us was, 'Well, we don't know what you can do, just tell us what you would like to do,' and so on and so forth. I put down all the things I had learned: airplane mechanics, machinist, and radio operator.

I didn't get to go anyplace I asked. Next thing I knew, I was on a train to Fort Sill, Oklahoma, for field artillery. I said, 'Oh my goodness, I'm not going to learn how to fly.' But then, I committed a cardinal sin in the military. I didn't go through channels! See, in the military, if you're one of the lower ranks and you want to do something, you go to your squad commander, and he passes it on to the company commander, and if the company commander sees fit, he will forward it. I wrote this letter to the commanding general of the

Air Corps! That's against the law [*laughs*]. I bypassed everybody, and in headquarters I think they realized I made a mistake. They wrote my father but not me. He told me that they had said not to worry, because they knew where I was. When the field school was finished and my class was called, they would cut orders and have me sent to Tuskegee.

Well, meanwhile, I didn't mind the field artillery because it was fun shooting those big guns, 155mm howitzers. I think I shot every gun type that the military had at the time, at least the ground troops—all kinds of machine guns. They had pistols from the cavalry, the kind that you see, those long-barreled pistols, in the movies. We had those kinds of pistols, and shotguns, and tank weapons. When my orders came through, they came through on a Friday evening; no, I think they came during the day. But my company commander didn't tell me until after retreat on that Friday. I think he was kind of angry with me because I had taken a lot of math in high school; I used to aim in my section, my howitzer section. To aim those big guns, they have what they call an aiming stick, which is behind the gun. There was a periscope-type thing on the breech of the gun. You look through that periscope back at the aiming stick to traverse the gun. They called down the elevation that they wanted you to fire the gun at. I was made chief of section because I had pretty a good math background and didn't have any trouble with triangulating a gun.

I turned him down on [becoming second lieutenant] because through the 'scuttlebutt' I had heard what had happened to second lieutenants in the field artillery—they made them forward observers! They sent them to places, especially over the Pacific. The Japanese would figure out who was calling down fire on them. They search out the forward observers, and, naturally, they didn't last long. So we knew all this stuff and I turned him down. And he was disappointed because he thought I would jump at the chance to become an officer and second lieutenant. I told him, 'No, I am going into the Air Corps.' Well, he didn't believe me, but I did get my orders. He waited until after retreat on a Friday, and I had to go to Oklahoma City to catch a train to go to Tuskegee.

Tuskegee

I had a lot of friends. They said, 'Oh, we will help you out.' They went up to the office and forged signatures and got me transportation to get to Oklahoma City to catch a train to Tuskegee. They of course could have gotten court marshaled for it. [*Laughs*] I arrived at a little town called Cheaha at about two o'clock in the morning—it was way out in the boonies. There was a telephone pole with one little light that looked like a sixty-watt bulb. [*Laughs*] It was raining and not really a train station, but out in the boonies. Pretty soon there came about three 6x6 trucks. They put us in the trucks and took us out to the field.

Before I left Fort Sill I tried to give my overcoat back. I told the quartermaster, or the guy that worked in the quartermaster's section, that I didn't need it anymore because I was going to southern Alabama where it was nice and warm. He made me keep my overcoat. When we got to the field there was nobody who had been designated to start a fire in the furnace in the barracks. They were brand-new barracks. So we had to sleep in our clothes the first night. The next morning when we woke up they had these big water barrels at the corner of each barrack. There was ice about an inch thick on the water of those barrels. I guess they were supposed to be in case of a fire, to help put a fire out. I learned about the South that it can get just as cold down there as it does up in the north! I was glad I had that coat.

Eventually, they got us settled down. Some of us were transferred to the campus of the Tuskegee Institute for our ground training, to learn navigation and communications and stuff like that. I didn't have any trouble because I had had the experience of radio and so forth. Eventually, while we were there, after we passed our tests in ground school, they would truck us each day out to Moton Field, the field which I told you is going to be a national [park] monument. We trained in PT-17s, which were biplanes built by Stearman Company.[75] It was the thrill of my life!

PT-17 trainer. 'Spirit of Tuskegee.' Credit: Rennett Stowe

When I was going to the ground school, I used to work at Harris Hill during the summer. They used to have the world gliding contests. But I had never been off the ground. My first flight, there was nothing like it. My instructor says to me, 'You know the way back to the field?' 'Oh yes!' And hotshot me, I pointed and he laughed. He turned the plane up in a vertical and he pointed right over to the

[75] *PT-17s*- Most Tuskegee pilots first trained in PT-17 Stearman aircraft; 'PT' meant 'primary trainer.' Though 10,000 were built in the 1930s and into the 1940s by Boeing, only two are now known to exist. www.collingsfoundation.org/aircrafts/boeing-pt-17-tuskegee-stearman/

home field. I was really embarrassed. [*Laughs*] Eventually I went through training, and the day came when we taxied out in the middle of the field. He says, 'Okay, take it around and don't break up the airplane.' That was when I soloed. First time in the air by myself, and the greatest thrill I ever had! The people who even learn to fly today, the first time you are turned loose, you fly by yourself, and it is a big thrill.

Then they transferred us to the Army Air Corps field for basic and advanced training. Our basic trainers were BT-13s, Vultee Vibrators as they were called, where we learned instrument flying and night flying. I had a little trouble in my basic training, because learning to fly instruments, it's like learning to walk blindfolded. You had to navigate and control the airplane solely by your instruments. One particular day I couldn't do anything right. I couldn't hold a heading, and I couldn't hold an altitude. When we came back I had tears in my eyes because I knew that I was washed out. I told the instructor what he could do with his airplane, which wasn't nice. [*Laughs*] When you come back with your instructor, you usually have to stand there and you critique your flight. You have to salute him and then go back to the ready room. I didn't even give him the benefit of that. I just turned on my heel, and like I said, I told him what he could do with his airplane! I went back up to the barracks and started packing my clothes because I knew I had washed out. The next day my name was on the board, and I went back and had a good day. I went to advanced training in T-6s.[76]

---

[76] *advanced training in T-6s*-Mr. Dart continued: 'My kids gave me a ride in a T-6 last year. Remember the airplanes that were advertised that were flying out of the field down in Ballston? They had T-6s down there. I forgot how much it cost, but it must have cost them three or four hundred dollars. My kids gave me a ride in a T-6 after all those years. I got to do a few aerobatics and whatnot. I got to do rolls and loops. It was fun and I appreciated it.'

North American AT-6C-NT Texan trainer, 1943. Credit: USAF, public domain.

When I first got to advanced training, the instructor I had was a real short guy. He was just a little over five feet six inches. He was demonstrating how safe the airplane was. He rolled it on its back. The T-6s didn't have an inverted fuel system, so the engine quit. I'm strapped in this seat and the ground is coming up. He is gliding this thing upside down. I see the trees coming up! Pretty soon he flips the airplane back over. He restarts the engine and said, 'See, you had nothing to worry about, because the airplane is safe.' [*Laughs*] For about five minutes I was questioning his method of teaching me to fly. He was a good instructor, and, in fact, our training group was the only one to do formation aerobatics—nothing exotic like you see at air shows, but loops and formations.

I finally graduated from advanced, and eventually I got my commission on November 3rd, in 1943. We transitioned into P-40s. That was an experience, because in the military in those days, when you transitioned into another airplane, they just showed you how to start the engine and gave you some of the air speeds that you should fly at for approach and take-off. And away you go; there is no instructor in there with you! Nowadays in the military you have to go to school and simulators. That's why they require everyone to have a college education in the Air Force today—because it is very complicated. There are lots of buttons to push. If you ever get to see the cockpit of those fighters nowadays, you just wonder how the guys ever have time to do anything but just watch all these little screens [*laughs*] and push all these little buttons and whatnot. Doing the things they have to do is very complicated. My class [size] fell as we graduated. We took our transitioning into this one beat-up P-40 that they had there.

Curtiss P-40Fs near Moore AAF, 1943. 'The lead aircraft in a formation of P-40s is peeling off for an 'attack' in a practice flight at the Army Air Forces advanced flying school. Selected aviation cadets were given transition training in these fighter planes before receiving their pilot's wings.' Credit: USAF, public domain.

Then we were sent to Selfridge Field outside of Detroit, Michigan, for overseas training. From there, every day we used to fly up to a field called Oscoda, which is north of Detroit, in the wintertime. That was an experience, because they didn't have very good snow removal systems up there. Sometimes coming in to land it was really an experience if you weren't lined up, if you were a little off line; the next thing you know, you would be going down the runway 'round and 'round like the cars do on the Northway![77] [*Laughs*] It was fun. But a lot of times we'd fly back in snowstorms, so our instrument training was very valuable to us.

To North Africa and Italy

After that we were sent to Patrick Henry and were transferred overseas. We had the good fortune to be on a luxury liner that had been converted to a troop transport, so we had good meals, except that we ran into one big storm, and, well, it wasn't funny, because this one time in the middle of the storm the ship started to roll. Then it got worse, and the next thing you know, the chairs and tables, they weren't bolted down, people were sliding from one side [*laughs*] of the ship to the other; oh, what a mess! You could hear the crockery and the plates falling on the floor, breaking! Well, after about a couple hours of that, we got out of the storm into calmer water, and after nine days we landed in Oran, Morocco. We were sent to the edge of the desert to train for a while.

North Africa and the Mediterranean had been cleared by the summer of 1943, although the opening of a second front in Italy had been hotly debated among the Allied high command. Churchill famously characterized Italy as the 'soft underbelly of Europe,' arguing that it was imperative to take down Mussolini and knock Italy out of the war, and also buy time before the massive cross-channel invasion from England. Hitler would be forced to divert troops to Italy from Russia, and the oil refineries of Romania and industrial targets in southern Germany would be more

---

[77] *like the cars do on the Northway*-Interstate 87 in upstate New York, during treacherous winter conditions.

accessible for Allied air power flying out of Italian bases. Others, such as the U.S. Army Chief of Staff George C. Marshall, opposed it as drawing off too many resources for the cross-channel invasion. The Italian campaign would rage for over 500 days, with the Allies suffering over 300,000 casualties, slogging it out against the Germans up the 'bloody boot'; the Germans would lose more than 430,000 killed and wounded.

The 99th Fighter Squadron, which I was eventually transferred to, had come over earlier. They had fought with the 12th Air Force with the 79th Fighter Group and they had moved to Italy. We got a chance to do some dive bombing and strafing there on the desert and flying under a bridge, which we were told not to do, but we all did it anyhow, just the thrill of it, you know. [*Laughs*] There was nobody around to tell us really what to do. There were no officials, so to speak, except for the people running the field there, so once we got out of sight, [we had fun].We used to do the same thing at Tuskegee; we used to buzz the people picking cotton in the fields [*chuckles*], stuff like that. There were all kinds of complaints, but people just didn't know how to report us, because if they got a number off the airplane or something, you know, you'd be washed out right away.

Combat

The 99th Fighter Squadron got their first taste of combat in North Africa in April 1943. From there, they moved to Sicily to support the invasion of Italy, and then to the mainland to support combat operations there.

We were put on a C-47 to catch up to the 99th at Capodichino [Field] outside of Naples, Italy, on the day before Vesuvius erupted.[78] Just the weight of the ashes out of that volcano destroyed nearly every airplane on the field, broke the wings off, the tails off; it was a mess. So we didn't have any airplanes to fly, and we had to wait, oh, I guess it was over a week, and they flew in replacements for us. Then they moved us to a little town outside of Naples called Cercola, and we were based there for the first few months. That's where I started my combat career.

*

The first time you find people trying to kill you, it puts you in a different phase in your life. You know, when I was a kid, I used to read all these romantic stories about 'G-8 and his Battle Aces,' about air duels in WWI, when the Germans were flying the Fokkers and the Allies were flying Spads, Sopwith Camels, and stuff like that. Well, our job [at that time] mainly was to do dive bombing and strafing, so we were never more than two or three thousand feet in the air, and you would have to come down from that anyhow to strafe, except when you were dive bombing.

I think it was on my fifth mission when we got a call to relieve some GIs who had been pinned down by the Germans. They told us to go give them some help. We had a new flight leader, and he should have known better, because he had been there about a month or two ahead of us. So he put us in trail, like in a gunnery school formation, you know, everybody nose to tail, but with, you know, some space. So we spotted the target—we went around the first time firing at, I think it was, a German machine gun nest; no return fire, so we went around the second time. I said, 'This isn't right,' because in the rules of combat, if you make the first pass and

---

[78] *the day before Vesuvius erupted*- Mt. Vesuvius most famously erupted on August 26, AD 79, destroying and burying the Roman cities of Pompeii and Herculaneum. Quite active in history many times since, the last major eruption on March 18, 1944, destroyed over six dozen USAAF aircraft and damaged many others.

you don't get any return fire, you just keep going, you come back another day. Well, we went around a third time and the ground opened up—it was like the best Fourth of July sight you've ever seen! They threw everything at us, and it wasn't long before I heard a big 'bang' and the cowling on my plane started peeling off, like somebody peeling a banana. Then another 'bang' and a hole opened up between my feet and the rudder pedals, and another 'bang' behind the cockpit, and the next thing I knew I was counting blades![79] There was a three-bladed prop on the P-40s; they shot out my fuel lines, oil lines, coolant lines, and the engine quit. And since we were strafing, I think I was down under five hundred feet! So I couldn't jump out, because the kinds of 'chutes we had in those days, if you weren't at least two thousand feet, your chances of landing safely weren't too good, because they were kind of slow opening. They didn't pop open like the parachutes do today. So I had to find a field to put the thing down. I figured I had picked a good field—I thought it was a good field; from the air it looked like it was kind of smooth—but it turned out it was a plowed field. So I knew I was going to have to belly land this thing. I reached down, pushed this little lever that locked my harness, and glided toward the field. One wing dropped. I think it was the right wing that caught the ground, and the airplane cartwheeled—a really rough ride. When it came to a stop, I was sitting there, kind of dazed, in the cockpit. I saw these guys running over this wall into the field. It turned out they happened to be GIs—but not from the place where we were relieving. This was another group of guys, who said the Germans had moved out of this field about an hour before. I was sitting there just in the cockpit because both wings were broken off, the engine was out of the mount, and the tail was broken off, and they got me out of the

---

[79] *counting blades*-the engine quits, the propellers slow their rotation to become visible to the pilot

cockpit! They had a medic with them who fixed up my few scrapes and bangs; well, they got me transportation back to my base. I was on crutches I think for about three days, because I was a little sore, before I was back in the air.

*

Nothing else happened until May of 1944, when we had another mission. The Germans had this big railway gun going—I don't know if you ever heard of it, it's on display down at, I forget that place in Maryland, just outside of Washington, where they have all these exhibits of WWII.[80] But anyway, it's a big railway gun, and the Germans would hide it at night in this railway tunnel, which was up over the beachhead at Anzio, and our job was to try to collapse the tunnel and keep this gun bottled up in there.[81] So we started on our run, because this was going to be not a dive, it was going to be to try to skip the bomb into the mouth of the tunnel. Just as we got about halfway there, I heard a 'bang,' and I didn't know what it was, but I found out pretty shortly afterwards, because the next thing I know, I could see flames coming out from under the cowling. Then I said, 'Uh-oh, I better put this down on the emergency field,' back at beachhead there, on the beach. I could see this big black cloud trailing behind me as I made my turn, and the guys were yelling at me to get out, but I couldn't; it was too low to jump out. So I made one circle, and I figured I'd put it down in a bunch of saplings. I thought to cushion my impact, but just as I was approaching, all of a sudden I looked and I saw these 155 'Long Toms' [British artillery] in the midst of the saplings—they were using that as a camouflage spot. And I had to drop my bombs safe, but thankfully I didn't pull the arming wires—there's a wire that goes in

---

[80] *all these exhibits of WWII*- The U.S. Army Ordnance Museum, Fort Lee, VA.

[81] *keep this gun bottled up in there*-To the GIs, this monster gun was known as 'Anzio Annie.' It had a crew of 85 men, sported a barrel more than 70 feet long, and could fire its 283mm 550+ lb. shells over 40 miles.

the little propeller on the end of the bomb that sets up the firing mechanism; when the bomb impacts, its pin pulls and the bomb explodes. Well, I dropped them safe, but I think the guys thought that I was going to bomb them [*laughs*], but the bombs didn't hit them. I found a little dirt road going east of there. I put this thing down on the road. I thought the fire had died down enough, but as soon as I hit, the fire flared up! Also, I had rolled the canopy back and locked it into a detent—that's the way you hold the canopy open on a P-40—but the impact, I guess, dislodged the handle. The canopy slammed forward and jammed, and I said, 'Uh-oh, I'm in trouble.' But I managed to get out of my harness, I got my feet under me, and with my back I popped that canopy off the airplane and I was down the road about an eighth of a mile before it blew up. Again I was rescued, so to speak, by some GIs, and they came out with a 6x6 truck. They took me to the beachhead where the Americans were using this big granary, which the Italians used to store their crops when they harvested them, but they were keeping their trucks inside. That doggone gun came out that night and fired at the ships in the harbor! We were supposed to have destroyed it; I don't know why the guys didn't finish the mission, but that gun was firing that night. Every time one of those shells went off, the truck would jump about six feet off the floor because those shells were about the size of a Volkswagen Beetle, and that's the kind of shells that that gun was firing. They were firing at the ships that were supporting the beachhead. So the next day, of course, the gun wasn't firing, because they pull it back into that tunnel.

The GIs had a beat-up P-40 that had landed there before, and they tried to get it started, but they couldn't get it started. So they gave me a ride back to my base about 50 miles down the coast. I got back to base, I wasn't too banged up this time, and I was back flying the next day.

Anyway, I got back through Rome. Mark Clark had taken Rome, liberated it, and the Germans were on the run.[82] I got back to my base and flew a few more missions. Then, in June, they brought over three other squadrons. Meanwhile, Colonel Davis had gone back to the States; he was my commanding officer early, but they [ordered] him back, because there was a lot of criticism about us—of course, it was all made up, just like it was before we got trained, when one senator said he had done a study and he found out that black people's cranial cavity was too small to hold the knowledge to fly an airplane![83] But, see, he didn't know that black people had been flying ever since everybody else had, because there were two schools in the country, one in Chicago and one in Los Angeles. When they brought the other three squadrons over, we got brand-new P-51s like the one in that picture [*points to photograph on the table*].

---

[82] *Mark Clark*-Commander of the U.S. Fifth Army. Rome was liberated on June 4, 1944, the first Axis capital to fall.

[83] *Colonel Davis*-Benjamin O. Davis was only the fourth black officer to graduate from West Point. As the commander of the Tuskegee Airmen, he had to deal with early Army criticism of underperformance, with the suggestion that black pilots were not capable of performing on a scale with whites. This argument was put to rest when in January 1944, the 99th Pursuit Squadron shot down 12 German fighters in a 2-day period. Benjamin Davis went on to become the Air Force's first black general. See www.greatblackheroes.com.

(L-R) Tuskegee Airmen Clarence Dart, Elwood Driver, Hebert Houston, Alva Temple discuss kill of Me-109, summer 1944, Italy. Courtesy Clarence Dart.

Now this was a P-51 'C' or 'B,' not the 'D's that everybody thinks of [*points to photograph again*] when they talk about P-51s. These were the Razorbacks. But they were good airplanes. In fact, I liked them better than the newer 'D's—to me, they were more maneuverable, it was more like a Spitfire—because the 'D's were heavier and they didn't feel as agile as the 'C's were and I felt comfortable, because I thought you weren't as exposed in these airplanes. In the 'D's you had that bubble canopy, you had that 360-degree view, but, like I said, it was heavier, and I didn't like it, but eventually I was given one and told I had to keep it, and they gave my airplane to my wingman! But anyway–

Our time was up for the day. We talked Mr. Dart into coming back again for another session, right before our Christmas holiday break. He was happy to oblige.

Clarence Dart, Part II

Mr. Dart again drove up to our high school from Saratoga Springs, twenty minutes' drive northward. Some of my senior students had expressed a desire to go to Saratoga themselves and pick him up; others noted that if he could fly a P-40 in a blinding Michigan snowstorm, he could probably make his way back. He did not disappoint, and picked up right where he left off, discussing life on base between the missions in wartime Italy.

Life Between Missions

Hygiene was handled by taking the liners out of our helmets [*gestures to his head*] and getting some stones, and putting the metal helmet on some rocks and starting a little fire to warm up the water for our hygiene. During the summer, what we'd do is take jerry cans of water and sit them out in the sun and let the sun heat up the water. Then we had a contraption that we made that was up on two poles with a rope on it, and when the water heated up, you put the can [*motions upwards, like putting can on the top of the poles*] up there and take the rope—and this is all outdoors—and pull it to get a brief shower. Eventually the Corps of Engineers came around and they erected some tents—they used their water wagons and we got a real good shower, they had a way of heating the water—but that only happened once that I can remember. Most of the time we were on our own as far as our hygiene was concerned.

Of course, maybe you have heard your grandfather or somebody that was in service talk about the meals, about K-rations, C-rations, and 'tropical butter' and 'tropical chocolate'—horrible stuff! [*Smiles*] The butter was just about like axle grease, so it wouldn't melt. The tropical chocolate, I defy anybody [*chuckles*] to put one of those bars in your mouth and try to bite off a piece of it; it was hard! I don't think it even melted in your mouth, but you could grind on it for a while until you got the effect of a candy bar. But also, we got a chance, oh, about every two or three weeks, to travel over to the Mediterranean side, and we could go down to the harbor in Naples and beg ice cream from the sailors. They were very cooperative; sometimes they slipped us a steak or something like that. So it wasn't too bad, except for the K-rations and the C-rations. I guess now they have what they call the 'Meals Ready to Eat' [MREs] for guys that are over in Iraq and Afghanistan, places like that. But I think they are a little better set up than we were.

When the weather started getting kind of rough, in order to keep ourselves warm we made little stoves. We would steal copper tubing [*chuckles*] from down on the line, and [*uses hand motions to depict the setup of the stove*] coil it up, and hook it up to a can of gasoline. As it came down through the tube, we would have a little fire down at the bottom that would heat it up and give us pressure, so that would keep the tent warm until it went out. But it didn't last too long, so you would try to get in your sack as soon as possible. Also during the summer, I remember, of course we had mosquito nettings and stuff like that, but once in a while we would get a visitor, somebody that liked to enjoy our [*chuckles*] sacks with us. You know what a gecko is? They used to have a lot of those things over there, and if the nights got kind of cool, when you go to get into bed, you might have a visitor. You get used to things like that.

But the biggest thing that I remember about Italy, outside of combat—did I mention about the kids? I didn't? Well, in the mess times, those kids would come around with little pails that they had made from discarded cans or something like that. [*Pauses*] Before we put a stop to it, they had been going into these fifty-five gallon drums where all the garbage was thrown, or where we would scrape our mess kits in after dinner. Of course, that was our one big meal during the day; most of the time, we didn't even get breakfast. But it bothered me, and the other guys too, that these kids were diving into that mess of, you know, coffee grounds, grease, and bread crusts, scavenging in there to get something to eat, and if they got a good piece of meat I guess they would take it home. So the way we finally put a stop to it—and it was against the rules, but we didn't care—after we had our meal, we would go back for seconds and rake our mess kits into these kids' little cans. We just couldn't stand to see them diving into all that mess just to get something to eat—that is how horrible it was for a lot of the people over there. After the war got going good, I guess they lost most everything, they couldn't grow anything. It was just horrible to think what war does to people, especially people on the losing end, and they lose practically everything.

*

The missions evolved with the nature of the war as the Allies gained more ground, and the airmen found themselves assigned to escort heavy bombers deep into enemy territory. The pilots were ordered to stay close to the bombers at all costs, and soon earned a reputation for not turning away to chase after enemy 'kills,' at great peril, in many cases, to themselves. While the myth that they 'never lost a bomber to the enemy' persists (due to sensationalistic wartime journalism and subsequent repetition), the fact is that they lost far fewer than other fighter escort units.[111]

'You'll go with the bombers'

But that was when we were based at Cercola a few miles away from Naples. That was when I was in the 12th Air Force and we were flying dive bombing and strafing missions until the middle of, I think, June of 1944, and then they transferred the group over to the other side, the Adriatic side, where our field was at Ramitelli. This was when we started flying long-range escort for the bombers, which was a whole new aspect of the war for us, because we hadn't been trained or told about how to escort bombers. But we soon figured it out, because a lot of things we had to learn on our own, just like I told you about dive bombing and strafing before.

The reason why we got our reputation was when we first got over there [to Italy], we used to take the bombers to the 'IP,' which is the Initial Point, where they start the bomb run to the target, and then pick them up when they came off the target. We wouldn't go all the way to the target, but then Colonel Davis said, 'From now on, you'll go with the bombers through the whole mission,' because the Germans were sending their fighters up into their own flak—they were getting desperate. Our mission was to keep the fighters off the bombers, and not to disrupt the formation, because when the bombardier took over the airplane at the Initial Point, he flew the bomber through the Norden bombsight. Once he started on a target, he couldn't deviate because he's figuring out the wind drift and everything, so the bombs will hit where they're supposed to; that Norden bombsight was flying the airplane. They couldn't deviate from the course because once they were on the line to the target, they were compensating for wind drift, all that kind of stuff, so that when they dropped the bombs, they would be as close to the target as possible. Large targets, like railroad yards and stuff like that, the accuracy wasn't as important, but sometimes if they were trying to hit a specific target, like a building, that the intelligence had pointed out was a prime target, they tried to be as close and accurate as possible. There were a lot of stories about that Norden bombsight, where they can drop a bomb from so many thousand feet into a pickle barrel. Well, that didn't happen; they missed a lot of times.[84]

The flak around the oil fields and the factories was very intense. After the first mission, Colonel Davis told us, 'From now on you are going to go with the bombers all the way through the mission.' [*Long pause*] It didn't always work, but that was our mission—we kept the Germans off the bombers. At first they didn't want us, but toward the end, they started asking for us as an escort, because we protected them to and from the missions. Of course, we couldn't do anything about the flak, though. In fact, we lost some of our own guys getting hit by flak.

I'm trying to think how I can describe escorting bombers through the flak. It made for a very intense, intense situation. Of course we were always maybe two or three thousand feet—well, maybe not quite that high—above the bombers. But you could hear the bursts of the flak [*pause*], and you could see the bursts, and you were just wondering when you were going to get hit. You could see some of the bombers when they got hit, especially before they drop their bombs [*pause*]—it was a horrible sight. Well, you didn't see anything except a big bright flash, then you looked again, but there

---

[84] *Norden bombsight*-The physics involved in dropping a bomb from thousands of feet to hit a target on the ground are astoundingly complicated. Carl Norden, a Swiss-born engineer, developed a 50 lb. analog computer that was so valued by the U.S. military that it invested 1.5 billion in 1940 dollars in it (for comparison, the Manhattan Project came in at around 3 billion). Bombardiers went to school for months to learn how to use it; it was installed in the bombers under armed guard and set to self-destruct upon the crashing of the aircraft. Unfortunately, its accuracy was highly questionable, given all of the combat conditions and high altitudes; the bombardier also had to be able to visually sight the target.

is nothing there. Sometimes, if the bomber didn't blow up, you would see guys jumping out, or sometimes when you did get a good look at some of the bombers, all you would see is just, like, streamers, you know, when you go to Fourth of July and you see these things blow up in the air. That's just what you'd see from the bombers, you know; ten or twelve guys are gone.

Our main mission was to keep the German fighters off the bombers, because early on, the Germans were taking a big toll because they had a very good air force. They had the experienced fliers, ones who had fought through the Spanish Revolution and their attacks on troops in Russia and Poland.[85] But after our bombers started blowing up their oilfields and whatnot, they were getting short on supplies. But we never did blow up all the manufacturing facilities, because the Germans were smart enough to move them into the mountains and places where the bombers couldn't reach them.

*

Our missions started getting longer—we started flying into Poland and Romania. Well, Ploesti was in Romania, and that was one of the worst missions I have ever flown. That was a long mission, a little over six hours. [*Pause*]

Have you ever seen a cockpit of an airplane? Do you know how much room is in there? Not a lot. I had to explain to some little kids one time that you can't get up and walk around like a commercial airline or something. It was very confining; you had a lot of stuff on, especially in the wintertime. There was hardly any room to move your arm sometimes. The parachute packer, he put that cylinder for the dinghy packs in the middle, but just squirming around in the cockpit trying to get comfortable, that thing would wind up

[85] *through the Spanish Revolution*-The Spanish Civil War, 1936-1939, where the Germans assisted the forces of General Francisco Franco and his fascists, testing their air force and refining their tactics.

in one corner [*chuckles*], and when you got back from a mission, you were pretty sore because it always seemed to come up at an angle at you; it seemed like you were always sitting on the rim of it!

I remember one time a kid asked how we went to the bathroom. Well, we had what is called a 'relief tube.' In the summertime you could access the darn thing, but in the wintertime, when you had all the stuff on, you couldn't access it. So you tried not to have too many liquids in your system when you went off on a mission because you couldn't reach the relief tube. It was uncomfortable, and if you couldn't make it you had to suffer the consequences [*chuckles*]; you didn't smell too good when you got back to base.

It was very cold when you got up to around 25,000 feet; you know, the higher you go, the temperature would drop. We had some heat; we had switched over from P-40s to '51s when we went into the 15th Air Force—there was some heat in the airplane from just one side, I think it was from the left side. That foot would be warm, but after about a half hour or so your right foot would have no feeling in it! So you would just cross it over to the left side [*laughs*] until you got your right foot thawed out. Also, there was another thing. The parachute packer would pack the dinghy—there was a, we called it a dinghy, but it was an inflatable boat in a pack under the parachute. It was blown up by a CO^2 cylinder. If you had to ditch in the water, and you survived the impact, you would grab this little lanyard and pull it and that would allow this CO^2 cylinder to blow up the dinghy. You would crawl in that until somebody came to rescue you. But in the '51, not too many survived the impact because the airplane was just like a submarine; once it hit, it would just go right under. [*Chuckles*] I came very close. That is why I believed somebody was watching over me. I'm trying to make this as cohesive as possible. [*Pause*]

Flying up there, especially in wintertime, going up over the Alps, sometimes we would have to break up the bomber formations and have them circle and take the bombers through the pass, just to get them to the other side of the Alps, because we would get into what they call 'ice fog.' You couldn't see anything, and if you couldn't fly instruments, you didn't know up or down. A couple of times I saw contrails that were going straight down [*makes a downward hand motion*], and you begin to wonder, 'Was that guy going straight down or the way you should be going?' But I was pretty good; after my experiences in training, I got to be a pretty good instrument pilot. So I never had to succumb to vertigo. Some people would, you know, just lose their sense; if they didn't know how to fly instruments, they would lose their sense of whether they were up or down or making a turn, and we lost some people that way. They lost their sense of direction, and the airplane would stall out on them or something, and you would see this contrail going straight down, and in the Alps, you know, it didn't take long before you hit something. But once we got on the other side of the Alps, we would finish the mission.

*

Ploesti's oil refineries were a major source of the lifeblood of the Reich. In 1943, low-level Allied raids from North Africa ended in disaster for B-24 bombers and their crews. Allied planners realized there would be no quick knockout blow; rather a 'rinse and repeat' approach had to be cultivated. As the Allies advanced towards more accessible airfields in eastern Italy, the distance lessened but the risk did not.

We were talking about Ploesti a few minutes ago. That was one of the worst missions I have ever been on. The Germans had about two rings of anti-aircraft guns around the oil fields there at Ploesti, and when the smoke from the flak blew together, there was just one big black cloud in the sky. You could see the bomber formations going in one side, and then there would be big holes in the formation as they came out the other side, and you knew that a lot of them got hit. After they got off the target, we would have to go around and round up the bombers that had straggled away from the formations, and take the long trip back home. Like I said, those missions were at least six hours.

Then we had a strafing mission in Athens, Greece—that was a long mission; we lost a couple guys on that mission. Intelligence would tell us where the headquarters of the German group was, and that was our job to strafe those places. I did not like strafing missions too much. I remember we had one mission around the shores of Lake Balaton.[86] The Germans were retreating, and what they would do was have civilians in the long line of guns and whatever they were moving, as they were trying to get back to Germany. Of course, our orders were to hit anything moving, and we would go down there and make a pass, and they would have horses pulling some of their artillery pieces, and you would see the horses lying on the ground and kicking and whatnot. You can imagine what kind of sound that was. I think we must have hit some of the civilians too, but it was our job to do it, and I had to be sort of counseled; because I didn't think that if they had civilians in those convoys that we should be strafing them. But they tell you this is war. I can remember one time, before I became a flight leader, I was flying wing with a guy who was a flight leader and we hit a motorcycle, one of those side-car motorcycles. I can remember that thing looked like somebody just took it and tossed it up into the air [*makes upward hand motion*]. We got to see the results of that; we got a Jeep and went back up the road. This was when we were flying P-40s. But I just think about how horrible war is, and what you are forced to do against your own will to accomplish a mission.

You just have to adopt a fatalistic view about what you have to do and what is going to happen to you, like I told you last week

[86] *Lake Balaton*-Western Hungary.

about my two crashes and getting shot down twice. I remember one time coming back after we had been on a mission to Vienna—and this time it was just a milk run, because although we had flak, we didn't run into any enemy fighters or anything.[87] So we were coming back, we go to the edge of the Adriatic on the Yugoslavia side, and we were just getting ready to tell the bombers that we were going to leave them. We were on the left side of the bombers, so I dropped down and slid under the belly of the lead bomber—to come up beside the pilot side, because we couldn't raise them on the radio—to tell them we were leaving, and that they were safe to go back to their base. I felt a shudder, and I told my wingman, I said, 'Cut the playing around out!' Because just for stress relief sometimes, we tapped wingtips or something like that, which is against the rules! [*Chuckles*]

But my wingman said, 'I wasn't doing anything, I am back where I am supposed to be!'

So when we got back to the field, my crew chief said, 'Oh my goodness, you guys were in it again today.'

I said, 'No, it was just a milk run.'

He said, 'Well, look at this!'

I don't know how I didn't see it in the air, but there was a line of bullet holes from the [*points left*] left wing tip on a diagonal right across down the wing behind my cockpit [*points behind him*] and the tail sections! My airplane was out of commission for about two weeks until they got new parts. In fact, they had to put a whole new tail section on it. I think when the sleepy belly gunner or one of the guys in one of the Plexiglas side windows had seen me or the silhouette of my airplane, he thought maybe I was an Me-109 or a

---

[87] *just a milk run*-in World War II airman lingo, a milk run was an easy round-trip mission with little or no enemy resistance, an analogy taken from the old-time dairy practice of the milkman delivering bottles of milk to one's door.

Focke-Wulf 190 and he let me have a burst! [*Laughs*] I still don't know to this day what caused him—he must have been asleep and woke up, and all of a sudden, the reflex, you know—to take a shot at me. I put in a complaint, but nothing was ever done about it. Those were things that happened all the time in the war—friendly fire. You read the things in the paper about in Iraq, about the guys getting in trouble by killing or dropping bombs on their own troops. But war is a dangerous thing, and I have always said when I got back, I said something has got to be done. People should not be doing this, because too many people get killed for no reason at all. A lot of civilians, especially the civilian population, especially when you hit targets in populated areas, you don't always hit the target that you are supposed to hit. Sometimes you are killing people that do not deserve to be killed.

*

Let me tell you some of the dumb things that I did. We were coming back from a mission one time, and it was a nice sunny day; we did not have any encounter with the enemy. We were letting down from about 25,000 feet, and in a '51, what you were supposed to do every now and then is gun the engine to clear the plugs, otherwise they could foul out, and this is what happened to me. We had just gotten to the Adriatic side by Yugoslavia, and then all of a sudden the plane got real quiet and I started counting blades—naturally, the engine had quit! I just had not cleared the engine, because, you know, after a while, I guess you get kind of lackadaisical about things. The engine had quit and we were just starting to go across the Adriatic! Now the P-51 is a nice airplane and it glides for a long ways, but to this day, I just say the Lord was on my side, because I fought that engine all the way across the Adriatic! Now I was not supposed to glide that far, and just as we got to the other side, the engine finally caught on! Meanwhile I had dropped my gear to let the Germans below know I was going to land on the beach and

I was going to be a prisoner of war. Well, that did not mean anything to them! [*Laughs*] Just as I got the engine started there was a big BLAM, and so I took off [*makes a peeling away motion to the left*] to go back to our base, which is on the other side of the Adriatic, there at Ramitelli. Our runway ran right down to the water's edge [*gestures across body at a diagonal motion*]. When I landed, my crew chief said, 'Oh, you've been in it again!'

I said, 'No!'

He says, 'Well, look at this!'

There was a hole about the size of a basketball [*uses hands to show size of hole*] in the wing wood that could have caused that wing to fold up, but I just think the Lord was with me that day.

Berlin

Another time, my last mission was to Berlin. This was March 23, in 1945.[88] They had 'maximum effort,' where every airplane in the 15th Air Force was up that day—all the bombers and all the fighters they could get in the mission to Berlin. We were assigned to a group of bombers, and when we reached a certain point, we were supposed to leave and go back to base and another group was supposed to come up and relieve us. Well, they never showed up, so we had to continue on to Berlin with this group of bombers. The

---

[88] *This was March 23, in 1945*- This dramatic mission was actually on March 24. *'Forty-three P-51 Mustangs led by Colonel Benjamin O. Davis escorted B-17 bombers over 1,600 miles into Germany and back. The bombers' target, a massive Daimler-Benz tank factory in Berlin, was heavily defended by Luftwaffe aircraft, including Fw 190 radial propeller fighters, Me-163 rocket-powered fighters, and 25 of the much more formidable Me-262s, history's first operational jet fighter. Pilots Charles Brantley, Earl Lane, and Roscoe Brown all shot down German jets over Berlin that day. For the mission, the 332nd Fighter Group earned a Distinguished Unit Citation.'* Source: www.everworld.com/tuskegee/332dfightersquadron.htm, via en.wikipedia.org/Tuskegee Airmen.

Germans sent over their jet fighters that they had developed, the Me-262s, and you could see them coming [*uses swooping hand gestures to depict the position and movements of Me-262s*].[89] They were way up above us, and then, when they started down to attack, the exhaust from their engine was just like a streak of black in the sky. So they hit a few bombers, and I got on the tail of one of them. I dropped my tanks, and then all of a sudden I realized my engine had quit; I'd forgotten to switch to my internal tanks![90] [*Laughs*] I was right on the tail of this guy, and I guess he sensed I was back there. All of a sudden there was a big cloud of black smoke and he was gone—he just disappeared! That's how fast those things were.

Messerschmitt Me 262A at the National Museum of the United States Air Force. Credit: USAF, public domain.

But our group shot down three of them that day, because they made the mistake of slowing down to fight with us. Their turn radius was so large at speed that in order to fight with us, they had to

[89] *the Me-262s*- Messerschmitt Me 262, the world's first combat jet-powered aircraft.

[90] *I dropped my tanks*- auxiliary fuel tanks carried by aircraft externally on long-distance missions; they would be jettisoned to reduce drag and provide 'catch-up' power.

slow down, but then it was to our advantage. When they slowed down—because our airplanes could turn inside their circle—we shot down three of them that day. Of course, I wasn't one of them; I was a dummy. I just got so excited because I hadn't seen a fighter, a German plane, in so long, and just that one little mistake in that short length of time cost me [a possible kill]!

After we got back to the base, my commanding officer says, 'You've had it, you've been over here long enough, you've had enough excitement, you've got to go home.' But I told him, 'No, the war's almost over, I want to finish the war,' you know? [*Pauses*] He said, 'No, you've got to go home.' [*Shakes head*] So I said okay; I packed up my kit and got a ride on the 6x6 back to Naples, where the replacement depot was, but I didn't sign in. I went AWOL [*chuckles*].[91] So I was roaming around Naples, you know, and I was getting ready to go someplace else. One of the guys who was back at the base happened to come over—I guess he was going to a rest camp—and he said, 'They're looking all over for you—if you don't hurry up and sign out and go home, they're going to court-martial you!' [*Laughs*] And so I signed in, and I got a C-47, no, it was a DC-4, and I went to LaGuardia in New York in April of '45. I got leave to go home for a couple of weeks, and then they transferred me back to Tuskegee, where they made me an instructor—an instrument instructor. That only lasted a couple of months, because they closed the field at Tuskegee and sent everybody up to Columbus, Ohio, at Lockbourne Field. And there things really slowed down and it was very boring, because, since our group was still overseas, there was no place for us to go. There were no jobs on the base—I mean, there were a few jobs, but the other groups weren't accepting us.

So, I finally went home and went to school: Aero Industries Technical Institute, out in Oakland, California. And when I finished

---

[91] *I went AWOL*-absent without leave, a punishable offense.

there, I came back home and went to work. Well, I didn't get a job right away. I got married, and then I went down to General Electric. I walked in the door, and the receptionist said, 'We don't have any jobs for you.' I had just gotten inside the door and that's what I was confronted with! I didn't even get a chance to ask her, you know, were they hiring anybody. [*Laughs*] One of the interviewers just happened to be walking by and he heard her, so he caught my eye and he beckoned me with his finger, and I followed him into his office. He said, 'Let me see what you've got.' I had my portfolio with me, and he looked at it, my school records and everything, and said, 'When can you start?' I said, 'As soon as possible.' He said, 'Okay, show up Tuesday morning.' Well, Monday was a holiday, but I got paid for it—my first day at GE and I didn't even work and I got paid for it, because it was a holiday! That was in April of 1948. I went to work for GE and stayed there for almost 40 years.

I had several positions at GE. First I went to work for the General Engineering Lab, and then they transferred me to Flight Test. I couldn't wait to get to work in the morning. That's the best place I'd ever worked in my life. It was a very interesting place. We did all kinds of things there. They had all kinds of airplanes—B-29s, B-17s, B-35s. They had a jet that was designed by the British, but Martin Aircraft was building them under license, and we were doing some work on that, and improving. And I was at Flight Test for I guess two years, and then they closed the place. We were doing a lot of repair work, along with other test work, which we were doing for customers. In fact, we had one of the early 707s, and my job was to design a stable platform for it. This was like a telescope, but it was a device that would read the signatures of missiles coming through the atmosphere so that you could tell whether it was really a missile, or a decoy. But in examining the airplane—the airplane had just come from a place down in Birmingham, I think it was—and they did some repair work, and so we called a pilot and showed him what had happened; those guys had put rivets in that were too long, but instead of heading the rivets, like you were supposed to do, they just bent them over! [*Laughs*] And the blood just drained out of that fellow's face, because, well, it was really a hazard. If any real stress had been put on that airplane, it would've come apart in the air.

After Flight Test, I was transferred to Knolls Atomic Power Lab outside of Ballston Spa, where they run test reactors for either submarines or ships. Very interesting work, but for the years that I worked there, you didn't dare get caught talking about what you did there. Well, like I said, I retired, and so, that's it. That's the end of the 'Clarence Dart' saga. [*Laughs*]

*

It was time for a question and answer session with the students.

Student: How did you feel about Eleanor Roosevelt before you went overseas?

Oh! She was one of the reasons that they finally decided to train black pilots. Our chief, Chief Anderson, he gave her a ride in a Piper—I think that's what it was, a Piper Cub. But she went back and she told Franklin that we could fly just like anybody.

I don't like to get into a lot of arguments about what black people can do or what they have done. But, if you do the research, just like all the war pilots I've told you about, black men have served in every war that this country has ever fought—from Crispus Attucks on up to this day.[92] Back in the Civil War, there were 18 Congressional Medals of Honor given out to black soldiers. But people conveniently forget all of that stuff—from Bunker Hill to the Spanish-

[92] *Crispus Attucks*-victim of the Boston Massacre, March 5, 1770.

American War—and of course you saw the movie about the Massachusetts 54th?[93] In fact, even during World War I, there was a destroyer that was manned, officers and sailors, by blacks. Of course, there's a lot of black history. We did the first open-heart surgery with Dr. Daniel Hale Williams, and the guy that invented the most annoying things to people who drive cars—the stop light—Garrett Morgan. And he also invented the first breathing device that they used to rescue some people when they were putting in a water line out in, I think it was Cleveland, Ohio, out into the lake—they rescued some guys that were in the tunnel; they used his breathing device! And what about the doctor who invented the way to preserve blood plasma? But over the years, people like that knuckle-headed senator, who said that black people's cranial cavity was too small to hold the knowledge to fly an airplane, well, he demonstrated that he was way behind the times, because we had people that had flown cross-country trying to prove that black pilots should be trained for the war and World War II! And it continues to this day—

Interviewer: What about the white bomber crews that you escorted?

Well, early on they didn't want us, because they had listened to the propaganda, but when they found out that they weren't getting shot up by the Messerschmitts and 190s when we were escorting them, then they started requesting us for coverage. In fact, a couple of times—you know what photo reconnaissance is? They had a stripped down P-51, and I had to escort two of those things on two different times. You were all by yourself, deep in enemy territory. But those guys, their airplanes were very fast, because they were all

---

[93] the Massachusetts 54th-*Glory,* 1989 winner of three Academy Awards, depicting an all-black regiment's assault on a Confederate stronghold.

stripped down, and all they had were cameras in them, and it was tough trying to keep up with them—once they got their pictures, they just took off, of course, and myself and my wingman, we would just be left out in the middle of Germany someplace, trying to get back home. [*Laughs*]

Student: Were you restricted from any white establishments?

Well, that was the norm back in those days—up to World War II. In fact, it didn't end until, let's see, 1954.[94] With my background, being brought up in Elmira, New York, we didn't know what [segregation] was, because in my neighborhood, everybody was mixed. We had white kids that came to my house for dinner, or I'd go to their homes for dinner, and there was never any of that kind of stuff, you know, generally. Not until we got below—well, I can remember, going south in the summer to visit my cousins, of course; my father worked on the railroad. He could get passes to go on different railroads. When you got to Washington, D.C., whatever car you were in, you had to go get in one separate car for black people [*pauses*] to go south of Washington, across the Mason-Dixon Line. You couldn't ride on the sleepers, and you couldn't go into the dining car. So my mother and grandmother, what they would do was fix up a basketful of food that would last for a day and a half to travel to South Carolina. That was in those days—

Student: Was there any difference in the way you were treated here and when you were in Italy?

---

[94] *it didn't end until 1954*-The armed services were officially desegregated in 1948; Mr. Dart refers to the landmark Supreme Court decision of *Brown v. Board of Education of Topeka* in which the Court declared state laws establishing separate public schools for black and white students to be unconstitutional, paving the way for further desegregation.

Well, the Italians, they weren't prejudiced. Prejudice was only in this country. In fact, when the war was over, and they brought everybody back by boat, and they got off the boat, there were signs saying 'Coloreds,' you know. You'd been overseas for almost two years, you'd go to an army base, and the German prisoners of war were treated better than you were; it was a hard pill to swallow. [*Pauses, expressing sadness*] Because even if you went to a movie theater—this was back in '45 and later—you'd go to a theater and they'd have a place for black soldiers to sit, you know, in the movie theater. And you couldn't use the PX. You'd have to use a different PX; they had one for blacks and one for whites.[95] In fact, they had formed a bomb group, the 477th Bomb Group, B-25s, and it was somewhere out in the Midwest, in Kentucky or someplace, and these guys weren't going to have any of that nonsense. They went to an officers' club, and even in those days the army had said that anybody who was an officer could go into any officers' club. But at this particular field, I think it was Freeman Field, the guys went to the club, and they tried to keep them out, and they went in anyhow. And because one guy happened to rush past one of the officers at the club, they court-martialed thirteen of them, I think it was. But the people who held on to that segregation eventually were court-martialed themselves. Plus, their orders were sent around to all the military bases that there was not to be any segregation of all officers.[96]

---

[95] *you couldn't use the PX*-Post Exchange, or the place on a military installation where consumer goods could be purchased.

[96] *there was not to be any segregation of all officers*- The Tuskegee Airmen of the 477th challenged the all-white officers' club at Freeman Army Air Field in Seymour, Indiana. Scores of black officers were arrested and three were court-martialed over several incidents in April 1945. Forty years later, their records were expunged; the incidents were regarded as an important step in the eventual integration of the military, and a spark for the fledgling civil rights movement.

Student: How do you feel about the new war—the war in Iraq. How do you feel about that?

Oh! We shouldn't be there—we shouldn't have gone without the cooperation of the United Nations. Now, it hasn't been that long ago when the president said that Iraq was a direct threat to the United States, and I looked at my wife and I said, 'What's he talking about?' And I said, 'You know Saddam Hussein was a bad guy, but he doesn't—after the first Gulf War—he doesn't have a navy, he doesn't have an air force. He's probably got a big army, but how can he reach the United States? He doesn't have any missiles. And I don't know how he could be a direct threat to the United States. I said, 'All they're going to do is get a lot of people killed for nothing.' And we did—we went over there, and of course, with our airplanes and technology, it didn't last long. Two weeks, I think it was? I think it lasted for two weeks, but look at what's happened since then—because I think we should have insisted that the UN, that since Saddam is guilty of all those things against, what do they call it?

Student: Crimes against humanity.

Yes. Since he committed all these things, then it's up to the UN to take care of it. We shouldn't be the policemen of the world. Our military is spread so thin now, if a couple other big countries wanted to jump on us, we'd be in big trouble! We've got people in Afghanistan, Korea—all over—islands, Guam, et cetera. We shouldn't be spread like that. And my basic thing that I tell my young grandchildren, I say, George Washington, in his Farewell Address, at one point he said, 'Beware of foreign entanglement.' I think those were the last words he said—'Beware of foreign entanglement.' But

I don't know what's happened in this country. We've exported out technology, and you go to buy something in a store, you look at the labels—all our textiles and clothing are coming from overseas. It shouldn't have been that way! But the CEOs, you've seen what's happened to a lot of these CEOs, like the guy that gave his wife a million dollar birthday party, and built, I don't know, five or six million dollar homes around the world, but he was a big crook![97] I remember when the president of SONY came over [from Japan], and he said, 'You're paying your CEOs too much money.' Now this was by a man that has one of the biggest electronic firms in the world. He said, 'You're paying your CEOs too much money!' Look at what [a famous CEO] got when he retired from [a Fortune 500 company] [*laughs*]—he did give back some of it, of course; his wife, I guess, got the other half for her shenanigans. [*Laughs*] What—why do they deserve that? If you run a large company, sure, you set the goals and you hire people to help you attain those goals, but why should one guy get as much money as it would take to hire maybe a hundred workers? It's not fair, you know, for a lot of money to be all in one, or among certain groups of people. But I'm not a communist or anything. [*Laughter in room*]

I got so mad at professional sports too, a while back, and so I don't watch football and basketball like I used to. And especially the rappers—I saw a piece in one of the Sunday papers where one guy is a billionaire already! You know, of course he branched out into a line of clothing and whatnot, but, I know my kind of music, and what kids like today—

Student: What kind of music do you like?

[97] *but he was a big crook*- Mr. Dart may be referring to the Enron scandal, which broke in 2001; our interview was in 2003.

Oh, I'm a jazz man. You know, Duke Ellington, Count Basie—

Student: You'd get along with my grandfather.

Yes, [*laughs*] I don't laugh at the kids nowadays, but when I was growing up, the Elks Club used to have dances for teenagers a lot, and you'd learn how to dance, you'd learn how to dance with a girl. [*Laughter in room*] You [*pointing to male students*] take a girl to a dance and you might not find her until the evening is almost over; you're out there, jumping up and down [*jerks shoulders and arms up and down repeatedly, to much laughter*] in one spot! That's not dancing! When I was in the cadets, we used to go to the Institute when they had dances for the cadets, and, of course, the rule was, 'no buckle-polishing'—you couldn't dance close, more than six inches closer to a girl [*shows distance with hands*]. But at least you could dance with her and talk to her, and put a bug in her ear, or something, you know... [*much laughter in room*] Well, I mean romancing, you know. Convince her that you were the one for her! But I know times have changed—I've raised eight kids, I know what it's like; six girls and two boys. The only hard thing was putting them through college.

Student: Did you take advantage of the G.I. Bill when you came back from the war?

Most people with half a brain, that's what they did, but some people didn't.

Student: Why didn't you try to be an airline pilot, or wouldn't they let you?

Oh, no; we tried. But [my reasoning on it] was that they had a lot of bomber pilots coming back, guys that had flown multi-engine airplanes. We did have two guys that were vice presidents of airlines—one guy was vice president of Eastern Airlines, and another guy was vice president of another airline, I've forgotten which one—but we had a lot of guys who were doctors and lawyers, bank presidents. [*Pauses*] Yes, there were a lot of successful people who took advantage of the G.I. Bill. Well, it was the only thing to do, the smartest thing to do. I don't know if they offer that to the guys coming back from Iraq. [*Someone answers in the affirmative*] They do? I'm glad to hear it, because veterans for the most part have gotten the shaft, especially as far as health care is concerned. That's kind of tragic...

Now out of time after two days of conversation, we wished Mr. Dart and his wife and family a Merry Christmas and holiday season. It was the last time that we saw him. On March 30, 2007, he and his fellow surviving Tuskegee Airmen were presented with the Congressional Gold Medal by then President George W. Bush, who gave them a long overdue salute. Clarence Dart passed away at age 91 in February 2012.

After Mr. Dart passed, I had the opportunity to speak with his son, Warren Dart, who drove up to my classroom to meet me to share more stories and photographs of his dad.

'Though my dad liked to talk to young people, there were some things he couldn't share. Once, he told me of a time when he was returning from a mission to base and spotted a German truck parked behind some trees. He circled around, dove in, and opened up on them. As he attacked the German soldiers, it occurred to him that they had pulled off the road to have their lunch. They were killed, and it's something that probably bothered him for the rest of his life.'

The Tuskegee Airmen Fight Song

Contact –
Joy stick back –
Sailing through the blue
Gallant sons of the 99th –
Brown men tried and true
We are the Heroes of the Night –
To hell with the Axis might
FIGHT! FIGHT! FIGHT! FIGHT!
Fighting 99th.
Rat-tat, Rat-tat-tat –
Down in flames they go
The withering fire of the 99th –
Sends them down below
We are the Heroes of the Night –
To hell with the Axis might
FIGHT! FIGHT! FIGHT! FIGHT!
Fighting 99th.
Drink up, Drain your cup –
To those daring men
Flying torch of flame, Oh GOD–
Red White and Blue – Amen.
For We Are –
Heroes of the Night
To Hell with the Axis might
FIGHT! FIGHT! FIGHT! FIGHT!
Fighting 99th WINGS![112]

*

John Weeks holds a photo portrait of himself and four of his friends, captioned, 'THE FIRST FIGHTER ESCORTED PHOTO RECON MISSION TO BERLIN'
(L to R) Lt. Schultz, Lt. Belt, Lt. Weeks, Capt. Batson, Lt. Davidson
13th Photo Recon Squadron – Mt. Farm Airfield, England
Credit: Wayne Clarke, NYS Military Museum.

CHAPTER TWO

The Reconnaissance Man

John Weeks sits in a chair in a public library where he volunteers to teach business investment classes at night. He appears with an aura of contentedness at being able to share his experiences, certainly grateful for the opportunity to remember his friends, generations after they were all 'touched by fire.' To the camera he holds up a framed photograph. Five young men are smiling for the camera, posing in front of a plane, standing on a perforated steel Marston Mat. 'Three out of the five men in this photograph did not survive the war; there was only one other survivor besides myself.'

In 1994, John was contacted by 'two gentlemen who run a museum in Plzen, Czech Republic, which is very active in gathering artifacts and information on World War II historical events that took place over their country, including the fate of airmen that were killed and perhaps missing in that area.' They got his name from his former commander.

'These men were particularly interested in a mission I took on April 26, 1945—which may very well have been the last photo reconnaissance mission of the war. I'm not sure why they were so very interested in that

particular mission, but I have the feeling that one of them may have been flying one of the jets that came up after me on that mission.'

*

John G. Weeks

I was born on March 7, 1922, and brought up in western New York State in a little town called Lyons. My father was a fruit farmer there and I worked on the farm, of course. After high school, I attended college in Grove City, Pennsylvania, where I majored in industrial engineering, which was a combination of business and engineering. I went into the army during my junior year.

I was 19, and I was playing bridge at college with some fraternity brothers of mine, and we had the radio on and we heard about Pearl Harbor. We couldn't believe it. I don't think we had any idea of the significance of what was happening, but, as I say, it was just kind of an unbelievable thing; we even wondered if it was a fake or not.

Shortly thereafter, after being turned down by the Marine Air Corps and the Navy Air Corps because of a misalignment of my back teeth, I was accepted and enlisted in the Army Air Corps. I was sworn in at the post office in Pittsburgh and immediately left for basic training at Miami Beach, Florida—where I had my first introduction to the war. We lived in one of the big hotels on the beach, and every morning when we got up, we looked out over the ocean and there would be black smoke on the horizon. It was a little sobering to learn that smoke came from ships that the Germans had torpedoed the night before out in the Gulf Stream right off the coast of Florida. The reason they were able to do that was because we didn't have a blackout in Miami Beach, and so that highlighted the targets that the Germans were after and it made it easy for them. Later, that was corrected.

After about six weeks in Florida, we were shipped to Wittenberg College in Springfield, Ohio. We spent about two months in Wittenberg, where we took a concentrated course—mostly in mathematics, from arithmetic through calculus. I have never worked so hard on academics before or since. Many of the budding cadets washed out at this point. From Wittenberg, we went to Santa Ana Army Air Force Base in California. We spent about six weeks here, with great concentration on astronomy for celestial navigation, and aeronautical engineering—including hydraulics, electrical systems, aerodynamics, and navigation. We also went through altitude chamber training, where they put you in a tank and sucked the air out to simulate altitude, as well as other equipment training. Then we went to Ryan Field in Tucson, Arizona, where we were going to learn to fly at last; I have never had such a thrilling good time in my life.

We flew a Ryan PT-22, which was originally designed in 1930. We had to have nine hours of instruction before we could solo—I had nine hours and three minutes. What a thrill! I just loved it. I had really found a home in the Air Corps.

Then we went to Marana Army Air Field in Arizona, where we flew the BT-13. It was 'affectionately' known as the 'Vultee Vibrator' because it shook so hard in a spin. I never liked the airplane very well, and I don't think many other cadets did either. It was very poor in acrobatics.

From Marana, I was sent to Williams Field in Chandler, Arizona, for my final advanced phase of cadet training. Here we flew the AT-6, which was a delightful plane to fly—very good at acrobatics. We also took a heavy concentration of ground school at Williams Field, where we had already been assigned to fly the Lockheed Lightning P-38—which simply delighted me; that was the plane I wanted. Ground school concentrated almost exclusively on the various systems on the P-38. After a couple of months at

Williams, I graduated as a bright new 2nd lieutenant and had a very coveted pair of pilot's wings.

I stayed right at Williams Field for my transition training into the P-38. We flew lots of lesser airplanes to get used to handling two engines—AT-9s, C-45s, UC-78s, B-25s. Because the P-38 was a single-place plane, the day finally came when they put you in one and simply said, 'Go!' It was quite a transition from 600 horsepower to 3,500 horsepower, from 160 miles per hour to 400 miles per hour in one jump—and all alone!

After Williams, we went to Will Rogers Field in Oklahoma City. Here we learned how to perform our specialty, photo reconnaissance, most of which was done at high altitude—25,000 feet or higher. You see, our mission was much different than that of the ordinary fighter pilot—we flew all alone in planes with no guns, only cameras, and had to survive only on our skill as a pilot and the speed of our planes to evade the enemy. Our training here was a combination of pinpoint navigation and high altitude photography. I think I photographed every tiny little town in the Midwest.

From there we went to Coffeyville, Kansas, for our combat training. I thought I was a pretty good pilot until I got to Coffeyville. Here our instructors were all pilots who had completed their combat missions and had returned to the States as instructors. They were really good. We practiced day after day doing nothing but evasive maneuvers and mock combat; it was very hard work. Our training was cut short, however, because the loss of reconnaissance pilots in Europe was so great during the Normandy invasion that they needed replacements badly.

Overseas

We were rushed overseas on the ocean liner *Île de France,* which made the crossing, unescorted, in five days, landing in Glasgow. We were processed very quickly and rushed to the Mt. Farm air base near Oxford, England.

The reason for the rush was immediately evident. The 13th Photo Recon squadron, to which I was assigned, had only 13 pilots left out of a full complement of 25, and those thirteen were exhausted. There were only five of us replacements—which meant that even with us, the squadron was still far below its full complement. Our mission was to photograph bomb damage of the major cities in Germany and France at that time, also ground movement of troops and so on—we were just trying to keep track of what the Germans were doing, and our bombing missions were based on the photographs that we took.

Our training time was brief, out of necessity, and consisted of very little flying. It was assumed that you knew how to fly and that you knew how to navigate and take pictures, so most of our time was spent talking tactics with the more experienced pilots. Because we flew alone, everybody developed their own tactics, so from talking with them, you sorted out what you thought made the most sense and determined to follow that course. We were also quite short of planes, because whenever you lost a pilot, you lost a plane.

Our early missions were shorter and less dangerous so that we could get the feel of things. I flew nineteen missions, and they were all over.

Reconnaissance P-38 with bold black and white invasion stripes during the Normandy Campaign.
Credit: USAF. Public domain.

I was assigned an older P-38J, which still had its invasion stripes painted on it. I never liked the plane—it was slow and was not equipped with dive breaks like the newer models. But because the loss of reconnaissance planes was so consistently high, the army tried to keep us equipped with the very latest model planes and equipment. Early on I got a brand-new P-38L with larger engines, dive flaps, rear-facing radar—the whole ball of wax. It was a wonderful airplane—very fast, very maneuverable, and quick to handle.

Let me explain a little about the dive flaps. The P-38 was so powerful, heavy, and streamlined that it would, in a dive, quickly go into compressibility, which made the plane curl under, which would eventually tear the tail off. Once it got into this condition, there was no recovery. The dive brakes were under the leading edge of each wing and were only about two feet long and about two inches wide. When extended with a push of a button, they would immediately pull the nose up and out of compressibility. They had an added bonus, too. In combat, if you were in a tight turn with an enemy plane, the turn would be tightened markedly when you popped these brakes. I'm sure that scared the devil out of many an enemy pilot, because he didn't know for sure whether you had guns or not, and that maneuver would put you right on his tail.

Flying High

I mentioned that each pilot developed his own tactics. Mine developed gradually, of course. I would fly as high as possible, with my limit being 39,000 feet or the bottom of the jet trail [condensation] level—you didn't want to create a jet contrail, because it would point right to you [like a finger]. Though the plane could go higher, thirty-nine thousand feet was my personal limit. Our cockpits were not pressurized, so my body would swell and get very uncomfortable because of the lack of air pressure. My legs would fill out my pants completely, my stomach would become much extended, and my neck would fill up my shirt, even with the top button undone. It was also dangerous because even though we had a pressurized oxygen system, if anything went wrong with it, you wouldn't be able to stay conscious but for a very few seconds—you would never have time to get down to a safe altitude. On the plus side, there were very few enemy planes that could get above you, and flak couldn't touch you that high. So while it was uncomfortable and dangerous, I felt most secure being way up there.

German Messerschmitt Me 163B Komet rocket-propelled fighter at the National Museum of the United States Air Force, Dayton, Ohio. Credit: USAF. Public domain.

It became more and more precarious as the war proceeded, however. First the Germans developed the Komet, the Messerschmitt 163, solely for the purpose of shooting down photo reconnaissance planes. This was an amazing rocket-powered plane that could climb at 40,000 feet per minute at a 70-degree angle and was very comfortable above 39,000 feet. The one saving grace for us was that it only had an eight-minute fuel supply, which meant that it could fly only by using its engine in short bursts and had to land without fuel. It was very vulnerable to our fighters in its glide mode. I was never attacked by an Me-163 and only saw one at a distance a couple of times.

The only time my plane was hit by enemy fire was on a mission to the Hannover area. If I was lucky enough to have thick clouds at high altitude, my tactic would be to fly just above the tops, quickly dive into the clouds in case of trouble. That was the situation on this day. When I was well over enemy territory, I saw a single plane off to my right going in the opposite direction. The British flew Spitfires on photo recon missions all alone, just like we did; I thought probably that was what the plane was. But it was a long way off, and German Me-109 fighters looked a lot like a Spitfire at a distance. I didn't want to take the chance that it was an Me-109 trying to circle around behind me, so I watched him very carefully.

German ground crew pushes Me-109 onto tarmac, fall 1943, France. Credit: Bundesarchiv, Bild 101I-487-3066-04 via Wikimedia Commons.

All of a sudden I saw tracer bullets going by my canopy! I looked up in my rear view mirror, which was fastened to the canopy about three inches above my head. He was firing at me from behind; I saw him for only a fraction of a second when my rear view mirror disappeared—it had been shot off! I quickly dove into the clouds right below me and made a turn. I flew along for a while and came up for a peek, and my adversary was nowhere in sight. Needless to say, I was much more careful to look all around, all of the time, after that.

About this time, things got really bad, because the Germans had come out with the Me-262 jet fighter. This plane could climb much faster and much higher than our P-38s. Our losses increased alarmingly, mostly due to these new jet fighters. It was at this point that the Air Corps provided us with P-51 fighters to escort the P-38 recon planes. They did not provide us with trained fighter pilots, but told us we would have to do our own escorting. So some of the recon pilots elected to fly the fighters as escort rather than fly the P-38 recon planes—they trained themselves. We used to laugh that the self-trained fighter pilots really weren't all that good, but I'm sure they looked formidable to the enemy. I didn't like the P-51 so elected to stay with the P-38 flying recon.

My worst mission was taken on Christmas Eve 1944. This was during the Battle of the Bulge. The weather had been very bad for about two weeks, and the troops were taking a terrible beating on the ground. On the day before Christmas, the sky cleared completely.[98] Both sides had had two weeks to make repairs on all of their planes, so when things cleared, it was a 'maximum effort' on both sides. It has been estimated that there were 7,000 planes in the air on that day. My mission was to Cologne and then back to the Bulge area. I was alone and was 'jumped' six times on that one mission.

[As I stated] we had very heavy losses; the Germans knew that if they saw one P-38, they pretty well knew that it was a photographic plane and they'd go after us. Sometimes if it was a 'black star' priority, which was a major 'do-or-die' type mission, they

---

[98] *Battle of the Bulge*- Hitler's last gamble to counterattack between the advancing American and British forces in northern France and the Low Countries began on Dec. 16, 1944. After the Normandy landings, the incredible magnitude of American industrial capacity dictated to Hitler that somehow the supply lines had to be cut, and he chose the Ardennes Forest for the avenue of attack in the hopes of reaching the port of Antwerp, combining the elements of surprise, rough ground, and bad weather for a quarter-million man offensive. On December 16, 600 tanks broke through the thinly manned American lines after a tremendous artillery barrage, creating a bulge or pocket they hoped to exploit to the sea, and sowing desperation, panic, and confusion. The weather cleared just before Christmas, and American air power helped to turn the tide as temperatures plunged to the coldest in European memory during the winter of 1944–45.

would send two photographic planes with P-51 escorts, the idea being that at least one would get back. A 'black star priority' mission might be perhaps on an oil refinery, or ball-bearing factories, sometimes a bridge. It would be varied, and actually, the pilot didn't necessarily know the specific target, but was told to take in the area, and it would include whatever they were after.

Toward the end, I was made commanding officer of the outfit of 2,500 men. The regulations required that the commanding officer of a combat squadron be a pilot, and at the age of 22, I was the oldest and most experienced pilot in the squadron!

The Last Mission

The last mission I took was on April 26 of 1945; I think that may have been the last mission of the war. My buddy Tom Vaughan from Texas also had a mission that day, and I can't remember who took off first or who landed last, but I believe that it was the last mission of the war, and a bad one at that. It was to Prague, Czechoslovakia, and when we got over there, one of the targets was an airfield. As we went over the airfield—and usually when we took pictures we were at about 25,000 feet, but going in and coming out, my personal tactic was to be much higher, as high as 39,000 feet—I looked down and I saw two fighters taking off from that airfield. The airfield had black marks on it, which meant that it was a jet field. We were terrified of these jets because they were at least a hundred miles an hour faster than we were and they could go higher. I had four fighters escorting me, and in a very short time I realized that the German jets were at our altitude! I called them out to my fighters and we all kept a very sharp lookout. In a surprisingly short time, I saw two specks in my rear view mirror at our altitude, and so I turned so that they would come in having a 'deflection shot' at me. I told the fighters to ram them, but this was not as dramatic as it sounds, because the closing speeds were over a thousand miles an hour, and to try to hit something [was next to impossible]. I called them out to my fighters and told them that when I said 'Break,' we would all turn into [the German jets]—it was very important that we convince them that we were trying to hit them, because if we didn't scare them off, they could make mincemeat out of us. What I did know was that the [German flight command on the] ground was listening to our conversations and was advising [the German pilots], and I thought that what we were saying would scare them. I counted on the fact that they knew the war was almost over, and that they were not anxious to get killed at this point, either.

It worked. We did come awfully close to them, but they only made one pass—the lead man, of course, was after me because I was the photographic plane, and he went under me. I could see him very plainly in the cockpit as he went under me, and he turned and went down, and that was the last we saw of them.

We had a range I would say of 1,200 or 1,300 miles. Fuel was always a problem coming back, but there were emergency fields in England down near the White Cliffs of Dover where we could land and refuel. Also, late in the war, there were airfields in Germany and in France. One of the times that I came back very low on fuel I ran into a thunderstorm over Holland, and I didn't know whether I was going to make it across the Channel or not. I didn't have much choice, so I went on to a field called Manston, which was a huge square paved field made especially for emergency landings; it was 10,000 feet square and so you could land in any direction and get a lot of runway. I landed there at the end of that mission. When I went to taxi in, I put the throttles forward a little bit, and both engines quit!

War's End

When the war ended, I'll tell you it was the greatest relief I've ever had in my life. I can remember that a sergeant came to me—we knew it was coming, probably a week or even more before, we just didn't know exactly when—he wanted to know if it was all right if they went out and bought some beer. I said I thought that was a wonderful idea, and so they went out and they bought six barrels. Now I'm not talking about a little 10-gallon thing, I'm talking about a barrel. Six barrels appeared and they brought them in on a 6x6 truck, and I had them put them in the ammunition dump, which was guarded 24 hours a day. The ammunition dump was also the coolest place because it was underground. When Churchill made his announcement that the war was over, we sent the trucks down there and they rolled the beer up onto the trucks and brought it to the squadron, and by the way, other squadrons had done something similar. We rolled the barrels out on top of the bomb shelter, which was elevated and could easily be tapped right there, and you never saw so many drunk guys in your life!

I didn't return home until May 26, 1946, which was about a year later. I stayed over there and I flew—I hate to admit this, but I signed up to fly for what at that point was 'Air Transport Command.' I was a multi-engine pilot, so I qualified, and frankly, the reason I did it was because I didn't want to go to the Pacific. I had had the war up to here [*gestures with hands*], and I was terrified and I was a nervous wreck. I knew that I could stay in Europe, so I signed up for a year. [Of course, when I did get home], there was a family celebration; I was met at the train by my folks, my aunt and uncle, and it was very emotional.

I went back to my college for one day. I hadn't even signed up yet, but I could get in, I knew, and I was at the dormitory and my roommate was sixteen years old! He was wet behind the ears, and I couldn't stand him in the first hour; I spent just one day there. I just knew that I would never be able to concentrate on college, so I left there and went up to Lockport, and very fortunately I got a very physical job at a cotton bleaching plant. My first job for a long time was to haul bales of cotton like a donkey from the warehouse into the plant, and that was the best thing that ever happened to me, because of course I had lots of trouble sleeping at that time. I can tell you that if you haul cotton all day, you will sleep [at night]! I stayed there for about a year and a half, and it was a wonderful transition for me. After that I got married and went to work for a box-making factory in Newark, New York, and I was near my hometown and [my life] took off from there.

I think [my experiences in World War II] made me a much better person. One of the experiences that I didn't mention was that at the end of the war, I had a mission, and I don't remember where it was to, but I was all alone and on the way back I ran low on fuel. I landed at Munich, Germany— the Munich area had just recently been [taken]; I remember the runway was all bombed out, and I had difficulty landing. They didn't have any aviation fuel, so I had to spend the night. When I got out of my plane, the first person I bumped into was Captain Cook, the [former] head of our military police at our base [near Oxford], and he had been transferred to Munich to keep order there.

He took me in his Jeep downtown to where I was going to spend the night, and by the way, my roommate that night was a Russian, so the conversation was very sparse. But Cook then took me to Dachau concentration camp and it had just been liberated. It was the most shaking experience of my life. We went in, and I can remember the first thing that struck me as we went through the gates in his Jeep was the smell; I vomited right as we went into the gate. We drove around the compound, and we had to drive very slowly because these people were in such terrible shape that they couldn't get out of the way very well. And they would come up and they would touch us on the shoulder and say 'Danke,' 'thank you.' We went to one area where they had dug a trench with a bulldozer—oh, it must have been eight feet wide and a hundred feet long—and they were pushing bodies into this common grave with a bulldozer, believe it or not. And that was a horrible experience as far as I was concerned, something I will never ever forget, very difficult.[99]

John Weeks enjoyed a long career in business and later in life settled into the communities surrounding Hometown, USA, volunteering in hospitals and medical centers and as a hospice caregiver in Washington County. He passed away on October 21, 2015, in Glens Falls, at the age of 93.

---

[99] *something I will never ever forget*-Dachau was liberated on April 29, 1945, by U.S. forces. I speculate that Mr. Weeks was there in the week that followed; it was a traumatic experience for GIs. This topic is dealt with extensively in my book *A Train Near Magdeburg*.

Richard Faulkner, World War II.

CHAPTER THREE

The Evadee

Richard Faulkner was born on October 8, 1924, a couple hours' drive west of Hometown, USA. He graduated from high school in 1942. He became a ball turret gunner on a B-17 in the 100th Bomb Group, nicknamed 'The Bloody Hundredth' for losing many aircraft and crews. In Richard's case, he was miraculously his crew's only survivor of a mid-air collision with another B-17 of the 100th Bomb Group, only a few hours into their very first mission. He then spent twenty-nine days evading the Germans in France with the help of the French Underground, eventually being picked up by boat off the coast of France. In crossing the English Channel, his rescuers came under fire by German fast attack boats, and one of the British gunners was killed. Faulkner manned the fallen gunner's weapon, and they made it back to England.[113] 'I don't go to the reunions of my bomb group because there's hardly anybody there that I knew. I mean, I was only there nine days. I was in France longer than I was in England.'

*

Richard J. Faulkner

My father died when I was 12. I was one of five children [growing up in the Depression], and we all had to pitch in to help.

[On December 7, 1941] I was [listening to] a Chicago Bears football game when it broke in with the news about Pearl Harbor. I was surprised and I didn't even know where Pearl Harbor was.

I enlisted two days after I turned 18, in October 1942. And when I went into the service, I immediately signed up for benefits for my mother, to help her out financially. But they didn't take me until December 11, 1942.

I went into the Air Corps because I wanted to fly. I wanted to get into the pilot program, but I didn't pass it. I went to Miami Beach, spent two weeks at Miami Beach, and then to Goldsboro, North Carolina, to airplane and engines school, and spent two months there. From there I went to gunnery school in Fort Myers, Florida, for two months, and then to Dalhart Army Air Base in Texas, where I was assigned to the group training. We got ready to go overseas, and my pilot didn't pass the proficiency test. So we went to Pyote, Texas, for another month.

Then we got ready and went to Grand Island, Nebraska, and picked up our airplane, a B-17G. We flew to Grenier Field, New Hampshire, then to Goose Bay, Labrador, to Iceland, and to Stornoway, Scotland. From there we were processed, and we went to further gunnery training at the Wash in England.[100]

I was in the same crew all the way through training and flying over to England, and we were assigned to the 100th Bomb Group. We wanted to name our plane *Esquire Lady*, but we didn't last that long. We were shot down on our first mission.

---

[100] *the Wash in England*- the square bay and estuary on the east coast of England, among the largest in the UK.

Richard Faulkner and his crew, World War II.

We were going to Augsburg, Germany, and to Munich. We were in the part of the group that was assigned to Munich, and we flew the plane that was assigned to us that day, the *Berlin Playboy.*

We were delayed an hour for takeoff because of the fog. We got airborne, and soon after crossing the Channel, the plane above us got hit. And it came down and hit us, broke us into two pieces. I was in the ball turret, and I had a parachute in there; being small, I could get one in there.

The airplane broke into two parts right behind the wing. The tail part flipped over. I was with the tail, with the tail gunner and the two waist gunners. And the other part [of the B-17] had the radio man, the bombardier, navigator, pilot, and co-pilot. But they just couldn't get out, evidently, and on the other plane, there were only two people that got out. So, nine plus seven—sixteen people were killed.[101]

---

[101] *nine plus seven—sixteen people were killed-* On this mission, the 100th Bomb Group lost 3 airplanes and thirty men. This incident claimed over half

[When the tail] turned upside-down, [the ball turret where I was] was now on top. I got the door handles open—it can only open in the stowed position from the outside, and it just happened to be that way. I was just lucky it was in the position where I could open the door. I had the chute hooked on my harness, so when I got out of the turret, I hooked the rest of it on the way down.

I was in a free-fall. When I could make out objects on the ground, I pulled the ripcord. I pulled the D-ring and nothing happened. So, there are three little snaps that cover the pilot chute. I got those unsnapped, and fished the pilot chute out. And luckily it pulled out, and it pulled the rest of the parachute out. I landed in a heap by some woods on a hillside, in a pasture.

The Farmer

I gathered up my chute and carried it over into the woods, and found a bunch of leaves and berry bushes, and I hid everything in there. The goggles and the helmet, the parachute and the harness, the whole works. I saw that there was a farm nearby, so I started for there. But I could see the Germans coming. So I got back and buried myself in the berry brambles, in the leaves. And when they came through, they didn't want to look in the berry bushes, so I didn't get found out.

---

of the men and 2 out of three of the planes. The technical details are as follows for RIchard's crew: Killed in Action, Munich, 18/3/44-Pilot: Paul Martin, Co-pilot: Tom Cryan, Navigator: Tom Hughes, Bombardier: Albert Racz, Flight engineer/top turret gunner: Levi Tonn, Radio Operator: Russ Longdon, Waist gunner: Lonnie Albin, Waist gunner: Veryl Lund, Tail gunner: John Howley. MIA-Ball turret gunner: Dick Faulkner (evaded capture); mid-air collision with 42-37913 (100BG); crashed Frevent, near Haudricourt, 16 miles SW of Poix, France. Missing Air Crew Report 3234. BERLIN PLAYBOY. Source: Imperial War Museum, www.americanairmuseum.com/aircraft/7212.

That was about noon, and then that evening, when it started to get dark, the farmer came, and I told him that I was an American. I couldn't speak French, he couldn't speak English. So he motioned for me to wait until the sun went down. So I waited and he came and got me after dark. My ankles and my knees were banged up, and he put me in the barn to begin with. And when he figured the Germans weren't looking for me, he took me in the house and put me in the bed, giving me some hot towels to soak my knees and ankles to get the swelling down.

But he kept motioning to me that there was something wrong. [I did not know what he meant], so somebody got the idea to get a mirror. And I could see I was all bloody—my face was all covered in dried blood; I had cut myself somehow coming out of the plane. And so they got that cleaned up, and the next day they moved me to another place, because the people got nervous. They thought that the Germans knew I was there, so they hustled me out after dark to another place. I heard later that they executed that family because the Germans were pretty sure I was there, because somehow they knew that there were ten people in the bomber, and only nine bodies [must have been found].

The French Underground

I went to another place, and I stayed there for about a week. Then they shipped me to another place, took me for another week or so, and then I was transported on the back of a motorcycle to another location, and we got a flat tire, right under a German machine gun outpost! And the Germans were up there laughing at us for having a flat tire, and I thought, 'If you only knew, fella, that this is an American down here.'

They had me in civilian clothes. And from there I went to Paris, where the [French Underground] was going to get a new picture and make up a false ID. They made it up, and it said I was a fifteen-year-old deaf-mute. We always laughed about it—the Germans were kind of slow, because there were so many deaf-mutes running around with IDs. [*Laughs*]

So I got the pictures taken, and they took me around sightseeing, Champs-Élysées and all that. And I was so scared, I thought all the Germans were watching me; all of them were walking around there, but it was probably the best thing [to be 'hiding'] right out in the open.

Leaving Paris

So when we got ready to leave, we were going to go on the subway. And there were two other fellas in the apartment with me. One was a big redhead, and the other was a Southerner from Houston, Texas.

The fellow in the Underground went down the stairs. When he got to the bottom, I started down, and the others followed suit, in the same way, in single file. I waited until [the leader] got to the corner of the street, then I came out of the building, and then I got to the corner, and then he was at another corner. But I didn't see any of the other fellows coming behind me, so I threw my hands up like, 'What do I do now?' And he motioned for me to come forward.

I ran into those two fellas much later, back home, after the Germans surrendered. The Gestapo picked them up as they came out the door, and they were held prisoner until the end of the war! But [I guess I blended in better]; I was short and dark like a Frenchman.

We got on the subway. The man in the Underground got in one door, and I got in another. When he gets off, I would get off. But I was standing right next to a colonel in the SS—he had a satchel handcuffed to his arm with a guard with a Sten gun. The train started up, and the SS colonel bumped into me. And he turned around to me and said, *'Pardonne-moi.'* I thought, 'Oh, my God.' I thought I was done right then and there! [*Laughs*]

[They put me] on the train going from Paris to Morlaix [on the coastline in Brittany], where I eventually exited France. I had a magazine—if you're holding that up in front of your face like you're reading, most people don't bother you. When I got to Morlaix, they brought me to a deserted French farmhouse.

P-47N flying over the Pacific during World War II.
Credit: USAF. Public domain.

There were other people from the Underground there, and also a P-47 pilot who had been shot down. His name was Ken Williams and he had flown 63 missions. I asked him how he got shot down.

He said, 'I shot myself down. I was strafing a German bomber, and it blew up under me and blew both wings off my P-47. I ditched it, and I started running across the field. And I'm trying to hide, and I look down, and I've got the bright Mae West [life jacket] vest still on!' [*Laughs*]

Pretty soon, into the farmhouse came two ladies and two other men. One was a captain in the British intelligence, and the other fella was losing his mind, and so they tried to get him out of there before he got caught. The two ladies had just been broken out of jail. They were Underground workers, a mother and daughter. So we waited, and pretty soon they distributed some handguns to two of the Underground guys and they went out; I found out later they were to go out and watch the German machine gun [outpost]. If the Germans spotted us, they were to shoot the Germans, but if not, they were to just leave them alone, because the Underground would use the route again.

We went out and they told us to watch for the phosphorus dots in the trail and follow them—'Don't get out of the track, because it's a minefield.' So we went across the minefield, and went down the bank, down to the shore. We waited down there, and at about 4:00 in the morning they flashed a flashlight from the shore to out at sea, and the British rode in with two rubber dinghies to pick us up. They brought the pilot and me out to something like a PT boat, a British gunboat. The others were put on another one.

We were put in the hold, in the crews' quarters. We started up and got moving, and we could hear gunfire, we could hear rounds hitting the boat. The captain opened the hatch up, and he said, 'One of you guys a gunner?'

I said, 'Yes, I am.'

He says, 'Well, I just had a gunner get killed, and I need a gunner!'

I went up on top. We pulled the guy's body away and they put me on one of those .303 machine guns.[102] We kept on in the gunfight for a little while, and then two British Spitfires showed up and chased off the German E-boats. So we had quite a time out there.

Well, we got into England, and they had us put on British uniforms. When we got to London, we were issued American uniforms. I think they were trying to hide the fact [that we had been rescued] from the German [spies], but I don't think it worked.

---

[102] *.303 machine guns*-the Vickers gun, a water-cooled British machine gun with a reputation for great reliability.

I was shot down on the 18th day of March, 1944, and I was picked up April 16, 1944. [They had notified my mother.] I still have the telegram that my mother received. *'Regret to inform you that your son, Richard J. Faulkner, is missing on a mission over Germany.'* And no other details. My mother wrote to the adjutant general and everybody she could write to. My chaplain on the base wrote his condolences to her.

When I got back, they had a form for a telegram to send my mother. And what it said was, *'Am feeling fine, having a swell holiday.'* So she got the message [that I was okay], but that's how she found out.

*

The long anticipated D-Day invasion was imminent, and Richard was able to convey important information about the enemy.

The Underground told me that in Metz, there was a German reinforced tank battalion that could go wherever they were needed. I told [our intelligence officers] about the configuration of the minefields that we went through, and all about the machine gun posts that we saw along the road. I noted the railroad stations that had anything of importance, where the Germans had troops with guns. I told them how many I thought were in each town that I was in. But I never tried to learn the names of the people who were helping me, because if I got captured, I didn't want to have any information I could give the Germans. If I didn't know anything [about them], I couldn't tell about them.

When I got back to my group, coming back across the Channel, General LeMay—who afterwards turned out to be the head of the Air Force—[summoned] me and two other fellas who had just returned. He wanted to know what he could do to change anything, or what needed to be done, [for guys who landed in enemy territory in the future].

I said, 'Well, somebody [has just put] an order out to tie a new pair of shoes on your harness so you have a good pair of shoes [if you have to bail out]. That would never work, because the Germans would notice those new shoes right off the bat.'

He said, 'I'll rescind that, Sergeant. I'll put good old pair of shoes.'

But the first thing I asked General LeMay about [had to do with my mother].

I said, 'What about my allotment?' Was my mother getting her money while I was gone?

He said, 'Sergeant, I have a mother that I have an allotment for, too.'[103]

*

I had a 28-day 'survivor leave.' I went to Atlantic City, New Jersey, and they processed me there. Then they sent me to the hospital in Nashville for rehabilitation—my knees and ankles were pretty weak. And so I was there for a month, and the army sent me to B-29 school in January of '45. There were nine of us who were combat returnees, and the army wanted to send us to the Pacific, but we said we didn't want to go. By then there were a lot of other people who had never been in combat, so the army didn't make an issue of it, and they put us in a mobile training unit for airplanes and engines. And I stayed there in that unit until I got discharged on October 27, 1945.

*

I ran into the guys who were captured by the Gestapo after I left the hospital in Nashville. I was in Amarillo, Texas, and I was in the

---

[103] *General LeMay*- General Curtis LeMay (1906-1990) was one of the developers of the 'combat box' formation of the 8th Air Force over Europe, often flying with his lead crews on the most hazardous bombing missions. In the Pacific Theater, where the combat box formation style was not applicable, he became the major architect of the controversial strategic firebombing campaign, discussed in my first book, *Voices of the Pacific Theater.* He was later Chief of Staff of the United States Air Force from 1961 to 1965.

PX. [The two of them were there, recognized me, and] hollered at me. My wife always said, 'Don't rob a bank, because everybody remembers you.' [*Laughs*] And they were kidding me about [how I got away and they were captured]. They told me about how as PoWs, the Germans kept moving them as the Americans kept getting closer, that they had them march on the outside of the formation, so if anybody was going to get shot, they were it. They were getting low on food and everything, but they made it out. They got through it.

I saw the P-47 pilot, Ken Williams, after he moved to Rochester, New York, after he retired. He became a lieutenant colonel. I found his name on a list of an 'escapee-evadee' association I joined. I called him up and I went up to see him in Rochester. My wife said, 'Look at the two of you. [For escapee-evadees], you're like two midgets! You're supposed to look like John Wayne.' [*Laughs*]

I sent a letter to him a year ago, and I got no answer. So I have no idea what happened to him, whether he moved away. His wife was a teacher. I got an idea that maybe they moved when she retired.

*

My wife and I took a trip to France two years ago, and we got to Normandy, near the cemetery where my crewmates were buried. I only had about fifteen minutes, but I found three of the fellows who were in the plane with me. The other six, they sent their bodies back home, evidently. But those three, they were still there.

*

On January 14, 2014, Richard Faulkner was officially awarded his Purple Heart by his congressman in the company of his family and 100 others gathered to witness the event. In 1944, he had turned down the medal.

'I don't think you can understand. I'll always have a guilty feeling that asks, 'Why me? Why did I get out, and nobody else? Why should I still be

around, and not them?' But I have talked to other people, survivors, and they feel the same way. It makes you appreciate being alive an awful lot. I just appreciate everything; it just amazes me how lucky I was.'

Richard Faulkner passed away on August 29, 2014, at the age of 89.

CHAPTER FOUR

The P-38 Pilot

George T. FitzGibbon was born in Staten Island, New York, on October 23, 1921. He joined the U.S. Army Air Corps in January 1942, shortly after the bombing of Pearl Harbor. After graduating from flight training in October 1942, he flew the P-38 Lightning and was shot down in June 1943, parachuting into the Mediterranean. Captured and held for a short time by the Italians, he was transferred to Stalag Luft III in Poland. He was a prisoner of war for 22 months. 'The day after Pearl Harbor, I was out at the airfield applying for my cadet training, and I was accepted. I went into the Army Air Corps Program.'

*

George T. FitzGibbon

At the time of the Pearl Harbor attack, I was a student primarily trying to get enough credits so I could get into the Army Air Corps Flying Cadet Program. That was my goal all along, so I had just about completed half the credits for the degree I needed, and Pearl Harbor was attacked.

I was in a restaurant called the Hobby House in Fort Wayne, not far from where I was living at the time. It was about 1:00 in the afternoon, and I was having a nice big hamburger. It was announced over the speaker system in the restaurant that Pearl Harbor was attacked. My first question was, 'Where is Pearl Harbor?' A Navy guy lived in our house, so he enlightened me as to Pearl Harbor. Boy, we got talking about this fast. 'Boy, this is going to be serious business.' Anyway, I used it as a catalyst to get into my flying program. Flying just always appealed to me since I was like 15 or so. I didn't have any experience other than riding in the backseat of a little open cockpit plane a couple times. I read a lot about it and thought that was what I wanted to do. This just provided the means for me to do it.

I went down to Maxwell Air Force Base in Alabama. Then after the basic training there, I went to primary flying school at Decatur, Alabama, [to learn with] a PT-17, a Stearman biplane. Then I went to Greenville, Mississippi, for basic training. That was the Vultee BT-13. Then back to Selma, Alabama, for advanced, a North American AT-6. The last 10 hours were in a World War II fighter. They had three different types. They had a P-36, a P-39, and a P-40. You drew to see which one you were going to get, and I drew the old P-36. Anyway, I flew my last 10 hours of flying school in a P-36, [but] it was the most sophisticated thing I'd flown so far, so I thought a lot of it. It wasn't as good as a P-40, I don't think, but I got 10 hours in it, and it helped me a lot. Then I graduated and proceeded from there.

I was assigned to Pinellas County Airport down in Florida, where we had P-40s, and I flew the P-40 down there for a couple of months. I was commissioned as a 2nd lieutenant, and then got shipping instructions to New York City and then a boat over to England. We went on the *Queen Elizabeth*, unescorted except for the first 500 miles. They went fast, and they changed course every three minutes. That was their evasive action, I guess, and we didn't have any problem. It was a rough-weather trip, but it took five days. We ended up in Glasgow, Scotland. We were assigned to a little base and airfield up there in Northern England called Shaftesbury. That was about the 24th of November of '42.

The trouble with Shaftesbury is it was a nice little military base, but it didn't have an airfield. We were about a dozen replacement pilots. They also didn't have any P-40s in England, which we were all prepared in, so we hung around there and played cards and went down to the pubs and things like this for a couple months until they asked. They wanted five volunteers to go down to North Africa. That was all they could tell us about it, it was down in North Africa, so I volunteered. I sailed in a convoy this time, and I think one of our ships got torpedoed. We saw the smoke, but that was about all I could tell. We came in through the Strait of Gibraltar, a nice calm Mediterranean Sea. I said, 'Oh, what a heavenly place for submarines.' [*Laughs*] We didn't have any problem.

We went into Oran, stayed overnight there, and then we went to a little pasture-type airfield about 20 miles out of Casablanca called Berrechid, Morocco. We had a couple old trainers there that we flew for a while. Then we found out they were bringing P-38s into Casablanca by ship, partially disassembled, but they'd reassemble them right there in Casablanca Airport. About five of us finagled getting checked out in the P-38; they used us to fly airplanes up to the front, after they were assembled. We did that for four or five trips, then we got orders to stay up there and join the 82nd Fighter Group.

P-38J flying over Southern California. Credit: USAF. Public domain.

The P-38 was wonderful, a dream machine. The only disadvantage was it was slow to roll. If you wanted to roll into a steep turn or steep bank to evade the enemy for instance, it took a little more time to get into that position than you wanted it to. With a single-engine fighter, you just hit that stick right over there and whip it right up. Anyway, it never adversely affected me.

Combat

Then I was assigned to the 96th Fighter Squadron flying missions right away out of Telerghma in North Africa. We'd go out over the Mediterranean, sometimes escorting bombers to Sardinia and Sicily; sometimes we'd go out on a shipping sweep. You could attack any ships you saw on the Mediterranean, because you didn't have to worry about identifying the enemy—anything you see out there is the enemy. We'd strafe boats and ships and drop bombs on them. I'd go down when I'd strafed a ship, and it looked like all those tracers are coming right between your eyes. We carried one 500-pound bomb on one side and a fuel tank on the other side, for equalization. The trouble was, you couldn't release one. You couldn't drop your empty fuel tank without dropping the bomb, too, so you'd keep them both until you got ready to drop the bomb and then punch the button. I don't think we ever did much damage with a bomb—we didn't have a bombsight. You just dive down and hope you're somewhere in the ballpark.

Following the Axis defeat in North Africa, the Allies pursued them to the island of Sicily. On July 10, 1943, U.S. and British forces began Operation Husky, an invasion of the island using troops deployed by gliders, parachutes, and landing craft.

When we got around Sicily, especially, we ran into a lot of fighters, Italian fighters and Focke-Wulf 190s, German fighters. I shot down a Macchi 202 Italian fighter that I got credit for. The day we invaded Sicily, enemy fighters were flying down to the southern tip of Sicily and strafing our troops. Then they'd go back to refuel, so we were on them when they came back to take on more fuel.

An Italian Macchi C.202 fighter at Wright-Patterson Field outside Dayton, Ohio, for United States Army Air Forces evaluation.
Credit: USAF. Public domain.

I was on my 25th mission and we got involved in a big dogfight there. I had a Focke-Wulf 190 in my sights, and I was shooting at him with everything I had—parts of him were just coming off. Just then something hit me in my left engine, and it was on fire. Black smoke just poured in through the wing root, right up into the cockpit, and all of a sudden, I couldn't see a thing, just the sky straight up. My little world was coming to an end.

A captured Focke-Wulf Fw 190A. Credit: USAF. Public domain.

I don't know [if it was part of his airplane that hit me]; I've been trying to figure that out for years. Possibly it was [another] fighter, but we were only about 200 feet off the ground, and I thought that I saw fire coming from places on the ground. We checked this out after the war, and nobody in Western Sicily reported shooting down a P-38 that day. I think it was ground fire. Anyway, it didn't make much difference. The smoke [was too much]; there was nothing I could do but get out of the plane. I pulled it up and released the canopy and unhooked my seatbelt and rolled it over. I pushed on the wheel and I fell out.

Now I'd say I was at about 800 feet. I was wearing a seat pack, and the seat pack caught on the canopy hinge back there, so I was hanging there out of the airplane. I couldn't do anything except kick my feet a little bit, and pretty soon it broke loose. Then I watched the airplane go by, and I pulled the ripcord. I pulled it and nothing happened. I pulled it again a little harder. Sure enough, that did it, so I landed in the Mediterranean Sea about 200 yards offshore.

Captured

I hit the water fast. When I was coming down, I didn't have much altitude to lose. You're supposed to get yourself undone out of this harness before you get in the water if you can; [I couldn't get out of it completely].Then the parachute fell over, and I was able to get my hand onto that, and I got it undone. I had a rubber boat in my seat pack and I had a Mae West life jacket on, but the water was only up to here [*gestures chest-high with hand*], and I was 200 yards offshore. I stood on the bottom and looked inshore. There's these three guys in there that were waving me to come in, so they fired a couple of shots on each side of me to get my attention, I guess. Anyway, I walked in. It was like a spit out there, because as I walked in, it got deeper, and then the bottom came back up again. I had a .45 sidearm right here [*gestures under left arm*], and didn't know what I was going to do with that, so I took it out and laid it on the bottom of the Mediterranean Sea, and I walked in. The guy says, 'For you, the war is over.' He was pretty near right, even though there was a lot of war left yet.

These were Italian soldiers. We walked to the village of Castelvetrano and went to a place that I think was an officers' club. It was like 7:00 in the evening. The place was loaded and they all had drinks in their hand. I guess the commanding officer was the guy they took me to. [Other than that], there was no conversation or anything. He gave the guy some instructions, and they took me down the street and put me up on the second floor of this little building, right in the middle of the village, and left the guard there with me. About an hour later, a guy came with a dinner for me, a nice piece of Salisbury steak, some spinach, and maybe a little spaghetti and some wine in the bottle. I said if I'd known the food was going to be this good, I could have come sooner, because we were eating C-rations where we came from. [*Laughs*] I stayed there about a couple of nights, I guess, and then I was loaded on a bus, and we drove up to Palermo. There were five guards and me and we stayed right in the airport operations building, Palermo Airport, second floor, with one guard with me all the time.

That night, I had to go to the restroom. The guard was sitting there on the bed, leaning on his rifle. He's dozing like this [*mimics drowsiness/sleep*]. I indicated that I was going to the restroom. All the window openings had no glass or anything like that. I jumped out of a window onto a landing, and I took off around two o'clock in the morning. He didn't hear me or anything—nobody saw me, so I walked west for half a mile or so. I went up through the city and there were no people around—everybody was asleep, I guess. I walked maybe three miles or so; now I was starting to think it's going to get light pretty quick and I'd better find a place to situate myself during the daytime.

Before I could decide on exactly what to do, I walked right into an Italian gun position. They were covering the road coming up from the south, with this big gun up on the top. First thing I knew, I hear this sound of metal clicking, and this big searchlight comes on. I put my hands up. I was right in the light, so I was recaptured again. Fortunately, they didn't shoot. They sure had the drop on me that time, though I was so close to General Patton's army, which would be coming through there in just two or three days' time. While Montgomery went up the east coast, Patton came around the other way, but I was back to being a PoW again.

The Allied 'finish line' in the battle for Sicily was Messina, which fell to General Patton's army in a spectacular conclusion in mid-August 1943. Unfortunately, more than 100,000 Axis forces escaped to mainland Italy across the Straits of Messina, taking Allied prisoners with them by boat.

Then we were put on a bus and taken to Messina. Messina had just been attacked, [but had not yet fallen]; they were still in the war there in Messina. There were a couple of civilian bodies lying right out on the street, not military; I don't remember if we could hear the guns there or not. There were now about five or six of us, all American pilots like me, and the Italians loaded us in a launch and took us across the Straits of Messina right in the middle of the day. I was worried we were going to get strafed out in the middle of the straits, but we made it across.

*

We walked. You do a lot of walking as a PoW. We got to a railroad, and they loaded us in a couple of boxcars. By now, there were 66 of us; they put 33 of us in each boxcar, and we took off.

We got up to the south of Salerno. The Salerno marshalling yards were all bombed out, so they pulled [the railcars] off on a siding and unhooked the engine, and the Italians went their own way. The guards just sat out there and laughed and had a big time talking. They had their own provisions. Nobody seemed to be putting any effort into getting us something to eat. We sat there for seven days, I think. The fourth day, they came around with a big kettle of some kind of brothy soup. It wasn't very good, but it tasted like heaven at the time. Then the Germans evidently heard that we were there, and they came down with three lorries and loaded us all on those three trucks and drove us around Salerno to a place called Capua, just northeast of Naples. It was a barbed wire camp, and we stayed in there a week or two. Now they're getting the prisoners all together. They must have had several hundred by then. Funny thing, only about a quarter of a mile from us was this brick factory, sitting right out in the open. It turned out to be a small arms factory. One day the B-25s came over and bombed that thing—that was exciting. It blew up for like 12 hours, boxcars and all. You just kept hearing one big blast. We'd say, 'Well, that's it for now.' Then another one!

Boy, it lasted a long time. They had masonry ceilings in our buildings, and the masonry came down and cut up a lot of guys.

We were prisoners of the Italians for like three months. We left that camp and got up to a place called Sulmona, which is east of Rome, in what had been a civilian prison. It had big 15-foot masonry walls, and it made thoughts of escape very difficult. Italian guards would be walking the top of that wall, until one day in September, they were gone, and the German paratroopers were up there. That's how we found out that Italy had capitulated.

On July 25, 1943, Benito Mussolini was dismissed as prime minister by the Fascist Grand Council. King Victor Emmanuel III had him arrested and then appointed the 'Hero of Ethiopia,' Marshal Pietro Badoglio, who promptly signed an armistice with the Allies on September 3. A furious Hitler disarmed the Italian army fighting with the Germans and sent 600,000 into slave labor.[114] *Mussolini, being held at a mountaintop resort, was later rescued in a daring SS glider raid ten days after Italy broke from Germany. The German war machine now poured into Italy and dug in.*

A couple weeks later, the Germans marched us down to the railroad and got us loaded in the boxcars, and we went up north. We had several stops along the route. They'd just stop for a couple hours, right out in the open, but they wouldn't let us out of the cars. Finally, we got into Bolzano, up in the Alps, right at the southern end of the Brenner Pass, at about 10 minutes to noon. We could hear our bombers almost before the train stopped. At the 12:00 bombing time, it turned out their targets were this railroad bridge and the [marshalling] yards right at the southern end of Bolzano! Somebody ran up and down and opened all the boxcars; the PoWs did this, not the Germans. You have a choice you have to make. Everybody is running like crazy. Do I go right or left? It scared the heck out of all of us.

I went left into the city of Bolzano. If I had gone right, there were some open lots out there, and then the river was out there, so I might have had a better chance to escape if I'd gone to the river because I can swim good. Anyway, I went left with another fella with me. People were all in the bomb shelters, so there was nobody out, except a German guard here and there to try to keep us contained a little bit. We saw this guard down the middle of the street, so we zipped into a building. We went up the stairs; everybody else was in the basement. We got to the top and went over another building, and we came down on the far side of this guard. Then we walked up the street, maybe a half a mile, right in the city. The third wave of bombers had already come over, and people were now coming out of the shelters, and the streets were getting full of people. We said, 'What are we going to do now?' We look like Americans right off the bat, you know, so we'll have to pull into one of these estate-like places, like a one-acre property with a lot of hedges and shrubs around. We pulled into one, got in behind the hedges, and we're sitting there, figuring we'll wait until dark and then get out of there. A German guy comes out with a Luger, and he says, 'Komm her,' so somebody had seen us going in there. We were recaptured and returned back to the rest of the troops.

We went back on the same train, went up north through the Brenner Pass, up to Munich. From there, we walked up to Moosburg, a big barbed wire camp. Later, towards the end of the war, we were back in Moosburg again, and there were like 30,000 of us in there. Anyway, we got in there, and we stayed there a couple of weeks.

Then we went back on the train again, and we went up north. We went all the way to Sagan, I guess. That's about 90 kilometers southeast of Berlin on the Oder River. That was where Stalag Luft III was, and we moved into there.

We stayed there for a year and a half. That's where *The Great Escape* [movie took place], and [that compound] was just over the fence. We couldn't see any of this, and we didn't even know it was going on. We had tunnel projects of our own. In fact, we had three going on in our barracks. It was Barracks 55, and we were in a corner, fairly close to the fences, but you had to tunnel a long ways. It was all sandy ground. That's where all our bed slats went, to holding up the sand [tunnels] from collapsing.

We developed a system after a while. The Germans would know that you had tunneling going on. They'd wait a while, and then they'd come in all of a sudden and search for the tunnel. We had two tunnels that we called 'diversionary tunnels.' They were the ones that were supposed to be found by the Germans. Then the other one was the main event, and hopefully they wouldn't find that one, but they did in our case. Eventually, they found it, but it gave us something to do.

[To conceal it], we had a stove. It was the same way as it was in Stalag 17. Did you ever see that in the movie? They had a stove, a little potbelly stove. We did a little carpenter work under it, and we made it so the stove would sit there, but you could take the whole thing down in a flash and move the stove over and pull the whole panel up. Then you go down about 10 feet, and there's your tunnel. Anyway, it kept everybody busy. If you did nothing else, you had to carry sand around in your pockets and unload the sand somewhere. We used to dump it around shrubs and stuff like that, but the sand was real white. The surface sand was brown, so it was hard to conceal. The Germans knew we were doing it all the time. Eventually, we just went into the outhouse and dumped the sand right down the holes.

We played a lot of bridge; played bridge all winter and played softball all summer. And if it wasn't for the Red Cross, we'd have been in dire straits. The Germans would give a bowl of soup on

Thursday. Maybe you'd get a potato or two per person for the rest of the week. You never could tell what day you were going to get it. Every six weeks, they'd give you a piece of the reddest, most luscious-looking steak you ever saw, but it was horsemeat. It was so tough you could hardly eat it. You could take a little bite of that, and you could chew it for an hour, which we did. Anyway, the Red Cross parcels, you're supposed to get one per person a week. We were getting about one parcel for six or seven guys there for the first year or so, but then as the war started winding down a little bit, after we were on the continent, things started picking up a little bit. I think the Germans started getting worried about who was going to get blamed for mistreatment, and stuff like that. The camp commander wasn't any dummy. He was going to protect his ends, so we ended up getting one parcel for four people the last few months, so that was good. There was some sugar and a can of either Spam or something like that, cocoa. Our cooks made some great things.

Oh, we did get bread. That's the main thing the Germans gave us was bread, like a pumpernickel loaf. It was not big, and it was black. We [heard] that the sawdust content was reduced to 10%, so I don't know what it was before that. Anyway, you could cut a slice of that about an eighth of an inch thick, and hold it right on the edge; it wouldn't even bend. [*Laughs*] Good stuff. I was a great bread eater all my life, and it was great. We'd get one-eleventh of a loaf of bread per day, per person. For breakfast, you'd have a piece of bread with some margarine on it. You'd get margarine in the Red Cross parcels. The Red Cross really saved us.

The guards were older. Most of them had been on the Russian front. They'd been wounded, and some of them were a little bit crippled from their wounds, a limp or an arm that they couldn't straighten out or something like that, and all [seemed to be] older guys. Yeah, we got along well with them. We didn't do anything to antagonize them. They were just hoping the war would be over soon, same as we were.

They had speakers in the camp, and we'd get German news broadcasts every afternoon. That was slanted, of course, and you didn't always get the truth from them. I remember when Cassino fell. It took them about four days to admit on the German broadcast that the Battle of Cassino... They never did say they lost it, but they say, 'We moved back to better defensive positions during the night,' or something like this.[104] Some ingenious Englishman there built some kind of radio that he could get the BBC broadcasts from. He kept it hidden. Nobody knew where it was, and nobody in our camp knew where it was. He copied that down every morning and sent it out on a piece of paper to somebody who was authorized to travel from one compound to another. They'd come in. The guy would come in with his piece of paper, and he'd brief everybody in the barracks on it after we posted guards to make sure that no Germans were around, so we'd get the BBC within 24 hours. We knew when the [D-Day] invasion occurred, and we heard all the high points: Saint-Lô and Caen and all those.

*

My mother received notification that I was a PoW about two to three months after I was captured, but my brother was in the 1st Armored Division. He came through our area there in North Africa when they were going back to rest camp after Tunisia fell. He met some of the guys in my squadron. Lo and behold, later he ran into

---

[104] *Battle of Cassino*-The Allies waged a months-long struggle in the first half of 1944 to dislodge Germans entrenched at a centuries-old monastery in the mountains on their way to Rome. At the time it was considered a paramount objective, and the Benedictine abbey was reduced to rubble by American heavy bombers—which ironically gave German paratroopers greater flexibility and cover in its defense. Monte Cassino fell on May 19, 1944, after over 50,000 Allied casualties and 20,000 Germans killed or wounded.

one of the same guys, probably at rest camp, too. This guy told my brother that I had been shot down, but they told him I bailed out, and they thought I was all right, so he wrote my mother. Everything was pretty good until she got that telegram.

My mother could write to me. I don't think she was restricted on how often she could write to me, but she was restricted on things she could send me. She could send a little box about every 60 days. I'd write about once a week to her, once a week to my girlfriend. After we got communicating, which took like six months of back and forth before we got our records straight, then she was sending me long winter underwear and socks. The box would be opened, and I'd go through everything. As far as I know, everything was there. I ended up with two sets of long winter underwear. When we marched out of that camp, I had both sets on. It was January 1945, and there was six inches of snow.

Marched Out

We marched south. I can't remember the little villages we passed through, but our terminal was a town called Cottbus.[105] It was about 45 or 50 miles, and it took us five days to get there because there were 10,000 of us. The winter conditions didn't help any. The first night out was absolutely wicked. You're all spread out, 10,000 guys. Some guys probably had good accommodations, relatively. Our group ended up in a stable. We slept on a concrete floor of this stable that didn't have any windows in it or doors. The wind whistled through there. We each had one blanket. This fellow from Wisconsin and I bunked together, so it gave us one blanket below and one above. It was a miserable night. Then we were out walking again the whole next day. We ended up in a factory, the second

[105] Cottbus is the second-largest city in Brandenburg, Germany, about 125 km southeast of Berlin, and a major railway junction.

floor of a factory.[106] The heat was pouring up in that place so much you could hardly... What a contrast, you know? It almost drove us right out it was so hot, one extreme to another.

Colonel Spivey was our camp commander, quite a wonderful gentleman. I'm sure he did a lot of things that I wasn't aware of, but he also did a lot of things that we all weren't aware of. I can't think of anything specific right now, but he was protecting us all the time and fighting with the German kommandant. There again, the story went that he got easier to fight with as the war progressed. Anyway, then we got on the train at Cottbus and took off, and we got in Leipzig just before midnight. Sure enough, we just got in there, and the air raid sirens went off, but we didn't have to wait too long, and they pulled the train out. What did happen was 10,000 guys had just had this soup, or some damn thing that the Germans served us and called it soup. We didn't know what was in it, and we hadn't had any solid food to speak of. I had a little bit of bread and margarine and cheese, but I was rationing that to myself, so we were all very hungry, and we ate this soup.

We got in Leipzig, and everybody needed to go to the bathroom. They opened up the doors. I think there were like 2,000 in our group on this train. We took one look around. There were women and kids. There are no men, just the guards. One of the sights of the war was watching 2,000 men go to the bathroom right out there in the open, I guess, with all these people watching. We had no choice.[107]

---

[106] *We ended up in a factory*-this march is further discussed in the chapter entitled 'B-17 PoW Reunion'; they were evacuated away from the rapidly advancing Russian armies. The factory refers to a pottery factory, and the fact that these freezing, sick prisoners were given shelter there saved many lives on the evacuation march.

[107] *We had no choice*-the men were probably suffering extreme intestinal discomfort due to the contaminated 'soup.' This incident is also recounted in the chapter entitled 'B-17 PoW Reunion.'

We got out of Leipzig and went down to Munich. Then we walked back up to Moosburg, and we spent the rest of the war there. There were 30,000 prisoners there then. A lot of them were Hungarians and Greeks and Romanians, people from that part of Europe. I know we had some civilians in there. Anyway, we were separated a little bit from them, not completely.

Liberation

We'd walk around for exercise. I got to be a good walker. That's what I did in Stalag III, I'd walk around that compound I don't know how many times. It's a thousand yards around, and I'd get my legs in shape. That really helped me when we marched out of there, I can tell you that. So I was walking around with a friend one morning. I think it was the 28th of April, and we could look up there on the hill. We could see something coming out of the woods, and we didn't know what the heck it was. It turned out to be a Sherman tank!

We got it on the radio that General Patton's army had got to Nuremberg, and elements of his army had turned south. That's what they said, so sure enough, here comes some of his army. Pretty soon, there were six tanks up there. Then the small arms fire started right in the woods, right next to us. We didn't even know there was anybody out there, and all this machine gun fire was starting up! We all piled into the trench we had and tried to watch the war [in front of us].

The village of Moosburg had a couple of church steeples, and the Hitler Youth went up in the church steeples with machine guns. They were shooting up the road, so the tanks blew those churches right down, both of them.

[The guards] were exiting. I think a couple of guards got hit by gunfire, but all the rest of them were gone, and we never saw another German. This all started about 9:30 in the morning, and at 12:30, a Sherman tank came rolling right into the camp. It got a tremendous welcome. Then they put our own military police around the place so people couldn't get out, which was reasonable. We don't want to turn 30,000 people out in the roads right behind the front that had just barely gone through.

This guy, Red Hanson from Iowa, he says, 'Let's get out of here.'

I said, 'I'm with you.'

We went out under the fence that night with our own guards on the fences—figured that if they saw us, they wouldn't shoot. Anyway, nobody saw us. It was pretty slim guarding, I guess, so we got out. We go down on the road, and it took us two days to get to Nuremberg. It was probably about 100 miles or so. We hitchhiked with American Jeeps and stuff, anybody who happened to be going along. Every time we got [a lift], we'd have to prove ourselves. We looked like hell, you know. I had an Eisenhower jacket on and British woolen pants and some kind of English woolen hat, a military hat, no rank insignia, nothing whatsoever, no dog tags. They were all gone. None, nothing, absolutely nothing. The first guy who stopped had his pistol right out. He was a captain. We were really sad-looking, so he asked us a lot of questions about Brooklyn Dodgers and all this. Finally, we convince him we're Americans, and he gave us a ride up the road. Then we had to go through it all again; it took us two days to get to Nuremberg. We went to the wrong airfield first, but then got to the right airfield where there were C-47s bringing 50-gallon drums of gasoline in for the tanks, and we convinced the operations officer that we were Americans, even though we looked like bums. He gave us a tent to sleep in. We got on that C-47 the next day, and we flew back to Le Havre [France], and we were met there by some Red Cross ladies, who hugged us even though we looked so bad.

We went to Camp Lucky Strike. We were either among the first to go through there, or there was a lull in operations, because they had a thousand pyramid tents out there, and there were only about a half a dozen occupied.[108] We showered. Man, that was great; something as simple as a shower is awful good when you don't have any. Then they deloused us—a guy came around with what looked like a flamethrower on his back and a big hose. Boy, he blew us in places we didn't even know we had! [*Laughs*] Then they issued us new clothes. They put us on five meals a day but with restricted quantities, which was okay, because we probably would have ruptured ourselves if we'd got into all of the mashed potatoes and gravy and stuff. That worked out good.

I was only there about three days and they announced they had some openings on one of the ships going back in a 26-ship convoy to Boston, so I got on a troop ship. Actually, all the ships went to New York, but my ship went to Boston. I can't remember the name of it, but I remember we weren't on a restricted five meals a day [regimen] anymore. Boy, did I eat! [*Laughs*] I think I gained 20 pounds on that trip.

[At Boston] we got on a train and went out to Fort Devens and stayed overnight, and the next morning we were on a train again and went down to New York City, then out to Fort Dix, where I was processed out. I wasn't forced out. I had a choice. I could stay in if I wanted to, but I elected to get out, not knowing any better. I

---

[108] *Camp Lucky Strike*- The so-called 'Cigarette Camps' were located in the Le Havre, France, port area, set up immediately after the liberation of this area following D-Day as depots and supply camps for combat staging. Mr. FitzGibbon arrived as they were transitioning over to repatriating American GIs and PoWs. Camp Lucky Strike was probably the largest of these, a tent city that reached nearly 60,000 at its peak. Other camps included Old Gold, Chesterfield, Pall Mall, and five others. The code names were designated primarily for security reasons. See www.skylighters.org/special/cigcamps for a good discussion.

got out and got transportation back into Manhattan, where my mother was living at that time. My train pulled into Penn Station, evidently before my mother could get everyone there. I headed for the nearest barbershop, where I had a shampoo, a shave, and a haircut. She had my old foot locker there with all my old uniform clothes in it, so I had everything except the tie, so I got all my uniform on except the tie. Soon she arrived, followed by my Aunt Lil and Uncle Fred and Bob and Shirley, who are my cousins. We had a big rendezvous with the family and walked down to this big restaurant in Greenwich Village and had dinner. I was treated like a hero. For George FitzGibbon, the war was over.

As a reserve officer, George FitzGibbon was recalled during the Korean War when they needed pilots. He stayed in the Air Force, retiring in 1969 as a lieutenant colonel, the operations officer of the 41st Air Refueling Squadron at Griffiss Air Force base in New York. He passed away at the age of 93 on May 5, 2015.

Charlie Corea (center) and GI buddies, World War II.
Photo: Corea family.

CHAPTER FIVE

The First Engineer

Charles P. Corea hailed from Rochester, New York, just north of where I went to college before returning to Hometown, USA to begin my teaching career. I did not actually have the opportunity to know him personally, but felt he shared a kinship with many profiled in this book, especially since he served in the 100th Bomb Group, 'affectionately' known by its members as 'The Bloody Hundredth.' He was trained as a flight engineer on a B-17 but did double duty as the top turret gunner on some of his missions, including his final one the day he was shot down. This interview took place just seven weeks after the September 11, 2001, terrorist attacks.

'We're all in the same boat. We all did what we had to do. I was telling this to a friend of mine the other day, that when we entered the service back in 1942, right after Pearl Harbor, all my friends and buddies and classmates, we went in and there was no doubt about what we had to do. I've never seen that much cooperation and patriotism until September 11th. That's the only good thing that came out of September 11th, the country coming together like it did back in 1941.'

*

Charles P. Corea

My godfather owned the creamery in Macedon, and my father was a cheese maker, and that's how I happened to be born in Macedon, New York. He came to this country back in the late 1800s, 1898 or 1901, and I was born there in 1921, and at the age of 18 months, we moved to East Rochester, where he worked for the dairy there. And that's how I became an 'East Rochesterian,' and I've been there ever since. Grew up in East Rochester, married the police chief's daughter—he gave me an offer I couldn't refuse, [*Laughs*] one of those things, and we've been living in the same house she was born in since then.

I graduated from East Rochester High School in 1940. For a short time I worked in the Merchant's Dispatch Transportation Company, making box cars and rail cars.

I was living with my mother and dad, and Pearl Harbor was on a Sunday. East Rochester on Friday and Saturday nights was a busy town. It was a working man's town. I used to do a little work for this fella who ran the hotel, like a gopher for the guys that played a little poker, so I generally got up a little later on Sunday morning. I remember getting up. I don't know what time of the day it was. I heard it on the news that Pearl Harbor had been bombed. Being a youngster, that was not as serious, in my estimation, as the recent happenings of 9/11 were, because the implications actually seemed a lot less to me as a person at the time. [But] the war had begun.

I remember playing cards that evening, and there were a couple of guys [who were anxious] to sign up. Wc were the first ones there at the draft office about 6:30 the next morning. I got called up in September of '42.

'Colorblind as a Bat'

We went to Fort Niagara and we took some aptitude tests. At the time I was gung-ho, I thought maybe I'd get into the [Air Force] cadets. I'm a young kid, I thought maybe I'd get one of those P-40s and play around with it, right? When you're young, you think you can do anything. I took a written test and passed that okay. Then I had to take a physical. At the time Fort Niagara was busier than heck. I took my eye test, passed that okay, and I was walking out the door and the guy called me back and says, 'One more test.'

That test was for color vision. He said, 'What did you see? See any numbers there?'

I kept wincing and stuff and he kept flicking the pages over. He put me down, 'Failed.' He said, 'You're colorblind as a bat!' He threw me out.

I got back [to the barracks] and the major said, 'Why'd you take the test if you knew you were colorblind?'

I said, 'I'm not colorblind. That guy was [too busy] and pushed me through like crazy.'

He picked up a yellow pencil and says, 'What color is that pencil?'

I says, 'Yellow.'

'You want to take the test over again?'

I said, 'Sure.'

The next day I got shipped out to Atlantic City. That was the end of my second test, but it turns out I am colorblind, browns and greens and stuff like that. Yellow, blues, and solid colors I can get away with.

I ended up in Atlantic City and I was with a couple of friends of mine. We stayed together, we all went in together. I remember we passed an aptitude test on whether you were a good candidate for radio or armament or photography. Having a decent education I had my choice of about seven or eight different qualifications. I remember talking to my buddy, who wanted to go to radio school, into switching over to go to photography school. I said, 'That way we'll get to do photography and we'll still get to fly around taking pictures instead of something else.' I talked him into that and he switched his number one choice from radio to photography. When I made my first choice, photography, the guy asked me, 'What do you want for a second choice?'

I said, 'I don't care.' We put down aircraft mechanics.

Well, the next call up was for aircraft mechanics, and I went and said, 'Hey, Jerry, why aren't you packing?'

He says, 'I wasn't called up.' The irony was that he ended up going to Denver to become the photographer! I ended up going down to Seymour Johnson Field in North Carolina, helping build that airfield because it was new in the war. I ended up being a mechanic for that duration they taught us. Then when we finished that particular school, they asked us, 'Who wants to take some examination for aerial gunnery?'

I says, 'I do, but I'm colorblind.'

He says, 'Go down and take it anyway.' They needed gunners pretty badly, and I passed that; instead of 20/20 I was 20/15, and he was very easy on me when I started going through the chart: 'Take your time, read the chart.' I ended up only missing four or five out of twenty. He passed me okay.

We became aerial gunners. We went down to Fort Myers, Florida, and went to school there and did some practice flying and shooting at targets. Then they took us from there and sent us to Lambert Field in St. Louis. It was at the Curtiss-Wright [plant]; they put us in that technical school. There were only 30 or 40 of us, and we had civilian instructors and they really taught us like you were going to a legitimate [military] school, the aerodynamics and the systems and the whole thing. We were the only Army personnel in the school. I got corporal stripes at Fort Myers gunnery school, and after getting out of that St. Louis school, they gave me sergeant stripes.

*

The war in Europe was going badly for bombers and they needed the B-17s. Everybody that had any knowledge of gunnery and stuff, they put them on B-17s. We went to Salt Lake City to get put on crews. Because of my training, they made me first engineer on a B-17. I had been carrying around this big technical book all the time about hydraulic systems [from the previous school], and I get on B-17 and it's all electrical. They gave me an assistant engineer who didn't know as much as I did, you know what I mean? But they needed personnel, they needed numbers.

They sent me up to Moses Lake, Washington. We trained there for quite a while forming groups: pilots, copilots, navigators and bombardiers, and the rest of the crew, which was ten people. We did some high-altitude missions and some hedge hopping. It was a fun time, because now we're flying, we're going down the Columbia River Basin, hedge hopping along the river and over the bridges and stuff like that. Here you are, twenty-one years old, and you've got the world pretty good. We'd go to places like Wenatchee, which only had about 50,000 people; we were the only Air Force personnel there. We couldn't buy anything; the people would just go to the bar, they would buy you a drink, or you'd go to the restaurant and they'd pay for the lunches. That was about the time that the Philippines was lost, and I don't know if you remember [a hero from that period] in history, Colin Kelly. Colin Kelly dove his B-17 into a Japanese destroyer, got the Congressional Medal of Honor for killing himself, and now the people were all gung-ho.[109] It's just like the euphoria that we have now with the September 11th deal.

---

[109] *Colin Kelly*-Colin Kelly, Jr. (1915-1941) piloted bombing runs against the Japanese navy in the first days after the Pearl Harbor attack. He ordered his crew to bail out during an attack shortly before his bomber exploded on

We trained and trained and trained, and now we're ready to ship out. We've got this group formed, overseas training group formed, and the next thing you know I've got to take another physical. I go in and everything's the same, and, boom, this time they give me a color test with yarn. They have different colored yarns. Well, Christ's sake, dark green, light green, brown, just flunked me again. They grounded me!

I'm saying to them, 'Hey, I've got all this training. Why the heck do I need [to see] colors? I'm going to be in a plane; all I'm going to do is shoot some [colored] flares.' Anyway, this buddy of mine got grounded because he had to go home; his wife had an emergency operation, so he lost his crew. We were chumming around before we got placed in another group, because he was a first engineer too.

He says to me, 'Go in and tell them that you were in the sunlight and the light bothered you and ask them for another test.' When they called me in for another test, he went in and took it for me.

I went in and I remember Major Barry put a waiver on my records, waived the color vision. Ray keeps telling me he took the test for me; [later] he wrote a letter about doing this for me. Anyway, to make the story chronological, I got on the crew. First thing you know, we did our training, we were flying overseas in January of '44.

Going Overseas

We had a real pilot. He was a very quiet type of guy. He never said much of anything. The copilot and the bombardier and myself, being up in front all the time, we got closer together than I did with

---

December 10, 1941, killing him. It was the first American B-17 to be shot down in combat. He was posthumously awarded the Distinguished Service Cross, and a Liberty ship was named after him.

the rest of the crew. When we got to England, we would chum around together.

I had to do a lot of jobs as the engineer. In normal duties, I logged everything. I logged the pilots, copilots, the names, the time, and all the crew. I put everything in a log: when we took off, and all the pertinent things. [I also did odd things], like during combat I remember a couple of times I had the tail-wheel pin sheared off. I had to crawl back in there and put a screwdriver in there so it would stay straight when we landed. A couple of times you had to turn the landing wheels manually to put them down; sometimes you get a little jam up in there or something like that. That was my job. In combat, I was also the top turret gunner.

We went to a place called Thorpe Abbotts.[110] It's about 99 miles north of London. It was great, but I wasn't there long enough to really enjoy it. What happened is we got there in January, but after our training we didn't get to the group until February, and they put us right into the thick of things. Everything went along pretty good until you got shot, until you went down, or until you got killed. The 'Bloody Hundredth' is probably one of your more famous groups; we ended up with [very high] casualties.

The Fifth Mission

I was shot down on March 6, just my fifth mission. It was the first daylight raid where the whole 8th Air Force got to Berlin. We tried to get there a day or two earlier and we had to abort because of bad weather conditions. A couple of wings did a couple of 180s

---

[110] *Thorpe Abbotts*- Home of the 'Bloody Hundredth.' The base was under USAAF control from June 1943 to the end of the war. Some of the airfield survives today, and it is the home of the 100th Bomb Group Memorial Museum. Source: Imperial War Museum, American Air Museum, www.americanairmuseum.com/place/373.

right into each other and we lost something like 31 planes—you couldn't see where you were going or anything. Worst feeling in the world; that was probably even hairier than the day I was shot down.

Anyway, we were in the lead group, and on the previous mission, we had lost one engine and we had to borrow a different squadron's plane to go on this particular mission on the 6th of March. If you had a crew able to go, and another squadron had a plane that was in mechanical good condition and yours wasn't, you went up in the other plane. It happened to be an 'all-out effort,' so General Doolittle didn't care who he sent up there; he sent us up there, 810 bombers, I think, and it was like 150 fighters or something like that. Out of those 810 bombers, we lost 69. Out of our group alone, we lost 15; most of that was due to German fighters.

Our group had taken off with thirty-six planes, six of which aborted because of mechanical problems. Out of the thirty that continued on, only fifteen got to the target. Out of those fifteen, I guess only a handful ever got back to our base, because they all scattered to different groups.

Our fighter support went a short ways with us, but they weren't there at that time. We were lead group. When you have that many planes in the air and that few fighters, you couldn't get them all. We got shot down around noontime by a Messerschmitt. I was in the top turret shooting at them, and I could see [their faces] as clearly as I'm looking at you. They wiped us out completely.

Our particular squadron, the 349th, was lead squadron that day, but when we borrowed this particular plane from the 351st, they stuck us with that squadron. We filled in on the triangle of the 351st; they put us in the last plane in their squadron because we didn't belong to them. You can visualize the lower element being four planes. [*Gestures with hands*] One, then two on the side, and one on the bottom. That's where we were, and on the Messerschmitt's first pass, he knocked out those first three planes! Also, he hit the lead plane, knocked it out—hit the tail. The guys survived and got back to England, but the fighter knocked up their dorsal fin. They came in, they didn't care; they were just very [bold] because they didn't want us to get to Berlin.

'They just devastated us'

Now this is noon, March 6, a very clear, bright, sunny day, very cold. Being the last plane in the element, of course, I was panning behind us, and as I'm turning I can see some flashes out of a waist gunner from one of the planes above in the upper element. I whipped the gun around as fast as I could from the back of the plane to the front of the plane, my twin .50s, and I just caught the fighters coming in, right out of the sunlight; they came swooping in wingtip to wingtip. You see, they had learned different tactics. Earlier in the war they would just dive in one after another. Well, one after another you could shoot each one at a time, but coming in this way they just strafed the whole group. They just devastated us.

Anyway, as I'm firing the top turret at them, they're coming over, and we're the last ones, so now he's pulling up. As he's pulling up and making his turn, I'm following him the same way. God as my witness, as I'm following for a split couple of seconds or so, he's banking this way, I'm banking with him. I'm looking at him and he's looking at me. You could see him looking over with his mask on, and he could see me obviously. I'm following him with the damn turret and you could see bits of the plane coming off his tail section, but not enough to bother him. As I'm turning, the electrical cord on my flying suit got caught underneath the swivel of the turret. As it got caught on the swivel of the turret, I couldn't turn it anymore.

The first thing I needed to do was to get down and untangle it. I ducked down, I untangled it, and right beneath the flight deck, the canvas over the gyro-equipment was on fire from a tracer round from the enemy. I took an extinguisher and I put the fire out. This couldn't have taken any more than two or three minutes, whatever it was. I put that out. Now I got back into my turret. Fellas, the turret wasn't there anymore. That son-of-a-gun who had been eyeing me came in and he hit his 20mm gun, took the top of that Plexiglas and tore it right off! Now I get up there, my guns are immobilized, and there's no turret! That's when I say, 'Oh boy.'

I got down; now I'm helpless. Now we're defenseless. The planes ahead of us have been shot down, we're lumbering along at 180 miles an hour, and these fighters were just [warming up] for target practice.

I got up between the pilot and copilot where I generally stand. I said to Lt. Coper, the pilot, 'Hey, Cope, I see some clouds down there about 10,000 feet below us. Dive down for those clouds.'

In the meantime my bombardier comes down, and he's just a step down to the front of the plane. He's a big fella, about 6'1 or 6'2. He says, 'Hey, Charlie, what are we going to do?'

[In the heat of things], I forgot about him, completely forgot about him. His flying clothes were all shredded like a cat had scratched him, from shrapnel, but he wasn't injured. I looked at him. I said, 'What the hell do you want from me? Bail out!' After I saw him in the [German] hospital later, he told me he kicked out the navigator's hatch right then, which was fortunate for him because when it was time for me to jump, I couldn't get out of the plane because the plane was in a spin.

I'm there for another three or four minutes when the fighters make another pass. In the meantime, they hit a couple of our engines; I think number three was on fire. Finally, they made another pass and they shot away our controls! We peeled off into one of these spirals—you've seen them on television where the plane will come over on its back and just spiral into the ground. That's when

I decided it was time to get out; [the whole time before] I figured we'd get back home—you know, optimistic. I didn't figure we were going to [crash].

We were at 21-22,000 feet when this happened. Anyway, I grabbed a hold of a chest pack parachute, because in a turret you can't wear a chest pack, there's not enough room. Trees are coming up at me, and I can't get the damn thing situated! The plane kind of gave a lurch, and all of a sudden I got it snapped on. I had my hand on the ripcord and out I went, headfirst.

Ordinarily the navigator's hatch is a couple of feet behind the number two propeller. Because we were spinning in, you're going down, so now you're actually going into the prop. I did half a flip; my foot was out and the prop caught my foot, split my foot right down the middle!

I pulled the ripcord as soon as I went out, and the chute opened immediately, and I said to myself, 'I don't want to drag my foot.' I landed, and as God is my witness, I landed just like I stepped off this chair, into a plowed field. Never had a chance to look up at the parachute silk or even down at the ground. My copilot went out right after me and he landed about 50 feet away, and about another 100 feet from him was where the plane crashed. That's how close to the ground we were; [none of the others got out of the plane in time]. Now I'm on the ground and this foot is split wide open. I hobble over to my parachute silk, and we're trying to tie a tourniquet around my leg when the bombs start popping. We were carrying twelve 500-pounders. There were some trees in between us, and every time they would go off, the shrapnel would come down like rainfall.

Anyway, we had just missed this farmhouse. We were in this field in northern Germany. The people from the farmhouse, they had little shelter. They had dug a four-foot square hole in the back of their house where they were staying. The only male in the whole contingent was a guy probably running the Home Guard or whatever he was. He came down, and the first thing he asked was if we had a 'pistola' or something. They issued us .45s, but I never carried one. I said, 'Nah, no pistola.'

'That's not Holland, buddy'

You've got to remember this was three months before the invasion, so the whole continent was occupied by the Germans. This was northern Germany. You come over the Channel and you fly through Holland and then you go east into Berlin. Anyway, Gordon, my copilot, the first thing he asked the guy, 'Where are we? Where are we?'

The guy kept saying, 'Deutschland, Deutschland.'

He said, 'Hey, Charlie, we're in luck. This is Holland.' Get this, the queerest thing about this is the copilot was of German descent, but he didn't understand a word of German. I said, 'Nice going, Gordon. That's not Holland, buddy.'

Now I'm bleeding pretty good, and these bombs start to go off, and I said, 'Well, we've got to get the hell out of here.' I start hobbling up towards the farmhouse. I jumped on one foot and I had my arm around my copilot. My foot would go this way and my toes would go that way. It was like a squirt gun, blood was coming out so bad. Anyway, I got up there and I was still trying to tie a tourniquet around my ankle where the bones are protecting your veins; I started up there where you've got more access to your veins. I'm starting to lose quite a bit of blood. As a matter of fact, one time, blood was squirting out so bad it would be like a water pistol from here to you. It just squirted right out of me, and that's how it was. I had to put my finger on the vein to stop the thing from squirting. The plane's on fire and the bombs are going off and I'm saying, 'We're about to get killed by our own damn bombs.' I turn around and try to say something to Gordon. Next thing I know, one of the bombs goes off and he's in that trench with those old ladies, lying down. I says, 'So much for help from him.'

I hobbled over to this farmhouse, which was maybe fifty feet away from this trench. It was an old farmhouse with a big barn attached to the kitchen. I got into the kitchen and they had some ladder back chairs. I took two of the ladder back chairs, turned them around, leaned back, and had my foot elevated, and it was enough to make me come back to my senses a little bit because I was starting to feel real faint. A short time later, two German soldiers came in, and I remember one was real sympathetic and the other was a little hard-nose, which wasn't too bad, because one out of two ain't bad.

One guy was saying, 'We'll take you to see a doctor.'

I said, 'Well, please.'

The other guy was telling me, 'Well, you should have thought about that before you took off,' or something like that.

Anyway, this one guy, here he sees my foot, so he starts sprinkling this sulfanilamide powder on it. At least he got it on there, right? They took me to a little crossroads in this little farm country.

Now you've got to remember, we were one of the lead groups; this was at noon, and we're still flying over. You've got eight hundred and ten B-17s and B-24s. If you were standing there watching the lead group go by for the whole mission, it would take you three hours before the last plane would fly over that particular position. That's how many planes came over; it was an 'all-out effort.' We had little spaces in between but you would have that many planes. Later on, as we got control and they produced more planes, the missions got a little heavier where you had thousand-plane raids. You've got all the German Air Force shooting, and it's like the Fourth of July. From the ground, it's noisier than hell, and then everything they shoot up comes down again, the artillery and flak and everything else. You could see why the people are really desperate down below.

The Operation

They took me to this little infirmary, and they had me on this metal operating table, and some guy with a flak helmet comes in. He severed my toes and tied the foot up. My big toe and the next toe were lying there by themselves in an enamel pan, but even then I was grateful. They did it without any anesthetic, which didn't bother me, because I didn't know what the hell this was about. Those German doctors that operated on me March 6, I never had anything else done to that foot since then, so it had to be pretty good. Today, similar circumstances with the toes still hanging on, they probably would have done microsurgery and probably would have stitched them together, but you've got to remember this goes back 56, 57 years.

They wrapped it up and they put me in an ambulance, sent me to a hospital in Oldenburg there, which was a secondary hospital. We were practically the first prisoners that they ever saw, and this was March 6, '44. They operated on me [again]. Of course, I had anesthetic then; they gave me some ether and stuff. I remember the two surgeons that did the operation, one was a captain and one was a first lieutenant, and they were both graduates from Heidelberg Medical School. I thanked them later on, and then I remember the younger guy sitting next to me while I was lying there. 'Well, we're first doctors,' he says, 'then we're soldiers.' Which meant he was going to take care of us.

He also asked me how many missions I was on. Of course, I said, 'Ah, that was my first one.' It didn't make any difference. They knew more about me than I knew about myself.

About thirty days later I was interrogated down there in Frankfurt. I remember the ride in this railroad car. For the last couple of days we hadn't had anything to eat, and we got into this interrogation center. One of the guards there put me in this little room, little cell. I said to him, in German, 'Hey, buddy.' I'd been there long enough to know a couple of words in German. I evidently got through pretty good with those few words, because he hollered over, 'Hey, we've got a German from Brooklyn here.' [*Laughs*]

I said, in German, 'I'm just hungry.'

He said, 'Okay, I'll take care of you.' He made me believe that.

I went in and got interrogated; this first lieutenant interrogated me. He spoke English quite well. He could have been reading the list of my whole crew.

I said, 'Hey, wait a minute. Tell me, did these guys pass through here?'

He wouldn't answer me, but they didn't. I was asking him questions whether or not some of those boys were there. Of course, they weren't. They were all killed; just the three of us got out. There was no way for them to get out. I was fortunate to get out because I was in front of the hatch and we were up front, but in the back it was whipping pretty bad. In other words, he knew my whole crew and all their names and previous records before I even took off. They asked me different things, and I asked him more questions than he asked me.

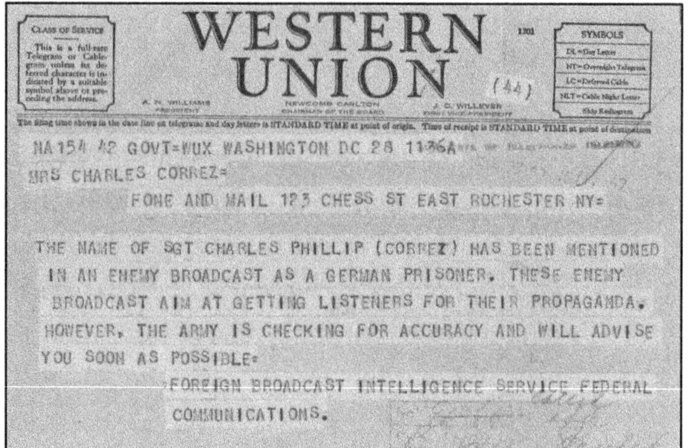

WESTERN UNION

NA154 42 GOVT=WUX WASHINGTON DC 28 1136A

MRS CHARLES CORREZ=

FONE AND MAIL 123 CHESS ST EAST ROCHESTER NY=

THE NAME OF SGT CHARLES PHILLIP (CORREZ) HAS BEEN MENTIONED IN AN ENEMY BROADCAST AS A GERMAN PRISONER. THESE ENEMY BROADCAST AIM AT GETTING LISTENERS FOR THEIR PROPAGANDA. HOWEVER, THE ARMY IS CHECKING FOR ACCURACY AND WILL ADVISE YOU SOON AS POSSIBLE=

FOREIGN BROADCAST INTELLIGENCE SERVICE FEDERAL COMMUNICATIONS.

Misspelled notice to Corea family giving update on Charlie's PoW status. Photo: Corea family.

Stalag 17

They sent us to Stalag 17-B, the world famous Stalag 17. They made a movie about it.[111] It was down in Krems, Austria, 40 kilometers west of Vienna. They had some of the first PoWs of the war—there were some there who were captured in North Africa. [But] most of us in our compound were all Air Force, non-commissioned officers, mostly 8th Air Force but 15th Air Force too. They also had French, Italians, and Russians, but they had different compounds.

We had an upper and lower level, with the center being the washrooms. Of course, they had double bunks. I was up in the infirmary for about 10 months, which was a break in that respect. The regular compound had these barracks—big washroom, lower barracks. Then they had a big, open field and they had a big latrine that took care of different barracks in the center. Then, of course, they had the main compound where you could walk around. Of course,

[111] *Stalag 17*- 1953 Oscar-winning film which tells the story of a group of American airmen in this PoW camp.

you were way out in no man's land; there was nothing but farmland around you.

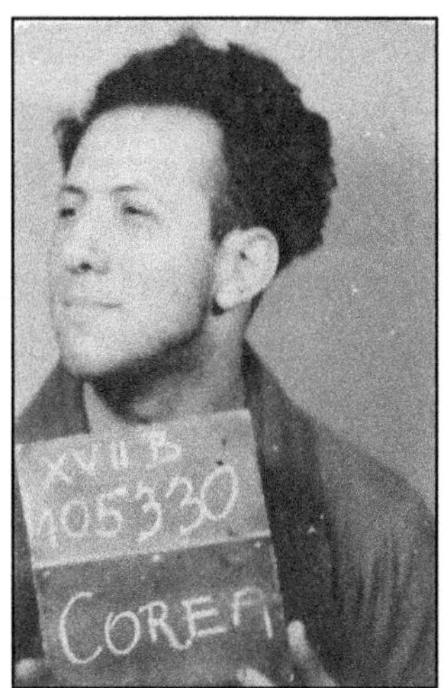

Charlie Corea, photo in captivity.
Photo: Corea family.

The conditions inside the barracks were kind of barren. I didn't get down there until about 10 months after I was a prisoner. They had some crystal sets that they were getting some information through BBC at night. What they would do is, after they turn the lights out, they would connect the antennas to the electrical circuit and use the electrical circuit as a big antenna. Then they would have this happen in maybe just one barrack or so. Then whatever news, they would come around and somebody would read it to us, that the war's going this way or that way. That was it, and, of course, we weren't allowed to work and we ended up with these parcels that the Red Cross gave us. We were fortunate, being down in Austria, close to Switzerland; that's where they were being distributed, through Switzerland. For the most part we were getting one package a week, and that took care of us pretty good. Later on, as things got a little hairy, you got maybe one package for two people. I don't know if you're familiar with it. It had a can of Spam, a ration of biscuits that looked like graham crackers, only very highly concentrated, and a good-size package of that. They had a two-ounce can of instant coffee, a larger can of dry milk, called 'Klim,' which is milk spelled backwards. It had a quarter-pound bar of cheese—sometimes you'd get Velveeta, sometimes you'd get American—along with a two-ounce can of jam or jelly, grape or strawberry or whatever. Five packs of cigarettes, and two D bars. D bars were like these great big Hershey bars, only they were thick and heavily concentrated—we used to have contests of how many you could eat before you threw up or something like that. [*Laughs*] Anyway, we used those D bars, they were our medium of exchange. The D bar was our gold standard and it was pretty good, like a can of strawberry jam, which was probably the most popular jam. If somebody wanted something, he may say, 'Look, I'll give you a D bar or a pack of cigarettes for it,' or something like that. The cigarettes were great, especially for bartering. I was a smoker, but not that much of a smoker. These Russians were in the compound next to us, and, of course, there was about three rows of wire between us. We could yell over, and they had a warning wire and everything else. They were workers. They would send them out to the farms and they would work in the fields, and, of course, they would bring home a package of onions, carrots, molasses, and stuff like that. I don't know where they got the molasses, but we would trade, and, of course, they didn't have no smokes at all. We'd fling over a pack of cigarettes, and they'd fling over a bag of onions or package of onions or carrots or potatoes; whatever they had, you know.

The Germans didn't mind too much, but the unfortunate thing was, you know, later in the war, some of the guards were a little younger and immature. I remember one of the times somebody threw over a pack of cigarettes towards the Russian barracks. This guy was in the window and he didn't quite get it, and it fell down below outside the barrack, which was inside the warning wire compound. Of course, the Russians had a more ruthless life anyway. The guy thought nothing of jumping down and picking it up and jumping back in.

Well, this particular day, this one young guard was over there, and he fired from the hip and happened to hit the guy as he was crawling back into the window. Killed him and let him lie there for half a day or so. The Germans transferred the guard the next day.

What we would [normally] do if something happened where a Russian would throw a bag of onions, say, and we had 20 feet of warning wire [and it fell short], we would bribe the guard to kick it over. You know what I mean? He'd say, 'What the heck.' It didn't bother him, so you'd give the guard a couple of cigarettes or something like that.

I never received any mail. For some reason it never got to me, but some of my mail got to my folks; I still have them. You didn't write too much, and I wouldn't worry my mother, just 'everything's fine and I'm okay.' They would block out anything else anyway. That part of it. I know my family was telling me that they would, back in those days, they'd go up to a place like Sibley's Department Store, and they used to have these packages for PoWs, and they would send whatever they got there; [I didn't see it]. But there were people who got their mail.

The End of the War

[Near the end of the war], the Germans were fighting a defending action against the Russians, along the Danube Road there. We were just north of the Danube. They decided to move the American prisoners out of camp towards Linz, Austria. Linz was the dividing line that passed down the agreement between Russia and the

United States that General Patton couldn't go any farther than that. He was at Linz, Austria, which was 60 kilometers northwest of us.

These last remaining Germans who were in charge of camp, they didn't want to be taken over by the Russians, naturally. They moved [everyone] out of the camp except for us wounded non-ambulatory people that were left, about 80 of us. They moved them out and marched them out of camp. We, of course, said goodbye. We figured, 'We'll see you. We're going back with Uncle Joe,' you know, Joe Stalin; we were naïve enough to think that he was a great guy. [*Laughs*] 'We'll see you when we get back,' and all that. When they moved a camp out and all the German officers left, a couple of guys went up to the headquarters and got some records. They got my service record and they got a little radio that was up there, and we got listening to the news.

We were all bunched up in this one part of the infirmary up on the hill. Of course, [the Germans] had supplies that Red Cross had sent and the mail up there that had never been distributed. There were packages that were sent to the prisoners [who were now evacuated], and I remember ending up with a couple boxes of Philly cigars and a brand-new baseball uniform that the Salvation Army had sent! Here they are, these beautiful white flannel baseball uniforms, pure white; I ended up wearing one of these white flannel uniforms, and I had a cigar. Then in marched some Russian or Jewish slave labor, I don't know what, to take the barracks that had been evacuated. We're on this side of the fence and we're watching these people come in. I'm a hell of a sight—here I am smoking a Philly cigar in a white baseball uniform, throwing cigarettes at these poor bastards who were coming across. You're twenty-two years old, what the heck. [*Chuckles*]

Anyway, these Russian troops came over into camp, and we were on the hillside, and they camped just on the high side. Our smiles went away pretty fast, because now [the Germans] are shelling the Russians from the top of the hill, and the Russians are going to shell them, and we're right in the middle! You've got about 80 Air Force guys trying to dig a foxhole! [*Laughs*] That was kind of scary, because the night that our GIs moved out, what they couldn't carry they decided to burn out in front of the barracks— planks, I don't know why. They just decided to burn what they couldn't take with them. So, of course, that night the ashes were smoldering. The Germans were still fighting this retreating action, so some night fighters see this, strafed the hell out of us. They could see these flickering lights, and the Russians are only a mile or two down in the same area. It got a little hairy, and that's when they even killed a couple of Germans, our guards.

The next day, we were in the top part of the barracks. Dangling out of the ceiling were all these cluster bombs that didn't go off. They looked like Christmas ornaments; that's how close it was! It got a little hairy right about then, because here we are, the war's over. We listened on BBC that night, I think May 7. *'At twelve o'clock the war will be officially over.'* No sooner had [the announcer] gotten that out of his mouth, this night fighter comes over and drops these cluster bombs like crazy [again]!

*

[The war's over.] For three or four days, we're in limbo here. The guys who went out to [try to arrange] our transportation, they didn't show up. What happened was they got to Linz and reported in, [told them] to pick up some American prisoners, so a convoy of three or four trucks was sent out to pick us up. They never notified the Russians. The treaty was 'don't go beyond that [line on the map].' The Russians knocked out the convoy! Then [our guys] had to go back and regroup the convoy—it was a week later we finally got taken out of there, and it's only 60 kilometers.

I got to go into the little town [near the camp] and visit some of the local people there; the Russians had come over by then. They were in the field and we walked right by them; they hardly looked up at us. Some of those cannons they had were horse-drawn. Couldn't believe it! They were sitting there eating whatever they had in their hand.

We were looking for maybe a bottle of wine; we asked the local people. I remember one family asking us to stay overnight. It's kind of funny. We found out the reason was they had a couple of young women there, their daughters. They figured if the Americans stayed overnight those scrubby Russians wouldn't come in and do who-knows-what to them. I don't remember if we stayed the night; I don't think I did.

Finally, we got out of there and got to Linz, Austria. We were flown out of Linz, Austria, to Camp Lucky Strike. We were supposed to fly home, but we finally went home by boat. We went home by an old cruise ship, the *Manhattan* or *American* or something like that. Anyway, there were a lot of experiences in between, naturally, but I could stay here for a week and talk to you about it.

*

'That's how I feel about it'

It's a funny thing when you get me talking about stuff like this. I can remember experiences, but if you ask me something that happened two days ago, like my wife will ask something, and I say, 'I don't remember.' That's what happens when you're eighty years old. You have old memories....

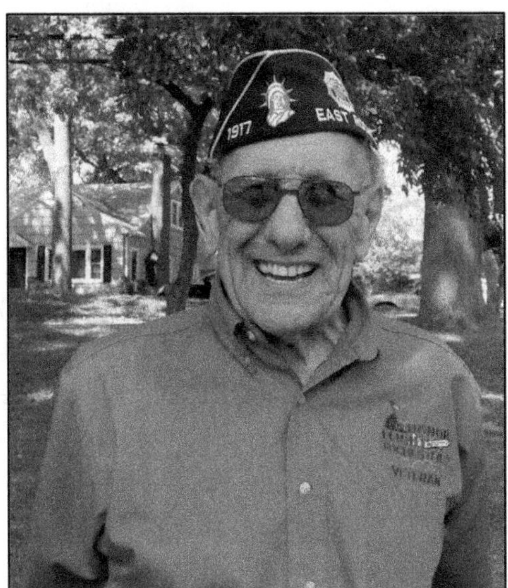

Charlie Corea.
Photo: Corea family.

I think I was very fortunate. Like everything in the military, you can get a medal for this, and a medal for that—it's just a matter of being in the right place at the right time, or in the wrong place. Like I just said, I received some awards, and the last one I got was for a state award. A young girl reporter asked me something about the war, about why did you get this.

She says, 'Well, you know you're quite a hero.'

I said, 'I'm not a hero. I have seven guys on my crew that were killed. How can I be a hero? I was lucky to get out. I was just a victim of circumstances.'

We got on talking about how I was lucky when I got out. The Germans operated on me and saved my foot and all that.

She said, 'Why would they do that?'

'Well, what do you mean?'

'Why would they take care of you?' That's how naïve these youngsters are.

I said, 'Well, there's a Geneva Convention that they had, and we take care of their prisoners and they hopefully take care of ours.' She couldn't understand.

'You're over there bombing them, and now you want them to take care of you.'

I said, 'Well, that's just the way it is. Stupid war. It's just the way it is. You get medals stupidly. You happen to be in the right place, you get a medal.'

That's how I feel about it. This is one of the very few times where I even talk about this... I get 30% disability. I'm sure if you saw my foot, I could probably get more. The system is there to be plucked if you want to pluck it, but I worked hard making a living while I was raising four children. You know what I mean?

[I look around today and] to me, sometimes I think it isn't worth it. [But then again], and I was telling this to a friend of mine the other day, when all my friends and buddies and classmates entered the service back in 1942, right after Pearl Harbor, there was no doubt about what we had to do. I've never seen that much cooperation and patriotism until September 11th. That's the only good thing that came out of September 11th, the country coming together like it did back in 1941. That's the closest feeling that I had to that, since.

[My friends and I], we went into the service, got out, we went on to college [or work]... I ran a little business, I published a paper, 39 years. I raised a family, put them through school, boom, boom—and all of a sudden we're eighty years old. I don't feel 80, but I'm 80. You'll find out as you get older, how fast time goes. You already realize that, right?

"I read The Greatest Generation. *I read three or four chapters of that. I put the book down. Somebody said, 'Why didn't you finish? Didn't you like it?'*

I said, 'No, I didn't finish, because everything he said was true and I already knew about it.' We all did the same thing; we all did what we had to do."

Charlie Corea passed away at the age of 92 on August 26, 2014.

Earl Morrow, Sam Lisica, Jerry Silverman. July 2001.
Credit: Author.

CHAPTER SIX

B-17 PoW Reunion

Earl M. Morrow was born in 1921 and was featured in Vol. II, detailing his early missions and all about the day that the B-17 bomber he was commanding was shot down, and his experiences that followed. In the summer of 2001, two of his World War II buddies came to his house to celebrate his 80th birthday. Earl asked me if I wanted to meet them, and I grabbed my video camera and headed over to sit with the three of them around Earl's dining room table. I interviewed him and the others, Sam Lisica of Pennsylvania and Jerome Silverman of Long Island, all formerly of the 457th Bomb Group of the U.S. Eighth Army Air Force during World War II.

All of them had been taken prisoner on November 2, 1944, near Volkstedt, in Germany, when their planes were shot down. Earl was the pilot and Sam was the bombardier on the B-17 'Delores' #4337766; Jerry was aboard the lead plane as the lead navigator for the mission that day and was picked up on the ground by enemy forces, winding up in the same German transport vehicle as Earl, where they met for the first time. This meeting was the first time in seven years that Earl and Sam had seen each other; Sam, who had bunked with Jerry in the PoW camp, had not seen Jerry since the end of the war. We sat at the dining room table at Earl Morrow's home. I set up my video camera; Earl, the pilot, was in another room, searching for some photographs. I began the conversation by asking some questions. It would turn out to be their last time together.

*

Together Again

Earl Morrow, pilot, 80
Sam Lisica, bombardier, 80
Jerry Silverman, navigator, 82

Matthew Rozell, interviewer: You were in the U.S. Army Air Force?

Sam Lisica, bombardier: The United States Army Air Corps, [in the beginning].

[*Earl Morrow enters the room with a crew photograph*]

Earl Morrow, pilot: We got lucky; I found it.

Sam, bombardier: That's the one we got in 1944.

Interviewer: You each got one?

Earl, pilot: Yes.

Jerry Silverman, navigator: Well, I don't have it with me. I showed a picture like that [to a young girl], and I said, 'You know when you see the parades and you see all these old people, these people marching with the flags and the hats and all? When you pass the cemetery and you see all the old people, grandmas and grandpas in the cemetery? Well, all those graves, the kids were 18, 19 and 20 years old...' Then I [showed the photograph], and I said, 'Next time you see a parade of old geezers, this guy here was 18, flying combat, this guy was 19, flying combat...'

Earl, pilot: [*points to picture*] This man here was 18.

Sam, bombardier: Yes, he just came out of high school. He was the waist gunner; he died the day we went down.

Earl, pilot: These three were killed the day we went down. This one retired in the 1980s as a brigadier general.

Interviewer: Which one are you?

Earl, pilot: [*pointing*] This is me, this is Sam, Bob; George is gone, Bill is gone, he was shot up real bad, but we got him out and he survived and he died in about 1978 or 1979—he was playing golf and he had a heart attack. George, the one next to him, he just passed away two years ago.

Crew photograph. Front row far left-Earl Morrow. Far right-Sam Lisica. Courtesy Earl Morrow.

Jerry, navigator, to interviewer: See that picture? Every crew had a picture like that; the army did that. The four in the front were generally the pilot, the copilot, the bombardier, and the navigator, or vice versa. These would be the enlisted men here [*pointing to top row in crew photo*]. See, these are the enlisted men, [and in the front], these are the officers.

Earl, pilot: [*pointing*] Radioman, waist gunner, top turret gunner, waist gunner, ball turret gunner; these two switched off and on and they were both killed. This other guy was qualified as an engineer also, but he didn't go with us that day. This is the tail gunner...

Sam, bombardier: We had ten men, but only nine flew, so every mission, someone would [sit it out]. Did you just have ten men in your crew?

Jerry, navigator: Oh yes.

Earl, pilot: In our group, they always pulled one waist gunner and left him home. One crew member stayed home.

Jerry, navigator: Never with us; we always had ten. I never flew a mission with nine people. Back when I was leading, we had two or three navigators [aboard one plane].

Earl, pilot: Well, they probably needed them, with you. [*Laughter*]

Jerry, navigator: If you're leading a group, it's one thing, but if you're leading a division or a wing, that's another one.[112] One was the lead navigator, one was the DR navigator, and one would just read our radar.[113]

Earl, pilot: You see, when we got over there, we always left one guy home, because we pulled the gunner off the radio, so if you get under attack, he goes back to the waist...

Jerry, navigator: You always have two waist guns, always.

Sam, bombardier: We had one.

Earl, pilot: [*pointing*] See, that's why Bellinger wasn't with us the day we were shot down.

---

[112] *leading a group, it's one thing, but if you're leading a division or a wing, that's another one*-Silverman refers to the size of the strike force a lead crew would be responsible for. A B-17 'squadron' might be six planes; by 1943, a heavy bomb 'group' included nearly 300 officers and 1,500 enlisted men to fly and service 48 B-17 bombers. Their 'wing' included 3 such groups.

[113] *DR navigator*-dead reckoning is the process of calculating one's position by estimating direction and distance traveled by using a previously determined 'fix' (position) and advancing that position based upon estimated speeds over time and course, rather than by electronic navigation methods.

Jerry, navigator: I was amazed at how many rounds I could shoot off. We went onto the back of the ship; you could kill yourself on all the shells all over the place—they're like marbles all over the place! You have to remember at this point I was the lead navigator and I didn't have any clue who I flew with; I didn't know any of these guys.

Earl, pilot: Yes, well, you flew in lead crews; it didn't pertain to you, what happened to us.

Jerry, navigator: My original crew had long since went home; the co-pilot and I came back for a second tour, but he and I didn't fly together because he was on a new lead crew, and he was on a crew that flew together.

Interviewer, referring to Jerry: You were the navigator, right?

Sam, bombardier: Group navigator.

Jerry, navigator: No, I was not a group navigator.

Earl, pilot: Squadron navigator.

Jerry, navigator: And I wasn't a squadron navigator.

Sam, bombardier: Lead navigator?

Jerry, navigator: No, not at that time.

Earl, pilot: What was your title then?

Jerry, navigator: I was a specialist navigator, but I navigated as a lead navigator. He's got more experience. They put you more forward—to lead the pack—because we always went in groups. There was the lead navigator, and the lead bombardier. We had to fly the target and help the bombardier fly close to the target.

Earl, pilot, to interviewer: And all we really needed to do was to follow the lead ship.

Jerry, navigator: We had to look at the [reconnaissance] pictures and see what the Germans were doing. A river would be like this [*mimics bends in a 'river' by snaking his hand across the tabletop*], and the target would be here [*gestures to a point on his 'river'*]. Many times we would have problems with clouds under us because we flew

20,000 to 25,000 feet. There would be a hole in the clouds, and [the Germans] would set up a whole city, a dummy [*decoy*].

[*Interviewer looks at him with incredulous expression*]

Really! If you see a hole in the clouds and you see this, you think this is it, that this is the target. It's a bend in the river the same as this; they'd duplicate it! There was a movie, *Command Decision* with Walter Pigeon, and it's exactly what happened to the navigator! They thought they hit the target and they got all excited, and then the navigator says that it's 'gross error.' He says, 'That was a dummy I hit.' It's in the movie.

And I'll tell you one thing, and this is documented. The Eighth Air Force—I don't know about the others, but I imagine the same thing—we would never turn back from a raid.

Interviewer: *Why not?*

Sam, bombardier: If we were told to go, we just went.

Jerry, navigator: The only time we turned back was because of really bad weather. That was the only thing. We had a recall for weather.

Earl, pilot: We couldn't see the ground unless we had the new radar, which they were just coming in with. There was no way to hit the target.

Jerry, navigator: Well, we still bombed; we just bombed through the clouds. On those days there was never really bad opposition from flak or fighters. We in the Air Command would say, 'We can't back up.' In the Air Command, it's not like the infantry; you can't say, 'Let's back up and regroup.'

8th AF B-17 Flying Fortresses, 396th Bomb Group, 1943.
Credit: USAF. Library of Congress, public domain.

Missions

Jerry, navigator: When we were in the air, we never turned back. They would put up so much flak, and we would never go around it before we hit another target. We went through the flak, straight for that target—we never dodged it. Each time we went through, we lost 50, 60, 70 bombers at a time, each carrying 10 men, and at the end of 1943 and three raids, if we had two more raids like that, we would have had no more Air Force. We would have been completely wiped out. So they just stood down.

Sam, bombardier: The RAF thought we were crazy; we thought they were crazy. Always doing it at night...

Jerry, navigator: They had a whole different conception; they bombed at night, but they weren't as heavily armed as we were.

They carried heavier bomb loads—we would never fly at night, it is dangerous as hell! They would never fly in the daytime; they would say you'd get killed doing that.

I copied [our high casualty rate] out of the book about the Eighth Air Force. The author said the Air Force had the highest casualties of any branch of service! I was stunned to read this in another book too, that the Eighth Air Force had more casualties than all of the Marine landings in the Pacific! And that really shook me up—the author states, 'You guys are heroes,' and we're not heroes, but when I read this, I decided, 'I am a damn hero.'

Interviewer: You must have lost a lot of friends. How did you deal with that?

Jerry, navigator: The way it was dealt with in many cases with the officers and the enlisted men—they were together, and then these guys finished up [*gestures to Sam and Earl*], and my guys finished up. And I went home after so many missions, 'rest and recuperation,' 'R&R,' which we called 'return and regret'—but anyway, we got through the thing. What happened when a crew went down, and replacements came through, was that word started getting around— 'Don't get friendly with these guys because it breaks your heart,' you know, so no one talked to anybody. But anyway, we got through the thing.

*

Interviewer: When you went over to England, who flew with Earl before you all got shot down?

Sam, bombardier: [*points to Earl, pilot*] We were the crew men on that plane.

Interviewer: Clarification—you two guys were on the same crew, that's why I have you in this photograph, and you had 17 missions before you got shot down.

Sam, bombardier: He had 17; I had 23.

Earl, pilot: There was a little period there where I got grounded.

Sam, bombardier: They were going to shoot him. [*Laughter*]

Earl, pilot: I tore up two airplanes one morning—wrecked them while we were taking off. It's simple, I just caught the tail section of the airplane in front of me with the wing tip, because we came up this taxiway and there was a portable tower sitting there, and we got into our right turn behind the next airplane, and we had no brakes—everything was gone! The tail wheel was turned, to keep us turned to the right. Well, we don't want to really tear up that tower there, and the airplane's in front of me and the tail's wrong, so at the last second, just to save everything we could, I had to gun the hell out of the two right engines and swing her around, and my wing tip caught the tail of one of the planes in front of me.

Sam, bombardier: Took the rudder off.

Earl, pilot: The problem was, the night before, someone came in and landed and took a building off its foundation! And the colonel said, 'Next time there is an incident, it'll be pilot error, one hundred percent,' and it was me. I fall into those things...

Jerry, navigator: The commanding officer of any unit is responsible, no matter what, and the pilot is responsible. Now if the mechanic does something wrong and the pilot, he's sleeping, and the mechanic is working at two o'clock in the morning, working on that airplane to get it ready, if something goes wrong, the end result in all commanding officers' opinions is that he's the pilot [*points to Earl*], he's responsible. In other words, Harry Truman later said, 'The buck stops here,' and that's what happened. Unfortunately, he had something mechanically wrong, but even though he didn't know anything, [in the colonel's eyes], it's going to be pilot error; otherwise some general's going to say, 'Colonel, what's going on?' He would then 'pass the buck.'

Earl, pilot: The co-pilot makes a mistake, and it's my fault for letting him make it. So you know when you get up there, you take the guff. So that's why we didn't come up with the same number of missions.

Jerry, navigator: [agreeing] That's why you didn't have the same number of missions.

Earl, pilot: Another reason is when I first got there, when I went on my first mission, I went out as a co-pilot with an experienced crew. The next day I went out as pilot, and I got all my crew, except my co-pilot; I got an experienced co-pilot. On the third mission, the crew was on its own.

Jerry, navigator: I came over before he did. When a group came over originally, you came over in one group. As you lost people, you got replacements. They [*Earl and Sam*] came over as another crew, as a replacement crew.

Interviewer: Were you at the same base?

Jerry, navigator: Same base, same squadron, same everything. So a whole crew got shot down, they put another crew in their beds.

Interviewer: *Did you know them at all before?*

Jerry, navigator: No, I never knew them. I had been there a while; I had never set eyes on them. Anyway, I came home; I've completed one tour, came home on what they call 'rest and recuperation.'

After 25 missions I could go home on leave. I could fly five more and stay home for good, or I could fly 25, go on leave, and come back again. If I chose to fly to thirty, I figured I could get killed on number 26, 27, 28, et cetera. I figured 'take what you got', you know, 'take your winnings and get off the table.' So I went home, and then I came back. Now I didn't come back [to my original] crew. I came back as a lead navigator, and I was put on as a lead crew navigator. They have crews who were trained to lead, they have other guys that come in to navigate. On the lead plane they had two guys navigating, one guy looking out the window, another guy doing the paperwork, the third guy was on the radio to make it as good as we possibly could get it.

I came back onto my second tour, and each time I flew, I flew with different people. I didn't even know the people I was on the plane with that day, but that's just the way it works. You know, when you fly, you have specialists: you have a special bombardier; the best bombardier in a crew, that sort of thing. What happened was here we are in a group of 36 aircraft in our combat box. We had twelve and twelve and twelve, so we were in the same unit. It was called a 'low box'; they called it a box because twelve [*points up*], twelve [*points middle*], and twelve [*points low*]—high box, lead box, and low box. When the Germans came, they came from behind, and they hit the low box and they took out seven planes, plus two more from our squadron.

*

Shot Down

Interviewer: And what was the target when you were shot down? It was November of '44, right?

Earl, pilot: It was November 2, 1944.

Jerry, navigator: Merseburg.

Earl, pilot: Merseburg synthetic oil field.

Interviewer: You were brought down by fighter planes?

Jerry, navigator: Fighters, yes. We got hit from behind—I never saw them. I heard the crew yelling, then the shooting, everything going on back there—I'm up at the front of the plane, this is going on in the tail. The Germans, at this point—previously they used to come in and attack individually—but at this point in the war they didn't have the gas to train their pilots, number one; number two, they didn't have a safe place to train them because our fighters were ranging all over, so they had inexperienced pilots. So they would take a few good pilots and tell the rest of the guys to 'String out and stick with us,' so they just hit us in waves. And the first thing I knew,

I see little 'cotton balls' in the air, which are 40mm cannons exploding, which I haven't seen before, and then an airplane hit ours, or one of their fighters hit our wing. I didn't see it happen, but I felt the whole airplane shake, and I said, 'What happened?', and something hit our wing—the plane was on fire, and we bailed out.

Sam, bombardier: I was hurt. When I hit the ground, I bruised my left knee. It was huge and it was all swollen, and I walked with a limp. I don't know if you were with me [*points to Earl*].

Earl, pilot: No, it wasn't me.

Sam, bombardier: Who the hell was it? I walked across the field, and they made me pick up my chute and carry it, and they took me to the burgermeister's house.

Earl, pilot: The first one I saw on the ground was our tail gunner, and he was the happiest guy on earth to see me. He was afraid that he had bailed out, and the rest of us had gone back to England. When he saw me, he knew he had done the right thing.

Interviewer: He didn't know that the plane blew up?

Earl, pilot: Well, no. But he knew to get out, because he saw the other crew up forward and he motioned for them to go. One guy was left standing there, and he just shook his head. He wasn't going.

Sam, bombardier: And he died. That was one of the guys that died on the plane.

Earl, pilot: And I still think that was strictly a case where—[*reaches for photograph*] Do you see these two small guys here? This guy was in the ball turret. This other one was standing here on the waist gun, and these guys would switch off in the turret. I think they had a deal between them—'If I'm in the turret, you don't leave until I'm out!' And Joe would always stand there and wait for him to get out. And the escape door was gone, and I think Lindquist must have gotten out, and I think he probably was wounded, because when we were on the ground, the Germans came back and told us 'Komrade bleeding,' but they wouldn't let us go to him.[114]

'How to bail out of the Flying Fortress.' B-17 training manual, U.S. Government. Source: www.cnks.info/b17-flying-fortress-interior

Jerry, navigator: I remember that one. When our plane was hit, it goes with what he's talking about [*points to Earl*]. Our pilot pushed the 'bail out' alarm button and a bell or something rang, and it meant you were supposed to bail out. So I started to bail out and my feet were already hanging out, and I realized that the plane was still flying straight and level. Everybody knew that many a time half the crew bailed out, and the rest of them somehow got back to England! So I figured, this thing is still straight and level. So I came back into the plane and hooked up to the interphone, I got an oxygen bottle, and I called the pilot and said, 'What's wrong with the airplane? We're still going straight and level.'

He said, 'We're on fire.'

---

[114] *the Germans came back and told us 'Komrade bleeding,' but they wouldn't let us go to him*-Radio operator Charles Lindquist, 20, of Iowa, Joseph Salerno, 16, of Michigan, and Robert Koerner, 22, of Kansas, are listed as KIA November 2, 1944.

I said, 'Where?'

He said, 'The waist.'

I crawled through the bomb bay and back, and I haven't crawled through a bomb bay since then, and I don't know how the hell I ever did it the first time, because you can't get through that bomb bay today; maybe I'm a little bigger now, I don't know. But anyway, I opened the door in the back and I see flames—from the radio room on back, it was just solid flame! I closed the door, came forward, curved straight over, and I bailed out. They tell me that the airplane blew up about a little after the last parachute was seen. The part that I forgot was that we were in this big room, and this was three or four hours after we landed, and then I got the shakes [*shakes his hands vigorously*], you know, my nerves were such—up until then I was perfectly normal, as normal as I am sitting here now, and about four hours later it was uncontrollable! I guess it must have been a delayed reaction.

Interviewer: Did all of your crew make it out of the plane?

Jerry, navigator: Everybody got out of our airplane. But the tail gunner that day... He was a lieutenant in the lead plane; the copilot flies in the back position and he polices the formation, he calls off whatever he sees, telling other planes [over the radio] to tighten up their formation. He was the eyes in the back of the pilot's head. He became a 'streamer,' which means he bailed out and popped his parachute, and the parachute came up, but it didn't blossom. It just streamed, so he went down. His name was Ford. I don't know his first name, but his name was Ford.

B-17 Flying Fortresses 486th Bomb Group near Merseburg, November 1944. Credit: USAAF, public domain.

Earl, pilot, to interviewer: [pointing at photo in National Geographic Magazine] You saw this picture, didn't you?

Sam, bombardier: That was the same day we got shot down.

November 2, 1944.

Earl, pilot: That's it. That's the day we were shot down. My wife was looking at it and said, 'That's you.' That's what we were going through.

Interviewer: You guys had already dropped your bombs, right?

Earl, pilot: Yes. We had already dropped ours and were five minutes out when we were hit and went down.

Sam, bombardier: That's what happens when you become a bomber. [*Looks up toward heaven with hands clasped*] If you get out, you say, 'Thank you, Lord, for letting me go.'

*

On the Ground

Jerry, navigator: When I got on the ground, he [*points to Earl*] was having his own problems in his plane and they bailed out. When I was on the ground, I got picked up by some civilians. Well, not civilians; they were coming towards me, but there was one guy who was police and they say get in the hands of the police or the military, don't let the civilians get a hold of you, because they have pitchforks and they were pitching things other than hay. I didn't see them, luckily, but there were American fliers hanging by the necks from telephone poles and trees because of what we were.

When we got picked up, they put us on a train and took us to [where] there was a railroad station. That's where we got on a train to go back west of Frankfurt, which was the interrogation center. So they had a number of us, I'd say maybe 15, 20, 30, something like that, and we were guarded by the Luftwaffe. We came into this railroad station and all these Germans were there, and the next thing you know, there was a mob of people screaming and shouting, and the Luftwaffe had their guns and they protected us. That's when we first found out...

Earl, pilot: They finally had to lock us in the building in a room in the basement to keep us away from the civilians.

Jerry, navigator: Had it not been for that, we would have been lynched right there. We would have been lynched right there! Now these are the same people that, come April [1945], when they could smell borsht on the Russians' breaths on one side, and onion on the Americans' breaths on the other, you know, then all of a sudden [*imitates German civilian, shrugging shoulders, palms up*], 'What could we do?' You know, [as if to say], 'What would you do if you were in the same position? You'd do the same thing...'

Earl, pilot: They said, 'If you get shot down, you get under military control as soon as you possibly can.'

When we were shot down, the only reason I had a .45 strapped to me was that they made sure you had it when you left. And they put some rifles in the back of the airplane in case you crash-landed so you could protect yourself with it. And at the end of all the discussion, when they were telling us how to use this stuff, they said, 'Save a bullet for yourself.' And I would never do that, but I mean, that's the way it was. The civilians were really going after the Air Force.

Sam, bombardier: They did all the killing of the American airmen when they were captured. Not the soldiers, the civilians did that. Strung them up on telephone poles...

Jerry, navigator: It seems to be worldwide. Nobody seems to like the American airmen. The worst thing about being airmen is being caught by the Viet Cong, caught by the Koreans; they'd torture the airmen.

Earl, pilot: I went to an Air Force gathering recently, that's where I met Clarence Dart [*local Tuskegee Airman*]. But beforehand I saw in the paper that there was going to be a German Luftwaffe pilot who was going to be a speaker, and I didn't want to go. So I called and talked to the director of the program, and his wife said, 'Well, forget your problems and come on out and have a good time.' So I went and I stood there when [the former Luftwaffe pilot] made the speech. Now his speech kind of turned me off, because he spent a lot of time explaining that he was not a combat pilot, and at the end of the war he was flying scientists out of the eastern zone back to the western zone so [the Americans] could get them, and so on and so forth. And he was backing himself up that he was a 'good guy.' So then I flat-out asked him, 'Well, tell me this, when our planes were shot down and our guys were in parachutes, why was the German Luftwaffe shooting at our guys with the parachutes?'

'It couldn't have happened,' he said.

'Well, it did happen,' I said. 'I was there and saw it!' And that kind of turned me off... and since I got on him pretty heavy about those German fighters shooting our guys in the parachutes, he kind of avoids me now.

Jerry, navigator: Well, I can prove to you that what he [*points to Earl*] is saying is correct because when I bailed out, I could see two or three other parachutes and about three or four of us were in a group. I heard the chatter of machine guns, and I got terrified and said, 'Oh my God, they're shooting us, they're going to come around and shoot us in our parachutes.' Now, if the story wasn't around, I wouldn't have thought of that, but it just so happened that all this [machine gun] chatter I heard was not them shooting parachutes; it was what they called a 'Lufbery circle,' which was developed in the first World War after a pilot by the name of Lufbery. [*Motions with hands*] Here's an Me-109, he's on the tail of a P-51, who was on the tail of a 109, who was on the tail of a P-51, and if you break out, you've got to try and turn inside [*motions again with hands*] so they can't get at you. All the while they're trying to get inside and shoot you. So the circle gets tighter and tighter and they're all firing at each other, so I couldn't wait to get down from that cloud level and disappear into the clouds below. But up above I could hear the shooting. And when I came through and I saw the planes, the first thing I thought was that they were shooting at the parachutes. And if I didn't think that, then where did I get the thought? From the stories that go around that they did do these things.

Earl, pilot: Well, they found a guy who was shot through the leg down there and he was still in his parachute. I didn't see any American fighters down there, either. Things were rather hectic.

Jerry, navigator: One thing came back to me yesterday that I hadn't thought about for a long time. By the time I got on the ground and we were picked up and put in a building, which Sam remembers and reminded me about—he's the first guy I've seen in years that was in that same building; I've met a lot of PoWs and I never found a guy that was in that building—and he remembers that I was one of the two guys who weren't wounded. Everyone was wounded, one way or another, and some guys were all burned and blackened like chicken.

Interviewer: It must have been terrible.

Jerry, navigator: Well, it wasn't good. Now this is what I'm talking about; I went off on a tangent and I forgot the damn point.

Earl, pilot: Were you going to talk about the first aid kits? They snatched them so quick, we had nothing to take care of our wounded with.

Sam, bombardier: [*referring to the kit*] The German soldiers would come with a knife and cut the whole thing off. It had iodine and bandages, and they took it for their troops. We had nothing for ours.

Interviewer: You said you were one of the two guys who weren't wounded?

Jerry, navigator: Yes.

Sam, bombardier: He and I were trying to figure out how we were going to take care of the rest. We would look for the packs, and there weren't any there. So I would take off my shirt and my undershirt, because I always wear an undershirt, and we cut that up and used it for bandages. Finally we got the Germans to bring us some stuff for wounds. Like the paper you dry your hands with—that's what they were using for bandages! They brought us some grease, and we put as much on our guys as we could. One guy landed on a roof and it collapsed, so he fell 35 feet to the ground and hurt his back and couldn't move. Every time we tried to move him, he was in pain.

Earl, pilot: He was the one I carried across Frankfurt, on my back, and I don't know if he got used to the pain or what, because he never uttered a cry or anything.

*

Prisoners of War

Interviewer: So it was the same exact day, the same mission you were on?

Jerry, navigator: Yes—then we were collected and put with other guys, and then put on a train, and each section was a whole story in itself, what happened here, what happened there. When I got picked up, two German soldiers came around in a Volkswagen, which was like a Jeep, and he [*points to Earl*] is sitting in the back of the thing, and that's where I met him.

Interviewer: What happened when you were on the Jeep?

Jerry, navigator: Well on the Jeep, this one German, the guy riding shotgun, had a patch on his eye. He was a big guy, and he took his watch [*points to Earl*], he took my high school ring, he said he would keep it so some other guy wouldn't just come and steal it from me, and I would get it back after the war.

I'm not going to argue with the guy. He goes over to him [*points to Earl*] to get his pilot wings, and this big dumb jerk [*referring to Earl*], he's pushing the German away, and I'm saying, 'These guys have guns, for God's sake, give him the damn wings before they kill us.' And he said, 'They're not getting my wings,' so I repeated, 'Don't be so damn stubborn, give him the damn wings!' And he wouldn't give him the wings and the guy backed off. But if this guy was in another frame of mind, you [*points to Earl*] wouldn't be here, and I wouldn't be here, and Sam wouldn't be here. He could have just shot us, and nobody asks questions, then. So that's where I met him.

Then they would collect us and we would go to central point, and they would ship you across the country to a place called Dusseldorf, which is an interrogation center. And they keep you there a few days while you get interrogated. And depending on what happened, they would send you to another place, until they got enough people together so they could try the freight train, or passenger train, or something, and then they send you off to your destination. That's how we all ended up in the same camp.

The camps were set up this way. If you were in the army or an infantryman, you were a prisoner of the German army. If you were in the navy and got picked up by the army some way or another, you are a prisoner of the navy. We were Air Corps people, so we were prisoners of the Luftwaffe, and I think we were treated better than anyone else. Because the British had so many Luftwaffe pilots in their camp, and Herman Goering would make sure the British would take care of his boys. We didn't have a picnic, it wasn't exactly the Hilton and it wasn't Hogan's Heroes, but we were much better off than anyone else in Germany. We got the same rations that [the guards] got, but they didn't really have all that much either, to tell you the truth. The German population, if you were a farmer you ate; if you lived in the city, you didn't get much either.

We didn't get much. We had Red Cross parcels come to us, but they kept saying, 'No parcels this week, your bombers hit three things—schools, hospitals, and supply trains with Red Cross parcels.' That's all our bombers ever hit. [*Laughter*]

The Red Cross parcels you are supposed to use to supplement rations they gave us, which was potatoes and soup and our lard or something. Everybody lost weight—I went from about 160 down to 129. They [*points to Earl and Sam*] would have to tell you what they lost, but most lost from 30 to 40 pounds. But we were still much better than those poor guys who ended up in Japan; there is no question about it. When they say, 'Geez, you were a prisoner of war, you had it tough,' I have kind of a guilty conscience because I knew guys that were in Japan.

Interviewer: Did you know any of the British troops or flyers in the PoW camps?

Sam, bombardier: We weren't up to their status; they didn't have anything to do with us.

Interviewer: They looked down on you?

Sam, bombardier: Oh yes, they looked down their noses on us.

Jerry, navigator: Can you say that again?

Interviewer: The British flyers, any contact with them or any conversations during the war?

Jerry, navigator: Well I got a chance to fly, not a mission but a practice. And I can't remember how it came about; we were talking about the other day. Some flew with us; it was sort of an exchange thing—they flew in and we talked to them.

I had great admiration for the Royal Air Force, they don't take the backseat to anybody. They had more guts when they were prisoners of war; if they could have had an [opportunity to] escape, they did. The British were taking the crème of the kids from the college, and putting them in the RAF. They were the crème de la crème. So when they got there, they had guys that could print, could forge, and could do this. They had engineers. You know, they could build tunnels, but they knew how to get air through it. When we got down to Moosburg, I see them with this little thing [*motions hands in a circular motion*]; they got a little blower with a duct going down there and you turn a few things on, and they had a red-hot flame going! The British had the ingenuity. I was watching this little thing, and I asked, 'What's that?' They devised all kinds of things—these guys were all experts in their own fields, and they knew how to forge documents, they knew how to do things with their time. They took uniforms and re-cut them and re-sewed them and made them into civilian clothes. And they got a hold of the train schedule and arrived at daylight out of the forest!

I can tell you another story about a PoW in our chapter who could speak seven languages. He was in our camp. He told me his name was Alex M.—about a year or two ago the Russian Ambassador gave him a medal down in Washington; it was in the papers. Now this guy was a prisoner in the camp that communicated with London. London dropped tons of cigarettes, which we used for currency. The Germans got a lot, but we got a lot in the camp. Alex got all of them; he had an apartment in Munich in which he was hiding, because he could speak the language; how the hell he got in and out of the camps, I have no idea. And he has Russians in this apartment, a whole story on its own, fantastic thing. [This is one of the ways] we got radio parts—cigarette companies sent tons and tons of cigarettes over. For every 5th or every 10th or every 100th carton or shipment, there was one pack, or in one cigarette, it had a part for a radio, and when it came we gave it to whomever we were supposed to give it to. Given enough of those, we'd get radios. We'd get cameras and we'd get parts and we'd sneak things in. So it was a very, very complicated thing.

Interviewer: Speaking of colonels, didn't you tell me that one time they dropped an officer, maybe a colonel, into your camp?

Earl, pilot: Yes, in our camp the colonel was running the camp. What was his name, the old fellow?

Sam, bombardier: He was a colonel in the B-24 group.

Earl, pilot: Yes.

Jerry, navigator: Once you were behind the barbed wire, the Germans said you were in the military organization, and the officers would run things, so that they don't have to. We have to tell our officers what we wanted. We had rules, very strict rules. You couldn't escape if you felt like it. You had to go to the escape committee, because you might do something to screw up somebody else's [escape plan], but anyways, let's not get into that yet.

In our compound, the west compound, there was a colonel. A fighter pilot, Jack Jenkins was his name, a Texan. He was the officer in charge. A story I knew about him is that he was standing outside when they have a roll call; they call it once at morning and once at night. They lined everybody up with space, and then two Germans go down and they count. They see that each line is complete and then they count up the lines [*counts in German*]. Then they count up this one and write it down, and add that one to make sure everybody is there. Well, that opens up a whole bunch of stories. However, this one particular day, we stand there, the counters are right; we were just standing there two hours. Something was said, and the colonel and the counting man came together, you know, and the next thing we know, they're standing there and there is a big argument. And the story as I got it was this—they said they wanted a list of all of the Jewish PoWs.[115] So the next day, we came out there and there's this big argument, there was raving and ranting. Jenkins says, 'That's it!' After all this standing around, we said, 'Well, what happened?' and the story filtered back. The German says, 'Give me a list of the names of the Jews!' Well, they all took the pledge that night, like they all had converted, like everybody was converted to Judaism. They would not give him the list of Jews! There was a 'hoo-ha' about it. The rumor was they wanted to take the Jews and hold them hostage up in the Alps. The next rumor that went around, I guess, maybe a month later, when they started to march a whole pack of us out. The story was they were going to take us as hostages to the Alps and use us as bargaining chips. Another story, which I've seen in print, one German general after the war said that Hitler had said he wanted all of the Allied airmen shot, because they

---

[115] *Jewish PoWs*- Jerry Silverman was Jewish.

were being coddled by Goering. We weren't, if you want to put this into perspective. Hitler said he wanted all the airmen shot [*pounds table with his fist for emphasis*], and they did not follow his orders. You know, we came this close [*gestures with his thumb and index finger very close together*], God-knows how many times. But that was one of the stories about Jack Jenkins, the fighter pilot from Texas. What made me cry was this is a guy from Texas, and even if he didn't like blacks, or he didn't like Jews, or Catholics, or whoever, no German was going to tell him what to do—no general was pushing him around! He says, 'We are Americans in this camp, and we are all the same.' There was another PoW camp for Allied officers in the North Sea, and a colonel was the head of a fighter group. The same thing happened up there. They asked him for a list of all Jews, and he said, 'You're not going to get it—if you're going to shoot them, you're going to shoot us all, because we are not going to tell you which ones to pick out.' So these are the things that make me feel damn proud to be an American.

Earl, pilot: I saw this colonel stand up to a German general. Prisoners were tearing the boards off the building down there in Nuremberg. A general came in there and says, 'The man who tears the next board off, we are just going to shoot him.' And the colonel just stuck his chest out: 'Anytime you want to start, start with me!' He had been on the march with us, but they had him in a wagon because he couldn't walk. And he was screaming at them back there because the Germans wouldn't let him up front with his troops. He was the same one that was at Sagan.

Jerry, navigator, to interviewer: 'Sagan' is Stalag Luft III—'Stalag' is 'prison camp,' 'Luft' is 'air,' 'Three,' it was the third one, and Sagan was a village nearby. [*To Earl*] Was he the fellow that wrote a letter about the bad conditions in the camp?

Sam, bombardier: Colonel Davenport?

Earl, pilot: Yes.

Sam, bombardier: I have it at home; it's twelve pages.

Earl, pilot: He wrote a letter on the conditions and slipped it to the Red Cross. And it went through.

Interviewer: Why were you tearing boards off the buildings?

Sam, bombardier: Heat. That was our heat.

Earl, pilot: Yes, we didn't have any other.

Sam, bombardier: Burned anything that would burn; we were freezing.

Earl, pilot: Yes, that same night, you could hear the boards being torn off.

Jerry, navigator: This was in Nuremberg.

Earl, pilot: Yes.

Earl, pilot: In Sagan we were using boards to make the tunnels.

Sam, bombardier: We were taking the boards off to make tunnels.

Earl, pilot: We were taking the bed stakes out of the beds.

Jerry, navigator: Next thing you know you were sleeping on three boards.

Interviewer: For escape?

Earl, pilot: Yes.

Sam, bombardier: That is when they were digging the tunnels.

Earl, pilot: So I was saying, you see, you had to shore up for every inch you made.

Sam, bombardier: And when the guys touched down straight so many feet, they had to shore it up with the wood. Then they'd start this way [*motions with hands*], and every time they'd move they'd have to shore it up. They made a gadget that they had to carry the dirt. They made a rope that they put wheels on. The guy had only room to go through. He could not turn around, you see. When he came out, he had to come out backwards.

Earl, pilot: At first they had to bring the dirt out in stockings, but they had gardens, see. They'd mix the dirt in with that [out in the garden]. Well, then the Germans stopped the gardening business.

So then they figured it out and we had a whole bunch of people go out in the field and drop the dirt.

Jerry, navigator: [*stands up, points just below the knee, walks around, demonstrating*] The stocking is right on his leg, tied with a string, and you walked out and pulled the string. But the dirt is going to look different; so they put a little out, then they walk, and mix a little up… They claim that the field there was raised six inches! The Germans drove a tank, and a little would collapse and we would have to dig deeper.

Earl, pilot: That happened when they brought a load of potatoes in Sagan, and about three days later, before they came and checked it. In the first camp that we were in north of Berlin.

The German soldiers were not supposed to think for themselves, and they drove across this tunnel, it caved in, so they got another wagon and unloaded that one and moved it on out. Then the officers came and spotted it, and of course I heard this story from other guys in there, because I'm not privileged to everything, but by then our tracks were all covered up and they didn't know anything about tunnels.

Jerry, navigator: Let me tell you about the escape committee. Every prisoner of war was expected to escape at all times—the reason being you tie up more German troops guarding you, it keeps them away from the lines—but if everyone tried to escape at once, it would mess up the other guy. So if you wanted to get out, they would help you, but you needed a plan to get over the fence. Once you got over the fence, they would get you clothes, timetables for trains, tickets, you know, maps, the whole bit. They could get you this stuff, but you had to go to the escape committee.

Let's say [a guy] wants to escape and has a plan. The committee would review it, and say, 'Okay, go, we will try it such and such night,' then they will try to find the weather report, for good cover. Two or three days before his plan of escape, somebody goes out of the barracks at night, and they clip some wires and make some tracks, and return. The Germans get up in the morning and they see this, they count, you know, and [they think] one guy is missing! But he's not missing—I'm up in the attic somewhere [*points to the ceiling*]! So then they line everybody up and you go through, past the desk, and they check your number and your picture and identify you and say, 'Silverman is missing.' That's the guy we're looking for, but I'm up in the attic. Three days later, one of the guys planning to escape goes out in the honey wagon[116] or potato wagon or to the hospital, and he gets out. Now I come down from the ladder, or the attic, and I'm standing where I'm supposed to stand; it doesn't make any difference—they don't know he's gone, you see? They're still looking for me! So until he goofs and gets caught on the outside, he is still free. This is why they had an escape committee. You know, just an example of how they did things.

Interviewer: You had to organize it.

Earl, pilot: And you did not try to escape on your own. It had to be approved by the committee.

Interviewer: Now how many men were on the committee? Were there officers?

Jerry, navigator: One guy was called 'Big X.' I don't know who he was; he was number one. His assistant was called 'Little X,' and I think you can find that in the movie *The Great Escape*, what went on in that camp. It was only across the wire from where we were in the next camp. We had towers there, they were the guards: all Germans were called 'goons'—so they called them 'goon boxes.' And there were little wires about this high [*motions about six inches with his hands*] called a 'warning wire,' and if you stepped over it, you were shot. If you were playing ball and the ball goes over, you wave to

[116] *honey wagon*- a cart or vehicle for carrying human excreta to dump or distribute elsewhere

the guard and point. You'd hop and if you pick up the ball and went back, it was okay, but if you go the other way, they'd start shooting. Then there was a barbed wire fence; it was a big fence, and then there was another fence. Between these two fences there were German Shepherds running around, you know, walking back and forth in case anybody went through. Also between the fences there were goon boxes up there. They had German guards we called 'ferrets'.[117] The barracks were put on the blocks, so that they could see through, go underneath, so you couldn't dig a tunnel, theoretically. There were always people standing around, saying, 'Goon up!' You know, that meant if you're doing anything, put it away, there's a German in the area; they might walk through the place, they might go under, they might hang around, they might listen, so consequently, with the American sense of humor, funny incidents would take place. I didn't see this, but I heard about it. Every [barracks] had twelve guys with pails; each guy had a pail of water. One day one of these ferrets would go underneath [the barracks crawlspace] and start snooping around, and they'd say, 'Okay, fellas, let's do it today!' They'd go down with scrubbing brushes—'Scrub your floors, men!' —and on the command, '1-2-3,' everybody would dump their buckets, and this wet rat comes out yelling. 'Oh, so sorry, Hans, we didn't know.' [*Laughs; Earl and Sam chuckle*]

Interviewer: *Where would the tunnels be?*

Jerry, navigator: They had ways of getting tunnels. They would dummy up things, latrines or...

Sam, bombardier: They took the stove. Remember the stove?

Jerry, navigator: I can't ever get how they linked the stove down to the tunnel below. They went through the stove, probably through the space, and then they'd have a pallet of some sort covering the tunnel, which they would cover with dirt. There must have

[117] *German guards we called 'ferrets'*-special anti-escape guards

been some way to get through this stove and get underneath their building. They'd lift this thing up and start digging their tunnels.

Earl, pilot: See, at first, the building sat on the ground and everybody was digging. It was later that they [built them] up on stilts. In the washroom, it was concrete, so I think the one in the *Great Escape*, they went down through the manholes in the bathrooms.

Jerry, navigator: They had three tunnels: Tom, Dick, and Harry. I remember that.

*

The March

Over a quarter million Allied prisoners were under German control by 1945. Between January and April, in a scene to be played out all over the Reich, hundreds of thousands of slave laborers, concentration camp victims, and PoWs were force-marched out of their camps to other locations to escape being liberated by the advancing Russian and western Allied powers. On January 27, Hitler himself ordered the captured airmen out of Stalag Luft III to camps west of Berlin.[115] *On the same day, Soviet forces overran Auschwitz death camp, less than 250 miles to the southeast; the Russians were also closing in hard less than a hundred miles away to the north and south of the PoW camp. With little, the men shuffled out into the cold and snow towards Bavaria. The rumor mill had it that they were going to be executed or simply marched to death, on Hitler's orders, or that they were going to be held as bargaining chip hostages in the Bavarian Alps, where the SS planned to make a last stand.*

Some of these forced marches indeed lasted for weeks in some of the harshest winter conditions of the 20th century. Men fell ill with typhus and dysentery, often contracted by resting in the same places along the march.[116] *Many men died from exposure and hunger; some were beaten to death when they fell, while in other situations, guards found themselves little better off than the prisoners they were to guard, as time went on.*

Some townspeople, fearful of the Russian advance, gave assistance to them, while others angrily pelted the prisoners with rocks and debris as they wearily shuffled into a new town.

Interviewer to Earl, pilot: You said you thought you had the best crew over there. Do you still think that?

Earl, pilot: Yes.

Jerry, navigator: Who said that?

Earl, pilot: Me.

Sam, bombardier: And I second that.

Jerry, navigator: [*joking*] And who gave you the authority?

Sam, bombardier: [*pointing to Earl*] Him.

Interviewer: [*pointing to Sam*] Is this the bombardier who had the amnesia?

Earl, pilot: Yes.

Interviewer: After you were shot down?

Earl, pilot: This was on the forced march.

Jerry, navigator: To this day he's got amnesia. [*Laughter*]

Earl, pilot: [*pointing to Jerry*] He was on the march, too. There were about 10,000 of us on the march.

Interviewer: What about the forced march?

Earl, pilot: Well, they have heard my version of it, let someone else give them their version of it.

Sam, bombardier: Well, this is in January 1945. The Germans didn't want us to be liberated in any way, shape, or form, so they were moving us all, going west through the forest.

Interviewer: Because they wanted you as bargaining chips.

Jerry, navigator: Well, that's the rumor; the prisoner of war camps are the greatest rumor factories in the world.

Interviewer: Sure, you don't have any information.

Sam, bombardier: Well, we did have good information.

Earl, pilot: We had a radio.

Sam, bombardier: Yes, we had a radio; the Germans could never find it.

Earl, pilot: They would ask, when we were moving, 'Taking your radio with you?'

Interviewer: *Where did you hide it?*

Sam, bombardier: You took it apart and put it together: everybody had a little piece.

Jerry, navigator: In our camp, it was in an accordion. I always heard about it, then a book got published ... and in it they had the picture of the accordion and I start jumping up and down like a maniac. I said, 'By God, I heard about that thing!' and here it is, there is a picture of it. The guys are sitting around and the Germans are taking everything apart, and one guy is sitting there playing 'Home on the Range,' and the radio is inside the accordion that this guy is playing.

Earl, pilot: And the BBC[118] knew it too, because they beamed stuff to us.

Sam, bombardier: We used to have a map on the wall, this big map the guys have drawn, and we knew where everyone [invading armies] was in the war. Where the French were moving up, where the Russians were, where the Germans were. They used to come to us to look at our map to find out what the hell was going on. But the radio always picked up from outside, always like a newscast. And there it was, we would have it.

Earl, pilot: And on that same map, it would have our line where we knew it was, marked. Then we would have their line where they advertised marked, and they didn't agree at all.

Jerry, navigator: In many cases they agreed, but the interesting part was we would get interpreters and we would get the German news. And, of course, we would get our own news from the BBC,

---

[118] *BBC*- British Broadcasting Corporation

and the Germans would say that, 'All victorious troops strongly defended this particular town,' then the next day, 'All victorious and glorious and loyal Nazi troops successfully beat down two platoons of American infantry at this town.' But now they were back over here! The next day they beat the hell out of us over here, and then they beat the hell out of us over here, then over there. When we look at the map, we laugh at the thing, but they haven't won a battle and they are slowly losing the war.

Sam, bombardier: They're backing up and backing up. Funny how they came in one day and said, 'Everybody get packed because we are going to move out!' So everybody starts packing and it started to snow in the afternoon. It was more like flurries and there was probably only an inch of snow on the ground, but as it got later in the day, the snow got heavier. And we had to go, so when we left there the snow was about four inches deep, when we went out.

Jerry, navigator: Middle of the night, midnight.

Sam, bombardier: And everybody has their sack, everything they could carry.

Earl, pilot: We really didn't have any idea where we were going, or anything.

Sam, bombardier: We were back six to eight buildings from the front, and as we went along, we could see where guys would be dumping stuff along the side of the road: they took extra food, we had a warehouse for canned food, and they were taking the sugar. Because while you were walking you wanted energy, so you would eat the sugar. So I packed, I would say, probably 200 cubes of sugar in my pockets, and that is what I ate as I went along.

We walked and walked, and I found it getting cold, and everybody is getting tired, and we keep going. It's like five, six, seven o'clock in the morning. It's getting colder out. I had a scarf around my face and it was just a ball of ice; I would have to reach up and break it so I could get air to my face. My feet were frozen.

Interviewer: How many hours had you been walking?

Jerry, navigator: About three days, [at that point].

Sam, bombardier: And you never got warm, we just kept going and going, we couldn't even change socks if you wanted to, so we had wet socks in cold weather—so as far as I'm concerned, that's what happened to me.

The next day we marched almost twenty-some hours, so now we were coming up to some town, now everybody is falling over. Then I did something that I didn't even know I did. I was in a group where everybody made a pledge to watch each other. I found myself off the side of the road and I lay in the snow and I said to myself, 'Wow, this is so warm.' I was so damn cold, I could hardly do anything. In the meantime, when I lay over, some guys saw me—one was a captain and one was a major—they saw me walk over and lie down, and they grabbed me. They stood me up and shook me, they asked me questions, and I—I didn't know anything, so they picked me up and made me walk. We got to this town and that's when he [*points to Earl*] came around; he was looking for me and he was hollering my name.

I was standing there and he comes over to me: 'Sam.' And I knew: 'You're Earl, you're the pilot.' When they had questioned me, I didn't know my name or anything, or where I lived—I was gone! The only thing I knew was [*points to Earl*]: 'You're Earl, you're the best goddamn pilot in the whole Air Force.'

Interviewer: Well, how many days had you been there?

Sam, bombardier: Well, that was after some 20 hours, we froze walking.

Earl, pilot: I went right to him [at that point]. I had gone through the same procedure as Sam—I actually sat down in the snow and they came to me... so I got up and I moved again. At about this time they're yelling, 'Sam Lisica,' and I woke up and got hold of him; I was all right by then. When you see someone worse than you are… I kept him moving then.

Sam, bombardier: When I started getting all mixed up, I do remember I knew I was walking fast, but I guess there were five, six, or seven barracks [of men in our group]. We went out in barracks, so everybody stays together—[but then] I walked through these guys, and all of a sudden, I'm the leader. I'm out in front of everybody, and that's how they saw me take off to the side of the road [to lie down].

Interviewer: *How many people would be on this march?*

Jerry, navigator: From the camp…

Earl, pilot: They estimated about ten thousand, didn't they?

Jerry, navigator: Stalag Luft III had a north compound, a south compound, a west and an east compound: we were in the west, this was the newest one. The north compound was the one that was all British, and that's where the famous *Great Escape* occurred: where they all went through a tunnel and 50 of them were caught and were murdered.

Jerry, navigator: And I guess three guys made it to, I think, Sweden: they made a movie out of that, Steve McQueen, there's another movie coming out about the same compound we were in. Bruce Willis is in it, which is going to be interesting, because nobody in the place was as old as Bruce Willis is right now.[119] [*Laughter*]

But anyway, when they took us out, one of the compounds went directly from there all the way to a place called Moosburg. The rest of us went on the march we were on, about a week, a week and a half, we took stops—we had no idea, no recollection of them. We eventually marched for about three days to the next town, we were going to stop—the next town, it was bitter cold. They kept us in a church one night, on marble floors. If you want to freeze to death,

---

[119] *as old as Bruce Willis is right now*-actor in *Hart's War* (2002).

I'll tell you what, that's the place. Another ten would come out [die], and another two, you know.

Then, some miracle happened. They put us into a factory, it was a pottery factory, and the floors were warm, actually warm. All the time in Germany we never felt warm; we were always freezing to death, and they kept us there for three days! I'm thinking that's what saved a lot of our guys who would have died from pneumonia or whatever. We got our chance to get our strength back.

The pottery factory was worked by Polish and French slave laborers. In the basement were the kilns, which operated day and night, warming the floors above. This reprieve indeed saved many; by this point, the line of prisoners extended nearly 30 miles.[117]

From there they marched us a day or two, then they took us to a place called Spremberg, and they put us into boxcars, 55 to 60 guys in a boxcar. Which only really held 40 or 8, 40 men or eight horses. We had 50, 55, 60 men, depending, with only one little slit for everyone to look through. Everyone could not sit down at the same time, and we were trapped in this thing for about three days.

Interviewer: Was the train moving?

Sam, bombardier: Oh yes, they were taking us west.

Jerry, navigator: They were taking us down to Nuremberg. Then we would end up in a prison camp in Nuremberg.

Sam, bombardier: That's when we all had discipline.

Jerry, navigator: This was between the train ride and the marching. Then one thing, then another, and the train having to stop to wait for the German soldiers to move so the train could continue moving again; the rail lines were all plugged up. Our train was strafed, lucky for us but unlucky for the guys at the other end—they were hit by our own P-47s. The Germans did not go through the trouble of putting red crosses on the trains with prisoners, but they did on their own troop trains.

The remnants of the Volkssturm[120] *were still streaming eastward in a futile effort to stem the tide of the Soviet advance, clogging the roads and railways as masses of humanity surged past them in a desperate attempt to outrun the Russians. At Spremberg, near the beginning of February, the men were finally issued some black bread, having walked over sixty miles in five days.*[118] *Then they were crowded into the boxcars, where many of the men suffered indignities again in freezing temperatures.*

Sam, bombardier: Then we all got dysentery. They stopped one time, and everybody had to go, and they would open the door. Everybody would run out, sitting by the railroad track...

Jerry, navigator: I've been waiting for years to hear from somebody of one of the funniest things I saw in the war. There were so many of us out of the train at one time, and we were on this track. The train was standing still, a bright, sun-shining day, the German guards were in the field with their guns and everything, and the guys came out to relieve themselves. About 150 guys sitting there with their pants down, all sitting straight, mooning the guards. [*Laughter*]

Sam, bombardier: When you've got dysentery, you could knock a fly dead from 50 paces because all the pressure and water and—zoom! The best part was when we were done, we would come walking by and they would say nothing to us. [*Laughter*]

The men arrived at Stalag XIIID at Nuremberg, an area that was a favorite target of their previous bombing raids due to its location near the railroad marshalling yards. Conditions here were abysmal, with rotten and vermin-infested food.

Jerry, navigator: You talk about the American sense of humor, if it wasn't for the American sense of humor... We always had funny

---

[120] *Volkssturm*-the national militia, composed of units of conscripts between age 16 and 60.

names for people; you could always find a funny moment. There was an air raid and one of our own bomb group came at us; they were dropping bombs around Nuremberg, and turning away, but one plane didn't, and it was coming straight at us! I did see this happen—some [American] guy grabbed hold of a guard and started shaking him, yelling, 'Where's the Luftwaffe, where's the Luftwaffe!' [*Laughter*]

Interviewer: And he was an American?

All: Yes.

Sam, bombardier: He told him to take out that bomber so it would not drop bombs on us! [*Laughter*]

Sam, speaking to Earl: Do you remember the day we were marching, we pulled off of the march and into the farmhouse, and we went up and knocked on the door? We asked them if we could wash our faces and shave, because me, I was taking a shave every day—no matter where I was, I shaved.

Jerry, navigator: I always shaved.

Sam, bombardier: So anyhow, you talked sign language and whatever you thought you knew in German, until you strike a deal. And then she says, 'Okay, wash up.' Their stoves were big cast iron stoves and on their sides they had water tanks, so they were cooking over here [*points to the right*], and the water stayed hot all the time. So they'd just pick up the lid, dunk the cup in, and give us a bucket of hot water. She said, 'Go out behind the barn, and there's a wash basin and a mirror.' And she even gave us towels. And she had two little kids, and we went out there and we got washed and came back and brought the stuff back. We came in, and there were four plates. We had fried bacon, fresh eggs, and she had just finished making rye bread in the oven. That was the breakfast I got on that march, the four of us got. So, anyhow, we said, what the hell can we give her? I had some leftover sugar cubes in my pocket, and I had a couple pieces of candy, and she had these little kids. We were talking, and all of a sudden, we made sense to each other. She was saying she was a widow, her husband was killed on the eastern front, and she had these kids and I think she had her mother living with her on this farm. I don't know how they worked it, but anyhow, we sat down and we gave her this and that, but she didn't want it. Anyhow, we got up to leave, and she turned to each of us—we were in our 20s and she was probably about 47 years old. She came over to us and gave us a big hug and said, 'Good luck.'

Interviewer: Now, is this after the war ended?

Sam, bombardier: That's when we were prisoners and we were marching from...

Earl, pilot: From Nuremberg to Moosburg...

Interviewer: How could you do that? Would the Germans let you do that?

Earl, pilot: We actually were bribing the guards to stay with us, because there were SS troops in the area—and a bunch of Americans walking without guards, you'd have problems. But now, along the same line, I didn't get into a deal that you got into [*points to Sam*]. I got into a store that a couple of ladies were running. They let about 15 or 16 of us in there and locked the door, and the guards pulled the shade. And the guards were outside beating on the door trying to get in. She let us get what we wanted and she'd sneak us out the back door.

You see, this was at the end, and I actually saw three women converge on the commandant of the camp. A big old fat major, he was at Sagan, then he was down in Nuremberg, and he was riding a bicycle on that march. I saw three women, two of them from each side and one of them from in the front, caught him on his bicycle and dumped him right out there in front of all of us. And then all the civilians wanted to know when the Americans were going to get there. Because, see, the Russians were coming too. They just wanted Americans. All the civilians, by then, on that march, they were with us. They wanted us there; they wanted the Americans there before the Russians got there.

Jerry, navigator: I told this story yesterday. I did eventually about 10 years ago meet one of the guys who was in this room with me, and he remembered everything as I did, because sometimes you think, 'I'm not sure if this happened or I heard it or what.' But this is what happened. It was on my birthday, the night before was a Saturday. They put us in a barn and made a big fuss about all these displaced workers, and they told these girls they were to fix up beds for us. So they made hay and got a blanket, you know, they took care of us and that was nice. But the next day he invited us into his kitchen. We came into the kitchen, large kitchen, larger than this room, and they cooked over in that area and the family sat there. We sat at a table for six over here [*pointing about the room*], so I had mixed emotions about this, which I'll tell you about at the end. They gave us pigs' knuckles, they boiled potatoes, and after the meal we sat at the table and he came over with a pad and said, 'I would like you to write a note to your commanding officer of the unit that occupies this area.' This would introduce 'Herr So and So,' who's the burgermeister, the mayor of the village here, and 'that he had the six of you there, treated you well, gave you breakfast, took care of you, and gave you good quarters, clean quarters in the barn, and kept you warm.' Because it was April—April 15 was my birthday, so it's etched—it was a Sunday, and he asked us if anybody was Catholic, and if we wanted to go to church with the family and so on. And they didn't go, and I said, 'I'm not signing anything like that.' The reason I didn't want to sign was because I remembered when they were winning in 1941, 1942, it was all, 'Our boys, our boys,' and I didn't see anybody say, 'Oh, this is terrible!' They were cheering, you know? Now that they were losing all of a sudden they turned their faces around. So I said, 'I'm not signing it.' Another guy said, 'I'm not signing it.' And then one guy said, 'Let me write it. I'll write it.' He got annoyed at the mayor, so he said, 'Let me write it.' So he writes it, and this is what he wrote: 'To the commanding officer...' And then he added one more part, and said, 'Please do the undersigned a favor and *take care* of this guy,' and then he signed it.

Sam, bombardier: 'Take care' meant different than take care of your welfare.

Jerry, navigator: What does it mean to an American? 'Take care of this guy.' So I've often wondered. I'd like to go back to find out whatever happened to him.

Earl, pilot: See, that's the only thing that really bothered me when I got back. On the march we had in January, the civilian crowd, they weren't with us at all, and then in April, boy, between January and April, they were going from this way to that way [*points from left to right*].

*

Liberation

Interviewer: Do you remember if you were liberated on the same day?

Earl, pilot: Yes; we were in the same camp, but we didn't all get out on the same date.

Interviewer: That was when General [George S.] Patton came through?

Sam, bombardier: He came in on his tank with his pearl-handled pistols; they were .38s he wore on his waist.

Interviewer: Did you all see him?

All: Yes.

Sam, bombardier: There were supposed to be 100,000 to 120,000 people in this camp at a time and they had other nationalities. They had Russians, they had Greeks, and they had Italians. I know they had a lot of Italians. The main gate was over here, and there was an abbey and there were buildings like this [*motioning with his hand*], and there was another gate and the Canadians were in there. The first thing we knew, our planes were coming overhead. One of the great experiences I remember now, and I hope these guys remember, two fighter planes with their contrails were making a great big '8' in the sky [*motioning in the air*], and the other one made a '9' for the Ninth Air Force, and [*motions with arm raised in air*] that's our boys! I mean, they were sharp! A P-51 would come by like this, you know, and we'd cheer and the Germans would get upset.

Anyway, we heard small arms fire one day. Now I'm air crew; I don't know anything about small arms. But when I see dirt hopping around, I figure something's up, so we scooted! And there was a battle; you could hear 'crackity-crack.' That's what I remember, and the next thing, people are looking out, and someone said, 'Look down there at the main gate!', and the American flag was flying and we went berserk, we just went berserk! We were looking at the goon tower and there's no goons there, there are Americans up there! And we saw the American flag, I mean—to this day I start to well up when I see the flag... [*Gets emotional*]

About three days later, word came that Patton was coming in, so by this time you could go from one compound to the other. I was on a roof peak of a building; there were only about six or eight of us, [but guys on rooftops all over]... there were French on that side, Canadians on this side [*motioning with his hands*]. Here comes this flying wedge of tanks, and here's General Patton, with his chest breaking the ice because he's like the icebreaker! And I'd known of him since Pearl Harbor—he's got these pearl-handled guns, so he's walking through, and the British salute, and we heard a French guy say, 'Mon General,' and there's an American next to us who says, 'Hey, Georgie, where the hell have you been, what took you so long?' He used an expletive that I'm not going to use: 'Where the bleep have you been?' George Patton, the first guy he acknowledged, was him! [*points at Earl, who laughs*] That's my memory of

George Patton. You can say what you want about George Patton; he liberated me, that's my boy.

Interviewer: So that was the beginning of May?

Sam, bombardier: That was April 29, 1945, a date that is etched in my memory.

Interviewer: You got a salute out of him, Earl?

Earl, pilot: Yes! See, these guys were more mobile than me; I had this bad knee and I wasn't getting around too fast, but I got up and ducked around the building, and there he was! I threw a salute at him, and he returned it; I just happened to be there all by myself, coming around that building. And he was upset. He said, 'You guys are all officers, and this is what they did to you?' Patton didn't hang around long; he made his little speech and he was gone.

Sam, bombardier: They sent up a field station, and we hadn't had nothing good to eat for months and...

Earl, pilot: Bread would look like angel food cakes, it was so white. We were used to that 'sawdust' bread.

Sam, bombardier: But the best thing was the Russian prisoners; they left the camp, they went out and killed some cows [and brought them back] on their shoulders: 'Gonna roast some beef!'

Jerry, navigator: That's right...

Earl, pilot. They got [food] from the guards, too...

Sam, bombardier: And they made the guards scared. So they went to the railroad yard and broke into a boxcar; they found condensed milk in gallon cans. And the Russians brought them to us in our tent where I was staying. They brought us the condensed milk and the army started to deliver the bread, and we looked at that bread and we were afraid; it looked so good, it looked like angel food cake. Everyone just looked at it, then we started eating it; we put the condensed milk on it. Then they started making food and we got good food. There must have been 50 guys in our tent.

Jerry, navigator: We had big white tents, far more than 50 guys...

Sam, bombardier: Great big tents, circus tents …

Earl, pilot: We had hay to lie on, clean hay, so it wasn't like back in Nuremberg; boy, Nuremberg was horrible…

Jerry, navigator: One thing about the Russians cobbling up the livestock was that the farmers got a hold of some American officer, because the Russians were killing off all the sheep. And they'd just cut off a couple steaks they wanted, and discard the rest of it, and then they'd move along. So he said, 'We're going to need this food, to feed you guys and us, our people.' But by the time he convinced this particular officer [to try to prevent the wanton slaughter of his animals], the farmer came back and said, 'Forget it!' [*waves his hand*]. His herd had been wiped out.

We spoke with some Russians who had some broken German, and Russians with some of our Polish guys, you know, we had sort of communications with them. At this point, we were at this [airfield], a German fighter base, and we were waiting for C-47s to come and get us. We hung around and exchanged some stories; we would tell the Russians how we were getting out of this, and ask, 'Incidentally, how are you guys getting out of this?' They said, 'We are walking home, we walk to Turkistan.' That name sticks in my mind, 1,200 or 1,400 miles, and me and the other fellows, we asked, 'Well, aren't they coming to get you, so you can go home by truck, or fly home?' Now that the war was over, Moscow didn't give a damn about them, and if they were going to go home, they were going to have to get out on their own [*motions with thumb, as in hitching a ride*]. They said, 'They do not recognize that we were prisoners of war—we were written off as dead, we were supposed to die.' You know, 'We either go forward or die, we cannot go back.' That's what they were up against.

*

'Thank God every day'

Jerry, navigator: I say that any person today, or any kid today who's growing up, should get on his hands and knees every night and thank God that he was born in the United States of America. Because even today you could be born in Africa, you have a fifty-fifty chance of getting to be twelve years old. You have AIDS all over, you've got one group murdering the other, you know, within their own country, killing each other, and all the while this is going on and on... in Israel, Syria, and Lebanon, and such. I mean, you can't even go to school without being afraid your bus is going to be machine-gunned or blown up. And people that live in this country have no idea how lucky they are.

In Mexico they're having a terrible time. They're coming by the droves to come over here and work. Same thing with the Canadians, they should be damn glad and thank God every day that they were born in that country. And I don't think anybody knows it! There's a quote by George Santayana, and it's posted at the Air Force Museum, and I can't recite it verbatim but it says, 'Those who do not learn from history are condemned to relive it,' to live it again—and nobody knows!

We spoke about this the other day [*pointing to Earl*], you know, they want the Olympics in China, and the pros say, 'Well, you know, we'll get in there and we'll do good, and they'll realize that they have to become more democratic.' And it can't be that way with their people, we don't learn from history—in 1936 they held the Olympics in Munich, now didn't that make Hitler the nice guy? Imagine what he would have been if they didn't have the Olympics, how bad it could have been?

Everybody is worried about himself and nobody is worried about the United States. Nobody is worried about his or her country. They want their vans, their boats; they want their summer cottage, you know? They want their retirement plan, you know; they want 'theirs.'

Sam, bombardier: It makes you laugh.

Jerry, navigator: In the meantime this stuff is using up gas and oil. You know, there's only so much juice in an orange, and there's only so much oil. Now, where is the oil right now that's being used up? Arabia? They want to take off a few yards of oil up here and some in the U.S. When this is done, who's going to have the oil? Russia, China, and India! [*To Earl and Sam*] So, boys, plan ahead! [*Chuckles*]

Sam, bombardier: We don't have anything to worry about. We're not going to be here.

Earl, pilot: Yes, well, you worry a little bit about your kids and grandkids.

Jerry, navigator: What you get out of the prisoner of war experience, it's amazing—I haven't seen this guy for 50 years [*points to Sam*], and politically, economically, and everything else, we're like twins. And you see any [former PoW]—that's why it broke my heart when John McCain dropped out [of the 2000 presidential race], because the guy is a former PoW. And I know—when you're a PoW, you suddenly realize what's important and what's not important. That's one thing you find out. The next important thing is that we've got to take care of this country first, and nobody seems to be giving a damn.

Interviewer: Have any of you been back to Germany since the war?

Sam, bombardier: Not me.

Jerry, navigator: They have tours—'do you want to go to the old prison camps,' you know, that's hot stuff. [*Sarcastically*] I get out of Sing-Sing[121]—after 15 years, do you think I'm going to go back and take a tour of the place? [*Laughter*]

Interviewer: So you have no desire to retrace those steps?

---

121 *Sing-Sing*- a maximum security prison in New York State.

Sam, bombardier: I wanted to go to just let my wife see England and France, but she'd get sick. You know? So, I can't do nothing, I was lucky to get here.

Interviewer: So what about German people today? Do you know any? Do you have any desire to know any?

Sam, bombardier: The men that I knew were the civilians, the ones who were left behind. We got to talk to them and I thought most of them I met were pretty nice people.

Jerry, navigator: I can tell you a story about that. If you're old enough, you have a story for everything.

I used to be in the driving school business. When I first got in, I worked for the summer and took it as a temporary job, and I was teaching a woman by the name of Katie G. She was a German woman, and also a nice woman. I just didn't get around to telling her that I had bombed Germany, you know, my job was to teach her how to drive. And she was married to Max. And Max is a salesman for a German company that makes hardware for operating, such as scissors, scalpels, etc. And in the course of discussion with him, it turned out that he was a German fighter pilot. We started to compare notes, and probably, we were mixed up, and we were flying every day, so he must have been flying when I was there, because he was flying in that period of time, and he was in an Me-109. Now this is the nicest guy in the world, I mean, we got along very well. They invited my wife and me, we went over, had dinner there, they wanted something done to their building and our scout master was a contractor, so I fixed it up with the scout master and he got the job. She was a chief housekeeper in a hospital in Hempstead [Long Island] nearby, and whenever anyone was in the hospital that I knew, I'd go in and see them, and then go down and see Katie. Katie saw to it that they got a little extra of this and that, that kind of thing. They were the nicest people in the world. Here's a guy doing his job for his country, I'm a guy doing my job, we were trying to kill each other, and 30, 40 years later, I don't see anything wrong with this guy.

But I'm not judging the German people or the German frame of mind; I'm judging Max G., individual. Now, I'm Jewish, and this guy's Luftwaffe, and he was fighting for the Nazis. He should have said to his wife, 'What? You let him teach you to drive?' Never happened. I taught Arabs, by the way, and if they pass, they think you're the greatest instructor in the world. If they fail, you're a bum. [*Laughter*] So anyway, they're passing and I'm getting a lot of these Arab people, and I'm getting them from Lebanon, I'm getting them from Syria, and I'm getting them from Israel itself, they're Palestinian Arabs. So one day I asked one guy, his name was Habeeb, I said, 'You guys know I'm Jewish. With all of this that's going on in Palestine, how come you're using me?'

And he said, 'That's Palestine, this is here. You're a good teacher; we want you.'

So if you go on a person-to-person level—and I've taught people in that area from all over—everybody wants the same thing. They want a good job, they want a clean house, they want a roof that doesn't leak, they want their bellies full, they want their kids clean, behaved, kept out of trouble, they want their kids educated, they want to enjoy Jones Beach just like everyone else, on a person-to-person basis. But when you get a rabble rouser that whips up the crowd [*waves hand in the air*], you know, I could mention a few of ours right now, whenever they set up a camera, bingo!—they are there. I'm not going to mention any names, you know who I'm talking about...

Some of the things that shake you—my younger son, I used to look down on him, now he is looking over me. I've found the packet with my old record and ID and so on from about 1943. I was 5' 10 ½". I think I'm about five feet even right now!

Sam, bombardier: They say you shrink, gravity's pushing us down. My kids all called me 'Shorty'; their mother's short. They're all over six feet.

Jerry, navigator: I used to have three sons and a daughter, now I've got three fathers and a mother.

[*Interviewer laughs*]

Jerry, navigator: Your day will come, don't snicker, your day will come...

Sam Lisica passed away at age 85, five years after this roundtable interview. Jerry Silverman died at age 89 in 2008, two years after Sam. I invited Earl to my high school again in 2011, where I had the honor of introducing him to the granddaughter of his liberator, General George S. Patton.

Earl M. Morrow, World War II Memorial, Washington, D.C., June 2016. Photo: Jessica Morrow Brand.

EPILOGUE

Trails in the Sky

I waited on the tarmac as the crew prepared the airplane for takeoff. A high school friend had let me know that the B-17 was coming to town, and I was going up in it for a thirty-minute ride over Lake George, New York, the 'Queen of American Lakes.' I hurried to the airport and filled out the pre-flight paperwork, and was briefed along with seven others on the 'dos and don'ts' of a once-in-a-lifetime ride aboard an authentic World War II Flying Fortress.

Once inside the narrow midsection, we were strapped along the fold-up metal seats for takeoff. Passengers were advised to insert the orange earplugs provided, but as the engines spat and coughed to life, I left mine out. I wanted all of my senses intact for my time in the belly of the bird.

We were off, lumbering down the runway and into the air. Our cruising altitude was probably less than a thousand feet as we headed north, the shadow of the bird plain as day over the golf course greens. From the top turret position I looked back on French Mountain and the city of Glens Falls, the hub of the nationally recognized 'Hometown, USA' activity 75 years ago. Moments later, from the waist gun windows, I could see the waves and pleasure craft on Lake George only a few hundred feet below. We banked over the Sagamore Hotel and Resort in Bolton Landing, completing the 180-degree turn to return via the lake southward over Lake George Village. People on summer holiday looked up and waved; a friend dining on the lake texted to ask if I was aboard, but at the time I was too absorbed in my thoughts and my surroundings to look at the message.

I looked at my fellow passengers—a red-headed teenager, riding solo with his father's blessing, another man about my age, seemingly as absorbed as I had been, a younger touristy woman, jaws working furiously to process a wad of chewing gum as she snapped miles of cell phone video and photographs. Certainly it was an experience that was photo-worthy. I took a few shots myself, and somehow captured the essence of serenity upon an older woman's face as she gazed out of the left waist gun window, not looking down at the lake, but drifting through the sky. Was she trying to live the moment of a special somebody: a brother, a father, or perhaps even a late husband? I didn't speak to her, but her serene look spoke volumes to me. Here I was, nearing the end of my own career as a teacher, knowing full well that my old friends who had once braved the skies over Europe were leaving me. In one of the most destructive machines of war, this lady just radiated peace, a level of contentedness and gratitude and everything else that I noted in the faces of some of these grizzled veterans sitting down for the first time in front of the camera. And I think they knew it too, opening up as they did for their interviewers, both young and old, students and professionals. They had a story to tell, before it was too late.

*

I last saw my friend Earl a few weeks ago. His daughter got in touch to say she would be in town, so I drove over to the old farmhouse where he grew up, bringing him a copy of my recently released first *War in the Air* book, where he is also prominently featured. His wife passed away a few years back, his PoW friends are gone now as well, but after turning 96 he is still plugging along, one day at a time. He might not get around like he used to, but he was excited to hold the book in his hands, and as he thumbed through it, he pointed excitedly to the B-17s he once commanded in a world that seems so long ago.

*

How soon we forget.

Our World War II veterans gave us a nation that for all of its imperfections survives as a model for others, a lesson in what it means to stand together during the tough times, often against seemingly insurmountable odds, in spite of our differences or innate biases. It may help us to recall that democracy is not only very fragile, it is also hardly even out of the cradle in the backdrop of world history. But as a wise philosopher-historian once told me, what sets democracy apart from every other experiment in history—in its pure form and in theory—is its defense of minorities. That doesn't exist yet, but maybe this form of government needs to be protected, and nourished. And maybe this is what the airmen, Marines, sailors, soldiers, and merchant marines who participated in the greatest cataclysm in the history of the world were fighting for.

The world does not have to be united, and, in fact, it never has been and never will be. We argue and we disagree all of the time. That is as it is, and as it should be; it's even part of what the Allies were fighting against: a 'New World Order.' But when the chips are down, the actions of this generation remind us of who we are as a nation, what we aspired to and achieved not so long ago, together. And that should be celebrated, fêted, and honored, while our veterans are still with us, and long after the last one departs.

The Airmen featured in this book

Clarence W. Dart: After the war, Clarence Dart married and he and his wife raised a large family in Saratoga Springs, New York. He worked nearly four decades for the General Electric Company and was a reservist in the New York Air National Guard, retiring with the rank of lieutenant colonel. Mr. Dart was inducted into the New York State Veterans' Hall of Fame in 2011. He passed away on February 17, 2012, at the age of 91.[119]

John G. Weeks: Following his military service, John briefly flew for commercial airlines. He then started a long career in business, concluding as a consultant to businesses trying to avoid bankruptcy. He and his wife had four children, and in retirement, he founded a mushroom farm in Washington County, New York. He was involved in his church and many civic organizations. He passed away on October 21, 2015, at the age of 93.[120]

Richard Faulkner: Richard Faulkner married and raised three children, working as a mechanic and then for 35 years at New York State Electric and Gas Company as a lineman. He was a member of American Legion, 100th Bomb Group Association, and the Air Forces Escape & Evasion Society. He passed away at age 89 on August 29, 2014.[121]

George FitzGibbon: As a reserve officer, George FitzGibbon was recalled during the Korean War when they needed pilots. He and his wife raised three children. He retired from the Air Force in 1969 as a lieutenant colonel, the operations officer of the 41st Air Refueling Squadron at Griffiss Air Force base in New York. Later he settled in Binghamton, New York, serving as the chief pilot for New York State Electric & Gas. He passed away at the age of 93 on May 5, 2015.[122]

Charles Corea: Charlie settled back in his hometown and married, raising four children with his wife of 68 years before his death. He was active in many civic organizations, and retired in 1984 as owner and publisher of the East Rochester Shopping Guide. He passed away at the age of 92 on August 26, 2014.[123]

Earl M. Morrow: Earl Morrow was a career airline pilot for American Airlines. He and his wife retired to the family farm in Hartford, New York, after his career, where he volunteered to transport fellow veterans to the VA hospital in Albany and was a sought-after speaker in local schools and community events.

Sam Lisica: Sam Lisica married and returned to Pennsylvania, retiring after 40 years with the Pittsburgh Forgings Steel Company. He and his wife raised four children; Mr. Lisica passed away on October 11, 2006, at the age of 85.

Jerry Silverman: After the war, Jerry married and raised four children on Long Island, New York, and founded his own driving school, where he worked for 25 years. He was active in civic organizations and the Northport VA, where he served as a driver for disabled veterans. He was also an active member of the Nassau/Suffolk Chapter of the American Ex-Prisoners of War. He passed away on October 4, 2008, at the age of 89.[124]

****

****

If you liked this book, you'll love hearing more from the World War II generation in my other books. On the following pages you can see some samples, and I can let you know as soon as the new books are out and offer you exclusive discounts on some material. Just sign up at matthewrozellbooks.com

Some of my readers may like to know that all of my books are **directly available from the author, with collector's sets which can be autographed** in paperback and hardcover. They are popular gifts for that 'hard-to-buy-for' guy or gal on your list.

Visit my shop at matthewrozellbooks.com for details.

Thank you for reading!

I hope you found this book interesting and informative; I sure learned a lot researching and writing it. What follows are some descriptions of my other books.

Find them all at matthewrozellbooks.com

THE NEXT BOOK IN THIS SERIES

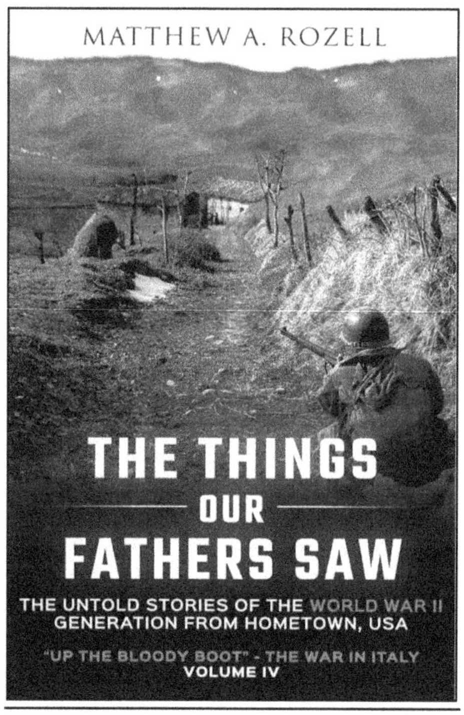

The Things Our Fathers Saw—The Untold Stories of the World War II Generation-Volume IV: 'Up the Bloody Boot'—The War in Italy

Volume 4 in this series will take you from the deserts of North Africa to the mountains of Italy with the men and women veterans of the Italian campaign who open up about a war that was so brutal, news of it was downplayed at home. The war in the Mediterranean, and particularly the Italian Campaign, is one that for many Americans is shrouded in mystery and murkiness. Yet it was here that the United States launched its first offensive in the west on enemy soil, and it was here that Allied forces would be slogging it out with a tenacious enemy fighting for its life in the longest single American Campaign of World War II.

—"There was an old French fort there, and we could look down on it during the day. We gauged the way we would hit that place so that the moon would set right between two mountain peaks; we timed it so when we got there, that moon would silhouette them, but not us... We carried out the first and only bayonet charge [of the war] by our Rangers; we didn't fire; very few people knew that we carried out an overnight bayonet attack. I'll tell you, that's something. You see that, it'll shake you up real good." ***—U.S. Army Ranger, WWII***

— "We attacked another hill, and I shot a German soldier. And then the Germans counterattacked on the hill, and I could not escape, so I decided to just lay down on top of that soldier and make believe I'm dead. They passed me by, I got up and [this German I shot] starts talking to me in English, he says he's from Coney Island, in Brooklyn; he went to visit his mother in Germany and they put him in the army. And he was dying, and he says to me, 'You can take my cigarettes; you can take my schnapps.' Then he died right underneath me. And I imagine he knew I had shot him...."
—U.S. Army scout, WWII

— "So there was a terrific fight going on in a place called Santa Maria, south of Rome. While we were going through, in transit, we stopped at a big Italian barn; they had a kitchen set up, and we had our own mess kits. As we were going through the line, we saw this huge rack of shelves with American Army duffel bags packed on there. And Hendrickson said to me, 'Hey, Tony, you know what? My brother must be in the area someplace. There's his duffel bag.' The name was stenciled on. So I said, 'That's nice.' [But] I was thinking, why is his duffel bag there? Well, there was a military policeman guarding these bags. I went back to the MP. I said to him, 'What are these bags doing here?' And I told him about Hendrickson. 'Well,' he said, 'I don't know if you want to tell him, but these guys are all dead. They were all killed at Santa Maria.'" ***—U.S. Army map maker, WWII***

ALSO FROM MATTHEW ROZELL

"What healing this has given to the survivors and military men!"-Reviewer

FROM THE ABC WORLD NEWS 'PERSON OF THE WEEK'

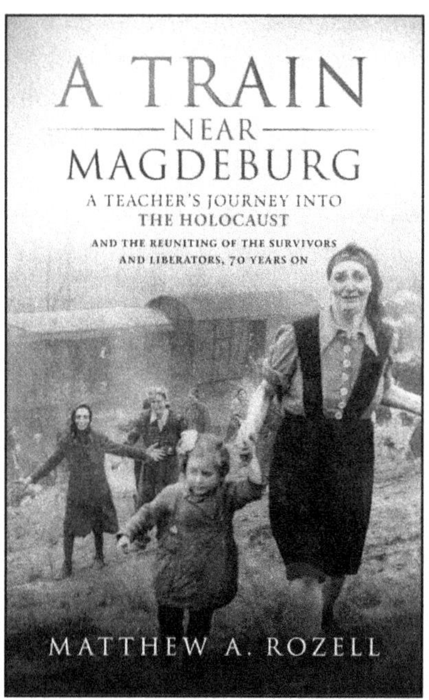

A TRAIN NEAR MAGDEBURG:

THE HOLOCAUST, AND THE REUNITING

OF THE SURVIVORS AND SOLDIERS, 70 YEARS ON

–Featuring testimony from 15 American liberators and over 30 Holocaust survivors

–73 photographs and illustrations, many never before published; 10 custom maps

–500 pages-extensive notes and bibliographical references

BOOK ONE—THE HOLOCAUST

BOOK TWO—THE AMERICANS

BOOK THREE—LIBERATION

BOOK FOUR—REUNION

THE HOLOCAUST *was a watershed event in history. In this book, Matthew Rozell reconstructs a lost chapter—the liberation of a 'death train' deep in the heart of Nazi Germany in the closing days of World War II. Drawing on never-before published eye-witness accounts, survivor testimony, and wartime reports and letters, Rozell brings to life the incredible true stories behind the iconic 1945 liberation photographs taken by the soldiers who were there. He weaves together a chronology of the Holocaust as it unfolds across Europe, and goes back to literally retrace the steps of the survivors and the American soldiers who freed them. Rozell's work results in joyful reunions on three continents, seven decades later. He offers his unique perspective on the lessons of the Holocaust for future generations, and the impact that one person can make.*

A selection of comments left by reviewers:

"**Extraordinary research** into an event which needed to be told. I have read many books about the Holocaust and visited various museums but had not heard reference to this train previously. The fact that people involved were able to connect, support and help heal each other emotionally was amazing."

"**The story of the end of the Holocaust and the Nazi regime** told from a very different and precise angle. First-hand accounts from Jewish survivors and the US soldiers that secured their freedom. Gripping."

"**Mr. Rozell travels 'back to the future'** of people who were not promised a tomorrow; neither the prisoners nor the troops knew what horrors the next moment would bring. He captures the parallel experience of soldiers fighting ruthless Nazism and the ruthless treatment of Jewish prisoners."

"**If you have any trepidation** about reading a book on the Holocaust, this review is for you. [Matthew Rozell] masterfully conveys the individual stories of those featured in the book in a manner that does not leave the reader with a sense of despair, but rather a sense of purpose."

"**Could not put this book down**--I just finished reading *A Train Near Magdeburg*. Tears fell as I read pages and I smiled through others. I wish I could articulate the emotions that accompanied me through the stories of these beautiful people."

"**Everyone should read this book**, detailing the amazing bond that formed between Holocaust survivors likely on their way to death in one last concentration camp as WWII was about to end, and a small number of American soldiers that happened upon the stopped train and liberated the victims. The lifelong friendships that resulted between the survivors and their liberators is a testament to compassion and goodness. It is amazing that the author is not Jewish but a "reluctant" history teacher who ultimately becomes a Holocaust scholar. This is a great book."

—Book Excerpt—

A TRAIN NEAR MAGDEBURG

A TEACHER'S JOURNEY INTO THE HOLOCAUST

Matthew A. Rozell

WOODCHUCK HOLLOW PRESS

Hartford · New York

A TRAIN NEAR MAGDEBURG

Battle-hardened veterans learn to contain their emotions, but it was difficult then, and I cry now to think about it. What stamina and regenerative spirit those brave people showed!

— GEORGE C. GROSS, LIBERATOR

Never in our training were we taught to be humanitarians. We were taught to be soldiers.

— FRANK W. TOWERS, LIBERATOR

[After I got home] I cried a lot. My parents couldn't understand why I couldn't sleep at times.

— WALTER 'BABE' GANTZ, US ARMY MEDIC

I cannot believe, today, that the world almost ignored those people and what was happening. How could we have all stood by and have let that happen? They do not owe us anything. We owe them, for what we allowed to happen to them.

— CARROL S. WALSH, LIBERATOR

I grew up and spent all my years being angry. This means I don't have to be angry anymore.

— PAUL ARATO, HOLOCAUST SURVIVOR

It's not for my sake, it's for the sake of humanity, that you will remember.

— STEPHEN B. BARRY, HOLOCAUST SURVIVOR

Farsleben train, moment of liberation, Friday, April 13, 1945. Two American tank commanders and their major liberate the train, deep in the heart of Nazi Germany. Stunned survivors come to the realization that they are saved. Major Benjamin snaps the photo.
Credit: Major Clarence L. Benjamin, 743rd Tank Battalion.

Author's Note

A photograph taken by an Army major seventy years ago flickers to life on the screen. In it, a profound drama unfolds before the eye. The caption on the museum website reads:

A female survivor and her child run up a hill after escaping from a train near Magdeburg and their liberation by American soldiers from the 743rd Tank Battalion and 30th Infantry Division.

Record Type: Photograph
Date: 1945 April 13
Locale: Farsleben, [Prussian Saxony] Germany
Photographer: Clarence Benjamin
Photo Designation: LIBERATION –
Germany: General
Train to Magdeburg/Farsleben
Keyword:
CHILDREN (0–3 YEARS)
CHILDREN/YOUTH
SURVIVORS
TRAINS
WOMEN

The picture defies expectations. When the terms 'Holocaust' and 'trains' are paired in an online image search, the most common result is that of people being transported to killing centers—but this incredible photograph shows exactly the opposite. And there are many things about this story that will defy expectations. Fifteen years after I brought this haunting image to the light of day, it has been called one of the most powerful photographs of the 20th century. It has been used by museums and memorials across the world, in exhibitions, films, mission appeals, and photo essays. Schoolchildren download it for reports; filmmakers ask to use it in Holocaust documentaries. Yad Vashem, the Israeli Holocaust Martyrs' and Heroes' Remembrance Authority, even employed it as the backdrop for Israel's state ceremonies in the presence of survivors, their president, prime minister, the entire government, top army brass, and the chief rabbi in a national broadcast on the 70th anniversary of the liberation and aftermath of the Holocaust. I know, because they reached out to me for it—me, an ordinary public school teacher, six thousand miles away.

For over half a century, a copy of this photograph and others were hidden away in a shoebox in the back of an old soldier's closet. By spending time with this soldier, I was able to set in motion an extraordinary confluence of events that unfolded organically in the second half of my career as a history teacher. Many of the children who suffered on that train found me, and I was able to link them forever with the men who I had come to know and love, the American GIs who saved them that beautiful April morning. A moment in history is captured on film, and we have reunited the actors, the persecuted, and their liberators, two generations on.

*

It is a cool spring morning. In the background, down the hill, are two cattle cars. If we look closely, we can see a figure sitting on the edge of the opening of a boxcar, perhaps too weak to climb out yet soaking up some energy from the warming April sun. In front of him, a wisp of smoke seems to rise from a small makeshift fire that others have gathered around. The sound of gunfire is echoing nearby; a metallic clanking sound is growing louder at the top of the hill.

This is an appropriate backdrop for the marvel unfolding in the foreground. Now only a few steps away, a woman and perhaps her young daughter are trudging up the hill toward the photographer. The woman has her hair wrapped in a scarf and is clutching the hand of the girl with her right hand. Her left arm is extended outward as if in greeting; her face is turning into a half smile in a mixture of astonishment and enveloping joy, as if she is on the cusp of accepting the belief that she and her daughter have just been saved.

In contrast, the little girl is shooting a sideways glance away from the camera. Her expression is one of distress—she looks terrified. So what is really happening, and what are the amazing stories behind the picture?

On this morning in Germany in 1945, she may very well be responding to the two Sherman tanks that are now clattering up to the train behind the photographer, who is in the Jeep with the white star.

Following the mother and daughter up the hill towards the soldiers are two other women. One welcomes the tanks with outstretched arms and a wide grin as she moves up the hill. The other follows behind her. She appears to be crying.

It is Friday, the 13th of April, 1945. Led by their major scouting in a Jeep, Tanks 12 and 13 of 'D' Company, 743rd Tank Battalion, US Army, have just liberated a train transport with thousands of sick and emaciated victims of the Holocaust. In an instant, Major Clarence L. Benjamin snaps a photograph so fresh and raw that if one did not know better, one might think it was from a modern cellphone, although it will be soon buried into his official report back to headquarters.

But what have they stumbled upon? Where have these people come from?

And what do the soldiers do now?

*

In this educator's narrative, you will learn of the tragedies and the triumphs behind the photograph. You will enter the abyss of the Holocaust with me, which the United States Holocaust Memorial Museum defines as 'the systematic, bureaucratic, state-sponsored persecution and murder of six million Jews by the Nazi regime and its collaborators.' You will meet the survivors of that train as they immerse you in their worlds as civilization collapsed around them. We will visit the camps and authentic sites together, and we will trace the route of the brave Americans who found themselves confronted with industrial-scale genocide. And I will lead you safely out of the chasm as we witness the aftermath, the miracles of liberation and reunification, seven decades later.

In many respects, this story should still be buried, because there is no logical way to explain my role in the climactic aftermath. I was born sixteen years after the killing stopped, a continent away from the horrors and comfortably unaware of the events of the Holocaust and World War II for much of my life. I was raised in the sanctuary of a nurturing community and an intact family. I am not Jewish and had never even been inside a synagogue until my forties. I'm not observantly religious, but I am convinced that I was chosen to affirm and attest to what I have experienced. In this book I rewind the tape to reconstruct how indeed it all came to be—the horrors of the experiences of the Holocaust survivors, the ordeals and sacrifices of the American soldiers, and the miracles of liberation and reunification.

As the curtain descends on a career spanning four decades, consider this also one teacher's testament—a memoir of sorts, but more a story of being caught up as an integral part of something much bigger than myself, driven by some invisible force which has conquered the barriers of time and space. I too became a witness, and this is what I saw.

Matthew Rozell
Hudson Falls, New York
September 2016

LIBERATION

'We Keep the Faith'

–Motto of the 743rd Tank Battalion

For the first time after going through sheer hell, I felt that there was such a thing as simple love coming from good people—young men who had left their families far behind, who wrapped us in warmth and love and cared for our well-being.

–Sara Atzmon, Holocaust survivor

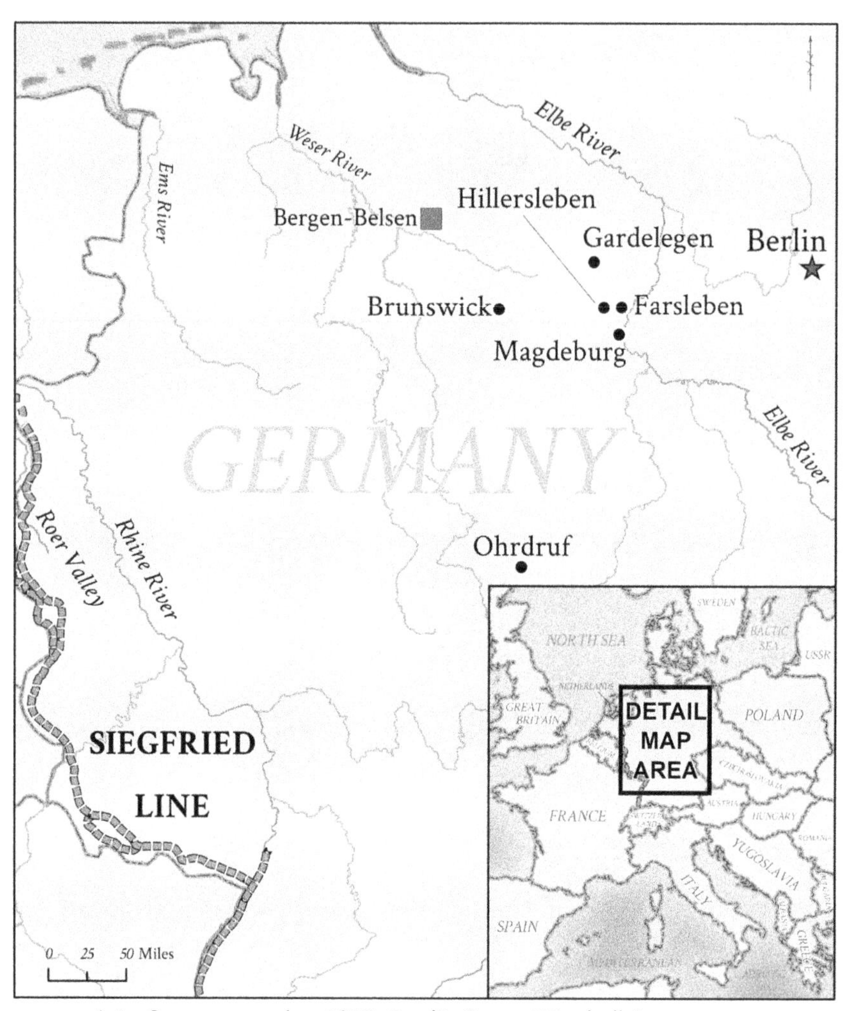

Into Germany, spring 1945. Credit: Susan Winchell-Sweeney.

What the Soldiers Saw

April 13, 1945/Central Germany

On April 13, 1945, World War II was in its sixth year. As Allied troops closed in on the crumbling Reich from all directions, the war continued everywhere. On this day in the Pacific, Tokyo would burn, again, after 327 B-29s dropped their payloads on the arsenal there. The battles for Okinawa and the Philippines were raging with no end in sight. The US Eighth Army Air Force was heading out on its 945th mission over enemy territory and Allied troops continued to slog it out against the retreating Germans in the north of Italy. Advance units of the 30th and 83rd Infantry Divisions reached the Elbe River and were preparing to cross it, although Eisenhower was now dictating that Berlin was a political prize which he would leave to the Russians, seeing no purpose in putting more American lives at risk when faced with the enormous tasks already at hand. Vienna fell to the Red Army and Soviet troops were also moving onto the Elbe River and closing in for the kill on Berlin even as

Hitler celebrated the death of Roosevelt, his own death by his own hand only a few weeks off.*

The American Ninth Army, to which the 30th Infantry Division was attached, had now nearly cut Germany in two, spearheading towards the Elbe River. The First and Third Army closed in on Austria and Czechoslovakia. Resistance in the industrial Ruhr Valley was rapidly collapsing, and Allied supply lines were stretched to the limit, compounded by the German forces now surrendering literally in the hundreds of thousands, all of whom had to be fed in the hastily erected compounds. Thousands more Russian, American, and British POWs shuffled along on forced marches where many dropped from exhaustion, starvation, dysentery, and outright murder at the hands of their captors. And all over the Reich, inmates of hundreds of concentration camps were also on the move as the Germans tried haphazardly to shift and destroy the evidence of their crimes. In the northwest, the British Second Army closed in on major ports and the town of Celle, where a nearby camp called Bergen–Belsen was putting out feelers for the peaceful transfer of power to the Allies.

Into this churning cauldron of suffering we now pour the nearly incomprehensible element that was thrust onto the shoulders of the young American soldiers—the overrunning of the hundreds of concentration camps and subcamps, euthanasia centers and prisons—an overall tapestry of horror that unfolded on an hourly basis throughout the collapsing Reich from the first part of April 1945 forward.

On April 12, General Eisenhower reached Ohrdruf, one of the more than 80 subcamps of Buchenwald, joined by Generals Bradley and Patton. It was the first Nazi camp liberated by US troops, and

---

* The Red Army launched its final assault on Berlin on April 16. In the two weeks that followed, it suffered over 350,000 casualties.

here, for the first time, the commanders themselves came face-to-face with the horrors of the Holocaust; General Patton got sick behind a shack. When aides pressed Ike to move on, he told them he was not to be rushed. He then ordered, 'I want every American unit not actually in the front lines to see this place. We are told that the American soldier does not know what he is fighting for. Not at least, he will know what he is fighting against.'

Later, he would cable Washington:

> The things I saw beggar description. While I was touring the camp I encountered three men who had been inmates and by one ruse or another had made their escape. I interviewed them through an interpreter. The visual evidence and the verbal testimony of starvation, cruelty, and bestiality were so overpowering as to leave me a bit sick. In one room, where they were piled up twenty or thirty naked men, killed by starvation, George Patton would not even enter. He said that he would get sick if he did so. I made the visit deliberately, in order to be in a position to give first-hand evidence of these things if ever, in the future, there develops a tendency to charge these allegations merely to 'propaganda.'[125]

*

On the 13th, just 40 kilometers to the north of where the men of the 743rd Tank Battalion and 30th Infantry Division were now setting out towards their final battle, over one thousand Jewish slave laborers were herded into a large barn by SS guards and locals. The doors were closed and the guards stationed themselves on the perimeter. Gasoline-soaked straw was then lit, and as the conflagration spread, nearly all of the prisoners burned alive and others were shot to death as they tried to burrow under the barn walls to escape the flames. Two days later, the Gardelegen Massacre was discovered as US troops reached the still smoldering barn.

*

Now, it was the tankers' turn. Shortly after the war ended, Pfc. Wayne Robinson, the author of the 743rd Tank Battalion's official history, composed the soldiers' dramatic introduction to the Holocaust, even before it had a name.

> There was another sidelight to the death of fascism in Europe. Only a few of the battalion saw it. Those who did will never forget it.
>
> A few miles northwest of Magdeburg there was a railroad siding in wooded ravine not far from the Elbe River. Major Clarence Benjamin in a jeep was leading a small task force of two light tanks from Dog Company on a routine job of patrolling. The unit came upon some 200 shabby looking civilians by the side of the road. There was something immediately apparent about each one of these people, men and women, which arrested the attention. Each one of them was skeleton-thin with starvation, a sickness in their faces and the way in which they stood-and there was something else. At the sight of Americans they began laughing in joy-if it could be called laughing. It was an outpouring of pure, near-hysterical relief.
>
> The tankers soon found out why. The reason was found at the railroad siding.
>
> There they came upon a long string of grimy, ancient boxcars standing silent on the tracks.

In the banks by the tracks, as if to get some pitiful comfort from the thin April sun, a multitude of people of all shades of misery spread themselves in a sorry, despairing tableau. As the American uniforms were sighted, a great stir went through this strange camp. Many rushed toward the Major's jeep and the two light tanks.

Bit by bit, as the Major found some who spoke English, the story came out.

This had been-and was-a horror train. In these freight cars had been shipped 2,500 people, jam-packed in like sardines, and they were people that had two things in common, one with the other: They were prisoners of the German state, and they were Jews.

Henry Birnbrey was part of an advance party that was one of the first to reach the train. As a German Jew, Henry had the good fortune to be sponsored for immigration to the United States before the war broke out; he applied to join the U.S. Army and was sent over with the 30th Division as a forward artillery spotter scouting positions in the lead-up to the final battle at Magdeburg; it was the advance parties which had probably radioed back to the command post the information about the existence of the train just ahead of the rest of the 30th Infantry Division.

Henry Birnbrey

I was a forward observer from the 531st Anti-Aircraft; we were searching for gun positions. We moved on to the Braunschweig

(Brunswick) area. Here, along the highway, we encountered ditches full of dead concentration camp prisoners who had been marched from one camp to another, and were shot before they had a chance to be liberated.

All of a sudden, I was attracted by this terrible odor and we could not figure out where it was coming from. I told my jeep driver to head 'over there.' Suddenly, I see these freight cars with people coming out of them. When I got out of the jeep, I realized what it was all about, and actually spoke with some of the people. Most of them, the first word out of their mouth was in Yiddish, 'Ikh bin a id,' which means, 'I am a Jew.' That was about the extent of our conversation—they only spoke Yiddish, and my Yiddish was very limited because German Jews hated the Yiddish language; my father would not allow it in our house. I communicated with a few people as best I could.

The sub-human conditions which these people were subjected to had reduced them to a very sorry state. We did not know how long they had been in those cars; they looked like walking skeletons and could barely speak. Unfortunately, we had no food to share with them, which gave us a very helpless feeling; headquarters was notified... I was very frustrated because I saw these people were starving, and I had nothing to share with them; all I had was my canteen with water. I had no K-rations; I had nothing to give them. I had an awful helpless feeling. I stayed about an hour and then I had to do my job that I was supposed to be doing.

I was in a state of shock; I had never seen people look that bad in my whole life. I was terrified. My biggest frustration was that I had nothing to help them with. I was reminded of the words of the prophet Ezekiel—

'He took me down in the spirit of G-d and set me down in the valley. It was full of bones.'

The train, Friday, April 13, 1945. Credit: George Gross.

George C. Gross

Major Benjamin led our two tanks, each carrying several infantrymen from the 30th Infantry Division on its deck, down a narrow road until we came to a valley with a small train station at its head and a motley assemblage of passenger compartment cars and boxcars pulled onto a siding. There was a mass of people sitting or lying listlessly about, unaware as yet of our presence. There must have been guards, but they evidently ran away before or as we arrived, for I remember no firefight. Our taking of the train, therefore, was no great heroic action but a small police operation. The heroism that day was all with the prisoners on the train.

Carrol 'Red' Walsh

We were coming down this dirt roadway, as I remember. I had no idea what we were approaching or where we were going or what was going on. I can remember just approaching this area, and all of a sudden, ahead of me I saw this train. It was stopped. In my mind I can still see it, and I could see how long that train was, that long, long string of boxcars and the engine in the front. There were no SS guards around it at the time that we came upon it. I can remember swinging my tank to the right and proceeding alongside of the train. I didn't know what was really on that train until that tank stopped. Then I saw what the train held.

Q. Did you see the doors of those boxcars open at that time?

Yes, I believe they were. I believe that they were open; some of the people were up. But I still remember peering into those boxcars and seeing those people just huddled and mashed together inside those boxcars.

Did you know at the time that these were prisoners, or had been prisoners, or that they had been held? Did you have any idea what they were doing there?

No, I had no idea. I had no idea who they were, where they had come from, where they were going—nothing. No idea. All I knew was, here's a train with these boxcars, and people jammed in those boxcars. No, I had no idea. And as I look back and I contemplate that thought, I suppose we were too busy in combat to think of anything except what we were doing at the time. And of course, you know, we were not privileged to hear any news. We did not know really what was going on. We did not know whether we were successful in our own [*chuckles*] endeavors or not! So, no. I was not aware of the extent of the horror that was perpetrated on the Jewish people. No, I had no idea at the time of the extent of the concentration camps.

The train, April 14, 1945. Photographer unknown, probably U.S. Army. Credit: USHMM, courtesy of Flora Carasso Mihael.

George C. Gross

Major Benjamin took a powerful picture just as a few of the people became aware that they had been rescued. It shows people in the background still lying about, trying to soak up a bit of energy from the sun, while in the foreground a woman has her arms flung wide and a great look of surprise and joy on her face as she rushes toward us.

Reports After/After Action, April 1945, Cont'd:

The photograph inserted below was taken by MAJOR BENJAMIN at the moment the first of the refugees at the train became aware of their liberation and started to move up the hill toward our troops.

There were 12 German military guards including the train commander who gave up without a fight when they saw our tanks. There 2500 pitiable, oppressed people from all over Europe, starved, beaten, ill, some dying, but all of whom were wildly happy and grateful to their "liberators." The tank crews passed out what food and cigarettes they could to help the sufferers. These people,

The original photograph inserted into the official After Action Report. Credit: Major Clarence L. Benjamin. Source: After Action Report, April 1945, 743rd Tank Battalion S-3 Journal History, p. 118.

In a moment, that woman found a pack left by a fleeing German soldier, rummaged through it, and held up triumphantly a tin of rations.* She was immediately attacked by a swarm of skeletal

---

* *that woman found a pack left by a fleeing German soldier*- The woman in the Benjamin photograph has been *possibly* identified as Sara Spitzer-Rubinstein of Havasmezö, Hungary. She died in Brooklyn, NY, at the age of 97, but others have made claims regarding the identity of the woman, and the little girl clutching her hand, as well.

figures, each one intent upon capturing that prize. My yelling did no good, so that I finally had to leap from my tank and wade through weak and emaciated bodies to pull the attackers off the woman, who ran quickly away with her prize. I felt like a bully, pushing around such weak and starving fellow humans, but it was necessary to save the woman from great harm. The incident drove home to me the terrible plight of the newly freed inhabitants of the train.

I pulled my tank up beside the small station house at the head of the train and kept it there as a sign that the train was under American protection now. Carrol Walsh's tank was soon sent back to the battalion, and I do not remember how long the infantrymen stayed with us, though it was a comfort to have them for a while. My recollection is that my tank was alone for the afternoon and night of the 13th.

Carrol 'Red' Walsh

What are we going to do with these people? How can we handle this situation? Fortunately, there was another attached unit with the 30th Division. They were in the area. The 823rd Tank Destroyer Battalion immediately went around the neighborhood there, getting food from the local farmers and bringing it to the people. And then overnight or the next day, there were other units that arrived to assist these people and find shelter for them. That first night they stayed around the train.

George C. Gross

A number of things happened fairly quickly. We were told that the commander of the 823rd Tank Destroyer Battalion had ordered all the burgermeisters of nearby towns to prepare food and get it to the train promptly, and were assured that Military Government would take care of the refugees the following day. So we were left to hunker down and protect the starving people, commiserating with, if not relieving, their dire condition.

*

Colonel Dettmer of the 823rd Tank Destroyer Battalion, also attached to the 30th Infantry Division, set up his command post in Farsleben, a small German hamlet of 500, now suddenly invaded by several hundred more desperate skeletal figures. The swarm of refugees, many of whom had broken into the town's two bakeries, reported to him that they had had nothing to eat for days. Dettmer immediately summoned the mayor, and ordered the bakeries to bake throughout the night, for cattle and sheep to be slaughtered, and for families to open their homes to the survivors. When the burgermeister began to protest and made a display of reluctance, the battalion commander drew his sidearm, put it to the mayor's head, and calmly asked him to recite his instructions.[126] The following day, the 823rd's surgeon, Captain Baranov, spent the entire day setting up a makeshift hospital to try to contain a typhus epidemic that was rapidly escalating among those rescued. The Military Government was arranging to transfer the survivors to a Luftwaffe base and proving grounds recently captured; Dettmer's command post moved out, and shortly thereafter the burgermeister unceremoniously murdered his wife and committed suicide.[127]

The logbook for the 105th Medical Battalion of the 30th Infantry Division was kept by T/4 Sgt. Wilson Rice, who interjected colorful personal commentaries when typing up his reports.

Wilson Rice

April 13, 1945

Farther on down the road, when the convoy was halted again, Major Marsh from the Military Government drove up to Col. Treherne's jeep. He told him about a train of civilians that were prisoners of the Germans. Our jeep pulled out from the convoy and went to Farsleben, Germany, where the train was located.

Also in this town was the command post of the 823rd Tank Destroyer Battalion, and we stopped there to pick up Capt. Baranov, the 823rd Battalion surgeon. He took us down there, and it was something that you've read about, but couldn't believe. They were people that looked of being very refined and cultured; it is said that among them was the French Consul to Germany.

Some great minds were among these people. There were two doctors that were members of the train, and they were caring for the people the best they could without any equipment. Capt. Baranov's men came up with a few drugs, bandages, etc. to use until they could get more. It was about the same as nothing, but it was to go to the women and children first. About 75% of the members of this train were Jews, so the drugs were given to the two doctors and the rabbi for distribution.* Major Lowell and Major Huff told them to get all of the contagious and seriously sick to be segregated into cars by themselves. These cars that they were traveling in were boxcars. Sanitation was terrible and the people had been traveling in them for eight days and nights, without food or water. Most of the sickness was due to malnutrition. There were only two typhus cases.

As all of the business was being transacted, a beautiful little girl, about eight years of age, came up to my side. She was very sweet and her complexion was very clear. I looked at her, smiled, and patted her on the head, and she smiled back. As Tommy and I were standing there, I soon felt a little hand slip through my arm. As I looked down, a big lump came in my throat.

As we were leaving, a man came up to our jeep. He was one of the American citizens and was from Detroit, Michigan. He was taken prisoner two years ago in Warsaw, and his family is still now in Detroit. He was a sick man, but there was nothing we could do for him, as we were not prepared for such things. The Military Government is taking care of things as fast as they can.

---

* *About 75% of the members of this train were Jews*- This statement, along with the one about the rumor of the French Consul to Germany being among the prisoners, were some of the speculations circulating among the soldiers that day. Probably all of the passengers were the Jews from the exchange camp, and no trace of a French consul has been substantiated.

This is what I mean when I say that warfare such as this was not planned for by the Army. Things are going too fast. This man told us about the 33 American citizens*. He went on to say that he knew our circumstances, knew we had to take care of the troops first, knew that everything possible will be done for them as fast as possible, and went on to say, 'We know how busy you guys are, what you will do for us, maybe one week, maybe two weeks, but even if nothing else is done, there is one thing we truly and dearly thank you for, and that is for our liberty.'

There was a break in this man's voice, and I knew how he felt. There was a lump in my throat.

Get The Book Here: matthewrozellbooks.com

---

* *33 American citizens*- The doctor probably refers to Jews with American papers, real or assumed identities.

ABOUT THE AUTHOR

Photo Credit: Joan K. Lentini; May, 2017.

Matthew Rozell is an award-winning history teacher, author, speaker, and blogger on the topic of the most cataclysmic events in the history of mankind—World War II and the Holocaust. Rozell has been featured as the 'ABC World News Person of the Week' and has had his work as a teacher filmed for the CBS Evening News, NBC Learn, the Israeli Broadcast Authority, the United States Holocaust Memorial Museum, and the New York State United Teachers. He writes on the power of teaching and the importance of the study of history at TeachingHistoryMatters.com, and you can 'Like' his Facebook author page at MatthewRozellBooks for updates.

Mr. Rozell is a sought-after speaker on World War II, the Holocaust, and history education, motivating and inspiring his audiences with the lessons of the past. Visit MatthewRozell.com for availability/details.

About this Book/ Acknowledgements

*

A note on historiographical style and convention: to enhance accuracy, consistency, and readability, I corrected punctuation and spelling and sometimes even place names, but only after extensive research. I did take the liberty of occasionally condensing the speaker's voice, eliminating side tangents or incidental information not relevant to the matter at hand. Sometimes two or more interviews with the same person were combined for readability and narrative flow. All of the words of the subjects, however, are essentially their own.

Additionally, I chose to utilize footnotes and endnotes where I deemed them appropriate, directing readers who wish to learn more to my sources, notes, and side commentary. I hope that they do not detract from the flow of the narrative.

*

First, I will always acknowledge the hundreds of students who passed through my classes and who forged the bonds with the World War II generation. I promised you this book someday, and now that many of you are yourselves parents, you can tell your children this book is for them. Who says young people are indifferent to the past? Here is evidence to the contrary.

The Hudson Falls Central School District and my former colleagues have my deep appreciation for supporting this endeavor and recognizing its significance throughout the years.

For helpful feedback and suggestions on the original manuscript I am indebted to my good friend and trusted critic, Alan Bush. Alan always offers solid advice, diving into the narrative as soon as it arrives in his inbox, saving me perhaps a good deal of anguish with his timely and trusted comments. Additionally, Sunny Buchman was one of my early champions and worked to arrange interviews with the folks at her retirement community, The Glen at Hiland Meadows. My wife Laura re-typed some of the seventy-five-year-old letters and reports. My friend Rob Miller traveled to my hometown to take some very special portraits of our veterans and participate in some of our events recognizing them. The Folklife Center at Crandall Public Library in Glens Falls helped with background information on the *LOOK Magazine* series that profiled the Glens Falls–North Country region as 'Hometown, USA' during the war. To my good friend and classmate Paul Dietrich, thanks for finally getting me on board to experience firsthand a deafening, lumbering B-17 flight up Lake George and back.

Naturally this work would not have been possible had it not been for the willingness of the veterans to share their stories for posterity. Andy Doty graciously allowed me to use excerpts from his well-written war autobiography. All of the veterans who were interviewed for this book had the foresight to complete release forms granting access to their stories, and for us to share the information with the New York State Military Museum's Veterans Oral History Project, where copies of most of the interviews reside. Wayne Clarke and Mike Russert of the NYSMMVOP were instrumental in cultivating this relationship with my classes over the years, and are responsible for some of the interviews in this book as well. Please see the 'Source Notes.'

I would be remiss if I did not recall the profound influence of my late mother and father, Mary and Tony Rozell, both cutting edge educators and proud early supporters of my career. To my younger siblings Mary, Ned, Nora, and Drew, all accomplished writers and authors, thank you for your encouragement as well. Final and deepest appreciations go to my wife Laura and our children, Emma, Ned, and Mary. Thank you for indulging the old man as he attempted to bring to life the stories he collected as a young one.

NOTES

Volume I Notes

A Sunday Morning

The chapter title was inspired by a heading in Studs Terkel's Pulitzer Prize winning The Good War: An Oral History of World War II (1984), undoubtedly the primary influence on my career in narrative history and on this work. A must-read for anyone who enjoyed this book. http://bit.ly/goodwar.

Map, *'Extent of Japanese Control in the Pacific, 1942'* by Susan Winchell-Sweeney, Matthew Rozell, Editor [2015] after Donald L. Miller, *The Story of World War II.* New York: Simon & Schuster, 2001. Digital data sources: Esri, HERE, Delorme, USGS, Intermap, increment P Corp., NRCAN, Esri Japan, METI, Esri China (Hong Kong), Esri (Thailand), TomTom, MapmyIndia, OpenStreetMap contributors, and the GIS User Community.

[1] Testimony of Stephen Bower Young, cited in Miller, Donald. *The Story of World War II.* New York: Simon & Schuster, 2001. 90. In this work, I have leaned heavily on Donald L. Miller. I had searched for months for a good 'textbook' to use with high school seniors. In addition to Terkel, mentioned above, this book fit the bill and I have used it in the classroom for over a decade.

[2] After Action Report. USS Oklahoma, Reports of Pearl Harbor Attack. 20 December 1941. Department of the Navy-Navy Historical Center.

[3] "World War II-Valor in the Pacific National Monument". National Park Service, U.S. Department of the Interior. http://www.nps.gov/valr/index.htm.

[4] Morton, Louis. *The Fall of the Philippines, Chapter V: The First Days of War.* CMH Pub 5-2. US Army Center for Military History. 1953. www.history.army.mil/books/wwii/5-2/5-2_5.htm

The Defenders

Map, *'Route of Pvt. Joseph G. Minder in the Philippines, Oct. 1941-May 1942.'* by Susan Winchell Sweeney, Matthew Rozell, Editor [2015]. Digital data sources: Esri, HERE, Delorme, USGS, Intermap, increment P Corp., NRCAN, Esri Japan, METI, Esri China (Hong Kong), Esri (Thailand), TomTom, MapmyIndia, OpenStreetMap contributors, and the GIS User Community.

[5] Tenney, Lester I. *My Hitch in Hell: the Bataan Death March.* London: Brassey's, 2001. 38. Lester Tenney, a Bataan Death March survivor and POW slave laborer at a mine in Japan, filed a pioneering lawsuit against the Japanese company he slaved for while a POW in Japan. In 2000, it was dismissed in a California court at the urging of the U.S. Government. In 2003, the U.S. Supreme Court turned aside this case and dozens of other POW slave labor claims.
[6] "Malinta Tunnel." Corregidor: The Island Fortress. http://www.corregidorisland.com/malinta.html.
[7] Ward, Geoffrey C. and Burns, Ken. *The War- An Intimate History.* New York: Alfred. A. Knopf, 2007.38.
[8] Miller, *The Story of World War II.* 105,111.
[9] Burr, Patten. "John Parsons, Local GI, Recounts Jap Tortures", *The Glens Falls Post-Star,* Jan. 30, 1946.
[10] Sloan, Bill. "Corregidor: The Last Battle in the Fall of the Philippines." HistoryNet. http://www.historynet.com/corregidor-the-last-battle-in-the-fall-of-the-philippines.htm.
[11]"Defenders of the Philippines." *92nd Garage Area.* http://philippine-defenders.lib.wv.us/html/92nd_garage.html.
[12]"Defenders" of the Philippines." *Cabanatuan.* http://philippine-defenders.lib.wv.us/html/cabanatuan.html

[13] Holmes, Linda Goetz. *Unjust Enrichment: How Japan's Companies Built Postwar Fortunes Using American POWs.* Mechanicsburg, PA: Stackpole Books, 2001. 13.
[14] Miller, *The Story of World War II.* 125.
[15] Keegan, John. *The Second World War.* New York: Viking, 1990. 275.

A TURNING POINT/GUADALCANAL

Map, *'Guadalcanal, Sept. 1942'* by Susan Winchell-Sweeney, Matthew Rozell, Editor [2015], after Hoffman, Major Jon T., *From Makin to Bougainville: Marine Raiders in the Pacific War.* National Park Service website. Digital data sources: Esri, HERE, Delorme, USGS, Intermap, increment P Corp., NRCAN, Esri Japan, METI, Esri China (Hong Kong), Esri (Thailand), TomTom, MapmyIndia, OpenStreetMap contributors, and the GIS User Community.

[16] Ward, Geoffrey C. and Burns, Ken. *The War,* 49.
[17]Alexander, Colonel Joseph H. *Edson's Raiders: The First Marine Raider Battalion in World War II.* Annapolis: Naval Institute Press, 2000. 49.
[18] Alexander, *Edson's Raiders.* 32.
[19] Alexander, *Edson's Raiders.* 60-63
[20] Alexander, *Edson's Raiders.* 102.
[21] Mr. Jones continued: "Matter of fact, he wanted me to stay out there and work for them. One day, he came to me and said—they were high society— he said, 'There's going to be a debutante coming-out party. We always like to have a few service men present, so it doesn't look too bad.' He asked if I would go with his friend's daughter. I said yes. He said it wasn't a romance or anything. I told him I would accompany her. Her name was Anne Folger, the coffee people, from Folgers coffee. Anyway, they took pictures of this coming-out party, and that's one of the pictures that was in *LIFE Magazine*… [*shows clipping*] That's me with Anne Folger… At the table were the Spreckles, they were the big sugar people [on the west coast]. One of them was married to Clark Gable, the movie actor. I was in way over

my head.... Incidentally, you don't remember the Mansons, do you? How his people murdered Sharon Tate, and Anne Folger...she was one of the girls that they murdered!"

[22] Alexander, *Edson's Raiders.* 112-115.

[23] Alexander, *Edson's Raiders.* 153.

[24] Miller, *The Story of World War II.* 151.

[25] Manchester, William. *Goodbye, Darkness: A Memoir of the Pacific War* (Boston: Little, Brown) 1987. p. 175, 209.

[26]I asked Gerry West, of Washington County, New York, how fellow Raider Bob Addison, originally from Ohio, came to be reacquainted with him. "Well, the funny thing was, after I retired from the military in March of '62, that summer Bob got transferred in [to work at the fledging Adirondack Community College] and came into Sears [store where Gerry worked] to buy his appliances. He looked over at me and walked over and said, 'I know you from somewhere.' I knew the face, and I mean you're talking twenty years, because the last time I had seen Bob was in 1943 in Camp Elliott. So it was like 19 years later! We got talking, and the minute he said, 'Marine Corps,' then I remembered."

[27] Wagner, Richard. *Richard Wagner War Diary* cited in Larson, Don, *Lucky's Life.* 2014. Privately published.

Sea Action

[28] Interview with Alvin Peachman, June 16, 2003.

Captivity—Year 2

Source: Minder, Joseph G. *World War II Diary of Joseph G. Minder, 1941-1945.*

[29] Burr, Patten. "John Parsons, Local GI, Recounts Jap Tortures", *The Glens Falls Post-Star,* Jan. 30, 1946.

[30] Supplemental information from "Memorial Day- Three Wars, Three Vets Remember". *Writings From Main Street*, https://dadoonan.wordpress.com, May 17, 2007.

ISLANDS OF THE DAMNED

The chapter title was inspired by R.V. Burgin's World War II Marine memoir of the same name.

[31] Berry, Henry. *Semper Fi, Mac: Living Memories of the U.S. Marines in World War II.* New York: Arbor House, 1982.
[32] Carola, Chris. "US Survivors of WWII Battle Recall Saipan Attack." *Associated Press.* July 6, 2014.
[33] O'Brien, Francis. *Battling For Saipan.* New York: Ballantine Books, 2003. xi.
[34] Carola, Chris. "US Survivors of WWII Battle Recall Saipan Attack." *Associated Press.* July 6, 2014.
[35] Miller, *The Story of World War II.* 379.
[36] Hough, Frank O. *The Seizure of Peleliu.* USMC Historical Monograph. Historical Branch, G-3 Division, Headquarters, U.S. Marine Corps. 94.
[37] A *Glens Falls Post-Star* clipping dated Jan. 13, 1945, indicates Mr. Murray was wounded at 'Palau Island in the South Pacific area.' This is technically incorrect, but not surprising. Little was known about the battle for Peleliu back home at the time it was being fought, and it was soon overshadowed by larger campaigns. Hearing the division commander's pronouncement that the operation would take three days at the most, few of the press corps were on the scene, many opting to travel with MacArthur to the long-awaited re-conquest of the Philippines. John's narrative has been excerpted from a private account written in 1995.
[38]Taken from a series of classroom interviews with Dan Lawler and James Butterfield over several years, beginning in May 2000.

CAPTIVITY—YEAR 3: THE HELLSHIPS

[39] "Defenders of the Philippines." Hellships. http://philippine-defenders.lib.wv.us/html/hellships.html.
[40] Blakeslee, Robert B. Unpublished interview conducted in 1945.
[41] Burr, Patten. "John Parsons, Local GI, Recounts Jap Tortures", *The Glens Falls Post-Star,* Jan. 30, 1946.

The Sands of Iwo Jima

The chapter title was inspired by the famous film of the same name.
[42]*World War II: Time-Life Books History of the Second World War*. New York: Prentice Hall, 1989.

Captivity—Year 4: The Copper Mine

Source: Minder, Joseph G. *World War II Diary of Joseph G. Minder, 1941-1945.*
This particular mine was owned by the Kajima Corporation. "Working conditions were dangerous and mistreatment a daily occurrence. Most slave labor was for the Fujita-gumi Construction Company." Source: "Hanaoka Sendai #7-B", *Center for Research, Allied POWS Under the Japanese.*
www.mansell.com/pow_resources/camplists/sendai/sendai_07_hanuoka/hanaoka_7_b.html.

A Rain of Ruin

The chapter title is inspired by President Harry S. Truman's Aug. 6, 1945, admonition that the Japanese would face a "rain of ruin from the air" if they did not surrender.
[43] Miller, *The Story of World War II.* 441,448.
[44] Miller, *The Story of World War II.* 458-61.

The Kamikazes

[45] "MacArthur's Speeches: Radio Message from the Leyte Beachhead", *American Experience*: *MacArthur*
www.pbs.org/wgbh/amex/macarthur/filmmore/reference/primary/macspeech03.html
[46] Miller, *The Story of World War II.* 415.
[47] Miller, *The Story of World War II.* 416.
[48] Crossing the 'T' illustration, Stephan Brunker 2004. Courtesy Wikimedia Commons.

Typhoon of Steel/Okinawa

[49]Interview with Bruce Manell. Interviewed by Kayla Cronin, Dec. 18, 2003.
[50]Interview with James Butterfield. Interviewed by Matthew Rozell, Veterans' Symposium, May 29, 2001. Sara Prehoda and Jackie Quarters helped with the transcription.
[51]Classroom interview with Dan Lawler and James Butterfield. Interviewed by Matthew Rozell, Nov. 24, 2003.
[52]Sloan, Bill, *The Ultimate Battle –Okinawa 1945 –The Last Epic Battle of World War II.* New York: Simon & Schuster. 2007. 257.
[53] This segment was taken from a classroom interview with Dan Lawler, James Butterfield, and Mary Butterfield on Jan. 11, 2007. Elizabeth Maziejka did work on the transcription.
[54]Miller, *The Story of World War II.* 151.

Redemption

[55]"Operation Downfall", *American Experience: Victory in the Pacific.* PBS. www.pbs.org/wgbh/americanexperience/features/general-article/pacific-operation-downfall/
[56] Hillenbrand, Laura. *Unbroken: A World War II Story of Survival, Resilience, and Redemption.* New York: Random House, 2010. 198-199.
[57] This incident is confirmed at "Hanaoka Sendai #7-B", *Center for Research, Allied POWS Under the Japanese.* www.mansell.com/pow_resources/camplists/sendai/sendai_07_hanuoka/hanaoka_7_b.html. Joe Minder's name can also be found on the POW roster there.
[58]Interview with Admiral Stuart S. Murray, U.S. Naval Institute Oral History interview, 1974. "USS Battleship Missouri Memorial", https://ussmissouri.org/learn-the-history/surrender/admiral-murrays-account.

[59] Sides, Hampton. *Ghost Soldiers: The Forgotten Epic Story of World War II's Most Dramatic Mission.* New York: Doubleday, 2001. 329.

Resurrection

[60] "World War II-Valor in the Pacific National Monument". National Park Service, U.S. Department of the Interior. http://www.nps.gov/valr/faqs.htm

[61] In late July 2015, as this book went to press, the Defense POW/MIA Accounting Agency began the exhumations of the 388 unidentified victims at the National Memorial Cemetery of the Pacific in Honolulu. Modern forensics should help with the identifying of 80% of the crew.

Additional Source Notes

[62] Interview with Gerald Ross. Interviewed by Matthew Rozell, Hudson Falls High School World War II Living History Project, Veterans' Symposium, May 19, 2001. Also, classroom interview, 1998. Mary Bancroft and Cameron Rigby worked on transcriptions.

[63] Interview with Joseph Fiore. Interviewed by Katelyn Mann, January 13, 2004.

[64] Interview with Dante 'Dan' Orsini. Interviewed by Shea Kolar, Dec. 8, 2005. Also, Mikayla Orsini, Jan. 7, 2012, and classroom interviews.

[65] Source Notes: Minder, Joseph G. World War II Diary of Joseph G. Minder, 1941-1945. Unpublished manuscript. Joe Minder's diary was reformatted in the spring semester of 2015 for use here by my 12th graders as a class project. Alanna Belanger, Sean Daley, Jessica Hogan, Emma Kitchner, Zoe Muller, Brendan Murphy, Ruthie Rainbow, Jack Roche, Nathan Smith, Kylie Tripp, and Alexis Winney all played a role in piecing it together.

[66] Interview with Major Richard M. Gordon-Bataan Death March Survivor. HistoryNet. www.historynet.com/world-war-ii-

interview-with-major-richard-m-gordon-bataan-death-march-survivor.htm. Major Gordon also wrote a well-received memoir titled *Horyo: Memoirs of an American POW*. Saint Paul: Paragon House, 1999.

[67] Burr, Patten. "John Parsons, Local GI, Recounts Jap Tortures", *The Glens Falls Post-Star*, Jan. 30, 1946.

[68] Interview with Dorothy Schechter. Interviewed by Kaitlyn Barbieri and Matthew Rozell, Jan. 5, 2007.

[69] Interview with John Leary. Interviewed by Matthew Rozell, Veterans' Symposium, May 19, 2001.

[70] Interview with Robert Addison, Interviewed by Ayme Baumler, Dec. 6, 2005. Addison commentary also taken from our veteran symposiums, May 19, 2001; May 24, 2002. Sara Prehoda and Jackie Quarters helped with the transcription.

[71] Interview with Gerald West. Interviewed by Laura Heil, Dec. 20, 2005. West commentary also taken from our veteran symposiums, May 19, 2001; May 24, 2002.

[72] Interview with Thomas H. Jones, Interviewed by Phillip Kilmartin, Jan. 16, 2009. Also Ashleigh Fitzgerald, Dec.31, 2009.

[73] Interview with Alvin Peachman, June 16, 2003. Interview by Matthew Rozell. My interview conducted with him at his home occurred 25 years after having had him as my high school history teacher. Shannon Bohan, Naomi Borlang, Kate Mann, and John O'Hara helped with the transcription.

[74] Ralph Leinoff was interviewed on various occasions. He developed close relationships with his student interviewers and his remembrances throughout this book were from interviews with Jillian Casey, Dec. 7, 2010; Matthew Dumas, Jan. 7, 2009; Matthew Rozell, Jan. 14, 2009; and John Trackey, Jan. 2, 2010. In the interview with Jillian Casey, Jillian noted the following: "At the time the bombs were dropped, Mr. Leinoff had four landings in the Pacific and he said he 'wasn't looking to do a fifth one.' He stated that [in 1945] he didn't care what happened to the Japanese. I wasn't expecting what followed: 'Since then, I have questioned—I don't have answers—I have questions about the way it was done, why we had to do it.' "

[75] Interview with Walter Hooke. Interviewed by Anthony Rosa, Jan. 9, 2008.
[76] Interview with Nicholas H. Grinaldo, Interviewed by Michael Aikey, New York State Military Museum, September 26, 2001.
[77] Interview with John A. Sidur. Interviewed by Wayne Clarke, New York State Military Museum, October 1, 2010.
[78] Dan Lawler visited my classroom several times. Lawler's reminisces for this book were also recorded and analyzed by Kristyn Wagner in an interview she did on Dec. 4, 2005, at his home. As a side note, Lawler remembered an incident as they were preparing to land at Peleliu that reminded him of home: "As we left for this island, I boarded a landing ship. There wasn't enough room in the mess hall for all of us, so we ate our meals topside. One afternoon while eating lunch, a friend of mine hollered to me if I was from New York, and I said, 'Yes!' He then asked if I knew where 'Hudson Falls' was. This big machine that we were sitting on was made at the Sandy Hill Iron and Brass Co.; there was a nameplate on the side. It was a big winch. My father helped make this machine! I asked a sailor what it was used for, and he said that after the ship has unloaded, this winch, which was attached to the anchor, would pull the ship off the beach."
[79] John Murray's narrative of his experience on Peleliu has been excerpted from a private letter written to his son in 1995.
[80] James Butterfield and Dan Lawler visited my classroom many times over several years, beginning in May 2000. Their interviews are noted elsewhere in the Notes.
[81] Blakeslee, Robert B. Unpublished interview conducted in 1945.
[82] Interview with Sanford Berkman. Interviewed by Michael Russert and Wayne Clarke for the New York State Military Museum, September 26, 2007. Also, incidental information gleaned from Murphy, Tyler, "WWII Marine commander recalls wounds of Iwo Jima", *The Altamont Enterprise,* July 31, 2013.
[83] Art LaPorte was interviewed on many occasions for this project. Mary Lee Bellosa and Heather Aubrey worked on the Oct.

1998 interview I conducted. He was also interviewed by David Elliot on Jan. 9, 2004.

[84] Interview with Herbert Altshuler. Interviewed by Marissa Huntington, Jan. 8, 2012; Mark Ostrander, Fall 2008; Britneigh Sipowitz, Dec. 18, 2010. I also interviewed Herb in 2009.

[85] Source Notes: Doty, Andrew. *Backwards Into Battle: A Tail Gunner's Journey in World War II.* Palo Alto: Tall Tree Press, 1995. Used with author permission.

[86] Interview with Bruce Manell. Interviewed by Kayla Cronin, Dec. 18, 2003.

[87] Interview with Katherine Abbott. Interviewed by Elizabeth Conley, January 11, 2007.

[88] Interview with John Norton. Interviewed by Troy Belden, Jan. 15, 2008.

[89] Interview with Joseph Marcino. Interviewed by Brooke Goff, Dec. 17, 2004.

VOLUME II NOTES

[90] Bailey, Ronald H. *The Air War in Europe.* Alexandria, Virginia: Time-Life Books, 1979. 28.

[91] Bailey, Ronald H. *The Air War in Europe.* Alexandria, Virginia: Time-Life Books, 1979. 29.

[92] Bailey, Ronald H. *The Air War in Europe.* Alexandria, Virginia: Time-Life Books, 1979. 30.

[93] Miller, Donald L. *The Story of World War II.* New York: Simon & Schuster, 2001. 38

[94] Bailey, Ronald H. *The Air War in Europe.* Alexandria, Virginia: Time-Life Books, 1979. 28.

[95] Tooze, Adam. *The Wages of Destruction: The Making and Breaking of the Nazi Economy.* London: Allen Lane, 2007. Location 7803

[96] Miller, Donald L. *The Story of World War II.* New York: Simon & Schuster, 2001. 257.

[97] *45,000 people were killed and 400,000 left homeless* -Miller, Donald L. *The Story of World War II.* New York: Simon & Schuster, 2001. 259.

[98] 'B-17 Flying Fortress', Boeing http://www.boeing.com/history/products/b-17-flying-fortress.page

[99] Ambrose, Steven. *The Wild Blue: The Men and the Boys Who Flew the B-24s over Germany*. New York: Simon & Schuster, 2001. 23

[100] Miller, Donald L., *The Story of World War II.* New York: Simon & Schuster, 2001. 483.

[101] Source Notes: **Duties and Responsibilities of the Airplane Commander and Crewmen** B-17 Pilot Training Manual -1943. United States Government (declassified, public domain). The responsibilities for those in the heavy bombers of the U.S. Army Air Forces are outlined at the start of many chapters. See 'B-17 Crew Requirements and Standard Operating Procedures', www.303rdbg.com/crew-duties.html. Also, 'Air Crewman's Gunnery Manual, 1944; Aviation Training Division, Office of the Chief of Naval Operations, U.S. Navy in collaboration with U.S. Army Air Forces,' www.ibiblio.org/hyperwar/USN/ref/Air-Gunnery

[102] Joiner, Steven. *Mission to Ploesti: B-24 Liberators*. Air and Space Magazine, Feb. 11, 2015.

[103] Source Notes: **Andy Doty**. Doty, Andrew. *Backwards Into Battle: A Tail Gunner's Journey in World War II.* Palo Alto: Tall Tree Press, 1995. Used with author permission.

[104] Source Notes: **Richard Varney.** Interviewed by Emily Thomson, December 16, 2003. Hudson Falls, NY. Deposited at NYS Military Museum.

[105] Source Notes: **Richard G. Alagna.** Interviewed by Michael Russert and Wayne Clarke, September 18, 2002. Rockville Center, NY. Deposited at NYS Military Museum.

[106] Source Notes: **Kenneth R. Carlson.** Interviewed by Michael Russert and Wayne Clarke, March 18, 2003, NYC. Deposited at NYS Military Museum.

[107] Source Notes: **Earl M. Morrow.** Interviewed by Wayne Clarke, September 4, 2009. Hartford, NY. Deposited at NYS Military Museum.

[108] Source Notes: **Martin F. Bezon.** Interviewed by Wayne Clarke, March 27, 2012. Port Henry NY. Deposited at NYS Military Museum.
[109] Source Notes: **Seymour 'Sonny' Segan.** Interviewed by Matthew Rozell, November 3, 2002. Glens Falls, NY.

VOLUME III NOTES

[110] For an excellent discussion of the Tuskegee Airmen, see the CAF Red Tail Squadron website, http://www.redtail.org. "The CAF Red Tail Squadron is a volunteer-driven organization dedicated to educating audiences across the country about the history and legacy of the Tuskegee Airmen, America's first black military pilots and their support personnel."
[111] CAF Red Tail Squadron website, www.redtail.org.
[112] CAF Red Tail Squadron website, www.redtail.org.
[113] Imperial War Museum, Richard J Faulkner. www.americanairmuseum.com/person/182944
[114] Miller, Donald L., *The Story of World War II.* New York: Simon & Schuster, 2001. 217.
[115] Miller, Donald L. *Masters of the Air: America's Bomber Boys Who Fought the Air War against Nazi Germany.* New York: Simon & Schuster, 2006. 493.
[116] Nichol, John, and Rennell, Tony. *The Last Escape: The Untold Story of Allied Prisoners of War in Germany 1944-1945.* London: Viking, 2002.
[117] Miller, 495.
[118] Miller, 496.
[119] Source Notes: **Clarence W Dart.** Interviewed by Matthew Rozell, December 2003.
[120] Source Notes: **John G. Weeks.** Interviewed by Michael Russert and Wayne Clarke, May 22, 2002. Deposited at NYS Military Museum. Also, John G. Weeks' unpublished memoir, '*The Story of a Photo Reconnaissance Pilot during World War II.*'

---

[121] Source Notes: **Richard Faulkner.** Interviewed by Michael Russert and Wayne Clarke, September 24, 2003. Auburn, NY. Deposited at NYS Military Museum.
[122] Source Notes: **George FitzGibbon.** Interviewed by Michael Russert and Wayne Clarke, May 18, 2002. Johnson City, NY. Deposited at NYS Military Museum.
[123] Source Notes: **Charles Corea.** Interviewed by Michael Aikey and Wayne Clarke, November 20, 2001. Rochester, New York. Deposited at NYS Military Museum.
[124] Source Notes: **Earl M. Morrow, Sam Lisica, Jerry Silverman.** Interviewed by Matthew Rozell, July 31, 2001. Hartford, NY. Deposited at NYS Military Museum.
[125] Hirsch, Michael. *The Liberators: America's Witnesses to the Holocaust.* New York: Bantam Books. 2010. 99-102.
[126] *'the battalion commander drew his sidearm, put it to the mayor's head, and calmly asked him to recite his instructions* - 'Towers interview with author, 2008; Jacob Singer interview with author, 2008. Singer was a four-year-old child but remembered this event and relayed it to the author. He also noted that he remembered the liberation because this was the first time in his life that he remembered 'seeing adults smile.' In an email communication to interviewer Jerri Donohue, Towers wrote, *'Yes, the German civilians, as well as their Nazi Burgomaster, were very reluctant to offer any assistance to these 'Jew pigs'!!! I actually did not witness any of this unwillingness, but only heard it from another liaison officer from the 823rd Tank Battalion, Lt. Floyd Mitchell, who was a close friend, and he saw this firsthand. It was his C.O., Lt. Col. Dettmer, who held a pistol to the head of the Burgomaster, and ordered him to get his civilians of the town to cooperate. Reluctantly they acted accordingly.'* A similar incident is recounted in Cornelius Ryan's classic book, *The Last Battle*: 'The psychological effect of the camps on officers and men was beyond assessment. On the Ninth Army front in a village near Magdeburg, Major Julius Rock, a medical officer with the 30th Infantry, came up to inspect a freight train which the 30th had stopped. It was loaded with concentration camp inmates. Rock, horrified, immediately unloaded the train. Over the local burgomaster's vehement protests, Rock billeted the inmates in German homes–but not until his battalion commander had given a crisp command to the complaining burgomaster. 'If you

refuse,' he said simply, 'I'll take hostages and shoot them.' As an additional sidenote, in 2009 Major Rock's daughter contacted the author; you can see more here: bit.ly/MajorRock.

127 United States Army, After Action Report, 823rd Tank Destroyer Battalion, April 14, 1945.

CPSIA information can be obtained
at www.ICGtesting.com
Printed in the USA
BVHW060909010321
601309BV00001B/1/J

9 781948 155120